DEVELOPING *and* ADMINISTERING
Early Childhood Education Programs

Shauna M. Adams	Amy S. Kronberg	Michelle L. Donley	Ellen M. Lynch
Associate Professor, University of Dayton	*Early Childhood Education Consultant Adjunct Professor, University of Dayton*	*Director, Bombeck Family Learning Center, University of Dayton*	*Associate Professor, University of Cincinnati*

Tenth Edition

Australia • Brazil • Canada • Mexico • Singapore • United Kingdom • United States

CENGAGE

Developing and Administering Early Childhood Education Programs,
Tenth Edition

Shauna M. Adams, Amy S. Kronberg, Michelle L. Donley, and Ellen M. Lynch

SVP, Higher Education & Skills Product: Erin Joyner

Product Director: Jason Fremder

Product Manager: Lauren Whalen

Product Assistant: Dallas Wilkes

Content Manager: Sharib Asrar and Sibasis Pradhan, MPS Limited

Digital Delivery Lead: Beth Ross

Director, Product Marketing: Neena Bali

Marketing Manager: Ian Hamilton

IP Analyst: Ashley Maynard

IP Project Manager: Kelli Besse

Production Service: MPS Limited

Designer: Chris Doughman

Cover Image Source: Rawpixel.com/ ShutterStock.com, iStock.com/ FatCamera, iStock.com/sturti

For product information and technology assistance, contact us at
Cengage Customer & Sales Support, 1-800-354-9706 or support.cengage.com.

For permission to use material from this text or product, submit all requests online at **www.cengage.com/permissions.**

Library of Congress Control Number: 2021905059

ISBN-13: 978-0-3575-1320-0

Cengage
200 Pier 4 Boulevard
Boston, MA 02210
USA

Cengage is a leading provider of customized learning solutions with employees residing in nearly 40 different countries and sales in more than 125 countries around the world. Find your local representative at **www.cengage.com.**

To learn more about Cengage platforms and services, register or access your online learning solution, or purchase materials for your course, visit **www.cengage.com.**

Notice to the Reader

Publisher does not warrant or guarantee any of the products described herein or perform any independent analysis in connection with any of the product information contained herein. Publisher does not assume, and expressly disclaims, any obligation to obtain and include information other than that provided to it by the manufacturer. The reader is expressly warned to consider and adopt all safety precautions that might be indicated by the activities described herein and to avoid all potential hazards. By following the instructions contained herein, the reader willingly assumes all risks in connection with such instructions. The publisher makes no representations or warranties of any kind, including, but not limited to, the warranties of fitness for particular purpose or merchantability, nor are any such representations implied with respect to the material set forth herein, and the publisher takes no responsibility with respect to such material. The publisher shall not be liable for any special, consequential, or exemplary damages resulting, in whole or part, from the readers' use of, or reliance upon, this material.

Printed at CLDPC, USA, 06-21

Honoring the Legacy Authors

Dorothy June Sciarra
and Anne G. Dorsey

We would like to honor the work of the original authors of this book, Dorothy June Sciarra and Anne Dorsey, whose contributions to the field of early childhood education are profound. Their work with the University of Cincinnati's Early Childhood Program has impacted decades of educators and the children and families they served. Their passion for the field and generous donations of their time and expertise has benefited the early childhood community locally, nationally, and internationally. They will be dearly missed, but their legacy of dedication to the field will live on in those of us who had the good fortune to know them.

Dedication

To Stan, my husband, partner, and best friend, who inspires me to see the glass as half full—without your love and support I would be truly lost. To my daughter, Meredith and son Ian, who add much joy to my life—thank you for allowing me to share your stories in my teaching and my writing. To my colleagues and the teachers, staff, children, and families of the Bombeck Family Learning Center, your work inspired my contributions to this book.

S.M.A.

To Jon, my partner in life, who reminds me of the importance of balancing the care of others with the care for myself; without your love and support, none of this would be possible. To my "assistant" and sweet boy Grayson, who greets each day ready to take on the world and teaches me patience, joy, and laughter along the way. To my parents, Dennis and Anna, and my sister, Sarah, whose encouragement makes my heart smile and keeps me moving forward. To Shauna, thank you for bringing me along on this journey and keeping me inspired through it all.

A.S.K.

To my husband, Scot, for your love and encouragement, and pushing me to continue advocating for what I believe in. To my children, Sam, Sawyer, and Scarlet, who remind me each day of how grateful I am. To my school family for your endless support and inspiration. To my coauthors: Thank you for the opportunity to add my voice to this book. It is truly an honor to collaborate with those who share a desire to lead the way into the future of our profession.

M.L.D.

In memory of my parents, Jean and Rex, whose lives were a model of strength and faith; to my husband, Dennis, whose unending patience and thoughtfulness never cease to amaze and support me; to my children Heather and Josh, who fueled my personal and professional interest in childhood; to Kaitlyn and Taylor, whose spirits continue to change my life so powerfully, absolutely, and unexpectedly; and to my coauthors whose knowledge of early childhood education and commitment to ethical practice are unparalleled.

E.M.L.

Brief Table of Contents

Contents

Preface

The tenth edition of *Developing and Administering an Early Childhood Education Program* focuses on honoring our past while we embrace the future. Our goal is to provide professors of early childhood education and their students an understanding of the need for well-prepared directors who come to their role with a background in child development, an appreciation of how learning occurs, and knowledge of the significant changes early childhood education has undergone and how they impact basic business practices and are necessary to run a quality early program.

State of the Directorship

As more attention is given to the importance of the early years of child development and learning, early childhood programs also face increased scrutiny. Educators, legislators, funders, program administrators, staff, and parents all want the best for children. But, of course, wanting the best, knowing what children need, and being able to provide it doesn't come easily, and the ongoing pandemic show how fragile this system can be. Progress is evident based on the work of individuals such as Paula Jorde Bloom, who for many years has written about leadership and provided programs in support of directors' development. Roger and Bonnie Neugebauer have provided bimonthly information specifically for directors in their *Exchange* publication for more than 30 years. Most states have Quality Rating and Improvement Systems (QRIS) and have established early learning and development standards. In addition to the 2011 revision of the Code of Ethical Conduct, these efforts are now supported by a series of new foundational documents for the profession of early childhood education and include the 2020 revision of the Position Statement on Developmentally Appropriate Practices; the 2019 revision of Professional Standards and Competencies for Early Childhood Educators; and a new Position Statement, Advancing Equity in Early Childhood Education, all of which can be found at the website of the National Association for the Education of Young Children (NAEYC) at https://www.naeyc.org/resources/position-statements/. Also, the efforts of 14 national organizations committed to serving young children and families culminated in a unifying document that provides a vision for the field of early childhood education that transcends where, when, how, and by whom services are provided. The Power to the Profession: Unifying Framework developed by the Power to the Profession Taskforce in 2020 should serve as guidance for directors and can be found at http://powertotheprofession.org/wp-content/uploads/2020/03/Power-to-Profession-Framework-03312020-web.pdf.

We recognize that one book alone will not prepare directors for their role. We rely on our field's professional organizations and their work to inform directors of current trends and research. The most current positions statements are woven throughout this text. Our goal is to help future teachers and directors understand the importance of the director's role for early childhood staff, children, their families, and the community. We hope that our text will also help those who are designing director licensure move more quickly to that goal.

Our Audience

The tenth edition of *Developing and Administering an Early Childhood Education Program* was written for college students interested in early childhood education. They may be preparing to be teachers of young children or they may be planning ahead to become administrators. Our intention is to depict the role of director, whether starting a new center or administering one already in operation. When teachers understand this role, they are more likely to recognize why their director has certain expectations of teachers and what teachers' responsibilities are as they plan and implement a flexible, interesting program for the young children in their group. Students in associate, baccalaureate, and master's programs need this information. As they study these chapters, they begin to realize that in an early childhood education career, the roles of the director are varied and interdependent.

Conceptual Approach

When the director is competent to engage in a wide range of human interactions as well as manage the center's business components, the center will function well. When the director's background in one or both components is weak, the center is likely to close or, even more disturbing, the program will continue in a way that is not productive for the children it serves.

Above all, we see the director as a well-prepared, ethical person who is authoritative and dedicated to meeting the needs of young children and their families. We emphasize adopting and using the NAEYC's Statement of Commitment, Code of Ethical Conduct, and the Supplement for Early Childhood Program Administrators whenever puzzling situations arise that may be of an ethical nature. We see the director's responsibility as educating staff and families about the code and how it can be used appropriately.

Using the Text

In each chapter we include boxes that illustrate the points discussed in that section of the chapter. Called "Director's Corner," these vignettes clarify the material with examples described from a director's experiences. Throughout the text are features called "Growth Mindset Moments," which are designed to give readers an opportunity to pause and consider their understanding of the points being made in the text. These boxes often relate to an experience a student may have had. Each chapter ends with a summary followed by one or more activities labeled "Try It Out!" in which directions for individual, partner, or small-group activities are included. Content in the chapter is often supported by the "Director's Resources" that follow the "Try It Out!" activities. Frequently, the "Director's Resources" are used in the "Try It Out!" activities.

Appendixes in our book provide a wealth of updated lists for both instructors and students. These include sources of materials, equipment, and supplies; early childhood professional organizations; early childhood periodicals and information sources; and copies of many NAEYC standards and position statements.

When presenting material from *Developing and Administering an Early Childhood Education Program*, instructors may choose to follow the existing order of chapters, or they may decide to depart from that order. Every chapter is self-contained, so either approach works well. Some instructors use the content as the basis of lectures, adding examples from their own experiences or inviting local directors to meet with the class to discuss a particular topic. Others assign students to interview directors on topics addressed in the text.

Many students enrolled in an administration class are involved in or will have completed an early childhood field experience. Many may be working in early childhood programs. Because the focus of college-level students may be primarily on the classroom, instructors may have students reflect on those experiences to determine how a director influences a program. For example, how does the director's work affect the health, safety, and nutrition of the children in your center?

Some instructors use the "Growth Mindset Moment" feature found throughout the text as a starting point for class discussions or as a topic for writing assignments. The "Director's Corner" feature, which presents quotes from directors on the chapter topic, can also be used this way. Other instructors use the "Try It Out!" exercises to stimulate discussion or reflection on personal experiences or feelings. These activities may take the form of role-playing, debates, or other authentic problem-solving activities.

Most students are comfortable with the reading level of our book. Terms that may be new are explained in context. *Developing and Administering an Early Childhood Education Program* lends itself well to related field experiences. Advanced students may be assigned as interns to work with directors, much as student teachers work with mentor teachers. Other instructors may assign students to form teams to create their own center on paper. This assignment may include creating an imaginary site, a mission statement, a funding plan, a tuition schedule, a budget, a marketing plan, a staffing plan, a policy and procedures manual, and a salary schedule. The assignment may be limited to one or more of these components. Instructors may assign students to write a paper or prepare a class presentation on one of the topics discussed in the text using related resources listed in the appendixes or at the end of each chapter.

What's New in This Edition: An Overview

The tenth edition of *Developing and Administering an Early Childhood Education Program* presents completely updated and expanded content. Here are some of the major revisions to both the text as a whole and for each chapter:

This administration text includes a focus on curricular leadership that emphasizes the administrator's roles in supporting high-quality curriculum selection and implementation. In this thoroughly updated edition, the authors seek to prepare readers for the vast number of changes in the field of early childhood education. The text addresses NAEYC's (2020) new statement on Developmentally Appropriate Practice as well as the recommendations for administrators in the new position statement, Advancing Equity. This revised edition weaves the Power to the Profession Unifying Framework throughout most chapters. Since the last edition, the world has changed significantly. A new chapter describing leadership during times of change and crisis provides strategies for facilitating change and supporting staff, children, and families as they deal with the trauma.

New! The 2020 Position Statement on Developmentally Appropriate Practice is included throughout the textbook.

New! The Unifying Framework developed by the Power to the Profession Taskforce (2019) serves as the catalyst to changes in the title of the text and the new verbiage used to describe the profession of early childhood education where early childhood educators work and administer early childhood programs. This framework seeks to advance the profession and should change how leaders view the field.

New! Quality early childhood education has been shown to be key in advancing equity for all children and families. Recommendations from the position statement, "Advancing Equity: Recommendations for Administrators," are woven throughout the text.

New! Material on biases, both implicit and explicit, is added with case vignettes designed to have readers think critically about their own biases and the impact on relationships with children, families, and coworkers. Interventions that can help staff members grow in their ability to reduce the impact of biases on practice will be shared.

New! To address the increase of stress and trauma in the lives of staff, children, and families, a new chapter has been added titled "Leading in Times of Change and Crisis."

New! The material on finance and budgeting has been streamlined into one chapter. The new sample budget provides a realistic view of costs based on the recommendations from the Power to the Profession's Unifying Framework.

New! Features titled "Crisis: An Opportunity for Positive Change" provide an opportunity for readers to examine their perspective and instructors with real-life examples for class discussion and student reflection.

New! Appendixes include the latest versions of standards and position statements from NAEYC.

Key Revisions and Additions to Each Chapter

Chapter 1—The Effective Director

Additional focus on the need for computer literacy in managing today's programs and the importance of understanding the administrative roles played by directors

Chapter 2—Assessing Community Need and Establishing a Program

Additional information on the importance of advocacy

New information on using online surveys to complete needs assessments

Chapter 3—Licensing, Credentialing, and Accreditation

Updated information regarding licensing and accreditation of programs

Updated information related to Quality Rating and Improvement Systems

Updated and expanded information about the various types of credentialing and credentialing bodies

Inclusion of a new Director's Resource related to developing a plan of operation for a new child care program

Chapter 4—Organizing Program Structure and Working with a Board

Additional focus on the use of technology to communicate with the board and its committees

New information related to the benefits of diverse board membership

Updated information on orientation of new board members

Inclusion of a new Director's Resource related to completing articles of incorporation

Chapter 5—Handling Financial Matters

Updated information about the importance of staff input in establishing budget priorities

New information on using technology-supported budgeting tools

Updated figures on wages based on national comparisons

New information about the Affordable Care Act

Additional information related to seeking funding beyond what is needed for a current year's operation

Updated information on employer-supported child care and on government funding of early care and education

New information on establishing an integrated system of child care

Chapter 6—Developing a Program Facility

New information on planning centers based on universal design

Inclusion of a new Director's Resource related to the way a program's mission and goals might impact the planning of an early childhood facility

Chapter 7—Equipping the Program

Expanded information related to technology needs in equipping the center and digital literacy

Updated information related to equipment list resources

Updated information related to playground safety concerns

New information related to safety concerns for infants and toddlers

Expanded information on purchasing equipment for children with disabilities

Chapter 8—Staffing the Program

New information related to growing leadership from within

New information related to using LinkedIn and other web-based systems to recruit and manage the hiring process

New example of a program handbook included as a Director's Resource

New example of a staffing schedule included as a Director's Resource

New example of a performance valuation included as a Director's Resource

Chapter 9—Recruiting Children

New information about including children with special needs

Expanded information about creating a quality website to recruit children and families

Chapter 10—Supporting Quality Curriculum

Expanded information on the theoretical basis for quality curriculum

Expanded information about the role of the director as a curriculum mentor

Expanded information about the effective use of technology with young children

Chapter 11—Managing the Food and the Health and Safety Programs

New information challenging students to consider how food is used in their program

New information related to the national Farm to School movement

Expanded information on how technology can be used to manage the food program and maintain the health and safety of children and staff

Updated information on legal issues related to health and safety in early childhood programs

Chapter 12—Leading in Times of Change and Crisis

This new chapter includes strategies for directors who are required to pivot to address required change and address the self-care and response strategies for leaders during times of crisis.

Chapter 13—Working with Families, Volunteers, and the Community

New information about comprehensive communication systems

New information about communicating with families through web-based portfolios

Inclusion of a new Director's Resource related to evaluating of the program's family engagement system

Chapter 14—Providing for Personal and Professional Staff Development

Expanded information on job-embedded professional development

New information on online professional development

Chapter 15—Evaluating Program Components

New information on developing assessment policies for programs

Expanded information on the use of portfolio assessment with children

New information on the use of electronic portfolios in evaluating children's progress

Updated information on cultural competence self-assessments in early childhood programs

Inclusion of a new Director's Resource related to annual staff performance reviews

Chapter 16—Marketing the Program

New focus on word-of-mouth marketing

Expanded information on using social media

Updated information on marketing the program to digital natives

New section on the characteristics of a quality child care center website

Updated references to support website development

Appendices A through H

Completely updated

Ancillary material

Accompanying Teaching and Learning Resources

Online Instructor's Manual

An online Instructor's Manual accompanies this book and contains information to assist the instructor in designing the course, including sample syllabi, discussion questions, teaching and learning activities, field experiences, learning objectives, and additional online resources. Additional online resources and assessments include:

- TeachSource videos of teachers teaching and children learning in real classrooms, accompanied by case study questions to assess students' understanding of the video concepts.
- Case scenarios requiring students to analyze typical teaching and learning situations and create a reasoned response to the issue(s) presented in the scenario, reflecting about and justifying the choices they made within the teaching scenario problem.
- Digital Download resources.

PowerPoint Lecture Slides

These vibrant Microsoft PowerPoint lecture slides for each chapter assist you with your lecture by providing concept coverage using images, figures, and tables directly from the textbook!

Cengage Learning Testing Powered by Cognero

Cengage Learning Testing Powered by Cognero is a flexible online system that allows you to author, edit, and manage test bank content from multiple Cengage Learning solutions; create multiple test versions in an instant; and deliver tests from your learning management system, your classroom, or wherever you want.

About the Authors

Shauna M. Adams is a professor of early childhood at the University of Dayton, where she also serves as the executive director of the Center for Early Learning. Dr. Adams has taught graduate and undergraduate students in such courses as child development, preschool methods, primary methods, and early childhood advocacy, research, and leadership. In her role as the director of the Center for Early Learning, Dr. Adams promotes opportunities for the Bombeck Family Learning Center to serve preservice and in-service early childhood professionals as a demonstration school and forum for professional development. She also advocates for children and families by serving on local and state committees that support quality early care and education and serves the university's mission by providing support for Catholic Early Childhood programming.

After teaching as an intervention specialist in public schools for 10 years, Dr. Adams became a school psychologist, working with children in preschool and the primary grades. She earned her doctorate in Early Childhood and Special Education from the University of Cincinnati. Dr. Adams became immersed in early childhood education through her work with the Bombeck Family Learning Center and has established partnerships with Head Start, Public School Preschool, child care, and a variety of agencies that support young children and families. In addition, Dr. Adams worked with community partners to develop the University of Dayton's online Early Childhood Leadership and Advocacy programs, which were designed to address the need for leadership in early childhood while also supporting the early childhood career lattice. She is also the lead author of the ACCESS Curriculum and has produced many articles, conducted presentations, developed websites, and pursued other outlets to share this curriculum with the field of early care and education.

Amy S. Kronberg is an early learning consultant and adjunct professor at the University of Dayton. Mrs. Kronberg began her work in early childhood education at the University of Michigan–Dearborn Early Childhood Education Center, immersed in an environment emphasizing personal and professional growth, early childhood mental health, playful learning, child-centered curricula, and the important connection between programs and families. She pursued further learning about advocacy, policy, and research at the University of Dayton, where she earned her Master's of Science in Education and has all but completed her dissertation for a doctorate in Educational Leadership.

Mrs. Kronberg worked alongside Dr. Adams to create courses focused on infant–toddler development and early childhood mental health, adapting coursework to bridge the theory–practice gap for current and future early childhood educators. She continues to embrace opportunities to bring playful learning experiences to the Greater Dayton area as an early learning consultant with Learn to Earn Dayton, a local nonprofit, to provide families a platform to inspire playful interactions with their young children.

Michelle L. Donley directs the University of Dayton's Demonstration School, the Bombeck Family Learning Center. After teaching infants, toddlers, and preschoolers for Head Start and at the Bombeck Center for 20 years, Michelle earned a master's of science in education in Early Childhood Leadership and Advocacy from the University of Dayton. She has directed the Bombeck Center for 5 years where she guided the program through NAEYC Accreditation and has maintained the highest rating in the State Quality Improvement and Rating System. Michelle believes in advocating for change in the profession for increased investments and she understands the need to improve the early childhood education system for children, families, and practitioners. Michelle is a member of the National Association for the Education of Young Children and the National Coalition for Campus Children's Centers. As a director, Michelle continues to evolve and mature in her leadership and management skills and her experiences leading a program during a time of change have been critical in making this edition of the text relevant to today. Her passion for the field is grounded in research, reflection, and ensuring sustained continuous improvement by empowering each program team member to find their true potential.

Ellen M. Lynch is now retired as an associate professor of early childhood education at the University of Cincinnati. Her doctorate is in special education with a focus on early childhood special education. She has been active in local and state early childhood organizations, including the Ohio Association for the Education of Young Children (OAEYC), for which she served as chair of the Children with Special Needs Committee; the state Board of Directors; and the Division for Early Childhood of the Council for Exceptional Children. In addition, she served as president of the Ohio Coalition of Associate Degree Early Childhood Programs. Dr. Lynch's current scholarly interests include engaging in the scholarship of teaching and learning and exploring the use of technology to support learning among preservice teachers. She is both an editor and reviewer for several problem-based learning journals. She has presented widely at local, state, national, and international levels on a variety of aspects of teaching young children, teacher education, and best practices for teaching in higher education.

Acknowledgments

Our book is the result of continuous support from friends and colleagues who have helped us immeasurably, even when they didn't realize the contributions they were making. We particularly want to thank the directors, who helped us understand their day-to-day work from a wide variety of situations and perspectives. We are indebted to the teachers, staff, children, and families of the University of Dayton's Bombeck Family Learning Center who shared their practice so that it might be captured in our words and photographs and used in real-life examples. We also thank our photographers—Jenna Williams, Jessica Pike, Meredith Adams, and Murless Harris.

We also would like to express our gratitude to the following reviewers, who offered valuable suggestions:

Jeanne Barker, Tallahassee Community College

Jennifer Barry, University of Mary

Yvonne Beirne, North Shore Community College

Jo Ann Burnside, Richard J. Daley College

Deb Farrer, California University of Pennsylvania

Colleen Fawcett, Palm Beach State College

Lisa Godwin, Central Piedmont Community College

Jill Harrison, Delta College

Joanny Iaccino, Los Angeles Valley College

Mary Janowski, Gulf Coast State College

Willie Jones, Tougaloo College

Janiece Kneppe, Red Rocks Community College

Debra Lawrence, Chestnut Hill College

Mary Lowe, College of the Albemarle

Vicky McBride, Northampton Community College

Maureen O'Neil, Tallahassee Community College

John Ronghua Ouyang, University of North Florida

Beatrice Paul, Salem State University

Donald Roberts, Cochise College

Joan Robison, Cloud County Community College

Jacque Taylor, Greenville Technical College

We hope our readers will find here the technical information they need to direct a quality program. Our greater desire is that they will recognize the significance of the leadership role of the director and the challenge and personal satisfaction derived from creating and implementing an excellent early childhood education program for young children and their families.

Shauna M. Adams
Amy S. Kronberg
Michelle L. Donley

The successful director and center personnel work to learn to build their organization in a way that is satisfying to them and to their clients, and that creates a true system of learning.

Chapter 1

The Effective Director

Standards and Recommendations Addressed in This Chapter

ADVANCING EQUITY RECOMMENDATION 6 Provide a regular time and space to foster a learning community among administrators and staff regarding equity issues.

PROGRAM STANDARD 1 Relationships

PROGRAM STANDARD 10 Leadership and Management

LEARNING OBJECTIVES

After reading this chapter, you should be able to:

1-1   Describe how the work of the Power to the Profession Task Force is transforming the field of early childhood education.

1-2   Identify the occupations in the early childhood education profession within the early childhood education field.

1-3   Explain the purpose of the NAEYC Code of Ethical Conduct and Supplement for Early Childhood Program Administrators.

1-4   Describe the systems that make up the field of early childhood education.

1-5   Discuss the competencies that program administrators must possess to be successful leaders.

1-6   Describe tools that enable the director to blend program management and people leadership.

Each and every child, beginning at birth, has the opportunity to benefit from high-quality early childhood education, delivered by an effective, diverse, well-prepared, and well-compensated workforce across all states and settings.

—Power to the Profession Task Force (2020, p. 1)

This vision statement, which was developed by a task force of experts from all segments of the early childhood education profession, represents a field that has been united and redefined. As a leader in an early childhood education program, your work must reflect a deep understanding of this vision and the impact that task force recommendations will have on the field of early childhood education and the program that you lead.

1-1 • New Vision, New Vocabulary

In the past, the profession included early childhood educators who did the same work but were called different names, had different credentials, and earned different salaries. Even the profession was referred to differently, depending on location, affiliation, and purpose. The Power to the Profession Task Force, in partnership with organizational stakeholders and thousands of individual educators, advocates, and allies, worked to establish common language to describe who we are and what we do. Its purpose was

> to establish unity and clarity around the career pathways, knowledge and competencies, qualifications, standards, accountability, supports, and

Where we are going: Our audacious vision for the profession of tomorrow

- Each and every child, birth through age 8, across all settings, is supported by early childhood educators who have recognized early childhood degrees and credentials.

- Early childhood educators at all professional designations (Early Childhood Educator I, II, and III) are valued, respected, and well compensated for the important roles they play.

- Educators with lead responsibilities across settings and age bands are prepared at the Early Childhood Educator III designation (earning a bachelor's degree in early childhood education) at a minimum.

- Anyone who wants to become an early childhood educator at any designation has equitable access to affordable, high-quality professional preparation and development that supports them in developing the agreed-upon set of knowledge, skills, and competencies needed in any setting.

- Early childhood educators at all designations are well compensated in accordance with the complex and demanding work they perform as part of a system that recognizes the cost of quality and finances early childhood education as the public good that it is.

Source: Power to the Profession Task Force. (2020). Unifying framework for the early childhood profession. Washington DC: NAEYC.; Link for Reference: https://powertotheprofession.org/wp-content/uploads/2020/03/Power-to-Profession-Framework-03312020-web.pdf compensation to define the early childhood education profession within the broader early childhood education field, associated scope of practice, expected level of professional preparation, and expected level of mastery of the Professional Standards and Competencies for Early Childhood Educators. (Power to the Profession Task Force, 2020, p. 5)

Learning to lead an early childhood education program during a period of transformation and change requires not only the knowledge and skills associated with leadership but also a personal growth mindset (Dweck, 2006). Crisis is stressful but can also provide an opportunity for growth. The unprecedented challenges of this decade certainly provide an opportunity to move beyond "what we do and what we have always done" to a focus on the possibilities of better practice to better serve children and families (Ashford, Sytch, & Greer, 2020; Brockner & James, 2008).

Learning about the management and leadership of early childhood programs is important for staff and for current and prospective directors. The role of administrator requires knowledge and skills in early childhood education and development as well as in business practices. With expertise in both areas, whether demonstrated by an individual or by a team, the program is likely to be successful for children, families, staff, and other stakeholders.

An effective director of an early childhood education program is involved in all the jobs that will be described in this text from enrolling children to evaluating staff, from budgeting to taking inventory, and from maintaining a physical plant to bandaging a child's scraped knee. The director's job includes doing or overseeing all aspects of program management and leadership. To do any one of these tasks, a director must have skills and knowledge; to do all of them requires

stamina, understanding, and organization; and to do all of them effectively demands exceptional interpersonal skills as emphasized throughout this text. These characteristics and abilities enable the director to bring the best to parents, children, staff members, board members, and the community. In turn, serving as a model of these skills encourages those same people to give their best to the program. The effective director realizes that an early childhood education program can never be a one-person operation. A network of caring and learning together transcends day-to-day chores and makes being part of a program worthwhile.

1-2 • Making a Commitment to Diverse Stakeholders

When you agree to become a director, you take on a tremendous responsibility to a diverse group of stakeholders, including the following:

- children enrolled in the program (and those seeking enrollment);
- families of those children;
- all program personnel (and those who apply for positions);
- the program's board, funders, and other agencies and administrators to whom you report or with whom you interact;
- the community; and
- yourself.

How can you possibly make a commitment to all of these individuals and groups? Perhaps you believed that you would be responsible for seeing that the early childhood educators in your program did what they were supposed to do. Perhaps you thought there might be a problem with one or two of them, but you felt confident you could handle that type of situation. Maybe you thought there would be one or two parents who expected special treatment, or a child who frequently hurt other children. And maybe you thought, "Sure, I can handle that."

Being an administrator entails much more than *handling* people and situations. The director must recognize that her constituency consists of the six components just listed. She must become familiar enough with all of them to know what is important to each constituency.

Growth Mindset Moment

Take a minute and think of your life during the novel coronavirus pandemic. This was a stressful and challenging time for most, but there were some silver linings in what many would call a cloud of despair. Did this crisis provide you with opportunities for growth? Did you learn new cooking techniques? Did you spend more time with your family? Did you become more organized? Did you develop new technology skills? What were your silver linings?

The early childhood education profession within the early childhood field

1. Each and every child, birth through age 8, across all settings, is supported by early childhood educators who have recognized early childhood degrees and credentials.

2. Early childhood educators at all professional designations (Early Childhood Educator I, II, and III) are valued, respected, and well compensated for the important roles they play.

3. Educators with lead responsibilities across settings and age bands are prepared at the Early Childhood Educator III designation (earning a bachelor's degree in early childhood education), at a minimum.

4. Anyone who wants to become an early childhood educator at any designation has equitable access to affordable, high-quality professional preparation and development that supports them in developing the agreed-upon set of knowledge, skills, and competencies needed in any setting.

5. Early childhood educators at all designations are well compensated in accordance with the complex and demanding work they perform as part of a system that recognizes the cost of quality and finances early childhood education as the public good that it is.

**The Early Childhood Education Profession
within the Early Childhood Field**

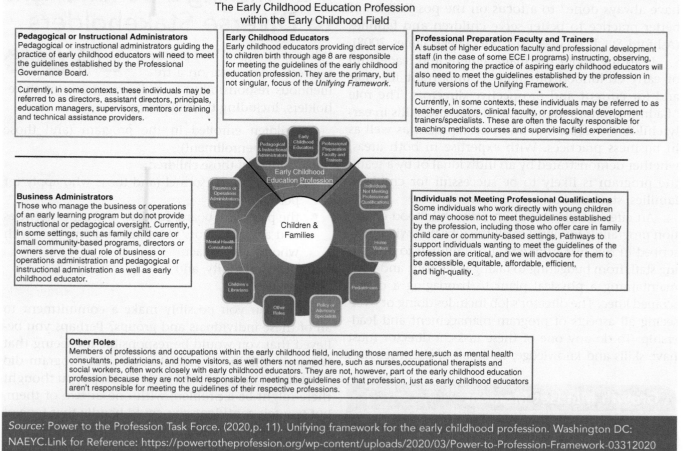

Pedagogical or Instructional Administrators
Pedagogical or instructional administrators guiding the practice of early childhood educators will need to meet the guidelines established by the Professional Governance Board.

Currently, in some contexts, these individuals may be referred to as directors, assistant directors, principals, education managers, supervisors, mentors or training and technical assistance providers.

Early Childhood Educators
Early childhood educators providing direct service to children birth through age 8 are responsible for meeting the guidelines of the early childhood education profession. They are the primary, but not singular, focus of the *Unifying Framework*.

Professional Preparation Faculty and Trainers
A subset of higher education faculty and professional development staff (in the case of some ECE I programs) instructing, observing, and monitoring the practice of aspiring early childhood educators will also need to meet the guidelines established by the profession in future versions of the Unifying Framework.

Currently, in some contexts, these individuals may be referred to as teacher educators, clinical faculty, or professional development trainers/specialists. These are often the faculty responsible for teaching methods courses and supervising field experiences.

Business Administrators
Those who manage the business or operations of an early learning program but do not provide instructional or pedagogical oversight. Currently, in some settings, such as family child care or small community-based programs, directors or owners serve the dual role of business or operations administration and pedagogical or instructional administration as well as early childhood educator.

Individuals not Meeting Professional Qualifications
Some individuals who work directly with young children and may choose not to meet theguidelines established by the profession, including those who offer care in family child care or community-based settings, Pathways to support individuals wanting to meet the guidelines of the profession are critical, and we will advocare for them to be accessible, equitable, efficient, and high-quality.

Other Roles
Members of professions and occupations within the early childhood field, including those named here,such as mental health consultants, pediatricians, and home visitors, as well others not named here, such as nurses,occupational therapists and social workers, often work closely with early childhood educators. They are not, however, part of the early childhood education profession because they are not held responsible for meeting the guidelines of that profession, just as early childhood educators aren't responsible for meeting the guidelines of their respective professions.

Source: Power to the Profession Task Force. (2020,p. 11). Unifying framework for the early childhood profession. Washington DC: NAEYC.Link for Reference: https://powertotheprofession.org/wp-content/uploads/2020/03/Power-to-Profession-Framework-03312020-web.pdf

You may be wondering why the director's constituency includes those *applying* for enrollment or positions at the program. Policies, procedures, and interactions in *every* aspect of the organization's work are included.

Therefore, although the director may not have an opening for a child or may find that a job applicant is not appropriate for the role, she or he is expected to treat each in accordance with the program's philosophy.

The profession's commitment to advancing equity (NAEYC, 2019a) adds additional emphasis to inclusivity and calls on administrators to provide a regular time and space to foster a learning community focused on equity issues. This important value needs to be shared among all staff so that it is also communicated consistently to stakeholders and the broader community.

1-3 • Meeting Challenging Situations Based on Ethical Principles

Any individual who assumes respon-**naeyc** sibility must recognize that challenges will arise. Some of these are easily met, but often there is no clear-cut solution. As you ponder what to do in such situations, you may wonder, "Is this a policy issue, one for which I, as director, should take action and maintain the policy, or are there other factors that make this a moral or an ethical issue?"

You can expect to be challenged by ethical issues as you work to meet the needs of a wide range of constituents. Fortunately, you have valuable tools at your fingertips: The National Association for the Education of Young Children (NAEYC) Code of Ethical Conduct and the Statement of Commitment as well as the Supplement to the Code for Early Childhood Program Administrators (NAEYC, 2011) are on the NAEYC website and are included in **Appendix A**. Becoming familiar with the code and the supplement now will help you when you are faced with a dilemma.

Both the code and the supplement begin with statements of core values. All individuals who work with young children should be expected to commit to holding and acting on those values. For example, directors should value and be committed to the belief that "the well-being of the children in our care is our primary responsibility, above our obligations to other constituents" (NAEYC, 2011b).

Both the code and the supplement contain ideals that "reflect the aspirations of practitioners" and principles that "guide conduct and assist practitioners in resolving ethical dilemmas" (NAEYC, 2011a, 2011b). For example, one ideal maintains that administrators "design programs and policies inclusive of and responsive to diverse families." A related principle suggests that directors "shall work to create

Core values

Standards of ethical behavior in early childhood care and education are based on commitment to the following core values that are deeply rooted in the history of the field of early childhood care and education. We have made a commitment to

- Appreciate childhood as a unique and valuable stage of the human life cycle
- Base our work on knowledge of how children develop and learn
- Appreciate and support the bond between the child and family
- Recognize that children are best understood and supported in the context of family, culture,* community, and society
- Respect the dignity, worth, and uniqueness of each individual (child, family member, and colleague)
- Respect diversity in children, families, and colleagues
- Recognize that children and adults achieve their full potential in the context of relationships that are based on trust and respect

_____
* The term culture includes ethnicity, racial identity, economic level, family structure, language, and religious and political beliefs, which profoundly influence each child's development and relationship to the world.

Core values of the NAEYC Code of Ethical Conduct

a respectful environment for and a working relationship with all families, regardless of family members' sex, race, national origin, immigration status, preferred home language, religious belief or affiliation, age, marital status [or] family structure, disability, or sexual orientation." Note that the documents do not purport to provide specific answers; rather, they serve as guides for decision makers who are facing unique situations.

Directors must be familiar with the code and the supplement and help staff and families understand their importance. Distributing copies to staff and families as part of their handbooks and then holding discussion sessions enables everyone to become familiar with why the program espouses the use of the code and the supplement. In the dialogue with others, be sure to include the importance of *reflecting* on an ethical dilemma and seeking guidance from a trusted professional when needed. As in all other aspects of early childhood work, confidentiality is essential.

The importance of the Code of Ethical Conduct for the staff is determined by how the administrator holds them accountable for knowing the code's content and committing to its use. Having all early childhood educators read and sign the Statement of Commitment is another way of emphasizing its importance.

1-4 • Considering the Program's Systems and Subsystems

Leaders of new or redeveloping businesses often begin their work by calling staff together to create a vision. But the vision can only be achieved when everyone in the organization is committed to it. Often most people do not realize that all businesses operate as systems, whether they are operated to design and sell automobiles or to support children's well-being. We know that each of our

naeyc

bodies is a system, and we are usually well aware when something goes wrong with our bodily system. We know, too, that this system is composed of many systems: the digestive system, the respiratory system, and

---

Growth Mindset Moment

After you have read and thought about the Code of Ethical Content and the Supplement for Early Childhood Program Administrators, reflect on situations you think would be most challenging for you. Have you encountered any ethical dilemmas where using the code might have been helpful?

Statement of Commitment*

As an individual who works with young children, I commit myself to furthering the values of early childhood education as they are reflected in the ideals and principles of the NAEYC Code of Ethical Conduct. To the best of my ability I will

• Never harm children.

• Ensure that programs for young children are based on current knowledge and research of child development and early childhood education.

• Respect and support families in their task of nurturing children.

• Respect colleagues in early childhood care and education and support them in maintaining the NAEYC Code of Ethical Conduct.

• Serve as an advocate for children, their families, and their teachers in community and society.

• Stay informed of and maintain high standards of professional conduct.

• Engage in an ongoing process of self-reflection, realizing that personal characteristics, biases, and beliefs have an impact on children and families.

• Be open to new ideas and be willing to learn from the suggestions of others.

• Continue to learn, grow, and contribute as a professional.

• Honor the ideals and principles of the NAEYC Code of Ethical Conduct.

---

* This Statement of Commitment is not part of the Code but is a personal acknowledgment of the individual's willingness to embrace the distinctive values and moral obligations of the field of early childhood care and education. It is recognition of the moral obligations that lead to an individual becoming part of the profession.

Source: From the National Association for the Education of Young Children (2011a, p.1) so forth. We can see patterns emerging. For example, a pattern of overeating and lack of exercise affects one or more systems and can lead to obesity. Most of us are becoming more aware of environmental systems as well. Destroying the habitats of various species can lead to their extinction. To work effectively in any business, including the early childhood education business, we must recognize that each of us plays a role in that system. Each of us must engage in systems thinking.

Senge (2006) defines systems thinking as "a conceptual framework, a body of knowledge and tools that has been developed over the past 50 years, to make the full patterns clearer, and to help us see how to change them effectively" (p. 7). A body of knowledge and tools for working together exists in each early childhood program. New members join that program with many of the beliefs, theories, and practices common to the field, but they must grow together with their colleagues to create the unique system that enables their program to function successfully.

Because each early childhood program operates as a system, whether the system is visible or not, the director and staff must work together to recognize the characteristics of that system. Periodically, a review must be conducted of the overall system on which a program's operation is based that answers questions such as these: Who are we as a program? What is it that makes us the XYZ program? What premises do we hold that guide us in our work? Are those premises valid? Are some of the program's operating methods still in place simply out of habit? Today, some programs are curtailing or eliminating independent playtime for preschoolers and substituting group instruction. Program personnel need to discuss the reasons for these actions and ensure that such changes support the program's vision.

1-4a • Subsystems in Early Childhood Programs

The system for an early childhood program consists of several subsystems. Some of these subsystems, which will be addressed in other chapters, include the finance system, the systems for securing and managing facilities and equipment, and the personnel system. The subsystems each make a contribution to the whole, and together they create a whole that is greater than the sum of the parts.

Those who create systems base them on what they believe to be important. For example, presumably you have a system for planning curriculum. As program personnel gather to review curriculum, you may find that an early childhood educator says, "We have always had our own way of doing things. Let's just leave it at that." However, in systems thinking, the willingness of each group member to meet and share thinking, to be open to each other's ideas, and to be willing to search for the best solution enables group members to learn together. Establishing such group openness takes time, a willingness on the part of the leader to also be open, and a commitment to implementing the plan to which the group agrees.

In an early childhood education program, several key systems are external to the organization and beyond the direct control of program personnel. Consider that diverse family systems affect the program's operation. Family members want what is best for their children. Family members interact with other systems, such as those at their places of employment. Those systems affect family members' ability to participate in the program and how the program views the role of families. For example, family members may not be free to attend conferences and programs at the program.

Director's Corner

We have six center-based programs within our corporation, widely spread over the local area. Each center-based program has its own identity. The populations we serve at each site differ. However, everyone who works here shares the same basic beliefs about children's learning and development.

I meet with the six directors as a group every month. We all look forward to that, and each of us benefits. Each of the directors is at a different stage in her development as a director, yet as a group, we share our thinking and support one another. Each director goes back to her program and has a meeting with her staff. Together they learn how to create the kind of program that we and they believe is supportive of children and families.

Several schools and companies have asked us to create and operate programs at their sites. We're choosing carefully where we'll expand and under what circumstances. We must follow the principles that we have agreed on in order to operate.

—*Executive director, not-for-profit multisite corporation*

The director and staff find ways to support each child's development and to help each child learn.

The regulatory system, whether required (such as licensing) or optional (such as accreditation or a state quality and improvement rating system), is another external system that interfaces with early childhood programs. Regulatory systems have different requirements, some of which may coincide with the way the program wants to function and some of which may not.

An important aspect of the director's role in working with the overall system and the related subsystems is establishing an understanding among all personnel (including the director) that they are colleagues rather than a hierarchy. This process is challenging because the difference in daily responsibilities is quite apparent and necessary. However, when all personnel have

developed trust in one another, they can learn to suspend the hierarchy for the sake of discussion. The challenge is to learn how to learn together (Senge, 2006).

1-5 • Administrative Styles and Roles

Although all directors are responsible for administering a program, their administrative styles are unique, so the outcomes of their programs differ. Some of the differences are based on the roles assigned to the directors, whereas others are based on their personalities, knowledge, skills, and attitudes. Their effectiveness in supporting the development of a "we" feeling—group spirit—is a key factor in the success of the organization. Each member of the team must be ready to work in a way that contributes to the overall organization. Other early childhood programs may follow trends—real or imagined—such as, "Kindergarten teachers expect us to have these children prepared to read, knowing how to print all the letters, and able to sit and complete worksheets for a half hour or more." Although that may be the case in some schools, many kindergarten teachers see each child as an individual and work with the child accordingly. The

Crisis: An Opportunity for Positive Change

During the pandemic, electronic forms of communication became a primary form of staying connected. Early childhood educators who may have avoided the use of technology in their work were called upon to conduct Zoom meetings. Although uncomfortable at first, many in our field develop expertise in conducting meetings with families, with their teaching team, and with the program staff, and they even have access to professional development. These new skills have made it easier for families to connect with the teaching team and also for staff to collaborate when it is not possible to meet face-to-face.

Making the Case for Qualified Administrators

Becoming a successful administrator of an early childhood program requires a complex set of skills and abilities. Understanding yourself and others, as well as your roles and responsibilities, is key to your ability to direct a program for young children. Preparation for an administrative position is vital! Reflect on the following questions:

1. What abilities do you possess that will enable you to address the many roles you will fill as a director?
2. What educational preparation and experience are required in your state to become an administrator of an early childhood program? How do these compare to the competencies identified in the NAEYC program administrator definition and competencies? (See **Appendix C**.)

administrator plays an important part in helping early childhood educators, children, and families recognize the role of the current system and how it relates to future systems in kindergartens and above.

1-5a • Styles

Individuals who head an organization often start out using a managerial approach. They determine what has to be done, how it is to be done, and who should do it. The assigned staff member is expected to report back to the manager when the task is completed or at intervals along the way. If that does not happen, then the manager takes responsibility for checking up on the staff member and commenting on the staff member's work or lack of success. This style may be appropriate when many staff members are relatively new in the field and have little background to draw upon. Even in that situation, however, staff members often exceed expectations when given opportunities. Or they may begin to feel like a cog in a wheel, going round and round and never really having an opportunity to be involved.

Other managers use a more laissez-faire approach, leaving much of the decision-making to the staff. Little or no overall structure may leave staff members with no support for decisions they make and confused about how the many independent decisions fit together. The administrator's interest may be directed more toward building outside relations for the benefit of the program. Although building relations beyond a business locale is essential, building a knowledgeable staff that understands the vision and goals cannot be minimized. This approach certainly does not support the development of a program-wide system, although staff members may develop an effective system on their own. There is such a variety of managerial styles that it is impossible to describe each one.

Some directors are natural leaders rather than managers. Others become leaders over time and with mentoring, reading, and studying. As the leader, the director looks to the staff for ideas, initiative, and implementation. Certainly, the leader does not turn over the running of the program to any staff member who steps forward. Rather, the leader supports and encourages staff to become part of the team that will help the program and its programs thrive. Directors realize that they must balance day-to-day reality with the vision that the program's stakeholders

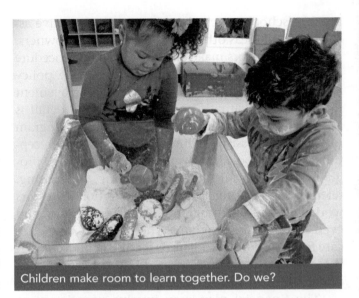

Children make room to learn together. Do we?

have prepared. The director whose leadership skills include the ability to accept and welcome ideas from others demonstrates competence and confidence. (To read more about becoming a leader, see Bruno, 2012; Carter, 2014; Covey, 2013; Sciarra & Dorsey, 2002.)

1-5b • Roles

If all the directors of programs in one state or county were to gather and discuss their roles, the job descriptions would undoubtedly cover a wide range of categories. Some directors teach, perhaps spending half of every day in their own classrooms. Others never teach but are responsible for several programs; they travel between the programs, keeping abreast of two or more sets of circumstances, staff members, children, families, equipment lists, and so forth. Some may be responsible to an industry, a corporate system,

Director's Corner

I had no idea how complex my role as director would be. Such a wide variety of people seem to need me immediately for such a wide variety of reasons. Meeting them all would probably be impossible (and maybe not even wise), but at the end of the day—most days—I know the challenges have been worthwhile. All it takes is one little pair of arms hugging me or one early childhood educator smiling and saying on her way out, "See you tomorrow, Chris!"

—*Director, large suburban preschool*

a public school principal, or a parent cooperative association, whereas others are proprietors and owners.

Some directors make all the policy and procedure decisions; others are in settings where some policy is set by a school system or corporate management team. In other situations, every procedural detail is administered by a board. A director in a large program may have an assistant director, a secretary, a receptionist, and a cook; however, a director of a small program often does all the record keeping, supervising, telephone answering, and meal preparation. Directors work with half-day programs, full-day programs, and even 24-hour care programs. The programs may offer care for infants and toddlers or for older children both before and after school. Sick child care or care of children with major special needs also may be provided.

The financial plan may involve proprietary or agency operations and may or may not be organized to make a profit. Program goals range from providing a safe place where children are cared for to furnishing total developmental services for children, including medical and dental care; social services; screening and therapy; and activities that promote intellectual, motor, emotional, social, and moral development.

Both the program clients' expectations and the community's expectations affect the program director's role. Some communities appreciate directors who actively participate in the affairs of their community council, in lobbying for legislative reform, and in helping to preserve the cultural backgrounds of the children. Others prefer a director who focuses strictly on program business or on preparing children to deal with the demands of elementary school. Directors must blend their personal philosophies with those of the community to achieve a balance. This blending can occur only if a potential director and a board explore each other's philosophies before agreeing on the responsibility for administering a particular program. If the philosophies of the director and those of the program truly are incompatible, then one or the other must be changed.

Sometimes, the director is confronted with a conflict between the two roles. The job description and the expectations of the people connected with the program may dictate that the director be present to greet early childhood educators, parents, and children each day and to bid them goodbye each evening. In between, the director may be expected to be present in case an emergency arises. Simultaneously, however, obligations to the profession and to the community must be met. The director may be asked to speak at a luncheon meeting of a community group that is ready to make a contribution to the program, to attend a board meeting of a local professional association, or to provide information at a session called by the diagnostic clinic to plan for one of the children with special needs who attends the early childhood education program.

Directors, especially those with experience, also have a responsibility to serve as child advocates.

Directors perform many roles, including observing staff and greeting families.

Although the NAEYC Code of Ethical Conduct calls on all who work with young children to "acknowledge an obligation to serve as a voice for children everywhere" (NAEYC, 2011a), directors are more likely to have opportunities to see the broader picture of events in the community and beyond. They can keep informed about important legislative issues and about conditions affecting children and families by reading professional journals and newsletters and by being knowledgeable about local and national news.

Many advocates are working for an all-encompassing system of early childhood programs. For example, when you type "NAEYC" in a search engine, you will receive a list of NAEYC sites with wide-ranging information about the organization. You can also subscribe to online mailing lists such as Exchange Everyday, sponsored by Child Care Exchange, and updates from the Children's Defense Fund. Share your findings with others interested in early childhood, and you will quickly find dozens of sources of related information. As with any website, however, it is important to check legitimacy.

Because directors are leaders and models, not only in their own programs but also throughout the community, staff, parents, and others often look to them for information about advocacy issues. Some directors may post information for staff and parents; others may make a concerted effort to involve people in an action plan. Some may write letters to editors or to legislators, whereas others may testify before various governmental groups. In determining participation in advocacy efforts, each director must weigh the responsibility to be an advocate against the responsibility to the program, as well as consider personal time.

Although many directors work more than a 40-hour week, it is unreasonable and unwise to expect them to regularly devote evening and weekend hours to their jobs. Directors who spend too much time on the job may become physically and emotionally exhausted, leading to ineffectiveness. As models for staff members, directors must demonstrate a balance of personal and program needs. As you study this text, you may wonder how directors do it all. Knowledge, disposition, organization, and support all contribute to their success.

1-5c • Personal Qualities

Directors may become enmeshed in unreasonable workloads because they have become personally involved in the program's work. An effective director should be involved closely with the activities of the program while maintaining distance, which is a difficult combination to attain. The primary reason for the difficulty in achieving this balance is that good directors assume their roles largely because they care about people. Caring is apparent when the director assumes the role of learner as well as early childhood educator and stays abreast of current research while providing this information to staff when it is relevant. Caring is demonstrated by paying attention to detail, such as spelling an unusual name correctly, ordering the special food an early childhood educator would like for a project, and seeing that each board and staff member is notified of an early childhood lecture being held in the community. Caring is regarding the operation of the program in a serious manner, yet maintaining a sense of humor.

For some people, caring is shown in an exuberant manner with lots of enthusiastic conversation, hugging, and facial animation. Others who are just as caring are quiet, seem somewhat reserved, and perhaps move into relationships more slowly. Directors may have other combinations of personal qualities, but the genuine and essential ability to care is the one that makes the difference.

An interesting aspect of caring is that it may be misunderstood. Because they are concerned for others, directors sometimes may have to adjust the style in which they relate to the diverse people with whom they interact. For example, some individuals may be uncomfortable with being touched; if the director unknowingly puts an arm around people who feel this way, they may be annoyed or insulted and be unable to accept the care and concern that is intended.

Being a caring person in the face of all the responsibilities of directing a program can be difficult. At times, a director may feel overwhelmed. The caring director is constantly helping others by listening and providing emotional support for both children and adults, and the director may well need people to respond in kind. Those individuals who become effective directors usually enjoy giving to others—and they seem to thrive on it. However, because they are seen at the program as the source of so much giving, they must seek sustenance from either the caring network at the program or a relative or friend outside the program. Even those people who freely and happily give of themselves sometimes need to receive support and encouragement through recognition and understanding.

Directing can be stressful because the director, although surrounded by people, is in a real sense an isolate. She has no peers in the program and, no matter how loved and respected, is "the boss." This feeling can prevail even when all personnel, including the director, have come together to form a learning system. Overdoing the caring component of the director's role can be damaging to staff, children, and families. The director's role is to support others rather than oversee and manage their comfort. Furthermore, the director is still ultimately responsible to the owner, the board, the main office, funders, and others.

Confiding in one particular staff member would be inappropriate because some of the information with which the director works cannot be shared with anyone at the program. Some directors have established a network of other directors. They meet, perhaps monthly, for a relaxing lunch and conversation. There is reassurance in knowing that other directors have to report child abuse, experience staff turnover, have too many forms to fill out, and have considered quitting. As a group, directors can create ways to solve problems, to support one another, and to heighten community awareness regarding the needs of young children and their caregivers while maintaining confidentiality.

Directors realize they have the power to create healthy, supportive communities for children, families, and staff, but they also recognize that their early childhood training and classroom experiences have not prepared them to carry the vast array of responsibilities of running a program. Until relatively recently, little attention was paid to credentialing directors. Depending on the size, scope, and type of program, directors find they have duties as varied and complex

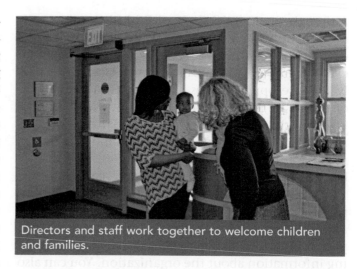

Directors and staff work together to welcome children and families.

as those of major corporate leaders. Yet they have had little or no preparation and often have no opportunity to prepare for the job. Limited mentoring is available.

To be effective leaders, directors must ensure that their own needs are met. Being a martyr—even a cheerful martyr who never takes vacation or sick days—may lead staff to feel somewhat guilty when they recognize and meet their own needs. Competent directors serve as models of balance.

1-6 • Managing the Program

Although directors may have a broad range of roles that bring a variety of personal qualities to these roles, every director is responsible for program maintenance. Completing this task, whatever its parameters, is possible only when the director is skilled and knowledgeable. Throughout this text, the information essential to doing the work of a program director is discussed. When combined with some teaching and administrative experience, this information should help you meet the responsibilities that are required for appropriate program maintenance and enhancement. As with every other professional role, directors need to continue learning and developing. A list of typical responsibilities is included here.

Depending on the organizational structure of your program, some of these responsibilities may be carried out by other personnel. However, the director is responsible for ensuring the following duties are carried out appropriately.

1. Develop goals and objectives in relation to the program's philosophy, placing emphasis on the needs of clients.

Director's Corner

Although I had been assistant director at the program, my role did not go beyond visiting the classrooms to see that all was well. When our director and her family moved to another state, I was offered the director's position. Little did I know how much I had to learn! Where is there a copy of the budget? Do we have enough money? What is expected of me? Do we have to pay taxes? What if someone doesn't pay tuition? Uh, oh, my computer isn't working. How can I get it fixed?

Note to self:

1. Begin creating a program manual.
2. Recruit and train assistant director.

—*Director, nonprofit program*

2. Develop and maintain knowledge of standards created by professional and regulatory groups. Ensure that standards are being addressed appropriately throughout the program.
3. Work with staff to plan a curriculum to meet the objectives of the program.
4. Visit each classroom frequently, preferably daily.
5. Develop a positive working relationship with the board of directors and its committees, placing emphasis on communicating the program's accomplishments and needs to the board.
6. Establish policies for program operation, or become familiar with policies established by the program board, parent corporation, board of education, or other sponsor.
7. Draw up procedures for implementation of policies.
8. Prepare and maintain a manual for board and staff members.
9. Work with licensing agents to meet applicable licensing regulations.
10. Provide adequate insurance coverage.
11. Comply with all local, state, and federal laws relating to the program's operation.
12. Establish and operate within a workable budget.
13. Keep accurate financial records.
14. Pay bills and prepare payroll.
15. Collect tuition.
16. Write proposals and seek other funds for operation of the program.
17. Locate and maintain suitable physical facilities for the program's program.
18. Order and maintain equipment.
19. Develop and maintain a marketing plan.
20. Enroll and group the children.
21. Employ appropriate staff.
22. Provide staff orientation.
23. Coach the staff.
24. Develop knowledge levels and skills of the staff members so that upward mobility within the profession is feasible.
25. Evaluate the program, the staff members, and the children's progress.
26. Develop an effective communication system among staff members through regular staff meetings, conferences, and informal conversations.
27. Provide in-service training for staff and volunteers.
28. Fill roles of other staff members in emergency situations.
29. Plan and implement a family program that is responsive to needs and interests.
30. Explain the program's program to the community.
31. Participate in professional organizations.
32. Become an advocate for children.
33. Continue professional development through reading and attending pertinent courses such as workshops, conferences, and lectures.
34. Provide a regular time and space to foster a learning community among administrators and staff regarding equity issues. Successful program maintenance requires that the director be organized. Just as the director expects early childhood educators to have a plan for the year, month, week, and day, so too must the director have plans. Whether the plans are on a handheld device or on paper, they must be followed to a reasonable degree. Document organization is also essential. Although some paper forms are necessary, computerized systems often simplify documentation. If backed up and stored appropriately, they can be easy to locate, use, and modify. At the same time, discarding items that are no longer needed will make it easier to find working documents.

As you read other chapters of this text, you will notice the many types of files directors are expected to keep, including policy manuals, staff records, child records, and financial data, as well as numerous others. Most, if not all of these, can be made available online if access is restricted to those who have a right to see them. As with all important documents, it is essential to have a backup copy in a safe place. You will find additional information about essential documents on the child care licensing website for your state.

1-7 • Serving as Curriculum Leader

An important responsibility of a director is that of curriculum leader.
Early childhood teacher-preparation programs have at least one course devoted to curriculum. Directors who do not have an adequate early childhood

Working Smart with Technology

Computer Literacy

Today's successful director must be computer literate. Like nearly every other business, the management of child care programs can be greatly enhanced and somewhat simplified through the use of technology. Directors can use technology to organize, store, and complete paperwork; manage finances; apply for program licensing; communicate with parents, staff, and board members; provide staff-development resources; and complete online educational opportunities. For additional information related to the use of technology in today's early childhood programs, check issues of the *Young Children* journal and *Exchange* magazine.

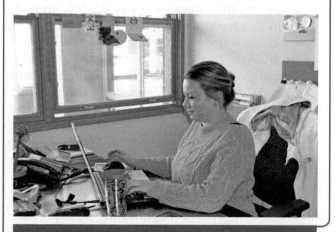

Today's directors must be familiar with the ways in which technology can be used to simplify, organize, and complete numerous tasks.

background should expect to complete at least one course in early childhood curriculum. A section in an administration textbook and course will not suffice, however, because directors as well as early childhood educators must continue to develop their understanding of curriculum and its relation to child development. Read Chapter 11 on the director's role in leading curriculum to learn more about the importance of this topic.

Numerous books are available to help with updating curriculum information. Directors must assume responsibility for becoming familiar with curriculum for the young child, including its sources, goals, and implementation approaches (see the Director's Library in **Appendix H** for suggested reading).

The director is responsible for instituting and maintaining a high-quality curriculum. Consulting with the early childhood educators is expected, but the director must ensure that the goals and philosophy of the program are reflected in the curriculum. Directors who employ new early childhood educators or early childhood educators with little or no background in child development and early childhood education will need to provide detailed coaching (Curtis, Humbarger, & Mann, 2011; Skiffington, Washburn, & Elliott, 2011).

The director must recognize that a curriculum claiming to have already done all the planning and provided all the necessary materials is highly unlikely to be effective. Such programs are usually costly. They may also be unaesthetic, with "art" that should not appear in classrooms. Most important, it is impossible for the best teacher to plan every day's curriculum a year in advance. Such a plan cannot take into account the changing needs of the children. Nor can such a plan address the children's specific cultures, individual backgrounds, or current interests. In short, a preplanned commercial curriculum should be examined carefully to determine whether it addresses the outcomes and uses a theoretical base that fits your organization's mission and that will be significant for children's learning. Recall that when developmentally appropriate practice was first being discussed, hundreds of manufacturers labeled their products, books, and curriculum kits "developmentally appropriate." Today, with the emphasis on research or evidence-based curricula, curricula are being labeled "research based." Before adopting a curriculum on the strength of that claim, make sure you see the research. Find out who the subjects were, what was done, and what the results were. Determine whether the results relate to your program's mission and goals.

Carter and Curtis (2010) remind directors of the importance of having a vision that goes beyond a high score on a state or national evaluation or getting new equipment. They encourage directors to envision how the program and experiences of staff and children *could* be. Directors can help staff, children, and families go beyond "cookie-cutter" environments, equipment, and activities. But first, the director and staff members must reflect, read, and believe in the goal of becoming what they would really like to be, going beyond today's criteria for success.

Because directors can get mired down in day-to-day tasks, turning to resources that focus on *what should be* can renew their delight in the roles of director, staff member, and child.

1-8 • Leading People

Directors sometimes acquire program-management skills and stop there, failing to realize the importance of the skills of leading people. Programs can and do run, at least for a while, without people leadership; however, programs that lack program management quickly close their doors. People leadership and enrichment are at the heart of a worthwhile early childhood education program. Without it, program quality begins to disintegrate, and staff turnover may become a major problem.

Directors can enhance their effectiveness at leading a diverse group of people by developing an understanding of their own interpersonal styles. They also will benefit from studying various approaches to leadership, analyzing their own administrative styles, and determining their strengths and weaknesses in these areas. Most directors have had limited opportunities to acquire this information because they often move into administrative roles because of their effectiveness as early childhood educators. Fortunately, many seminars, books, videos, and DVDs are available to enable directors to learn about interpersonal styles and management approaches.

Many agencies such as Child Care Aware of America (formerly the National Association of Child Care and Resource and Referral Association) offer coaching programs for early childhood educators and directors. Coaching has also become an important component of the Quality Rating Improvement Systems in many states that seek to improve the quality of early childhood programs (Smith, Robbins, Schneider, Kreader, & Ong, 2012). Typically, the director or early childhood educator is observed, followed by discussion with the coach. Although many athletic teams have provided this service for their players for years, it is relatively new in early childhood programs.

The professional director understands that the role involves leadership as well as management. Beginning directors usually have to grow into the leadership role, but with motivation and support, they can acquire the characteristics that will help them develop the entire program's organization as a learning system. Their major contribution will be creating and supporting a team whose members work effectively, efficiently, and positively with one another and with clients. For more information on this topic, see Bruno (2012).

The program's board of directors may be willing to fund some training opportunities for the director, particularly if board members understand and use this type of information. Possibly, a board member could furnish training or related materials.

1-8a • Addressing Conflict Resolution

Another option is to provide total staff or joint board–staff coaching in an approach such as conflict resolution. If well done, this approach to professional development leads to confirming the director's role as leader while establishing the responsibility of each staff member for the success of the program. The sessions can also emphasize the responsibility of the director to see that staff members are involved in decision-making and that their ideas are valued and accepted.

However, satisfaction obviously does not mean that everyone's demands will be met. For example, an early childhood educator may be unhappy about working with a particular assistant whom she regards as lazy. When the early childhood educator approaches the assistant with directions about what is to be done, the assistant does not complete the assigned tasks. In such a case, the director can facilitate a discussion between the early childhood educator and assistant. However, had the early childhood educator and assistant been coached in conflict resolution, they might have solved the problem themselves. This situation certainly does not preclude the director from making a decision about retaining the assistant. However, helping a teaching team learn to work together is often more productive than terminating someone and bringing in a new person. The decision to terminate should only be made when the director is convinced that termination is in the best interest of the children and staff.

Because conflict in any organization is inevitable, preparing people to address it in a straightforward, rational manner can lead to satisfaction. Such an approach also goes a long way to eliminating gossip, dissension, and rumors. Everyone connected with the program—directors, board, staff, families, and children—realizes that their ideas will be respected. They begin to recognize that when disagreements occur, a people-programmed approach to a solution is possible. The director does not have to be the judge in most situations. Individuals are empowered to work together to solve problems.

The basic ideas include bringing together the people who are experiencing conflict. This may be two individuals, the staff and director, or any other combination. When the people who are concerned are together, have them each state what the problem is. Depending on the situation, it may be helpful to write the results of each step for everyone involved to see. If two early childhood educators want to use the playground at 10:00 a.m. and there is room for only one group of children at a time, the problem is stated as a question: "How can playground time be scheduled to everyone's satisfaction?" (Notice how similar this is to the problem of two children wanting the same toy at the same time.)

Next, brainstorm solutions. All solutions are presented for consideration. No comments about a potential solution are appropriate at this point.

Examine the suggestions one at a time, eliminating any with which either party disagrees. Continue until a solution that is agreeable to each party is reached. Agree to try the solution for a set period of time and to renegotiate at the end of that time if necessary.

In summary, the process is as follows:

1. State the problem.
2. Generate solutions.
3. Select a solution agreeable to all.
4. Implement the planned solution.
5. Check after an agreed-upon time to determine whether the solution is working.
6. If it is not working, return to step 1 and continue the process.

The staff and board members who agree to commit to a conflict-resolution type of philosophy use the concept that their customers (children and families) are their first priority as a starting point. By extension, one of the director's priorities must be staff satisfaction, and the board's priority must be a successful outcome for the operation of the program. This approach works well when everyone understands it and accepts this basic principle.

Directors who are quite comfortable with an authoritarian role may find it difficult or impossible to relinquish that role, just as early childhood educators who are convinced that an early childhood educator–directed approach is the only appropriate way to work with children may be unable to provide choices for children. Directors willing to invest time and effort in learning about management usually find they are far more able to lead the staff and clients in ways that are more satisfying to everyone and that the responsibility for the smooth running of the program no longer rests primarily with one person.

The staff-oriented director plans time each day to visit each classroom, greet each staff member, and acknowledge their efforts and successes. He coaches and supports them as they develop new understandings and skills, and he provides honest, sensitive feedback. The staff-oriented director remembers and relates to events and incidents that are significant to staff, children, and families. It may be as simple as commenting to an early childhood educator about how well she managed a frightened child during a thunderstorm by describing specifically the effective approach the early childhood educator used. Perhaps the director stops to greet a child who is proudly bringing his rabbit to school for a visit. Maybe the director telephones a father to thank him for organizing a book fair to benefit the program.

Tending to the personal and professional development of the people associated with a program's program is seminal to the program's success. The manner in which the director carries out tasks that support people is a major contributing factor in program maintenance and vice versa. There is a delicate balance between successfully dealing with the mechanics of efficient program operation and simultaneously creating a caring environment for adults and children.

A director can exhibit human relations skills, care for others, ask for their ideas and opinions, encourage

TeachSource Video Vignette

Leadership Practices in Child Development Programs: Personnel System

This video provides an overview of the many roles that directors of early childhood programs must play. As you view this video, reflect on the following questions:

1. What strategies does this director use to ensure that morale among staff members is maintained?

2. What are the characteristics of a successful director?

them to try new methods, and provide positive feedback. But if that same director does not have the skills and knowledge to accomplish the huge amount of work required of an administrator, the program cannot succeed. Similarly, the director who is task oriented, skilled, and knowledgeable may conduct a program that provides services but never really addresses or satisfies people's needs. Obviously, the director must combine work-orientation skills with communication skills. If skills in either area are lacking, precious time will be wasted doing jobs or rebuilding relationships. Meanwhile, the children will not receive the excellent care they deserve.

Throughout this text, you will read many more details about both program management and leadership, which are required of all directors. You will begin by learning to manage a range of circumstances and tasks. Gradually, as you work at being a manager, if you are committed to developing your abilities and those of the staff, you will find yourself analyzing situations that occur in a child-development program. As you reflect on what you do, why you do it, and the

outcomes of your decisions, you will be creating new knowledge and understanding for yourself—something that no text or instructor can give you. You will be well on your way to moving from the role of manager to the role of leader.

Realizing that you may be feeling overwhelmed at the magnitude of the director's job, we turn now to a discussion of management tools to help you manage a challenging role.

1-9 • Management Tools

Every director has a limited amount of time in which to do numerous tasks and develop many relationships. This work can be accomplished most effectively if the director is well organized. Then, when the inevitable unexpected event occurs, the director will be in a stable position to withstand the demands of the crisis. For example, the director whose financial records are in order may not have extra cash available to replace a broken water heater but at least is better prepared to adjust other budget categories to provide the funds. The disorganized director may not even know the income and expenses anticipated within the next few months in order to adjust the budget to meet the financial crisis. An efficient director can comfortably take time to listen to a group of excited children who burst into the office describing all the worms they found on the sidewalk. But a disorganized administrator may be too busy planning menus that are already overdue. Obviously, administration will not always run smoothly for any director; however, the director who knows about appropriate techniques and uses them is certainly better prepared to cope effectively with the hubbub that often is evident in a child care program.

The use of several management tools can enable directors to administer programs effectively. Key tools for beginning directors include policies and procedures manuals and time-use skills.

1-9a • Policies and Procedures Manual

A manual containing all the program's policies and procedures facilitates the administrator's job.

Generally, when there is a board involved, the board members make the policies, and the director develops the procedures for implementing those policies. For example, the board may establish a policy to admit any child between ages 3 and 5 who can profit from the program. The director then establishes the procedures necessary to accomplish the child's enrollment such as plans for informing the community, distributing and receiving enrollment forms, and notifying parents that their child has been accepted or that the program is full. The director also designs the necessary forms and includes copies in the manual.

When procedures are overly detailed or cover self-explanatory material, they become burdensome and even may be neglected or circumvented by staff members. For example, early childhood educators may be required to fill out a lengthy form to request permission to purchase something for which they will be reimbursed; they also might be required to fill out another form after having purchased the item. At this point, some early childhood educators may decide not to bother with purchasing needed items for their classrooms. They can carry their reaction one step further by disregarding the otherwise accepted procedures for using materials from the central storeroom. Naturally, some established procedures will be unpopular with the staff, but if directors are open about why the procedures are important and are careful about limiting the number of procedures to be followed, they will find that staff members are willing to comply.

Staff input before the establishment of procedures is common, although the director still may need to make some independent decisions. When directors focus on their own need for power instead of on establishing procedures to ensure an operation runs smoothly, it becomes impossible for the staff to feel respected. Staff members for whom every procedure is spelled out have no freedom. How can they be expected to offer freedom to the children with whom they work?

1-9b • Other Contents of the Manual

In addition to policies and procedures, the manual contains the program's bylaws, job descriptions, salary schedules, and information about the program such as philosophy, goals, sponsorship, funding, and perhaps a brief history. Each of these should be dated with the adoptive date. If the manual is large, a table of contents and an index are essential. Placing all materials in a loose-leaf binder enables staff members to add and delete pages as necessary. Each staff and board member receives a manual when first joining the program. It is the holder's responsibility to keep the manual up to date and to return it to the program when vacating the board or staff position.

1-9c • Using Technology

Taking advantage of current technology can be a major time-saver and organizer. Directors who are not already comfortable using computers will find that the initial learning period may be time-consuming. After gaining some confidence in their use, however, the benefits will accrue.

One question often encountered when applying for financial assistance is "How will your company's financial records be maintained?" Financial record keeping and report generation are essential and time-consuming components of the director's role. Completing these tasks using software saves time and promotes accuracy after the data are properly entered. Available software can provide computations for payroll deductions, billing, attendance, inventory, and a range of additional tasks. Most directors have access to a computer and use it for word-processing tasks, but many do not use other components that can be helpful. You may choose to contract with a specialty business for payroll, fiscal reporting, and other functions and yet find it reasonable to manage child information on paper. Nonetheless, analyzing staff time in terms of cost plus the cost of contracted services compared with software cost and reduced staff time to generate comparable information may be surprising. Admittedly, the initial learning time will increase costs. Another important consideration is the professional appearance of computer-generated reports.

To find a software company that fits your program's needs, perform an online search for "child care software." Read information provided by various purveyors and then contact them to ask for a demonstration. You can also check professional journals for reviews of child care software. *Child Care Information*

Growth Mindset Moment

Imagine you have planned to spend the evening writing a term paper that is due the following day. A friend telephones. He is terribly upset about his wife's illness. Think about what you might do.

Now imagine that at 3:00 p.m., you, an early childhood program director, are greeted by an early childhood educator who is leaving for the day and wants to talk about her husband who has just lost his job. You had planned to spend the rest of the afternoon working on the major equipment order that is needed for a board committee report the following morning. You may choose one of the following:

- Listen to the early childhood educator.
- Tell the early childhood educator you do not have time to listen because of the report you must prepare.
- Schedule time the following afternoon to listen to the early childhood educator.
- Choose some other plan.

Any of these choices may be appropriate; the director must make the best choice. But the directors who always find themselves too busy to listen and those who always find themselves spending so much time listening that they must work all evening must analyze why their scheduling problems recur. Think about your own reaction to this situation.

Exchange and *Young Children* are potential sources, as are other directors who are experienced users of business software. At regional and national conferences, ask for demonstrations of software packages. Take a list of questions with you and jot down the answers and your impressions.

Consider which features you would like and which are essential. Ask whether you can buy components if you do not want or need a comprehensive package. Many software companies will offer a complimentary trial disc or access to an online trial.

Your staff may also benefit when you add computer technology to your program. Aside from paperwork (child records, assessments, and curriculum planning) that they may be able to complete more easily and professionally on a computer, they may also use the computer for continuing education courses. The director can set up a calendar of tasks to be completed, appointments, and so forth. Explore these and other uses and packages thoroughly before buying.

1-9d • Time-Use Skills

Some directors study time management as a tool to allocate available time wisely. The board may provide tuition or released time for a director to attend a time-management course or seminar. Several time-management techniques can be acquired easily and put to immediate use.

1-9e • Analyzing Use of Time

As a beginning, directors can analyze how they spend their time by writing down in detail everything they do for several days and how much time is spent on each task. The next step is to make a judgment about which activities have not been enjoyed, have not been done well, or have not been related either to the director's personal goals or the program's goals. When time is frittered away on such activities, less time is available to invest in other, more productive activities. The individual alone can decide which activity should take priority. In some businesses, listening to a client discuss an emotional problem is considered a waste of the administrator's time. In early childhood education, with its focus on children and families, time that the director spends listening may be the most effective use of the available administrative time.

Voice mail, email, and other computer communication approaches help the director keep in touch while controlling the use of time. However, directors must be careful to avoid communicating with families and staff solely through technology. The sensitive director is alert to the need for a live human contact and a handwritten note in some situations.

Although some of the director's tasks may not be appealing, they may need to be done. A director can at least recognize how much time must be devoted to undesirable tasks; then this amount of time can be put into perspective. The director also may decide to devise ways to make tasks more manageable. Of course, if the majority of tasks seem undesirable, the director may choose to change jobs.

The director checks in daily with teachers and children.

1-9f • Grouping and Assigning Tasks

The director who needs to economize on time also may decide to make an effort to read and answer all mail, place outgoing telephone calls, and record financial transactions at a specified time each day. Directors who allocate time for these types of chores and establish the policy that they are not to be disturbed during that time will probably have more time for meeting people's needs during the rest of the day.

Directors also should consider which jobs they must do and which they can delegate. For example, could the janitor let the director know on a regular basis what supplies are needed instead of the director checking on supplies? Perhaps the receptionist can be trained to respond to the general calls for information about the program instead of involving the director in a routine conversation about when the program is open and the age range of children the program serves.

When the program's operation is reasonably under control, additional staff members can be prepared to fill the director's role in her absence, thereby allowing the director to move into the wider community on occasion. It is not appropriate to insist that other staff people do the director's work, but it is appropriate to coach them to assume the role of director temporarily. In this way, both parties can benefit professionally.

1-9g • Planning a Time Line

One of the ways a director develops efficiency is by developing a time line. Jobs that must be done on a regular basis are scheduled, and the director then completes them according to the schedule.

This simple concept curtails procrastination by helping the director recognize that when she postpones a job scheduled for this week because it is distasteful, time and energy are spent thinking about it anyway. Because the job must be completed eventually, no time is saved by waiting until next week; nor does the job become easier. In fact, the director then may be in the uncomfortable position of having to apologize.

Each director must develop a time line based on the personal responsibilities unique to the type of program and the clients' needs. No matter which jobs and time frames are included, writing a time line gives the director and others a clear picture of the work to be done. The time line can be flexible when circumstances warrant, but the basic goal is to adhere to the plan so that regularly scheduled tasks will be completed, and time will be made available for working with people.

Throughout this book, you will learn how important the director's interpersonal relationships are and how they set the tone for the program. Now, as you prepare to learn more about the director's role, you will see this theme reemphasized. It may seem impossible that a director really could focus on establishing a "we" feeling when most of the chapters present an almost overwhelming set of director responsibilities. Nonetheless, directors who know what is involved in the job, who work to acquire the necessary knowledge and skills, and who use a managerial approach

The director ensures that the physical plant is well maintained.

that reflects an understanding of the needs of staff and clients are found in nearly every community.

These competent and successful directors know that being a director is exhausting, and frequently challenging, sometimes frightening, never boring, sometimes lonely, many times hectic, and, yes, even fun.

They also know that being a director—*a really good director*—a leader, a manager, a model, a coach, and a supporter is hard work and time-consuming.

And being a director just often enough is deeply satisfying, even exhilarating, and richly rewarding!

Summary

Effective directors of early childhood programs combine skills, knowledge, and caring to accomplish the following:

- understand their role in the profession of early childhood education within the field of early childhood education;

- understand their responsibility to a wide variety of stakeholders;

- are familiar with the NAEYC Code of Ethics, which provides important guidelines for professional decision-making and practice;

- recognize that early childhood programs operate as complex systems and that the director and staff must work together to identify the characteristics and interworking of systems and subsystems;

- be aware that although directors fill a variety of roles in countless styles, no effective director can let either the management and operation of the program or the care of and communication with people occupy an inappropriate proportion of time;

- identify and be able to perform the numerous responsibilities that directors have as managers of a program;

- understand that the director is responsible for instituting and maintaining high-quality curriculum and ensuring that early childhood educators are able to appropriately implement the curriculum;

- be aware that performing one's role as a leader of people can require a significant amount of skill, time, and energy, but this must be balanced with the management of the program; and

- use a wide variety of tools that support both program management and people leadership.

TRY IT OUT!

1. Discuss with a classmate the personal qualities you possess that might impact your ability to successfully manage an early childhood program. Which of these qualities might prove useful as a director? Which qualities might present challenges to being an effective manager or leader?

2. Discuss the kind of director you would like to be with three members of your class. Review the director's responsibilities as described in the chapter. On which of the director's roles would you like to spend the most time? Which of the roles would you find more challenging? Why would this be the case? Compare and contrast your ideas with those of your classmates.

3. If you were the director, which of the tasks in the director's responsibilities could you assign to someone else? Why would it be appropriate to do so?

REFERENCES

Ashford, S. J., Sytch, M., & Greer, L. L. (2020, August 20). 6 ways a crisis can help you cultivate a growth mindset. *Harvard Business Review*. https://hbr.org/2020/08/6-ways-a-crisis-can-help-you-cultivate-a-growth-mindset

Brockner, J., & James, E. H. (2008). Toward an understanding of when executives see crisis as opportunity. *Journal of Applied Behavior Analysis, 44*(1), 94–115. https://doi.org/10.1177/0021886307313824

Bruno, H. E. (2012). *What you need to lead an early childhood program: Emotional intelligence in practice.* Washington, DC: NAEYC.

Carter, M. (2014). Leadership for sustainable organizations. *Exchange, 215,* 8–12.

Carter, M., & Curtis, D. (2010). *The visionary director: A handbook for dreaming, organizing, and improvising in your center.* St. Paul, MN: Redleaf Press.

Covey, S. (2013). *The 8th habit: From effectiveness to greatness.* Rochester, NY: Free Press.

Curtis, R. R., Humbarger, J. A., & Mann, T. E. (2011). Ten tips for coaching adults: An emotionally healthy approach. *Young Children, 66*(1), 51–54.

Dweck, C. S. (2006). *Mindset: The new psychology of success.* New York, NY: Random House.

National Association for the Education of Young Children. (2011a). *Code of ethical conduct and statement of commitment: Guidelines for responsible behavior in early childhood education.* Washington, DC: Author.

National Association for the Education of Young Children. (2011b). *Code of ethical conduct and statement of commitment: Supplement for early childhood program administrators.* Washington, DC: Author.

National Association for the Education of Young Children. (2019a). *Advancing equity in early childhood education position statement: Recommendations for administrators of schools, centers, family child care homes, and other early childhood education settings.* Washington, DC: Author.

National Association for the Education of Young Children (NAEYC). (2019b). *Professional standards and competencies for early childhood educators.* Washington, DC: Author.

Power to the Profession Task Force. (2020). *Unifying framework for the early childhood profession.* Washington, DC: National Association for the Education of Young Children.

Sciarra, D. J., & Dorsey, A. G. (2002). *Leaders and supervisors in child care programs.* Clifton Park, NY: Thomson Delmar Learning.

Senge, P. M. (2006). *The fifth discipline: The art and practice of the learning organization.* New York, NY: Doubleday.

Skiffington, S., Washburn, S., & Elliott, K. (2011). Instructional coaching: Helping preschool teachers reach their full potential. *Young Children, 66*(3), 12–19.

Smith, S., Robbins, T., Schneider, W., Kreader, J. L., & Ong, C. (2012). *Coaching and quality assistance in quality rating improvement systems: Approaches used by TA providers to improve quality in early care and education programs and home-based settings.* New York, NY: National Center for Children in Poverty. http://www.nccp.org/publications/pub_1047.html

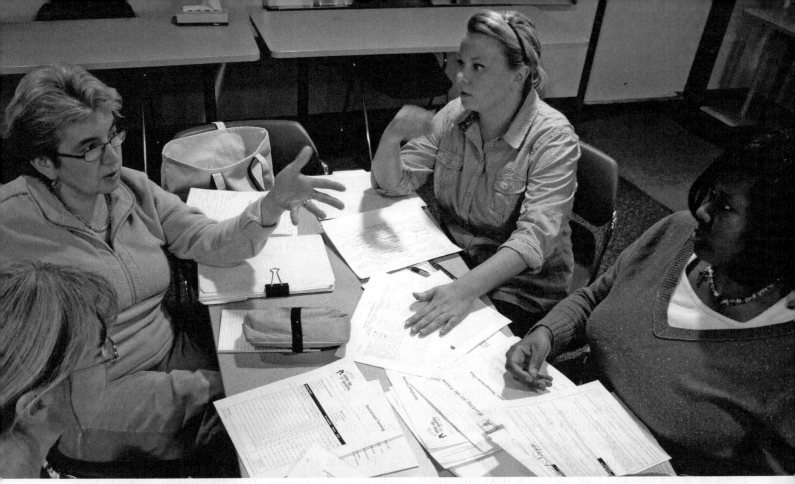

The decision to start a program is best conceived when the voices of multiple stakeholders are heard.

Chapter 2

Assessing Community Need and Establishing a Program

naeyc

Standards and Recommendations Addressed in This Chapter

ADVANCING EQUITY RECOMMENDATION 1 Provide high-quality early learning services that demonstrate a commitment to equitable outcomes for all children.

PROGRAM STANDARD 8 Community Relationships

PROFESSIONAL STANDARDS AND COMPETENCIES: STANDARD 2 Family-Teacher Partnerships and Community Connections

PROFESSIONAL STANDARDS AND COMPETENCIES: STANDARD 3 Child Observation, Documentation, and Assessment

PROFESSIONAL STANDARDS AND COMPETENCIES: STANDARD 6 Professionalism as an Early Childhood Educator

LEARNING OBJECTIVES

After reading this chapter, you should be able to:

2-1 Identify information that will help determine the types of child services needed now and in the future.

2-2 Develop a mission statement that reflects the program's core values.

2-3 Determine the various types of child care needed by families in the region.

2-4 Recognize where the standards of quality practice can be located and how they should be used when determining the program's core values.

2-5 Describe the director's role in obtaining funding for an early childhood program.

2-6 Classify the sources of funding and how they match to the type of program being established.

Creating a new program is an exciting challenge that requires abundant creativity and energy and can be overwhelmingly complex. The process requires program planners to consider multiple factors in a stream of ever-changing priorities. Planners need to be agile decision makers and problem solvers, considering the priority of the day and shifting to the next important decision as needed to get a complete picture of both program and community needs. Clearly, there must be a need for the program. And there must be some driving force in the community, whether an individual or a group, that will generate the creative energy to

- examine the need,
- develop the program mission and values statements,
- decide about the type of program that will fit the need and available resources, and
- identify sources for funding based on the type of program being established.

These major activities will be taking place simultaneously, and each will influence the program that is developed as well as how it will be funded.

The driving force for developing the program might be an early childhood professional with a desire to open a program, or it might be a group of parents who have an interest in providing child care services for their children. Sometimes community agencies choose to expand their services to include early childhood education program. Perhaps there is a need for an expansion of both employer- and public-school–sponsored early childhood education programs. These are a few of the common catalysts for developing a program, and as the need for care continues to increase, it is important to be aware of new forces that impact how a program might be sponsored. The planners, whether an individual, an agency, or a corporation, must be prepared to carry out all preliminary tasks until a director is hired, including dealing with funding issues, undertaking public relations campaigns, and carrying out the needs assessment.

Program sponsors examine what services can be delivered realistically without diluting quality. Usually, it is unrealistic to set up a program that will be responsive to every demand and meet every need. The same can be said for expecting to start a new program and have it fully enrolled immediately. Bringing a new program up to full enrollment can take several years to accomplish, and the fiscal aspect to establish a new program can be daunting. It is better to begin on a small scale, carefully weighing the assured need against the services that can be delivered under the existing financial and resource constraints. Overextending by trying to meet everyone's needs or by providing a large-scale operation that overtaxes the resources is dangerous. Problems also arise when the need is overestimated, and a program is set up that is underenrolled. In either case, program quality diminishes, and children become the victims of impoverished environments. As a result, families do not trust the program to deliver the promised services, and it is doomed to failure.

Director's Corner

I projected it would take us three years to reach capacity in this new program, which is licensed for 115 children. We are now at the beginning of the third year of operation and we are about two-thirds full—so my prediction was on target.

—*Director and owner, franchised program*

2-1 • Assessing the Need

To ensure that the planned program is properly scaled to meet both the size and nature of the community need, doing a needs assessment during the preliminary planning period is important. The assessment can begin before or after a director is designated or hired, but it must be completed before any financial or program planning begins. The purpose of the needs assessment is to determine the number of families and children that will use an early childhood education program service and the type of services desired by those who will use it (see **Director's Resource 2-1**).

2-1a • What Must You Know about Need?

The first step in the needs assessment process is to determine what you need to know. After that has been decided, procedures for collecting the data can be worked out. In some situations, there may be a group of stakeholders who have an interest in the program's success and how it is configured. This group can be helpful in informing the fact-gathering process, but it cannot replace more comprehensive data collection.

2-1b • Number of Families and Children

One way to start the needs assessment is to determine the number of potential families and children that could be served. It is useless to go beyond the earliest planning stage unless families are available to use the service. Simply assessing the *number* of children is not sufficient because number alone tells only part of the story, leaving out the interest, need, or ability to afford to pay for care. If you currently are running a program for preschool children but get many calls for infant, toddler, or school-aged early childhood education program, you are alerted to a need to expand your program offerings. However, between the time you assemble your waiting lists and accomplish the program expansion, many of those families on your list will have made other early childhood education program arrangements. One quick and informal way to decide whether to proceed with a needs assessment is to find out if other programs in the vicinity have waiting lists.

Some planners overestimate the number of families who need early childhood education program and fail to consider how many of those families will use or pay for enrollment in any provided early childhood program. Although the numbers of preschoolers in early childhood education program whose mothers work outside the home has increased sharply over the past six decades, determining who cares for the children of these working families is difficult. As of 2008, "more than 60 percent of children under age [6] and 70 percent of school-age children in 44 states and the District of Columbia have all parents in the labor force" (Children's Defense Fund, 2014, p. F-3). In 2019, this percentage increased to 72.3 percent (U.S. Bureau of Labor Statistics, 2020), and the need for quality early childhood programs has also increased. Unfortunately, many early childhood programs closed during the pandemic, making access to quality early childhood programs even more difficult. Many of these children are with friends or family members, thus making it difficult to determine how many of these working parents would choose early childhood programs or home-based programs for their children if they became available.

One resource for planners is the Early Childhood Longitudinal Study, Birth Cohort, which was sponsored by the U.S. Department of Education's National Center for Education Statistics, Center of the Institute of Education Sciences (Flanagan & McPhee, 2009). This study collected national data on the early home and educational experiences of children from infancy to entering kindergarten. **Table 2-1** shows the type

Table 2-1 Primary type of nonparental care arrangement before kindergarten entry

	Number of Children (Thousands)	Percentage Distribution of Children
No regular nonparental arrangement[1]	699	20.9
Home-based care program	711	21.2
Relative care	499	14.9
Nonrelative care	212	6.3
Center-based care early childhood program	1,850	55.3
Multiple arrangements[2]	84	2.5

[1]The type of nonparental care in which the child spent the most hours.
[2]Children who spent an equal amount of time in each of two or more arrangements.
Source: U.S. Department of Education (2011).

of care and education that 4-year-olds use during the year before kindergarten in the United States.

2-1c • Socioeconomic Level of Families

Many families may be interested in naeyc early childhood education program services but are unable to cover the cost of the services they choose or need. For example, "In 2011 center-based care for infants was more expensive than public college in 35 states and the District of Columbia, and 4-year-old early childhood education program was more expensive than college in 25 states and the District of Columbia" (Children's Defense Fund, 2014, p. 63). When families are unable to pay the high cost of quality early childhood education program outside the home, operators cannot depend on tuition but must seek outside sources of funding if planned programs are to succeed. It is important to know how many families that express a need for assistance actually qualify for state or federal subsidy. When families are able to pay, determining what they are willing to pay for enrollment in an early childhood program or home-based programs is important. It is reasonable to expect that many families can afford to pay up to 10 percent of their total incomes for an early childhood

TeachSource Video Vignette

Prekindergarten Funding Cuts

This video provides an overview of the importance of the impact of state and national policy on the availability of prekindergarten (pre-K) for all children. View the video vignette titled *PreK Funding Cuts*. Reflect on the following questions:

1. Why is it important to know what is happening at the state and national levels in terms of policy, funding, and legislation related to the early childhood profession?

2. How do state and national policies impact local need?

Making the Case for Advocacy

As the need for quality early care and education has become widely accepted by both major political parties in the United States and the push for universal preschool remains a political talking point, it finally seems possible for all young children to have access to rich learning and development experiences before they start school. Although external support is important, there is also a need for those in the field to inform advocacy. Well-intentioned advocates who do not know the complexities of the field can support decisions that ultimately do more harm than good or spend limited resources in ways that do not support children and families effectively. As programs become increasingly diverse and issues of equity are at the forefront of discussions, it is imperative directors ensure their voice is heard. Policies do not always support the needs of the children within our care, and politicians are not the ones working with children daily to understand their need (O'Leary, 2018).

Decisions about how to fund early childhood programs are made quickly and require a commitment from early childhood professionals to inform the decisions being made. To support effective advocacy, directors need to do the following:

1. Seek out ways to become more politically connected and aware of trends in the field. Become a member of email distribution lists such as those associated with the U.S. Department of Education, the National Child Care Resource and Referral Association, the National Institute for Early Education Research, and other organizations that inform the field.

2. Be aware of the local champions for early care and education. Know the local organizations that are advocating for young children and stay connected with them. These organizations will notify stakeholders when there is a call to action.

education program. However, low-income families could be forced to pay as much as 25 percent of their income for an early childhood education program.

2-1d • Ages of Children to Be Served

The ages of participating children affect all program planning considerations and can make a considerable difference in the cost of delivering the service. Determine the number of families who expect to have infants or toddlers participate in the group care program outside the home. Although early childhood education programs have traditionally served 3- and 4-year-old children, the increase in the number of one-parent families and the number of working mothers has increased the demand for infant and toddler care for before and after school as well as for year-round programs for school-aged children. Therefore, when doing the needs assessment, inquire not only about 3- and 4-year-olds who may need care but also about older children and those under age 3.

2-1e • Type of Service the Families Prefer

In assessing the need for a program, one of the first things you must find out is whether families prefer full-day early childhood education program or a half-day program. Working families must have full-day care, and they often will need it for children ranging in age from birth through school age.

Although the demand for half-day programs has decreased because of families with all parents in the workforce, those families who choose half-day programs may use a program for toddlers and 3- and 4-year-olds (sometimes called *preschoolers*) but may prefer to keep infants at home. These families might select a five-day program for preschoolers but often prefer a two- or three-day program for toddlers. Parents who want to become involved in the program may choose to place their children in a cooperative early childhood education program. Other parents may not have the time or the interest in becoming directly involved in the school program.

In some situations, home-based programs may be more suitable than an early childhood center-based program because they can serve a broad range of needs, be available for emergency care, and provide evening and weekend care. The home-based program involves parents taking their children to someone else's home and paying for early childhood education program on an hourly, daily, or weekly basis. These arrangements usually are made individually, although there is often some regulation of the number of children for whom care can be provided in a given home. In a few cases, satellite programs are set up that coordinate home-based programs by an early childhood professional or an employer. Parents make arrangements through the early childhood program or the employer referral service for placement of their children in an affiliated home-based programs. They make payments to the program or make use of this employer benefit. The program or employer, in turn, pays the caregiver and provides the parents with some assurance that the home and the caregiver have been evaluated and that placement for the child will be found if the caregiver becomes unable to provide the service because of illness or other reasons. When the need for care is immediate and critical, it may be useful to locate and organize a few home-based programs while the planning and financing of an early childhood program is underway.

2-1f • How Do You Find Out about Need?

After you have determined the kind of data necessary to substantiate the need for a program, you are ready to decide how to collect the data. Some information for long-range planning can be obtained from census figures, chambers of commerce, or data on births from the health department. However, planners in most communities have access to information from their Child Care Resource and Referral Agency (CCRRA). These agencies are funded through Child Care and Development Block Grants issued to the states through the U.S. Department of Health and Human Services and were created to support families and providers who are interested in affordable and quality early childhood education program. CCRRAs provide technical assistance for a variety of early childhood education program providers, including family early childhood education program, early childhood programs, and after-school programs. They support programs that serve infants, toddlers, preschoolers, and school agers. Many CCRRAs will generate zip code–specific program planning reports that can include the number and type of early childhood education program slots available as well as the number of children by age in an area. Child Care Aware of America (formerly the National Association for Child Care Resource and Referral Agencies) serves as a professional organization and useful resource for early childhood education program. It is important to be connected with the CCRRA that supports your area.

Although the CCRRA should be the first stop for data collection, other detailed information for decision-making will likely be needed to answer all necessary questions.

Data must be collected, recorded, compiled, and analyzed so that the need for the program can be explained to anyone who is involved in initial planning, including members of a sponsoring group or funding agency. The data-collection process might be formal and wide in scope to cover a broad potential population, or it can be informal and confined to a small group of parents and community representatives. Possible methods of collecting needs assessment data include mailed questionnaires, telephone or online surveys, and informal small group meetings.

2-1g • Use of Questionnaires

When a large group of potential clients is sampled, it is wise to develop a questionnaire that can be completed online or can be returned in an enclosed, addressed, and stamped envelope. Questionnaires provide specific data that can be recorded, compiled, and analyzed. These data are usually quite accurate; however, some families may indicate interest in early childhood education program and then no longer need one or decide not to use an early childhood education program when it becomes available. In some communities, the use of online survey tools such as Survey Monkey or Google Forms might be appropriate. Many online tools are free, easy to use, and can design surveys that collect both open-ended and forced-choice data.

The use of online surveys can reduce the cost and also increase the percentage of returns. The task

Working Smart with Technology

Online Surveys

Online survey development tools such as Survey Monkey and Google Forms can provide opportunities for directors to send out surveys to a broad audience. Because online surveys are easy to access and can be returned by clicking the submit button or embedded right into an email message, the return rates are often much higher than pencil-and-paper surveys that must be returned by mail. Online surveys are easy to develop and can include a variety of multiple-choice, true-and-false, and open answers and can include demographic questions. Some free online survey development tools limit the number of questions that can be included. Surveys that limit the number of questions to 10 are more likely to be returned. Another benefit of using online surveys is that they typically include a tool that allows the user to create charts and graphs, which can be useful when presenting survey results to stakeholders. These electronic surveys can be sent out via email quickly and efficiently, and they have tools built in for summarizing, analyzing, and compiling data quickly and easily.

Photograph by Tara Koenig.

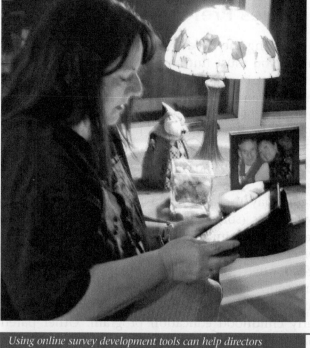

Using online survey development tools can help directors gain insight from a variety of stakeholders quickly and inexpensively. When individuals can access surveys anytime, anywhere, the return rate is much higher.

of developing a good questionnaire or survey can be challenging, and getting the survey into the hands of the right group of people requires thoughtful consideration. Those who determine that a traditional paper-and-pencil survey is best for their project will need to plan for the cost of mailing the survey with an enclosed addressed and stamped envelope to increase the number of returns. They should plan on a lack of response and realize that unreturned questionnaires often create more questions because it isn't clear whether those families are not interested in the service or remain interested but neglected to return the questionnaire. Creating a database to collect and combine both paper-and-pencil surveys and electronic surveys is essential for getting a full picture of family needs as well as information about how families prefer to receive communication.

When developing a questionnaire, it is best to share the intended questions with a smaller group of individuals to ensure the questions are free from bias, use easy-to-understand language, and yield the responses you intend. Having a smaller group review the questions provides the opportunity for meaningful feedback as you develop the survey questions, which in turn is likely to minimize confusion while maximizing meaningful responses and input.

Whether using a pencil-and-paper or online version, developing good surveys or questionnaires can be difficult. The questionnaire must be brief and understandable by the recipient, and the items included also must be carefully selected to provide the precise data that are important to the needs assessment for any given program. Therefore, if you are involved in drafting a questionnaire, it is imperative to analyze the potential audience first so that items are covered in terms the audience understands and that it is family friendly; then you must be sure to include inquiries about *all* the information you need while keeping the form brief.

Before planning the location, type, and size of the program and the ages of children to be served, it is helpful to ask for the following information:

- number of adults in the household,
- number of those adults employed,
- number and ages of all children in the household,
- number of children cared for outside the home,
- number and ages of children with special needs,
- estimate of family income,
- estimate of how much is or could be spent on an early childhood education program,
- days and hours early childhood education program needed,
- preferred location of early childhood education program, and
- whether the family will use the proposed early childhood program when it becomes available.

2-1h • Use of Telephone Surveys

In the past, the use of telephone surveys was a viable option for collecting data. Today, telemarketing has come under public scrutiny, with many households opting out of being called at home by signing up for the National Do Not Call Registry. Although it is unlikely that conducting a needs assessment survey would fall under the Do Not Call Registry guidelines,

Director's Corner

At the beginning of our planning process, we worked with our neighborhood elementary school and received permission to sponsor a booth at the school's fall open house. The booth included some information on the importance of quality early childhood education program and some enticing trinkets that brought children to the booth with their families in tow. We asked visitors to fill out an interest survey and provided both a pencil-and-paper version and an online version of the survey using a laptop computer. We were somewhat surprised to see how many people preferred to use the computer to complete the survey, and many took a card with a link to the survey website with them so that others not at the open house could complete the survey. We were also able to talk with the principal who offered to include a link to our survey and a short article in the school's electronic newsletter, which generated a lot of interest and greatly increased the number of completed surveys. When it came time to compile the data, we were able to input our pencil-and-paper data into the online version. The online survey automatically analyzed our results and presented our data in a series of colorful and easy-to-understand charts and graphs, which we used as we presented our findings to potential funders.

—*Director, private nonprofit program*

the public's annoyance with telemarketing calls is clear, and many families use caller ID to screen their calls. Many families also rely on cell phones versus landlines, which makes acquiring lists of accurate phone numbers challenging. When an existing phone list is available and a telephone survey is determined as the option of choice, then be prepared for a time-consuming and costly task, especially if you expect to include a large number of families. One way to reduce both cost and time is to call a sample of the large potential population to obtain fairly accurate information about the total group without calling each family. If you are involved in an extensive needs assessment program, you should consult a marketing specialist about appropriate sampling techniques. On the other hand, if you have access to a group of volunteers who can do some telephoning and the population to be contacted is small, then calling prospective families may yield accurate data, provided that the questioning is conducted uniformly and that the data collected are what you need to know.

To ensure uniformity, telephone surveys also must use a questionnaire. The survey caller verbally asks the questions and fills in the questionnaire. The same considerations that apply to mailed or online questionnaires apply to those used in telephone surveys: understandable wording, complete coverage of data, and brevity.

Growth Mindset Moment

Think for a moment about being called by someone doing a telephone survey. What was your reaction to the call? Was the call at a convenient time, or did it interrupt your study time or dinner? Did the caller get to the point quickly or waste your time, inquiring about your health or if you were having a good day? What led you to agree to participate in the survey or decline and hang up? Recalling your reaction to a telephone survey can help you gain insights into how parents might respond to a needs assessment telephone survey.

Now consider an online survey that you have taken. How did this experience compare to the telephone survey? Did you complete the online survey at a time that was convenient to you? During which experience were you more likely to provide complete and accurate information?

2-1i • Small Group Meetings

Holding informal group discussions with families who express interest in having their children participate in a program is a good way to obtain information about need. Small group meetings are practical when the potential client population is defined (for example, church members, apartment-complex dwellers, employees of a particular company) or when the size of the community or neighborhood limits the number of families who might use the program. Informal meetings have the advantage of establishing a basis of trust and open communication between the service providers and the families who will use it. Without the constraints of a specific questionnaire, parents are free to discuss their values and goals for their children, their unique needs and desires in terms of their family situation, and their feelings about different types of programs that might become available. However, this informal data-collection process yields information that is often not as valid, is less reliable, and is more difficult to tabulate and analyze than questionnaire data. You may find it beneficial to work out a combination of the informal discussion and formal questionnaire procedures by holding a series of small group meetings in which parents fill out a brief questionnaire at the close of the meeting. Needs assessment data that are collected through both formal and informal channels can both provide the basis for the decision about whether or not to have a program and furnish information about family values and goals that will enter into formulating the program philosophy. Of course, the values and the educational interests of the program planners and the director also will have a significant impact on the philosophy.

2-2 • Program Mission and Values Statements

The characteristics of an early childhood education program should emerge from the mission and values of the program. Developing the mission and values statements is part of the planners' strategic planning process. These carefully crafted statements guide directors' decisions about hiring new staff and designing appropriate professional development to ensure that all staff members are prepared to implement a program consistent with those statements. These statements should also be included in the program handbook, providing families and personnel with details about how the stated mission and values are present throughout all aspects of the program. For a specific example of a mission and values statement, see the Program Handbook example provided in **Appendix E**.

2-2a • Decisions about the Mission and Values Statements

Mission statements must reflect the principles of our profession and provide the indicators of quality that define good practice. Decisions about the mission of a program will also emerge from the data that are gathered in the initial planning process. If the data suggest that a full-day, 12-month program is needed for preschoolers of middle-class professional families who work from 8:00 a.m. to 5:00 p.m., then the mission of the program will reflect this need. A quite different mission statement would likely be developed for:

- children of military families who are frequently deployed overseas,
- children of schoolteachers who need 9 or 10 months of care, and
- children whose families are in poverty and work split shifts.

The cultural, educational, and socioeconomic levels of the child and families are among many factors that impact how the mission statement is developed. Understanding the construction and purpose of mission and values statements is important for planners engaged in the strategic planning process.

Growth Mindset Moment

Think about the three different groups of children and families previously described. How might the mission of each group be crafted to reflect the needs of the children and families to be served?

Growth Mindset Moment

Think about a program that you have taught in or observed. Identify the assumptions about how children learn in this program. Try to formulate an example from that classroom experience that supports the assumption about how children learn. Think about activities you may have planned or behaviors you encouraged, and try to determine the area of development you most value. What are your assumptions about how children learn?

2-2b • Mission Statements

A mission statement briefly defines the focus or purpose of the organization. It appears on numerous program documents, including personnel policies, the parent handbook, brochures, newsletters, the program website, all promotional and fundraising materials, as well as stationery and news releases. Having a well-developed mission statement is an indicator of program quality. Sections in both the Accreditation Standards from the National Association for the Education of Young Children (NAEYC) and the Program Administration Scale (PAS) require a mission statement. Under "Documents Needed," the Program Planning and Evaluation section of the PAS indicates that programs must have a mission or vision statement. Vision or mission statements are mentioned in the NAEYC Accreditation Criteria for Leadership and Management Standard.

2-2c • Developing a Mission Statement

A mission statement should clearly and concisely state the purpose and business of the program in a manner that resonates with the current staff and stakeholders. Radtke (1998) recommends that mission statements be revisited every 5 years to "ensure relevance" and should also answer the following three questions:

1. What are the opportunities or needs that we exist to address? (the *purpose* of the organization)
2. What are we doing to address these needs? (the *business* of the organization)
3. What principles or beliefs guide our work? (the *values* of the organization) (Radtke, 1998, p. 2)

Figure 2-1 shows an example of how one university-affiliated program answered Radtke's three questions to develop a mission statement.

Developing a mission statement

What is the purpose of the organization? To provide a high-quality early childhood program of care and education for young children and professional development for early childhood college students and practicing professionals.

What is the business of the organization? To provide opportunities for a highly qualified staff of early childhood educators to work together to learn about, critically reflect on, and collaboratively develop and deliver high-quality and research-supported programs to young children and seek opportunities to share their practice with students and practicing early childhood professionals.

What are our values? The staff early childhood educators and stakeholders value high-quality care and education programs for young children within a curriculum framework that is child centered and supports intentional teaching, integration, and inquiry. We value curriculum that:

- is created jointly by children and adults;

- is assessment supported versus assessment driven;

- is emergent at times and negotiated at others so that children investigate important topics in authentic ways;

- is intentional so that development and learning are supported throughout the daily routine and environment; and

- integrates early learning content, developmental domains, and family culture in personally meaningful and socially relevant ways.

The mission of this program is to:

- provide a high-quality early childhood program care and education for young children while demonstrating an assessment-supported, child-centered, emergent, integrated, and science-focused curriculum;

- work together as reflective decision makers who seek to improve the quality of care and education of early childhood programs for young children by mentoring early childhood graduate and undergraduate students and sharing research-supported practice with the larger early childhood community

FIGURE 2-1

2-2d • Decisions about Core Values and Value Statements

Establishing the core values that will serve as the foundation of the program is a critical step in establishing a meaningful and well-justified program. Core values come from a sound understanding of child development and the best practices in the field. The value statements are important in determining the curriculum and teaching strategies that reflect the program's core values. Suppose a group of program planners identify one of its core values as "children learn through inquiry," meaning that children come to understandings about things and people in their world through the process of inventing ideas and developing hypotheses. A value statement that reflects this core value might be developed that identifies children as autonomous investigators. In turn, decisions about how classrooms are set up would support this core value. A classroom guided by this value statement would replace planned activities set up to teach letters or numbers with a print-rich environment that includes many books, charts, and a writing center, and children would enjoy the use of math games, measuring tools, and simple machines such as pulleys and pendulums. Consider **Table 2-2** and note how core values are transformed into value statements.

Table 2-2 Sample core values and value statements	
Core Values	**Value Statements**
Children are:	Therefore we provide:
Social beings	Opportunities for children to work and play with each other and with responsive adults.
Independent learners	Environments where children make choices about their learning with adult support when needed.
Problem solvers	Children with a variety of open-ended experiences and authentic materials that prompt a sense of wonder.
Communicators	Opportunities for children to communicate about their wants, needs, and wonderings within a respectful and responsive environment.
Literate learners	A print-rich environment where children see a purpose for letters, words, and numbers and have opportunities to use this emerging knowledge in meaningful ways.

Having a director who fully understands and supports the core values is important because he or she will be the educational leader responsible for the implementation of a program that supports these values. When the planners have highly specific ideas about either mission or values or a new director is hired for an ongoing program, then the new hire is expected to operate within the program's adopted framework. Frustrations over incompatible values or philosophies can create unworkable teaching situations for dedicated staff members who need the support of the new director (Kuykendall, 1990, p. 49). If the core values of a program are based on the philosophical assumption that the child is born a *tabula rasa* (meaning the mind at birth is a "blank tablet" to be written on by experience; the stated goal of education is to fill that tablet with experiences), then it is helpful if the program director is committed to that same philosophy. A director with a cognitive developmental or constructivist point of view who does not accept the tabula rasa premise will find it difficult to develop or direct an educational program that reflects the stated program philosophy. For a discussion of constructivism and a comparison of programs sharing the cognitive developmental orientation, see DeVries and Kohlberg (1988).

Value statements typically emerge from a philosophical position. The need for a philosophical position as a base for program design seems clear (Decker, Decker, Freeman, & Knopf, 2009). Whether it is based on developmental theory, social learning theory, the notion of multiple intelligences, or behaviorism, a well-grounded philosophical foundation gives substance and validity to the program. The program philosophy underlies most programmatic decisions. It should reflect the values, beliefs, and training of the director as well as the wishes and interests of the program planners and families who will participate in the program. When administrators attempt to implement programs for which they are unable to state a philosophy nor substantiate their curriculum and accompanying pedagogical strategies in terms of that philosophy, they risk internal confusion, lack of unity, loss of teamwork, and an inability to help parents understand their true purpose.

2-2e • What Is the Basis for Choosing a Philosophy?

When programs are planned and implemented, the curriculum content and teaching strategies either consciously or unconsciously reflect a philosophy that is based on:

- assumptions about how children learn,
- values of the program planners and the families involved, and
- views of the planners regarding basic issues in education.

Although the three areas that influence the philosophy of the program can be discussed separately, they interact with one another and, in reality, are almost impossible to identify and delineate.

2-2f • Assumptions about How Children Learn

In the broadest sense and most simplistic terms, assumptions about how children learn fall into three major categories: environmental, maturational, and interactional. The environmental position assumes that the child's learning depends on extrinsic motivators in the form of tokens, compliments, smiles, gold stars, and so forth. The adult decides what the child is to learn and then plans lessons designed to teach content and skills. One of the basic assumptions of this position is that anything worth teaching is also observable and measurable. Attempts to relate this particular assumption about learning to some theoretical base usually lead to the mention of people such as Thorndike, Watson, and Skinner.

Goals based on the environmental assumptions about how young children learn in preschool classrooms might include the following:

- Children learn to recite the alphabet through alphabet songs and stories.
- Children practice rote counting during group time and while at play.
- Staff help children with letter recognition by using flash cards and word games.
- Group-time activities include color recognition and color-naming exercises.

The maturational position assumes that there is an internal driving force that leads to the emergence of cognitive and affective systems; this, in turn, determines the child's readiness for mastery of developmental tasks. Mastery of the task is itself rewarding, so the reinforcement is based on intrinsic satisfactions derived from accomplishment and task mastery.

Learning is controlled by an internal growth force, and the child selects from various offerings, thereby learning what she is ready to learn. The theorists associated with the extreme maturational position are Freud and Gesell.

Goals based on maturational assumptions about how young children learn might be that children in the program:

- show interest and choose to work in various interest areas in the classroom,
- choose activities based on their interests and their rhythms, and
- show evidence of satisfaction after having mastered a task (verbally, with actions, or with body language that communicates pleasure in the accomplishment).

The interactional position assumes that learning results from the dynamic interaction between the emerging cognitive and affective systems and the environment. The interaction with both the material and the human environment is driven not solely by an internal force but also is nurtured, facilitated, and intensified by the timely intervention of significant adults in the environment. The child is intrinsically motivated to select appropriately from the environment, but the adult is responsible for preparing the environment and for timely and appropriate questions and ideas to alert the child to the learning opportunities in each situation. The adult facilitates the development of intellectual competence. The impetus for the interactional approach came from Jean Piaget's work. Additional insights into the interactive theoretical perspective come from Lev Vygotsky's work in which he emphasized the important connection between a child's social and psychological worlds for cognitive development (Bodrova & Leong, 2006, p. viii).

Goals based on interactional assumptions about how young children learn might be that in all classrooms the following is true:

- Play is cherished, and play spaces are rich with learning opportunities.
- Children are encouraged to explore and create.
- Children enjoy successes that lead to greater self-confidence and independence.
- Staff members value and are responsive to each child's special abilities, learning style, and developmental pace.

2-2g • Beliefs, Values, and Attitudes in Action

Additional considerations in developing a mission and vision statement involve how the organization embodies these statements in daily

Crisis: An Opportunity for Positive Change

During the COVID-19 global pandemic, many early childhood programs were required to temporarily shut down over health concerns. Several programs evolved to accommodate the needs of families, including reducing ratios, expanding the ages of children eligible by applying for additional temporary licensure, and adapting programming in the center to meet health and safety needs. As you begin to make plans for opening up a center and draft a handbook, it is important to consider what contingency plans will be considered for families; this is also true of natural disasters, community emergencies, or other situations that can dramatically change the look of daily practice. Although not all changes can be planned in advance, it is a good idea to consider including some possible emergency plans as you draft your mission and vision statements within the handbook.

Growth Mindset Moment

Have you ever thought about how you believe young children learn? This is a critical question to ask yourself as a leader in your program and leader in the field. Do you view yourself as a traditionalist, where children are passive recipients of knowledge and work independently at their own speed? Or do you view yourself as a constructivist, where children actively construct their own understanding and knowledge and learn through social interactions with peers? Many early childhood programs make the decision to focus on either developmental or academic outcomes, reflecting the differences between these two ideals. What implications do these values have on your thoughts about creating a program?

operations and in its relationships with families. Puig, Erwin, Evenson, and Beresford (2015) describe how guiding values and beliefs was a common theme among families enrolled and had an impact on the relationship between families and early education programs. Four key areas to contemplate are planning, instructing, assessing, and implications for daily practice. When establishing a handbook that connects values to practice, ask the following questions:

- Planning
  - How will we plan for ways to assess student learning?
  - What do meaningful learning experiences in the classroom/program look like?
- Instructing
  - How will lessons be implemented?
  - How do we ensure children are learning in meaningful ways?
- Assessing
  - Through what means is learning documented?
  - What tools are used to measure children's growth, development, and learning?
- Implications
  - What systems or practices support teacher reflection?
  - How are those reflections used to plan future experiences?

These questions get to the heart of the beliefs, values, and attitudes inherent through each classroom. The effective director takes on a leadership position in supporting curriculum development as well as ensuring that daily operations run smoothly. It is imperative that all staff members have a common understanding or shared belief in how children learn, what values are inherent in those beliefs, and the attitudes in action that impact realizing the mission and vision of the organization.

This process of determining beliefs, values, and attitudes and how it will impact daily programming and curricular practice is sometimes referred to as a *backward design*. Wiggins and McTighe (2007) describe how "given a clear and robust mission and guiding principles for learning, the particulars of schooling—curriculum, assessment, instruction, roles of staff, policies, structures, use of resources— are derived from the results desired" (p. 5). In essence, to achieve the desired destination as a

> ## Growth Mindset Moment
>
> Think about the following mission statements. How well do they answer Radtke's three questions?
>
> - Mission—To develop and operate a model professional early childhood education program that meets the diverse needs of the children and families in the communities we serve.
> - Mission—To enhance the cognitive, social, and emotional well-being of the young children in our program and to serve the diverse needs of their families.

program, you must start by examining your beliefs to chart a path to success.

Although many people argue that decisions about how programs operate, missions are developed, and visions are refined simply by developmental standards determined by individual states, that is not the case. Wiggins and McTighe (2007) describe how state standards may reflect a few of the goals of a program, content-specific benchmarks should not be the sole focus of programming, especially in the early childhood profession. Reflecting on how you believe children learn, along with establishing a collective vision with your staff, provides a whole picture for development and early learning supported by the programming you will provide to children and families.

2-2h • Values of the Program Planners and the Families

The program philosophy is influenced by the priorities parents and planners set for the children. When questioned, most administrators state that they value the optimum development of the whole child: her or his social, emotional, physical, language, aesthetic, and cognitive development. However, when the philosophy or the ongoing program is analyzed, it may become clear that priorities actually do exist. Concern for the development of the whole child is the stated position, but careful analysis reveals that cognitive outcomes are given priority over social and emotional goals or vice versa.

2-2i • Views on Basic Issues in Education

Several basic issues in education are implied, if not directly addressed, in its philosophy and its value statements. One of these issues is content versus process, which is sometimes interpreted as school orientation versus human orientation. Those who subscribe to the content orientation support the notion that the goal of education is to provide children with content that enables them to succeed in school as it exists. Their focus is on preparation for the next step in schooling; achievement is evaluated by relating each child's progress to norms or grade level. The goal of education for those who support human orientation, or what might be viewed as the developmental point of view, is the upward movement of the child as an independent learner to higher levels of intellectual competence. The process of learning and the development of problem-solving skills are more important than content mastery. Autonomy, collaboration, and cooperation are valued, and the years in school are considered an integral part of life itself. The major goal is for children to become autonomous problem solvers (Kamii, 1982). Schooling is not viewed as either preparation for later school or preparation for life. Achievement is not dependent on reaching a norm or the next grade level but on the ability to cope with the here and now.

Today, planners and program directors must find a way to be consistent with their philosophical orientation and also develop a program that is both content and process focused. The reality of the school readiness movement, the need to overcome the achievement gap, and accountability pressures from federal, state, and local funders call upon leaders in early care and education to find a way to advocate for childhood as a unique and valuable stage in the human life cycle while providing all children access to rich and challenging experiences that support early learning content. These demands do not need to be mutually exclusive; with careful planning, it is possible to put a framework in place for curricular decision-making that allows early childhood educators to reflect both a grounded philosophy of how children learn and to develop with the realities of societal demands for school readiness, content knowledge, and accountability.

As the federal government has become more involved in policy and decision-making over the past several decades, the discourses about kindergarten readiness have intensified. With increased accountability in the primary grades, a debate among early childhood professionals has surged. This debate about whether school should be developmentally focused or academically focused is a fundamental one in the field of early childhood education: Should kindergarten readiness and, in turn, early childhood program practices emphasize social-emotional skills or more easily measured academic skills? Little and Cohen-Vogel (2016) provide an analysis of how this debate has changed since 1965, and conclude the vision for both foci—developmental or academic—is the same playful, child-centered program we expect though the emphasis on learning outcomes lies exclusively with those who have an academic focus.

At first glance, discussions about philosophy may seem unrelated to the problems of starting a program or to taking over as director of an ongoing program. However, making program decisions is impossible without a commitment to an agreed-upon philosophy. Identifying the elements of this philosophy will be addressed in more depth in Chapter 11.

2-3 • Types of Programs

After the need has been assessed and **naeyc** the mission and values statements are written, another major item to be determined is the type of program to be offered. After deciding on the type of program in terms of sponsoring agency and funding, the decision about ages of children to be served must be made before making arrangements for site selection, licensing, budgeting, staffing and equipping the program, and enrolling the children.

Decisions about the type of program will depend on the assessed need, the development of the mission and values statements, the sources of available funds, and the source of the impetus for the program. Not-for-profit programs receive financial support through government funding or subsidies from sponsoring agencies, whereas proprietary programs are supported by capital investments of individuals or corporations. Many different terms such as *preschool, nursery school, child care center,* and *early education center* are used when referring to early childhood education programs, but there is nothing inherent in these labels that identifies what type of program or philosophy is practiced in the program. As mentioned in Chapter 1, the profession of early childhood has moved away from using such terms in an effort to establish clarity around the career pathways and elevate the view of our work as a whole (Power to the Profession Task Force, 2020). A wide range of program philosophies, including Waldorf, Reggio Emilia, and those based on Piaget's or Maria Montessori's teachings, to name a few, can operate under any of the program types discussed in the following section.

2-3a • Not-for-Profit Programs

Public and private not-for-profit programs (sometimes called *nonprofit*) range in size and scope from the small cooperative preschool to the large, complex, agency-sponsored early learning program. Although *not-for-profit* and *nonprofit* may be differentiated for legal reasons in some states, the terms are used interchangeably in most places.

2-3b • Individual Cooperative Programs

Cooperative programs, often called *parent co-ops*, are owned and operated by a group. Parents are expected to help in the classroom, so the small co-op usually functions with one or two paid staff members, one of whom is usually a teacher or director. Costs are kept at a minimum, and tuition is lower than in other programs. Most co-ops are half-day programs because they require parent participation; however, some co-ops are organized as full-time early learning programs.

2-3c • Agency-Sponsored Programs

Many not-for-profit early childhood education programs are sponsored by community agencies such as church groups, labor unions, service agencies, neighborhood houses, and United Way organizations. These programs may be set up as full-day early education programs for working families or as half-day enrichment programs. Such programs are found in both rural and urban areas and can serve both low- and middle-income families, depending on how much support is provided by the sponsoring agency. Agency-sponsored programs sometimes receive partial support from a sponsor such as United Way and obtain the remaining support from tuition, government funds, or grants.

2-3d • Government-Sponsored Programs

Head Start is perhaps the best known of the federal government-sponsored, early childhood education programs and is the nation's leading investment in early childhood profession. Head Start provides a range of comprehensive education, health, nutrition, parent involvement, and family support services, and it has primarily served at-risk children and their families since 1965. Head Start actually consists of two programs: Head Start and Early Head Start. Head Start is a comprehensive early childhood development program primarily serving at-risk preschool-age children and their families (National Head Start Association, 2011).

Head Start is administered by the Administration for Children and Families in the U.S. Department of Health and Human Services. Head Start funds are sometimes distributed through and monitored by the local Community Action Agency. Funding for Head Start programs may go to public school systems, universities, and public or private not-for-profit agencies. Larger grantees such as public schools or universities often find creative ways to partner with other agencies to provide opportunities for more families to receive the benefits of this comprehensive government-sponsored child care program. For example, a public school may set up a partnership with a church child care program that serves low-income families. The church, in collaboration with the public school, can offer Head Start income-eligible families various health and social service benefits with the help of a Head Start family advocate. The Head Start funding also helps the church cover program expenses for these families. Many unique collaborative arrangements are being worked out between and among various types of child care agencies across the country, all in an effort to better serve children and families.

Head Start programs may be based in an early childhood or home-based program and may provide child care on a full-time or half-time basis. Formerly just for preschool children, Early Start, a part of Head Start, is now available to children under age 4. Those who receive funds from Head Start (grantees) are mandated to serve children with disabilities (10 percent of enrollment opportunities) who must be mainstreamed and receive a total care package through direct services from the grantee or from other resources in the community.

The Department of Defense and the Department of Veterans Affairs also sponsor child care programs in some regions of the country, as do some state governments. Of course, there are many military programs (see the "Military Programs" section).

2-3e • Government–Community Partnerships

A recent expansion of government-supported, not-for-profit programs include partnerships between early childhood programs and community-supported efforts. Seattle, for example, has established the Early Childhood Education and Assistance Program, which is funded by the state of Washington's Department of Early Learning alongside the city of Seattle and provides a variety of choices for a full year of enrollment in an early childhood program for eligible 3- and 4-year-olds. In Dayton, Ohio, a partnership between local philanthropic organizations along with an increase in local taxes was established to provide a full year of affordable, quality preschool to all age-eligible entrants. As awareness for the importance of quality early learning experiences increases, so does the community interest and investment in these types of programs. Conducting a needs assessment for the community and working with community partners can determine if this type of partnership is right for your community.

2-3f • Public School–Sponsored Programs

Most states are funding some prekindergarten programs, and many of these are in public schools (Neugebauer, 2003). Full-day or half-day public school programs are staffed by people hired through public school personnel offices, and the programs are housed in public school buildings. Local school boards, public school administrators, and teacher unions typically have a voice in making policy as well as in teacher and program evaluation. The building principal is the appointed instructional leader, and these programs fall under the jurisdiction of the superintendent of public instruction or the commissioner of education at the state level.

Practices in public preschools tend to focus on academic success, school readiness, and standardized testing, but advocates for quality programming in preschools are challenging this academic readiness position of some public school instructional leaders. With the current trend toward universal prekindergarten, additional government funds are flowing into public schools to support the interest in offering a prekindergarten experience for all children. The aim in some states is to increase the amount of state funding that comes to those systems offering prekindergarten programs.

This could potentially lead to prekindergarten programs that focus on instruction and dilute the caring dimension of the daily interactions between early childhood educators and children. Some states are making an effort to combine public and private funding, which may be a way to have a system that allows for a combination of education plus the caring and emotional support that young children require. Although this could potentially lead to a "pushing down" of academic expectations from kindergarten to 12th grade into the prekindergarten classroom, it provides an opportunity to narrow the gap between early learning and formal school experiences. Directors and administrators working within these systems must advocate for the most effective practices, ensuring that responsive relationships and care for the development of the whole child drive decision-making.

Before- and after-school programs for school-aged children often are housed in public schools. Some are also public school–sponsored, and others are run by community agencies or service groups such as the Salvation Army and YMCA. The public school–sponsored programs may be staffed by teachers in the building or by high school or college students who are free during early morning and late afternoon hours. Often the person in the school system responsible for the preschool programs also oversees these

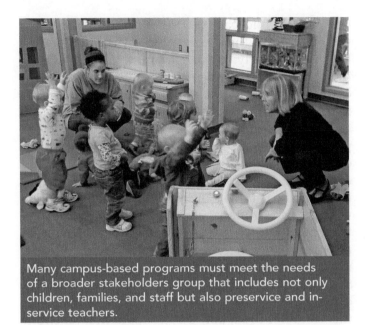

Many campus-based programs must meet the needs of a broader stakeholders group that includes not only children, families, and staff but also preservice and in-service teachers.

before- and after-school programs and other wrap-around programs, and the building principal is the on-site administrator in charge.

2-3g • Campus Child Care Programs

Laboratory (or demonstration) schools and child care programs for children of students, faculty, and staff are two types of programs found on college campuses. The programs may be sponsored and subsidized by the college or university or by government funds. These programs often provide facilities for research, observation, and teacher training. They may be full-day or half-day and may charge full or, in some cases, partial tuition for those affiliated with the university. In places where student groups as well as the university itself offer support for the care of students' children, the students pay minimum tuition for their children, and the program hours are flexible to accommodate the students' course schedules.

2-3h • Privately Sponsored Not-for-Profit Programs

Many large industries, hospitals, and apartment complexes include early education programs in their facilities and offer services for the children of their employees and residents. These not-for-profit programs are set up for the comfort and convenience of the employees and residents. The hours are often flexible; in some cases, fees are on a sliding scale to encourage full use of the available facilities. The fees for hospital- and industry-operated programs may be part of an employee benefit package implemented through the use of vouchers, direct payment to the caregivers, or a child care allowance to the employee (see **Director's Resource 2-2**).

Some employers offer a *dependent care assistance program* or *dependent care reimbursement program* that allows employees to set aside a certain amount of their yearly pretax salary for child care expenses, thereby providing a substantial tax savings to the employee.

Employers are realizing they cannot meet the challenge of fulfilling employees' child care needs on their own and are reaching out to the early learning community for help in managing on-site programs. Some employers contract with programs for a reduced fee or funded slots for employees, whereas others prefer to contract for information and referral services in the area but are not involved in service delivery.

2-3i • Profit-Making Programs (Proprietary)

Although much is written about not-for-profit programs such as Head Start, United Way centers, and public school programs, a large majority of the early childhood education programs in the United States are proprietary. These programs are set up to provide a service that will make a profit.

2-3j • Independent Owner

Many full- and half-day child care programs are owned and operated by solo individuals or small groups (partnerships or small corporations). In the case of the proprietary program, tuition is usually the only source of income, and the operators frequently have budgeting and financial problems, although some proprietary and nonprofits can obtain supplementary funding from other sources, including state funds. The proprietary operators may be able to draw a salary from the tuition that is paid by families using the service, but the operators rarely make a profit over and above that because of the high cost of operating a quality program. Sometimes, proprietors open more than one program in a community or region and begin a small chain operation. Although it is difficult to make a profit from the small chain, quantity buying and shared service costs sometimes can reduce the cost per child and increase the possibility of making a profit over and above operating expenses.

2-3k • Corporate Systems

Large, for-profit child care organizations are operated by a parent company that develops a prototype and sets up a number of programs throughout a state or region or across the nation and into Canada. Some of these corporations have gone public, and their stock is traded on the New York Stock Exchange. These national child care chains operate under a central administration that furnishes the financial backing and is usually powerful in setting the policy and controlling the program. There often is a prototype building and program that are publicized by identifiable slogans, logos, brochures, and advertisements. Some corporate systems operate all programs carrying the chain name, whereas others work on a franchised basis. In the latter case, an individual purchases a franchise from the parent company for a basic purchase price and then pays the company a percentage of gross intake for the ongoing use of the name and the program. In addition, the parent company supplies guidelines for fees, sample documents, brochures, advertising materials, and the like. Some of these sample documents must be changed by program operators to meet local regulations or be in line with local practice. The parent corporation often monitors the franchised programs to maintain the company standard of quality control. Because company policy often controls the program, directors are usually expected not only to adopt the program as outlined by the corporate body but also can adjust some practices based on their own philosophy.

2-3l • Employer-Sponsored Programs

There is an increasing demand for employer-sponsored child care. Employers are analyzing the benefits of child care services and seeking creative ways to meet their employees' identified needs. During the early 2000s, among the top players in child care management organizations involved in employer-sponsored care was Bright Horizons, which has changed names several times over the past decade in an effort to clearly communicate the services they provide. The company accounted for the lion's share of the phenomenal growth in employer-sponsored care in the late 1990s. Much of its growth resulted from contracts to take over programs that employers were previously managing on their own in addition to some acquisitions of other independent child care providers. The concept of employer-sponsored care is not new. In the 1940s, during World War II, the Kaiser Shipbuilding Company on the West Coast provided care for the children of women who were called into the workforce to support U.S. troops in the war effort. Companies such as Stride Rite and Levi Strauss also were pioneers in the on-site, employer-sponsored child care business. The availability of child care management corporations is relatively recent.

Demand by big industry for services provided by the leading employer child care management organizations leveled off in the first years after the turn of the 21st century for some of the large for-profit child care providers. However, business held and improved slightly for Bright Horizons even as it leveled off for others in this group. These companies continue to find that the families who use their early childhood programs demand additional customized services, such as backup and sick child care, therapy services for children with special needs, crisis intervention, and many extracurricular programs, including karate, gymnastics, music, and dance. Other creative ways they serve families are offers to pick up dry cleaning, UPS deliveries, and gourmet meals as well as provide haircuts for children. In most cases, parents contract with these special service providers, and the program is the appointed location for deliveries and pickups. Early childhood programs are not involved in billing or receiving payments for these special services.

When unemployment is low, growing numbers of employers begin to view child care as a recruitment and retention tool. For example, hospitals sponsor on-site programs to help recruit and retain nurses and other technical personnel. Employers also look for child care solutions that will work for the employee who telecommutes from home as well as some who work at small satellite offices away from the main campus. Although many employer-sponsored programs are run by the large management organizations, some employers seek out public or private groups such as universities or the YMCA to run early childhood programs for them. In some cases, the employers provide generous subsidies by building new facilities that are rent free or by offering low-cost leases for ground on which to build. Employers who not only strive to keep fees down for their employees but also value quality care and want fully qualified staff as well as low teacher-to-child ratios will subsidize their programs to make up the deficits.

When universities or other nonprofits such as hospitals or YMCAs are called on to manage programs for large for-profit corporations, it is important for the early childhood program director to be prepared for many discussions with the corporate partners to clarify the mission and goals of the new program. Of course, families and children are always the focus of those who manage and staff the program. However, keep in mind that recruitment, retention, employee productivity, and morale are major goals of the corporation that subsidizes and sponsors the program. Directors know they have many customers, including families, children, and staff, but now directors must also realize that one of the most important customers is the sponsoring corporation. When issues and questions arise, the position of corporate customers must be considered. They may have questions about curriculum or hiring practices, but they are likely to accept the decisions of the early childhood professionals they hired to deal with those aspects of the program. For the director, this is no different from handling the usual inquiries and concerns from parents in any type of program. But a business sponsor may need to make decisions about hours of operation, changing schedules for children by the week (or even the day), backup care, sick child care, late day or night care, and weekend care to keep employees who work different schedules. Corporate sponsors respect the early childhood professional and value the beautiful classrooms and rich programming offered the children. However, to meet the expectations the corporation has for its employees, early childhood staff members may have to reconsider what they view as best for the children and adjust to the interests and schedules of their sponsor without compromising the integrity of their own ethical and professional values.

Enigma/Alamy Stock Photo

Programs that serve military families must be prepared to meet the sometimes intense needs related to having a loved one deployed for long periods of time. These programs need to have close connections with the social services offered on the base and also need to be tuned in to the sometimes exceptional emotional needs of the children and families served.

2-3m • Military Programs

The Department of Defense (DOD) operates child care programs at military installations across the country. Financed by a combination of government appropriations and sliding-scale parent tuition fees, the programs may be full-day, early childhood program-based care; part-day preschools; drop-in care; and, in some places, evening and weekend care. Some of this is program based and some is in home-based programs.

Director's Corner

I have been the director of an on-site program sponsored by a not-for-profit organization for almost 20 years. When that organization contracted with a large for-profit corporation to manage a new program they were ready to build, I was made the director of both programs. The corporation selected us because we had been the recipient of a national award and were well known for the quality program we offered in the on-site program. One of my greatest challenges when I began to work with the point people from the large corporate sponsor was to realize that they were now a customer of my not-for-profit employer. It really forced me to stretch my thinking and rethink what I valued and where I would draw the line on issues and not compromise.

—*Director of two large employer-sponsored programs*

Each of the military services—Air Force, Army, Marines, Navy, and Coast Guard—operates its own child care service, but all must follow the mandates of the Military Child Care Act of 1989. The act addresses program funding, required training for staff, competitive pay rates for staff, and an internal inspection system. To meet the demand for child care services, the DOD has expanded preschool and school-aged child care options by increasing the number of programs on military installations. It accomplished this by using existing resource and referral programs to help families locate available child care and by contracting with off-installation programs to guarantee spaces for DOD children.

2-3n • Home-Based Programs

Family child care is reminiscent of an extended family, with a small group of children being cared for in the home of an early childhood professional (Gordon & Williams Browne, 2011). Although this type of child care service is most popular for infants and toddlers, these home-based program providers also care for preschool children and offer before- and after-school care. The provider may be an employee of a system but most often operates independently, contracting directly with families who choose home-based programs over the care provided in early childhood programs. These providers run their own businesses. In some states, home-based programs must be licensed, whereas in other places they are certified or registered by a community agency authorized to pay for children of low-income families who are in the home. Many providers join employer or community agency information and referral registries that take calls from parents seeking child care. Registered home-based programs may or may not be subject to inspection by a responsible community agency. In some places, inspections are made only after a complaint has been filed.

2-4 • Standards of Practice

All child care programs of every type listed in the previous section are expected to provide high-quality programs for young children. These programs are assumed to meet local licensing requirements because programs are not permitted to remain open for business without a proper license. However, to provide the very best for children and to meet the accepted standards of quality based on expectations of fellow professionals, directors are expected to go beyond meeting minimum standards established by the states and strive for higher standards of quality.

The best-known and most widely accepted standards for quality practice for any and all programs for children, birth through kindergarten, are those developed by the National Association for the Education of Young Children (NAEYC). School-age programs are accredited by the National After-School Association, while family child care programs are accredited by the National Association for Family Child Care (NAFCC). In some places, programs receive accreditation from the National Association of Child Care Professionals. (For additional information on accreditation, see Chapter 3.) There is also a quality movement in many states that involves rating early care and education programs based on a series of quality indicators. These systems serve to increase awareness of the importance of quality.

2-4a • Establishing Funding for the Program

All directors, whether previously experienced in business or not, must understand the finances of operating a program. Even the director who does not have day-to-day responsibilities for the financial component of the early childhood program's structure must have financial knowledge and understanding. Directors who have moved up from teaching must remember that as early childhood educators they were authoritative rather than authoritarian. They knew what was appropriate for children and classrooms. Now they must also become authoritative about business.

A major component of the director's responsibility is ensuring sufficient funds to establish and operate the program. Although this assignment is ongoing, responsibilities mount when a new program is created, a new facility is needed, or components are to be added to an existing program. Of course, every director annually addresses the upcoming year's funding, and experienced directors recognize the need for long-range

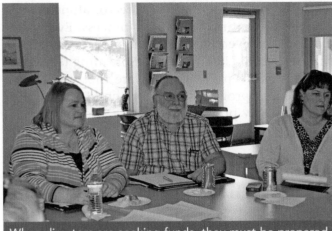

When directors are seeking funds, they must be prepared to explain their requests to bankers or representatives of a foundation.

fiscal planning. Certainly, seeking additional funding is important, but carefully shepherding existing funds is essential. In child care, there are no dollars to waste or lose through carelessness.

An important consideration in seeking funding, especially within the first few years programming is offered, is the type of program you will be establishing. Where funding comes from is determined by whether you choose to open a not-for-profit or a proprietary or for-profit program. Additional funding in subsequent years, including grants, support from businesses, local organizations, or government agencies depend on early fiduciary decisions. In addition, the type of fiscal reporting required of each type of program differs as well, which will be discussed in Chapters 4 and 5. Establishing a sound business plan and identifying key sources of income are critical for short-term survival and long-term success.

2-5 • Getting Started in Raising Funds

Typically, the director's role in an early childhood education program is demanding in time, energy, and talent. Throughout this text, you will read about the wide range of expectations placed on the director. When it comes to funding, it often is wise to obtain needed assistance in one of several ways. To begin with, the director must understand that "few

organizations are successful in raising funds from their communities without significant and sustained involvement by the board" (Bergman, 2010, p. 19). One beneficial approach is to establish a board to provide insight into a variety of elements, which will be discussed in more detail in Chapter 5. That is one reason for creating a board with a broad community and business base rather than a collection of outstanding early childhood educators: The more diverse the representation of members on the board, the more informed business-related decisions will be.

Everyone involved with the program should play a fundraising role, directly or indirectly. For example, the director may assign other staff or enlist the aid of one or more volunteers to assume some additional responsibilities, such as organizing equipment orders or conducting inventory, thereby providing time for the director to engage in fundraising. A well-trained volunteer may conduct program tours for prospective clients; an enthusiastic parent may do an excellent job of pointing out things that parents are especially interested in knowing. A volunteer may answer the telephone one afternoon a week to provide the director with uninterrupted time to write a proposal. Finally, volunteers may participate in the fundraising process in myriad ways that will be discussed throughout the chapter.

Early childhood programs with several sites may be able to afford a full- or part-time funding specialist. Directors of several programs may support each other by creating a joint fundraising plan. They even may be able to hire a fundraising consultant to guide their efforts, particularly if they have limited knowledge of the process. In the long run, such an expense may be quite productive.

Growth Mindset Moment

Consider all of the elements of an early learning program: There are business aspects, health and safety concerns, curricular decisions, legal processes, furnishing the program, and enrolling families, just to name a few. Which of these do you have experience with or are qualified to address? What type of professional would you need to assist with the others? When considering establishing a board of directors or advisers in beginning to make programming decisions, make sure there is a voice in the room that can speak to all of these elements.

An example of such cooperative planning and funding occurred when several program directors, together with their local CCRRA, were involved in monthly discussions. They were interested in supporting children with social and emotional needs beyond those expected in typical development. As a result, they formed a consortium specifically to work together on funding and implementing the program they all needed. They wrote proposals and received grants. A team of specialists was employed, and a volunteer teacher coaching program was implemented. Many children, families, early childhood educators, and directors are benefiting from this collaborative approach, yet each program maintains its identity. No matter which approaches to funding you decide to take as director, it is es-sential to recognize that the director alone cannot manage the entire fundraising process. Every staff member and every family member of the program's children should be involved. "Spreading the word" is one way. Keep everyone aware that you have a high-quality program for young children and that a high-quality program requires a strong financial position.

2-6 • Funding a New Early Childhood Program

Obviously, starting a new early childhood program or expand-ing an existing one requires a significant amount of planning and money. Before seeking a loan or investing personal assets, remember that you are starting a business. The U.S. Small Business Administration (SBA) and the Service Corps of Retired Executives are good resources. Some business textbooks provide easy to understand and detailed descriptions of start-up funding (see Greene, 2012; Hatten, 2011).

A prospective program developer who does not have a strong business background should seek assistance. Before you start a business, the SBA recommends you answer the following questions:

What niche or void will my business fill?
What services or products will I sell?
Is my idea practical, and will it fill a need?
Who is my competition?
What is my business's advantage over existing firms?
Can I deliver a better-quality service?
What skills and experience do I bring to the business?
What will be my legal structure?
How will my company's business records be maintained?
What insurance coverage will I need?
What equipment or supplies will I need?
How will I compensate myself?
What are my resources?
What financing will I need?
Where will my business be located?
What will I name my business?

▶ TeachSource Video Vignette

Financial Planning for Early Childhood Programs: Establishing a Budget

This video provides an overview of the issues that must be considered when planning a budget for your program. You are planning to show the video to members of your program's fundraising committee. Reflect on the following questions:

1. What information is provided that would enable your fundraising team to better understand the expenses associated with operating a child care program?

2. Mr. James comments that "there may be instances where cutting too much could jeopardize the very core of your program." What does he mean by this statement? What examples could you provide to members of the committee to help them understand this idea?

Another possibility is purchasing an existing business. Such a purchase involves real estate, possibly equipment, the name of the program, and the goodwill the program has established (if that is the case). (See Greene, 2012, to find out what to look for.) Linsmeier (2003) explains how a child care business is valued. As a buyer, you will need to research the value that the seller uses and how that amount was calculated. At the same time, maintaining confidentiality is essential so that the current enrollment is not diminished based on parents' anxiety about changes in ownership. You would not want to buy an early childhood program whose status was being compromised by rumors.

In any case, check with your state department of labor about specific policies that will govern your business. (You'll read about other business requirements in other chapters.) You may need to register your business name and get a business license and sales tax number, and you must definitely open a separate business bank account. You will need to know the federal and state laws governing employees and stay current with business publications in your area. Gather data on whether the market for child care is growing or declining in the area in which you are planning your business. Your local chamber of commerce or child care resource and referral agency may be able to help with information and may provide valuable contacts. Even when your business is going well, stay current with your community and its needs.

To obtain money, you must know exactly how much you need, why you need it, when you will need it, and how you will pay it back. You must also commit sufficient capital such as a second mortgage on your home. If you are working as an incorporated company, the corporation will need to demonstrate its sources of funding in addition to the loan being sought. The lender will obtain your credit report, so it is wise to check your own credit report or that of the corporation before applying for a loan.

Can you convince key people in your community of the importance of a new child care and education program? Are you and your board confident that your new program is what your community needs so that preschoolers can have the experiences and support they need to learn and develop?

Working Smart with Technology

Using Technology to Find Funding Source

Finding funding sources is one of the most important challenges faced by early childhood program owners. Your computer can be a tremendous help in surveying many of the grant opportunities available to you. Federal program information can be accessed at the GRANTS.GOV and Small Business Administration websites as well as on the Resources for Child Care Providers section of the Office of Child Care website. Information about the Child and Adult Care Food Program that provides reimbursement for meals can be found on the USDA Food and Nutrition Services website. One of the largest databases of grant sources can be found on the Foundation Center's website. And do not overlook your local library system. Search the library's website to see if it offers services related to locating and writing grants, including free workshops. Also note that many libraries are partners with the Foundation Center. This means that you may be able to access the foundation's resources through your local library.

Directors of programs should become familiar with the many funding sources available to them online.

2-7 • Start-Up Funds

Start-up capital is the money that must be available before the program is opened and for some time thereafter to support the initial program operation until the flow of tuition and other funds is sufficient to support the ongoing program. After a director is hired, it takes a *minimum* of 2 to 3 months (much more in some cases) to complete the necessary preliminary planning before the program begins. Money for space, equipment, office supplies, and some staff salaries must be available during these early months before the program opens. Programs often are underenrolled during the first few months of operation. Checks from funding sources are sometimes delayed until the program operation is well underway. Therefore, it also is wise to have sufficient capital on hand at the outset to operate the program for at least 6 months. These operating monies that need to cover costs for both the planning period and the initial operation of the program are in addition to the capital needed to finance the purchasing or remodeling of a site and to purchase equipment and supplies for the children's program. In other words, it takes a considerable amount of money to start a program, and it is important to make careful calculations to ensure that the start-up money is adequate to cover the costs until regular operating funds become available.

A director who has been a teacher and is now planning to open a program will notice that lenders, suppliers, inspectors, and insurers will not ask about what kind of relationships she plans to establish with children and families, what the curricular objectives are, or what kinds of special activities will be provided. They are interested in *business*. The director will have to have or develop this new focus while continuing to focus on the needs and interests of staff, children, and families. Although the director may have a close relationship with families because both of them care about their children, she is still the administrator. She must be careful to avoid crossing an invisible line. At some point, the director may have to follow up on a slow tuition payment. A family may decide to dispute the way an injury was handled or to complain about the food being served. The director must maintain an objective and ethical stance. (See the NAEYC Administrators' Code of Ethics Supplement in **Appendix A.**)

At the same time, the board and the director must seek out the leaders in their community who can be shown the need to go beyond a bare-bones program. Help them see that young children aren't "just" playing and that the learning that is occurring will be a foundation for continued learning and development. The process of cultivating individuals and businesses that can help is ongoing. Keeping the program and its importance in the forefront is a major job. The results can be quite rewarding for the program, children, and families.

Most agency-sponsored early childhood programs are nonprofit, and many are eligible to receive

Director's Corner

The bank wouldn't lend me the money to start a program. They said it would take too long to show a profit. Finally, we put our house up as collateral and we got the loan. But I didn't get any salary for three whole years. We're in good shape now after five years and we're expanding.

—*Director, private for-profit early childhood program*

funding from other community or governmental agencies after there is an established, ongoing program to fund. To get started, however, the agency may need to apply to foundations or other sources for funding. A sample grant application is shown in **Director's Resource 2-3**.

You may be preparing grants for much larger amounts of money for bigger projects, but this example provides an idea of how a proposal looks. Often, agencies conduct campaigns, soliciting first from their own board members, who are expected to contribute. Next, businesses and others who have expressed interest in the work of the agency are approached. Some corporations that operate many programs, or a large program, obtain funds from investors. Operators of small proprietary early childhood programs that are established for profit or that have no sponsoring agency must invest personal capital or arrange for a loan to get started. Foundation money is rarely offered to proprietary programs; it is reserved for serving particular populations chosen by the foundation that meet specific foundation-determined goals.

2-7a • Community and Governmental Support

When the community expresses great interest in getting a program started, it may be possible to promote a successful fundraising program. However, only relatively small amounts of money can be obtained through raffles or bake sales. Established philanthropic groups such as Kiwanis, Lions, various community groups, and fraternal organizations sometimes are willing to donate money to cover start-up costs such as equipment or to support a capital improvements fundraising campaign. They may fund specific activities such as field trips. Like other funders, however, they seldom provide operating expenses.

A company may provide start-up funding for an early childhood program for its employees' children with the understanding that the director will need to secure adequate funding for operating costs from other sources, including tuition. If the company makes something the program could use such as diapers or packaged food products, it may offer a continuing supply to the program. Other companies may offer a flex plan, a benefit that allows employees to set aside before-tax income to pay for child care. This benefit makes child care more affordable for families. In turn, it provides relatively reliable tuition payments for programs because employees must show a paid receipt from the programs or caregiver to collect their own before-tax dollars. If the employee has not used all of his child care benefit fund by the end of the year, the money reverts to the employer.

Early childhood programs in public schools are usually funded through special government grants, and the central administration may manage the budget. In some cases, public schools offer government-supported programs for children, sometimes specifically for children with special needs. However, families within the community are encouraged to enroll and are expected to pay for children who are typically developing, thus creating a diversified class. In the case of large chains of programs, the corporate office secures investors and then funds the start-up of new programs based on its market research. It may also arrange for franchises, finding individuals who are interested in contracting with the corporation to be a franchisee. (You may be familiar with family restaurants, ice cream stores, or dry cleaners that operate as part of a franchise system. You may also find franchised early childhood programs in your area.)

Programs not connected with other institutions or programs usually need a major source of income beyond tuition. When an early childhood program is operated day to day on tuition and small funding campaigns such as raffles or cookie sales, the board and the director will come to realize that a major pool of funds is needed to make any real changes, handle an emergency such as water damage from a broken pipe, or cover a sudden drop in enrollment, such as if parents lose jobs and can no longer afford their children's programs. That is one reason for choosing members of the board of directors carefully. When the board has members who have "connections" to people and companies with major resources, they may be able to organize and implement a campaign for a children's program. Such plans must be made well in advance, using a rationale that will appeal to a wide range of contributors. Simply saying "Our family program needs financial help" won't sell well. But creating a slogan that ignites interest can be quite effective. Programs that start without a sufficient funding base are in fiscal trouble from the outset. Maintaining a balanced budget for an early childhood education program is extremely difficult. Therefore, it is paramount to keep a balanced budget at the outset by finding enough capital to cover start-up costs as well as to plan for unexpected needs and to enhance the program in a major way when needed.

Summary

Many decisions must be made concerning how needs should be assessed, what philosophy will be most representative of the thinking of the planners and the prospective director, what type of program is feasible in terms of financing, financial resources available to fund the program, and so forth. All directors must also understand their fiduciary responsibilities related to operating an early care and education program. To conduct an effective needs assessment, directors must do the following:

- identify information that will help determine the types of child services needed now and in the future,

- develop a mission statement that reflects the program's core values,

- determine the various types of child care needed by families in the region, and

- identify where the standards of quality practice can be located and how they should be used when determining the program's core values.

Investigate the roles that the director plays in obtaining funding for an early childhood program.

Be familiar with the numerous local, state, and national sources, both private and governmental, that are available for providing funding, and develop some skill in writing applications and proposals.

TRY IT OUT!

1. Review the sample needs assessment questionnaire in **Director's Resource 2-1** and adjust it so you could use it for a 10-item online survey.
   a. How would you introduce the survey in an email that encourages potential program users to answer the questions?
   b. What incentive would you offer to encourage participation in the survey?
   c. What follow-up message would you send to those who participated in the survey?
2. Consider a program that you would most like to direct and use Radtke's three questions to develop a mission statement. Be sure to describe the type of population that would be served by this program.
3. In groups of four students, discuss and record the thinking of the group about the following questions:
   a. What are your assumptions about growth and development?
   b. How does learning or the development of knowledge come about?
   c. During the early years of a child's life, what is the adult's role relative to
      • physical development?
      • social development?
      • emotional development?
      • cognitive development?
      • language development?
      • moral development?
   d. What goals do you have for the children in your care?
   e. What is your belief about how families impact development and how they should be served in your program?
4. Assume you have been hired as a director of a new early childhood program. Write a list of core values and corresponding value statements for your new program.
5. Investigate who provides funding for early childhood education in your community.

Are any programs funded by the federal, state, or local governments? United Way? Private individuals? Chain or franchised programs? Universities or colleges? Businesses or proprietors? Is anyone else funding early childhood education in your community? Your instructor may assign one student or a group to explore each potential resource and provide a written or oral report for the class. Identify the purpose of the funding, conditions for receiving funding (e.g., start-up, operating, or special project funds), potential amount available, and the procedures that must be followed to apply for the funds.
   a. Contact or invite to class a rural or inner-city early childhood program director (not a Head Start program). Inquire about the funding base.
   b. How much tuition do parents pay?
   c. How much of the total budget is covered by tuition?
   d. What outside funding sources are available to support the program, and how much money is available through those sources?
   e. How were outside funds obtained?
   f. Discuss your findings in class. Do the resources seem adequate? What else might the program director do to secure funding for the program?
6. With one or two classmates, examine the sample grant application in **Director's Resource 2-1**. Identify the individual sections of the proposal and discuss the following:
   a. What is the purpose of this particular grant application?
   b. How much funding has been requested?
   c. What information has been provided to justify the request for funding?
   d. What is the importance of the Statement of Agency Commitment?
   e. Identify the type of information included in the Statement of Need.

Director's Resource 2-1

SAMPLE NEEDS ASSESSMENT

1. How many adults are there in this household?

2. Do all adults in the household work? Yes ☐ No ☐
   If yes, ☐ part time How many?_____ ☐ full time
   How many? _____

3. What is the total number of children under the age of 16? _____

4. What is the number of children under age 6? _____
   Check ages of children under 6

   ☐ Under 1   How many? _____
   ☐ Between 1 and 2   How many? _____
   ☐ Between 2 and 3   How many? _____
   ☐ Between 3 and 4   How many? _____
   ☐ Between 4 and 5   How many? _____
   ☐ Between 5 and 6   How many? _____

5. Does any child in this family, younger than school age, regularly spend time away from home? ☐ Yes ☐ No
   If yes, how many? _____

6. Do any children in the family have special needs?
   ☐ Yes ☐ No
   If yes, how many? _____
   If yes, does the condition require attendance at a special school or program? ☐ Yes ☐ No
   If yes, describe program(s) needed:
   _____
   _____

7. Is/are your child(ren) regularly cared for every day in your home by someone who does not live with you?
   ☐ Yes ☐ No
   If yes, is the caregiver a relative? ☐ Yes ☐ No

8. How many children over 5 regularly spend time away from home before or after school? _____ What are their ages? _____
   Describe type of program: _____
   _____

9. For statistical purposes only, please give the total family income in this household:
   ☐ $0–$15,000
   ☐ $15,001–$20,000
   ☐ $20,001–$35,000
   ☐ $35,001–$50,000
   ☐ $50,001–$75,000
   ☐ $75,001–$90,000
   ☐ over $90,000

10. Approximately how much do you pay every week for the care of all your children? Give that figure in column A. In column B, mark how much you would be willing to pay for quality care for all of your children. Mark with an X.

A	B	
_____	$0–50	☐
_____	$51–75	☐
_____	$76–100	☐
_____	$101–125	☐
_____	$126–150	☐
_____	$151–175	☐
_____	Over $175	☐

11. Parents have a difficult time arranging for the care of their children. Indicate what has been your experience.
    ☐ Easy
    ☐ Not very difficult
    ☐ Difficult
    ☐ Extremely difficult
    ☐ No opinion

12. If you had a choice of arrangements for the care of your child, what would be your first choice?
    ☐ Care in child care program for 4 hours or less
    ☐ Care in child care program for more than 4 hours
    ☐ Care by another mother or someone in her own home
    ☐ Care by a sitter in your own home
    ☐ Care in a program before and after school

13. If you could have the type of arrangement you prefer, how many days per week would you want your children to spend there (insert number of days)? Infant _____
    Toddler _____ Preschooler _____ After school
    _____ (Age _____)

14. Where would you prefer to have your child(ren) cared for?
    ☐ Near where you work
    ☐ Near where you live
    ☐ Other location: _____

15. Generally speaking, in selecting an ideal child care arrangement, which is more important to you? (Assume that quality is equal.)
    ☐ Cost more important
    ☐ Closeness to home more important
    ☐ Closeness to work more important
    ☐ No opinion

16. If an early childhood program opens across the street from your office (insert home, church, factory, as appropriate), for which age child would you be likely to use it?
    ☐ Your infant
    ☐ Your toddler
    ☐ Your preschooler
    ☐ Your school-age child(ren)

Director's Resource 2-2 ////

SAMPLE SLIDING FEE SCHEDULE

Parent pays (%)	20	30	40	50	60	70	80	90
Infant ($/week)	30	45	60	75	90	105	120	135
Toddler ($/week)	25	37.50	50	62.50	75	87.50	100	112.50
Preschooler ($/week)	20	30	40	50	60	70	80	90

TeachSource Digital Download

Director's Resource 2-3 ////

SAMPLE GRANT APPLICATION*

(for use with Try It Out! 2-3)

Doe Learning Center Inc. is a nonprofit corporation that operates four child care programs in the greater metropolitan area. The programs provide quality child care for children ages 3 months through 5 years and also offer school-age care at two of the sites. As a United Way agency, the programs' common goal is to work toward alleviating the current crisis of child care, as outlined in the Long Range Plan for Child Care of the United Way in 2000. This study shows that there is an urgent need for quality programming for children identified as having special needs. Doe Learning Center Inc. has responded to this need by operating four programs whose common goal is the inclusion of all children.

Statement of Agency Commitment

Metropolitan Learning Center (MLC) is located in the central area of the city. The program serves 67 children ages 3 months through 5 years. In the summer, we enroll an additional 20 children in our school-age program. Established in 1984, MLC was the first full-day program in this city to be accredited by the National Association for the Education of Young Children.

Largely based on the theories of Piaget and Erikson, the program's philosophy reflects a focus on the development of the whole child and the formation of strong, trusting relationships. The developmental constructivist approach holds the belief that children develop sequentially from one stage of development to another. Because of this, we believe that children must be provided with opportunity that will challenge them and aid in their progression from one stage to the next. It is a necessity that learning be based on actual experience and participation. Talking without doing is largely meaningless to young children.

We believe that for children to grow, they must be placed in a setting that meets their basic needs. Therefore, it is our utmost concern that our program provides a nurturing, comfortable environment that is specifically structured to meet the physical, emotional, and cognitive needs of each individual child.

*Names of people and places are fictitious.

Director's Resource 2-3 (continued) ////

This philosophy was the foundation for the development of the agency. Due to this commitment, the question of inclusion was never discussed, only how to do it well.

In this time of severe staff shortages in the early child education field, MLC feels fortunate to have an outstanding quality and quantity of professionals:

- four preschool head educators (MEd);
- one toddler head educator (associate in early education);
- two infant educators (bachelor's in education) and two infant teachers (associates in education); and
- Dr. John Jones, professor emeritus at the Metropolitan University, who has been consulting with our agency for three years. This past year, Dr. Jones has been working strictly at MLC, coordinating our educational services.

MLC has worked extensively with the Early Childhood Education Department, Metropolitan University. The program has been a training site for the past 5 years and works with an average of three to four students per quarter.

According to Washington County Child Day Care: The State of Today and Plans for 2010: "Special needs children are still at a great disadvantage. Most child care providers feel ill equipped to serve children with developmental problems and physical disabilities." MLC has successfully integrated approximately 25 children identified as having special needs. One family called more than 60 early childhood programs before finding a placement at MLC for its child with cerebral palsy. The program has served many children with a wide variety of special needs, including but not limited to pervasive development disorder, fragile X syndrome, autism, mild mental retardation, receptive language disorder, and visual impairments, to name a few.

One primary goal of the organization is to meet the needs of the family, parent, and child. MLC has identified its ability to meet these needs as follows.

Needs of the Child

- Placement in a program meeting the standards of developmentally appropriate practice
- Master-level staff capable of identifying and working with high-risk children

Needs of the Family

- Providing high-quality care for its children
- Providing quarterly parent education and training programs
- Providing assistance in identifying (or working with existing) available services (e.g., early intervention) for their children

MLC has been identified in the community as a program that will not only serve children with special needs but also give them access to the services they need or support the work of other service providers as part of the daily program. Metropolitan University acknowledged the endeavors of the program by placing students from the Special Education department under the guidance of our experienced staff. We have worked with many agencies to provide more comprehensive services to these children. These agencies include the following:

- Washington County Department of Human Services
- Special Education Regional Resource Center
- Cerebral Palsy Services Center
- Center for Developmental Disorders
- Speech and Hearing

Director's Resource 2-3 (continued)

- Speech Pathology
- Child Advocacy Center
- Association for the Blind
- Metropolitan University—Early Childhood and Special Education Department
- Foster Grandparent Program
- The Council on Aging
- The Single Parent Center

Statement of Need

There are currently eight children enrolled in the program who have been identified as having special needs. There are several children who are integrated into the environment and are receiving services from support agencies. MLC feels confident that we can meet their needs without additional services. Two children pose challenges to our existing program. One child is currently enrolled in our infant program; he is 20 months old and has cerebral palsy. When we enrolled Ed, we assessed that we could meet his needs in the infant program. Although Ed is nonmobile and nonverbal, he uses smiles, cries, and coos to communicate with his caregiver.

To continue serving Ed:

- We need to be able to meet the challenge of facilitating his growth through experiences with the toddlers.
- We need to acquire the equipment to encourage his further development.
- We need release time for his caregiver to meet with his therapist to learn how to use specialized equipment and participate in his individualized education plan (IEP) meeting.

Our second child has been identified with pervasive developmental disorder and mild characteristics of autism. Communication has been the primary barrier in the progression of Ryan's development. This aspect of his disorder carries over into other areas of his growth, including the development of self-control. Ryan has been enrolled in our program for 1 year and within that period has gone from single-word utterances to communicating in four- to five-word sentences. Because of this increased ability to communicate, the agency believes that a transition to the oldest preschool classroom is the next step. The goal of this move is to place Ryan in an environment of his same-age peers where he might benefit from the modeling of age-appropriate behaviors and participation in activities. Any changes in daily schedule and transition times are extremely difficult for Ryan, and separation from his current classroom teacher will be a tremendous undertaking.

Our belief is that to best aid in this transition, MLC will need the assistance of an additional staff person for the following reasons:

- to meet the needs of Ryan during the period of transition so that classroom staff may continue to meet the needs of his peers;
- to act as a facilitator, giving Ryan assistance with social interactions so that he might form relationships with his peers and staff; and
- to give the classroom staff opportunity to focus on forming trusting relationships with Ryan without concern that the experiences of his peers are being limited

Purpose of Funding/Budget

The purpose of our funding breaks into three categories: equipment, consulting and training, and additional staff to decrease ratios.

Director's Resource 2-3 (continued)

Equipment

Type	Purpose	Cost
Outdoor swing		126.95
Floor sitter	Seat for severely challenged student allows a nonmobile child to interact with peers but have necessary support	150.00
Button switch toy		42.00
Jelly bean switch toy		42.00
Circus truck		27.00
Bumper car		25.00
Brontosaurus		29.50
Oversized ball	Easier to manipulate than typical ball 18"	24.35
	34"	69.50

Consulting and Training

Topic (we would like to open these to the public)

How to adapt "typical" equipment to meet the needs of physically challenged children	100.00
How to use switch toys	80.00
How to write an appropriate IEP and how to make the IEP meeting work for the child	100.00

Consulting

How to arrange the toddler environment to meet the needs of a physically challenged child	100.00
How to encourage positive peer relationships with typical and atypical children	50.00

Support Staff

Enrolling a physically challenged child into the infant program was within the abilities of our staff. Allowing time for this child to interact with peers of his own age and slowly transitioning him into the toddler room will be a challenge for us. We need time for his caregiver to visit the toddler room with him, and then time for the toddler teacher to have one-on-one time for him. This cannot be done without additional staff. Any choice we make with the current staff situation will either shortchange Ed or the other children enrolled. We are requesting a part-time assistant for 6 months.

Cost	$6,656.00.

Having children that model age-appropriate behaviors has been the most vital ingredient to Ryan's development. To continue his progress, it is imperative that he be surrounded by children exhibiting the behaviors that Ryan is striving for. As previously mentioned, any transition is very difficult for Ryan. To continue servicing Ryan and meet his needs by transitioning him to be with children of his own age, we will need additional staff.

We are requesting a part-time assistant for 6 months.

Cost	$6,656.00.
TOTAL REQUESTED	**$14,278.30**

Expected Outcome

This grant will enable us to purchase equipment that will
- allow physically challenged children to become more accessible to the other children by being positioned near them on the floor,
- provide stimulation and encourage peer interaction, and
- lessen isolation so that relationships with peers will increase.

This grant will enable us to provide sufficient staff to
- allow challenged children to be surrounded with children of their own age providing appropriate models,

Director's Resource 2-3 *(continued)* ////

- allow staff to meet the requirements of our children with special needs without denying other children the attention they need,
- facilitate smooth transitions that encourage success with meaningful relationships with other children, and
- make inclusion a successful experience that will encourage staff to include additional children.

This grant will provide technical assistance that will

- give the staff and management the knowledge to include these children and additional children in the future.

Director's Resource 2-3 *(continued)* ////

- encourage other early childhood programs to attend these training sessions and build support through networking with other early childhood educators participating in inclusion.

We will be asking staff who are working with Ed and Ryan to fill out a short questionnaire before we provide additional services and then again after. We would like to see if these support services change any possible insecurities or feelings of being overwhelmed that had previously occurred.

TeachSource Digital Download

REFERENCES

Bodrova, E., & Leong, D. J. (2006). *Tools of the mind: The Vygotskian approach to early childhood education* (2nd ed.). Upper Saddle River, NJ: Prentice Hall.

Bergman, R. L. (2010). *Not just small change: Fund development for early childhood programs.* Redmond, WA: Exchange Press.

Children's Defense Fund. (2014). *The state of America's children: 2014 Report.* Washington, DC: Author.

Decker, C., Decker, J. R., Freeman, N., & Knopf, H. (2009). *Planning and administering early childhood programs* (9th ed.). Upper Saddle River, NJ: Prentice-Hall Merrill.

DeVries, R., & Kohlberg, L. (1988). *Programs of early education: The constructivist view.* New York, NY: Longman.

Flanagan, K. D., & McPhee, C. (2009). *The children born in 2001 at kindergarten entry: First findings from the kindergarten data collections of the early childhood longitudinal study, birth cohort (ECLS-B)* (NCES 2010-005). Washington, DC: National Center for Education Statistics, Institute of Education Sciences, U.S. Department of Education. http://ies.ed.gov /pubsearch/pubsinfo.asp?pubid=2010005

Greene, C. L. (2012). *Entrepreneurship: Ideas in action* (5th ed.). Mason, OH: South-Western, Cengage Learning.

Gordon, A. M., & Williams Browne, K. (2011). *Beginnings and beyond* (8th ed.). Clifton Park, NY: Delmar Cengage Learning.

Hatten, T. S. (2011). *Small business management: Entrepreneurship and beyond* (5th ed.). Stamford, CT: Cengage Learning.

Kamii, C. (1982). *Number in preschool and kindergarten: Educational implications for Piaget's theory.* Washington, DC: NAEYC.

Kuykendall, J. (1990). Child development directors shouldn't leave home without it. *Young Children, 45*(5), 49–51.

Linsmeier, D. (2003, May). Valuing your child care business. *Child Care Information Exchange, 151,* 56–59.

Little, M. H., & Cohen-Vogel, L. (2016). Too much too soon? An analysis of the discourses used by policy advocates in the debate over kindergarten. *Education Policy Analysis Archives, 24*(106), 1–38. https://eric.ed.gov/contentdelivery/servlet /ERICServlet?accno=EJ1119327

National Center for Education Statistics. (2011). Early childhood longitudinal study, kindergarten class of 2010–11. Washington, DC: U.S. Department of Education. ECLS-K: 2011. https://nces.ed.gov/ecls/kindergarten2011.asp

National Head Start Association. (2011). *Basic Head Start facts.* Alexandria, VA: Author. https://www .headstartva.org/assets/docs/Basic_Head_Start_ Facts_rev02212011.pdf

Neugebauer, R. (2003). Update on child care in public schools. *Child Care Information Exchange: The Director's Magazine, 150,* 66–71.

O'Leary, A. (2018). Aha! Advocacy moment. *YC: Young Children, 73*(4), 4.

Power to the Profession Task Force. (2020). *Unifying framework for the early childhood profession.* Washington DC: NAEYC.

Puig, V. I., Erwin, E. J., Evenson, T. L., & Beresford, M. (2015). "It's a two-way street": Examining how trust, diversity, and contradiction influence a sense of community. *Journal of Research in Early Childhood Education, 29*(2), 187–201. https://researchwith .montclair.edu/en/publications/its-a-two-way-street -examining-how-trust-diversity-and-contradict

Radtke, J. M. (1998). *Strategic communications for nonprofit organizations: Seven steps to creating a successful plan.* New York, NY: John Wiley & Sons, Inc.

U.S. Bureau of Labor Statistics. (2020). Employment characteristics of families summary. Washington, DC: Author. https://www.bls.gov/news.release/famee .nr0.htm#:~:text=(See%20tables%201%20and%204, percent%20in%20the%20prior%20year

Wiggins, G. P., & McTighe, J. (2007). *Schooling by design: Mission, action, and achievement*. Alexandria, VA: Association for Supervision and Curriculum Development.

The primary function of the licensing agent is to ascertain whether a program complies with minimum requirements.

Chapter 3

Licensing, Credentialing, and Accreditation

naeyc

Standards and Recommendations Addressed in This Chapter

ADVANCING EQUITY RECOMMENDATION 2 Take proactive steps with measurable goals to recruit and retain educators and leaders who reflect the diversity of children and families served and who meet professional expectations.

PROGRAM STANDARD 1 Relationships

PROGRAM STANDARD 5 Health

PROGRAM STANDARD 8 Community Relationships

PROGRAM STANDARD 9 Physical Environment

PROGRAM STANDARD 10 Leadership and Management

PROFESSIONAL STANDARDS AND COMPETENCIES: STANDARD 2 Family–Teacher Partnerships and Community Connections

PROFESSIONAL STANDARDS AND COMPETENCIES: STANDARD 6 Professionalism as an Early Childhood Educator

LEARNING OBJECTIVES

After reading this chapter, you should be able to:

3-1 Explain the purpose of licensing.

3-2 Describe various types of licensing regulations and their specific purposes.

3-3 Identify the steps in the licensing process.

3-4 Discuss the role of the licensing specialist.

3-5 Compare and contrast licensing and accreditation of early childhood programs.

3-6 Describe the function of state Quality Rating and Improvement Systems (QRIS) and how they differ from accreditation and licensing.

3-7 Identify and explain the various levels of individual credentials available for staff in an early childhood education program.

3-8 Explain the relationship between career pathways and Power to the Profession early childhood educator levels.

The field of early childhood education has made great strides in improving the quality of early childhood education programs by defining quality, refining standards, and unifying the field (Power to the Profession Task Force, 2020). Almost all states have a Quality Rating and Improvement System (QRIS) that is designed to improve quality and inform families as they choose programs for their children. Program directors play an essential role to lead their centers toward the highest quality possible. Early childhood programs are responsible for understanding licensing, accreditation, credentialing, and other regulations pertaining to providing services for young children. Although standards are developed by professional organizations such as the National Association for the Education of Young Children (NAEYC), regulations are typically developed by a governmental body and have specific purposes. Directors must understand which standards and regulations apply to their programs and ensure that all requirements are fulfilled in a timely manner. They also must be prepared to pay the requisite fees.

In the future, people who assume responsible roles in children's programs probably will have to deal with more and more regulatory functions. This increase in regulation is related to the expanded use of public funds and the broader acceptance of the fact that programs for young children must provide care and protection for children and be educationally sound. Also, educational accountability points to greater focus on the need to ensure that the people responsible for children's programs have the required credentials as well as an understanding of the protection of children's health and safety requirements addressed through the licensing of programs. The term *licensing* may cause confusion because it is used to signify that a governing body is giving permission to do something. In this case, what is being permitted is the operation of an early childhood education program. Later in the chapter when we discuss the licensing of early childhood educators (also known as *certifying* or *credentialing*), what is being permitted is the opportunity to obtain a teaching position.

After programs comply with the minimum standards required for local or state licensing, they can move toward higher standards and gain some form of professional recognition. NAEYC works with early childhood education programs through the Council for NAEYC Accreditation of Early Learning Programs, which were established by NAEYC's governing board. As described on its website, it is "an independent body established to ensure the equity, integrity and accountability of NAEYC Accreditation of Early Learning Programs" (https://www.naeyc.org/accreditation/early -learning/council). The Association for Early Learning Leaders (formerly the National Association of Early Childhood Program Professionals), the National Early Childhood Program Accreditation Commission (NECPA), the Council on Accreditation, and the American Montessori Association also provide opportunities for accreditation. On-site directors and boards are responsible for determining which form of accreditation is required and which is aspirational. For example, most states require that early childhood education programs be rated using the state's QRIS (Alliance for Early Success, 2020), but other forms of accreditation such as NAEYC are optional. Directors and boards are tasked with being aware of the options and requirements and provide the necessary inspiration and leadership to improve the program. They work to move a program from compliance with minimum licensing requirements to meeting quality performance standards. Even beyond these standards lies the goal of dynamic development, which continues to produce a quality educational program. Model program directors are always working to refine their programs as they move toward the goal of excellence. The knowledge base in child development and early childhood education is constantly growing, so no program can afford to be complacent about its quality.

TeachSource Video Vignette

The Quality of Early Childhood Program

This video provides an overview of the importance of quality programming for children's development. View the video vignette entitled *The Quality of Early Childhood Program*. Reflect on the following questions:

1. How do quality care and education support children's development?

2. As a director, what factors should you consider to ensure quality programming for the young children in your care?

3-1 • The Purpose of Licensing

Licensing programs is required, but requirements vary from state to state.

For example, in some states, only full-day early childhood education programs are required to obtain a license, whereas in other states, all full-day, half-day, and home-based programs must be licensed. Depending on the type of program being planned and the geographical location of the program, both local and state requirements might need to be met. When federal funding is involved, there will be additional requirements. In some states, program sponsorship determines program licensing. For example, programs affiliated with public schools may be licensed by a state's department of education. Your licensing agent can provide updated licensing information. A directory of state and territory licensing agencies and regulations is available from the U.S. Department of Health and Human Services Administration for Children and Families Office of Early childhood program at https://childcareta.acf.hhs.gov/sites/default/files /public/licensing_regulations_agencies_web.pdf. To view an individual state's early childhood program licensure regulations, go to the National Resource Center for Health and Safety in Child Care and Early Education at https://nrckids.org/.

In 2020, Child Care Aware of America released the results of the *Child Care Licensing Benchmark Project*, which "marks an important step forward to help states not only gauge how well they align with federal requirements, but also guide them as they strive to increase the quality of their child care system" (Engelman, Dobbins, Veatch, & Tercha, 2020, p. 2). This project examined licensing standards from all 50 states, reviewed research-based indicators of quality, and developed licensing benchmarks (see **Figure 3-1**).

3-2 • Benchmarks

There are seven benchmark categories for both oversight and program. In addition, program benchmarks include specific criteria for child care centers and family child care where appropriate.

- Oversight benchmarks: Oversight benchmarks reflect state policies, procedures, and practices and the administration of child care licensing regulations.
- Program benchmarks: Program benchmarks reflect child care licensing regulations that

specifically apply to the programs that directly provide care to children (e.g., child care centers and family child care programs).

In addition to the broad benchmark categories In **Figure 3-1**, more comprehensive benchmark language can be found in **Appendix F**. Regardless of the work of the Child Care Licensing Benchmark Project, the licensing function is a result of legislation, and its focus has historically been on accountability for the health and safety of children and staff. Licensing requirements have typically been minimal, and enforcement practices in some localities are limited. As a result, program licensure does not guarantee quality of care or protection for children and rarely addresses the educational quality of the program. The licensing function is essential and valuable but often misunderstood. A license gives *permission* to operate but does not indicate quality. The Child Care Licensing Benchmark Project developed guidance for states that are striving for quality.

An estimated 312,254 licensed early childhood program facilities are operational in the United States (National Association for Regulatory Administration and the National Center on Early childhood program Quality Improvement, 2014). Approximately 34 percent of these are programs; the remaining 66 percent are licensed early childhood home-based programs or other types of facilities.

3-2a • Early Childhood Program

Early childhood home-based programs are places in which people care for one or more children in their homes instead of in a program or in the child's own home. Some states divide these into categories based on the number of children permitted. In larger early childhood program homes, perhaps 12 children may be cared for. At least two adults are needed, and building regulations should be required. Many families prefer this type of ca particularly for infants and toddlers, becau the smaller setting. Although family earl hood program (or *family day care* as it is called) has always been a frequently u early childhood program, its regulat relatively recent.

Oversight Benchmarks	Program Benchmarks
1. Licensing Requirements	1. Background Checks
2. Inspection Reports	2. Provider Qualifications
3. Monitoring	3. Professional Development
4. Program/Staff Ratio	4. Health and Safety
5. Licensing Staff Qualifications	5. Learning Activities
6. Background Check	6. Group Size and Ratios
7. Professional Development Implementation	7. Family Engagement/Access

FIGURE 3-1
Benchmark categories.

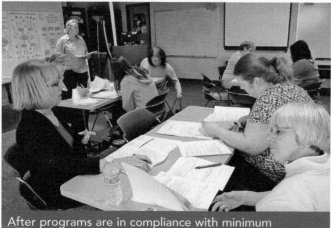

After programs are in compliance with minimum standards required for local or state licensing, they can work toward higher standards that may lead to accreditation.

Although more and more states have established preservice qualifications for family home early childhood program providers, the mandated qualifications related to early childhood training are limited. For example, much of the training may be in first aid, collecting fees, or completing forms for early childhood program food program reimbursement. Because of the limited hours available for training, information about young children's development and learning is minimal.

Early childhood program staff preservice training shows a trend toward emphasizing early childhood education. Although not part of the regulatory system for early childhood program, the American Association of Colleges of Teacher Education has called for all preschool early childhood educators to have a bachelor's degree. This proposal far exceeds licensing requirements but is consistent with requirements for kindergarten teachers. As a future early childhood educator or director, you may want to discuss this proposal with your peers or instructors.

In addition to the licensing department, the building department in most localities will review the plans, and the fire, building, and health or sanitation departments will send individual representatives to inspect the proposed space where the services for children will be offered. No matter what system is used in a particular state, an initial inspection and approval is required before the program can begin to operate. Even when the program is moving from one location to another, inspection and approval must

still be done. The regulating departments may be willing to send individual representatives to inspect the proposed space where the services for children will be offered. These inspections can alert the director to major and minor changes that need to be made. The decision about moving to a particular facility may hinge on the cost and time line for making these changes, as well as on the deadline for exiting the current premises.

The director must play an active role in the licensing process, which may include making frequent phone calls to agencies or emailing agencies if necessary. Communication breakdowns can occur, and directors must be proactive.

After initial inspection and approval, inspections and license renewals will be required on a regular basis. Directors are responsible for ensuring that their programs comply with regulations and for being familiar with appeal and grievance procedures if conflicts arise regarding compliance with the regulations.

TeachSource Video Vignette

Leadership Practices in Child Development Programs: The Regulatory System naeyc

This video provides an overview of the many responsibilities that directors of early childhood programs possess. As you view the *Leadership Practices in Child Development Programs* video, reflect on the following questions related to licensing:

1. What is the importance of regulatory compliance?

2. What steps can be taken to ensure that new employees are aware of licensing requirements?

3-3 • Licensing Regulations

Local and state licensing regulations typically cover building safety and requirements for physical space and establish base teacher-to-child ratios. Although licensing regulations vary greatly from state to state, most licensing regulations include the following points.

3-3a • Building Safety

Licensing regulations always include at least the minimum fire, sanitation, and building safety standards that apply to all private and public services. Fire regulations usually cover the type of building construction, ease of evacuation in the event of fire, alarm systems, smoke detectors, sprinkler systems, availability of fire extinguishers, and methods of storing combustible materials. Building codes usually cover wiring, plumbing, and building construction, including building materials. Health department regulations cover conditions in all areas of the building, with particular attention to the bathrooms and food service operations.

When infants or children who are nonambulatory are enrolled in the program, the director must be sure to meet licensing requirements for those groups. Typically, these requirements focus on egress in case of emergency. Housing these programs on the first (ground) floor is usually required.

3-3b • Physical Space

Licensing regulations usually specify the amount of space necessary for programs for infants, toddlers, and preschool children. The requirement for 3- to 5-year-old children is typically a minimum of 35 square feet of indoor space per child and 50 to 75 square feet of outdoor space per child. Because programs for infants and toddlers require cribs, feeding tables, and diaper-changing areas, such programs require more space per child than do programs for 3- to 5-year-olds. Levels and sources of light, levels of heat, sources of fresh air, fencing of outdoor areas, protection from radiators and low windows,

and numbers of toilets also are included in regulations covering physical space. These standards are minimal, and good programs usually exceed them. Providing more than minimal space, particularly for children who will be at the program all day, is likely to make both children and staff more comfortable. For additional state and national data regarding physical space requirements, see the collaborative report by the American Academy of Pediatrics, American Public Health Association, and National Resource Center for Health and Safety in Early Childhood Program and Early Education (2019).

3-3c • Teacher-to-Child Ratios

Some licensing regulations include minimum teacher-to-child ratios. These state or local ratios vary but in the range of 3 to 8 infants to 1 adult, 4 to 12 toddlers to 1 adult, and 6 to 20 preschoolers to 1 adult. The baseline licensing standards for child-to-staff ratios in early childhood programs in some states already meet the standards used by NAEYC, but most states are still below these significant ratios. Most regulations require that two responsible adults be on the premises at all times. The ratios are established to furnish a baseline standard for protecting the safety of children; however, group size is even more important and also is regulated by some states. A collaborative report from the American Academy of Pediatrics, American Public Health Association, and the National Resource Center for Health and Safety in Child Care and Early Education (2019) recommends the group size and child-to-staff ratios shown in **Table 3-1**.

Licensing standards seem to be coming closer to these guidelines. Following are the most common child-to-staff ratios required by licensing in 2017

Table 3-1 Recommended group size and ratio of children to staff		
Child Age	Maximum Group Size	Ratio of Children to Teacher
Infant	6	3:1
Toddler	8	4:1
3-year-olds	14	7:1
5-year-olds	16	8:1

(National Association for Regulatory Administration, National Center on Early Childhood Quality Assurance, 2016, 2019) for early childhood programs:

- infants—4:1;
- toddlers—6:1 (18 months of age) and 8:1 (27 months of age);
- 4-year-olds—10:1; and
- 5-year-olds—15:1.

3-3d • Staff Qualifications

Early childhood educators' training in child development and their interactions with the children are key factors in creating a quality program. NAEYC's standards continue to uphold the importance of well-prepared staff members and appropriate group sizes. These standards also call for early childhood educators who have completed considerable formal education and specialized professional preparation in early childhood. Check the NAEYC website for current information related to qualification guidelines for early childhood educators and directors.

Although licensing regulations sometimes address staff qualifications, requirements are often minimal. Fortunately, the Power to the Profession Taskforce (2020) has worked to identify the unique roles, educational requirements, and specific responsibilities for each of three designations of early childhood educator.

> Each designation, with names chosen in part because they can be incorporated and localized to support all settings, staffing, and supervisory structures, will have a unique role and be prepared for specific responsibilities. Establishing three different roles while keeping them together in the same professional structure will increase inclusivity and reduce stratification. This will help ensure that all individuals on an early childhood education team are explicitly valued, have a common identity, and are prepared to be effective in their specific practice. (Power to the Profession Task Force, 2020, p. 13)

The comprehensive effort of the Power to the Profession Task Force has only recently been released and efforts have yet to be fulfilled to overcome the limited requirements that early childhood educators be able to read and write or hold only a high school diploma to be hired as a teacher an early childhood educator, assistant, or aide. Most states require a director to have at least a high school diploma, and only a few states require some college training, which may or may not be in child development or early childhood education. Others, however, require specific training in early childhood education or attainment of the child development associate credential. The Power to the Profession Task Force (2020) has worked diligently to upgrade the criteria for early childhood staff as one component of the effort to improve quality and compensation. As the work of the task force becomes more widely known, we can expect licensing standards to continue to improve.

3-3e • Transportation

In programs that provide transportation, the service usually must meet the state motor vehicle department standards for school bus service. These standards regulate numbers of children, types of vehicle, types of lights on vehicles, proper identification on the vehicle, use of car seats and seat belts, and appropriate licensing and insurance coverage for vehicles and drivers. Even when it is not required, it is wise to provide drivers with training in child development and management so that time spent on the bus will be positive as well as safe for both children and drivers.

Having a second adult on the bus to assist in an emergency is also advisable. The driver, of course, should not leave even one child on the bus while seeking help or when walking a child to the door when that child's parent does not come out to meet the bus. Furthermore, some children have a difficult time leaving seat belts on. The driver, who must give full attention to the road, should not have to check constantly to ensure that all children are safely seated. The program also should establish a policy requiring the driver to check the interior of the vehicle thoroughly to be sure no child remains on board. This procedure should be in effect every time the driver leaves the vehicle. This procedure is required by law in some states.

3-3f • Other Standards

In programs serving infants, licensing usually requires detailed plans for diapering, including the surface on which the baby is placed, a plan for disposing of soiled and wet diapers, and handwashing by staff after each diaper change. Additional requirements for storing food, feeding babies, and washing toys also are included.

As you review this section on licensing regulations, it should become clear that, depending on the size, location, and scope of the program for which you are responsible, you could find yourself working with local, state, and federal regulatory agencies. At times, the regulations from the various bodies are not totally compatible, and they even may be contradictory. As director, you are tasked with handling all these regulatory agents so that your program is in compliance. If your program is not in compliance, you run the risk of having a fine imposed or of being unable to take full advantage of available funds and community resources. There also is the risk of having to delay the opening of a new program or having to close down an ongoing program because of failure to meet minimum licensing requirements. In some cases, noncompliance may jeopardize the well-being of children and staff.

3-4 • The Licensing Process

Directors who are seeking initial licensing should allow plenty of time for the lengthy process, which includes on-site visits and conferences with inspectors from all the departments involved. It is wise to allow *at least* 90 days to complete the initial licensing process, although some states suggest that much more time may be required. For example, in Ohio, a minimum of 150 days is recommended to complete the steps in the process. All departments must provide clearance before the license is issued. On rare occasions, programs are permitted to continue operation when they are out of compliance because licensing specialists are trying to help provide sufficient early childhood programs in the community. Regardless, the regulatory agencies constantly monitor the work being done to bring the program into compliance with the minimum requirements. The burden is on the operator, who must present data to show that the program qualifies for a

license or is working toward that goal within a well-defined, limited time line.

Total compliance with all regulations may be expensive, so it is important to have a clear understanding of the changes that are essential before a program can operate and those that can be made as money becomes available. For example, the fire inspector may not allow children in the building until all required fire extinguishers are purchased, mounted appropriately, and made accessible. The health department might allow an early childhood program to begin before a separate sink for handwashing is available in the food-preparation area, provided that adequate handwashing facilities are available elsewhere in the building and that a double sink is in the kitchen. Monies must be budgeted to move toward compliance in areas that require further work. Therefore, the director and any board members who are involved in budget preparation should be well informed about any aspects of the program and the physical environment that might need modification to comply with licensing standards. The time allowed for total compliance with all the licensing regulations will vary greatly and may be negotiable.

In general, the steps involved in the licensing process are as follows:

1. Request a copy of licensing requirements from the appropriate regulatory agency. Many agencies provide this information on governmental websites.
2. Complete any trainings specified by the regulatory agency that may be required of applicants for early childhood program licenses.
3. Ensure that the zoning authorities in the area have approved the land use; that is, does zoning allow early childhood program at the site you have chosen? Because early childhood program may be considered a business instead of an educational program or school, neighbors may be reluctant to allow a zone change. Some may be concerned about setting a precedent that would allow additional businesses to locate in that immediate area. Others may be unhappy about increased traffic and noise, as well as about the compatibility of the building with others in the area. Whether or not a zone change is needed, one of the first jobs of

Familiarity with Licensing's Use of Technology

The U.S. Office of Child Care (OCC) works with state early childhood program licensing programs to ensure they meet minimum health and safety requirements. The OCC has recommended to states that technology be used to as a means of enhancing efficiencies in their programs and improve quality (National Center on Early Childhood Program Quality Improvement, 2014). Specific suggestions for integrating technology to improve service include using mobile technology during monitoring visits, providing resources and alerts for providers, and permitting providers to apply online for a license. Directors of programs must become familiar with these enhanced strategies as they are implemented within states.

Directors of programs must become familiar with the ways that technology is being used by the licensing specialist and agency.

the director is to reach out to neighbors and establish the center as a cooperative part of the neighborhood.

4. Obtain information from the licensing agent about contacting the sanitation inspector, the fire inspector, the building inspector, and the public health office.
5. Arrange for conferences with and on-site visits from representatives of all necessary departments.
6. When all inspections have been completed and the inspectors have provided evidence of approval, complete the application for the license and send it with the required fee to the appropriate licensing agent. You may be required to submit a detailed plan for operating the program, including number of staff, daily schedule, equipment list, and program policies and procedures. (See **Director's Resource 3-1** at the end of the chapter.) You also may have to show copies of forms you will use for gathering required information such as health and emergency data.
7. On receipt of the license, post it in a conspicuous place in the early childhood program so that it is visible to families and visitors.
8. Check the expiration date and establish a procedure to ensure that the renewal process will be set in motion in time to eliminate the possibility of having to interrupt the provision of services to the children or having to pay a fine.

Some states and localities provide a one-stop licensing process. The idea is that a director can contact one person to set the licensing process in motion. Such a plan eliminates most if not all of the frustration directors may have experienced in the past when they tried to coordinate various departments and agencies. The goal of the various inspectors and the director is to ensure that the standards are met.

The director or, in special cases, a designated member of the board, is responsible for obtaining a license for the early childhood program. Renewals, although less time-consuming for both the director and the licensing agents, must be taken care of on a regular basis. The cost of a state or local license is minimal when considered in light of a total budget, but it is an item that must be included in the budget. Although some states do not charge a fee, others charge varying amounts based on the number of children served. Some states have additional fees for special services such as review of a particular building before deciding to obtain that building.

3-4a • The Licensing Specialist

The primary function of the licensing specialist is to ascertain whether a program is in compliance with the licensing regulations

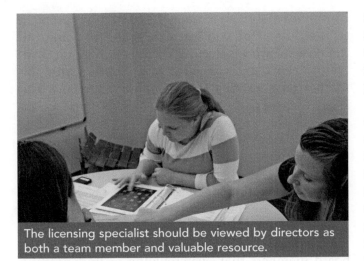

The licensing specialist should be viewed by directors as both a team member and valuable resource.

and to issue or recommend issuing a license to those programs that meet the minimum requirements. When programs do not meet minimum requirements, the function of the licensing specialist is to provide support and suggest resources that will help bring the programs into compliance rather than close them. The specialist's goal is to improve services for children and families. Licensing specialists are being viewed more and more as people who provide services instead of as people who simply issue licenses or close programs.

When combined with a thorough knowledge of the licensing regulations, knowledge of the community makes the licensing specialist a valuable resource for directors who are seeking training for staff, looking for educational program consultants, and exploring the best and least expensive ways to meet the fire, health, or building regulations. The licensing specialist also may be available as a consultant when a director is petitioning to have an unusual or unrealistic restriction varied or adjusted. In situations in which licensing regulations are inappropriate for children's programs, licensing specialists are available to support community efforts to have the regulations changed. Often specialists are not in a position to initiate an action to change a highly restrictive regulation. However, they may provide support and information to a group of laypeople or professional people who organize to bring about changes that will allow quality service for children while simultaneously freeing the programs from unrealistic restrictions. If you find yourself confronted with a local or

state regulation that seems impractical or unworkable, enlist your licensing specialist's help in making contact with other directors who feel as you do about the regulation and form a task force to investigate the process necessary to have the regulation changed.

In one locality in which all staff people were required to hold first aid certificates, program operators and licensing specialists worked together to adjust the requirement and make it more realistic without jeopardizing the health or safety of the children. Having a first aid license is valuable for everyone, whether at the program or elsewhere. However, when a program experiences high rates of staff turnover, paying for training and providing paid time to complete the training can be a major burden. In some cases, programs require staff to meet this requirement during their own time and at their own expense. The key is ensuring that appropriate numbers of staff are prepared and properly certified to administer first aid at the program, while children are being transported, and on field trips.

An unreasonable or outdated requirement may be included in licensing and may need to be changed, but the regulation may remain until some pragmatic and energetic director comes along who is willing to organize the forces necessary to create change. You may find yourself interested in doing just that with the help of other directors, related agencies, and your licensing specialist.

You also may find yourself in a situation in which the licensing requirements offer little effective protection of children. In this case, even though your program exceeds minimum standards, it is your responsibility to advocate for appropriate standards. Section IV of the NAEYC Code of Ethical Conduct (2011) calls out our ethical responsibilities to community and society and points out our obligation

Director's Corner

I spend a lot of time keeping track of paperwork. I know that I have to have all the staff and child medical records as soon as a new child or staff member comes to the program. That's one of the first things I do. I also make a calendar each year that reminds me when to apply to renew our license, to get our fire inspection, and our kitchen inspection.

—*Director, private not-for-profit program*

"to support policies and laws that promote the well-being of children and families" (p. 7). Often, licensing specialists support the need for more appropriate requirements, yet their authority allows them to enforce only the written rules.

The licensing specialist also can help you work through a grievance process if you encounter a unique problem with licensing. For example, one specialist explained a situation in which the fire inspector was holding to the letter of the law by requiring that an expensive, special type of glass be installed in the windows of a building that was not the required 30 feet from an adjacent building. The regulation requiring 30 feet is appropriate and necessary for adequate fire protection, but the program windows in this case were 28 feet away from an all-brick, fire-resistant building separated from the program by a grassy area. There was no real hazard to the children in this particular program. The licensing specialist provided special help to the director to expedite the grievance process, and the requirement was waived for the program.

In another situation, a new, all-day program was to begin for a 1-year period on an experimental basis. The kitchen facility was totally inappropriate for cooking lunches for children who were to stay all day. With the help of the licensing specialist, the director was able to obtain a temporary permit to operate the experimental program for 1 year by having the children bring brown-bag lunches. Bag lunches are strictly forbidden in this particular locality under the program licensing regulations, so this particular experimental program could not have been implemented without the understanding support of the licensing specialists. It was agreed that the conditions in the program's food service area would have to meet minimum standards if the program were to be extended beyond the first experimental year and that the bag lunches would have to be appropriately stored each day during that period. The program provided information to parents about appropriate nutritional content of sack lunches.

Licensing specialists are well acquainted with many directors and early childhood educators in the community, so they can serve as a communication bridge between programs by taking ideas and news from one program to another. For example, sharing the news about how a director in a neighboring community solved a budget or staffing problem (without breaking confidentiality) can be helpful to the director who is dealing with seemingly unsolvable problems and is isolated from contact with colleagues facing similar problems. The specialist can assist directors who are trying to effect budget adjustments or staffing changes but who are meeting resistance from board members or influential community groups. Occasionally, for economic reasons, some board members will pressure the director to overenroll a group to increase revenue. Overenrolling is a risk because there are days when all the enrollees appear, and the classroom becomes overcrowded and understaffed. It may be difficult to convince some board members that overcrowding or understaffing for a few days a month can be demoralizing for staff members and disruptive for children. In some states, overenrolling is even illegal.

Although some people prefer fewer government regulations, keep in mind that the quality of early childhood program would almost certainly diminish rapidly if state regulations were reduced or eliminated. If early childhood program licensing were not in place, an individual could assume responsibility for large numbers of children. This is an unsafe condition that would jeopardize children's health, safety, and development.

Making the Case for *Program Accreditation*

While licensing of early childhood programs addresses the minimal regulations for operation, accreditation entails meeting standards that in many cases far exceed the requirements of licensing. Some administrators may feel that accreditation is not necessary or is too costly or time-consuming. Reflect on the following questions:

1. What are the important similarities and differences between licensing requirements and accreditation? (Refer to **Appendix D** for an overview of NAEYC accreditation standards.)
2. How might the process of accreditation benefit an early childhood program, including the children, parents, staff, director, board members, and the community?

3-5 • Accreditation

While licensing implies meeting minimum standards, accreditation implies performing at a higher level and meeting additional standards. Directors volunteer to have their program reviewed by an accrediting agency, and those programs that are accredited are deemed worthy of the trust and confidence of both the private and professional communities. Approximately 11 percent of early childhood programs in the United States have achieved national accreditation (Child Care Aware of America, 2013).

The accreditation process varies, depending on the organization conducting the evaluation of the early childhood program. However, the process typically includes an extensive self-study of a program's facilities, staff, and programming that is followed by validation, which may include a site visit by professional early childhood educators representing the accrediting body. Programs usually must seek renewal of their accreditation after a specified period to maintain their status as an accredited program.

Engaging in the accreditation process is productive for the director, staff, parents, and, ultimately, the children. The self-study process may be revealing to the director because it requires reviewing all facets of the program's operation. The process can also provide opportunities for the director and staff to work together in achieving the quality they desire. Groups such as the American Montessori Society, the Association Montessori Internationale, the Child Welfare League of America, the Association for Early Learning Leaders, the National Early Childhood Program Accreditation Commission (NECPA), and the YMCA have various programs to ensure that their programs provide quality early childhood education. The Association for Early Learning Leaders and NECPA also accredit programs. The National Association for Family Child Care offers the only national accreditation system for family early childhood program providers. The most far-reaching effort is that of the National Academy for Early Childhood Program Accreditation, a division of NAEYC. One facet of this professional organization's attempt to improve the quality of life for young children and their families is the accreditation system, based on research and criteria developed over several years with input from a wide range of early childhood educators. Although many early childhood professionals and parents recognize the benefits of accreditation, individual states are beginning to recognize the value as well. For example, both Maine and Arkansas offer tax credits to families choosing to enroll their children in NAEYC-accredited programs (NAEYC, 2019). Additional information about NAEYC accreditation policies and procedures can be found on the organization's website. The NAEYC accreditation criteria can be found in **Appendix D**.

3-6 • Quality Rating and Improvement Systems (QRIS)

As previously discussed, most states have implemented a QRIS (Alliance for Early Success, 2020), which can be viewed as a "systemic approach to assess, improve, and communicate the level of quality" of early childhood programs. These systems build on licensing systems within states and seek to improve the quality of care in early childhood programs. Although not an accreditation system, the QRIS process provides a research-based framework of best practices that administrators and staff can use to evaluate and enhance programming. In addition, quality rating systems provide parents with another indicator they can use to select programs for their children.

QRIS include multiple tiers in which each level builds on the previous level. Each tier contains specific standards related to items such as staff–child ratios, administrator and staff education and experience, accreditation, benefits for employees, and implementation and assessment of research-based curriculum.

Most states have adopted a recognizable symbol that programs can use to advertise their program as having successfully completed the QRIS evaluation. For example, stars may be awarded to programs that have met criteria related to a specific tier. In Colorado, early childhood programs can earn up to four stars; in Ohio, those programs that reach the top tier are awarded five stars.

Although completion of a QRIS should not be viewed as a substitute for accreditation, the two systems can work hand in hand to help directors and staff members provide the most appropriate program possible for young children. In fact, some states provide support to programs seeking and maintaining accreditation, and many have included accreditation as part of their QRIS as an indicator of quality. For example, some systems provide points for having accreditation, and others require a program to be accredited in order to reach the top tier.

Additional information about QRIS can be found on the QRIS National Learning Network website at https://www.qrisnetwork.org/.

3-7 • Credentialing

The work of the Power to the Profession Taskforce (2020) emphasized the need to establish three distinct and meaningful designations: Early Childhood Educator (ECE) I, Early Childhood Educator II, and Early Childhood Educator III (see **Figure 3.2**). This task force states,

> Although these professionals will be prepared to work together in various configurations as part of a teaching team, each designation has an associated scope of practice, expected level of professional preparation, and expected level of mastery of the *Professional Standards and Competencies as for Early Childhood Educators*.
>
> To recognize these levels of mastery, all early childhood educators will hold a professional license to practice at the ECE I, II, or III designation based on: completing an accredited/recognized professional preparation program,

completing field experiences, and passing an assessment(s) of competencies. Licensure assessments must have multiple measures, be affordable, and not reinforce cultural, gender, racial, or linguistic biases, and educators must have affordable, equitable, efficient, and high-quality paths to licensure. (p. 13)

Individuals who work in a profession may be awarded a credential indicating that they have demonstrated the capabilities necessary for successful participation in that profession. Although licensing is required for an agency to operate a program, credentials are related to the educational preparation of individual staff members. Credentials may or may not be required by licensing, but they are an indication that an individual has had appropriate preparation for the early childhood profession. There are several types of credentials in the field of early childhood education.

3-7a • Staff Credentialing

State Teacher Licensure Licensing or certification of early childhood educators has been under discussion in many states for many years. Early childhood teaching licenses accredited by NAEYC are common throughout the country. Some states like Ohio have lost ground by discontinuing its early childhood pre-K to age 8 license based on NAEYC standards to a pre-K through fifth grade elementary license that responds to Council for Accreditation of Educator Preparation standards. Some people refer to the credential as a *certificate*, meaning a license to practice the profession of teaching, just as doctors, lawyers, real estate agents, or beauticians may obtain a state license to practice their professions. Although the term *certificate* was more widely used in the past, licensing is now considered to be the norm. A certificate may be earned from the National Board for Professional Teaching Standards, which indicates that the individual exceeds minimal requirements for teaching. This system is parallel to program licensing and program accreditation.

A teaching license is usually issued by a state's department of education. In some cases, the state provides enabling legislation; that is, the license is available but the state does not require that everyone who

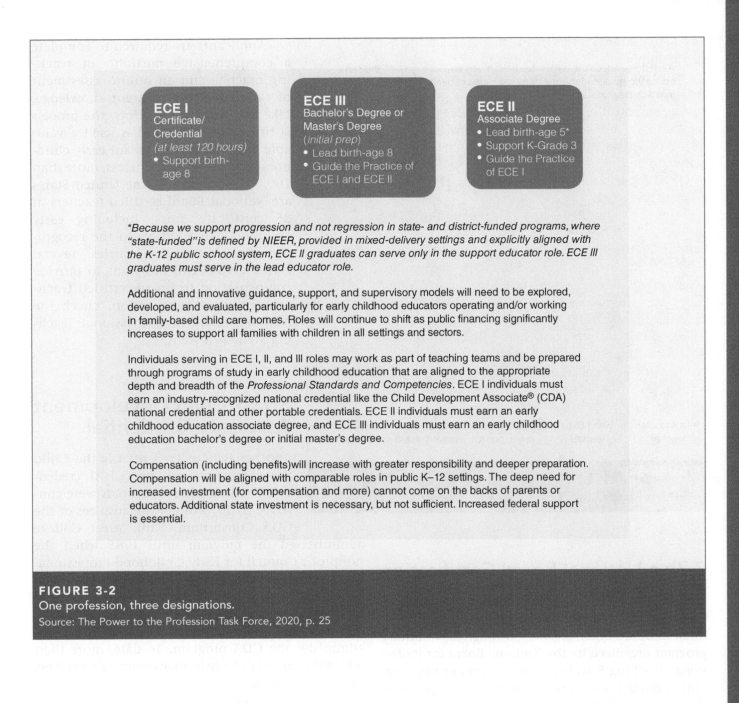

ECE I
Certificate/
Credential
(at least 120 hours)
• Support birth-
age 8

ECE III
Bachelor's Degree or
Master's Degree
(initial prep)
• Lead birth-age 8
• Guide the Practice of
ECE I and ECE II

ECE II
Associate Degree
• Lead birth-age 5*
• Support K-Grade 3
• Guide the Practice
of ECE I

*Because we support progression and not regression in state- and district-funded programs, where "state-funded" is defined by NIEER, provided in mixed-delivery settings and explicitly aligned with the K–12 public school system, ECE II graduates can serve only in the support educator role. ECE III graduates must serve in the lead educator role.

Additional and innovative guidance, support, and supervisory models will need to be explored, developed, and evaluated, particularly for early childhood educators operating and/or working in family-based child care homes. Roles will continue to shift as public financing significantly increases to support all families with children in all settings and sectors.

Individuals serving in ECE I, II, and III roles may work as part of teaching teams and be prepared through programs of study in early childhood education that are aligned to the appropriate depth and breadth of the *Professional Standards and Competencies*. ECE I individuals must earn an industry-recognized national credential like the Child Development Associate® (CDA) national credential and other portable credentials. ECE II individuals must earn an early childhood education associate degree, and ECE III individuals must earn an early childhood education bachelor's degree or initial master's degree.

Compensation (including benefits) will increase with greater responsibility and deeper preparation. Compensation will be aligned with comparable roles in public K–12 settings. The deep need for increased investment (for compensation and more) cannot come on the backs of parents or educators. Additional state investment is necessary, but not sufficient. Increased federal support is essential.

FIGURE 3-2
One profession, three designations.
Source: The Power to the Profession Task Force, 2020, p. 25

teaches preschool children be licensed. However, all 50 states and the District of Columbia require that public preschool educators be licensed. Many different licensure configurations are available, including birth to 5 years, birth to 8 years, 3 to 5 years, and so forth.

Individual program policies may require that early childhood educators be licensed, but the demand is much greater than the supply of licensed teachers who wish to work with young children. Although the job of the early childhood educator may be the same, the compensation across settings differs greatly (see **Figure 3-3**). Directors who require licensure as a qualification for their early childhood educators must be aware of the many kinds of teaching certificates. Preparation for elementary or secondary teaching licenses, for example, does not include attention to most of the knowledge, skills, and attitudes necessary for those working with younger children. Therefore, these licenses may not be appropriate criteria for early childhood educator positions.

All of these educators have a bachelor's degree. But even with the same education qualifications, their pay still varies depending on the setting in which they work.[ix]

FIGURE 3-3
Same job different pay.
Reprinted with permission from the Power to the Profession Task Force (2020, p. 8).

3-7b • National Board Certification

Early childhood educators who desire to demonstrate that they are accomplished in their field may apply to become certified teachers through a voluntary program organized by the National Board for Professional Teaching Standards. This nonprofit organization is governed by a board primarily composed of classroom teachers.

Eligibility for the certificate requires the applicant to have the following:

- at least 3 years' experience working with children ages 3 through 8,
- a baccalaureate degree, and
- a valid license or certificate in the applicant's state (in states where a license is not required, the candidate must have taught in programs or schools that are approved to operate by the state).

Applicants are required to complete a comprehensive portfolio of teaching practice and an online assessment of early childhood content knowledge. Like any worthwhile effort, the process is time-consuming and is itself a valuable learning experience for early childhood educators. Nonetheless, more than 100,000 educators in the United States are National Board certified teachers in 25 certificate areas, including early childhood. In addition to the recognition the certification carries, several states have begun programs to provide compensation to board-certified teachers. For more information, check the National Board for Professional Teaching Standards website.

3-7c • Child Development Associate Credential

Another type of credential is the Child Development Associate (CDA) credential. The first CDA credentials were conferred in 1975 under the auspices of the CDA Consortium. Bank Street College administered the program until 1985 when the nonprofit Council for Early Childhood Professional Recognition was established. The council was established by an agreement between the U.S. Department of Health and Human Services, Administration on Children, Youth and Families, and the NAEYC to administer the CDA program. To date, more than 300,000 credentials have been awarded to caregivers in four categories:

1. center-based infant care,
2. center-based preschool care,
3. home visitor care, and
4. family child care.

A bilingual endorsement for each type of credential is also available.

This national credential is included as one of the possible qualifications for directors or early childhood educators throughout the United States. Candidates for the credential demonstrate their skill in six competency goal areas, including 13 functional areas such as advancing physical and intellectual competence (physical, cognitive, communication, and creative). A combination of experience and training prepares candidates for assessment based on procedures established by the council. Now, almost 40 years since its inception, the credential is still tied closely to Head Start, the program that led to its creation. The CDA is widely recognized by the entire early childhood community as a valuable addition to professional development.

To be eligible to apply for assessment in the CDA process, candidates must:

- hold a high school diploma or GED or be enrolled in a career or technical program in early childhood education at the junior or senior level;
- be able to speak, read, and write well enough to perform CDA responsibilities;
- have 480 hours of experience working with children within 3 years before they apply;
- complete the professional portfolio within 6 months of application; and
- complete 120 clock hours of formal education in eight subject areas before they apply.

Candidates must be prepared to demonstrate their understanding of the following areas:

- safety,
- health,
- learning environment,
- physical development,
- cognitive development,
- communication,
- creative development,
- self (emotional development),
- social development,
- guidance,
- families,
- program management, and
- professionalism.

Although fees are associated with participating in this credentialing process, scholarships are available, and some agencies pay all or part of the fees.

3-7d • Certified Childcare Professional Credential

The Certified Childcare Professional (CCP) credential is offered by NECPA. The credential authenticates teaching skills and professionalism, particularly for those who do not have a college degree or are entering the field from another discipline. Candidates must have a high school diploma or GED, be 18 years of age or older, and speak, read, and write English at a level that will allow the candidate to complete the duties of a CCP. Moreover, an opportunity exists for candidates to obtain college credit for their work. Additional details and application materials can be obtained from the NECPA website.

3-7e • U.S. Department of Labor Registered Apprenticeship for Careers in Child Development

The apprenticeship program for careers in child development is offered by many agencies and organizations throughout the United States. Sponsored by the U.S. Department of Labor, this certificate program targets practitioners and requires both on-the-job training with a mentor and classroom instruction. Increased compensation for participants must be provided as they progress successfully through their apprenticeships. Additional information about the program is available from the U.S. Department of Labor's Employment and Training Administration website or your state's apprenticeship agency.

3-7f • Director Credentialing

Since 2000, a movement toward director credentialing has grown significantly. The idea evolved

Directors who are working toward a credential can review their understanding of child development by observing in the classroom.

through the work of advocates in the profession such as Gwen Wheeler at Wheelock College and Paula Jorde Bloom at the McCormick Center for Early Childhood Leadership. They understood the importance of specific training, education, and recognition of program leaders (Bloom et al., 2011). Director credentials certify "that an individual has met a defined set of requirements set forth by the grantor of the credential, usually related to skills and knowledge, and may include demonstrations of competence" (National Child Care Information Center, n.d., p. 6-2). The body that awards the credential may or may not be the same organization that delivers the training. A credential may be awarded by a professional association, a state agency, a higher education consortium, or other organization, and it signifies a consensus by those groups of the validity of the standards set forth.

Many states have established director credentials or are in the process of developing credentialing systems. Because this movement is evolving quickly, check with your licensing specialist to determine the status of your state's progress toward the credential.

Several organizations offer national director credentials or certificates. For example, the National Administrator Credential, sponsored by the NECPA Commission, focuses its efforts on the licensed private early childhood program community.

The McCormick Center for Early Childhood Leadership at National–Louis University offers the Aim4Excellence online director credential program that requires completion of nine self-paced modules. This credential was the first in the nation to be recognized by NAEYC as meeting the *relevant training and credentials* criterion for those directors seeking accreditation of their programs.

When seeking a credential or certificate, you must decide which program meets your needs and the requirements in your state. Typically, credentials are offered through states and reflect a more rigorous process of preparation than do certificates. Programs seeking accreditation from NAEYC must be able to demonstrate that teaching staff and administrators meet specific preparation and education guidelines. The organization does not offer a credential or certificate itself; however, it does provide credit for directors who have earned their NAEYC-approved state administrator credential. Administrator credentials are important because they

have the potential to increase the knowledge and skill level of administrators, particularly in the business and management roles they must assume. As a result, the quality of programs is likely to improve, and staff turnover under the leadership of a knowledgeable administrator may be reduced. The director makes the decisions that influence child outcomes while helping to create the culture of the program. Components such as creating suitable staff-to-child ratios, providing appropriate resources, creating partnerships with diverse families, and selecting well-qualified early childhood educators lead to high quality. Being credentialed creates value for the role of director and encourages individuals to consider this position as a career. Moreover, credentialing can promote both public and private support as the directorship becomes recognized as a valid professional role. Because much of the early childhood education programming being offered today is of poor quality, the need for well-prepared directors is receiving greater attention.

3-8 • Career Pathways

Credentials are important indicators of one's developing skill and competency; this is why they have been included in many states' early childhood QRIS and career pathways, which are also known as *ladders* or *lattices*. Career pathways provide clearly defined routes by which professionals can enhance their qualifications, recognize professional possibilities that exist in the workforce, and be compensated appropriately (LeMoine, 2008). Pathways include a variety of experiences such as completion of in-service trainings or college coursework and attainment of degrees, credentials, or certificates.

The career pathways efforts were based on the work of LeMoine (2008) and provided a foundation for the Power to the Profession Task Force in its efforts to "establish unity and clarity around the career pathways" (2020, p. 1). Career pathways will transition to the "knowledge and competencies, qualifications, standards, accountability, supports, and compensation" established by the Power to the Profession Task Force "to define the early childhood education profession within the broader early childhood education field" (2020, p. 1).

Summary

The director of an early childhood program is responsible for being familiar with licensing regulations, accreditation, and staff credentialing opportunities because these all work together to ensure quality care for young children. Specifically, the director should do the following:

- understand that licensing of programs provides the minimum standards for early education programs and focuses on the health and safety of children and staff;

- be familiar with licensing regulations and understand the purpose behind each requirement;

- know the steps in the process that are required by the local or state agency responsible for issuing a program's license to operate;

- recognize the important role of the licensing specialist as a resource and in ensuring that regulations are achieved and maintained;

- understand the differences between the licensing and accreditation processes and the role that each plays in providing quality early childhood education for young children;

- be familiar with the requirements of the QRIS in one's state and recognize that even though it is not a substitute for national program accreditation, the two can work together to provide high-quality programming for children;

- differentiate among the various credentials for program staff and how they can contribute to professionalism and quality programming; and

- understand the impact of Power to the Profession Task Force on the roles, responsibilities, career pathways, and compensation.

TRY IT OUT!

1. Invite the licensing specialist from your community to come to a class session to discuss all the services provided by the licensing agency. Before the licensing specialist visits, review the local licensing regulations. After the visit, complete the following activities in class with a small group:
    a. Review the licensing regulations and determine which sections of the code would help you do a more effective job as a program director.
    b. Evaluate the regulations and determine which sections (if any) should be revised so that more effective service could be delivered to children.
    c. Discuss what you consider to be the most challenging part of the licensing process.
2. Many states require that a detailed plan of operation or business plan be developed as part of the licensing process. Review **Director's Resource 3-1**, which provides a sample of such a plan. In a small group, discuss the information that must be addressed when planning an early childhood program. Visit your own state's website to secure information regarding the requirements for business plans. Compare and contrast your state's document to **Director's Resource 3-1**.
3. Divide the class into small groups to consider the pros and cons of licensure for an early childhood educator who teaches preschoolers.
    a. Can you think of any individuals or groups who provide services for young children who would be opposed to licensure? Discuss why.
    b. Does licensure guarantee quality service to young children? Discuss the reasons for your conclusion.
    c. What are the best ways to guarantee quality service to children? Report your conclusions and supporting rationale to the class.
4. You are the director of an early childhood program who is considering working toward NAEYC accreditation for your program. Review and discuss the four steps of accreditation with a small group. Draw a time line of the process that you can present at your next board of directors and parent meetings. You may obtain

information on program accreditation from the NAEYC website.

5. With a small group, compare and contrast program accreditation, quality rating systems, early childhood educator and director credentialing, and career pathways. How are they different? How are they related? How does each contribute to the quality of care and education of young children?

6. Review the career pathway, lattice, or ladder for your state or one provided by your instructor. Discuss the following questions with a classmate or small group:

   a. How does the existing career pathway align with the recommendations made in the Power to the Profession Task Force recommendations?

   b. What requirements must be completed to reach each level?

   c. How are the individual levels related to specific positions in early childhood?

   d. Given your current experience and educational background, in which level would you be placed in the pathway?

   e. Consider your long-term professional goals. Identify those criteria you would need to meet or complete to achieve your goal.

7. Working with a small group, review the three sets of standards that appear in **Appendixes B, C,** and **D.** Identify those standards and competencies that relate to licensing, accreditation, and early childhood educator and administrator qualifications. What are early childhood professionals expected to know and be able to do? Discuss your findings with the class.

Director's Resource 3-1 ////

OHIO DEPARTMENT OF JOB AND FAMILY SERVICES PLAN OF OPERATION FOR AN EARLY CHILDHOOD PROGRAM

Ohio Department of Job and Family Services
PLAN OF OPERATION FOR A CHILD CARE CENTER

Dates of Attendance		Do Not Write In This Space
Opening a Child Care Program (Available through OCCRRA)		Application Number
Initial Plan of Operation Orientation (Provided by ODJFS)		Assignment Number
Plan of Operation Review (Conducted by staff from the local licensing field office)		Date Plan Received

SECTION 1: GENERAL INFORMATION/SPACE

Name of Center		County	
Address		State	Address
Mailing Address (if different)		State	Mailing Address (if different)
Name of Contact Person			
Center Telephone Number		Contact Person's Telephone Number	
Proposed Date of Opening		Owner/Corporation	
Directions to the Center			
Proposed Hours of Operation	Proposed Days of Operation		Proposed Months of Operation

PLANNED ENROLLMENT

Age Categories	Number of Children Planned at Opening	Number of Groups Planned at Opening	Number of Children Planned at Capacity	Number of Staff needed at opening
Infants (0-18mo.)				
Toddlers (18mo-3yr)				
Preschoolers (3yr – school age)				
School age Children (5 yr - 14yr) Note: School age children present more than 4 hrs per day are considered fulltime during school breaks, holidays, snow days, etc.	Before school / After School	Before School / After School	Before School / After School	
	Fulltime	Fulltime	Fulltime	

Total Number of Child Care Staff Members Needed at Opening

Director's Resource 3-1 (continued) ////

INDOOR SPACE
(Rule 5101:2-12-13)

Draw a diagram of the indoor space used by the child care operation. Indicate the following:
- Exits
- Walls, partitions or half walls
- Walls, partitions, or half walls that are moveable
- Sinks and water fountains
- Emergency exits and exits to the outdoor play space
- Room assignments (i.e., infant room, toddler room, preschool room etc.)
- Restrooms
- Diaper changing area with sink
- Food preparation areas

Is center building occupied by any other persons or groups other than those of the child care center during hours of operation? Explain:

(Include what space is used by these persons as well as the children from the center.)

Will the center care for children under the age of 2 ½ years? If yes, describe how the center will keep these children separated from other groups older than 2 ½ years.

OUTDOOR SPACE
(Rule 5101: 2-12-14)

Diagram the space used for outdoor play.
- Include location of fence or barriers.
- Note gate locations, street locations, and parking lots.
- Sketch outdoor permanent play equipment which stays in space (i.e., slides, swings, sandboxes, etc.)
- Also include sidewalks, concrete, or blacktop areas.

If the play space is away from the center, diagram the outdoor space used.
If the center has no outdoor play space an indoor recreation area must be provided. Give dimensions of your indoor recreation area.

1) What type of protective fall surface will the center use on the playground? (Fall surface needed under slides, swings, climbers, bouncers, etc.)

2) How is the play area enclosed or otherwise protected from traffic or other hazards?

3) Describe how children will have access to bathroom facilities and drinking water during outdoor play time.

4) How will the center provide a shaded area when needed?

Note: When the playground does not meet the square footage requirement of 60 square feet per child, for all children at one time; then children will need to play in groups by staggered shifts.

Director's Resource 3-1 (continued) ////

SECTION 2: SAFE/SANITARY REQUIREMENTS

SAFE/SANITARY EQUIPMENT
(Rules 5101:2-12-15, 5101:2-12-15.1, 5101:2-12-15.3 and 5101:2-12-15.4)

1) Describe the center's plan to maintain and clean indoor and outdoor play equipment, furniture and materials. (Be sure your answer includes all parts of this question.)

2) What supplies will be used for cleaning and sanitizing? (Refer to Appendix A for Rule 5101:2-12-15 for more information.)

3) How often is equipment cleaned?

4) How often is equipment sanitized?

5) Who is responsible for cleaning and maintenance?

6) Explain how you will keep track of when cleaning/sanitizing is completed. (Describe your tracking system.)

7) Describe how and where cleaning equipment and supplies will be stored.

8) Will the center care for pets? ☐ Yes ☐ No   If yes, explain and indicate how pet shot records will be maintained?

9) Will the center use fans? ☐ Yes ☐ No   If yes, what safety provisions will be taken?

10) Is the center's water publicly supplied?
☐ Yes ☐ No   If no, sampling by the local health department must be completed.

11) When are cots cleaned?

12) When are cots sanitized?

13) Describe the location of the hand washing facilities for children over 2 ½ years old and explain when children wash their hands.

14) If center staff is permitted to smoke, what will be your policy? (Refer to 5101:2-12-15.3 for restrictions.)

15) Will children be provided the opportunity to brush their teeth while at the center?
☐ Yes ☐ No   If yes, explain how you will keep brushes sanitary.

Director's Resource 3-1 (continued) ////

SECTION 3: PROGRAMMING AND CENTER POLICIES

PROGRAMMING/EQUIPMENT AND COTS
(Rules 5101:2-12-16 and 5101:2-12-19)

1) Where will a copy of the daily program schedule for each age group be posted?

2) What provisions have been taken to provide enough equipment representative of all areas listed in Rule 5101:2-12-16? (Have you listed all categories? Have you listed all age groups?)

3) Who will monitor the equipment so sufficient quantities are maintained and replacements are ordered in a timely manner? (Describe your system.)

4) If you have school age children who rest/sleep at the center, what type of equipment will be provided?

5) How many cots are available at the center for daily use by toddlers and preschoolers?

6) How are cots assigned to the children?

7) What tracking system will be used to document when cots are cleaned and sanitized?

SWIMMING AND WATER SAFETY
(Rule 5101:2-12-17)

1) Will the center's program include swimming or water activities? ☐ Yes ☐ No   (If Yes, continue below, otherwise skip to Transportation and Field Trip Safety.)

2) Describe type of activity including the pool location if off the premises.

3) Describe the center's plan for supervision of children when they are out of the water and the system the center will use for supervising and tracking each child while in the water.

TRANSPORTATION/FIELD TRIP SAFETY
(Rule 5101: 2-12-18)

1) Does the center plan to offer: (Check all that apply)
☐ Field trips
☐ Routine trips

If the center will **not** take field/routine trips, skip to Supervision/Child Guidance and Management

2) Does the center provide transportation? ☐ Yes ☐ No

3) Describe the center vehicles or vehicles that are used (by a contracted agency, if applicable. i.e., mini-van, bus, car)

4) Explain the center's safety procedures in regards to transporting children.

5) What will be taken on trips?

Director's Resource 3-1 (continued) ////

6) How will identification for the children be provided?

7) How will permission be obtained?

8) Explain how the center will obtain verification of an appropriate valid driver's license for all drivers.

9) Who is responsible for obtaining an _annual_ vehicle safety inspection? See prescribed form JFS 01230.

10) Who will be responsible for providing the transportation safety training each year to any employees who will be driving or riding?

11) Who will be responsible for completing the _weekly_ vehicle inspection?

12) How will the administrator verify that any areas of concern, indicated on the weekly inspection sheet, will be addressed? (i.e., brake lights not working, low tire pressure, etc.)

SUPERVISION/CHILD GUIDANCE AND MANAGEMENT
(Rule 5101:2-12-20 and 5101:2-12-22)

1) Explain how all child care staff members will be made aware of the center policies.

2) Describe the center's procedure for taking attendance and maintaining attendance records.

3) Explain provisions made for compliance with staff/child ratios on occasions when staff is absent, late, or leave for breaks? (Describe your plan for each situation.)

4) Describe the center's plan for transitioning children into the next age group.

5) How will the transitioning child's whereabouts be tracked?

EVENING AND OVERNIGHT CARE
(Rule 5101:2-12-23)

1) Will the center be providing evening and/or overnight care? (Between 7:00 PM and 6:00 AM) ☐ Yes ☐ No
(If yes, complete the following questions otherwise skip to Center Administrative Policies and Procedures.)

2) Days and hours overnight and/or evening care will be provided?

3) Describe the center's security plan to ensure that access to the center is limited to parents and guardians of children in care and authorized persons.

4) Describe the center's sleeping arrangements, including how children will be grouped.

Director's Resource 3-1 (continued) ////

CENTER ADMINISTRATIVE POLICIES AND PROCEDURES
(Rule 5101:2-12-30)

This refers to your Parent Handbook that you will attach.
(See Sample Form JFS 01268 for guidance)

**ADMINISTRATION OF MEDICATION AND
FIRST AID SUPPLIES/PROCEDURES**
(Rules 5101:2-12-31 and 5101:2-12-36)

1) Describe the center's procedures for administering medication, and topical products or lotions. (Be sure to describe the plan for each type of product.)

2) Describe the center's procedures for administering food supplements and/or modified diets. (Describe the plan for each.)

3) Who is the designated individual(s) who will be assigned and responsible for the administration of medication?

4) How will the designee(s) document the administration of medication to assure accurate records?

5) Describe the procedure if medication is: not administered, delayed or incorrectly administered.

6) Describe the center's plan for safe storage of medication.

7) Describe the center's procedure for implementing standard precautions (5101:2-12-15.1)

8) Where will first aid supplies be stored?

MEDICAL, DENTAL AND GENERAL EMERGENCY PLAN
(Rule 5101:2-12-34)

1) Describe the center's plan for emergency transportation of children.

INCIDENT/INJURY REPORT
(Rule 5101:2-12-35)

1) Describe the center's procedure for completing incident/injury reports. (Use prescribed form JFS 01299)

2) Describe the center's procedure for notifying the appropriate licensing office when a serious incident, injury, illness, death of a child or unusual or unexpected event occurs.

Director's Resource 3-1 *(continued)*

SECTION 4: STAFF REQUIREMENTS
ADMINISTRATOR RESPONSIBILITIES AND QUALIFICATIONS
(Rule 5101:2-12-24)

1) How will the center assure the administrator will be onsite for a minimum of one-half of the hours that the center is in operation?

EMPLOYEE AND CHILD CARE STAFF MEMBER REQUIREMENTS AND STATEMENTS OF NONCONVICTION, CRIMINAL RECORDS CHECKS
(Rules 5101:2-12-25 and 5101:2-12-26)

1) Explain the procedures used to maintain employee's group assignments, work schedule and the date of employment. (How will the Employee Record Chart be kept up to date?)

Complete an Employee Records Chart, bold box only.

2) Describe the center's plan for providing the orientation training for staff using the prescribed online curriculum. Include when it will occur and who will provide the training.

3) Describe plans for the administrator to review the licensing rules, and to provide a copy of the Medical and Dental General Emergency Plan, and the center policies and procedures to each employee.

4) Where will the ODJFS Licensing Rules be located for staff?

5) Has the administrator submitted requests for both BCII and FBI criminal records web checks?

Be certain the results for owners/administrators are being sent directly to the appropriate child care licensing field office by the WebCheck agency.
6) Describe procedures for submitting requests for BCII and FBI criminal records web checks, for each child care staff member prior to employment. (What is the system for tracking this?)

Be certain the results for employees are being sent directly to the child care administrator/center by the WebCheck agency.
7) Describe the center's procedure for assuring that child care staff members are not left alone with children until the results of their criminal records checks are returned, and reviewed and approved by the administrator.

8) Describe the center's system for tracking results for all child care staff members/employees when the results are not received in a timely manner.

9) Describe the center's procedure if the results of the records check indicate that an employee has been convicted of a crime that prohibits employment. (Note: Review background check requirements and considerations for rehabilitation contained in this rule.)

10) Will the center use a non-employee as a second adult as required in Rule 5101:2-12-20? ☐ Yes ☐ No
If yes, describe the center's plan for obtaining the required information and describe the means to summon the second adult.

Director's Resource 3-1 *(continued)*

TRAINING IN FIRST AID, CPR, CHILDHOOD ILLNESSES, CHILD ABUSE PREVENTION AND INSERVICE TRAINING
(Rules 5101:2-12-27 and 5101:2-12-28)

1) How will the center assure that child care staff members who are trained in First Aid, Common Childhood Illnesses, CPR (for all the needed age groups), and child abuse prevention, will be on the premises during all hours of operation, and in all buildings?

2) What tracking system will the center use to ensure child care staff members have maintained current certifications in the areas above?

3) Describe the center's requirements for staff and annual inservice trainings.

4) What tracking system will the center use to ensure child care staff members meet inservice training requirements?

SECTION 5: CHILDREN'S RECORDS and FOOD REQUIREMENTS
CHILDREN'S MEDICAL STATEMENTS AND RECORDS AND CARE OF CHILDREN WITH HEALTH CONDITIONS
(Rules 5101:2-12-37 and 5101:2-12-38)

1) Describe the center's plans to ensure that all required children's medical statements will be secured within 30 days of each child's admission. (Be sure to note the difference in the medical requirements for school age children.)

2) What action will be taken if the child's medical examination records are not provided within the required time frame?

3) Describe the procedure the center will follow to assure medical examinations are updated as required.

4) Explain the center's system for obtaining and updating all required enrollment information for each child. (How often will information be reviewed?)

5) Describe how the center will obtain the medical/physical care plan, if needed. (How will these records be kept up to date?)

MEALS AND SNACKS
(Rule 5101:2-12-39)

1) List all meals and snacks that the center will be providing and the approximate serving times.

Director's Resource 3-1 *(continued)*

2) Will meals and snacks be prepared on site or brought in from another source?

3) Where will meals/snacks be eaten? Who will be responsible for getting the meals/snacks to the serving area? Who will serve the meals/snacks?

SECTION 6: INFANT/TODDLER CARE
INFANT DAILY PROGRAM/INFANT CAREGIVER
(Rule 5101:2-12-40)

1) Describe the center's procedure for assigning staff to groups of infants. How will parents be informed of the primary caregivers assigned to their infant?

2) Describe the center's procedures for assuring that necessary information regarding infant's care is exchanged among staff and between staff members and parents.

3) Describe how the cribs will be separated from the play space. What type of barrier will be used?

INFANT FORMULA AND FOOD
(Rule 5101:2-12-41)

1) Describe the center's process for feeding infants.

2) How will the center adapt the menu to take into account the developmental levels of infants?

3) Describe the center's procedure for obtaining written instructions from the parent(s) about serving food to infants.

4) How often will this be updated?

5) If formula is prepared by the center, describe the technique used.

6) Explain where this preparation of formula takes place.

7) How is the infant food prepared?

8) Describe the center's plan for safe storage of baby food, formula and breast milk.

Director's Resource 3-1 *(continued)*

9) How will formula be heated?

10) How will the center assure that extra formula, for all enrolled infants, will be on hand and available for use?

DIAPERING FACILITIES AND PROCESS
(Rule 5101:2-12-15.2)

1) If the center's hand washing facilities are located in a space other than where the infants/toddlers receive care, describe the location of the hand washing facilities and the center's plan to maintain supervision while diapering.

2) What separation material will the center use during diaper changes?

3) What will the center use to disinfect the changing station?

4) Describe the storage of soiled diapers/clothing.

CRIBS
(Rule 5101:2-12-42)

1) How many cribs will the center have available?	Porta Cribs	Full Size Cribs

2) When were the cribs purchased/obtained? (Do they meet the federal standards for cribs that were effective June 28, 2011?)

2) Describe the center's schedule for cleaning and sanitizing cribs. (If more than one infant will share a crib, how will the cribs be cleaned and sanitized in between children?)

3) Describe how staff will be trained on the safety requirements of this rule and who will provide the training.

4) What will the center's policy be on positioning infants when placing them in their cribs to sleep? (See prescribed form JFS 01235)

Director's Resource 3-1 *(continued)*

STATEMENT OF UNDERSTANDING

I understand that the department may revoke a license if:

- A center fails to comply with the requirements of Chapter 5104 of the Revised Code or Chapter 5101:2-12 of the Administrative Code.
- The center is found to have furnished or made misleading or false statements or reports to the department.
- The center refuses or fails to submit reports requested by the department within required time frames.
- The owner or administrator has pleaded guilty to or been convicted of an offense described in Section 5104.09 of the Revised Code and has not met the standards of rehabilitation set out in Rule 5101:2-12-26.
- A center has refused to admit the director's representative onto its premises.

I understand that the following must be obtained prior to an individual starting employment.

- A medical that meets the requirements of Rule 5101:2-12-25.
- Educational verification showing completion of high school or equivalency per Rule 5101: 2-12-25.
- Signed non-conviction statement per Rule 5101: 2-12-26.
- Fingerprint impressions/web check, the administrator must assure that child care staff members and employees have submitted fingerprint impressions to BCII and FBI per Rule 5101:2-12-26 prior to the first day of employment.
- A signed statement that the administrator has reviewed the licensing rules and all center policies and procedures to the employee per Rule 5101:2-12-25.

I have read and understand the requirements listed above.

Signature of Administrator	Date

Director's Resource 3-1 *(continued)*

SECTION 7	REQUIRED ATTACHMENTS TO THE CHILD CARE CENTER PLAN OF OPERATION
ATTACHMENT 1	If the center is owned by a corporation, attach a copy of the **incorporation papers.**
ATTACHMENT 2	A copy of the **Certificate of Occupancy.**
ATTACHMENT 3	A copy of the completed **fire inspection report** (JFS 01303.)
ATTACHMENT 4	A copy of the center's **food service license**, exemption and/or caterer's food service license.
ATTACHMENT 5	**Diagrams** of indoor floor plan and outdoor play space. (See page 2 for instructions)
ATTACHMENT 6	The **laboratory test** of the water supply from the local health department per Rule 5101:2-12-15, if the center's water is **not** publicly supplied.
ATTACHMENT 7	A copy of the **center's inventory.** Divide the inventory by all age groups, infants, toddlers, preschool, school age, and by category. Be sure to include the number of each item listed. (See Rule 5101:2-12-16.)
ATTACHMENT 8	A copy of each parent **permission form** that applies: field trip, routine trip, swimming and water activities.
ATTACHMENT 9	A sample **attendance form** which the center will use to record daily attendance of all children at the center.
ATTACHMENT 10	A copy of the center's **evening program schedule**, if applicable.
ATTACHMENT 11	A copy of the **administrator's qualifications and job description.**
ATTACHMENT 12	A copy of the **Parent Handbook.** (See Rule 5101:2-12-30)
ATTACHMENT 13	A copy of the center's completed **medical, dental and general emergency plan.**
ATTACHMENT 14	One week **menu** for meals and snacks.
ATTACHMENT 15	If the center will not prepare food but only **serves food brought by the parents**, attach: (1) a list of foods kept on hand to supplement lunches which do not meet the one-third daily dietary allowance, (2) a copy of the nutritional information given to parents (3) a description of the center's food storage plan for lunches.
ATTACHMENT 16	A sample copy of the center's **infant daily record and basic information.**
ATTACHMENT 17	A copy of the **Employee Record Chart** (JFS 01306) with the bolded box information completed.

Director's Resource 3-1 *(continued)*

**Portion Sizes for Meals Served at
Child Care Centers and Type A Homes**
(To be used when completing Attachment #14)

Meal	Component Age of Child	Minimum Serving		
		1 & 2 years	3-5 years	6-12 years
Breakfast	Fluid Milk	½ cup	¾ cup	1 cup
	Juice/Fruit or Vegetable	¼ cup	½ cup	½ **cup**
	Grains/Breads/Dry Cereal	½ slice ¼ cup or ⅓ oz.	½ slice ⅓ cup or ½ oz.	½ **slice** ¾ **cup or** 1 **oz.**
Lunch or Supper	Meat or Meat Alternative	1 oz.	1 ½ oz.	2 oz.
	2 Fruits or Vegetables	¼ cup	½ cup	¾ **cup**
	Grains/Breads/ Pasta/Noodles	½ slice ¼ cup	½ slice ¼ cup	1 slice ½ **cup**
	Fluid Milk	½ cup	¾ cup	1 cup
Snack	Meat or Meat Alternative	½ oz.	½ oz.	1 oz.
	Fruit or Vegetable	½ cup	½ cup	¾ **cup**
	Grains/Breads	½ slice ¼ cup or ⅓ oz.	½ slice ¼ cup or ⅓ oz.	½ **slice** ¼ **cup or** ⅓ **oz.**
	Fluid Milk	½ cup	½ cup	1 cup

Additional information on meal preparation and nutrition may be found at:
http://www.fns.usda.gov/cnd/care/ProgramBasics/Meals/Meal_Patterns.htm

Director's Resource 3-1 *(continued)*

Attachment 14

		Component	Monday	Tuesday	Wednesday	Thursday	Friday
Breakfast	One serving of each	Fluid Milk					
		Fruit or Vegetable					
		Grain/Bread/Cereal					
Meal	One serving of each	Meat or Meat Alt.					
		2 Fruits or Vegetables (one of each is recommended)					
		Grain/Bread/Cereal					
		Fluid Milk					
Snack	Two serving of the four groups	Grain/Bread/Cereal					
		Fruit or Vegetable					
		Meat or Meat Alt.					
		Milk					

- Only 100%, undiluted fruit or vegetable juice shall meet the fruit or vegetable requirement for meals or snacks.
- Children under 12 months of age shall receive formula or breast milk unless otherwise directed in writing by a licensed physician.
- Children 12 months to 24 months of age shall receive whole homogenized Vitamin D fortified cow's milk, unless otherwise directed in writing by a licensed physician.
- Children over 24 months of age shall receive fluid milk that is Vitamin D fortified. Lowfat and skim milk shall be Vitamin A and Vitamin D fortified. Reconstituted dry powdered milk shall be used only for cooking and shall not be used as a beverage.

Director's Resource 3-1 *(continued)*

Attachment 14
page 2 (if needed)

		Component	Monday	Tuesday	Wednesday	Thursday	Friday
Evening Meal	**One serving of each**	Meat or Meat Alt.					
		2 Fruits or Vegetables (one of each is recommended)					
		Grain/Bread/Cereal					
		Fluid Milk					
PM Snack	**Two serving of the four groups**	Grain/Bread/Cereal					
		Fruit or Vegetable					
		Meat or Meat Alt.					
		Milk					

Source: Ohio Department of Job and Family Services

REFERENCES

Alliance for Early Success. (2020). Washington, DC: Author. https://earlysuccess.org/

American Academy of Pediatrics, American Public Health Association, & National Resource Center for Health and Safety in Child Care and Early Education (2019). *Caring for our children* (4th ed.). Elk Grove Village, IL: American Academy of Pediatrics, Washington, DC: American Public Health Association, and Aurora, CO: National Resource Center for Health and Safety in Child Care and Early Education. https://nrckids.org/files/CFOC4%20pdf-%20FINAL.pdf

Bloom, P. J., Vinci, Y., Rafanello, D., & Donohue, C. (2011, January–February). Directions in center director training. *Exchange*, 18–20.

Child Care Aware of America. (2013). *Child care in America: 2013 state fact sheets*. Arlington, VA: Author. http://www.naccrra.org/sites/default/files/default_site_pages/2013/2013_state_fact_sheets_082013.pdf

Engelman, K., Dobbins, D., Veatch, & Tercha, J. (2020). *Child Care Licensing Benchmark Project*. Arlington, VA: Child Care Aware of America. https://info.childcareaware.org/hubfs/ChildCareBenchmarkLicensingProject-FINAL-11022020.pdf?hsCtaTracking=61cf9472-d1a4-437d-ad3d-7e73bf19bc7d%7C5428138c-ce9a-471f-bce5-0ec3b735e7eb

LeMoine, S. (2008). *Workforce designs: A policy blueprint for state early childhood professional development systems*. Washington, DC: NAEYC.

National Association for Regulatory Administration and the National Center on Child Care Quality Improvement, Office of Child Care. (2014). *The 50-state child care licensing study*. https://www.naralicensing.org/assets/docs/ChildCareLicensingStudies/2014CCStudy/center_licensing_trends_brief_2014.pdf

National Association for the Education of Young Children (NAEYC). (2011). *Code of ethical conduct and statement of commitment*. Washington, DC: Author.

National Association for the Education of Young Children (NAEYC). (2019). *NAEYC early learning program accreditation standards and assessment items*.

Washington, DC: Author. https://www.naeyc.org/sites/default/files/globally-shared/downloads/PDFs/accreditation/early-learning/standards_and_assessment_2019.pdf

National Center on Early Childhood Program Quality Improvement. (2014, August). *Use of technology to enhance licensing administration.* Fairfax VA: U.S. Department of Health and Human Services, Office of Early Childhood Program. https://childcareta.acf.hhs.gov/sites/default/files/public/001_1408_technology_licensing_final.pdf

National Center on Early Childhood Quality Assurance. (2016). *State and territory licensing agencies and regulations.* Fairfax VA: U.S. Department of Health and Human Services, Office of Early Childhood Program. https://childcareta.acf.hhs.gov/sites/default/files/public/licensing_regulations_agencies_web.pdf

National Center on Early Childhood Quality Assurance. (2019). Analysis of data from the 2017 Child Care Licensing Study. Unpublished data. Presented at the 2019 CCEEPRC Meeting in Washington, DC. https://www.researchconnections.org/files/meetings/ccprc/2019/D2-1.pdf

National Child Care Information Center. (n.d.). Vienna, VA: Author. https://ectacenter.org/~pdfs/calls/2009/sec619/nccic_elements_of_a_prof_dev_sys.pdf

Power to the Profession Task Force. (2020). *Unifying framework for the early childhood profession.* Washington, DC: Powertotheprofession.org. http://powertotheprofession.org/wp-content/uploads/2020/03/Power-to-Profession-Framework-03312020-web.pdf

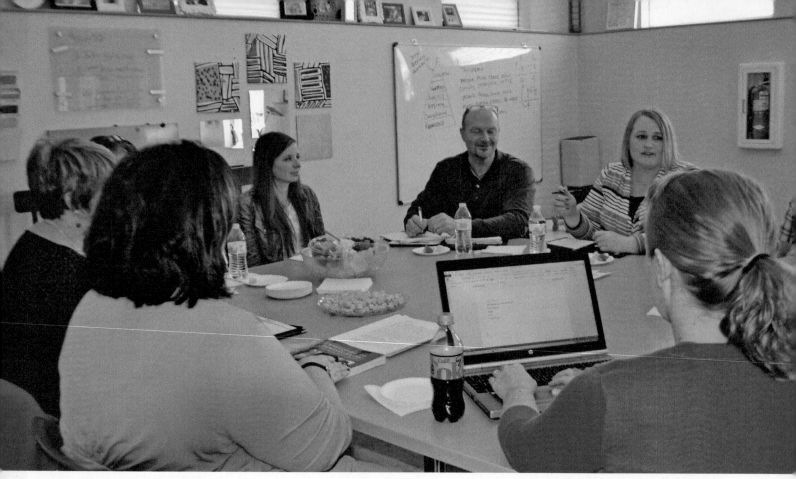

Board members can be extremely helpful to the director in carrying out the mission of the program.

Chapter 4

Organizing Program Structure and Working with a Board

Standards and Recommendations Addressed in This Chapter

ADVANCING EQUITY RECOMMENDATION 2 Take proactive steps with measurable goals to recruit and retain educators and leaders who reflect the diversity of children and families served and who meet professional expectations.

PROGRAM STANDARD 8 Community Relationships

PROGRAM STANDARD 10 Leadership and Management

PROFESSIONAL STANDARDS AND COMPETENCIES: STANDARD 6 Professionalism as an Early Childhood Educator

LEARNING OBJECTIVES

After reading this chapter, you should be able to:

4-1   Describe four types of business organizations and explain the advantages and disadvantages of each.

4-2   Identify circumstances under which a business must have a board.

4-3   Explain important considerations in the selection and orientation of board members.

4-4   List the responsibilities of a program's board.

4-5   Describe the various roles of board committees in conducting the work of the program.

4-6   Explain the rationale for maintaining open communication with and among board members.

4-7   Discuss the role that the board plays in the operation of the program.

4-8   Explore the types of reporting on finances and operations that need to be presented to the board.

4-1 • Organization of the Program

Before accepting the job, anyone considering a position as director of an early childhood program must determine how the prospective program is organized and for what purpose. The roles of directors vary widely based on the organizational structure of the early childhood program, the purpose of the program, the needs of the community, or the requirements of the owner. In some cases, a director may also be an owner. "The legal structure . . . will determine how much paperwork you will have to do, how much personal liability you will incur, how you will be able to raise money, and how your business will be taxed" (Pinson & Jinnett, 2014, p. 61). Let's look at the four main organizational structures.

4-1a • Sole Proprietorship

Individuals who create programs and maintain ownership are sole proprietors. They can make all the decisions and bear all responsibility. They provide the financing, often through bank loans using their own property as collateral. Some individuals may obtain loans from friends or relatives. This type of operation usually is rather small but may later grow, perhaps then becoming a partnership or a corporation. These business owners, also called *entrepreneurs*, establish new companies to fill unmet needs (Greene, 2018).

Being the decision maker has benefits but also can be lonely, particularly when a crisis hits. When the program's furnace must be replaced on the coldest day of the year, or the lead educator leaves and a replacement can't be found, the proprietor may second-guess the organizational decision. When the waiting list is long and a child gives the owner a hug, the decision seems just right. The owner is at risk, however, in the case of a lawsuit—for example, when a child is injured on the playground. All the owner's assets may be in jeopardy. Carrying liability insurance is essential, even for small proprietary programs.

Creating a sole proprietorship is relatively easy after the financial hurdles have been resolved. Papers must be filed with federal, state, and local governments. Usually a form indicating the name of the business is required. Even if Mary Smith decides to open Smith's Early Childhood Educator (ECE) Program, she should file the paperwork stating that she is doing business as (dba) Smith's ECE Program.

When the percentage of program income required for salaries is considered (see Chapter 5), it would seem almost impossible for an individual owner to make a profit. Nonetheless, over the years, many individual programs grow, with the owners gradually opening more and more programs. Soon regional chains are bought up by larger groups. Today, a corporation may oversee thousands of programs, some of which may have been started originally by individual owners.

Something to note when considering a sole proprietorship is the increasing standard of quality required by Quality Rating and Improvement Systems (QRIS) and even more so by the Unifying Framework developed by the Power to the Profession Taskforce (2020). This task force developed recommendations "to establish unity and clarity around the career pathways, knowledge and competencies, qualifications, standards, accountability, supports, and compensation to define the ECE profession within the broader ECE field" (2020, p. 1). Although critical to advancing the profession, two of the recommendations are likely to have a significant impact on the cost of operating a quality early childhood program. The Unifying Framework included recommendations for three professional designations, with distinct roles and responsibilities that will require educators to have credentials in ECE and not be assigned duties beyond their professional early childhood educator level. This means as these aligned indicators for quality are reflected in state regulations and QRIS, staff who do not have a credential but who have been affordable will be limited in their role. In many states, programs that are not QRIS rated will not be eligible for funding associated with public child care subsidies, which is another aspect of laws and regulations that impact the decisions that directors must make.

Also, in the Unifying Framework is a closely related recommendation for professional compensation that states that because early childhood educators are

> professionally prepared, [. . . they must] be professionally compensated. Compensation for early childhood educators will be comparable for those with comparable qualifications, experience, and job responsibilities, regardless of whether they work in a community-based program, elementary school, or family-based child care home. Compensation will include an adequate benefits package, increase commensurate with increased preparation and increased competency, and not be differentiated on the basis of the ages of children served.
>
> Power to the Profession Task Force (2020, p. 1)

The Power to the Profession Task Force also addresses the issue of unfunded mandates, which often financially cripple ECE programs. The Unifying Framework also states,

> We recognize that, to date, when policy makers have increased accountability for educators by raising expectations and educational requirements, they have frequently done so without sufficiently attending to or funding necessary supports and increased compensation. Because of these policy and financing decisions, current and future educators have had to make decisions as well—including deciding to leave the field or not to enter it at all. This is the reality that has led directly to the current crisis faced by families who can neither find nor afford high-quality child care and early learning. Investing in the education and compensation of those working in early childhood education program is the best supply-building strategy available to policy makers. (2020 p. 9)

With the release of the Unifying Framework, directors need to be prepared for rapid changes in the field, including new guidelines for staffing and compensation. They should also be aware of all opportunities for funding offered by their counties, states, or federal government.

In addition to center-based programs, another common type of sole proprietorship is the home-based program. Many of these providers do not consider themselves to be in business; in fact, they are unless they care only for relatives. They are subject to business requirements such as keeping records of attendance, receipts, expenses, and so forth. They may be eligible for the government food program and, in some communities, may receive visitors who provide information about how children learn, activities and supplies, and answers to the provider's questions. In many communities, home care providers are not licensed, and there is no oversight. Serious problems have occurred too often. To protect children and those home providers who are providing appropriate care, every state should have home provider licensing in place, just as every state licenses ECE programs.

4-1b • Partnerships

Sharing responsibility and finances is another possibility. One option is to form a partnership—that is, "an association of two or more persons to carry on as co-owners of a business for profit" (Hatten, 2020, p. 40). For example, two people might be equal partners or split the business 60–40 or some other combination. This decision usually impacts the amount of decision-making and responsibility each assumes and the amount of financial involvement of each. Being a silent partner—contributing financially but not being involved in decision-making—is also a possibility. When profits are available, they usually are allocated according to the percentage of investment. In case of a lawsuit, each partner is liable on a percentage basis, and personal assets are at risk. The liability issue is based on the way in which the partnership is legally constituted. A formal contract between or among those entering the agreement is signed to delineate their obligations and responsibilities (Hatten, 2020).

Having one or more partners provides additional capital and a relatively stable business life. Partners can both (or all) contribute to decision-making and share responsibilities so that each can have at least some free time (Cohen, 2006).

Because setting up a partnership is somewhat more complicated than setting up a sole proprietorship, employing a lawyer is essential. The paperwork must be prepared with care. Furthermore, even the best of friends or relatives may disagree and decide to end the partnership. Or one or more of the partners may decide that this is no longer the business investment desired. In addition, it must be made clear in writing what happens to the partnership in the event of a partner's death.

4-1c • Franchise

One way to have your own business using a model that has already been standardized is to invest in a franchise. "A franchise is an agreement that binds a franchisor (a parent company of the product, service, or method) with a franchisee (a small business that pays fees and royalties for exclusive rights to local distribution of the product or service" (Hatten, 2020, p. 109). The owner of the franchise sells the rights to use the logo, program, and company reputation to a buyer and may provide free management training. Buying and using the company supplies and equipment is expected. Because the franchisor sells large amounts to franchisees, the cost may be lower to the individual program. In turn, the buyer probably will be required to follow specific policies and procedures and to complete company paperwork. If the program loses money, the company is unlikely to share in the loss (Hatten, 2020; Pinson & Jinnett, 2014).

Parents can expect that each franchise will be the same as others of the same name with which they may be familiar. The franchisor ensures that the franchisee follows company policies and standards. You may be familiar with this model based on some of the fast-food restaurants you patronize. If you like certain foods prepared a certain way, you expect to find the same product at all franchises of that restaurant. Getting a burger that's not the way you like it isn't a major problem; however, the same cannot be said for ECE programs. If parents have had experience with a specific franchised program in the past, they will no doubt expect that all programs managed by this franchisor will offer equal quality. Getting involved with any major business opportunity requires careful checking in advance.

4-1d • Corporation

To form a corporation, articles of incorporation must be filed, usually with the secretary of state (see **Director's Resource 4-1**). Bylaws, also referred to as *regulations* or a constitution, must be adopted, and a governing body, usually called a *board of trustees*, must be formed to set policy and assume overall responsibility for the operation of the corporation.

A corporation is a business owned by one or more shareholders. The shareholders elect directors to manage the affairs of the corporation, and the directors, in turn, elect officers to handle the day-to-day business of the corporation. Both federal and state laws regulate registration of stock issued to shareholders. *Stock* refers to shares or parts of ownership of a corporation. A stockholder provides an amount of money to a company, often through a broker, thereby becoming part owner of the company. In exchange, stockholders experience the possibility of profit or loss in their own accounts.

Large companies have thousands of shareholders, whereas a corporate ECE program may be owned by a tiny number of friends of the program. Some ECE programs, however, become major corporations by creating or acquiring a large number of centers under one corporate name. Examples of large corporate ECE programs are KinderCare Education and Bright Horizons Family Solutions. These organizations serve thousands of children in hundreds of locations. When you go to their websites, you may see that they are encouraging early childhood program owners to consider selling their programs to one of the large companies.

Like large corporate groups, federal, state, and local branches of government are taking on a larger share of the ECE role. In some cases, a governmental body will provide funding for ECE programs. In other cases, a business will be chosen or created to run a tax-funded early childhood program. For example, a school board might hire a corporation that manages many children's programs. That corporation provides staff and equipment, usually at the school, and is paid to run the ECE program for preschoolers and a before- and after-school program for older children. Increasingly, public schools are offering their own ECE program for preschoolers, staffing them, and creating the curriculum. Many parents appreciate this, believing it is easier to have preschoolers in the same building as older siblings and feeling that the young child will not have to transition to a new place for kindergarten. The program may be partially or totally funded by tax dollars. One drawback may be that some programs operate on the typical school schedule, with no provisions for before- and after-school care or for holidays and vacations. In some cases, the program for young children and for after-school care may be primarily academic rather than focus on the whole child. Infants and toddlers are rarely included in public school programs. An exception occurs when a school creates a program for the young children of high school students, in large part to help the teens finish their education.

One aspect of the increased direct involvement in preschool education by public schools is the effect on ECE program businesses. Because the need for infant and toddler care will still be strong, programs may find that the high cost of care for the youngest children may no longer be balanced by the lower cost of care for 3- to 5-year-olds. As you read more about financing programs for young children in a later chapter, this idea will become clearer.

When a program is to be operated as a corporation, the board is responsible for initiating the incorporation process. Because laws vary from state to state, consulting an attorney is essential. The law does not require that ECE program incorporate, but it is desirable.

Growth Mindset Moment

Do you think you would like to direct a program in a large chain, or would you rather operate a program independently? Have you thought about working in an ECE program managed by an agency such as a hospital or faith-based group? What might be some of the pros and cons of each arrangement? Think about the programs with which you are familiar. How are they organized?

Although initially setting up a corporation is more complex and more costly than setting up a sole proprietorship or partnership, there are advantages. Corporations may attract funding more easily and be more stable if they are less dependent on the involvement of one or a few individuals. Nonetheless, a corporation can be quite small and consist of only a few family members.

One advantage that accrues to corporations is the limitation on financial responsibility. Because the liability of the corporation is limited to the assets of the corporation, individuals holding positions in the corporation are generally protected from personal liability for acts or debts of the corporation. A corporation can be sued and lose all of its assets, effectively putting it out of business. However, the personal assets of the director or owners are not included. On the other hand, corporate assets of small ECE programs often are obtained by using personal assets as collateral. In that case, individuals' assets are jeopardized.

4-1e • Profit or Not-for-Profit Corporations

When a program's management plan is to incorporate, the decision to be for-profit or not-for-profit must be made. In the case of a not-for-profit corporation, the corporate structure is different. For example, there are no shareholders in a nonprofit corporation. Instead, members elect trustees to manage the affairs of the corporation. The required number of trustees and officers varies by state. Once incorporated, the corporation must function in accordance with the state's laws, its articles of incorporation, and its bylaws.

Although it is a common belief that nonprofit entities are organized to provide some sort of charitable, educational, or religious function, the law does not require such a purpose. An organization can provide "almost any kind of good or service on a not-for-profit basis. . . . Some nonprofits are supported by donations, others depend on income from sales of goods and services, and many receive most or all of their revenues from government" (Hall, 2016, p. 3). Although nonprofits can receive funds from donors and foundations, only a small percentage of ECE program funding is from charitable contributions (National Council of Nonprofits, 2019).

Not-for-profit corporation status does not automatically result in tax-exempt status. Based on Internal Revenue Code 501, a corporation must apply to the Internal Revenue Service (IRS) for tax-exempt status and to demonstrate that the organization's purpose is educational or falls under one of the other IRS-exempt categories. A specified Department of the Treasury form must be completed accurately. This form requires a statement of the organization's sources of financial support, fundraising program, purpose, activities (past, present, and future), relationship to other organizations, and policies (for example, nondiscrimination). This lengthy form also requires a statement of revenue and expenses and a list of governing board members. The process is time-consuming and expensive, often taking months to complete and costing thousands of dollars. However, programs that operate on a not-for-profit basis are subject to fewer taxes. For example, with the proper documentation, they usually are exempt from sales tax as well as some federal taxes. Exemption from state and local taxes, including sales tax, is often tied to exemption from federal income tax, but application for exemption must be made to each taxing body.

Because tax law is subject to change, the director and board must keep abreast of new requirements. New directors moving in to existing programs must check to see that the documents are in order and that proper procedures are being followed. Every director must be informed about current tax and reporting requirements of the federal, state, and local governments. Not knowing is not an acceptable excuse for improper filing and reporting.

When donors make contributions to a not-for-profit program, they may be allowed to deduct the amount on their federal income tax subject to

No matter how the center is organized, individual attention to each child is essential.

applicable tax laws. It is common courtesy to send a written acknowledgment to all contributors, stating the amount of their contributions and any monetary benefits received. Furthermore, your letter may enable the contributor to document a tax deduction. In the event that a not-for-profit program ceases operation, its assets must be donated to another not-for-profit organization. Although nonprofits can obtain grants, writing grant requests takes time, effort, and skill. Typically, grants do not cover the capital needed to start a program or cover operating costs.

The profit versus not-for-profit issue is complex. Organizations are advised to consult with attorneys and tax advisers before making this type of decision. When there is a corporate program's board, it will have an important role in this decision-making.

Director's Corner

I operate an ECE program in a low-income neighborhood. Some families aren't eligible for vouchers, so I keep the tuition low enough for them to afford to send their children. It's a problem because the vouchers are worth $170 per child. But since I am charging families without vouchers only $130, the county gives me only $130 per voucher. If I raise tuition to $170, I'll get $170 for each voucher, but some families will have to withdraw their children. I'm losing money, and I'm going to have to make a difficult decision.

—Director, not-for-profit program

4-2 • The Early Childhood Program Board

Depending on the ECE program struc- **naeyc** ture, boards can be either advisory or fiduciary. Advisory board members are appointed based on their experience or expertise, but they do not have legal responsibility for the decisions that program administrator makes. A board of directors usually has fiduciary responsibility for the organization, and the program administrator typically reports to the board. Members of a board of directors can be appointed or elected. Board membership, board duties, committee structure, and board operations vary, depending on the size and type of program and on the relationship of the program to a sponsoring or funding agency. Despite the inevitable variation in the structure and function of program boards, directors will be better equipped to assist in establishing a board or to work with an existing board if they have some basic information about governing boards and how they operate.

The program's director, who is responsible to the board, implements the program as mandated by the board. The board's major role is financial but can also include making or approving policy. The director then creates procedures to carry out those policies. In practice, board involvement runs the gamut from heavy involvement with the program to deferment of all the work to the director. In the former situation, the board carries out all the functions described in this chapter and then charges the director with full responsibility to act on decisions that the board has reached. In the latter case, the board does not question the rationale or philosophical basis for the recommendations presented by the director for board review and gives carte blanche approval. Ideally, a board should function somewhere between these two extremes by carrying out some functions related to personnel, finance, facility, and program and by keeping in close contact with the director who also is working on fiscal and program matters. Although some proprietary programs operate without the guidance of a governing group, the organizational structure of most agency-sponsored and publicly funded programs includes a board of directors.

When the program is an arm of another agency, such as a church-sponsored ECE program or a university-affiliated ECE program, the agency board may serve as the governing board, sometimes with representation from the program. In other cases, an advisory committee for the program is formed. As the name implies, the role of the advisory committee is much less structured, and the committee has less authority than a board. When an early childhood program is part of a public school system, the principal often assumes many of the director's responsibilities and a lead educator assumes others. The actual board then is the elected board of education. Because of the great variation among organizations, program directors may have several administrative levels above them. Generally, they report to the director's immediate supervisor one level above. Decisions may be made at a higher level in some cases.

4-3 • Board Membership

Most well-planned boards consist **naeyc** of 10 to 20 members who are either elected or appointed to board positions. A board operates most efficiently when its size is small enough for members to know each other and feel comfortable about speaking out when issues are being discussed yet large enough for members to cover all the committee assignments required to conduct business without overworking any board members (U.S. General Services Administration Child Care Center of Expertise, 2016). Tenure for board members is specified in the bylaws. Requirements for board membership are based on program philosophy and needs, state laws, and sponsoring agency mandates.

When for-profit corporations involve much larger organizations, usually the parent organization manages all the programs by providing regional supervisors (a variety of titles may be used). In this case, because the corporation operates on a major business model and may be traded on a stock exchange, the board also operates commensurate with the rest of the organization. Board members are chosen from a national perspective and usually are paid. Shareholders vote for the board members, and their vote is weighted based on the number of shares they own. Shareholders are invited to the company's annual meeting, although rarely do small shareholders attend because of lack of knowledge, lack of influence, and inconvenience of travel distance. The boards described in the next sections refer to those affiliated with individual programs or small groups of programs. A program may also establish a local board when it is part of a much larger agency. Such a board usually will not have fiduciary responsibility and is often called an *advisory board* or *council.*

4-3a • Selection of Board Members

At the outset, boards may be made up entirely of appointed members. After the bylaws are developed and incorporation is accomplished, ensuing boards usually are elected by a regulated process required by law and stated in the bylaws. When a director, a board, or a nominating committee chooses people to be appointed or elected to an ECE program's board, the background and personality of the candidates and the current board composition must be considered.

The nominating committee should create a process that will allow it to fill board positions effectively and efficiently. The committee may begin by deciding the types of people who are needed on the board. As the organization's circumstances change, the kinds of board members needed also may change. Although a variety of professionals can be valuable board assets, their expertise should not be exploited. Their perspectives will help guide the board, but when particular professional advice is needed, the board should allocate funds and employ someone not on the board. For example, although it may be advisable to have a physician on the board, that person's role should be one of commitment to the whole program rather than only to health needs (Bess & Ratekin, 1999). When an organization and a board are small and in a start-up phase, some professionals may be willing to join the board and provide guidance that would not be needed for an established program. They may be serving out of friendship for the director or out of community spirit. Finally, consideration should be given to developing a board with diverse membership.

Professionals from the fields of health, education, finance, and law often are asked to serve on early childhood program boards. These professionals can provide support in decision-making in their areas and often volunteer time and expertise to help solve problems. For example, the physician who is a board member may direct the board to accurate

Making the Case for *Diverse Board Membership*

Our society is becoming increasingly diverse, and board membership should reflect this diversity. Having a diverse board sends the message to staff, families, and the community that your program is inclusive and values unique perspectives and personalities. According to the National Council of Nonprofits, when diversity exists, "each person will bring to his or her own personal and professional contacts and life experiences to their service on a nonprofit board. With a diversity of experience, expertise, and perspectives, a nonprofit is in a stronger position to face opportunities and challenges" (National Council of Nonprofits, n.d.). The council also notes specific benefits of diverse boards:

- Programs have greater opportunities to form relationships with potential donors or important policy makers in the community.
- Diversity of membership will increase the organization's ability to access resources in the community.
- When challenges or important decisions arise, the presence of diverse beliefs and perspectives will enable the board to identify potential risks and opportunities.

information about health practices in the program, or the accountant board member may help draw up the budget and prepare for an audit. A media specialist or a board member who can write effective proposals and has contacts with various funding sources can be a real asset. A person with knowledge of special education may support the board in its efforts to meet requirements of the Americans with Disabilities Act and may help the program's staff address issues related to inclusion of children with disabilities. A computer specialist also may be a valuable asset as a director ponders what types of hardware or software are best for the program. Some boards reserve a percentage of slots for parents, and an educator also may be a member, although usually a nonvoting one.

After the nominating committee has decided on the types of members needed, it may solicit suggestions from existing board members. After creating a master list, the committee begins contacting potential candidates, explaining that it is considering board and committee nominees to determine interest. The committee may send interested persons an information sheet about the organization, including the purpose and philosophy, as well as job descriptions of board and committee members. Each potential candidate may be invited to tour the program. Then the committee may interview several potential candidates and recommend putting them on the board slate or on a committee until a board opening occurs. No new board member should be surprised when asked to serve on a committee or when asked to contribute and solicit funds for the organization. Board members should be prepared to be active and committed to the organization.

Large agencies usually provide liability coverage for board members, but smaller organizations may be unable to afford this coverage. Nonetheless, board members usually are legally liable for the program's operation. Prospective board members should be informed that they will need to provide their own liability coverage if that is the case. Director liability is controlled by state law. Additional information on this important topic can be obtained from your insurance agent or attorney.

4-3b • Orientating Board Members

New board members should be expected to participate in an orientation program led by the chair of the nominating committee. Board officers may be asked to participate, both to welcome the new members and to explain their components of the organization. Before this session, each should receive a board book, preferably a loose-leaf binder, containing the following:

- welcome;
- board members' names, addresses, and pictures;
- mission statement;
- bylaws;
- strategic plan;
- board committees;
- minutes from the past year;
- fiscal statements from past year;
- current year budget;
- program's information, including philosophy, number of children and ages served, and calendar; and
- your state's guidelines for nonprofit board members.

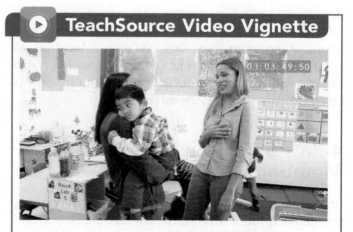

TeachSource Video Vignette

Leadership Practices in Early Childhood Education Programs: Orientation of Board Members

Effective boards typically comprise members from both inside and outside the field of early childhood. Although they bring their own professional experiences to the work, they do not necessarily have enough background in early childhood to be able to contribute fully. View the Video Vignette titled *Leadership Practices in Early Childhood Education Centers* as an example of what might be included in your board's orientation. Reflect on the following questions:

1. What segments from the video would be useful in helping board members obtain information about the complexities of managing a program?

2. What additional information would you provide board members at the orientation?

At the orientation, new members should learn about the role of the nonprofit agency board and be alerted to the differences between the roles of board and staff. As a result, new members should be ready for their first meeting with a basic understanding of

Director's Corner

The board treasurer keeps track of all the tax forms and other reports that are due. Once when we changed treasurers, we forgot to file a particular form and wound up with a big fine even though we hadn't owed any money. The board needed a lawyer on that one!

—*Director, not-for-profit incorporated program*

current and recent issues and decisions. They should enter the meeting knowing a few of the members and be greeted individually by others. This approach helps new members recognize that they are valued and that the board functions in a businesslike manner with positive interpersonal interactions (Bess & Ratekin, 2000).

Those who have not served on a program board previously may have the misperception that as volunteers they serve in an honorary or advisory capacity. As a result, the board orientation should include information about the specific leadership, fiduciary, and related legal responsibilities that accompany the position. Additional information about board membership can be obtained from the National Council of Nonprofits or your state attorney general's website.

4-3c • Terms for Board Membership

Continuity in board membership is important. Therefore, many boards elect members for a three-year term, allowing for one-third of the members to be new each year. To achieve this ratio, the initial board members draw lots to determine who will hold three-, two-, and one-year terms. This time frame may not be workable for parent members who may not feel comfortable about joining the board until their children have been at the program for a while or who may no longer be interested after their children have left the program.

Although continuity is valuable, stagnation may occur when board members serve for too long. Consequently, bylaws should contain a provision for a limited number of terms of board service. Provisions also should be made to replace members whose attendance is poor. When a board member resigns, an exit interview may provide insight regarding possible changes in board operation. Members who feel overworked or undervalued may choose not to complete a full term.

4-4 • Board Duties

Board members are responsible for the leadership and governance of the program and for "taking the care and exercising the judgment that any reasonable and prudent person

would exhibit in the process of making informed decisions" (Renz, 2016, p. 129). This legal responsibility is known as the Duty of Care. The Duty of Loyalty requires members to "consider and act in good faith to advance the interests of the organization" (p. 128). The third fundamental responsibility is to demonstrate the Duty of Obedience, "which requires obedience to the organization's mission, bylaws, and policies, as well as honoring the terms and conditions of other standards of appropriate behavior such as laws, rules, and regulations" (p. 130).

Board members must be ready to thoughtfully yet quickly modify the organization's mission and practices to meet their communities' changing needs and values. They must also be prepared to find funding that is commensurate with the growing recognition of the importance of providing well-prepared staff. More specifically, the board is responsible for drawing up the bylaws for the program's operation. Subsequently, the board makes policy decisions and provisions for the operation of the program.

4-4a • Drawing Up Bylaws

Bylaws for operation of the program are written by the board and should contain the following points:

- name and purpose of the organization;
- composition of the board of directors, including information about when and by whom its members are elected or appointed, their duties and terms of office;
- description of the process by which officers are selected, including terms of office, duties, and election or appointment procedures;
- policies related to the removal of directors or officers when necessary;
- frequency of meetings or minimum number of meetings to be held annually;
- standing committees and their composition and duties;
- relationship of staff to board;
- rules governing the conduct of meetings;
- provisions for an annual meeting;
- procedures for amending the bylaws; and
- procedures for dissolution of the corporation.

Other items may be added to meet the needs of a particular board.

Board members may be invited when a special activity is planned at the center, and they are always welcome to visit.

Bylaws should be extensive enough to meet legal requirements and to guide the board. However, when bylaws are too detailed, the board's operation is hampered. Furthermore, changes to bylaws appropriately involve rather detailed procedures that become burdensome if changes must be made frequently. For example, the bylaws should not list the specific month of the annual meeting or the exact number of board members.

Along with the establishment of bylaws, the board works on developing or revising (if needed) the organization's mission statement. The board may also create a vision statement, describing the future to be expected if the mission is carried out according to strategic planning.

4-4b • Making Policy

After the mission and philosophy have been established, the board sets goals for the program based on the organization's philosophy and purpose. If goals have already been established before formation of the board, the board formally adopts them. The board then informs the director and staff about the philosophy and goals that form the basis for establishing the objectives for the daily program. In some cases, a knowledgeable director can take a leadership role in guiding the board's decision-making about philosophy and goals that reflect sound theories. In any case, the board establishes policies, and the director uses these policies as the basis for formulation of

procedures. A *policy* is a course of action that guides future decisions. A *procedure* is a series of steps to be followed, usually in a specific order, to implement policies.

Creation of policies based on the program's philosophy should lead to a cohesive approach to the program's operation. This systemic approach facilitates staff commitment to the overall program because it has been made transparent. Ensuing decisions then will be consistent because they will be based on established policy.

Issues such as required orientation for all new staff should be in policy form and accompanied by procedures such as who will orient staff and what will be included. Regarding personnel, a policy might be, "Written personnel policies will be provided to all employees during their orientation." Procedures for signing in, getting a substitute, or holding parent conferences may be included. Policies regarding board membership and responsibilities should be in place in addition to the statements included in the bylaws. A policy regarding when the bylaws will be reviewed for possible revision should also be included. Because the policies should not be changed without serious consideration, the board should make them general and flexible enough that the director is able to implement them without disregarding program goals and without being required to request policy changes every time a new circumstance arises.

Procedures are more detailed than policies. Their purpose is to provide an implementation plan that is clear and uniform. Fire drill procedures or procedures for checking out material from the storeroom are good examples. Procedures also may be written for using the building after the children leave, for using equipment in the multipurpose room, or for filling a staff vacancy.

Policy decisions regarding personnel and program are ultimately subject to board approval; in practice, they are often made by the director with official board approval becoming a formality. Occasionally, an involved, knowledgeable board will scrutinize policies presented by a director, often asking for the rationale to support each policy. In some instances, staff and program policies are actually written by board members.

The type of program offered and the population served are both program policies subject to board approval. Decisions about the number and age span of children, the method of selection, and the population served are all board decisions. Examples include decisions about setting up the program schedule to include after-school care or care for children on a part-time basis. Although these policy decisions are usually based on the director's recommendations, the board makes the final determination.

Written policies and procedures are essential, but avoid creating so many that all creativity is eliminated. In fact, in a field such as ECE, it is impossible to predict exactly what will happen from day to day.

4-4c • Operating the Program

The board is responsible for making provisions for the operation of the program. The major decisions in this category are as follows:

- selecting a director;
- providing for appropriate staff members and for their suitable, in-service training opportunities;
- providing facilities and equipment;
- preparing or approving the budget and overseeing the finances of the program;
- writing proposals and obtaining funding, including setting rates of tuition;
- complying with local, state, and federal laws;
- evaluating the operation of the program and the work of the director, and assisting the director in the evaluation of other staff;
- arranging for an annual audit of financial records;
- arbitrating problems between the staff and the director that cannot be resolved by the director; and
- replacing the director, as needed, and dismissing the director as the situation warrants.

After provisions are made for operating the program, it becomes the director's responsibility to implement the program. At this point, the director becomes accountable to the board for the total program operation.

4-5 • Board Committees

Board work is usually done by committees. Each standing committee has a charge that is spelled out in the bylaws. When all the standing committees are in place and working, the basic board functions are carried out. As special needs arise, ad hoc board committees are appointed by the board chairperson to perform specific, short-term tasks and report to the board. When the task has been completed, the committee is dissolved.

The board chairperson appoints members to each standing committee based on their interest and expertise and makes an attempt to balance the membership on committees by gender, race, age, point of view, and type of skill. Some boards have special requirements for committee membership. For example, the bylaws may state that each committee must have a parent member or a community representative.

Board committees convene at intervals that correspond to meeting the demands of their workload. When a program is being formed, most committees are extremely active; however, in an ongoing program, some committees have activity peaks. For example, the building committee deals with building maintenance, which is fairly routine. But if a decision is made to remodel, relocate, or build a new facility, then the building committee becomes active.

Decisions about the number and types of standing committees needed to carry out the board functions are made when the bylaws are written. Some of the typical standing committees include executive, personnel, finance, building, program, and nominating.

4-5a • Executive Committee

The executive committee is composed of the board's officers with the program director often serving as an ex officio member. The executive committee advises the chairperson on actions to be taken, changes to be made, and committee assignments. This committee conducts board business between meetings and acts in place of the total board in emergency situations. However, it is critical that the executive committee plan far enough in advance to avoid as many "emergency" situations as possible, lest the way be opened for making important decisions without total board participation. Board members will become disgruntled and fail to contribute time or energy to board business if they find that crucial decisions are being made outside official board meetings. Whenever possible, board decisions should be made by the total board. In some situations, it may be illegal for the executive committee to make decisions.

4-5b • Personnel Committee

The personnel committee is responsible for hiring a director who will adhere to the philosophy of the program and implement the policies established by the board. To accomplish this task, the committee advertises the position, conducts the interviews, and prepares the director's contract. The personnel committee also is responsible for firing the director if that becomes necessary.

Personnel committee members usually assist the director in writing job descriptions, interviewing job candidates, and discussing the merits of each applicant. After these steps are completed, the hiring recommendations are made to the total board for final approval. Other boards set the basic criteria for staff members and set hiring and terminating employees as the director's responsibility.

In small programs where there is no evaluation committee, personnel committee members may be asked to conduct the evaluation process. In this capacity, the committee determines the method of evaluation, carries out the evaluation of the director, and monitors the director's evaluation of the staff and program.

4-5c • Finance Committee

Because they prepare the budget and appropriate the funds, finance committee members must understand the program's overall operation and the way in which the operation relates to the program philosophy. In situations in which the director prepares the budget and secures the funds, the finance committee approves the budget, monitors the record keeping, and arranges for the annual audit. In some programs, the finance committee sets salary schedules and reviews bids for major purchases. This committee also should teach board members how to read financial statements and what they mean.

4-5d • Building Committee

The responsibility for finding and maintaining a facility suitable for the type of program being offered rests with the building (or facility) committee. Before starting a program or establishing a new facility, the committee spends an extraordinary amount of time making decisions about purchasing, constructing, or

The director and the board treasurer meet to review the financial report.

leasing a building. The committee is responsible for locating a new facility or a construction site. Building committee members work closely with the architect when construction or remodeling is in progress and must remember to involve the director, who presumably has the most knowledge of what the program needs.

The building committee is responsible for seeing that the building and grounds are clean, safe, and attractive. Preventive maintenance and emergency repairs also are authorized by this committee. Although directors usually manage the details of applying for a license and arranging for necessary changes at the program to keep the program and facility in compliance with licensing standards, the building committee may be the one designated by the board to monitor licensing.

Many boards also assign the building committee responsibility for the program's equipment. The director must obtain the approval of the committee on major equipment orders, and the committee sanctions orders after considering whether the suggested purchases are suitable in type and quantity and within the budget. The committee members may also ascertain whether the equipment is properly stored, maintained, and inventoried.

The building committee makes long-range plans by considering questions such as the program's future building needs. It projects the type and amount of space that will be needed and plans for ways to meet those needs. Equipment needs are considered in a similar way. Long-range planning prevents the board from suddenly finding that a major addition or repair is needed when no funds are available. Long-range planning also enables the program to stagger the purchase of equipment so that the quality and quantity are constantly maintained at a high level and so that the budget is not suddenly unbalanced by the need to replace large quantities of worn-out equipment.

4-5e • Program Committee

The responsibility for all programs ultimately rests with the program committee; however, in practice, any work on the program is handled completely by the director and the staff. The children's program, the parent program, and the in-service program for staff all may be under the auspices of the program committee. The committee recommends policies to the board focusing on the enrollment and grouping of children, the hours and days of operation, and the offering of ancillary services such as health, nutrition, and social services. Some boards set up separate committees for medical services and social services if these are major components of the program. These separate committees are responsible for working with the director to determine what services are needed and where and at what cost they can be obtained. The committees also may help with transportation arrangements to the medical program, if required, and with recruiting volunteers to assist children and families needing special social or educational services.

4-5f • Nominating Committee

The nominating committee's function is twofold. Potential members of the board are screened by the committee, which also prepares the slate of board officers for election by the board. The process should be open, and the committee should check with prospective members for permission to nominate them.

A separate committee may be set up for the orientation of new board members, or the nominating committee may serve in this capacity. Continuing the process begun at nomination, the committee ensures that new board members understand their duties and the operating procedures of the board.

4-6 • Board Communication

From the committee descriptions, it should be obvious that the functions of the committees are interrelated and that communication among committees is essential. For example, the building committee must know what kind of plans the program committee is making in order to provide an appropriate facility. However, the building committee cannot choose a facility without an understanding of how much the finance committee plans to allocate for physical space. To avoid duplication of efforts, each committee's task must be delineated clearly. Sometimes, a board member may be assigned to two closely related committees to facilitate

Communicating with Board Members

Regular and deliberate communication with board members and committees is an important responsibility of the director, and technology can simplify this process considerably. Email distribution lists or listservs can be used to share program news as well as information related to ongoing management issues, committee work, and developing concerns. In addition, sending agendas and related background information before meeting dates enhances meeting efficiency. Make sure to check with board members to request the email address they want you to use for the purpose of sharing program mailings, and be cautious about flooding their inboxes with program mail.

Directors can use technology to communicate with board members on a regular basis to keep them informed of important management issues and decisions.

communication between them. Care must be taken to divide the work of the board equitably among its members and to see that every board member is involved in and aware of the operations of the board and the program.

The board shares responsibility with the director for maintaining open communication within the board itself and among the board, the sponsoring agency, the staff, and the families who use the program's services. The most successful boards are those whose members communicate effectively with the program's director and with each other. Both the board and the director have responsibilities here, and providing training in interpersonal communication for all concerned may be worthwhile. If staff and board members both attend the training sessions, communication skills are improved, staff and board members become better acquainted with each other's values, and the outcome is a greater sense of community among those people who are responsible for the program's operation. An obvious place to start is to make sure that new board members are introduced and that continuing board members also introduce themselves. Taking new board members on a tour of the facility and introducing them to the staff is another way to foster communication. When board members and staff members have developed effective communication skills, all will be expected to use the skills. Ideas will be expressed and considered openly; likewise, disagreements will be stated specifically and objectively. Board and staff members lacking these skills may be less willing to address problems directly, with the result that disagreements may not be resolved and factions may develop within the organization.

As with all good communication, correspondence between the board and the staff is two-way. The board informs the director of policies that have been formulated because the director is responsible for seeing that the policies are executed. The board also explains the reasons for its decisions and approaches any necessary changes in a positive way instead of in a dictatorial manner. The director, in turn, communicates to the board any difficulties the staff is having with the existing policies or suggests

Director's Corner

I know that our board members are really interested in our program, but they aren't early childhood educators. So I have to make sure they understand the needs of the program and of our staff. I put a lot of effort into making sure key persons are well informed. Maybe I'll have lunch with the board chairperson or talk about an idea I have over coffee. You definitely don't want to surprise your chairperson with a new idea during a meeting.

—Director, agency-sponsored early childhood program and education program

policy changes, providing reasons for these changes. For example, if the director finds a number of parents asking for a program for their 2-year-olds, the suggestion is presented to the board and is supported with arguments for and against the admission of 2-year-olds. Facts concerning the type of services that could be provided, the facilities available, the cost of such a program, and the advisability from an educational standpoint also should be presented to the board. Considering the data and the recommendation of the director, the board makes the final decision about the admission of 2-year-olds.

The board is responsible for using the director's recommendations and all other pertinent data in formulating or approving policy. Policy decisions must be based on sound data so that they are fiscally responsible, developmentally and educationally sound, and legal. They must also follow good business practice and be realistic. For example, a policy requiring the director to be on duty whenever the program is open may seem sound but will be unrealistic in practice in an early childhood program that operates for 10 hours a day. Similarly, a board policy requiring the director to hire only well-qualified educators with ECE bachelor's degrees would make the hiring task nearly impossible if available salaries are held at or near the minimum-wage level. Because the director is mandated to carry out board policy, the board ideally gives careful consideration to her or his recommendations to ensure that final policy is mutually agreeable and feasible.

The board serves as the communications liaison between the program and the sponsoring agency. The director keeps the board informed about the program's functioning by sending the board members copies of newsletters, special bulletins, and meeting notices; by reporting at board meetings; and by presenting a written report to the board at least annually. Board members may be invited when a special activity is planned at the program, and they are always welcome to visit. The board, in turn, communicates to the sponsoring agency by reporting regularly to the agency board. This type of communication is two-way in that the board also receives information from the sponsoring agency concerning the expectations of the sponsoring group. For example, a community group may provide partial funding for the program with the stipulation that it be used to provide training for a staff member or parent program, or a church sponsor may expect preferential admissions for members' families. As long as these stipulations and expectations are compatible with the program's philosophy and are legal, they should be fulfilled.

4-7 • Board Involvement in Program Operation

When a new program is starting up, the board must meet frequently—even daily—during the busiest planning periods. However, in ensuing years, boards may meet monthly, quarterly, or even annually. When the board is working closely with the director and is intimately involved in policy making, monthly meetings are essential. On the other hand, the board that assigns most of the decision-making to the director may meet only annually to receive the director's report, approve the budget for the ensuing year, and make any adjustments in goals, policies, or procedures that seem necessary. Notice how unrewarding service on such a board might be.

The board that meets frequently contributes to the operation of the program by working closely with the director and by using fully the skills of all board members. The board that meets less frequently provides the director with maximum freedom to operate on day-to-day matters, although within definite guidelines. Each board must decide which alternative seems to be more appropriate for the type of program being planned, and the director is chosen to fit into the selected method of operation.

Although each board has its own style, board meetings must be conducted according to recognized parliamentary procedures that may be covered in the bylaws. In large, formal organizations, a parliamentarian who is appointed or elected ensures that business meetings are conducted according to the procedures adopted. Although too much formality may be uncomfortable for some board members, total informality leads to loose practices, with disputes arising over decisions that are based on improper voting procedures or other points of order.

The board of an incorporated program is obligated by law to conduct its business in an organized manner and to keep accurate records of all transactions. In situations in which record keeping is not required by law, it is just sensible business practice to operate an agency in an orderly manner. Therefore, minutes of all board meetings, committee reports, and financial records must be kept. Copies of contracts and agreements, job descriptions, and correspondence also should be in the files.

4-7a • Program Enrollment Report

How many children are enrolled, and how many are on the waiting list? If the program serves various age groups, then the report should be subdivided

Growth Mindset Moment

REPORTING TO THE BOARD AND FUNDERS

Whether the funders are organizations providing support to assist needy families, stockholders investing for profit, members of a parent co-op, school board members, or individuals who own and direct the program, every funder needs to know how the business is doing. Accurate, timely, and understandable reports are essential. The director uses the daily transaction records to prepare monthly financial reports available to funders as well as for internal use in making budgetary decisions. (These reports also should be available to those staff members who choose to read them.) The director may present this information at a board meeting or mail it to board members and other concerned people. Either way, the information should be presented in a clear, neat, and concise format. Computer-generated reports can be revised readily so that the most current information is available. The director must be prepared to answer questions regarding the month's operating budget and justify the figures in the report.

Because the purpose of the report is to inform the reader, it is meaningless to present a highly technical report to a group with no background in reading such reports. On the other hand, large organizations may require that each program follow a particular reporting format. In any event, the information must be presented in such a way that the reader can grasp it easily. Brief comments may clarify various aspects of the report.

The director prepares or oversees the preparation of several types of reports.

into the various subgroups such as infants, toddlers, preschoolers, and those children in after-school care. The director also may project the number of children expected to move up to the next age group on a month-by-month basis. For example, if six children will no longer be eligible for the toddler group in March, will there be room for them, based on licensing rules, in the preschool classrooms?

4-7b • Accounts Receivable

The director should receive a report at least weekly of accounts receivable. In an early childhood program, this figure will consist primarily of tuition owed. Repeated billing on a specific schedule (usually weekly) is essential.

4-7c • Budget Comparison Report

This report may also be called the *budget variance report*. Each month, the director prepares or receives a report from the bookkeeper showing what was spent the preceding month in each category. The report also shows budgeted spending for that month, as well as actual and budgeted spending for the year to date. The director or board then can spot cash flow problems, analyze expenditures, project remaining expenses, and revise the budget if necessary. If a funder requires monthly reports, then the budget comparison report may be used.

4-7d • Statement of Financial Position

On an annual basis, a statement of financial position should be prepared that shows assets (what is owned) and liabilities (what is owed). This statement may be helpful as you seek additional funding.

4-7e • Income Statement

The director or accountant must create an income statement at the end of each year. This statement reflects the total of all revenue earned and all expenses incurred during the fiscal year. The difference between revenue and expense is *net income* if revenues are greater than expenses and *net loss* if expenses are greater than revenues. The income statement is widely considered the most important financial statement because it is a measure of how well a business is doing at the end of the year. The statement shows whether the company has generated a profit or is incurring losses. The income statement represents the actual figures for each of your previously budgeted categories. It can be used as a tool to evaluate monies allocated to specific categories on your budget. For example, if maintenance and repair expenses were actually $7,000 for the year according to the income statement but were budgeted at $2,500 on your operating budget, you would want to reevaluate your budgeted figure, provided that the dollars spent for maintenance and repair were not one-time, unusual expenditures. In addition to this latter example, the income statement can be helpful for other kinds of statistical analyses.

4-7f • Annual Report

At the end of the fiscal year, the director presents a final report showing the amount budgeted in each category and the amount actually spent. Up-to-date cash flow statements make it relatively easy to prepare the annual report, and the income statement may be used in this capacity. In some cases, the report will consist of income and expenses for a particular grant only. The annual report from the program or organization may be distributed to everyone who contributed, families, prospective donors, and local news media. The report should be designed to capture the recipients' attention. Information should be succinct while also conveying the accomplishments of the program. If your organization is large enough, you may want to employ a professional firm to prepare and mail the report.

Purchasing the software you'll need for processing your financial reports is essential. Invest in programs that will make fundraising presentations more interesting and informative.

Growth Mindset Moment

Consider how you might work most effectively as a director. Would you prefer a board that left the decision-making to you and expected an annual report about what you had done? Or would you prefer a situation in which you had to check back with people in authority on a regular basis to get the benefit of their thinking, after which you would follow their lead as you continued your work? You may be able to compare this idea to college classes in which you operated independently and received feedback from your instructor only on the final exam against classes in which you regularly submitted written work throughout the course and subsequently received information from your instructor about your work. It would be wise to give careful consideration to your own needs and administrative style before accepting a directorship.

Summary

There are key questions to be decided when new programs are being planned:

- What business structure will be selected for the new program: sole proprietorship, partnership, franchise, or corporation? Will this be a profit or not-for-profit program?

- Based on the type of program selected, will the program have a board of directors?

- What considerations exist when selecting and orienting board members?

- What responsibilities will board members be expected to carry out in supporting the work of the program?

- What board committees are required to assist with conducting the work of the program?

- How will open communication with board members be carried out by the director?

- What is the board's role in creating policy that results in a well-organized program?

TRY IT OUT!

1. Visit your state government's website. Search for information about serving on nonprofit organization boards. (In many cases, this will be the attorney general's website.) Discuss with classmates the following questions:
   a. What type of information is provided related to board member responsibilities?
   b. Based on the requirements and responsibilities, what types of people would be important for you to include as board members?

2. Interview (or invite to class) a director of an early childhood program that has a board of directors. Ask the following questions and then compare responses with members of your class:
   a. How are members chosen?
   b. What type of orientation is provided for new board members?
   c. How long is a member's term?
   d. What are the duties of board members?
   e. How often does the board meet?
   f. Are minutes of each meeting kept?
   g. What is the relationship between the director and the board?
   h. Is the director a voting member of the board?

   i. What challenges have you experienced working with a board?
   j. If the program does not have a board, who carries out the responsibilities that would have been met by the board?

3. Obtain a copy of the bylaws of an early childhood organization with which you are associated or of any type of community agency. (Consider your YMCA, your church group, PTA, and so forth.) In class, compare and contrast the bylaws of the group you select with the bylaws provided by other students.
   a. How are they similar in structure?
   b. What are the substantive differences?
   c. How do the differences in the documents reflect the differences in the purposes of the organizations?

4. Investigate the process that must be followed in your state to start a for-profit or nonprofit program for young children. Review the forms that must be filed to incorporate your program. (See **Director's Resource 4-1** for a sample.) You may find the information you need on your state's secretary of state website or by using library resources.

Director's Resource 4-1

INITIAL ARTICLES OF INCORPORATION – NONPROFIT

JON HUSTED
OHIO SECRETARY OF STATE

180 East Broad Street, Suite 103 (ground floor) • Columbus, Ohio 43215
Toll Free: (877) SOS-FILE (767-3453) Central Ohio: (614) 466-3910
www.OhioSecretaryofState.gov • busserv@OhioSecretaryofState.gov

Please return the approval certificate to:

Name: _____ (Individual or Business Name)

To the attention of: _____ (If necessary)

Address: _____

City: _____

State: _____ ZIP Code: _____

Phone Number: _____ E-mail Address: _____

☐ Check here if you would like to receive important notices via e-mail from the Ohio Secretary of State's office regarding Business Services.

☐ Check here if you would like to be signed up for our Filing Notification System for the business entity being created or updated by filing this form. This is a free service provided to notify you via e-mail when any document is filed on your business record.

Type of Service Being Requested: (PLEASE CHECK **ONE** BOX BELOW)

○ **Regular Service:** Only the filing fee listed on page one of the form is required and the filing will be processed in approximately 3-7 business days. The processing time may vary based on the volume of filings received by our office.

○ **Expedite Service 1:** By including an Expedite fee of $100.00, **in addition** to the regular filing fee on page one of the form, the filing will be processed within 2 business days after it is received by our office.

○ **Expedite Service 2:** By including an Expedite fee of $200.00, **in addition** to the regular filing fee on page one of the form, the filing will be processed within 1 business day after it is received by our office. **This service is only available to walk-in customers who hand deliver the document to the Client Service Center.**

○ **Expedite Service 3:** By including an Expedite fee of $300.00, **in addition** to the regular filing fee on page one of the form, the filing will be processed within 4 hours after it is received by our office, if received by 1:00 p.m. **This service is only available to walk-in customers who hand deliver the document to the Client Service Center.**

○ **Preclearance Filing:** A filing form, to be submitted at a later date for processing, may be submitted to be examined for the purpose of advising as to the acceptability of the proposed filing for a fee of $50.00. The Preclearance will be complete within 1-2 business days.

Director's Resource 4-1 (continued)

Form 532B Prescribed by:
JON HUSTED
Ohio Secretary of State

Central Ohio: (614) 466-3910
Toll Free: (877) SOS-FILE (767-3453)
www.OhioSecretaryofState.gov
Busserv@OhioSecretaryofState.gov

Mail this form to one of the following:

Regular Filing (non expedite)
P.O. Box 670
Columbus, OH 43216

Expedite Filing (Two-business day processing time requires an additional $100.00).
P.O. Box 1390
Columbus, OH 43216

Initial Articles of Incorporation
(Nonprofit, Domestic Corporation)
Filing Fee: $125
(114-ARN)

First: Name of Corporation _____

Second: Location of Principal office in Ohio _____
City _____ State _____
County _____

Effective Date (Optional) mm/dd/yyyy _____ (The legal existence of the corporation begins upon the filing of the articles or on a later date specified that is not more than ninety days after filing)

Third: Purpose for which corporation is formed
_____

**Note for Nonprofit Corporations: The Secretary of State does not grant tax exempt status. Filing with our office is not sufficient to obtain state or federal tax exemptions. Contact the Ohio Department of Taxation and the Internal Revenue Service to ensure that the nonprofit corporation secures the proper state and federal tax exemptions. These agencies may require that a purpose clause be provided.

**Note: ORC Chapter 1702 allows for additional provisions to be included in the Articles of Incorporation that are filed with this office. If including any of these additional provisions, please do so by including them in an attachment to this form.

Director's Resource 4-1 (continued)

ORIGINAL APPOINTMENT OF STATUTORY AGENT

The undersigned, being at least a majority of the incorporators of _____ hereby appoint the following to be statutory agent upon whom any process, notice or demand required or permitted by statute to be served upon the corporation may be served. The complete address of the agent is

Name

Mailing Address

City   State   Zip Code

Must be signed by the Incorporators or a majority of the incorporators

Signature

Signature

Signature

ACCEPTANCE OF APPOINTMENT

The Undersigned, _____, named herein as the

Statutory Agent Name

Statutory agent for _____

Corporation Name

hereby acknowledges and accepts the appointment of statutory agent for said corporation.

Statutory Agent Signature _____

Individual Agent's Signature / Signature on behalf of Corporate Agent

☐ If the agent is an individual and using a P.O. Box, check this box to confirm the agent is an Ohio resident.

Director's Resource 4-1 (continued)

By signing and submitting this form to the Ohio Secretary of State, the undersigned hereby certifies that he or she has the requisite authority to execute this document.

Required
Articles and original appointment of agent must be signed by the incorporator(s).

Signature

If the incorporator is an individual, then they must sign in the "signature" box and print his/her name in the "Print Name" box.

By

Print Name

If the incorporator is a business entity, not an individual, then please print the entity name in the "signature" box, an authorized representative of the entity must sign in the "By" box and print his/her name and title/authority in the "Print Name" box.

Signature

By

Print Name

Signature

By

Print Name

Director's Resource 4-1 (continued)

Instructions for Initial Articles of Incorporation
(For Domestic Nonprofit Corporation)

This form should be used if you wish to file articles of incorporation for a domestic nonprofit corporation.

Name of Corporation
As set forth in Ohio Revised Code §1702.05, the name must be distinguishable on the records in the office of the secretary of state.

Ohio Principal Office Location
Please provide the address in Ohio where the principal office of the corporation is to be located.

Effective Date
An effective date may be provided but is not required. Pursuant to Ohio Revised Code §1702.04(D), the legal existence of the corporation begins upon the filing of the articles or on a later date specified in the articles. The effective date cannot (1) precede the date of filing with our office or (2) be more than ninety (90) days after the date of filing. If an effective date is given that precedes the date of filing, the effective date of the corporation will be the date of filing. If an effective date is given that exceeds the date of filing by more than ninety (90) days, our office will return the filing to you and request that a proper effective date be provided.

Purpose
Pursuant to Ohio Revised Code §1702.03, a nonprofit corporation must provide a purpose in the articles. A nonprofit corporation may be formed for any purpose or purposes for which natural persons lawfully may associate themselves. **Note:** The Secretary of State does not grant tax exempt status. Filing with our office is not sufficient to obtain state or federal tax exemptions. Contact the Ohio Department of Taxation and the Internal Revenue Service to ensure that the nonprofit corporation secures the proper state and federal tax exemptions. These agencies may require that a purpose clause be provided.

Additional Provisions
If the information you wish to provide for the record does not fit on the form, please attach additional provisions on a single-sided, 8 ½ x 11 sheet(s) of paper.

Original Appointment of Statutory Agent and Acceptance of Appointment
Pursuant to Ohio Revised Code §1702.06, an Ohio Corporation must appoint and maintain a statutory agent to accept service of process on behalf of the corporation. We cannot accept articles of incorporation unless the statutory agent information is provided. The statutory agent must be one of the following: (1) an Ohio resident; (2) an Ohio corporation; or (3) a foreign corporation that is licensed to do business in Ohio and is authorized by its articles of incorporation to act as a statutory agent and that has a business address in Ohio.

If the statutory agent is an individual using P.O. Box address, they must also check the box below the address to state they are a resident of the state of Ohio. The statutory agent must also sign the Acceptance of Appointment at the bottom of page 2.

Director's Resource 4-1 (continued)

Signature(s)
After completing all information on the filing form, please make sure that page 3 is signed by the incorporator(s).

**Note: Our office cannot file or record a document which contains a social security number or tax identification number. Please do not enter a social security number or tax identification number, in any format, on this form.

REFERENCES

Bess, G., & Ratekin, C. (1999, May). Recruiting effective board members. *Child Care Information Exchange, 127*, 14–20.

Bess, G., & Ratekin, C. (2000, November). Orienting and evaluating your board of directors. *Child Care Information Exchange, 136*, 82–87.

Cohen, W. A. (2006). *The entrepreneur & small business problem solver* (3rd ed.). Hoboken, NJ: Wiley.

Greene, C. L. (2018). *Entrepreneurship: Ideas in action* (6th ed.). Stamford, CT: Cengage Learning.

Hall, P. D. (2016). Historical perspectives of nonprofit organizations in the United States. In D. O. Renz (Ed.), *The Jossey-Bass handbook of nonprofit leadership & management* (4th ed., pp. 3–42). San Francisco, CA: Jossey-Bass.

Hatten, T. S. (2020). *Small business management: Entrepreneurship and beyond* (7th ed.). Thousand Oaks, CA: Sage Publishing.

National Council of Nonprofits. (n.d.). *Diversity on boards*. Washington, DC: Author. https://www.councilofnonprofits.org/tools-resources/diversity-nonprofit-boards boards

National Council of Nonprofits. (2019). *Nonprofit impact matters: How America's charitable nonprofits strengthen communities and improve lives*. Washington, DC: Author. https://www.nonprofitimpactmatters.org/site/assets/files/1/nonprofit-impact-matters-sept-2019-1.pdf

Pinson, L., & Jinnett, J. (2014). *Steps to small business start-up: Everything you need to know to turn your idea into a successful business* (8th ed.). New York, NY: Kaplan Publishing.

Power to the Profession Task Force. (2020). *Unifying framework for the early childhood profession*. Washington, DC: NAEYC.

Renz, D. O. (2016). Leadership, governance, and the work of the board. In D. O. Renz & Associates (Eds.), *The Jossey-Bass handbook of nonprofit leadership & management* (4th ed., pp. 125–156). San Francisco, CA: Jossey-Bass.

U.S. General Services Administration Child Care Center of Expertise. (2016). *Board of directors child care resource book*. Washington, DC: Author. https://www.gsa.gov/cdnstatic/Board_of_Directors_Resource_Book_2016.pdf

The director must be aware of the needs of all the stakeholders in the center. Ongoing communication with teachers can provide insight into how well needs are being met.

Chapter 5

Handling Financial Matters

naeyc

Standards and Recommendations Addressed in This Chapter

ADVANCING EQUITY RECOMMENDATION 1 Provide high-quality early learning services that demonstrate a commitment to equitable outcomes for all children.

PROGRAM STANDARD 8 Community Relationships

PROGRAM STANDARD 10 Leadership and Management

PROFESSIONAL STANDARDS AND COMPETENCIES: STANDARD 6 Professionalism as an Early Childhood Educator

LEARNING OBJECTIVES

After reading this chapter, you should be able to:

5-1   Describe the process for creating a financial plan for an early childhood program.

5-2   Explain how to prepare and operate a budget.

5-3   Identify the financial responsibilities of a well-managed program.

5-4   Explain the purpose of a break-even analysis and how it can be useful in determining funding needs.

5-5   Differentiate between start-up and operating funds and how tuition rates may be determined.

5-6   Describe several external funding options.

The director's role as one who sets the tone for the program has already been established, but the director also must be a pragmatist capable of dealing with all the financial obligations of running a program. To meet the needs of children, families, and staff within a balanced budget, a financial plan must be in place. A well-constructed financial plan is comprised of two major components: a system for managing financial resources and a means of obtaining adequate funding. This chapter focuses on financial planning as well as methods of funding the program.

To effectively manage financial resources, the director must create policies and procedures that

- develop and follow a plan for using funds,
- keep records, including those mandated by law, and
- provide required documentation.

Every program needs both a long-range financial plan and a plan for the upcoming year. Poor financial planning and fiscal management can lead to a lack of funds, which will likely hinder personnel as they work to achieve program goals. High-quality care for young children is expensive, and funds must be allocated properly to provide a developmentally sound program on which children and parents can depend. No matter how well intentioned the staff, a program cannot continue to operate for long without a balanced budget and a reserve fund. Therefore, before publicity is in place, before staff are hired, and before detailed plans are made, the board must be sure that sufficient funds for start-up are available, keeping in mind that it may be many months before the revenue stream can offset the expense of a new early childhood program.

5-1 • Creating a Financial Plan

In a new program or one that is reorganizing, a decision must be made regarding who will be responsible for the program's financial management. In a sole proprietorship or partnership, the owner or director may assume these duties or delegate them to a financial designee. However, regular reports of financial status must be shared and reviewed. In a corporation, the board is responsible. A corporate system may have a regional or national financial officer for all of the system's programs. Franchisees manage their own budgets within company constraints such as any fees set by the parent company. No matter what the program's organizational structure, someone must ultimately be responsible for fiscal management. Throughout this chapter, therefore, we will use *director* to include others who may bear responsibility. We will also assume the program could have a financial officer. When that is not the case, the director may have to assume all fiscal duties.

Usually, the director has some responsibility for creating and managing an annual budget. If a board is involved, the members bear ultimate responsibility. When a program has multiple sites, a financial officer may be part of the staff. This person would be expected to keep day-to-day records, produce financial reports, and consult regularly with the director.

5-1a • Policies and Procedures

The policies and procedures manual must include a section on fiscal management. Although not all policies and procedures are reviewed annually, reviewing those related to finances helps everyone involved check to ensure that these requisites are being met. Following are some of the policies that must be in place:

- All financial transactions must be checked for accuracy.
- Standard accounting practices will be followed.
- The director will prepare a long-range fiscal plan.
- The annual operating budget will be prepared before the start of the fiscal year.
- The budget will be used as a guide throughout the year.
- Every financial transaction must be recorded in a specific location.
- Transactions must be recorded at least weekly, preferably daily.
- A business checking account must be used for all transactions.
- Personal funds and business funds must never be mingled, even if the owner is the director.
- All receipts must be deposited rather than used to pay bills.
- All payroll checks must be available to each employee on the expected date.
- All taxes must be paid by the required date.
- A budget variance report will be prepared at least quarterly.
- Money will be handled by two people—one to receive and record the funds and the second to deposit the funds and record the deposits.
- Amounts, due dates, and payment methods for tuition, as well as consequences of delinquent tuition, must be provided to parents.
- An income and expense statement and a balance sheet must be prepared annually.
- Reports to funders and requests for release of funds will be made on the required schedule.

This list is more detailed than most policy lists. Specific procedures for each of these policies must be written and placed in the policies and procedures manual made available for review by all staff. Spelling out financial requirements in detail can help avoid problems in the future. When staff members know what to expect, they are better able to implement policy and adjust their practice when needed.

Directors work with staff to prepare policies that are clear and workable. They may spend part of a staff meeting discussing this topic, ask staff to submit suggestions, or prepare the policies and procedures with the financial officer and make them available for staff information. Having all staff members spend time writing financial policies is a poor use of their time. Encouraging the staff to provide input lets them know that their perspectives are valued and will be taken seriously by both director and staff.

Growth Mindset Moment

You have just read a long list of items that must be carried out by the business manager or director. List the items that are unfamiliar to you. Check the item off as soon as you learn about it. If you cannot find an explanation, ask your professor to provide more information on the topic. Directors must understand the program's finances. Imagine how much easier it will be to learn now rather than when you are a director in the midst of setting up or reorganizing a program.

Making the Case for *Staff Input into Budget Priorities*

Highly effective directors are well informed about the needs of the program and consider staff input when constructing a budget. Obviously, the director is ultimately responsible for establishing the budget. However, staff members feel more empowered when they are able to provide input to define the priorities. When budgets are tight, staff need to have enough information to understand why financial decisions are being made. Problems with morale can be minimized if staff members feel they are part of the solution.

1. Provide staff members with an opportunity to state their needs as part of the budget-building process.
2. Keep staff informed of the general financial condition of the program. Directors will need to find a balance between maintaining confidentiality and providing enough information to keep staff informed.

5-1b • Establishing a Fiscal Calendar

Because there are so many important financial tasks, the director and the financial officer must work together when appropriate to create a calendar of due dates. Working backward, they schedule dates for reviews of drafts of the proposed budget. A review of the budget will be of interest to most staff members, so time should be allowed for their input. Preparation of items, such as submission of withheld taxes to government offices, can be done by the financial officer as a routine matter but should appear on the calendar.

If your fiscal year begins January 1, the budget for the coming year should be under way in October. The board will be able to review preliminary numbers based on those from the current year yet modified based on plans for the coming year. For example, a proposed staff raise might be included. By November, with recommendations for changes made, the budget should be resubmitted to the board with hopes of final approval. Because the financial records should be closed as of December 31, it is important that the new budget is ready for January 1.

5-1c • Managing Payroll

Many dates must be scheduled for payroll items. It is essential that staff receive paychecks on time. Preparing

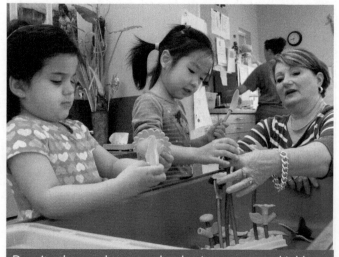
Despite the need to attend to business matters, highly effective directors recognize that the program exists to support children's development.

them is complex, however, even with advanced computer software. Each staff member's name, ID number, address, wage or salary (hourly, weekly, biweekly, or monthly), and local taxing district must be entered into the computer. The financial officer must contact federal, state, and local agencies to determine withholding rates, the current minimum wage, overtime laws, Family and Medical Leave Act requirements, and any other laws that may affect payroll.

The employer must obtain a federal taxpayer ID number from the Internal Revenue Service (IRS) because, before an employee is paid, the employer must make appropriate deductions from the amount earned. When submitting these deductions and the company's equal contribution, the company ID and the employee's ID are listed.

The financial officer is responsible for withholding from each person's pay the appropriate amount of money for various taxes as well as Social Security and other required federal, state, and local payments. The employer pays an amount equal to the percentage withheld from the employee's pay for Social Security and Medicare. The employer must also pay unemployment compensation and workers' compensation. These programs cover payments to the employee for job-related injuries, diseases, and disabilities that occur as a result of working conditions. These amounts must be put aside so they are available for submission to the respective governments on specified dates each quarter. The program may be charged interest and penalties if these payments are not timely or are for incorrect amounts. Your accountant can help you determine the taxes for which you are liable.

5-1d • Health Care Costs

Quality and affordable health insurance is an important employee benefit that contributes to maintaining a quality staff, and it also impacts the budget. The role of the employer in providing health care has been the focus of media attention since the roll out of the Affordable Care Act in 2013. Although expectations for employers have increased, the options for quality and affordable health insurance may have increased in some regions of the country. It is important for directors to understand the new law and its implications for the budget. The law has changed several times, and new information that impacts how the law is implemented always needs to be understood.

Supporting employees in obtaining health care insurance can be an incentive for a prospective employee to join your organization, whereas not offering health care or keeping employees at a part-time status to avoid the cost of health care is likely to be a detractor for highly qualified early childhood educators as they consider their employment options.

5-1e • Tax Forms and Pay Roll

Whenever new employees are hired, the financial officer must obtain form W-4 from the IRS that indicates the number of dependents an employee is claiming. Calculations for the amount of tax to be withheld are made on this basis. Each year, all employees may submit new forms if changes need to be made to the number of dependents. By January 31 annually, a statement of earnings and deductions must be provided to all employees who worked at the program during the year, even if they are no longer employed there.

When all the categories affecting pay are entered into payroll software, the deductions can be readily made. Nonetheless, because preparing the payroll accurately is challenging and time-consuming, quite a few programs hire a payroll company to take care of this aspect of their business. Still, the information must be collected and entered by the financial officer or by the contracting payroll company. The director is responsible for seeing that these requirements are fulfilled.

Program directors must ensure that they comply with the Fair Labor Standards Act (FLSA). Many complex issues and conflicting results of court cases make it difficult to determine who is considered an early childhood (EC) educator for the purposes of FLSA. This determination can make a difference in whether an employer is required to provide overtime pay and pay for hours spent at in-service training and parent meetings "after hours."

The U.S. Department of Labor regulations in the Fair Labor Standards Act (FLSA) rule that took effect on January 1, 2020 raises the current minimum salary level for exempt employees from $455 per week or $23,660 annually to $684 per week or $35,568 annually. This means that only those staff members who make $35,568 annually and whose work relates directly to the management or general business operations of the organization are exempt from overtime pay. These rules change frequently so it is important to seek professional advice especially when addressing complex legal matters.

Another major personnel policy relates to hours worked. Will staff be paid for break time, planning time, and required meeting time? Be sure to check labor laws before making this and other policies. Because many early childhood programs are open for 10 or more hours, no EC educator is in a classroom for the entire program day. Therefore, many part-time staff members are employed. Will they have paid time to meet with the lead EC educator? Will the program provide for an overlap in the schedules of the departing EC educator and the arriving EC educator so that the children's day is not disrupted?

5-1f • Planning Reports

Throughout the year, the director and others will need to know how close the program is to meeting budgetary projections. Is your enrollment on target? Is tuition being paid in a timely manner? Do you have enough cash on hand to meet payroll? Then, when the year is over, how did you fare? Was it a good year financially?

Reports that will help you determine the answers to these questions include a cash flow report, which can be prepared monthly; a variance report (monthly, quarterly, or annually); and an end-of-the-year balance sheet. Any report used by a program can be prescheduled on the annual calendar. We discuss their contents later in this chapter.

▶ **TeachSource Video Vignette**

Financial Planning for Early Childhood Programs: Establishing a Budget

View the video vignette titled *Financial Planning for Early Childhood Programs: Establishing a Budget*. Critical to the management of every well-run early childhood program is the development of the program's budget. The budget is a statement of the center's goals for 1 year stated in financial terms. Responsible fiscal management, in fact, starts with this important document. Watch this video to see Chief Financial Officer Clement James provide concrete and specific information about the development of a budget.

1. What is the difference between a variable expense and a fixed expense?
2. Which of these two types of expenses can be considered when a program needs to trim costs?

5-2 • Preparing and Operating a Budget

One major task of the director or finance committee is preparing a budget, which is a plan or financial forecast usually set up for a period of 1 year. One section of the budget contains a list of income categories and dollar amounts; the other section shows a list of categories and dollar amounts for expenditures. The director's goal is to balance income and expenses and, in most cases, show a profit. Recall that in a for-profit program, the

profit may be distributed to shareholders or used for the program. In a nonprofit or not-for-profit program, the profit stays with the program and can be saved to build financial reserves, reduce tuition, or spent on the program in some other way.

5-2a • Types of Budgets

Budgets are classified in several ways. They may be based on the stage of development of the program, or they may be categorized according to the stage to which the budget itself has been carried. The creation of a new program demands one kind of budget, whereas the ongoing operation of a program requires a budget of a different type.

The director prepares a budget by

- estimating the cost of the program (based in part on the program's goals),
- determining how much income will be available (see Chapter 6), and
- seeking more income to equal expenditures, adjusting expenditures to equal income, or doing both.

5-2b • Start-Up Budgets

The creation of a new program presents a crucial opportunity to test the financial aplomb of the director. When a program is being created, the director prepares *two* budgets: the start-up budget and the operating budget. The *start-up budget* consists of all the expenses incurred in starting the program. These expenses include initial building costs (down payment on the purchase of the building, the cost of building renovations, or rent deposit), the purchase of major equipment, the cost of publicizing the program, the director's salary for several months before the children's arrival, the deposit on telephone service, and the utility charges during the start-up period. Salaries for any additional personnel needed to assist the director of a large program also must be provided. Total start-up costs vary widely. When these costs are incurred, the usual sources of revenue ordinarily have not become available. In these cases, a special grant may be needed, or the organizers of the program may arrange for a loan or invest their own funds. When a loan is obtained, the cost of the interest must be recognized as a legitimate budgetary item.

Occasionally, suppliers will permit purchasers to defer payment for 90 days, and the program can schedule purchases so that the first tuition is received before the 90-day period ends. However, the first receipts certainly will not cover all the expenses. If receipts are due from agency or government funds, then those first payments usually are made after the services have been provided. In the meantime, suppliers may charge interest on unpaid bills. Therefore, it is important to obtain as much assurance as possible that funds for start-up will be available when needed. Searching for "GSA Early Childhood Program Startup" on the Web will provide you with a wealth of information, although specific costs are not provided.

Geographic area, projected size of the program, ages of children to be served, in-kind support (such as free or reduced-price space offered by a church), and amount of money to be borrowed all factor into start-up costs for new programs. Therefore, it is difficult to project the cost of a specific program. The Small Business Administration (SBA) recommends that those interested in starting a program create a business plan. Using this approach, prospective owners can determine whether their plan is realistic in terms of potential resources (loans and so forth) and potential success. More information about start-up is available online at www.sba.gov.

5-2c • Operating Budget

The *operating budget* consists of an income and expense plan for 1 year and is used when programs enroll children and begin the program and annually thereafter. The program may operate on a calendar year (from January 1 to December 31) or on a fiscal year, a 12-month period chosen for ease of relating financial matters to other operations of the program. Programs funded by agencies that operate on a fiscal year running from July 1 to June 30 find it easier to work on the same schedule as the funding agency, but many early childhood education programs choose September 1 to August 31 for their fiscal year because those dates relate closely to the start of their school year. After a program has selected its fiscal year, no change should be made without serious

reason. Planning 1 year's budget from January 1 to December 31 and then changing to a September to August fiscal year in the following year causes confusion and may need to be justified for tax purposes.

5-2d • Estimating Costs

The financial director's first task is to figure program cost. The task requires an overall understanding of the early childhood education program and its goals and objectives. It also requires reviews of the child care industry spending patterns nationally and locally.

At the local level, the director determines what is needed for children in the particular community and program and then analyzes the cost of meeting these needs. These data are essential in preparing a realistic budget. If other people are preparing the budget, the director works with them in interpreting program needs. Priorities should be established on the basis of the program goals, whereas the cost and the availability of funds determine the scope of the program. For example, a program may select improving salaries as a primary goal. If new playground equipment is also desirable, the decision about providing equipment in addition to improving salaries will be made based on the availability of funds, as well as on which is the greater need. If the planned primary goal is related to salaries, the program staff may work together to

In planning a budget, directors must be aware of the day-to-day needs of everyone in the program.

create workable playground enhancements until the desired equipment can be purchased. Nonetheless, in many cases, additional funding will be needed. The director must take a leadership role in implementing a plan for obtaining funding.

Another question that has an impact on both program and finances is the following: What is the population to be served? For example, does the program serve children from infancy through preschool age, and does it provide after-school care? If so, the director will have to recognize that costs for infant programs are considerably higher than costs for preschoolers, based largely on the staff-to-child ratio that infants require.

School-age children need fewer adults, and they are usually at the program fewer hours. Consequently, their care is less expensive.

Other questions include these: How many EC educators will be needed and for what hours? Will it be necessary to have aides? A cook? A janitor? A secretary? A bus driver? Answers to these and dozens of additional questions should be available from the people who are responsible for designing the program and will come primarily from the director. By using this method, the director keeps the goals and philosophy of the program paramount.

Some directors have difficulty with the initial phase of budgeting. Instead of starting with the goals and objectives, they start with the dollars available and attempt to determine what can be done with them. Such a program is truly ruled by the budget (or by the finance director), and maintaining an educationally and financially sound program under these conditions is extremely difficult.

Although program and financial decisions in a corporate system may be made at the national or regional level, the director of each program is responsible for implementing these decisions. The national or regional financial officer provides information about how much money is budgeted for each category; each local director then orders equipment and supplies through the main or regional office and is responsible for generating the required tuition. Some franchisees create their own budget, including fees paid for the right to use the franchised name and logo in the community.

Determining the dollar amount of a budget is a major part of the overall financial plan. This figure is arrived at by listing the items needed to operate the program for a year in categories such as salaries, rent, and equipment. Next, the budget director determines how much each category will cost with as much accuracy as possible. The sum of the costs for each category is the amount of income needed for a year. A sample budget in **Director's Resource 5-1** provides an idea of the costs of each category and of the costs of the total program for a hypothetical program. This sample budget is not meant to be used in the form presented here but may be used as a guide to budget preparation. In your area, costs may be much higher or lower. More important, the philosophy and goals on which you base your planning may differ widely from those used in this sample. Program directors and other professional groups and organizations in each community may provide helpful local information. Companies such as gas and electric companies, kitchen equipment suppliers, toy suppliers, and business associations can furnish more specific and relevant cost information for individual programs.

The following factors influence the total amount spent by a program and the ways in which that amount is allocated:

- number, ages, and special needs of children enrolled;
- EC educator-to-child ratio;
- staff training;
- type and location of building;
- amount of equipment already owned or available;
- type of program and services provided;
- section of the country in which the program is located;
- general economic conditions;
- amount and type of in-kind contributions; and
- special considerations such as free rent.

Growth Mindset Moment

It may be easier to think about the financial aspects of an educational program by looking at your own educational finances. Think about the following questions: How is your college course work being financed? If you are paying tuition, what percentage of the actual cost of your education do you pay? Who finances the balance? Taxpayers? Endowments? How are other school expenses (high school and elementary school) financed?

The sum of the costs for each category is the total cost of running the program for 1 year. Dividing this figure by the number of children to be served establishes the cost per child, a figure that can be further examined on a monthly, weekly, daily, or hourly basis. The cost of various program components such as infant or school-age programs can be figured this way also.

It is important to consider whether the program is a nonprofit organization or whether one of its goals is to make a profit. This question is sometimes hotly debated among early childhood educators, many of whom feel that early childhood education programs should not be operated for profit because someone then makes money at the expense of the children. Admittedly, early childhood education costs are high, and it is difficult to make a profit. Nonetheless, if a person or group can provide a good program, meeting the needs of both children and staff while showing a profit, there is no reason to discourage such a financial plan. The director is responsible for ensuring that children are not shortchanged in the interest of making a profit. Nor should EC educators receive inadequate pay and benefits. This ethical issue may become even more challenging if the director's salary is tied to the amount of profit.

5-2e • Adjusting Budget Figures

Although it is relatively easy to change the budget figures on paper, the budget must remain balanced. Expenses must not exceed income. Chronic budgetary problems will drain staff energy from the daily operation and will remain unless the program can actually pare costs to the level of income earned. When one budget category amount is increased, obviously another budget category must be decreased.

Each expense must be analyzed with an eye toward its relative importance to the overall program. Can the equipment budget be lowered by substituting some free or inexpensive materials? Can food costs be lowered by cooperative buying? Can the consumable supply budget be reduced without a major effect on program quality? What effect will a particular cut have on the quality of the children's program? How will the cut affect the staff?

At the same time, both new and current funding sources can be approached with clear documentation of the need in relation to goals because expenses must not exceed income. If professional early childhood

Crisis: An Opportunity for Positive Change

A recent example of being forced to adjust budget figures came with the COVID-19 pandemic, which caused many early childhood programs in the country to close unless they were serving the children of essential workers only. Many states required that providers apply for a special pandemic child care license. Ratios were greatly reduced, and many states provided subsidies to offset the reduced tuition income. In addition, teaching teams may have had to be reconfigured, and children reassigned to new classrooms. This sounds incredibly challenging and disruptive, doesn't it? Where is the opportunity for positive change?

As new teams were formed and decisions about safety were made, an effort to establish sound teaming and collaboration practices were required. What had become "this is how we do things here" practice became an opportunity to reexamine and make intentional decisions. Teams were required to discuss their philosophy about staging the environment, making decisions, planning, what to do when they felt challenged by a child's behavior, family communication, and conflict resolution. The pandemic forced critical reflection on practice.

educators take the approach that it is better to have a poor program than none at all, then the problem of adequately funding child care will never be solved. When a program's financial management is poor, the director may continue operating past this point without becoming aware that the inevitable outcome will be a poor-quality program or bankruptcy. If the year begins with a deficit budget (that is, expected expenses exceed expected income), it is highly unlikely

Director's Corner

Our needs assessment indicated that more than 100 children would use our program. Two major corporations in the neighborhood worked with us, and many of their employees expressed interest in enrolling their children. We were shocked when we spent the whole first year with only nine children enrolled. Luckily, we had strong financial backing, and we have now reached capacity enrollment.

—*Director, private not-for-profit program*

that the year will end with a balanced budget. For that reason, deficit budgets should not be approved.

5-2f • Analyzing Budget Categories

Even when a financial officer assumes major responsibility for preparing the budget, the director is still responsible for understanding and articulating what is needed to operate the program successfully. Many board members have limited knowledge of the actual cost of child care. The director must help them develop this understanding.

Some programs budget by function rather than simply by category; that is, administrative costs and the costs of each aspect of the program are budgeted separately. For example, if 20 percent of the director's time is spent working directly with the children and 80 percent on administration, then 20 percent of the director's salary would be allocated to the children's program salaries category and 80 percent to administration. A complex program may provide and budget several separate functions such as infant program, preschool program, and after-school program. This budgeting method clearly delineates the actual cost of the children's program. When coupled with a description of the services offered, it provides a mechanism for comparing costs with other programs and for including the value of the services provided in relation to the costs incurred. This method also provides information used in determining tuition. However, ever-changing tax laws make it essential for even small programs to have the services of an accountant to guide the director in setting up financial systems and to provide information about new governmental requirements. An attorney also may be needed to help ensure that the program is operating within legal limits. The cost of these services must be included in the budget.

Although requirements at each program vary widely, new directors may be given a general idea of costs if they consider the following rough estimates:

- 70 percent personnel;
- 10 percent facility, utilities;
- 5 percent equipment;
- 3 percent supplies;
- 3 percent food; and
- 9 percent other categories.

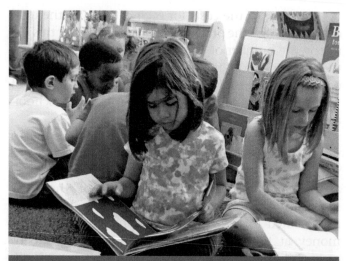

The director understands that all children need a wide variety of books from which to choose and thus provides adequate funds to maintain the program's collection.

Attempting to design a budget to fit these percentages, however, would be inappropriate because these figures are provided as general guides.

The following budget categories will provide a rough idea of the costs of early childhood education and the formats used for presenting a budget.

5-2g • Salaries

In any early childhood education budget, the major component is salaries. A program can expect to spend 70 percent to 80 percent of its operating costs for personnel. This figure includes salaries and wages for full- and part-time staff members (such as director, EC educators, cooks, janitor) and for substitutes. It also includes fringe benefits for the full-time staff. In determining the budget for salaries, the personnel policies should be consulted in regard to pay rates and fringe benefits. The salary policies may address issues such as staff members' education level, previous experience, or meritorious service. The director also must comply with the minimum wage laws, tax laws, and laws regarding employer responsibility.

Salaries are considered in budgeting as a cost of doing business. Of course, to the employee, salaries represent livelihood. Employees expect and are entitled to fair pay for the amount and type of work they do. Their job category is usually determined by the preparation and experience they bring to the role.

Director's Corner

Recently, a local employer built a brand-new on-site program and employed a director. She is a company employee. Her salary and all building costs, including rent, maintenance, and utilities, are covered by the company. We had to increase our salaries because we were losing staff to the new program, which could, of course, pay higher salaries. But it meant we had to raise tuition, and we really didn't want to do that.

—Director, full-day early learning program

By now, you are well aware that salaries in the demanding field of early childhood education are relatively low. Parents are paying higher and higher tuition. Why, then, aren't staff salaries higher?

In its Unifying Framework, the Power to the Profession Taskforce (2020) states,

> As a result of the nation's failure to adequately invest in high-quality child care and early learning over the years, children are not getting what they need; families are paying more for child care than for housing, if and when they can find and access that care; and the workforce is paid so little that nearly half live in families that depend on public assistance. (p. 7)

As you can see, directors today are out ahead of a wave of change with many unknowns. It does appear that the priorities of the nation around early childhood education are changing. However, the current financial realities must govern the development of a budget.

The Bureau of Labor Statistics of the U.S. Department of Labor regularly reports wages by occupation. The occupations related to early childhood programs still used by the Bureau of Labor Statistics represent the inequities identified by the Power to the Professional Taskforce (2020) as shown in **Table 5-1**. Salaries of "preschool teachers," "child day care workers," and "elementary school teachers" are separated for analysis and reported by mean (average) and annual dollar amounts. See **Table 5-2**. Although the current goals of the profession of early childhood education are not accurately represented in how the Bureau of Labor Statistics data are presented, the wages listed can be used as a point of reference.

The Bureau of Labor Statistics lists teachers, beginning with kindergarten teacher,

Table 5-1 Same job, different pay

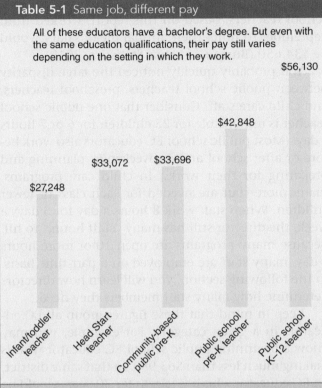

All of these educators have a bachelor's degree. But even with the same education qualifications, their pay still varies depending on the setting in which they work.

- Infant/toddler teacher: $27,248
- Head Start teacher: $33,072
- Community-based public pre-K: $33,696
- Public school pre-K teacher: $42,848
- Public school K–12 teacher: $56,130

Source: The Power to the Profession Taskforce (2020, p. 8).

Table 5-2 Comparison of wages by job title, May 2019

Job Title	Hourly Wage ($/40 Hours per Week)	Annual Wage ($)
Preschool teacher*	16.66	34,650
Child day care services	16.80	34,950
Elementary school teacher		*63,980

*Note that preschool teachers employed by public schools typically earn the same salary and work the same calendar as elementary school teachers.

Source: Bureau of Labor Statistics (2019).

by annual salary rather than by hourly wage. Kindergarten teachers were listed as earning a mean salary of $63,980. Mean annual salary for preschool teachers was listed as $34,650. The preschool figures appear to be based on a work schedule of 40 hours per week at 52 weeks per year. Because hourly rates are not provided for kindergarten teachers, one can assume that the annual salary is for the school year rather than for 52 weeks at 40 hours each. If preschool teachers, based on this report, worked from September to June, their annual mean salary would be $34,650 (Bureau of Labor Statistics, 2019).

You probably quickly noticed the large disparity between public school teachers, preschool teachers, and child care staff. Consider that one public school teacher is responsible for 25 children for 6 or 7 hours a day. (Most public school EC educators also work before or after school and on weekends, planning and preparing for their work.) In child care programs, many more staff are needed for each class of fewer children. When staff work 8 hours a day for 5 days a week, the director still has many "staff hours" to fill. Because many programs are open 10 or more hours a day, many staff are employed on a part-time basis. In the following section, you will learn how directors determine how many staff members they need.

Keep in mind that these figures group all EC educators in a given category. For example, you may know a beginning public school EC educator who is making much less than $63,980. In that same district, an EC educator who has taught for 30 years would be earning much more than $63,980 per year. Also, all the figures mentioned in this section were based on national averages. However, salaries vary widely from state to state and from program to program (Child Care Aware of America, 2019).

5-2h • Staffing and Full-Time Equivalents

As discussed previously, approximately 70 percent of your operating budget will be spent on staff salaries and benefits. But how does an administrator determine the number of EC educators that will be needed and the salaries that can be provided? One strategy you might employ involves computing the full-time equivalents (FTEs) or number of full-time employees that will be needed to meet EC educator-to-child ratios. The following is an example of how you could approach this aspect of the budgeting process.

Assume you are the director of an early childhood program that serves 140 children 12 hours a day, 5 days a week. Your program has an annual operating budget of $1 million. Based on the 70 percent figure, we can presume you will budget approximately $700,000 for salaries and

benefits ($1 million × 70%). Let's also assume that your state's teacher-to-child ratio and group size licensing requirements are less stringent than those found in the National Association for the Education of Young Children (NAEYC) standards. As a program that will be applying for accreditation, let's assume you have decided to try to meet and, in some cases, exceed the more rigorous guidelines provided by NAEYC.

You may love working with numbers and immediately want to explain **Table 5-3** to everyone else—or you may give up as soon as you see so many numbers in one place. In either case, proceed slowly so that you will gradually be able to plan staffing for one classroom and eventually move to a much more complex setting. Every director must understand this, even if he or she hires someone else to handle it. Showing it to parents, funders, and elected officials should help them appreciate that early childhood programs have complex financial needs.

Table 5-3 presents an overview of your program's staffing needs. You have planned for three groups of infants, four groups of toddlers, and five groups of preschoolers. Based on the caregiver-to-child ratios you have adopted, *each classroom* will require 24 "caregiver hours" each day (two EC educators three 12-hour days, which equals 24 hours per day). Each classroom will need 120 hours each week (24 EC educator-hours per day, 5 days per week). Note that this does *not* mean that EC educators work a 12-hour day. This number reflects the number of hours that must be covered by a staff person.

We know that there are 12 classrooms.

Each room needs the equivalent of two EC educators for 12 hours a day or 120 hours a week.

12 hours × 5 days × 2 EC educators = 120 hours

120 hours a week × 52 weeks a year = 6,240 EC educator-hours per room

6,240 EC educator-hours per room × 12 classrooms = 74,880 EC educator-hours per year

We can see that the total number of caregiver hours required in your program each year is 74,880. If all EC educators are full-time employees, then we can assume that they will work a total of 2,080 hours per year:

40 hours per week × 52 weeks = 2,080 hours per year

Table 5-3 Overview of center staffing needs

	No. of Children in Each Classroom	Caregiver–Child Ratios	No. of Caregivers Required to Meet Ratio	No. of Caregiver Hours Required Each Day (12-Hour Day)	No. of Caregiver Hours Required Each Week (5 Days per Week)	No. of Caregiver Hours Each Year (52 Weeks per Year)
Infants	6	1:3	2	24	120	6,240
Infants	6	1:3	2	24	120	6,240
Infants	6	1:3	2	24	120	6,240
Toddlers	8	1:4	2	24	120	6,240
Toddlers	8	1:4	2	24	120	6,240
Toddlers	8	1:4	2	24	120	6,240
Toddlers	8	1:4	2	24	120	6,240
Preschoolers	18	1:9	2	24	120	6,240
Preschoolers	18	1:9	2	24	120	6,240
Preschoolers	18	1:9	2	24	120	6,240
Preschoolers	18	1:9	2	24	120	6,240
Preschoolers	18	1:9	2	24	120	6,240
TOTAL	140		24	288	1,440	74,880

Source: Thanks to Dr. Ellen Lynch for contributing this activity and chart.

Therefore, your program would require a total of 36 full-time equivalents:

74,880 caregiver hours ÷ 2,080 hours per year = 36 FTEs

In other words, to maintain your caregiver-to-child ratios, you would need to hire the *equivalent* of 36 full-time EC educators.

Let's assume you are hiring EC educators at a mean hourly wage of $16.80. Therefore, a full-time EC educator would have an annual salary of $34,950 (2,080 hours × $16.80 per hour), and your annual budget for teaching staff would need to be $1,258,200 ($34,950 × 36 FTEs). Based on your original figure of $1,256,200 for salaries, it appears that you will not be able to cover your staffing needs. However, you must also consider that fringe benefits were not budgeted, and these may add approximately 30 percent to the salaries. Moreover, you must consider that this example does not account for administrator and support staff salaries or variations in wages based on the staff member's position (e.g., lead EC educator, classroom assistant, aide) or EC educator experience.

If, instead of thinking about EC educators' salaries, you wanted to provide *at least* the national average preschool teacher pay of $16.66 per hour, then what would your classroom staff cost be? As the program's director, it becomes your responsibility to balance the budget while addressing the needs of your staff and the children and families you serve.

Table 5-3 can be modified to meet your needs and can be used when you have some full-time and some part-time children. You may not need two EC educators in each classroom for the first and the last hour of each day, depending on how many children arrive and leave during those hours, but you must always have a minimum of two staff available at all times.

With this guideline, you can get a starting point in deliberations about the salary requirements for your program. However, you will still need to make your own chart showing each EC educator by name, assuming that each EC educator's salary is based on qualifications, years of experience at your program, merit, and other potential salary criteria included in your policies and procedures manual. You will also need to make a chart for each room showing what time each staff member arrives and leaves and when they are on break or have planning time. These charts will ensure that you have the desired number of staff in each classroom at all times. Your focus should be on maintaining consistency for the children and avoiding having too many different caregivers in one room over a 1-week period.

5-2i • Consultants

A second component of a program budget that is closely related to salaries is contract services or consultant fees. This category covers payments to people who agree to perform specified services for the program or its clients. Most programs have an accountant and an attorney available for consultation on a retainer or an hourly rate. Other possible consultants might be doctors, dentists, social workers, real estate agents, psychologists, nutritionists, and educational consultants. These types of professionals could be employees of a large program or system. However, they usually serve as consultants by agreeing, for example, to give dental examinations to all children enrolled in the program or to provide workshops for EC educators one day a month. When the program's staff is not well trained, or when a broad range of services is provided for children, many consultants are needed. Although some programs do not hire consultants, and most will hire only a limited number, the overall quality of the program may be increased by the services they provide.

When consultants come from out of town, their transportation, meals, and lodging may be additional costs. Sometimes, consultants are paid a per diem rate to cover meals and lodging. The current per diem rate of the federal government might be used in budgeting. Both the program and the consultant should agree in writing on all financial arrangements and performance expectations in advance of any services rendered. Under no circumstances should the director attempt to classify a staff position as a consultancy to avoid paying taxes and benefits. Serious legal ramifications may result.

5-2j • Plant and Equipment

The largest cost in the physical plant category is facility rental, lease, or mortgage payments. The costs for maintaining and repairing the building and grounds also are part of this budget component. When maintenance work is done on a regular basis, the costs usually will be lower in the long run. However, because it is impossible to predict all maintenance and repair needs in advance, a lump sum for this purpose should be allocated each year. A preliminary assessment of the main components of a building (foundation, roof, plumbing, wiring, heating and cooling system, termite damage, and so forth) will provide a rough idea of when major repairs may be expected. Periodic assessments must also be scheduled.

Also included in the physical plant category in the operating budget are utilities (heat, electricity, and water). In some cases, one or more of the utility charges may be covered in the lease, a point that should be fully understood and in writing before a lease agreement is made. Some programs also may have to pay for garbage removal. When utilities are not included in the lease, an approximate budget figure can be obtained by checking with previous tenants or the utility companies.

In budgeting for a new program, equipment for the children, the office, and the kitchen is a major part of the start-up budget. For a continuing program, the operating budget includes supplementary pieces, as well as repair and replacement where needed. Leasing and rental charges for equipment are included here. For example, a program may rent a carpet cleaner for a day or two or lease a copy machine for a year. The continuing equipment budget will be about 10 percent of the start-up equipment budget, so if the start-up equipment budget is $1,000 per child, the continuing equipment budget would be $100 per child per year.

Growth Mindset Moment

Think about purchasing a new car. As soon as you drive it away from the dealer's showroom, it becomes a used car and is worth less than you paid for it. Every year, therefore, it is worth less, partly because it is being used and gradually wearing out and partly because newer models with different features are being produced. At some point, it may be worth a lot more to you than to anyone else. You may continue to drive it. But if the cost of repairs becomes high, you will probably decide that it would be more economical to get a different vehicle.

Think about the building and equipment needed for a program. They, too, are depreciating.

5-2k • Depreciation

One of the costs of doing business that may be overlooked is depreciation of major equipment. When a program purchases major playground equipment or furniture such as tables, chairs, and shelves, it would appear that the program had added that amount of dollar value to its assets. However, after an item is purchased and put into use, its value begins to drop or depreciate. Let us assume that the children's furniture will last 15 years, whereas the computer and copy machine will have to be replaced in 5 years. Dividing the initial cost of the item by the anticipated length of its useful life yields the annual depreciation amount. A $2,000 computer divided by 5 years results in depreciation of $400 per year—that is, the computer is worth $400 less each year. **Table 5-4** depicts the annual value of the computer. Although the computer may still be functioning adequately, it now has little or no value. When you consider the assets of your child care business, this computer is no longer an asset even though you may continue to use it.

In listing assets, the annual amount of depreciation is deducted so that the value of the equipment is more realistic than if the full cost were listed. At the same time, wise directors build an equipment replacement fund so that when eight infant cribs must be replaced, the program is prepared for that expense.

5-2l • Supplies

Three types of supplies must be purchased: (1) office and general supplies, (2) classroom supplies, and (3) food supplies. The first category includes items such as pencils, stationery, toilet paper, paper towels, cleansers, and brooms. Construction paper, paint, crayons, pet food, and doll clothes are included in classroom supplies. Food supplies encompass all items available for human consumption. Usually, two meals and two snacks per child per day are served in full-day programs, with one snack offered in a half-day program. In any case, sufficient food should be provided so that EC educators can eat with the children. Food costs vary, depending on the availability of federal food subsidies and on factors in the economy. A nutritionist engaged as a consultant can aid the director in setting up a nutritionally and financially sound food plan. (See Chapter 12 for a discussion of nutrition and the U.S. Department of Agriculture.)

5-2m • Transportation

This category may include the purchase or lease of several buses for transporting children to and from school and on field trips. In such cases, insurance, gas, maintenance, and license fees must be budgeted. Some programs contract with a company to provide transportation for children, and others may rent a bus for special occasions. Vehicles must be equipped with child safety seats or seat belts, depending on the size and age of the child, and other governmental regulations regarding vehicles must be followed. Based on a ruling by the National Highway Traffic Safety Administration, buses rather than vans are to be used. They must comply with both federal and state laws. Your state may require that you transport children in vehicles meeting special school bus regulations and that drivers have special licenses. The many financial, safety, and liability issues involved frequently lead programs to require parents to provide the child's transportation to and from school.

Costs for staff members to travel to professional meetings, other programs for observation, and homes for home visits are included in the transportation category. The mileage rate for automobile travel reimbursement is usually based on the current federal government mileage rate.

5-2n • Communication

Telephone costs can be determined by checking with the telephone

Year	Worth ($)	New Value ($)
1	2,000–400*	1,600
2	1,600–400*	1,200
3	1,200–400*	800
4	800–400*	400
5	400–400*	0

Table 5-4 Five-year depreciation of a $2,000 computer

*$2,000/5 years = $400 depreciation per year.

company. In deciding on the number of telephones to order, consider the program's staffing pattern. For example, if a classroom staffed by one adult is located on another floor away from other classrooms, an extension or cell phone is needed to allow that EC educator to get help when necessary. When an EC educator is outside or on a field trip, even though at least one other adult is present, it is a good idea to provide a cell phone. In an emergency, the EC educator can get help. Licensing requirements in some states specify where a telephone is required. In any case, enough lines should be provided to enable parents and other callers to reach the program without undue delays. Although many people now use cell phones, some programs require that they be turned off in the program.

Getting emergency messages through immediately is a priority. Providing staff with access to a telephone for personal calls during breaks is a benefit

that recognizes their needs and helps them feel they are respected members of the organization. In fact, it is a requirement in at least one state.

Many programs rely heavily on email for much of their within-agency communication, as well as contact with families, colleagues, vendors, home offices, and others. The director and other staff also will use various websites for gathering information, contacting legislators in their roles as advocates, and marketing the center. The monthly charge for this access is included under the communication category. Directors may also subscribe to an online child care management tool to communicate with staff and families and track child attendance and store important information in child profiles.

Having a presence on sites such as Facebook and Twitter is a great public relations tool for some programs, whereas others have a policy of not participating and requiring staff to agree that they will not discuss the program online. Such policies must be carefully written. A director may not be able to have specific policies regarding staff using social media, but staff can still be held accountable for "diminishing the reputation" of the center, which is an essential to the educators commitment to the NAEYC Code of Ethical Conduct.

5-2o • Staff Training and Development

Even when a program is fortunate enough to have a staff of well- **naeyc**
prepared EC educators and assistants educated in the early childhood field, continuous in-service programs will be needed. Recognizing that learning is lifelong and that research continues to provide new information about children's development, both directors and staff members need opportunities to participate in conferences, classes, and visits to other programs. When staff members are underprepared, the director must begin their in-service program immediately. State licensing regulations may require a particular number of hours of training annually, usually a minimal level. The director is responsible for determining what is needed and facilitating the acquisition of that training or education. Some programs provide partial scholarships for classes and may reimburse the staff member on successful completion of a course.

Supplying art materials to allow children's creativity to develop requires careful budgeting.

Providing current professional journals and books in the staff lounge or supply room will support EC educators' growth and development as well.

5-2p • Insurance

In addition to health insurance, directors must also have other types of insurance. Insurance agents can quote rates and provide information about appropriate kinds of insurance. A program usually needs fire, theft, and liability insurance at a minimum. If the program provides transportation or owns vehicles, various types of insurance are required. A child accident policy is valuable and relatively inexpensive. If the program has a board of directors, then insurance for directors and officers is important. Be sure to read each policy carefully and ask questions about any items you do not understand. Find out whether your legal expenses would be covered if, for example, you were sued by a family who claimed you were negligent. What are realistic deductibles for your situation? What exclusions, if any, are written in your policy ("Does Your Insurance Coverage Fit," 2002)?

5-2q • Postage

Postage covers the cost of mailings to parents, prospective client families, and past and prospective donors. The cost of shipping and other business mailing is included. In some cases, fax or email may be appropriate and less costly, but a record of important communication should be maintained in every case.

Most programs use web-based program so that families can receive and pay bills online. Some programs establish the policy that payment is due on a particular date each month, and no bills are sent. Postage costs can be held down to some extent if information is distributed by creating a culture in which families expect regular communication through email. Many programs have adopted family communication systems like Moment Path, which provides a vehicle for sharing between EC educators and families. If you have a flexible software package, you should be able to accommodate each family's preferences.

5-2r • Marketing

Marketing includes newspaper and social media advertisements, brochures and fliers, and radio or television announcements. Some agencies design a logo and use it on products such as T-shirts, stationery, business cards, and mugs. Also included are promotional items such as open house events, announcements of staff activities (e.g., names of EC educators who recently attended a national conference), and information about a speaker coming for staff development. In fact, any opportunity to highlight the program without, of course, compromising the privacy of children, families, and staff can be considered *marketing* (see Chapter 16).

5-2s • Licensing

Information about licensing costs can be obtained from the licensing agent; these costs will vary according to the program's location. Other professional fees, such as those for NAEYC accreditation, also belong in this category.

5-2t • Audit

Yearly audits are essential. They assure the board and funders that the program's financial matters are being handled properly. You should ask your accountant for a cost estimate and build that into the budget.

5-2u • Miscellaneous and Other

This category includes funds for small items that do not fall under any of those previously mentioned. However, attributing expenditures to a particular category provides a more accurate picture of the program's financial status and eliminates slippage in expenditures. For example, if postage and advertising were both included under miscellaneous, postage expenditures could skyrocket and not be recognized as a budgetary problem.

5-2v • In-Kind Contributions

Some budget items are not received in cash and not paid for in cash. These are called *in-kind contributions* and should be shown in the budget so that the true cost of operating the program is known. For example, a program may rent two 600-square-foot rooms in a church building for $200 per month per room. The church may charge the program $4,000 for a 10-month program. If the fair rental cost is at the rate of $10 per square foot (a total of $12,000), then the church is, in effect, contributing $8,000 to the program. Note that the reverse is also true. Some church schools provide income for their church.

Consultants may volunteer their services, and such services also should be shown as in-kind contributions. For example, assume that a child development specialist conducts a half-day workshop without charging the program. If the specialist's regular fee is $300, her contribution is valued at $300.

Sometimes, directors expect staff to volunteer to work additional hours without pay. This practice is usually inappropriate and may be illegal. Many EC educators already spend time at home planning and preparing materials. Furthermore, staff salaries usually are alarmingly low. If staff members are expected to attend meetings and programs outside regular work hours, then these conditions should be spelled out in the job descriptions. Some programs include policies relating to staff caring for children who are program clients outside of work hours. At a minimum, staff members who are required to work more than 40 hours in a week must be paid overtime rates for the additional hours, unless they are exempt under U.S. Department of Labor regulations.

Working Smart with Technology

Technology Supported Budgeting Tools

The financial decisions facing the director of the 21st century require accuracy in accounting and the ability to complete "what if" financial modeling projections. A director who is faced with trimming the budget needs to know how closing a classroom might impact the bottom line. Another who is seeking a high rating on the state's Quality Rating and Improvement System (QRIS), needs to know if the monetary award offsets the additional expense of hiring a more qualified staff. In the past, calculating these impacts would be onerous. Today, technology-based budgeting tools allow directors to respond to "what if" scenarios with just a few clicks.

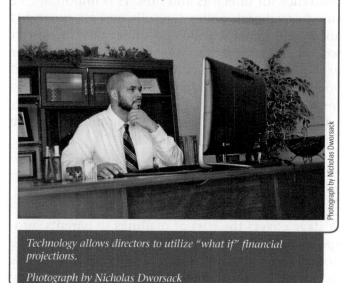

Technology allows directors to utilize "what if" financial projections.

Photograph by Nicholas Dworsack

5-2w • Using Budget Systems

After the sources and amounts of income have been determined, these facts must be written down along with the plan for spending discussed previously in this chapter. This written plan must be prepared in such a way that the people who need to read it will be able to understand it.

Small programs can use a simple format. Programs that are publicly funded may be required to use whatever system is designated by the funding agency. Many programs use budget codes or account numbers, assigning a code number to each budget category and using separate numbers for each item within that category. For example, if the budget item

equipment is coded as 110, then the subcategories might be:

111 office equipment
112 classroom equipment
113 kitchen equipment

Similarly, personnel might be coded as 510, with

511 salaries
512 Social Security
513 workers' compensation

Such a system enables the financial director to record transactions according to appropriate budget categories and ascertain quickly how much has been spent and how much remains in a given category.

Programs with a large number of classrooms, a range of age groups, or more than one site will certainly use a computer program to manage budgets. These may be modified to meet the program's needs.

An additional consideration in keeping accurate records is the responsibility to maintain ethical and legal practices. Having access to large sums of money is tempting to some people. If safeguards are not in place, then the director or an employee who has access to financial records may manipulate them in unethical and illegal ways. A system of checks and balances can deter this behavior. For this reason, board members should be tenacious in insisting on current and thorough financial reports and should not hesitate to question any items they do not understand.

5-2x • Approving the Budget

Before spending can begin, the budget must be approved by the board and the funding sources. The budget must balance—that is, income and expenses must be equal. When there is a surplus in the income side of the budget, it is categorized as profit or may be put in a reserve fund for large expenses that may occur in a future year. Because not-for-profit businesses obviously do not show a profit, such funds would be added to appropriate budget categories or put into a reserve fund. However, if the budget projects a loss, serious attention must be paid to immediate financial trimming. Believing that "something will turn up" is a poor way to conduct business and should not be accepted by a board or funders. At this point, conflict may arise among the board, the funding agency, and the director as each group may have varying interpretations of the program's goals and the means for reaching these goals. After a consensus has been reached and the budget approved, the budget becomes the working financial plan, and the director must see that it is followed.

5-2y • Budgeting for Subsequent Years

Several months before the end of the year, the director and members of the finance committee meet to review the budget prepared for the ensuing year.

For the second and subsequent budgets, the previous year's figures can serve as a guide. The new budget figures, however, are based on experience and program changes and will usually differ from those of the previous year. Still, income and expenses must balance.

5-3 • Financial Responsibilities

The budget is the major tool used by the financial director for management of program finances, but balancing income and expenses is only one aspect of an overall, ongoing financial system. The director has many continuing financial responsibilities, all of which relate ultimately to the budget.

5-3a • Managing Cash Flow

To be sure you will have enough cash on hand to pay staff and order budgeted equipment, you must keep track of cash flow. Often, budgets are divided into monthly components with the assumption that each month you will spend approximately one-twelfth of the annual amount. You can assume that income will be received in a similar pattern: One-twelfth of the annual income is expected each month. Realistically, some items are paid for annually, semiannually, or quarterly. Similarly, total tuition expected in summer may be lower because some children stay home with older siblings or with parents who work as EC educators and are home during the summer. The reverse may occur if you have a school-age program. Children who from September to June come before and after school may spend all day at the program during the summer, thus increasing program income. But suppose your budget includes $1,200 for classroom supplies. Does that mean you can spend $100 a month or can you place a $500 order in March? You need to know whether the cash will be available.

To accomplish this, you make a cash flow chart, showing each income and each expense item on a monthly basis. Often, these amounts are shown on a one-twelfth per month basis. At the end of January, you record the amount actually received and disbursed in each category. In another column, you

Growth Mindset Moment

You have $120 in your checking account. An item of clothing you have desired for a month has just gone on sale for $100. What factors will you consider in determining whether to buy it?

Now assume you direct a program. In examining your records for this month, you note the following:

- Income for March 2021 = $20,359
- Expenses for March 2021 = $15,250

As the director, can you purchase $5,000 of needed equipment for the program? Why or why not? If you have recorded that you had placed an order for $2,000 worth of equipment (even though the bill has not been paid yet), and if you also realize that several other major required expenses are coming up in the next 3 months, you would know that you had already encumbered (or planned for) $5,000 for equipment that hadn't arrived yet.

show the difference between what you expected to receive or spend in that category and what actually happened. Your accountant may refer to these as *accounts receivable* (money owed to you) and *accounts payable* (money owed to others).

You also may record year-to-date expenses and receipts, as well as year-to-date expectations. Assume you listed $100 each month for classroom supplies for an annual total of $1,200. If you spent $0 in January, $50 in February, and $0 in March, you would have a $250 favorable balance in the supplies line. It is not necessary to spend money only as it is available in that line. However, you must be sure you can meet all expenses and not exceed the annual amount allocated without either receiving unexpected or unbudgeted income or decreasing the amount to be spent for the year on another item. Recognize, too, that if you purchase items or services monthly before cash is available to pay for them, you may be faced with high finance charges. Using a good software package to help you keep these records will simplify your task. **Director's Resources 5-2** and **5-3** provide examples.

5-3b • Handling Salaries

After the budget is approved, the financial director informs the personnel committee of the allocation for salaries. In a new program, the committee may begin the employment process in accordance with the personnel policies. In continuing programs, pay raises should be considered.

The director keeps additional records relating to the budget category *salaries*. Professional staff may be paid monthly, biweekly, or weekly, but their salaries are a fixed expense regardless of the number of hours worked as long as those individuals remain on the payroll. Other staff members receive wages based on the number of hours worked during the pay period. Employees who are paid hourly must have some way to record the amount of time spent on the job if that is the basis on which they are paid. Some programs have employees record their working time on weekly time cards or sign in and out on a computer. These records are referred to when paychecks are prepared or may be recorded in one step by the software when the employee checks in and out. The director keeps a record of the sick days and the professional days used for all employees, including those who are salaried.

Payments are made to each individual employee on the basis agreed on in the employment contract. In small programs in which staff have the same schedule daily, time sheets may not be kept. In any event, the director is responsible for keeping track of hours worked, sick leave, and vacation time. Here again, entering this information into a computer database enables the financial officer to prepare up-to-date reports and facilitates preparation of the payroll.

Staff members also may be on unpaid leave. Current laws require that certain leaves be available to staff for circumstances such as childrearing. The returning staff member is not guaranteed the exact job but is guaranteed employment when the legal leave

Director's Corner

I thought we were in good financial shape. We were showing a solid bank balance, and we had full enrollment. What our cash accounting system didn't show was that we had several thousand dollars in bills that the bookkeeper hadn't paid yet. I learned that checking the cash on hand and even looking at how much we had budgeted for a category weren't necessarily appropriate ways to make decisions about what I could spend.

—*Director, for-profit proprietary program*

concludes. Programs also may create additional opportunities for leave. In any case, accurate records must be kept of leaves requested, granted, and used, and the director or designee is responsible for knowing and following related laws.

5-3c • Ordering Goods and Services

With an approved budget in hand, the director or purchasing agent (or someone else assigned to this role) can begin to order supplies, equipment, and services. The first step is to consult those who will use the item or services. The janitor may be consulted about a waxing machine, and EC educators should be involved in decisions about tables and chairs for the children. Both janitor and EC educators could participate in selecting carpeting for the classrooms. However, when it comes to actually ordering goods and services, as few people as possible—one is preferable—should be involved.

Several methods of ordering goods and services are used, depending on the nature of the purchase. Major purchases usually are approved by the director, the board, or a committee. If outside funding has been received, the program's contract may require that bids be submitted for large items or for large quantities of items such as food or paper goods. The purchaser writes out required specifications to suppliers or advertises for bids in the case of a large order. Then the purchaser examines the bids and contracts that each supplier offers. The lowest bid must be accepted unless the bidder does not meet the specifications. Specifications can refer to a description of the item in question (e.g., a commercial dishwasher), the performance of the item (with water temperature of 180 degrees), or its delivery date (to be delivered by September 1).

Smaller purchases or those that are routine, such as art supplies, may be ordered from a wholesaler. However, some programs require that price information on such items be obtained and that the item of appropriate quality having the lowest price be purchased. Sometimes, purchases are made with particular outlets because they allow credit, but this choice will be false economy if the quality is not satisfactory.

In some large cities, several programs may band together to purchase large quantities of items at reduced prices in a plan called *cooperative buying*. Each program may contribute to the salary of the person who manages the co-op and must transport items from a central location to its own program.

5-3d • Making Payments

The director (or someone so designated) is responsible for making all payments. When shipments arrive, they are checked and paid for as soon as possible within the terms of agreement. For example, if the vendor gives 30 days to pay, the program should use the money until the payment is due but should monitor bill payment carefully so that unnecessary interest is not incurred. In cases in which a discount is offered for prompt payment, that may be a wiser course to follow. Before paying for any item, it is important to verify that the items received are proper in quantity and quality and that the price on the invoice is correct.

A program should establish a checking account immediately so that payment for goods and services can be made promptly and safely. If the program is small, there may be the temptation to pay expenses directly from cash income. This practice is a major mistake because under such a plan, money can easily be lost or stolen, and errors or misunderstandings are more likely. Furthermore, no audit trail of these items is available. Most programs use checking accounts, and some programs require two signatures on each check, perhaps the signatures of the board treasurer and the director. In small programs or proprietary programs, the director signs all checks. Of even greater importance is the appointment of a person other than the bookkeeper to reconcile the bank balance. When procedures for money management are in place and followed, fewer errors are likely to occur.

There must be a specific place to store bills and a specific time set aside to pay them. In small co-ops, a parent may work at home recording transactions. In large, complex organizations, all finances may be handled through a central administrative office, which may be in another city or state.

5-3e • Recording Transactions

Whenever a financial transaction occurs, it should be recorded promptly in a specific form and in a specific place. Access to a personal computer and appropriate software makes this task relatively easy and provides clear, readily available reports that show the financial position of the program on a monthly, weekly, and even daily basis.

In fact, many directors who now use computers for record keeping wonder how they ever managed without these tools. At first, using this technology can be time-consuming, particularly if you are completely unfamiliar with the way these machines can work for you. However, after the system is set up, it takes no more time (and probably less time) to enter figures by means of the keyboard as opposed to pencil and paper. The result usually is easier to read, may be converted readily to chart form on the computer, and can be cross-referenced. For example, you can enter in each child's record the tuition received that month from that family and, without rewriting all the amounts, query the computer for the total amount of tuition received that year to date.

Billing can be easy, and child care management programs such as Procare, EZCare, Sandbox, and others can take data entered when enrolling a child and create an account that can collect payments, track accounts, show past statements, and other billing-related paperwork.

Although not directly related to the program's fiscal operation, you may want lists of program children or families by the child's birth date, health checkup due date, zip code, or class at the program. You can print out attendance reports (often required by funders), which is a task made even easier if the parent signs the child in and out using a computer. Clip art or your own creative graphics add zest to notices. Just remember, however, that you are directing a professional program and not a "Kutesy Korner."

Getting your payroll out on time can be much simpler with a computer. Once programmed with the hourly or monthly rates, the percentages to be withheld or deducted for various purposes, and other data to be recorded such as sick days used and available, your computer will do the calculations and print the checks. You'll have a record of the transactions, but, as with any other document, you'll make a backup disc or use an external drive and keep it in a secure place.

As you work on budgets, reports to funders, cash flow statements, and any other data, you can use a password that will prevent those who do not need or should not have access to the data from viewing or modifying it. For example, a parent may not want the child's address published on the class list.

Every year, hardware and software manufacturers develop new capabilities for this technology. If you are relatively new to computer usage, finding a knowledgeable board member, volunteer, or consultant to assist you is essential. Choosing computer components requires understanding how you will use your computer. Most programs can't afford to buy a more powerful computer than they will need in the next few years, yet buying strictly on price will probably prove to be false economy. If your computer cannot run the software you need, you may wind up with nothing more than an expensive typewriter.

Purchasing software also can be challenging, though not as costly as the hardware. Just as you can add hardware components as you acquire the need and the funds, so you can also add software packages. For example, you may add an accounts receivable package. You may also modify or customize existing programs, or you might purchase a basic program and create your own system.

When purchasing software, some of the items you'll want to consider include the following:

- What kind of hardware is needed to run this software?
- Can you try out the software?
- Does it do what you need?
- What kind of support is available and at what cost?
- Are seminars available? Where and when are they held?
- Is there a telephone help line? What are the hours in your time zone?
- Are upgrades provided?
- How long has the company been in business?

Because both computer hardware and software are changing so rapidly, it's a good idea to check with colleagues about what has worked effectively and what they would like to add. Professional journals such as *Child Care Information Exchange* provide regular reviews. Most reputable software companies will permit you to try out the software instead of watching someone else work with it and telling you about it as they go. ProCare Software and Softerware (maker of EZ-CARE2) are two of the most active players in this market. However, you also may find an excellent package developed by individuals who have been or are directors and have worked with computer programmers to design software that meets specific needs. Of course, whether a program uses computerized records or handwritten reports, these will be timely and accurate only when timely, accurate information is recorded.

5-3f • Summarizing Data

Shortly after a fiscal year ends, the financial director should prepare an income statement for that year. This statement shows all revenue and expenses for the past year and points out the net income or loss. **Director's Resource 5-4** provides an example of an income statement.

To monitor the program's financial position, the financial director lists all assets and all liabilities as well as the equity the owner or owners have in the program. Directors need this total picture to enable them to understand their total financial position.

For example, if the assets are much less than the liabilities, the program is obviously in financial trouble. Notice how important accrued accounting is in creating the statement of financial position. **Director's Resource 5-5** provides a sample statement of financial position.

Sometimes children enjoy and learn by using materials that do not appear in the budget. Nonetheless, the director must carefully plan and monitor the program's financial functions.

5-3g • Auditing

In most businesses, including early childhood education programs, an auditor reviews the books annually. The director makes the financial records, including the checkbook, canceled checks, receipts, and invoices, available to the auditor, whether on computer or in a ledger. The director or bookkeeper must keep these documents in an organized manner, and they must be regularly updated. Shoeboxes or laundry baskets full of invoices are totally unacceptable and certainly unprofessional. At the very least, such lack of organization leaves the impression that the financial transactions of the program are not accurately maintained.

Auditors can perform several levels of audit or verification that the financial operation of the program is based on generally accepted procedures. The board will determine which level is needed; in any event, the auditor will not verify each individual transaction. An annual audit protects the financial personnel of the program by making sure their job is being done according to procedures and protects the entire operation by ensuring that the use of funds is being recorded as planned and that procedures are being followed.

5-3h • Handling Petty Cash

There are several ways to operate the petty cash fund. Each EC educator may receive a specified sum of money to spend for the classroom, or the director may allocate a certain sum per staff member, paying cash when the staff member presents an appropriate receipt. Some programs use petty cash for all unexpected small needs. The director keeps a sum of cash on hand and gives it to staff members who present legitimate requests. For example, if the cook has run out of bread, petty cash may be used to purchase a loaf or two. Petty cash should be used as little as possible to avoid obscuring substantial program expenditures under its heading. If $20 worth of food is purchased weekly with petty cash, then the item *food* in the budget is underrepresented. All expenditures should be recorded (or allocated) to the correct account. This can be accomplished by the bookkeeper when the user presents receipt documentation. Some directors prefer to eliminate petty cash altogether.

5-4 • Break-Even Analysis

In determining the amount of funds needed, a break-even chart is useful. **naeyc**
You want to know how many children you need to enroll to break even financially as well as to make a profit or provide some funds for future initiatives. You and your accountant can prepare such a chart by first determining the fixed costs of operating the program, such as rent, utilities, and director's salary. These are costs that will remain at the same level, regardless of enrollment.

Variable costs are calculated. These are the costs for operating the program that change as enrollment increases or decreases. For example, when four or five children are added, the cook probably orders more food, more art materials are needed, and so forth. If you have several years of budget experience available for this program, you can figure the cost of food per child from the previous year by dividing the cost of food by the number of children. In the same manner, you can determine the cost of equipment per child and the cost of teaching staff per child. As prices rise, you will need to increase amounts accordingly.

Although you don't change the line every time an additional child is admitted, it is clear that the more children you enroll, the more expenses you will have. Some figures can be computed per child such as the amount of food or of disposable materials (crayons, paper, soap, etc.). However, when you have a sufficient number of children, you will need additional EC educators, furniture, and even an additional classroom, depending on the number of children added.

Let's finish the break-even chart so you can see what the financial effect might be.

At this point, the analysis becomes more challenging. Based on licensing requirements and program policies, when a certain enrollment is reached, an additional EC educator must be employed. For example, think of a program with 30 children in which a 1:10 ratio is required. When the thirty-first child is added, the program must provide an additional EC educator, even though the additional tuition generated by a single child surely will not pay an EC educator's salary. However, if six new children are added, it may be feasible financially to have four groups of nine children. Of course, if tuition from 10 children is required to pay an EC educator's salary expenses, then the director should not add children until she can ensure a class of 10 or realize that money will be lost on that class and must be made up by charging higher overall tuition.

The director or accountant can figure a break-even analysis—that is, how many children and what tuition rate will be needed to offset costs. To get an idea of how this works, use the following steps (Hatten, 2019):

1. Calculate fixed costs (see **Figure 5-1**). These must be paid no matter how many children are enrolled (see **Figure 5-2**). These include rent, phone, utilities, insurance, equipment, and salaries and benefits for director, cook, maintenance staff, secretary, and any other nonclassroom staff.
2. Determine the number of children you will serve.
3. Based on the number of children per EC educator, calculate the number of EC educators and the cost of EC educator and assistant salaries and benefits.
4. Based on the number of children, estimate the cost of food and supplies.
5. Add the costs to be incurred (items 1, 3, and 4).
6. Divide the total (from line 5) by the number of children.

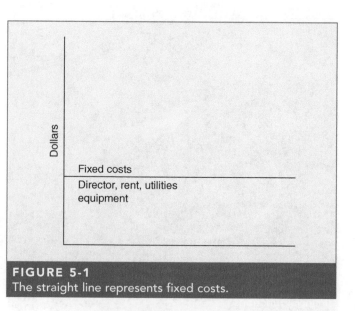

FIGURE 5-1
The straight line represents fixed costs.

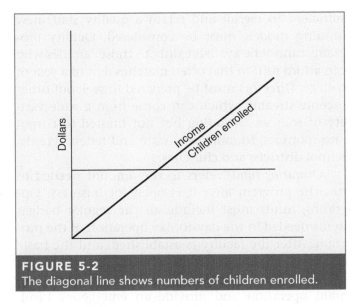

FIGURE 5-2
The diagonal line shows numbers of children enrolled.

The dollar figure in line 6 represents the amount you will have to receive in tuition to break even (see **Figure 5-3**). If, at any time, you do not have full enrollment, you will lose money. Therefore, you will want to build into your budget a cushion that will allow for underenrollment. One way to accomplish this is to charge higher tuition than required to break even. However, if any of your tuition comes from government vouchers, you may be limited to the current voucher rate, which will almost certainly be below your tuition costs.

Costs for infants and toddlers are higher than for preschoolers, while costs for school-age care are lower, based primarily on the EC educator-to-child ratio. Because infants require a lot more individual care and attention than older children, an EC educator can care for only three or four infants at the most. To determine break-even costs when you serve a variety of age groups, do the following:

Divide the fixed costs by the total number of children in all age groups (as described previously). The fixed cost for every child is the same regardless of age.

Calculate the variable costs for each age group separately (teaching staff, food, supplies).

Divide each age group's variable costs by the number of children in that age group to find the variable cost per child.

Add the variable cost per child and the fixed cost per child. This amount is the tuition that must be collected from that child to break even.

To carry this further, you may want to investigate how you would figure costs for a program serving 8 infants and 36 preschoolers. Notice that although the variable costs for infants will be considerably higher than those for preschoolers, the fixed cost for each child remains the same. Therefore, preschool tuition, although spread over more children in this example, must cover part of the cost of caring for infants. (A sample budget in Chapter 5 demonstrates that a program may lose money on infant care but cover that loss with tuition from preschoolers.) Nonetheless, infant care is

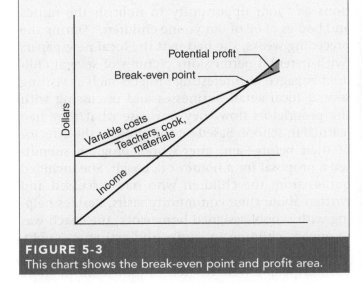

FIGURE 5-3
This chart shows the break-even point and profit area.

Teachers manage the number of children at an activity. To break even, directors must manage the number of children enrolled.

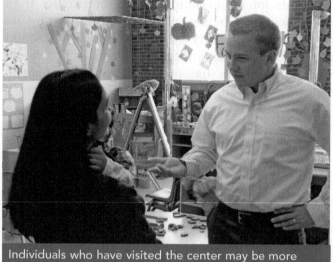

Individuals who have visited the center may be more likely to contribute to your fiscal campaign.

important for at least two reasons: (1) There is a major need for infant care in many communities, and (2) when children start in a program during infancy, the program hopes to retain them throughout their preschool years. If the number of preschool children in a program decreases, the cost of infant care may have to increase, or the fees for all children must increase.

By the same premise, school-age care can potentially balance the cost of care for younger children. Programs must carefully plan school-age tuition so that it is reasonable for families. However, because fewer staff are needed, before- and after-school care is less costly than preschool and may be financially helpful to programs serving preschoolers. The key factor remains retention of high-quality care for all age groups.

Using a break-even chart, the director projects the income based on the enrollment. She then looks for the points at which the total costs meet the income and checks to see at what enrollment levels that occurs (Cohen, 2006; Hatten, 2019).

5-5 • Operating Funds for New and Continuing Programs

At a time when the cost of early childhood education is too expensive for families and yet the wages and benefits are not sufficient to recruit and retain a quality staff, new funding models must be considered. Quality programs cannot be available only to those families who can afford tuition that often matches that of a year of college. Directors must be prepared to seek out other income streams, which can come from a wide variety of sources, including but not limited to corporate sponsors, foundations, state and federal grants, school districts, and churches.

Operating funds refers to the amount needed to run the program after it is open for business. Operating funds must include all the regular budget items needed in the day-to-day operation of the program. After the facility is established, and the basic equipment has been purchased using start-up funds, income must be adequate to both ensure daily program operation and provide an emergency fund. Many programs have depended heavily on government funds, United Way, and other charitable monies to provide most or all of their operating funds. An analysis of these sources for the 21st century indicates that it is unlikely that many will be sufficient to maintain the quality that programs must provide.

Fundraising for operating costs must be planned carefully in terms of the benefit to be derived from the contributor's dollars. Imagine a contribution being used to pay for rather mundane yet certainly essential categories such as utilities and insurance. Such usage may not encourage the giver. The creative fundraiser frames requests in terms of projected program accomplishments. One director in an annual fundraising letter labeled contributions as "your opportunity to nourish the minds and bodies of 62 of our young children." During the preceding weeks, she had sent the local newspapers (with parental permission) pictures of several children engaged in interesting projects such as visiting several local small businesses and discussing with the proprietors how they now use what they had learned in school. Based on this project, the director of their before- and after-school program submitted a proposal for a homework coach. She included quotes from the children who had discussed and written about their community visits. Besides helping with school-assigned homework, the coach was to engage children in games and activities involving logic, problem-solving, and creativity. The local businesspeople were invited to join them in these activities. As a result, this successful grant paid for a well-qualified staff member and a wide variety of materials.

5-5a • Tuition

When the program largely depends on tuition for operating funds, it will be necessary to balance the number of children to be enrolled, the amount of tuition their families can reasonably be expected to pay, and the amount of money needed to operate the program. The program will not always be fully enrolled; therefore, the budget should have at least a 3 percent to 8 percent vacancy rate built in. Programs just beginning may have only a few children enrolled for many months, necessitating close management of the initial budget and reduction of variable costs to the lowest possible level. Even some fixed costs can be reduced. For example, a director may employ one or two salaried EC educators until the tuition receipts warrant the addition of more staff.

Because the salaries of most preschool EC educators are unreasonably low and salaries are the biggest expenditure by far in an education budget, it is sensible to charge an amount that will provide the fairest possible salary to the staff. Therefore, the tuition rate should be based on facts, including the following:

the amount needed to meet professional commitments to staff,
the amount that is reasonable in terms of the type of program offered to families, and
the amount charged by comparable programs in the area.

5-5b • Adjusting Tuition

For many programs, payments by parents are the major source of income. There may be an application fee, which will be applied to the child's tuition when she enrolls. If the child is not enrolled, the program retains the application fee. To assist parents or to attract clients, programs may decide to offer 1 or more weeks' tuition free for vacation or illness for each child. If you decide to do this, remember to multiply the weekly tuition by 51 instead of 52 weeks or to divide the annual tuition by 51 weeks. Keep in mind that if parents pay 51 times a year, there may be a

week when you receive no tuition income. However, if you are following your budget, you will recognize that you should not be spending more than the total amount initially approved. You may specify in your enrollment agreement that the fifty-second week of the child's attendance is the week during which no tuition will be due. You may also decide to require 2 weeks' tuition in advance. If the child will be leaving the program, the parents are expected to give 2 weeks' notice to the director. They will then not pay for the last 2 weeks, but the director may have time to find a child to fill the spot.

You may also offer a discount to the second child enrolled from the same family at the same time. But remember, if Jamala's tuition is $5 less per week than that of the other children in her class just because her older brother is also attending the program, you still need to get that $5 per week from some source. If you have 10 children who have a sibling at the program,

When the center director can convince a funder of the importance of physical and motor development opportunities for children, he may be able to secure funding for outdoor equipment.

keep in mind that this means you are receiving tuition minus $50 each week.

$5 × 10 children = $50 less per week

$50 × 52 weeks = $2,600 less income per year

You then need to reduce the budgeted amount of tuition by $2,600 and reduce (by $2,600) the amount allocated to the expense side of your budget or find a way to acquire the $2,600 from some other source.

Similar situations arise when parents request that you hold a space for their child. For example, holding a space for a newborn who will be coming to the program in 2 months can mean that you lose 2 months of infant tuition. Working parents face the dilemma of finding infant care, whereas program directors face the dilemma of keeping full enrollment.

The director must balance this loss of income against the potential loss of enrollment and still make the initial tuition rate high enough to cover such factors. However, because these costs are quite variable depending on how many two-child families are enrolled in the program at a given time or how many infant spaces become available, they may add to budget instability.

Some programs charge tuition on a sliding scale based on the parents' ability to pay. Often these programs receive government or agency funds to supplement tuition income. A sliding fee scale formula is prepared that considers the amount of income, the number of dependents, and other circumstances such as extraordinary medical bills. However, whenever a family pays less than the actual cost of care, the difference must be either covered by making the top of the scale higher than the cost so that some families pay more than the cost of care or by securing outside funds. A sample sliding fee scale appears in **Director's Resource 5-6**.

5-5c • Scholarships

Many program directors encounter situations in which parents want to enroll their children but are unable to afford the tuition. You may want to plan for some sort of aid for either partial or full tuition. This can be accomplished by establishing a scholarship fund created by charging more tuition than the cost per child and using the excess for scholarships or by contacting individuals, agencies, and foundations to ask them to support full or partial scholarships.

Think about the purpose of a scholarship. Do you want to assist families who are temporarily unable to afford tuition, families whose income falls between eligibility for government support and the ability to pay tuition, children from other cultures, or children with disabilities? In any event, the purpose must be clear. To create a scholarship program, you will need an application process, a review process, and a thorough system for keeping records of funds that have been contributed and those that have been disbursed. If the tuition-assistance program is large, particularly in a multiple-site organization, additional staff time may be needed to maintain thorough oversight of the scholarship initiative.

Assume you need 100 children paying $160 a week ($16,000 tuition per week) to balance your budget. Think about having 10 children on partial scholarship. Of the $160 weekly preschool tuition, each of the 10 families is able to pay $70 per child. The $90 per week that those families do not pay ($160 − $70 = $90) has to come from somewhere:

$90 per week not charged × 10 children = $900
(weekly amount needed to compensate for
scholarships)

If no special scholarship funds are available, then the $900 weekly would effectively have been divided among the remaining 90 children. (Of course, this would be done before the tuition was announced to the parents.)

100 children total − 10 children at reduced
rate = 90 children paying full price

Calculating the Potential Effect of Scholarships on Tuition

$900 per week (scholarship money) ÷ 90 children = $10 per fee-paying child per week

$160 per full-paying child + $10 per full-paying child = $170 per full-paying child

Tuition for the year: $170 per week ×
90 children = $15,300

$70 per week × 10 children = $700

$15,300 + $700 = $16,000 per week tuition
for the 100 children at the program

Parents might not be aware that their $170 per week tuition is contributing to scholarships, or you may choose to tell them. Such a plan is effective unless the tuition rate becomes higher than nonscholarship families can or will pay.

5-5d • Tuition Rates

Tuition charges are set by estimating what families are willing and able to pay for services and by considering what rates are charged by competing agencies in the community. Local professional organizations or the local or state universities may have information about the amount of tuition that reasonably can be charged in a particular community. Unless a program offers something very different from that offered by nearby programs (such as NAEYC accreditation or top ranking in state QRIS programs), it may be difficult to convince parents to pay significantly higher tuition for one program over another; therefore, tuition rates must be reasonably competitive. On the other hand, if tuition is lowered to attract clients, it may be difficult to cover costs and compete with other programs in offering EC educators appropriate salaries and in hiring competent staff. Directors of quality programs often have to educate members of the community about the differences in program quality and, in particular, about the value of well-prepared and more costly staff.

Although most programs charge tuition, sometimes that charge is even higher than tuition at a college. A typical range for early care and education in a community might be $185 to $215 per child per week. Infant tuition is higher than tuition for preschoolers because of the higher EC educator-to-child ratio in infant rooms. Usually, parents of children needing child care have had limited opportunities to save for tuition because they are just beginning their careers or are working in low-paying jobs. College tuition is often supplemented by governmental support, endowments, and grants. Completing college is important for many people, but more and more attention is now being given to the importance of the early childhood years as the foundation for future learning. One factor influencing child care costs is the general cost of living in an area.

Employer-supported early childhood education has become much more prevalent during the past two decades. According to a Families and Work Institute study, employers are most likely to provide less costly support options such as dependent care assistance plans enabling workers to pay child care costs with pretax dollars as well as share information with employees about child care services near the worksite (Matos & Galinsky, 2012). In addition, the study showed that larger employers, when compared to smaller businesses, are more likely to provide access to child care at the worksite or offer vouchers to assist with child care costs.

5-5e • Community Resources

Many early childhood education programs are subsidized by local charities and church groups. These groups typically do not provide cash to help meet the operating budget. Instead, they provide in-kind contributions such as free rent, janitorial service, coverage of utility bills, volunteer help, and so forth. If the director and the board find themselves with an unbalanced budget at the end of the year because of unforeseen problems with enrollments or unexpected expenditures, some sponsoring agencies will cover the losses. This practice is particularly prevalent when one of the sponsoring agency's goals is to provide child care services to low-income members of the community. However, the director who is not managing her budget well is not likely to be bailed out more than once.

Boards and directors may want to respond to newly identified needs and to creative ideas. To meet these needs, seeking funding is almost inevitable. Occasionally, whoever funds operating costs also may fund special projects. More often, special funding must be sought. Consider the program that served several children—Mindy, Dashawn, and Ronnie—who had developmental delays. The EC educator observed that they seemed especially interested in caring for

Director's Corner

We really couldn't charge more tuition. Parents just couldn't afford it. It means that the board can't pay me for planning time. My contract calls for a 3 percent raise annually, but this summer, the board president said to me, "Jeanine, we're going to have to use your raise to cover the unexpected moving expenses. There's no other way." I know they tried hard to get other funds.

—*EC educator and director, incorporated not-for-profit program* classroom plants. She asked the director for gardening supplies and a section of playground so that her whole class could create a garden. Mindy, Dashawn, and Ronnie were to be assigned special responsibilities. Recognizing a creative idea, the director went to a local nursery for help. The owner not only contributed tools and seeds but also volunteered to help the class create the garden and joined them at circle time to discuss her job. Later, the class visited the nursery. Having been so delighted with the children's interest and the positive response from parents, several of whom later made purchases from her, the owner made a follow-up call to the director. She offered to provide a small greenhouse for the school so that the children could start plants earlier the following year. Imagine how much everyone benefited from one idea and one director's efforts to provide funding.

United Way funds, raised through a United Appeal campaign, are available for child care services in some communities. Usually, this is a grant for a specific purpose. Eligibility for these community funds varies depending on the locale, the amount of money available, and the demands placed on that source of funding.

As a director of a program that may need community support money, you should familiarize yourself with eligibility requirements in your community so that you can plan accordingly. Often, several preliminary steps must be taken before a program can be presented for funding consideration. Also, some United Way agencies will not give start-up money or operating funds to new programs. Eligibility requirements for funds typically include the following points:

The agency must be an incorporated, voluntary, nonprofit, charitable organization possessing tax-exempt status under Section 501(c)(3) of the Internal Revenue code. The IRS must be licensed by the appropriate authority; provide a needed health, welfare, or social service; and have a qualified and representative governing body that serves without compensation.

The agency must have and must implement a written policy of nondiscrimination and nonsegregation on the basis of race, ethnic origin, disabling condition, sex, or religion regarding its governing body, its employees, and the people it serves.

The agency must have been established and continued to function for a minimum of 3 years (number of years varies) before applying for funds.

The agency must be willing to cooperate in the United Way fundraising campaign and to abide by all the policies of the United Way agency.

After the minimum eligibility requirements have been met, the necessary steps for funding consideration must be taken by the director of the program or by a designated board member. The director usually is the only person who has all the necessary information for completing application forms and thus is the one ultimately responsible for filing the numerous ongoing attendance and financial records that most agencies require. If a board member assumes this responsibility, the director still must provide the necessary data. Therefore, the director must be familiar with the application procedures and clearly understand the ongoing requirements, including reporting requirements for funded programs *before* entering into any agreements with any funder.

The application for funding may seem intimidating to some directors and hinder them from applying for available funds. The process does become easier as the director gains more experience in applying and finds that many applications require similar information. After the information has been gathered, some of it can be reused in subsequent proposals. Nonetheless, directors must be prepared to spend a great deal of time and energy on routine reporting if they expect to use outside funds. Keep in mind, too, that some funders are targeting certain areas. The area may be a well-baby initiative or ensuring that all school-agers have a safe place to go after school. With national attention currently focused on early childhood education, you may find that an organization in your area will also support that initiative.

5-5f • Foundations

A *foundation* is a fund administered by trustees and operated under state or federal charter. Foundation funds sometimes are made available to program early childhood programs for major equipment purchases or for a special project. Occasionally, a foundation will provide funds for building or remodeling a facility or for training staff. Foundation support for a program depends on whether the trustees of the foundation have declared education or, more specifically, early childhood education, as an area of interest.

Large philanthropic foundations such as the Ford, Carnegie, and Rockefeller Foundations have broad-ranging programs with specific interest areas that change periodically. For example, there may be a general interest in funding innovative educational programs, but monies may be going into literacy or single-parent programs during one funding period only to shift to programs for preschool children with developmental delays or to innovative child care models during the next funding period. Smaller foundations may limit support to programs in a certain geographic area or to a given problem area that may change every few years, whereas other special-interest foundations limit support efforts to specific interest areas that do not change.

The Foundation Center is an organization with branches in several major cities. Free classes on various aspects of funding are frequently offered at its sites. In addition, individuals may register to receive regular emails from the center, which publishes research reports that you can view at its locations or its partners' locations or purchase online. The reports include helpful information for those interested in applying for grants, including national trends and priorities of foundation giving. The website also includes a large section labeled "Foundations Supporting Early Childhood Care and Education." Consider this source when you are looking for funds.

Money from corporate foundations is available in many communities. In smaller cities, it is wise to solicit funds from small, local corporations that often have some funds set aside for use by local agencies. Frequently, the small corporate funds are controlled by corporate managers who are sensitive to the public relations value of making a gift to local agencies that, in turn, will give due credit and recognition to the funder. The company name may be attached to the contribution, which is a reasonable expectation. For example, when the XYZ local branch of a department store funds new block areas in all your classrooms, you may install a small plaque that reads "Donated by the XYZ Company." You may submit pictures of a store official handing you a check, building with the children (with parental permission for the photo), or in some other way promoting the company and your program. You, your staff, and the program families may support the store with your business in return.

In an earlier example, a small-business owner recognized a creative and worthwhile idea. She was interested in helping children learn about plants and therefore responded to the program's request. Foundations, too, are looking for innovative ideas and approaches to solving problems. You can approach foundations with your opportunity for them to support a good cause (Mitchell, 1996). Mitchell's article, although written more than two decades ago, still offers excellent advice. Your well-prepared and enthusiastic presentation, as well as your strong interpersonal and communication skills, will improve your chances of obtaining funding. Keep in mind, however, that foundations provide only a small portion of the large amounts of money required to provide good child care.

When directors plan to approach a foundation for money, they must know precisely what they expect to do with the money and how they expect to do it. Their appeal for money must be tailor-made to the foundation's interest areas, and all funding requests must move through the proper channels. However, personal contacts with foundation trustees or other people connected with the foundation are considered extremely helpful. Perhaps a member of the program's parent group or a board member has personal contacts with a foundation or can help find the best channels to use for personal contacts.

Funds tend to flow toward challenging and interesting programs in well-run organizations rather than to needy institutions that are faltering. A few letters of reference from respected sources may increase your chances of receiving funds.

5-5g • Government Funding

Federal, state, and local governments all have some commitment to the care of the children of working mothers, with the federal government historically the forerunner of that movement as far back as the early 1940s. Although state and local government agencies have been involved in licensing and monitoring early childhood care and education programs for some time, the availability of state and local money for child

Director's Corner

When I write a proposal, I always try to think of something that will appeal to the proposal reader—a catchy title or an intriguing goal such as introducing preschoolers to good nutrition through 15 microwave cooking projects. In the long run, we not only meet the goal, but we still have the microwave to use for daily food preparation.

—*Director, agency-sponsored not-for-profit program*

care for working mothers is relatively recent when compared with federal monies available on a somewhat sporadic basis for more than 50 years. It should be noted that tuition rates vary from state to state (see **Table 5-5**). Government monies typically are available for programs that serve low-income families or those that serve children with special needs. Currently, the Head Start program and the proliferation of programs for young children with disabilities serve as evidence of the federal government's focus on these children's education. California was the first state to establish an extensive network of state-supported early childhood programs. However, many other states are moving to expand their state-supported systems. In 2011–2012, 40 states provided state-funded preschool at a cost of $5.1 billion. With more than 1 million children attending these programs, states became the largest source of public preschool (Friedman-Krauss et al., 2020). Then in 2010 and 2011, with prices rising and unemployment high, many states reduced funding for education at all levels. In 2012, state spending per child dropped below the $4,000 mark for the first time since the National Institute for Early Education Research began collecting data in 2002. The funding increased gradually until the pandemic created great challenges for the economy.

Many children are underserved or receive no services. Others receive no services because their parents do not enroll them for a variety of reasons.

Several major sources of federal funding were established during the 1960s and continue to provide some basic support for child care and for children with disabilities. Although some of these programs have ended, advocates for high-quality early education continue to work to find ways to provide qualified EC educators for every child and support for early childhood education and care programs. In addition, the current focus on providing universal early care and education in the United States may result in increased funding in the future from the government.

Some funders may send representatives to observe in classrooms, view center records, and confer with the director.

5-5h • Head Start

One of the most well-known federal early childhood initiatives has been Head Start. This large, well-funded program was created in 1965 as part of the federal government's War on Poverty. Designed to serve low-income children and their families, Head Start now focuses on two age groups. The original Head Start program serves low-income preschool children and their families. Early Head Start serves low-income children prenatal to age 3, pregnant women, and their families. Both programs are comprehensive early childhood development programs. Since Head Start's inception, more than 25 million children have been enrolled. Public Law 116-94, the Further Consolidated Appropriations Act (2020) included $10.6 billion for programs under the Head Start Act, which was an increase of $550 million over the fiscal year 2019 funding level.

5-5i • Child Care and Development Block Grants

Another source of federal funding is the Child Care and Development Grant Fund (CCDF). In 1996, to provide eligible low-income families with subsidies to help them afford child care, the welfare reform law consolidated several sources of federal funding to create the Child Care and Development Block Grant. In fiscal year 2012, this fund provided approximately

Table 5-5 Lowest and highest child care charges for 2019		
Lowest price for infant care	Mississippi	$5,760
Highest price for infant care	District of Columbia	$24,081
Source: The US and the High Price of Child Care: An Examination of a Broken System. https://www.childcareaware.org/our-issues /research/the-us-and-the-high-price-of-child-care-2019/		

$5.2 billion in federal block grants to improve the affordability, supply, and quality of child care in the United States and to enable low-income families to work, attend training, or enroll in education programs. States and territories use some CCDF funds to support child care start-up or expansion grants and loans to providers. In addition, many states have used block grant funding to help early childhood programs improve their star or quality rating level in the state's Quality Rating and Improvement System.

5-5j • Advocacy

Despite the best efforts of early childhood educators nationwide, the issue of funding early childhood programs presents several dilemmas. First, many parents simply cannot afford to pay the cost of care. Although governments already provide large sums of tax revenue, those amounts have never been enough to provide even basic quality for all the children who need care. Nor have governments provided for all the children whose parents want them to participate in preschool education. At the same time, by far the largest part of the child care budget goes to staff salaries. Yet most staff salaries are deplorably low. A plan for financing universal early care and compensation has been proposed by many early childhood educators. Major ideas include delineating a career lattice that would allow entry-level child care staff to begin work with limited previous training and then participate in professional development at no cost. Staff members with bachelor's degrees would be paid salaries in line with those of public school EC educators. All staff would be expected to continue to participate in professional development activities. Directors need to be aware of such initiatives, to contribute ideas, and above all, to work for improved quality in child care and education.

Legislation involving child care is often controversial. As more women work outside the home and more children grow up in single-parent families, child care has taken on new political importance. (See the U.S. Department of Education website for updated information regarding federal policies and initiatives related to early care and education.) Program directors need to keep informed of current and pending legislation and make their views known to state and federal legislators who can provide up-to-date information. Local and national organizations such as Child Care Aware of America (formerly the National Association of Child Care Resource and Referral Agencies) and NAEYC are good sources of information on legislation related to young children. You can easily find the names and contact information for your state and federal legislators online. The Children's Defense Fund provides a newsletter available through email. Regular updates and bulletins on pending legislation are provided. Governmental bodies, individual government officials, and myriad organizations related to funding, education, and similar issues are easy to locate on the Internet. Two publications addressing the overall issues of early childhood care and education are *The Pre-K Debates: Current Controversies and Issues Vision for Universal Preschool Education* (Zigler, Gilliam, & Barnett, 2011) and *Ready or Not: Leadership Choices in Early Care and Education* (Goffin & Washington, 2019).

Making the Case for *Adequate Funding of an Integrated System of Care*

As support for universal early childhood education increases, we find ourselves at a crossroads. The current system of prekindergarten education has developed in a somewhat piecemeal fashion, resulting in a wide variety of programming: public and private preschools, program-based and family home-based programs, and Head Start programs. Some educators and policy makers believe that as we move forward, public schools should serve as the foundation for all early childhood programming because they have the demonstrated capacity to provide affordability and quality (McCartney, Burchinal, & Grindal, 2011). Others contend that a mixed-delivery system of educating young children, which makes use of existing programs in modified configurations with adequate funding, will provide the greatest potential for quality education (Barnett & Ackerman, 2011; Gilliam, 2011). As the director of a program, you have the opportunity, and perhaps the responsibility, to become involved in this critical debate over the future of early education in our country. For additional information, see Zigler, Gilliam, and Barnett (2011). How have these earlier efforts informed the Unifying Framework offered by Power to the Profession?

Program directors are responsible for maintaining current knowledge of how federal, state, and local dollars are being allocated. They should make their opinions known to their legislators and determine whether their programs or the children they serve might be eligible for various types of funding. If so, they certainly should give serious consideration to applying for those dollars.

Some programs are funded almost entirely by state or federal government tax dollars. Although one might argue that 3-year-olds are just as entitled to government funds as 7-year-olds who attend public schools, relying on tax monies to support a program totally can be risky. Funding for some programs or individuals has been eliminated rather abruptly, and there is no guarantee that funds will continue from year to year. Many

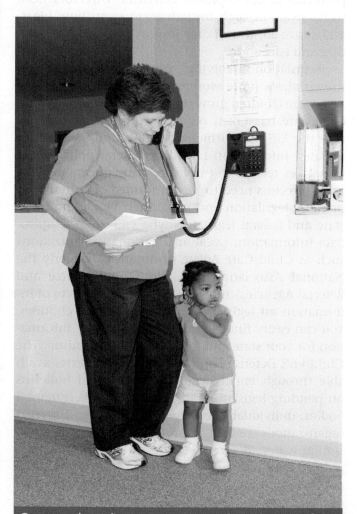

On some days, directors are expected to take care of the needs of homesick children, answer the phone, and also work on obtaining funds for the program.

public elementary and secondary schools engage in additional fundraising for aspects of the program that are usually considered integral parts of schooling such as music, athletics, field trips, and transportation to school. You must be prepared to participate in the universal preschools debate armed with information rather than relying solely on your personal opinions.

5-6 • Soliciting Funds from Corporations and Individuals

The fundraising we have addressed so far relates to major government grants and to relatively small amounts raised for a specific immediate purpose such as additional books for classrooms or cooking activities. Most programs require funding that far exceeds tuition paid by parents. Not all programs are eligible for government funding, and the owners of home programs prefer to solicit funds from nongovernmental programs.

Because most directors will need to be involved in annual and special fundraising from corporations and individuals, they must establish policies and procedures regarding this responsibility. These policies and procedures then can be used to create individual funding campaigns.

The first step of a funding campaign is to find the people who will be the fundraisers. If board members have been selected with this activity in mind, at least some will be able to contribute significantly, monetarily or in service, to the fundraising program. All board members should understand their responsibility to make a contribution to the program, no matter how small. Some board members may have connections with community members or corporations that are prospects for program support. All should be willing to ask for contributions.

5-6a • Preparing for Fundraising

Before beginning any fundraising program, the board and director must make sure that the program has been formally chartered by the state and has IRS exemption. Forms for the latter can be obtained from the IRS. This status permits individual donors to deduct the amounts contributed to the program as charitable contributions. Specific procedures must be followed depending on the size of the contribution and the value (if any) that the contributor receives in return such as a dinner, a book, or a ticket to an event. Written reports are required in these cases, and it is the director's responsibility to know and follow the law or to see that the person assigned to this task has complied. Many agencies disseminate this type of information in a special brochure. When the contributor does not receive the proper documentation from the agency, future contributions may be jeopardized.

Whether the program retains an attorney, relies on the volunteer services of an attorney who also is a board member, or keeps abreast of legal requirements in some other manner, the board is responsible for knowing and following the law. Professional organizations and journals are helpful in alerting directors to potential changes and to those that have been adopted. But not knowing the law is not accepted as an excuse for not following it.

After the agency is in a position to seek contributions, the board approves the plan to conduct a fund drive. Next, the director oversees preparation of attractive and informative materials that make the case for the program's current and future operation. The information must be free of jargon and accurate, not overblown or overly dramatic. Important points must stand out with clarity to aid the busy reader who initially may be totally unfamiliar with the program and its mission. Be sure to include the purpose of the request, the total amount being sought, and information on current funding. If the document is based on a request for proposals (RFP) created by a funder, the proposal must state clearly how the funds will be used and relate that information to the funder's goals. RFP guidelines must be followed closely, and meeting the funder's deadline is essential.

Many reference sources are available to help you plan your fundraising strategies and to help you target foundations, corporations, and government agencies that are likely contributors to your type of request. For one, *Not Just Small Change* (Bergman, 2010) provides detailed information about working with your organization's board to create and implement a fundraising program. Your public library is a good resource, as are websites related to foundations. Your board members are usually good sources of contacts, and you may want to engage a professional trainer to help you develop your solicitation plan.

5-6b • Requesting Contributions

The director is responsible for ensuring that board members are prepared to speak knowledgeably and enthusiastically about the agency and the fund purpose and that they know how to ask comfortably and specifically for funds. Board members (or whoever will request contributions) should determine who will be approached, by whom, and in what time frame. Then the designated person either telephones or writes for an appointment. The latter is usually more successful and may be followed with a brief letter of confirmation. Targeting a specific amount or range for an individual or organization gift is necessary. You may receive a "no" followed by "but I can contribute a lower amount." A request for a vague amount or for a contribution may net you $100 when a specific request for $1,000 may have produced that amount. Many people are uncomfortable discussing money, and even more cringe at the thought of asking someone else for funds. Good fundraisers focus on the value of the contribution to the agency's clients and on providing the prospective funder an opportunity to engage in important work. In most cases, the enthusiasm and sincere approach of the requesters go a long way toward eliciting a positive response.

Let us assume that you called on someone for funds. Whether or not the response was favorable, writing a brief thank-you letter will win friends for the agency and is common courtesy. If a contribution is made, your appreciation is certainly warranted, and if the prospective funder chose not to contribute, appreciation for the time spent with you is in order.

Growth Mindset Moment

Think about a time when you needed a loan from a bank, your parents, or a friend. Did you plan ahead what you would say and how you would explain your need? Did you mention the amount you needed and the purpose of the loan? How did you decide whom to approach for a loan? A director who writes a proposal must answer similar questions. A fundraiser seeking contributions must be equally well prepared.

Summary

Handling financial matters is a challenging but essential function of the director. Directors must develop a financial plan based on both priorities for meeting children's needs and available funds. The major tool used by the financial director is the budget, a plan for balancing income and expenses. The director is responsible for all other financial matters, including designing budget systems, ordering goods and services, making payments, recording transactions, and preparing the new budget.

To plan for and maintain a fiscally healthy program, the director must do the following:

- Describe the process for creating a financial plan for a program early childhood program.
- Explain how to prepare and operate a budget.
- Identify the financial responsibilities of a well-managed program.

TRY IT OUT!

1. Work with a partner. Create a plan for staffing two classrooms for 1 week. Show what time each staff person will arrive, leave, and be on break. Assume the program is open 10 hours a day. Compare your plan with others created by your classmates. How many full-time staff did you include? How many part-time? How many FTEs did you need?

2. Earlier in the chapter, a general idea of costs to be considered provided the following estimates:
   70 percent personnel
   10 percent facility, utilities
   5 percent equipment
   3 percent supplies
   3 percent food
   9 percent other categories
   How well does the early childhood program budget in **Director's Resource 5-1** align with the percentages in the estimate. How might you explain the differences?

3. Examine **Director's Resource 5-4**, Income Statement; and **Director's Resource 5-5**, Statement of Financial Position. What information can you obtain from each statement?

4. Find out who provides funding for early childhood education in your community. Are any programs funded by the federal, state, or local governments? United Way? Private individuals? Chain or franchised centers? Universities or colleges? Businesses or proprietors? Is anyone else funding early childhood education in your community? Your professor may assign one student or a group to explore each of these potential resources and provide a written or oral report for the class.

5. With one or two classmates, examine the sample grant application in **Director's Resource 5-3**. Identify the individual sections of the proposal and discuss the following:
   a. What is the purpose of this particular grant application?
   b. How much funding has been requested?
   c. What information has been provided to justify the request for funding?
   d. What is the importance of the Statement of Agency Commitment?
   e. Identify the type of information included in the Statement of Need.

Director's Resource 5-1

SAMPLE EARLY CHILDHOOD PROGRAM BUDGET

Income	Number	Funds per Week ($)	Number of Weeks	Total Income ($)	
Tuition Income					
Infant tuition	8	230.00	50	92,000.00	
Toddler tuition	12	220.00	50	132,000.00	
Preschool tuition	51	210.00	50	535,500.00	
				Tuition Income	$759,500.00
Other Income					
Food program	1	250.00	50	12,500.00	
Application fees	30	20.00		600.00	
Interest on					
Accounts	1	$600.00		$600.00	
Fundraisers	1	1,200.00		1,200.00	
QRIS grant award	1	25,000.00		25,000.00	
Corporate sponsorship	1	75,000.00		75,000.00	
				Other Income	114,900.00
				Total Income	874,400.00

Expenses	Number	Expense ($)	Wage ($)/Hour	Total Expense ($)	
Personnel expenses					
Director salary	1	50,000.00		50,000.00	
EC educators					
Level 3	5	31,000.00	17/hour	155,000.00	
Level 2	5	29,120.00	16/hour	145,600.00	
Level 1	5	27,300.00	15/hour 12/hour 20 hours/week	136,500.00	
Substitutes	1	49,920.00	12/hour, 20 hours/week	49,920.00	
Custodian	1	6,240.00	12/hour, 10 hours/week	6,240.00	
Nutrition specialist	1	28,000.00	15.38/hour	28,000.00	
Secretary	1	28,000.00	15.38/hour	28,000.00	
				Total salary	599,260.00
Benefits*		179,778.00	30% of salary	179,778.00	
				Salary and benefits total	779,038.00
Nonpersonnel expenses		36,000.00		36,000.00	
Rent		36,000.00		36,000.00	
Utilities					
Advertising		3,000.00		3,000.00	

Director's Resource 5-1 *(continued)*

Food		36,000.00		36,000.00	
Office supplies		3,000.00		3,000.00	
Custodial supplies		2,700.00		2,700.00	
Classroom equipment and supplies		6,000.00		6,000.00	
CPA and professional development		2,500.00		2,500.00	
Liability insurance		12,500.00		12,500.00	
Capital improvement fund/reserves		12,500.00		12,500.00	

Nonpersonnel expenses total	150,200.00
Total expenses	929,238.00
Total income	874,400.00
Total expenses	(929,238.00)
	$(54,838.00)

*Benefits include FICA, workers' comp, unemployment, and health care insurance.

TeachSource Digital Download

Director's Resource 5-2

HYPOTHETICAL BUDGET BY MONTH CREATED ON SPREADSHEET

Felton Family Preschool
Monthly Budget

	"Reasonable" Budget A3	September	October	November	December	January	February	March	April	May	June	July	August
INCOME													
Tuition	344,235	25,000	28,000	30,000	30,000	30,000	30,000	30,000	30,000	30,000	27,078	27,078	27,078
Fund-Raising	3,500	292	292	292	292	292	292	292	292	292	292	292	292
County Grant	27,000	2,250	2,250	2,250	2,250	2,250	2,250	2,250	2,250	2,250	2,250	2,250	2,250
Other	2,000	167	167	167	167	167	167	167	167	167	167	167	167
TOTAL INCOME	376,735	27,708	30,708	32,708	32,708	32,708	32,708	32,708	32,708	32,708	29,787	29,787	29,787
EXPENSE													
Payroll Expense													
Salaries-Staff	270,000	22,759	23,793	20,690	23,793	23,793	20,690	21,724	22,759	22,759	21,724	23,793	21,724
Payroll Taxes	24,300	2,048	2,141	1,862	2,141	2,141	1,862	1,955	2,048	2,048	1,955	2,141	1,955
Worker's Comp	13,500	1,138	1,190	1,034	1,190	1,190	1,034	1,086	1,138	1,138	1,086	1,190	1,086
Staff Benefits													
Health Ins.	27,250	2,271	2,271	2,271	2,271	2,271	2,271	2,271	2,271	2,271	2,271	2,271	2,271
Dental Ins.	4,000	333	333	333	333	333	333	333	333	333	333	333	333
Education Allow.	875	73	73	73	73	73	73	73	73	73	73	73	73
Rent	4,800	400	400	400	400	400	400	400	400	400	400	400	400
Janitor	6,000	500	500	500	500	500	500	500	500	500	500	500	500
Insurance													
Liability	2,914	243	243	243	243	243	243	243	243	243	243	243	243
Accident	1,575	131	131	131	131	131	131	131	131	131	131	131	131
Directors Ins.	944	79	79	79	79	79	79	79	79	79	79	79	79
Supplies	15,000	1,250	1,250	1,250	1,250	1,250	1,250	1,250	1,250	1,250	1,250	1,250	1,250
Utilities	2,835	236	236	236	236	236	236	236	236	236	236	236	236
Capital Improvement	2,000	0	0	1,000	0	0	0	1,000	0	0	0	0	0
TOTAL EXPENSES	375,993	31,461	32,640	30,102	32,640	32,640	29,102	31,282	31,461	31,461	30,282	32,640	30,282
SURPLUS (DEFICIT)	742	(3,753)	(1,932)	2,606	68	68	3,606	1,427	1,247	1,247	(495)	(2,854)	(495)

Source: From JACK, The Business of Child Care, 1E. © Cengage Learning.

Director's Resource 5-3

SAMPLE GRANT APPLICATION*

Doe Learning Center Inc. is a nonprofit corporation that operates four child care centers in the greater metropolitan area. The centers provide quality child care for children ages 3 months through 5 years and also offer school-age care at two of the sites. As a United Way agency, the centers' common goal is to work toward alleviating the current crisis of child care, as outlined in the Long Range Plan for Child Care of the United Way in 2000. This study shows that there is an urgent need for quality programming for children identified as having special needs. Doe Learning Center Inc. has responded to this need by operating four centers whose common goal is the inclusion of all children.

Statement of Agency Commitment

Metropolitan Learning Center (MLC) is located in the central area of the city. The program serves 67 children ages 3 months through 5 years. In the summer, we enroll an additional 20 children in our school-age program. Established in 1984, MLC was the first full-day program in this city to be accredited by the National Association for the Education of Young Children.

Largely based on the theories of Piaget and Erikson, the center's philosophy reflects a focus on the development of the whole child and the formation of strong, trusting relationships.

*Names of people and places are fictitious.

Director's Resource 5-3 (continued)

The developmental constructivist approach holds the belief that children develop sequentially from one stage of development to another. Because of this, we believe that children must be provided with opportunity that will challenge them and aid in their progression from one stage to the next. It is a necessity that learning be based on actual experience and participation. Talking without doing is largely meaningless to young children.

We believe that for children to grow, they must be placed in a setting that meets their basic needs. Therefore, it is our utmost concern that our program provides a nurturing, comfortable environment that is specifically structured to meet the physical, emotional, and cognitive needs of each individual child.

This philosophy was the foundation for the development of the agency. Due to this commitment, the question of inclusion was never discussed, only how to do it well.

In this time of severe staff shortages in the ECE field, MLC feels fortunate to have an outstanding quality and quantity of professionals.

- Four preschool head teachers—M.Ed.
- One toddler head teacher—Associate in Early Education
- Two infant teachers—Bachelor Education and two infant teachers—Associate Education
- Dr. John Jones, professor emeritus at the Metropolitan University, has been consulting with our agency for three years. This past year, Dr. Jones has been working strictly at MLC, coordinating our educational services.

Director's Resource 5-3 (continued)

MLC has worked extensively with the Early Childhood Education Department, Metropolitan University. The program has been a training site for the past five years and works with an average of three to four students per quarter.

According to Washington County Child Day Care: The State of Today and Plans for 2010: "Special needs children are still at a great disadvantage. Most child care providers feel ill equipped to serve children with developmental problems and physical disabilities." MLC has successfully integrated approximately 25 children identified as having special needs. One family called more than 60 child care centers before finding a placement at MLC for their child with cerebral palsy. The center has served many children with a wide variety of special needs, including, but not limited to, pervasive development disorder, fragile X syndrome, autism, mild mental retardation, receptive language disorder, and visual impairments, to name a few.

One of the primary goals of the organization is to meet the needs of the family, parent, and child. MLC has identified its ability to meet these needs as follows:

Needs of the Child

- Placement in a program meeting the standards of developmentally appropriate practice
- Master-level staff capable of identifying and working with high-risk children

Director's Resource 5-3 (continued)

Needs of the Family

- Providing high-quality care for their children
- Providing quarterly parent education/training programs
- Providing assistance in identifying (or working with existing) available services (i.e., early intervention) for their children

MLC has been identified in the community as a program that will not only serve children with special needs but also give them access to the services they need or support the work of other service providers as part of the daily program. Metropolitan University acknowledged the endeavors of the center by placing students from the Special Education department under the guidance of our experienced staff. We have worked with many agencies to provide more comprehensive services to these children. These agencies include the following:

- Washington County Department of Human Services
- Special Education Regional Resource Center (SERRC)
- Cerebral Palsy Services Center
- Center for Developmental Disorders
- Speech and Hearing
- Speech Pathology
- Child Advocacy Center
- Association for the Blind
- Metropolitan University—Early Childhood/Special Education Department
- Foster Grandparent Program
- The Council on Aging
- The Single Parent Center

Director's Resource 5-3 *(continued)*

Statement of Need

There are currently eight children enrolled in the program who have been identified as having special needs. There are several children who are integrated into the environment and are receiving services from support agencies. MLC feels confident that we can meet their needs without additional services. There are two children that pose challenges to our existing program. One child is currently enrolled in our infant program; he is 20 months old and has cerebral palsy. When we enrolled Ed, we assessed that we could meet his needs in the infant program. Although Ed is nonmobile and nonverbal, he uses smiles, cries, and coos to communicate with his caregiver. To continue serving Ed:

- We need to be able to meet the challenge of facilitating his growth through experiences with the toddlers.
- We need to acquire the equipment to encourage his further development.
- We need release time for his caregiver to meet with his therapist to learn how to use specialized equipment and participate in his IEP meeting.

Our second child has been identified with pervasive developmental disorder and mild characteristics of autism. Communication has been the primary barrier in the progression of Ryan's development. This aspect of his disorder carries over into other areas of his growth, including the development of self-control. Ryan has been enrolled in our program for one year and within that period has gone from single-word utterances to communicating in four- to five-word sentences.

Director's Resource 5-3 *(continued)*

Because of this increased ability to communicate, the agency believes that a transition to the oldest preschool classroom is the next step. The goal of this move is to place Ryan in an environment of his same-age peers where he might benefit from the modeling of age-appropriate behaviors and participation in activities. Any changes in daily schedule and transition times are extremely difficult for Ryan, and separation from his current classroom teacher will be a tremendous undertaking.

Our belief is that to best aid in this transition, MLC will need the assistance of an additional staff person for the following reasons:

- To meet the needs of Ryan during the period of transition so that classroom staff may continue to meet the needs of his peers
- To act as a facilitator, giving Ryan assistance with social interactions so that he might form relationships with his peers and staff
- To give the classroom staff opportunity to focus on forming trusting relationships with Ryan, without concern that the experiences of his peers are being limited

Purpose of Funding/Budget

The purpose of our funding breaks into three categories: equipment, consulting/training, and additional staff to decrease ratios.

Director's Resource 5-3 *(continued)*

Equipment

Type	Purpose		Cost
Outdoor swing			$126.95
Floor sitter	Seat for severely challenged student allows a nonmobile child to interact with peers but have necessary support		$150.00
Button switch toy			$ 42.00
Jelly bean switch toy			$ 42.00
Circus truck			$ 27.00
Bumper car			$ 25.00
Brontosaurus			$ 29.50
Oversized ball	Easier to manipulate than typical ball	18"	$ 24.35
		34"	$ 69.50

Consulting/Training

Topic (we would like to open these to the public)

How to adapt "typical" equipment to meet the needs of physically challenged children	$100.00
How to use switch toys	$ 80.00
How to write an appropriate IEP and how to make the IEP meeting work for the child	$100.00

Consulting

How to arrange the toddler environment to meet the needs of a physically challenged child	$100.00
How to encourage positive peer relationships with typical and atypical children	$ 50.00

Director's Resource 5-3 *(continued)*

Support Staff

Enrolling a physically challenged child into the infant program was within the abilities of our staff. Allowing time for this child to interact with peers of his own age and slowly transitioning him into the toddler room will be a challenge for us. We need time for his caregiver to visit the toddler room with him, and then time for the toddler teacher to have one-on-one time for him. This cannot be done without additional staff. Any choice we make with the current staff situation will either shortchange Ed or the other children enrolled. We are requesting a part-time assistant for six months.

Cost $ 6,656.00

Having children that model age-appropriate behaviors has been the most vital ingredient to Ryan's development. To continue his progress, it is imperative that he be surrounded by children exhibiting the behaviors that Ryan is striving for. As mentioned earlier, any transition is very difficult for Ryan. To continue servicing Ryan and meet his needs by transitioning him to be with children of his own age, we will need additional staff. We are requesting a part-time assistant for six months.

Cost	6,656.00
TOTAL REQUESTED	**$14,278.30**

Expected Outcome

This grant will enable us to purchase equipment that will

- allow physically challenged children to become more accessible to the other children by being positioned near them on the floor.
- provide stimulation and encourage peer interaction.

Director's Resource 5-3 *(continued)* ///

- lessen isolation so that relationships with peers will increase.

    This grant will enable us to provide sufficient staff to
- allow challenged children to be surrounded with children of their own age providing appropriate models.
- allow staff to meet the requirements of our children with special needs without denying other children the attention they need.
- facilitate smooth transitions that encourage success with meaningful relationships with other children.
- make inclusion a successful experience that will encourage staff to include additional children.

This grant will provide technical assistance that will

- give the staff and management the knowledge to include these children and additional children in the future.
- encourage other early childhood programs to attend these training sessions and build support through networking with other teachers participating in inclusion.

    We will be asking staff who are working with Ed and Ryan to fill out a short questionnaire before we provide additional services and then again after. We would like to see if these support services change any possible insecurities or feelings of being overwhelmed that had previously occurred.

TeachSource Digital Download

Director's Resource 5-4 *(continued)* ///

Office and paper supplies	3,300
Rent	16,000
Payroll service fees	1,420
Cleaning service fees	8,920
Custodial supplies	950
Equipment expense	2,800
Utilities and telephone expenses	11,300
Garbage removal	650
Advertising	850
Travel and field trips	1,600
Bookkeeping and audit service fees	11,500
Licenses	625
Maintenance and repair expense	5,920
Insurance expense	3,200
Total expense	425,225
Net income (net loss)	45

TeachSource Digital Download

Director's Resource 5-4 ///

SAMPLE INCOME STATEMENT FOR THE YEAR ENDED DECEMBER 31, 20XX

Revenues	
Infant program income	$70,500
Toddler program income	64,500
Preschool program income	247,120
Federal child care food program	41,500
Donations or contributions	500
Parent fundraising	1,100
Other income	50
Total income	$425,270
Expenses	
Salaries or wages	267,100
Health benefits	19,650
Employment taxes and insurance	21,840
Management services fee	15,000
Training or consultant fees	7,200
Food and beverage supplies	21,300
Educational supplies	4,100

Director's Resource 5-5

SAMPLE STATEMENT OF FINANCIAL POSITION AS OF APRIL 30, 20XX

(For use with Try It Out! 5-2)

Assets

Cash–operating	$7,000
Cash–payroll	8,000
Accounts receivable	11,200
Educational supplies	900
Office supplies	400
Property, plant, and equipment	42,000
Total assets:	$69,500

Liabilities ($)

Accounts payable	$11,000	
Wages payable	5,000	
Mortgage payable	32,000	
Long-term liabilities	11,000	
Depreciation	4,000	
Total liabilities:		63,000

Equity ($)

Capital	6,500
Total liabilities and equity:	$69,500

TeachSource Digital Download

Director's Resource 5-6

Center Enrollments in February

Currently Enrolled

Infants	10	Infants Transferring to Toddlers in:	
Toddlers	16	March	1
Preschool	24	April	0
		May	2
Waiting List		June	1
Infants	12	July	1
Toddlers	3	August	0
Preschool	0		

Toddlers Transferring to Preschool in:

March	0
April	1
May	0
June	2
July	0
August	0

TeachSource Digital Download

REFERENCES

Barnett, W. S., & Ackerman, D. J. (2011). Public schools as the hub of a mixed-delivery system of early care and education. In E. Zigler, W. S. Gilliam, & W. S. Barnett (Eds.), *The pre-K debates: Current controversies and issues* (pp. 126–129). Baltimore, MD: Brookes Publishing.

Bergman, R. L. (2010). *Not just small change: Fund development for early childhood programs*. Redmond, WA: Exchange Press.

Bureau of Labor Statistics. (2019). *National occupational employment and wage data estimates*. Washington, DC: Author. https://www.bls.gov/oes/current/oes399011.htm

Child Care Aware of America. (n.d.). The US and the high price of child care: 2019. https://www.childcareaware.org/our-issues/research/the-us-and-the-high-price-of-child-care-2019/

Child Care Aware of America. (2019). *Child care in America: 2019 state fact sheets*. Arlington, VA: Author. https://childcareta.acf.hhs.gov/ncase-resource-library/child-care-aware-americas-2019-state-fact-sheets

Cohen, W. A. (2006). *The entrepreneur & small business problem solver* (3rd ed.). Hoboken, NJ: John Wiley.

Congressional Research Service. (2019). *The Affordable Care Act's (ACA's) Employer Shared Responsibility Provision (ESRP)*. Washington, DC: Author. https://crsreports.congress.govhttps://fas.org/sgp/crs/misc/R45455.pdf

Friedman-Krauss, A. H., Barnett, W. S., Garver, K. A., Hodges, K. S., Weisenfeld, G. G., & Gardiner, B. A. (2020). *The state of preschool 2019: State preschool yearbook*. New Brunswick, NJ: National Institute for Early Education Research. http://nieer.org/state-preschool-yearbooks/2019-2

Gilliam, W. (2011). Preschool programs should be coordinated in the public schools with supports from head start and child care. In E. Zigler, W. S. Gilliam, & W. S. Barnett (Eds.), *The pre-K debates: Current controversies and issues* (pp. 120–126). Baltimore, MD: Brookes Publishing.

Goffin, S., & Washington, V. (2019). *Ready or not: Leadership choices in early care and education 12 years later* (2nd ed.). New York, NY: Teachers College Press.

Hatten, T. S. (2019). *Small business management: Entrepreneurship and beyond* (7th ed.). Thousand Oaks, CA: Sage Publications.

McCartney, K., Burchinal, M., & Grindal, T. (2011). The case for public preschool. In E. Zigler, W. W. Gilliam, & W. S. Barnett (Eds.), *The pre-K debates: Current controversies and issues* (pp. 116–120). Baltimore, MD: Brookes Publishing.

Mitchell, A. (1996). Fishing for dollars in philanthropic waters. *Child Care Information Exchange, 111,* 7–10.

Power to the Profession Task Force. (2020). *Unifying framework for the early childhood profession*. Washington, DC: Powertotheprofession.org. http://powertotheprofession.org/wp-content/uploads/2020/03/Power-to-Profession-Framework-03312020-web.pdf

Zigler, E., Gilliam, W., & Barnett, S. (2011). *The pre-K debates: Current controversies and issues*. Baltimore, MD: Brookes Publishing.

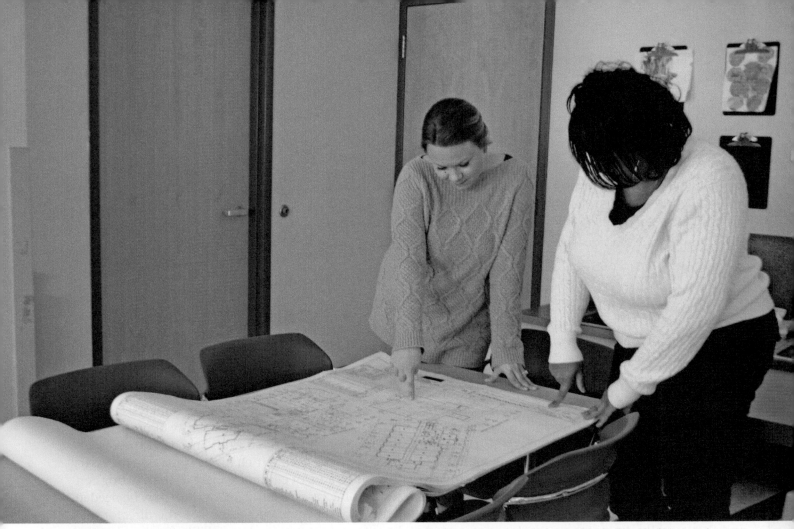

Directors work with architects and contractors before and during the building or renovation process.

Chapter 6

Developing a Program Facility

Standards and Recommendations Addressed in This Chapter

PROGRAM STANDARD 5 Health

PROGRAM STANDARD 7 Families

PROGRAM STANDARD 8 Community Relationships

PROGRAM STANDARD 9 Physical Environment

PROGRAM STANDARD 10 Leadership and Management

PROFESSIONAL STANDARDS AND COMPETENCIES: STANDARD 1 Child Development and Learning in Context

PROFESSIONAL STANDARDS AND COMPETENCIES: STANDARD 6 Professionalism as an Early Childhood Educator

LEARNING OBJECTIVES

After reading this chapter, you should be able to:

6-1   Identify and describe the many factors that must be considered when planning a facility that meets the needs of children, staff members, and families.

6-2   Explain the director's role in creating a new program.

6-3   Identify the individual consultants involved in planning an early childhood program facility.

An early childhood education program should be housed in a spacious, attractive facility that has been created or redesigned for children and that meets the needs of staff members and parents. The director is responsible for ensuring that appropriate space is available; therefore, space needs are analyzed carefully for both ongoing and new programs. The director may assume full responsibility for analyzing space needs, or this job may be done in cooperation with the board building committee or with staff members. Corporate systems often have a prototypical design for all centers in the system, and they usually designate an employee to provide and manage the physical facilities for the system's centers. Similarly, preschool facilities in public schools may be planned by central administration, although the principal may have a major decision-making role. In any case, the facilities must be well maintained. The director is responsible for developing a maintenance system and seeing that it is implemented.

In Chapter 2, we looked at how our beliefs, values, and attitudes are reflected throughout the program philosophically, and in this chapter we will reflect on the manifestation of those philosophies in the physical environment. In addition, it is worth noting the role of diversity—in race, culture, and abilities—as a necessary component of developing an engaging, positive, and welcoming program facility.

As we work to meet all the standards and requirements imposed for good reason, let us also reflect on the words of beloved early childhood educator and author, Jim Greenman: "An environment is a living, changing system. More than the physical space, it includes the way time is structured and the roles we are expected to play. It conditions how we feel, think, and behave; and it dramatically affects the quality of our lives" (Greenman, 2007, p. 1).

6-1 • Analyzing Space Requirements

In providing a suitable facility, the first task is to analyze its space needs. When a program is already in operation, this analysis is made periodically to ensure the availability of proper facilities for both current and future needs. If the center's program or enrollment changes, it may be necessary to modify, add, or eliminate space in the existing center. In some cases, a different location may be needed. Under any of these circumstances, the director may have to assume major responsibility for ensuring that appropriate facilities are provided. A thorough space analysis should be made before any renovation, relocation, or initial facilities choices are made.

Users of an early childhood education facility fall into three groups: children, staff, and families. An analysis of space requirements must be based on the needs of each group of users. Space needs are based on consideration for the users, program requirements,

---

Growth Mindset Moment

Think about a place you often go. Maybe it's a library, a store, or a college building. What kind of experience do you have as you approach the building? Is it easy to find the entrance? Is it accessible? Do you feel comfortable entering, or are you a little bit intimidated? After you enter, can you find the area you need? If not, is help available (receptionist, signs, computer information kiosk)? How do you feel when everything seems quite unfamiliar and no one seems to care that you have arrived?

How might a 3-year-old feel on his first day in preschool?

When we received funds to move out of a church basement, we designed our new center in two pods. Each pod has rooms for infants, toddlers, and preschoolers. Each pod has playground spaces, one for infants and toddlers and one for preschoolers. The large motor activity area, office, staff space, and area for visitors serve both pods. A few years later, when our enrollment continued to grow, we added a third pod. We find that the children, families, and staff identify the pod as "their" school, while the educators and families feel part of a school community as well as of a specific pod.

—*Director of an employer-sponsored early childhood program*

and governmental regulations. Therefore, the director must have up-to-date information in all these areas. One option for creating a space analysis is to chart the hours that the center is used by one or more persons. How many people will use each space, at what times, and for what types of activities? Of course, the desired number of children to be enrolled will be of major importance. The smallest centers may be more costly (per child) to operate, whereas those that serve hundreds of children may overwhelm the child. Large centers must be carefully designed so that children have private spaces. The facilities and people the child encounters each day must be manageable for each child.

6-1a • Basic Requirements

In its revised statement on developmentally appropriate practice, the National Association for the Education of Young Children (NAEYC, 2020) states that the "physical environment protects the health and safety of the learning community members, and it specifically supports young children's physiological needs for play, activity, sensory stimulation, fresh air, rest, and nourishment" (p. 17). The environment is required to support a daily schedule that "provides frequent opportunities for self-directed play and active, physical movement, regardless of the length of the program day or the ages of the children" (NAEYC, 2020, p. 17). The emphasis on the learning environment also includes outdoor experiences and daily interaction with the natural world. Program quality cannot be attained without intentional planning or the facility including both the indoor and outdoor environment.

Lella Gandini, official liaison in the United States for the administration of early childhood education of the municipality of Reggio Emilia in northern Italy emphasizes the importance of recognizing the "special qualities of local life." She also points out,

> One of the greatest challenges in designing institutions is to transform a physical plant into a human environment. One part of the transformation has to do with discovering ways to allow impersonal rooms and hallways to reflect the lives of the children and adults who spend so many active hours in that space. (Gandini, 1994)

Intentional decision-making about the environment includes the use of decoration, color, light, and other factors that can be calming or overstimulating. To avoid bombarding children and adults with stimulation, directors need to establish and communicate the center's guidelines for using decorations. The goal is to use decorations judiciously to minimize environmental "noise." For example, limit what is on walls and windows. Children's art and photographs, documentation of projects, and information for parents and staff are all legitimate items to be posted. When space surrounds a posting, it is more likely that someone will notice the item. When displays are changed frequently, the newness draws children and adults alike to inspect them. This will likely be a shift for staff who come from American school culture where walls and bulletin boards are adorned with primary colors, borders, and cute cartoons. Directors will need to be proactive and share the rules for decorating, identify the need for a culture shift, and explain what is now known about sensory overstimulation.

Because an early childhood program is planned primarily to meet the needs of children, all program facilities should be comfortable and convenient in terms of children's sizes, their developmental levels and needs, and their interests. Preschool children need space for active and quiet play, for naps, and for having breakfast, lunch, and snacks. The youngest infants need a play area that is safe from crawlers. And crawlers need plenty of space to move around and explore their environment without being stepped on by children who have just begun to walk.

Each child needs an individual space to keep outdoor clothing and a change of clothes. Infants and toddlers need separate storage areas for diapers and other personal items that are provided by parents. Preschoolers need a place to store special items they bring to show but not to share with others.

Programs for school-age before- and after-school programs require space for older children and must take into account the need for active play as well as relaxing, studying, and preparing and eating snacks. Children who spend 6 or 7 hours in a school classroom need a change of pace and should not feel they are in a schoolroom before and after school.

The building also must be comfortable and convenient for adult users. To work effectively with the children, staff members need a place designed for breaks and planning time. To feel comfortable in the program, families need a welcoming entry experience and a place to meet with other families and with staff.

The design of a diaper-changing station must take into account the child's needs as well as staff convenience and back health. Maintaining safe and sanitary procedures is essential.

The primary needs that planners must consider for each of these users are:

- health and safety,
- the accessibility of facilities,
- controlled traffic flow,
- personal space,
- opportunities for independence and growth, and the aesthetic character of all spaces.

Meeting the needs of each group of users has a cumulative and reciprocal effect because when the needs of one group are met, a step is taken toward meeting the needs of the other two groups. The dynamics of a human environment involve the impact of each group on the others. In a well-run program, the three groups interact effectively because each is involved in the joint, sensitive process of child development.

6-1b • Health and Safety

Program planners must be aware of the safety aspects above and beyond those stipulated in licensing regulations. A hazard-free building meets the needs of staff and parents, as well as children. Directors must stay abreast of environmental issues. For example, asbestos and lead paint, once considered appropriate building materials, are no longer used in early childhood programs. Some sealed buildings in which air is recirculated may be simply redistributing poor-quality air. Recently, several schools have extensively renovated sections of buildings in which mold had developed, usually from a leaking pipe. Although not ordinarily visible on the surface, mold may cause children and educators to become ill. The solution is to close off the area while qualified personnel remove contamination. In some cases, the director may be required to close the program while the work is done.

Governmental regulations usually determine the type of building and decorative materials (such as carpeting) to be used; the number and type of exits (including panic hardware and lighted exit signs); the number and location of fire extinguishers, smoke detectors, and fire alarm systems; and the location of furnaces and water heaters relative to the children's play area. All these regulations protect children and staff from dangers associated with fire. Choosing environmentally friendly materials whenever possible will ultimately enhance the environment and the health of everyone.

Children also must be protected from such hazards as tap water that is too hot, slippery floor surfaces, unsafe or unprotected electrical outlets and wiring, and poorly lighted spaces. Because of the hazards to both children and adults, smoking must not be permitted anywhere in the building or on the grounds. Covered convenience outlets or specially designed safety outlets are needed throughout the classroom for audiovisual equipment, computers, aquaria, and so forth. The director must ensure that the flooring is even; that there are no protrusions to cause falls; that stairs are provided with sturdy, low rails; and that protective screening is installed on all windows. Although the director is primarily responsible for establishing and maintaining a basic safety plan for the program, every staff member must remain alert to potential hazards and must teach children simple safety procedures such as reshelving toys and mopping up spilled water.

In public schools where older children use the hallways, plans for entering and exiting the building and moving about must be made so that young children experience minimal encounters with large groups of grade schoolers. Although older children can move about the building independently, additional staff may be required so that young children will have escorts when they go to the library, the office, or the restroom. Ideally, each classroom for young children will have its own adjoining bathroom.

In any building, many safety practices revolve around the enforcement of program safety rules, such as prohibiting children from climbing on window sills, but it is preferable to adapt the building itself so that it is a safe place for children. Placing locks on the furnace room door is less disturbing to everyone and far safer for children than telling them they must not enter the furnace area. Be sure, however, that security devices such as locks or gates do not block an emergency exit. Guidelines for fire safety can be obtained by consulting the fire inspector. All staff must understand and follow written procedure for everyone's safety. Situations that may require calm and immediate use of these procedures include fire, tornadoes, hurricanes, the presence of intruders, a building lockdown because of a situation in the area, and so forth.

For safety reasons, programs for children usually are housed on the ground-floor level of the building, even when licensing regulations do not require this. Stairways are dangerous obstacles to quick and safe building evacuation. In the event of a fire or other emergency that requires building evacuation, preschool children may become confused or frightened and will need individual guidance to reach safety. In such situations, staff members caring for infants, toddlers, and nonambulatory preschoolers will be able to remove only the one or two children they can carry. Some programs place several babies in a crib and roll the crib to safety. If children are on an upper floor, remember that it is unsafe to use elevators in an emergency.

Over and above promoting the ease of evacuation, other safety considerations make ground-level facilities immediately adjacent to fenced outdoor space advantageous. Licensing regulations require an emergency response plan to address procedures for emergency situations. For example, the state of Ohio requires a plan for the following: natural disasters and severe weather, fire, explosions, hazardous spills, gas leaks, bomb threats, intruders and active shooter lockdowns, loss of power, water, heath, medical emergencies, infectious disease outbreaks, epidemics, and other emergencies. Chapter 12 will focus on leading in the time of change, but it is important to consider how emergency plans align with the physical layout of the building and how people will be able to move about or adapt in different spaces when the need arises.

When children can go directly from their classrooms to a fenced outdoor area, the teaching staff can supervise both children who choose outdoor play and those who remain indoors. One early childhood educator would be outside with children there, and another would be inside with those children. An adult must be able to see every child at all times and to reach each one quickly and easily. The outdoor space is viewed as an extension of the indoor space. Fenced-in play areas prevent children from leaving the play space and prevent others from entering and damaging equipment, interfering with children's play, or leaving dangerous materials such as broken glass around the area. A covered outdoor space provides an additional advantage because it can be used on both rainy and hot sunny days. You may find it helpful to review the national standards for physical activity in group care presented in the *Stepping Stones for Caring for Our Children* report from the American Academy of Pediatrics, American Public Health Association, and the National Resource Center (NRC) for Health and Safety in Child Care and Early Education (2013). In 2019, the NRC revised its compliance and comparison checklist found at https://nrckids.org/files/Stepping %20Stones%20Compliance_Comparison%20 Checklist_.pdf. This checklist is a valuable resource for directors who must ensure the most current standards are being met.

All exits from the building and the outdoor playground should be in locations where supervision of whoever comes and goes can be maintained readily. Although the program may welcome community visitors, strangers should not be permitted to wander through the building. Similarly, children should not be able to leave unnoticed, either alone or accompanied by anyone other than authorized personnel. Panic hardware must be provided on all exit doors, but the doors should be locked so that visitors cannot enter without being admitted. Parents and staff probably will have to be reminded that holding the door open for an arriving visitor is unwise because that person's presence in the program may go unnoticed.

Crisis: An Opportunity for Positive Change

The COVID-19 pandemic changed how programs communicated with families because they were unable to enter the building. This was important to maintain the health of the staff and children by minimizing the spread of disease. Programs turned to using Zoom or other videoconferencing methods to communicate with families or community members interested in the program and required a variety of staff to safely escort children into the building for drop-off and pick-up. Although the pandemic brought to light many concerns about health and safety, communication was strengthened through the use of technology (email, videoconferencing), and building spaces were modified to ensure families were still connected to the program even outside of the physical building space.

6-1c • Accessibility of the Facility

All users must have easy access to the building. Many parents do not want to subject their children to long daily trips to and from the program, and they prefer one close to home. Others will look for a program close to the workplace so that they can visit the child during the day. Location near public transportation also is desirable for staff and parents.

Access to the program is increased when people feel comfortable about entering the building; therefore, the scale of the building is another consideration. As children approach the program, they should feel that it fits them. Even a large building should have some features that indicate to all children that the building is theirs. Entranceways and the areas surrounding them can be scaled to the children's requirements so that the children are not overwhelmed by a huge, heavy door or a stairway wide enough for a regiment.

Because parents and visitors often form opinions about a program on the basis of external appearances, the grounds must be well maintained, and the building itself must be inviting. A building welcomes people through its scale, color, texture, and design. When the building is compatible with other buildings in the neighborhood, the program can begin to establish itself as a positive force in the community and be considered as an integral part of the total community. Understandably, an ultracontemporary building might not be welcome in a traditional residential neighborhood.

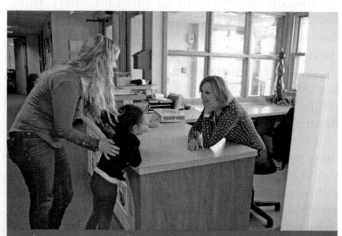

A pleasant greeting from a receptionist makes everyone feel welcome.

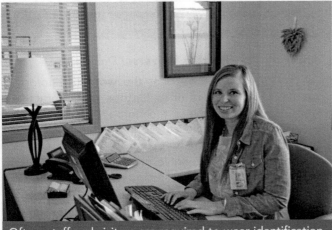

Often, staff and visitors are required to wear identification badges. Another important identifier of you and your staff is the warm greeting you give one another each day.

The parking area should be located near the program's entrance and be large enough to accommodate the cars of staff, parents, and visitors. A safe walkway from parking to entry is essential because many parents will arrive with several children, diaper bags, and favorite toys. Some children are so excited about arriving at their program that they may run quickly—but not safely—to the door.

6-1d • Building Entry

When an early childhood program is housed in a building shared by other users, the program should have a separate entrance that is clearly marked so that families and visitors can find it. Entrances used by older students, agency clients, or other tenants may mean heavy traffic that can intimidate children and may make supervision of their arrival and departure more difficult. Many programs now have entry systems requiring visitors to ring a bell; designated family members enter a code that unlocks the door. The code may be changed periodically for security.

Inside the building, there should be clear indications of where to proceed. Signs, supergraphics, or pathways incorporated in the flooring (such as tile arrows) can lead visitors to the proper place, even if no receptionist or secretary is available. A pleasant greeting from a receptionist is ideal, especially when the child and parent are called by name, but many programs are unable to afford a staff member to fill that role.

When the receptionist's or secretary's office has a large glass window overlooking the entry, visual contact can be made with people as they arrive, and parents or visitors will feel more comfortable about asking for assistance. In the office adjacent to the entry, the program staff can greet people and receive forms and payments from families. If parents or visitors find no one to communicate with when they enter the building, they may become disgruntled and leave, feeling that no one cares about their needs. Or a visitor may search out the classrooms and begin a conversation with a busy educator, disturbing activities there and probably inviting a cursory response that is detrimental to good public relations. The entry also should be accessible to the director's office so that he is highly visible and readily available. Furthermore, it is imperative that all visitors be screened to ensure that everyone who enters has a legitimate purpose.

Many programs require an access code to open the door of the building. As technological development continues, an even wider variety of options may be readily available to programs such as voice and fingerprint recognition. Although some programs have already installed surveillance cameras at exterior doors and in hallways, these may become more commonly used by programs. Some programs have these cameras in classrooms so that parents can access views of their children's activities from their places of employment. A simple safety feature such as well-lighted exterior doors makes it easier and safer for staff and parents arriving and leaving the program during early morning and evening hours.

In many programs, staff members wear identification badges. Visitors are given a temporary visitor badge. In other programs, parents sign their children in and out via computer, connected to the program's

Director's Corner

This morning, Mrs. Downing stopped in to see me. She just wanted to let me know how much she and Ralinda missed Marion, our receptionist, who has been home with the flu for a week. She said, "Marion always calls everyone by name. She greets us with a smile and, especially on days when I'm rushing, I really enjoy the welcome.

—*Director, urban program*

software package. More elaborate screening devices are used in the largest programs, requiring visitors to insert their driver's license into a machine that records the data with the exact date and time of arrival. To exit, the process is repeated.

In any case, the entry itself should say "Welcome." The colors used in the entry should indicate that this is a place for growth and vitality; grayness and drabness do not belong here. Lighting is as important here as it is in the classrooms. The area should be bright but not harsh. Glare can be prevented by using sheer window covers, awnings, or shades. Sunshine is ideal, but when that is not available, an artificially, brightly illuminated area with softer lighting in cozy areas sets the tone for the real warmth that children and families can expect to experience throughout the program. Entry surfaces also are important and must be designed to withstand muddy shoes or boots and dripping umbrellas. Although the entry should be large enough to accommodate several people without being crowded, it should not be too large because such space has minimum use but still costs about as much per square foot as areas that are heavily used. Furthermore, large entranceways may overwhelm a child or intimidate an unsure parent. Some children will interpret large open spaces as an invitation to run.

The required minimum number of entrances and exits is determined by local fire laws, but to determine the best locations for these doors, the planners should consider the traffic patterns of people who come to the building. Early childhood educators like to greet parents as they arrive with their children; therefore, locating the arrival point close to the classrooms helps parents and children as well as educators. Similarly, when the children leave, educators can see the parents briefly.

Just as children should be able to reach their classrooms without walking through long, uninteresting, and perhaps frightening hallways, adults should be able to get to their areas conveniently and without disturbing children's play. For example, deliveries to the kitchen or other service areas should be easy to make without having to negotiate stairs or move through the children's space.

Accessibility carries an additional importance for those who have special needs. The Americans with Disabilities Act (ADA) requires that facilities be designed so that all services can be used

Working Smart with Technology

Applying Principles of Universal Design

All too often when we hear the word *technology*, we may think of cell phones, laptops, and interactive whiteboards. However, technology has a much broader definition and can refer to the knowledge that is used to create items as well as the use of scientific principles to solve problems. In the 1990s, Ronald Mace and his colleagues began applying their scientific knowledge to the design and construction of buildings. Mace, an architect who used a wheelchair, coined the term *universal design* (UD) to refer to "designing all products, buildings and exterior spaces to be usable by all people to the greatest extent possible" (Mace, Hardie, & Place, n.d., p. 2). The goal of UD for buildings is to ensure that structures are planned from the beginning to be accessible to all potential users without the need for later retrofitting.

One foundational principle of the field of early childhood education is embracing diversity and celebrating difference. This important value can be seen in the facility we provide for young children. If we use our knowledge of the science of child growth and development as we plan with consultants from other disciplines, we can provide a welcoming facility that meets the needs of the diverse children, families, and communities we serve.

A facility with automated doors makes entering the center easier for everyone—children with and without disabilities, parents carrying children, and visitors making deliveries to the front desk.

by all clients and employees. Entrances and exits, traffic flow patterns, and facilities throughout the building and grounds should be designed for ease of use by people who have disabilities. People (children included) in wheelchairs or on crutches should be able to move about comfortably; to use bathrooms, drinking fountains, and telephones; and to participate in all aspects of the program. Seemingly small items such as the type of faucet on sinks or the handles on cabinets can be designed to facilitate use by people who otherwise would have to ask for assistance. The ADA requires these accommodations for most programs that meet certain conditions, but even in situations where the accommodations are optional, concern for the comfort of all individuals necessitates that efforts be made to modify buildings. Additional information on accessibility and UD in early childhood can be found on the University of Maine's Center for Community Inclusion and Disability Studies website (https://ccids.umaine.edu/).

6-1e • Control of Traffic Flow

Planners should consider the children's daily traffic patterns between indoor and outdoor spaces, as well as within those spaces. For example, children will move from classroom to multipurpose room and back, and from classroom to outdoor area and back. They may leave from the outdoor area if they are playing there when their parents arrive. A good floor plan accounts for the fact that young children should be able to go directly outdoors, preferably from their own classroom, or at least with minimal walking in hallways or in areas used for other purposes.

Coat storage should be near the door where the children enter. When coats are stored in the classroom, shelving may be used to create a coat area separate from the play space.

Well-planned children's areas are designed so that educators can supervise all areas from almost any vantage point without excessive walking and certainly without screaming at children. An educator in a room with an alcove may have to walk over to that area repeatedly to know what is happening there. An L-shaped outside area may be spacious, but such an area becomes difficult to supervise without extra staff because as soon as children turn the corner, they are out of sight and beyond the reach of their educator.

Decisions regarding how people move throughout a space are not entirely made based on feel or aesthetics or are completely random. Teachers and administrators use an environment rating scale to guide them in setting up the environment of a classroom or larger gathering space. The Infant/Toddler Environmental Rating Scale (Harms, Cryer, Clifford, & Yazejian, 2017) and the Early Childhood Environmental Rating Scale (Harms, Clifford, & Cryer, 2014) can be completed by the educators and administrators; an early childhood education coach or consultant can also be hired to complete the scales and meet with teachers and administrators while providing a valuable perspective for teachers to reflect upon.

6-1f • Food Service

Serving meals to children further complicates the traffic flow in the program. Because preschool children usually eat in their classrooms, there is no need for a separate cafeteria. In fact, in a public school, the noise and confusion of a cafeteria is inappropriate for preschoolers, and the furniture is too large to accommodate them comfortably. Preschool classrooms, therefore, must be large enough to contain tables and chairs for all the children and educators without crowding the play space. The kitchen should be nearby. Steps or doorways between the kitchen and the classrooms make moving food carts or carrying trays difficult, and long distances between the kitchen and classrooms may mean long walks for educators and long waits for children when something extra is needed during mealtime.

When educators sit at the table with children and eat the food that is served to the children, they model good eating habits and appropriate manners without lecturing children on how to behave and what foods are good for them. The program budget should include enough food for educators because this is part of their job. Some educators will prefer to provide their own lunch to be eaten during their break time. Nonetheless, those educators should still have lunch with the children and eat at least small amounts of the food served.

The kitchen must function primarily in relation to the classrooms and secondarily in relation to adult areas. The amount of kitchen space required varies according to the activities to be conducted. The program that uses a catering service for lunches may need little space, whereas the program in which hot lunches are prepared will require additional equipment and space. In the largest programs, a kitchenette

Growth Mindset Moment

Think about how the traffic pattern of a building you use frequently affects you. When you arrive at this building, which room do you go to first? Where is that room in relation to the door you use to enter the building? Think about the directions in which you move through the building during the day. Are there any places that could be rearranged to save you steps?

Classrooms can be arranged for variety and ease of traffic flow if areas within the room are clearly demarcated and exits are located so that traffic does not cross through many areas. Shelves for blocks are excellent room dividers that can be used to separate the block area from the housekeeping area and from heavy traffic areas, thereby providing a special space for undisturbed block building. Reading and writing areas can be separated from noisy carpentry or music areas by shelves or dividers; then children can find quiet, secluded spaces for solitude and concentration. Children can work comfortably without being disturbed when traffic patterns in the classroom are taken into consideration. One of your roles as director will be to help educators recognize the value of planned traffic flow.

may be provided for staff use and to prepare refreshments for various meetings.

6-1g • Bathroom Locations

Licensing laws regulate the number of toilets and sinks required, but the location of the bathroom is equally important. Children need bathrooms immediately adjacent to their classrooms, multipurpose room, and outdoor play areas so they can get to them quickly. Each of these areas may not need a separate bathroom, but planning can locate one bathroom to serve two areas. Prekindergarten boys and girls are comfortable sharing the same bathroom. However, the philosophy of some programs and the requirements of some governmental bodies now necessitate separate toilet facilities for boys and girls. Certainly these are needed for school-age children. As with all other areas, restrooms require adequate adult supervision.

The location of adult bathroom facilities is often determined by designing a plumbing core around which the bathrooms and kitchen are built. Although a plumbing core design is economical, it may not be practical in terms of the traffic pattern and the program needs because adult bathrooms must be placed appropriately to serve the people in classrooms, offices, meeting rooms, and the kitchen.

6-1h • Program Philosophy in Action

Think about going into a store: When you walk in, do you prefer the store to have things you can touch, feel, pick up? Or do you prefer it to be a place where you are afraid to move around, where staff constantly ask you to be careful or follow you around to make sure you don't need help? Would you rather make choices on your own, or be told directly what to buy, how to use it, and why you need it? This is a good parallel to the early childhood classroom: The first scenario suggests the freedom to discover your own interests, make your own choices, and be able to move around as you please. The latter suggests you need to be told what to do, what you need, and that you consistently need help. Which seems like a more natural feel—discovery or direction? Would you rather look at pictures or a catalog or see the merchandise in person, touching, feeling, and experiencing the pieces in three dimensions?

Consider a classroom environment that does not promote engagement, exploration, or positive interactions. Educators can be left feeling as though they are constantly moving around the classroom, policing behavior and providing directions throughout the day. Carefully planning an environment, which includes providing materials that provoke thought, creativity, and independence frees you from those constraints. It also gives an opportunity for early childhood educators to make connections with individual children, engage in play, and promote an environment that emphasizes thoughtful and meaningful learning. This is not something that happens overnight, but the underlying skill for this type of learning environment is intentionality. In their book *A Room to Learn: Rethinking Classroom Environments*, Evanshen and Faulk write that a program's or classroom's "physical environment tells a story about the type of learning that takes place" (2011, p. 30). This is how program philosophy becomes program practice—thoughtfully designing an environment where movement is natural, engagement is easy, and learning is embedded into each element of the building.

6-1i • Arrival Area

Figure 6-1 shows an example of a plan for a child care program. Because each program should be designed to meet the needs of its clients and staff, the plan is not meant as a model. Several of its characteristics are worth imitating, however. Note that as families arrive, the receptionist (or director) can greet them, and then they can go directly to the classrooms. (The arrow to the right on **Figure 6-1** indicates the entrance.) An observation booth is shown overlooking one classroom. When space is available, this feature may be desired for all of the children's spaces. Parents and visitors can observe without being seen by the children. Observation booths enable future educators to learn about children's development and related good teaching practices. Note, too, that each classroom has an adjoining restroom for children and that a multipurpose room is available for large-muscle activities.

6-1j • Staff Area

In planning for traffic flow, the staff's daily traffic patterns also must be considered with particular attention focused on which areas they use and in what sequence on a typical day. **Figure 6-1** shows the relationship of staff members' spaces to children's spaces in one program. Early childhood educators need a conveniently located general storage room to enable them to set up the day's activities efficiently. They must be able to move comfortably and quickly from the storage areas to the classroom, the outdoor area, or the multipurpose room, depending on where the equipment or the supplies are needed. Educators each need a locked cabinet or drawer in which to store personal belongings of value. In or near the classroom, they need a place to hang coats, gloves, and so on, which are needed when they go outside with the children.

Bathroom facilities for educators should be separate from those used by the children, and there should be a lounge area in which to have refreshments during break times. Work space includes places in which they work with children, places in which they prepare materials for classrooms, and places in which they do paperwork or hold conferences. Work space that meets the staff members' needs assists them in performing their duties well. Some personnel have specialized work spaces (maintenance staff, the cook, and specialists such as a

FIGURE 6-1
Hypothetical floor plan showing relationship of staff space to child space.

nurse, speech and language therapist, psychologist, or other consultants). Each workplace must be of suitable size for the activity in question. For example, full-time office staff each need approximately 100 square feet of office space. This space should be arranged to provide for some privacy and sound control so that work can be accomplished with minimal interruption.

Sometimes, with proper written documentation from parents and the child's physician, an educator will be asked to administer medication at school. Therefore, a locked cabinet is necessary in each classroom. A clipboard or notebook on which to document the administration of the medication should be in or next to the cabinet. This responsibility is critically important; making a mistake could be quite damaging to a child. Paying attention to licensing guidelines as well as program policies and procedures related to these issues is essential.

Office space sometimes is placed close to the classrooms so that immediate additional supervision can be provided in an emergency situation; however,

planners may decide to place the offices farther away from the classrooms to eliminate distractions for the director, off-duty educators, or other staff members. An intercom system can be installed to facilitate communication in emergency situations and to eliminate disturbances. The intercom or a telephone may be a necessity if a classroom or any other area used by children is isolated from direct contact with the rest of the program. For example, all classrooms may be located on the ground floor while the multipurpose room is a level above them. An early childhood educator using the multipurpose room needs a telephone to reach additional help if a crisis occurs. In any case, policies regarding the use of the intercom and telephone should be in place, largely to eliminate unnecessary noise and disturbance in the classrooms.

Figure 6-2 shows additional ideas for arranging program facilities. If you have ever browsed through magazines showing floor plans of various homes, you may have found yourself saying, "There's a feature

FIGURE 6-2
Hypothetical floor plan.

I like" or "I'd never want to have a room like that." Consider these floor plans in the same way. Examine them to see what you would like and why. Keep in mind that the ages and numbers of children to be served will have a major effect on the plan for the building and grounds. Geography and topography also will play important roles. For example, on a sloping lot, both the front and the back of a building may be at least partially at ground level, which is an important planning issue.

6-1k • Spaces for Children

When we talk about the environment, there are several different components to which we can refer: the physical environment, the social environment, and the temporal environment (Iris Center, 2015). In general, we have been describing the physical environment

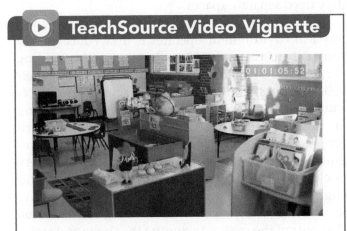

TeachSource Video Vignette

Space Planning, Equipment, and Facility Maintenance

The video titled *Space Planning, Equipment, and Facility Maintenance* provides an overview of the issues that must be considered when planning children's spaces for a facility. Reflect on the following questions:

1. How does the director meet the needs of different age groups of children?

2. How might you use this video with members of your board and fundraising committee to justify your request for maximum square footage, beyond that required by licensing, for your new facility?

throughout the center, but it is worth noting other components of the "environment" are present throughout the program. Describing a "facility" generally refers to the building and the tangible things in it. According to Clinton and a team of researchers and authors from the Ontario Ministry of Education,

> In educational discourse, the word "environment" usually refers to the physical environment, inside and outside. It will serve us well if we can expand this perception to include the context in general, including the relationships among the people and between them and the materials, the rules, the schedule. These contexts should be co-constructed by the adults and children because the impact on everyone is tangible. (Clinton et al., 2013, p. 11)

For the purposes of this text, we will first describe the physical environment and then touch on the social and temporal components involved in a program.

A comfortable and convenient classroom for young children includes enough space for each child to work and play without being disturbed by other activities. Thirty-five square feet per child is considered minimum, so a classroom for ten 3-year-olds must have at least 350 square feet, which measures some 18 feet by 20 feet. Fifty square feet per child is more realistic, and more space should be provided whenever possible. However, extremely large classrooms are difficult to supervise and may feel overwhelming to children. When determining classroom square footage, do not include permanent fixtures such as a sink in the classroom or immovable cabinets. Also keep in mind that when children's storage cubbies are in the classroom, the space immediately in front of the cubbies is rarely usable for classroom activities (except getting outdoor clothing on and off). Space in front of doors—entrances, bathrooms, and outside play areas—is also not usable for activities.

Rooms for infants require more space because of their cribs. Infants need a quiet area so that they can sleep on their own schedules. Infants able to play on the floor need space to practice moving from place to place by scooting, creeping, and crawling, while others are trying to roll from side to side, working on sitting up, and reaching a toy just slightly out of reach. Meanwhile, one of the caregivers may be rocking and soothing an uncomfortable child, feeding a hungry baby, or changing a diaper. Therefore, groups of infants are kept quite small with a 1:3 or 1:4 adult-to-child ratio and two adults at all times.

Toddlers are becoming a little more independent, more mobile, and more interested in exploring everything in the environment. They still need the support of and access to an adult frequently during their waking hours. Toddler rooms should also be a little larger per child than rooms for preschoolers.

In all classrooms where diapers are changed, a special area is needed with a changing table; access to supplies needed such as gloves for the adult, cleansing supplies, and clean diapers; and a place to deposit used diapers—all within the reach of the adult who is at the side of the child being changed to prevent falls. A sink immediately adjacent to the changing table is needed for adult handwashing. Keep in mind that while diaper changing is occupying one adult, the other adult must be alert to the needs of the remaining five to seven babies. One can see why infants and toddlers are placed in small groups!

All children need cozy places where they can relax while they look at books, examine interesting objects, or just daydream. These spaces should be small enough to promote a sense of privacy and intimacy yet large enough to be shared with a friend or two. For preschoolers, a loft can meet this need. It must be quite sturdy and have some kind of siding to prevent objects from falling to the floor and hitting anyone below. The space under the loft can be used for storage or small group activities. The educator must be able to supervise the area. Furthermore, a loft and all other spaces designed for children's use should be accessible to each child.

The classroom also must include a meeting area that is large enough for many children to gather for a story or special activity. Furniture can be moved for these occasions; movable shelving and furniture facilitate such rearranging. These movable pieces also will be valued when educators are placing cots for children's naps. Too much furniture moving detracts from the educator's real role, but most programs do not have a separate nap room and must consider how to place cots so that children will not be too close to one another (a requirement of many licensing rules). When cots are too close together, children may find it difficult to rest. Space also must be available for cot storage.

Some programs also offer care to children from kindergarten through third or fourth grade or older. These children come to the program for before- and after-school care and may even be transported between sites by a program bus. School-age children will treasure some personal space. Imagine spending 10 hours a day in a relatively small space with 30 people, primarily following someone else's directions. Although many adults do spend 8 hours in a work environment crowded with equipment and people, they have the opportunity to go out for lunch or take a short break. Children in schools usually are required to stay with their class for the entire day. After school, having some private space provides a welcome respite.

Before and after school, elementary-grade children also need spaces for organizing clubs and playing games, for informal sports, and for creating and carrying out their own wonderful ideas. They need both adult supervision and much more independence in organizing and reorganizing the space, perhaps decorating it so it is theirs. Because these needs are quite different from those of younger children, they need separate spaces.

An additional consideration outside of how the physical environment operates is how educators organize the classroom. This reflects an understanding of the ways in which children learn and embody their beliefs, values, and attitudes in action (Evanshen & Faulk, 2011). It also demonstrates an understanding of child development and developmentally appropriate practice. When designing the classroom and community spaces, it is important to consider a variety of elements that go into designing a welcoming and engaging space. Deviney, Duncan, Harris, Rody, and Rosenberry (2010) recommend looking at the unique elements of the spaces, including the shape and architectural features involved in the space. Consider also the largest furniture that will occupy the space and how children will move within a given area. It is important at each step in the designing process to circle back to how the space will be used and how people will move within it. Part of designing an inspiring, engaging, and positive learning space involves imagining all of the movement and how children will use (or sometimes misuse) given parts of the room.

6-1l • Family Space

Parents and visitors need a comfortable lounge area in which to wait for their children or to talk with each

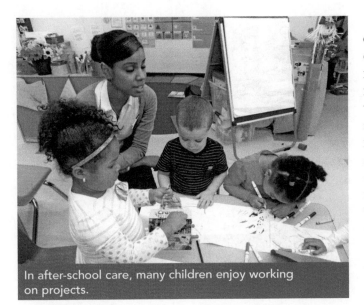

In after-school care, many children enjoy working on projects.

A setting that encourages independence also has classroom storage that is directly accessible to children, enabling them to find and reach all the materials and equipment they use. When such shelving is adequate, each piece of equipment is displayed so that the children can see it easily, remove it from the shelf without moving other items stacked on top of it, and return it to its proper place. Clearly marked storage space for children's personal belongings, located so that children can get to it, also will promote independence. In addition, however, storage space that is out of children's reach also is needed in each classroom so that educators can store materials and supplies they do not want the children to obtain such as gallon jugs of glue.

Single-purpose buildings allow programming to be based on users' needs (especially those of children) rather than requiring that the program be planned based on the needs of a range of occupants. A program allows educators to feel independent when the design of the facility enables them to plan programs for their children without constantly checking with other educators. For example, early childhood educator independence is curtailed when a preschool class is housed in a public elementary school where the young children must use the bathroom, lunchroom, or outdoor play space for specific time blocks because older children use these facilities at other times. Even if the children's needs suggest a deviation from this schedule, the educators may be required to follow it. Some educators in programs that move children from room to room for various activities find that they are not able to plan as independently if they have to direct children from the art room to the music room and then to the playroom on a daily basis at a predetermined, scheduled time rather than having the children move at their own pace. Children may feel frustrated at having to move to another area just as they are getting interested in writing a message or serving dinner in their "restaurant." Obviously, balance is needed. Children and educators usually have to stop at a particular time for lunch. And when it's time to go home, a parent may be able to spend a few minutes while her child finishes an art project, but then it's really time to leave.

The environment that fosters independence and growth is one in which variety is apparent, offering children an appropriate number of choices. They are

other. Parents also need a space that is large enough for group meetings and space that is small enough for individual conferences with an educator or the director. Even if a whole room is not available, programs can at least provide some seating in another area. Fire laws may preclude having furniture in hallways. Facilities for observing the classrooms, while going unnoticed by the children, represent both a convenience and a learning experience for parents and visitors.

Often, employer-sponsored early childhood programs are provided near the work site. Parents will appreciate an area in the classroom where they can spend quiet time with their own children sharing a book or puzzle. In infant programs, a private space for nursing offers a relaxing time for mother and baby.

6-1m • Opportunities for Independence and Growth

The facility should be planned to promote the independence of both children and staff. An environment for children fosters independence and growth when it is arranged so they can make decisions and solve many of their own problems. Such a setting has child-sized appointments, including sinks, toilets, and drinking fountains; doorknobs that children can reach and operate (where that is desirable); and wall decorations that are placed at the children's eye level. Planners must keep in mind that independence is equally important for children with special needs.

not overwhelmed with choices or bored with repetitive sameness in the design of space. If not overdone, variety in color, texture, floor level, and building materials can give children a sense of vitality that can be stimulating. Noise level is another area in which variety can be appropriate. Some spaces may be set aside for noisy play while others are retained for quieter activities. Although acoustical ceilings, carpeted floors, and curtains all absorb sound and contribute to the auditory comfort of everyone in the program, children still can learn to use appropriate sound levels in each space and to choose their activities accordingly. The environment leads to cooperation as well as independence. When staff members find themselves working in a well-designed, appropriate space, they are happier, which leads to a better program for parents and children.

6-1n • Aesthetic Character

An environment for children should be aesthetically pleasing to them. The factors relating to other users' needs and to program requirements can be designed so that they appeal to the children's sense of beauty. For example, it is just as easy to have an interesting painting in the classroom as it is to put up a fake window with curtains over the play sink. Both are intended to make the room more attractive. Children can enjoy a wide range of art, but the value of a fake window is limited at best.

Provide as much natural light as possible while avoiding glare. Artificial lighting should be bright enough for children's activities but also adjustable. Lamps that cannot be tipped over, ceiling lighting that can be controlled with dimmer switches, and area lighting all contribute to a feeling of physical and emotional well-being and help foster productivity, relaxation, and comfort. Incandescent lighting and full-spectrum lighting seem more appropriate than fluorescent. Consider purchasing energy-efficient lightbulbs, which, though initially more expensive, are longer lasting and environmentally friendly.

Wall surfaces can provide texture and color that contribute to the room's vitality. Garish decorations or "cute" wall coverings, emblems, or cutouts contribute little to children's appreciation of beauty. Carpets replete with numbers and letters add "busyness" to the environment and provide neither

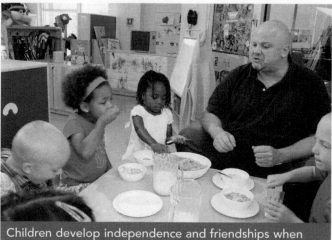

Children develop independence and friendships when they enjoy meals together. Teachers always sit with the children and share the meal.

aesthetic nor intellectual stimulation. Children and staff probably will be more inclined to take care of an attractive environment. It is easy to develop messy habits when the surroundings are poorly designed with inadequate facilities and unappealing spaces. It is equally easy and more satisfying for everyone to develop good habits and an appreciation of beauty when the facilities are well designed. Note that the touches an educator adds may be inexpensive or free: a single flower from her garden, attractively mounted pictures of the children at play, or a crystal hanging in the window to catch the light and project interesting colors and patterns throughout the room.

Having analyzed the facility requirements for a high-quality early childhood education program, and the information provided by a specific needs assessment, the director can determine the program's current facility needs and project the building and ground needs of the center for several years. This long-range planning is useful in enabling a

Director's Corner

Our entire staff spent hours discussing what our ideal program would look like. We listed all the criteria for each space, including details such as height and depth of classroom sinks, number of feet of shelving in the toy storage room, and types of doorknobs. We couldn't have everything we wanted because of the cost, but we all felt like we had helped design our new program.

—*Director, agency-sponsored program*

Making the Case for *Supporting Physical Activity*

We are in the midst of an obesity epidemic among children today. Early childhood programs have been found to be effective environments for encouraging healthy eating and physical activity to combat this epidemic (Lyn, Maalouf, Evers, Davis, & Griffin, 2013). When planning a facility, consideration should be given to providing children with physical activity on a daily basis. Reflect on the following questions:

1. What is the climate where you want to create a program? What do these conditions mean for you as you plan your facility that supports regular physical activity?
2. What do you know about the physical development of young children that should be considered when planning indoor and outdoor spaces for large motor activity?

program to coordinate program, facility, and financial decision-making. Whether the director is analyzing need in terms of possibly rearranging or remodeling the existing program's facilities or leasing or constructing a new program, the users' needs are kept in the forefront when working toward a decision.

6-1o • Programmatic Requirements

The director and building committee members must be thoroughly familiar with the early childhood education program before they attempt to evaluate an existing or proposed facility. They must understand the types of activities planned, the program goals, and the enrollment projections. For example, in contrast to a half-day program, a full-day program must provide a place for resting and for eating meals. Many children who spend the entire day at a program also need room in which to seclude themselves from the group for short periods of time—that is, a quiet place supervised by the educator but free from the intrusion of other children.

The program's philosophy influences the type and arrangement of space. If the philosophy places heavy emphasis on parent involvement, space will be needed for meeting rooms and a lounge, and

additional parking will have to be provided. For example, the Reggio Emilia philosophy emphasizes relationships, wherein the environment is the third teacher, with parents and educators being the first. This relationship-based approach implies spaces for families to gather in a physical space that involves collaboration, connection, and space for creativity (Biermeier, 2015). The prevailing climate also affects the type of building. If children are able to be outdoors most days on a year-round basis, they will need more outdoor space and slightly less indoor space. On the other hand, a program located in a region with temperature extremes will emphasize indoor areas and give major consideration to effective heating, ventilating, and air-conditioning systems. An appropriate floor-level temperature in the children's areas is critical because children frequently play on the floor.

Planning for carpeting and tiling sections of the classroom floor should be done with activities in mind. Cleaning is facilitated when art and food activities take place on hard surfaces, and educators will be able to focus on the children's needs instead of protecting the carpeting. A sink in the classroom is a much-used and much-desired convenience and also should be in the tiled area.

Keep in mind the importance of the outdoor environment. Just as children need to test ideas in the classroom, they also need to test ideas outdoors. They need opportunities to test what they can do physically as they explore an environment created to challenge and stimulate them. Similarly, children

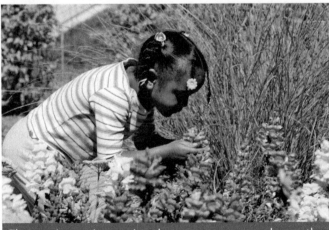

Flowers (nonpoisonous) and grassy areas can enhance the children's playground.

need time to try new ways of doing things—new ways of interacting with water, mud, plants, and people. As more and more information becomes available on the problems caused by childhood obesity, directors must plan for spaces and opportunities for children to engage in significant periods of large motor activity.

Children need extensive opportunities to interact with the green environment. Digging in the soil, planting, caring for, and enjoying what they helped produce provide important science learning. Walking and running on paths surrounding green spaces provides much more interest than running on a concrete surface surrounded by more concrete, metal, and wood equipment. When the outdoor environment is aesthetically pleasing for children and adults, well maintained, and designed with lots of movement in mind, it beckons them to come out and be involved.

6-1p • Governmental Regulations

In communities that have zoning laws, an early childhood education program that is operated for profit may be limited to locating in a business or less restrictive zone, whereas a nonprofit educational facility generally may be located in any zone. Local rulings may also limit nonprofit use of certain areas. Before signing a lease or contract to purchase property, the director must check with the local zoning board to see if usage of the particular piece of property complies with the zoning code. In some cases, a zoning variance may be allowed; that is, the director may petition to use the location for a program if it can be shown that the presence of the program will not have a negative effect on neighboring sites. Zoning ordinances also may include parking requirements, and off-street parking provisions may have to be made for program staff and visitors, including those who have special needs.

When a new facility is built or an existing building is renovated or put to a new use, current codes usually apply. For example, a building being used as a public school would be inspected based on the codes in existence when that building was put into use. However, if a child-development program leases the space, the owner will be required to meet the current regulations. When a building is renovated or a new facility is constructed, the ADA must be followed. Some requirements include access by means of ramps instead of, or in addition to, stairs; accessible restroom facilities; doors that can be opened by a person in a wheelchair; and lower-height drinking fountains.

Other governmental regulations pertain to licensing. These are discussed in Chapter 3 and include the number of square feet of space for children's use both indoors and outdoors, fencing, exits, building materials, and toilet and handwashing facilities. Before you purchase, lease, or renovate a building, ask your licensing agent to ensure that the facility complies with governmental regulations or can be renovated appropriately and at an affordable price. There may be a charge for this consultation. Also make sure that your lease and all conditions make it worthwhile for you to pay for the required changes to the building.

Sometimes, a church, community service organization, or school will permit or invite an early childhood education program to use its facilities at little or no charge. Available rooms also may be found in school buildings. This contribution is a major cost benefit to the program. Before agreeing to this use of the building, however, both the contributor and the program's board should have a clear, written understanding of the rights and responsibilities of each party. For example, both will need to know how liability and property insurance will be handled and exactly what is covered.

Get written answers to your questions, such as the following:

- Will the program be able to operate if the agency or school is closed for vacation or for a holiday, such as Presidents' Day, when many parents must still go to work?
- What maintenance responsibilities will the early childhood program have?
- How will the rest of the property be maintained?
- Will the agency or school be responsible for all grass cutting, snow removal, utilities, garbage collection, and recycling?
- Will the program area be wired for phones, computers, and other technology?
- How many parking spaces will be reserved for staff and parents?
- With whom can the director communicate if a problem occurs, such as a leaking roof?

Check details carefully. You don't want to be in a situation in which the agency's behavior leads to serious problems for the program. For example, suppose the agency neglected to pay the utility bills as agreed, leaving the program without heat or water.

6-1q • Cost and Quality

Cost is a factor in every aspect of facility development and maintenance. Using low-quality materials to save money often proves to be expensive in the long run. For example, inexpensive carpeting may be difficult to keep clean and may have to be replaced frequently. Many "cute" or unusual details put in place to attract parents may do that in some cases but add nothing to the quality of the children's experience. Examples include elaborate entryways, themes related to TV or film characters as part of the permanent decor, and so forth. Program directors have many opportunities to choose environmentally conscious materials, such as electrical appliances that use reduced amounts of energy. Ensuring that a building is well insulated can save many dollars on heating and cooling bills.

6-2 • Planning a New Program

In planning for a new program, the sole proprietor, the partners, or the corporate board will be the final decision makers. As discussed in a previous chapter, the director may also be an owner. In any case, it is the owners who must decide or agree that a new program is needed. They must also raise the necessary funds and employ appropriate contributors (realtor, architect, attorney, banker, and contractor). If the director is an employee, the owner may charge him with the tasks of performing a preliminary property search, providing a list of criteria for the building, and, in some cases, taking on the major responsibility of planning and implementing the entire construction process. To avoid conflict, wasted energy, and probable cost overruns, roles and responsibilities must be clearly delineated early in the planning stage. The decision may be to construct a building; to buy, rent, or lease an existing building; to renovate an existing facility extensively; or to locate space that

would be donated by the owner on a temporary or permanent basis.

Planning for a new program involves the same analysis of space requirements that is done when an ongoing program facility is assessed. The one item that usually stands out as being important in decisions about planning a new program is cost. Although cost is a major factor, the key concept is the value of the setting to children, staff, and families.

Let us assume that a new program is being created. The owners already have several programs in other cities. They are not early childhood educators, and they do not want to spend time on the details. Therefore, they have hired a director and given him the major responsibility of planning the program. He is to report to the designated owner on a weekly basis. The owners will make the final decision on all major issues.

The director starts facilities planning with a needs assessment in the community (recall that needs assessment was discussed in Chapter 2). The director must also obtain applicable information about zoning and licensing. These data, combined with the availability of a particular amount of money, are applied as criteria in the search for appropriate facilities. Some programs assess needs, locate facilities, and then mount a fund drive, anticipating that sufficient money will be obtained. The director or building committee must assess realistically the amount of money that will be available for establishing and maintaining the program facility and the amount of money that will be required to meet the assessed need.

The building committee works closely with the budget committee to determine the amount of money needed and available for constructing, purchasing, renovating, or leasing a building. Costs of real estate and construction vary widely, depending on geographical location; even within a given city, they vary from the inner city to the suburbs. Costs must be checked for each locale. Careful planning is essential because after construction starts, changes are costly.

6-2a • Considering New Construction

Both land and building costs must be considered. The lot must be large enough for a building of the required size, a playground of at least 75 square feet per child (groups of children may use this area at different times), and parking for staff, parents, and visitors. The cost of the building will depend on the size of the building, the quality and elaborateness of the materials used, and the intricacy of the design. A major advantage of new construction is that the building can be created to meet the specific needs of children. Furthermore, it can be designed to look like a place for children. If well designed, it will be a place in which the program can be delivered efficiently, effectively, and with a high level of comfort for all users. Talk with your architect about "going green"—that is, using environmentally friendly materials and design as well as taking advantage of the natural setting. Often a company that owns many programs will have a standard building plan that will be used no matter where the building is located.

6-2b • Using Existing Buildings

Costs involved with the use of an existing building are purchase price, lease or rent, and renovation. A program may incur none, one, or two of these costs, depending on the owner and on the condition of the building.

If funds are available, then a down payment on the purchase of a lot or a building, or plans for extensive remodeling, may be made. The board must be certain that funds for monthly payments, including interest as well as principal, will be available. A bank or savings and loan company can provide information on interest rates, length of mortgage, and payment procedures, as well as explanations of penalties, foreclosures, and insurance requirements.

6-2c • Renting or Leasing

Because purchasing a building involves high initial costs, many programs rent or lease all or part of a building. Both renting and leasing involve periodic payments. Under a lease, the lessor and the lessee agree that the space will be available and paid for during a specified length of time, usually at least a year. A longer lease is preferable because moving can be expensive, and clients may be lost if the program changes locations. Relocation costs include staff time spent in the following activities:

- fundraising,
- attending additional board committee meetings,
- locating a new site,
- negotiating the lease,
- arranging a loan for additional costs,
- communicating with staff and families about the move,

- arranging for required and desired renovations,
- planning logistics of the move,
- working with a licensing specialist,
- arranging for reaccreditation as needed, and
- managing the unexpected.

The following are direct costs of relocation:

- attorney fees;
- architect and contractor fees;
- materials needed for renovation;
- cleaning before the move;
- movers;
- changing address or other information on stationery, brochures, website;
- reaccreditation fee; and
- paying staff overtime to prepare the new site just before the program opens.

One of the most challenging aspects of moving a program is making the move so that service to children and families will be interrupted as little as possible. Another challenge is the possible loss of families if the new location is not as convenient for them. The director is then faced with recruiting new families quickly while managing the settling-in period in the new program. When a space is rented, the renter may have to pay only for the period during which the space is actually used. For a 9-month preschool program, this savings could be important and significant. Such a situation occurs primarily when renting from a church. The school's equipment may have to be moved out during the summer months or be used by other groups as part of the rental agreement. If you are renting space, try to negotiate limitations on rent increases.

A lease should spell out these conditions and include answers to questions such as the following:

- What are the beginning and ending dates of the lease?
- Is the lease renewable?
- If renewable, what limits, if any, will be set on a fee increase?
- Can the lease be terminated early?
- If terminated, what penalties apply?
- Can we sublet?
- Who is responsible for maintenance and repairs? What is included in maintenance and repairs? Who pays for it? Who provides materials, supplies, and tools? When will maintenance and repairs be done?

- Who is responsible for compliance with the building code?
- Who pays for utilities?

For example, if the board of health requires the addition of a handwashing sink (a permanent fixture), will the program or the landlord pay for the sink and its installation? The program cannot operate a program without the sink because a license will not be granted; but if the program should move, the landlord will still have the sink.

If the landlord is responsible for maintenance, can an agreement be reached that the grass is not cut during children's regular playground hours? Think about securing a written agreement about spraying for insects and rodent control. Insist that it be done when children are not present and that no residue harmful to children will remain.

If the facility is shared because the landlord uses part of it or rents part of it to someone else or because the program owns a building and rents or leases part of it to someone else, all the preceding items must be considered. In addition, the building committee or director will settle the matter of who has access to the building and when they may have access. For example, if a teenage group uses the building in the evenings, will it be allowed to use the playground during the late afternoon before all the children have left? Other points to be considered include the following:

- Who may have master keys?
- Who may use what equipment and supplies?
- Who is responsible for ordering and paying for shared equipment and supplies?
- Who pays the telephone bill? Internet service?

Other questions involve use of the program's space by other organizations or individuals when the children are not present, such as during the evenings or on weekends. The use of the facilities (their own and that of others) by program staff members and the parent group during evening, weekend, and holiday hours also must be considered.

It is easier to reach agreement on these issues before the building committee signs a lease and takes occupancy. If a lease has been signed, the program usually cannot be moved without financial penalty, which could mean that an uncomfortable situation exists for a number of months. When the lease clearly details the rights and responsibilities of each party, most questions can be settled amicably.

Director's Corner

When the renovation was initially being planned and the architects were working up the drawings, the chairperson of the committee and I went in and talked about what we would like to see happen. It seemed to break down after the initial meetings, and there were some outcomes that we were not that pleased with. Everything was ordered and halfway done before I realized what was happening. There wasn't any way that we could go back and ask for changes.

—*Director, preschool in a church facility*

6-2d • Renovating

Renovation costs also vary widely, depending on the location of the building and the type of work to be done. Complex changes such as relocating plumbing, rewiring electrical circuits, or installing exits, stairways, and fire-resistant surfaces are costly. The type and amount of renovation to be done will be based on the particular licensing requirements, including fire and building codes, and on the requirements of the planned program. If the program owns the building, renovation usually is a worthwhile investment.

6-3 • Working with Other Professionals

A variety of professionals outside the field of early childhood education can be helpful in planning a space for young children. Usually, the cost of their services is relatively high on an hourly rate, but in the long run the expertise they contribute to the program's development is worth far more than the actual expenditure. However, checking references and credentials before you sign an agreement with the individual or company is critical. Written agreements with each service provider also are essential.

6-3a • Licensing Agent

Because most programs must be licensed, the building committee contacts the licensing agent first. This specialist often provides free services and is funded through state or local taxes. Through this agent, the committee works with other professionals in the building, sanitation, and fire departments. Community planners also may be involved either at the governmental level or through community councils. Even though these professionals are not paid by the program, the licensing and inspection fees must be paid as required.

6-3b • Realtor

Whether you are looking for an existing building or land for a new building, a realtor may be able to save you a lot of time. Many realtors specialize in certain areas and may know of property that will be available but has not been advertised. They can also look for the type of property you need, keeping your price range in mind. The realtor can assist you in determining the zoning requirements in the area you select and may be able to help you determine whether a zone change or exception can be obtained. After you are settled into your new program, your realtor will be well aware of your program when home buyers ask about programs for young children in the area.

6-3c • Architect

During the earliest planning stage, retaining an architect can produce positive results. An architect can evaluate a site in terms of a program's needs or can examine an existing building and make recommendations about the renovations that are necessary for safety, efficiency, and aesthetics. And, of course, an architect can design a new building to fit your needs.

Ongoing architectural services can be contracted at an hourly rate, flat fee, or on a percentage (of building or renovation cost) basis. The contract should include the fee for services and the payment due dates. In addition, the architect should spell out clearly in the contract the services that are to be provided—such as survey, site selection, design, working drawings from which a building can be built or remodeled, building permit clearance, contractor selection, construction supervision, or final inspection.

Your architect also will assist you in selecting materials if that is part of your contract. For instance, gypsum wallboard (which is inexpensive) is readily dented, gouged, and subject to corner damage. It is usually not the best choice in areas used by children. If you are not familiar with building materials, then an architect's recommendation of an alternative material could save you money and repeated repairs in the long run.

When selecting an architect, choose someone with whom you feel comfortable. Some architects are unfamiliar with early childhood program needs, and you will want to choose one who is willing to listen to your concept and incorporate your ideas. Keep in mind, however, that architects have knowledge about design and construction that can help you attain a more attractive, more functional building within your budget. A few architects will want to put a great deal of emphasis on the exterior of the building, using such a large portion of the budget there that little money remains for finishing and furnishing. Listen to your architect with an open mind, but be willing to insist on components essential to your program.

Also be sure to let your architect know what kind of budget you are working with. You may have dreams of an elaborate program with all kinds of wonderful enhancements, but your budget may dictate that you have a much more straightforward approach. A good architect can help you get the most for your money. **Figure 6-1** previously in this chapter shows a simple, relatively inexpensive design. Only the essential spaces are included for this hypothetical half-day program. A rectangular building is often the least expensive to build.

When the plans are complete, asking a colleague to review them with you may help uncover details you hadn't considered. Changes made at this stage are relatively easy; changes made after construction begins may be impossible or quite expensive.

Generally, the architect will oversee the job, but the general contractor is responsible for scheduling subcontractors, ordering materials, and so forth. Some architects also serve as construction managers, and some contractors offer building design services.

6-3d • Contractor

A contractor may plan the construction or remodeling of the program's building and carry the work through to completion. Parts of the job, such as the electrical or plumbing work, may be subcontracted, but the contractor retains responsibility for the satisfactory and timely completion of that work. Nonetheless, the director must pay attention to the job as it moves along. Balancing frequent site visits with allowing the contractors to do their work is necessary, but asking questions is essential when you aren't sure about an aspect of the construction or when the work is not completed as promised. Sometimes, directors feel intimidated because they don't understand the drawings and specifications for the work. Part of the contractor's job is to ensure that the work is done to the client's specifications as determined by the written contract.

6-3e • Accountant

The building committee works with an accountant to determine the amount of money that can be invested responsibly in construction, purchase, or rental. The accountant also may help locate a lending agent and help the building committee find the best interest rate. Information about depreciation and taxes also may be provided. An accountant may charge an hourly rate or a flat fee for a particular piece of work. Some programs pay an accountant a monthly retainer in exchange for whatever services are needed, including preparation for the annual audit.

6-3f • Attorney

When the building committee decides to enter into a contract or sign a lease, its attorney reviews the document to ensure that the program's needs are being met and that all legal aspects have been covered. The attorney also participates in settling disputes in relation to payment, failure to perform work satisfactorily, and so forth. In a few cases, these disputes may be taken to court. In those special situations, the attorney would represent the program in court. The attorney may be on retainer or paid an hourly fee.

Summary

Whether it is a brand-new building or one that was constructed years ago for another purpose, directors or program owners must do the following:

- become familiar with the numerous factors to be addressed in meeting the needs of children, staff members, and families while at the same time satisfying all licensing requirements;

- understand the complex role played by the director in planning and building a new program; and

- be able to collaborate with a variety of professionals such as architects, contractors, and realtors to create a program that is best suited for carrying out the program for which it has been designed.

TRY IT OUT!

1. Work with a classmate to design a floor plan for an early childhood program for 44 children (six infants, eight toddlers, 14 three-year-olds, and 16 four-year-olds). Also show the spaces that are used by adults. Be prepared to explain your design to the class.

2. Work with a classmate to design a building plan for a half-day preschool for 14 three-year-olds and 16 four-year-olds. Make your drawing approximately to scale.

3. Compare the drawings in Try it Out! 6-1 and 6-2. Are any of the differences attributable to full-day versus half-day early childhood program? Explain.

4. Assume that you and your classmates are board members of an early childhood program for 60 preschool children located in a community center building. They had asked you to set up the program 4 years ago. Now the community center director feels he needs your space for additional adult activities during the day. You need to move out of the building in 30 days. What will you do? Consider all the options, and then make a plan.
   a. Consider children, families, and staff as you make your decision.
   b. If you decide to move, consider what you will do to avoid this type of occurrence in the future.

5. Examine **Director's Resource 6-1**. Discuss with members of your class the ways in which development of this program's facility might be affected by its philosophy and belief statement.

Director's Resource 6-1

PHILOSOPHY STATEMENT

(for use with Try It Out! 6-5)

We are dedicated to care for and educate all the children at the Bombeck Family Learning Center. We believe that positive experiences for infants, toddlers, and young children are critical to healthy development and that these experiences serve as the foundation for future development and learning. Our philosophy is based on the work of such classic early childhood theorists as Ainsworth, Bandura, Bowlby, Bronfenbrenner, Erikson, Gerber, Honig, Montessori, Partens, Piaget, and Vygotsky. We have learned from prominent early childhood approaches such as the Project Approach (Katz and Chard) and the programs of Reggio Emilia, Italy. We believe that children benefit from practices that are well grounded in research. We also strive to maintain a program where diverse children and families are welcome and engaged. We believe in the following developmental principles:

1. Each child's uniqueness is the result of interplay between genetic and environmental factors. Child development involves interrelated physical, cognitive, emotional, and social changes. Rates of development vary from one child to another, but the sequential progression of growth does not.

2. With these principles in mind, we believe that infants, toddlers, and young children are individuals in their own right and must receive the same respect and consideration afforded older children and adults.

Director's Resource 6-1 *(continued)*

3. We believe that it is our responsibility to provide responsive care and responsible guidance where strong social and emotional development is promoted and modeled. Furthermore, we are committed to providing a developmentally appropriate environment in order to nurture growth in all areas of development, while treating each child as a whole person.

4. We believe that it is the job of adults to provide children with enticing and accurate learning experiences that are based on sound content knowledge and developmentally appropriate practices. Our science-focused curriculum is intentional, integrated, inclusive, inquiry- based, and innovative.

Source: Bombeck Family Learning Center of the University of Dayton.

Director's Resource 6-2

SAMPLE SLIDING FEE SCHEDULE

Parent pays:	20%	30%	40%	50%	60%	70%	80%	90%
Infant	$30/wk	$45	$60	$75	$90	$105	$120	$135
Toddler	$25	$37.50	$50	$62.50	$75	$87.50	$100	$112.50
Preschooler	$20	$30	$40	$50	$60	$70	$80	$90

REFERENCES

American Academy of Pediatrics, American Public Health Association, and National Resource Center (NRC) for Health and Safety in Child Care and Early Education. (2013). Stepping stones to caring for our children (3rd ed.). https://nrckids.org/CFOC/Stepping_Stones

American Academy of Pediatrics, American Public Health Association, and National Resource Center (NRC) for Health and Safety in Child Care and Early Education. (2019). Stepping stones to caring for our children: Compliance/comparison checklist. https://nrckids .org/files/Stepping%20Stones%20Compliance _Comparison%20Checklist_.pdf

Biermeier, M. A. (2015). Inspired by Reggio Emilia: Emergent curriculum in relationship-driven learning environments. *Young Children*, *70*(5). https://www.naeyc.org /resources/pubs/yc/nov2015/emergent-curriculum

Clinton, J., Callaghan, K., Baird, L., Coughlin, A. M., Shanker, S., Wien, C. A., & Underwood, K. (2013). Think, feel, act: Lessons from research about young children. Ontario Early Years Policy Framework. Toronto, ON: Ontario Ministry of Education. http:// www.edu.gov.on.ca/childcare/research.html

Deviney, J., Duncan, S., Harris, S., Rody, M. A., & Rosenberry, L. (2010). Inspiring spaces for young children. Lewisville, NC: Gryphon House.

Evanshen, P., & Faulk, J. (2011). *A room to learn: Rethinking classroom environments.* Silver Spring, MD: Gryphon House.

Gandini, L. (1994, March). Not just anywhere: Making child care centers into particular places. *Child Care Information Exchange*, 48–50.

Greenman, J. (2007). *Caring spaces, learning places: Children's environments that work.* Redmond, WA: Exchange Press.

Harms, T., Clifford, R. M., & Cryer, D. (2014). *Early childhood environment rating scale* (3rd ed.) (ECERS-3). New York, NY: Teachers College Press.

Harms, T., Cryer, D., Clifford, R. M., & Yazejian, N. (2017). *Infant/toddler environment rating scale* (3rd ed.). New York, NY: Teachers College Press.

IRIS Center. (2015). Early childhood environments: Designing effective classrooms. https://iris.peabody .vanderbilt.edu/module/env/

Lyn, R., Maalouf, J., Evers, S., Davis, J., & Griffin, M. (2013). Nutrition and physical activity in child care centers: The impact of a wellness policy initiative on environment and policy assessment and observation outcomes, 2011. http://www.cdc.gov/pcd/issues/2013/12_0232.htm

Mace, R., Hardie, G. J., & Place, J. P. (n.d.). Accessible environments: Toward universal design. http://www .ncsu.edu/ncsu/design/cud/pubs_p/docs/ACC%20 Environments.pdf

National Association for the Education of Young Children. (2020). Position statement: Developmentally appropriate practice. Position S. Washington, DC: Author.

Supplying appropriate equipment contributes significantly to the success of early childhood programs.

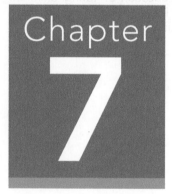

Chapter 7

Equipping the Program

naeyc

Standards and Recommendations Addressed in This Chapter

ADVANCING EQUITY RECOMMENDATION 1 Provide high-quality early learning services that demonstrate a commitment to equitable outcomes for all children.

PROGRAM STANDARD 2 Curriculum

PROGRAM STANDARD 3 Teaching

PROGRAM STANDARD 5 Health

PROGRAM STANDARD 9 Physical Environment

PROGRAM STANDARD 10 Leadership and Management

PROFESSIONAL STANDARDS AND COMPETENCIES: STANDARD 1 Child Development and Learning in Context

PROFESSIONAL STANDARDS AND COMPETENCIES: STANDARD 4 Developmentally, Culturally, and Linguistically Appropriate Teaching Practices

PROFESSIONAL STANDARDS AND COMPETENCIES: STANDARD 6 Professionalism as an Early Childhood Educator

LEARNING OBJECTIVES

After reading this chapter, you should be able to:

7-1 Identify the necessary equipment that will meet child, adult, and service area needs.

7-2 Identify and explain criteria for choosing equipment and vendors.

7-3 Describe the issues to be addressed when working within an equipment budget.

7-4 Describe a system for ordering equipment that meets program needs.

7-5 Describe a system for managing equipment over time.

Equipping an early childhood program is both challenging and rewarding. Your personality will be reflected in the physical environment you create as you strive to meet the needs of the children and their families and as you select components that enable the entire staff to maintain congruence with your program philosophy. Although many programs are being implemented with inadequate, unsuitable materials, supplying equipment that is appropriate contributes significantly to successful program implementation. Creating rich learning environments that are replete with abundant opportunities for children to be actively involved with age-appropriate and individually appropriate materials requires thoughtful, careful selection of classroom equipment and supplies. Furthermore, staff members are able to do their assigned jobs more efficiently and comfortably when they work in adequately equipped environments.

One component of your organization's systems approach (described in Chapter 1) will center on equipment. Establishing a program-wide value to the role of equipment and supplies in carrying out your mission will support staff members' decision-making as they develop curriculum, arrange their classroom environments, and support children's learning on a day-to-day basis. Whole staff discussions on the role of equipment in support of children's learning and development helps educators create a more cohesive, meaningful philosophy. As new early childhood educators enter the staff, they can observe the similarities across classrooms as well as the individual differences in equipment selection, arrangement, and use.

Establishing clear and pared-down policies and procedures for selecting, ordering, storing, and maintaining equipment and supplies will streamline this element of your system. Within the system and the philosophy it supports, staff members will be free to create classrooms they and their children find to be joyful and productive.

7-1 • Establishing Needs

Equipping an early childhood program is done in three major areas. With input from the staff, the director must determine the type and amount of equipment needed for each one. When the program is already operating, the educators will join in this decision-making. Following are the three areas to be equipped:

1. children's spaces, both indoors and outdoors;
2. adults spaces, including offices, waiting rooms, conference rooms, and lounge areas; and
3. service areas.

Equipment refers not only to furniture but also to appliances, computers, and other durable goods. Included in this budget are supplies, which are items that have a relatively short useful life or that are disposable. Examples are paper for the printer, finger paint, food, and paper towels. The equipment and supplies budgets should provide for initial purchases as well as for long- and short-term replacements of both basic furnishings and consumable supplies.

Directors entering an ongoing program begin by taking inventory of what is on hand, setting up a priority system for securing new equipment, replacing worn-out items, and replenishing supplies of consumable materials. Directors of new programs are confronted with the somewhat overwhelming task of equipping an entire early childhood program. Some companies will provide lists of equipment you will need and suggest room arrangements.

Child Care Aware of America (2018) has developed a series of self-assessments that can identify areas of strength and need. Another valuable source is Community Playthings, which produces sturdy blocks, wood trucks, and other accessories and furniture for children. This company can provide you with drawings of sample room arrangements and a description of materials needed for your classroom. The company also offers free floor plans and room-arrangement information for students who are preparing to be educators or for individuals needing information for grant proposals. Visit its website (https://www.communityplaythings.com/) to explore its products and resources.

TeachSource Video Vignette

Space Planning, Equipment, and Facility Maintenance

The video titled *Space Planning, Equipment, and Facility Maintenance* provides an overview of the issues that must be considered when planning children's spaces in an early childhood program. As you view the video, reflect on the following questions:

1. What domains of development should be considered when planning spaces for young children?
2. What factors should be considered when purchasing equipment for children's classrooms?

7-1a • Children's Spaces

Program philosophy and the needs of children dictate what will be ordered for the children's spaces in the program. Let's assume that every child comes with a parent or "comfortable-to-him" adult to visit the classroom before school starts or at a time when no other children are present. Think about what the room says to a child opening the door. Some children may be overwhelmed with delight as they quickly see a world of interesting walls, shelves, areas, and a new-to-him adult. Other children may be frightened by the magnitude of the space, the overwhelming variety of objects to see, and the sounds that they can't yet decode. Some children may take days, even weeks, to feel comfortable. Others can't wait to move right in.

Too much in a room can overwhelm a child, as well as his parents, even after they have been enrolled for months. Having everything in bold, bright colors can make a room seem "loud." Well-designed classrooms with uncluttered shelves, walls, floors, and tables help children find their way. Organizing space so that areas are somewhat separate helps children decide on a place to start. Everything needed for a particular type of activity should be available in that area.

When a building has a common storage area for classroom materials, educators can share toys, tools, or objects to be used by children. When children's interests change or educators want to present new materials to support children's learning, they can choose what they need from the shared storage area. Later, some of the same objects may be returned to the classroom as children become ready to use them in different ways. The director's role is to see how this system is working and to encourage educators to establish policies and procedures for using shared equipment and supplies.

Most early childhood programs provide basic interest areas in each classroom. These usually include areas for art, music, blocks, books, science, manipulative activities, and pretend play as well as spaces for math games and writing materials. All of these curricular areas require special furnishings and materials. Provisions also must be made for water, sand, and sensory play, carpentry, cooking, building, and large-muscle activities. Note that an interest area often addresses more than one content area. For example, puzzles in the manipulative area may depict characters from a book that the educator has read to the children. In the science center, children may be recording observations of an animal; in the block area, you may find a child working on developing symmetry; and in the music area, a child may be listening to a song sung in Chinese or Spanish. You'll read more about the director's role in curriculum in Chapter 10.

Furniture for working, resting, and eating is needed, including such accessories as clocks, planters, wastebaskets, and curtains. Most preschool groups gather together daily and need a space large enough so that everyone is comfortable. Children need spaces to work alone or in small groups. Low dividers can define spaces, but shelving is often used for the same purpose. Often a few rolling shelves are moved back to make the gathering space available. When quickly and easily locked by the educator, the shelves won't roll.

Children of all ages need outdoor play time. Almost every activity that can be done indoors can be moved outdoors as well. Infants can enjoy the swaying and rustling of leaves. Toddlers can feel powerful climbing a low grass-covered hill and running or rolling down it. Outdoor play also offers essential opportunities for gross motor activities and skill development such as climbing, swinging from rung to rung, running, jumping, and so forth. Some large equipment may be provided to encourage some of these motor activities, but plenty of space, along with cushioning material, must surround each piece of large equipment. Such equipment must be installed with firm, deep anchors that are below ground level and should be checked regularly for protrusions, splinters, or other potential hazards. It is important to follow the manufacturer's guidelines.

Although this type of equipment is found on many playgrounds, explorations of nature also appeal to children and help them begin to understand its importance in our lives. Running around curving paths and "hiding" in bushy alcoves easily supervised by an educator are exciting and fun for children. Planting and caring for their own gardens also interest and teach children. Even digging in soil and finding "treasures" such as a stone, a root, or an insect can fascinate children, especially those who live in areas where there are no yards. Walking in a summer rain, making and throwing snowballs, and crunching fallen leaves all go beyond going up and down a slide (although that is fun, too).

If the director is not familiar with early childhood curriculum and the associated equipment, room arrangement, and scheduling, the program definitely will need an education coordinator who has this knowledge and who is an experienced early childhood educator. She must also be familiar with programs for infants, toddlers, and school-age children if those groups are to be served. Taking courses in early childhood education curriculum and child development will also enable the director to develop a better understanding of why some materials are important and why others are not supportive of program goals and children's needs. Curriculum courses also provide information on how and why to integrate curriculum. Suggested books on curriculum and child development are included in the Director's Library in **Appendix H.**

Appropriate Environments and Arrangements

The video titled *Appropriate Learning Environments and Room Arrangements* provides an overview of the impact of appropriate equipment and room arrangement on play. View the video vignette and reflect on the following questions:

1. What environmental factors contribute to supporting meaningful play and appropriate behaviors in the classroom?

2. As a director, how might these factors affect the items you select for purchase?

7-1b • Adult Spaces

Adults working together to meet the common goal of providing rich, fulfilling experiences for children need space to meet together, think and plan together, and, at least briefly, relax together. They need space to write reports and converse with parents in private. Early childhood educators need access to a telephone for parent contacts and for personal calls when they are on break. The location of the telephone should allow for quiet talks and for privacy. Staff members also need a few comfortable chairs for lounging during breaks, a refrigerator and microwave for snacks, and any other amenities that the program can provide. A bowl of grapes, cherries, or even mini chocolate bars once in a while would be welcomed by most staff members, especially after a week of staying inside because of bad weather.

Even a small program at a minimum requires some office space with a locked file cabinet for records. Because adult desks are not used in classrooms for young children, some desk space for early childhood educators is essential. A resource library and a work table with a paper cutter, laminator, and storage for supplies such as poster board, scissors, and markers support educators in their work.

Almost every professional child care program director now relies on a computer for record keeping, billing, correspondence, writing reports, information gathering, and emailing. Many educators also use computers to maintain professional currency via the Internet. Therefore, purchasing appropriate hardware and software becomes a significant contribution to the smooth running of a program. If your knowledge of computers is limited, recognize that everyone has experienced this beginning stage, and avoid saying you understand if that is not the case. Other staff members can assist you, or you may find free courses at your library or online. Purveyors of software want you to like and use their material. Although it is not uncommon to find glitches in computer software, you still should expect the vendor to provide needed support in rectifying such a problem. Protecting against computer viruses with special software is essential.

Directors of large programs find that a copy machine is a worthwhile investment in terms of the time and money saved in duplicating newsletters, menus, forms, and interesting articles to share. Although these machines are initially expensive, they pay for themselves over time by saving staff time and enabling the program to produce materials of professional quality. At the same time, consider ways to avoid overcopying by using other ways to communicate whenever possible.

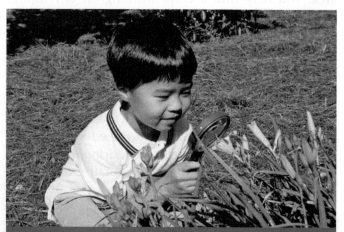

Experiences with nature allow children to enjoy and learn about their world.

When the families who are affiliated with your program have access to the Internet, you may want to send information via email. This process may be used for communicating with the entire program's population, with families from a particular classroom, or with an individual parent. Setting up a listserv with the email addresses of those families who choose to be included makes communication easy and quick. However, other ways of reaching those who are not using this technology must be provided. Remember, too, that personal, face-to-face communication is still highly desirable whenever possible. Look for ways to communicate in the language most familiar to the recipient. Parent or community volunteers may be available to facilitate translation, including through sign language. You may also want to communicate with members of the broader community by creating and maintaining a website. In some areas, this approach can be developed into a successful marketing tool.

In addition to communications tools, the staff needs a place for meetings. When staff meetings are held after children leave, the classrooms can be used. However, it certainly is more comfortable for the adults attending meetings to have a space furnished with adult-sized chairs and tables. Comfortable furniture should be provided for use by parents who come to the program for conferences and by consultants who come to meet with staff members. Bulletin boards and coat racks are convenient accessories for adult spaces. Consider the seating and other furnishings and equipment in terms of adults who may have special needs.

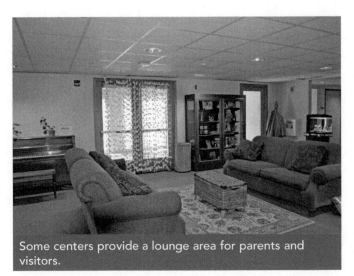
Some centers provide a lounge area for parents and visitors.

Some programs provide a separate lounge for parents and visitors. This area should have comfortable seating, lamps, tables, a bookshelf for pertinent reading materials, and perhaps facilities for coffee or other refreshments. Wall hangings or pictures, plants, a rug or carpet, and curtains all enhance the appearance of the space. A shelf of toys and books for visiting children indicates that the program is sensitive to children's needs. The goal is to let families know that they are valued and welcomed.

7-1c • Service Areas

Basic equipment in the bathrooms, kitchen, laundry room, and janitor's closet is usually built in and, therefore, is not purchased from the equipment and supplies budget. In a new facility, some appliances may be included in the equipment line. Consumables for service areas must be furnished, and appliances must be replaced over time. Dishes, cutlery, cooking utensils, and serving carts must be provided in programs where lunch is served. In large programs, special appliances such as commercial dishwashers, rug shampooers, heavy-duty automatic washers and dryers, and large refrigerators and freezers are needed. The local board of health may have highly specific requirements about the type of kitchen equipment that must be provided. The fire department will usually require alarm systems and may also require a fire-suppression system. A battery-operated radio with weather channel is an important tool to help the program prepare for weather emergencies.

Director's Corner

Our director has created a separate group email list for the families of each class. If we are working on something in my class, I can easily send a brief email to all the families telling them that the children have become quite interested in ants. Some parents will use this to start a dinnertime conversation with their child. Others will go outside and see if they can find ants together, watch them, and suggest that it would be a good thing to tell the other children the next day. It's a way for me to communicate quickly and positively with all my families.

—*Educator in a franchised child care program*

Flashlights in every classroom are also helpful. However, these items are useful only if you replace batteries regularly.

First aid supplies must be available in all classrooms, in the office, and in vehicles used to transport children. You may want to install an alarm system that would notify the police in the event of an emergency or a break-in when the program is closed.

If you have decided to provide child transportation, you will find many companies offering small buses equipped with seat belts and outfitted to accommodate car seats. Because the driver needs to focus on safe driving, a second adult should ride with the children to see that they remain in their car seats and are delivered directly to the previously agreed-upon adult.

When ordering cleaning supplies for your program, keep child friendly and environmentally friendly items in mind. Keep in mind also that some children or staff members may have allergies or asthma. Some states now require schools to use environmentally sensitive cleaning products. This requirement reduces exposure of children and staff to dangerous chemicals. Early attempts to regulate emission of formaldehyde used in producing some furniture may become law in some states. Find out from vendors of furniture, toys, and other equipment what kind of glue and paint are used

(White Hutchinson Leisure & Learning Group, 2007). Also check periodically with the U.S. Consumer Product Safety Commission (CPSC) to determine whether various products have been recalled. Directors have the ability to subscribe to a listserv in which the program is notified of all recalls (see https://www.cpsc.gov/Newsroom/Subscribe/).

Choose recycled paper and encourage everyone in the program, including children, to recycle. In addition to paper, glass, and plastic, ink cartridges can be recycled. Everyone in the program can learn to conserve water, and the director can ensure that leaky faucets are repaired quickly (Stoecklin, 2005).

7-2 • Using Selection Criteria

Selecting equipment should be based on a set of pre-established criteria that you have created as part of your system. The primary consideration is usefulness; that is, will a specific piece of equipment meet the needs of this program? Other criteria are versatility, safety, suitability, durability, ease of maintenance, attractiveness, and user preference. Some equipment for children should encourage and even necessitate cooperative play. All equipment should work the way it is supposed to and should be durable and economical. Although these criteria apply to all equipment purchases, this chapter primarily covers information about equipment that children will use.

The goals and objectives of a particular program will dictate purchases. That means that the director and all staff members must focus on the goals and objectives that have evolved from the program's mission. The recent emphasis in the media on preparing children for kindergarten has led some programs to focus heavily on academic content and may lead some directors to order materials suitable for older children as an approach to preschool learning. As director, you must assume responsibility for keeping current on developments within the early childhood field as well as within the broader population. Helping staff maintain familiarity with these issues enables them to speak knowledgeably with parents and community members and to offer a curriculum that meets the needs of children. For example, many elementary schools are reducing or eliminating

Making the Case for *Digital Literacy*

The inclusion of digital technologies in early childhood facilities is no longer considered optional. However, to make responsible choices about what should be purchased for new programs, administrators must first understand the technology being considered. The National Association for the Education of Young Children (NAEYC) and the Fred Rogers for Early Learning and Children's Media (2012) contend that educators "need training, professional development opportunities, and examples of successful practice to develop the technology and media knowledge, skills and experience needed" to meet the needs of children. It is also true that those making decisions about costly purchases must educate themselves about the technologies under consideration.

Equipment and supplies for maintaining cleanliness must be child- and environment friendly. Keep in mind also that some children or staff members may have allergies or asthma.

recess so that children will have more time to develop literacy skills. You can help staff understand how to explain the value of play, particularly outdoor play. One would hope that most staff could respond comfortably and professionally.

As director, you may feel pressure from parents and from observing how some early childhood programs operate, and you may begin to question your system's goals. Would it be better to use funds for prekindergarten workbooks? To find the answer, you must return to your understanding of how children learn. Is your program providing opportunities for children's development in all areas, including literacy? Consider the children's small motor development, understanding of recording a correct answer rather than choosing an interesting picture to circle, and the ability to work in silence in a group, all of

Working Smart with Technology

Identifying Technology Needs before Making Purchases

Equipping a program today must include reflecting on how technology and interactive media will be used in the program for children, families, and staff. As you contemplate your purchases of equipment, consider the following:

1. What types of computer hardware will be needed for children and staff members? Desktops, laptops, tablets with touch screens?

2. What software should be purchased to manage finances, the food program, children's records, licensing data, and so on? What software should be purchased for use in classrooms?

3. What devices will be used in the classrooms to provide opportunities for listening to recorded books and music or for taking photos?

4. What telephone, security, and alert systems (e.g., carbon monoxide, smoke, and fire) should be considered for your program?

5. Is closed-circuit television appropriate or financially possible?

6. Will you provide smartphones or other wireless devices to enable emergency communication among staff and families?

7. If you are including a separate space for parents in your facility, will you provide a computer for those who may not have access at home?

Managing today's early childhood program requires that directors and educators understand how to use technology to facilitate their work.

Growth Mindset Moment

As a student, you are required to spend a certain number of hours observing and assisting in a preschool classroom before student teaching. The educator starts the day with a drill on the sounds that letters make. (You wonder when was the last time she ever heard a letter make a sound. Oh well, it's her classroom.) Then the class practices counting from 1 to 30. You are surprised because yesterday, you asked two children who were playing a game, "Which is more—7 or 9?" Neither of them had any idea. You begin to wonder whether you will teach this way or you will do something different.

After you finish reading this, ask yourself what you plan to do in your own classroom. Why?

which are often necessary for completing required worksheets. Many people would agree that children entering kindergarten should be prepared and that the kindergarten system should be prepared for the children. When you are a director, your role is to determine how best to prepare children for kindergarten as well as for their lives in the here and now. You must base this on knowledge on how children develop, how learning occurs, and the needs and interests of each child in your class rather than on more narrowly focused goals such as readiness for kindergarten in a particular content area. Most kindergarten educators value children's age-appropriate social and emotional development as more important to them at the beginning of kindergarten than whether children are well versed in letter–sound relationships.

Today's standards-driven educational approaches require that administrators and staff become familiar with standards set forth by state departments of education and national professional organizations. In some cases, working to ensure that all children meet these standards will be mandated. For example, in some states, preschool programs that receive state funds are expected to be guided by the standards and to demonstrate how standards are met in each "lesson" or activity. More and more, children entering kindergarten are being tested to determine what they know, particularly related to specific literacy skills. Directors who have a good grasp of developmentally appropriate curriculum will be able to help early childhood educators work toward the standards

within the context of routines, schedules, and plans that meet each child's needs while supporting children's progress toward meeting the content standards. Eliminating play and the related materials and equipment is not an option.

How will such knowledge relate to purchasing equipment and supplies? You must think about how equipment will be used and how it will support children's interest in learning in all areas. For example, early childhood educators understand that providing blocks and offering long periods of time and space to explore ways to use them can help children learn in every content area (math, science, social studies, literacy) and in the arts (Chalufour & Worth, 2004; Dodge, Colker, & Heroman, 2016).

Knowledgeable directors realize that during block play, children also develop skills in planning, balance, organizing, cooperating, and persistence toward a goal. The other interest centers in an early childhood classroom lead to similar development with the guidance of a well-prepared educator.

Elsewhere in this book, you can read about the important role of the director in selecting and orienting educators who will support children's development. You'll also consider how the director supports educators as they develop more competent ways of enhancing children's growth and change in all areas. It is the director's responsibility to use a systematic approach, blending facility, equipment, staff, families, and finances to accomplish the mission related to children's care, growth, and development. Equipping a program is costly, and replacements are doubly costly when mistakes are made. Therefore, plan your purchases carefully by first assessing your needs, then developing criteria for equipment selection, and finally relating needed and desired items to your budget.

Many equipment suppliers will be happy to provide sample equipment and supplies lists. In addition, some states now provide online equipment lists that can assist owners and directors in planning purchases. For example, the Utah Department of Workforce Services, Office of Child Care (2012), provides a guide titled *Opening a Quality Child Care Center*. This document includes separate lists of equipment and materials needs for infants, toddlers, preschool–kindergarten, and school age. You may find local resource and referral agencies can provide information as well. For example, the American Academy of Pediatrics, American Public Health Association, and

National Resource Center (NRC) for Health and Safety in Child Care and Early Education (2013), *Stepping stones to caring for our children* (3rd ed.). https://nrckids.org/CFOC/Stepping_Stones by Child Care Aware of North Dakota (2013) includes excellent suggestions for planning equipment needs for young children.

These comprehensive lists are not intended as mandatory purchases but as guides to be adjusted and supplemented based on the needs of particular children, staff, and families. As new materials become available, they can be considered based on their appropriateness for the children who will use them. For example, although vinyl records and audiotapes were widely available in preschools some years ago, today programs are more likely to purchase CDs, DVDs, or digital music files.

Suitability of specific curricular materials is not discussed here because many texts include this information in the context of program development. See **Appendix G** for related books.

7-2a • Developmental Needs

The developmental levels, capabilities, and age range of the children enrolled influence what will be purchased. A program serving 2-year-olds will need some pull toys and small climbers that would not be needed if the youngest child were 3. Infants require special furnishings such as cribs and changing tables. Although younger infants are always held during feeding, infants who are able to sit independently

Growth Mindset Moment

Think of yourself as a director who is responsible for equipment purchases. Did you realize that you would pore over websites and catalogs for classroom equipment and materials and find yourself searching through office equipment and restaurant supply catalogs, websites, and ads? Your duties now have expanded from educator and administrator to purchasing agent. This responsibility probably seems overwhelming at the moment because many of you have been responsible for purchasing only personal items and, in some cases, basic household equipment. No doubt you are beginning to realize that the role of the director has many facets and requires a wide variety of special skills.

are also ready to help feed themselves and should be encouraged to do so. High chairs had been standard equipment for this purpose, but because of the danger of children falling from the chairs, they are usually replaced by low feeding tables, which are similar to high chairs but have shorter legs. An educator sits in a low chair opposite the children and helps when help is needed. Infants also require washable and chewable toys, bibs, sheets, blankets, and disposable diapers. Parents may be asked to furnish some of those necessary items and to take responsibility for their infant's laundry.

When program bathrooms have adult-sized toilets and sinks, children will need step stools to be able to use the equipment independently. Preferably, the program will have installed child-sized toilets and sinks at the appropriate height. Toddlers also need toys that provide opportunities for filling and dumping, big toys that can be carried during early walking stages, and lots of duplicates so that sharing will not be necessary. Toddler rooms are arranged in interest centers, but because many toddlers like to practice walking and carrying items in each hand, materials are often found in a variety of places. Preschoolers can understand that everything in their classroom has its own place, and they usually learn quickly to return things to their specified location. Many creative preschoolers find new uses for classroom items. For example, a child may take yarn from the art area to use as spaghetti in the house play area. Whether or not this creative use is encouraged depends on the philosophy of the program.

Preschool children need equipment and materials in all of the interest areas. Some of these materials will be specifically designed for children, and many others will be of interest to both children and teachers, such as items from nature, maps, and books and posters depicting and identifying birds, flowers, cars, or dinosaurs. Adult musical instruments often appeal to children, especially if the children are permitted to both listen and try their hand at bowing or strumming. Opportunities to prepare and eat most kinds of food provide chances to learn about nutrition, food from other cultures, heat and cold, textures, comparisons, contrasts, the safe use of tools and appliances, math, literacy, social studies, science, arts, turn taking, preferences, and sharing good times with friends.

School-age children in after-school care programs need games and crafts that are far too complex and frustrating for younger children. They also need well-lighted working areas for homework, larger furniture in which they can sit and work comfortably, and equipment for active, semiorganized sports and games. A place to store and eat snacks and an area to relax away from the group provide some feeling of independence.

Programs for school-age children should enable them to participate as fully as possible in activities that other children their age enjoy. When the program is well equipped to meet these needs, it will provide not only activities that the children could have been doing at home after school but also enriching group activities that encourage children to develop new interests and hobbies.

Children with special needs may require modified equipment or equipment designed to meet a particular need. A director with contacts at agencies serving people with disabilities can seek their assistance in providing modifications or special equipment. The equipment should allow the child to function as independently as possible. If the director is new in the area and does not have the necessary contacts, then one of her priorities should be to become familiar with the community and its resources.

7-2b • Usefulness

The usefulness of a piece of children's equipment is measured first by how well it meets the developmental needs of the children in the program and second by whether the equipment can be put to multiple uses by those children. When a piece of equipment meets both these criteria, a director may be able to convince a potential funder to support a request for funding. For example, a set of large, sturdy, wooden boxes can serve as cozy places to hide, as houses for pretend play, and as places to climb on and jump from; a wooden board added to the area can function as a stage, slide, or tent. Of course, all the wood needs to be well sanded and protected from weathering.

7-2c • Versatility

A piece of equipment that can be used in several ways is a bonus, both financially and in terms of enriching the learning environment for children. Such a piece

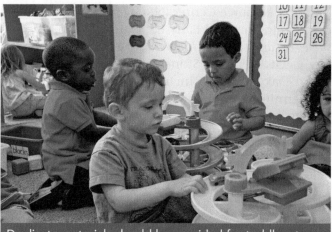

Duplicate materials should be provided for toddlers to minimize potential conflict.

The director who understands child development and ways of learning is prepared to equip classrooms appropriately.

saves space and money and gives children the opportunity to use their imaginations in creating different functions for one object. For example, the large, hollow blocks that can be used to make a puppet stage or a grocery store can serve as individual work spaces for children's small projects. A bookshelf can be a room divider and a storage facility. Two-year-olds may find the water table to be a relaxing place for splashing, whereas 4-year-olds may be more interested in using this equipment for constructing a water maze. Many pieces of equipment may be shared by two or more classes for the same or different purposes, eliminating the purchase of duplicate materials and freeing up money for other purchases.

Some equipment can be used both indoors and outdoors, a practice that is economical and provides a wider variety of learning experiences for children. Easels, water tables, and a workbench are a few items that may be moved outside if the building and play area have been planned to facilitate such indoor–outdoor movement. When that planning has not occurred, educators will not be able to leave the children in order to make several trips to carry equipment, and the children will not have access to those items. Perhaps a janitor, or even older children in elementary settings, may be able to help set up outdoor equipment. In some situations, equipment must be put away and locked up when children are not in the outdoor area.

7-2d • Safety

No matter how versatile, attractive, durable, economical, and suitable a piece of equipment may be, it must be rejected if it is not safe. A climber with protruding bolts, blocks of soft wood that splinter, and tricycles that tip over easily must not be used in the program. A kitchen appliance that requires a long extension cord is a hazard to the cook and should be avoided. All equipment used by the children must be made of nontoxic material and have no sharp or pointed edges. Safety is maintained by staff members who make a point of being constantly alert to the condition and the arrangement of the equipment that is placed in the learning environment (Aronson, 2012).

No one but a curious toddler seems able to spot a small button that has fallen from another child's clothing. Nonetheless, every classroom should be checked for safety hazards daily and throughout the day. Items used in infant–toddler rooms must not have small pieces that could be dislodged, such as the eyes of stuffed animals or small beads on a wire in a board counting book. Even some 3-year-olds are still mouthing small items.

However, a safety issue may be inadvertently overlooked. Three areas to which staff must give special attention are fall zones, entrapment, and protrusions (Wardle, 1999). Fall areas occur under climbers and swings. *Entrapment* refers to the possibility of a child getting a body part trapped in a piece of equipment (e.g., when fence slats are not close enough together to keep a child from getting an arm or a leg caught). Look carefully at elaborate climbing towers with tunnels. It is possible for a child to become

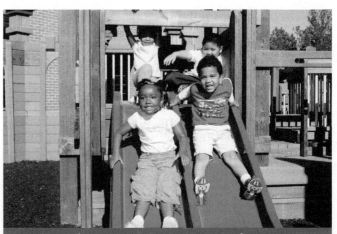

Providing safe equipment is an important first step to planning for playground safety. Positioning it with safety in mind is the next step, followed by regular evaluation of the condition of the equipment and vigilant supervision by the staff.

frightened while in the tunnel, yet the tunnel may be too long or narrow for the adult to reach the child. Protrusions also may pose safety issues. Sharp corners on furniture or screw heads extended from a flat surface may injure a child.

The U.S. Consumer Product Safety Commission provides voluntary standards for children's playgrounds as well as up-to-date safety alerts on its website. In addition, you can request email alerts or download the CPSC cell phone app. The 2009 CPSC update reported that the majority of injuries requiring hospital treatment during 2001–2008 resulted from swings, climbers, slides, and monkey bars. This does not mean that this equipment should be banned. Rather, they should be surrounded by appropriate and adequate cushioning material and should be located away from other activities to avoid having children run or ride through the climbing area. Other playground injuries result from hot surfaces, entanglement of clothing in the equipment, head entrapment in openings, and entanglement in ropes. Selection of appropriate equipment and close supervision on the playground are major factors in preventing injuries. Nonetheless, the active play, motor skill development, confidence building, and enjoyment that children experience on the playground should not be denied. An excellent resource for directors is the CPSC's *Public Playground Safety Handbook* (2015).

Some furniture may tip over and is particularly dangerous if a heavy object such as a computer monitor or aquarium has been placed on top. A child may try to pull or climb on the furniture, causing it to tip over.

It is not unusual for child care programs to have at least one potential safety hazard. This can include the use of clothing with drawstrings at the neck, lack of safe playground surfacing, and cribs with soft bedding. If you visit the CPSC website, you will find a lengthy list of toys that have been recalled because they use lead paint, are swallowing hazards, and so on. As program director, you may be diligent to purchase safe toys and equipment; however, a child may bring his own favorite toy to school. Some programs have policies encouraging children to show their toys at group time but to put them in their cubby immediately afterward.

Most directors know that lead paint has been banned for consumer use for many years, but they may not be aware of the lead hazard lurking in playground equipment. Older equipment that has been painted several times may still contain lead. Products from other countries, especially toys, should be checked for lead paint. Children need consume only small quantities on a regular basis to be exposed to a harmful lead level. In 2007, news media reported that millions of toys in homes and schools contained lead, small magnets, and other components harmful to children, leading to a massive recall. Be aware that even the surface under playground equipment may contain lead. Having a trained inspector check a playground periodically for lead and other hazards is a wise investment (Aronson, 2012). Paying attention to recalls is essential.

Purchasing equipment for infants and toddlers requires particular consideration regarding safety. The Consumer Product Safety Commission (2019) reports that in 2018, there were approximately 59,000 injuries treated in emergency rooms in children under 5 years of age that were associated with nursery products such as cribs and mattresses, high chairs, infant carriers, and strollers. Falls caused the greatest percentage of injuries. Note that in some instances, these injuries were not caused by the product itself and could have been prevented with greater supervision or other interventions. Additional information regarding the purchase of safe equipment can be found in the *Stepping Stones for Caring for Our Children* report from the American Academy of Pediatrics, American Public Health Association, and the National Resource Center for Health and Safety in Child Care and Early Education (2013).

7-2e • Suitability

Some equipment must be provided in several sizes to meet the needs of each user. For example, the secretary must have a standard, adult-sized chair, preferably ergonomically designed. Chairs for children are usually 10, 12, or 14 inches high, depending on the child's age and height. Chairs that are so tall that seated children cannot put their feet on the floor are not suitable for them. Children's chairs also should have a wide base so they will not tip.

For meals, school cafeteria tables and chairs are not at all suitable for toddlers and preschoolers. If these children are to use a school cafeteria, they must have low tables and chairs. Eating in their own classroom is often a better option. When older children are also present, the noise and activity levels may be distracting for preschoolers and toddlers. Children in before- and after-school programs should never be expected to use preschool-sized chairs and tables. They need furniture, space, and equipment designed to fit their needs.

7-2f • Stereotypes

Equipment must be chosen with the understanding that it may be used equally by all children. Staff members who plan curricula in a stereotyped way will need special guidance on this point so that boys are not relegated to playing with blocks and trucks, and girls are not always expected to dress dolls and play quiet table games. People with special needs should be depicted in books, puzzles, and classroom displays, and they should be shown participating in a variety of activities. Classroom materials should reflect many cultures and depict a variety of roles being chosen by members of various cultures and of both genders. For example, dolls of many races should be available. The play figures that are used as block accessories might include a female postal worker and a black doctor rather than depicting all white males. Books, music, food, and posters should be carefully selected to avoid any stereotyping and to depict the culturally pluralistic society in which the children live. This principle applies even when the program serves children from only one racial or ethnic group, a situation that may occur when students all come from a segregated neighborhood.

7-2g • Children with Disabilities

Educators today focus on planning a curriculum and environment that allows all children to participate. As discussed previously, the principles of universal design (UD) are important to providing an inclusive program and should be considered when planning equipment purchases. This idea does not mean that everyone does the same thing the same way at the same time, but that each child can participate in a meaningful way in understanding the activity, implementing it, and demonstrating what she or he is learning. Often, consulting a special educator or intervention specialist facilitates this type of planning.

In determining the suitability of equipment, you must consider children with special needs. A child who cannot walk, for example, may need easels and water tables that can be used while the child sits in a chair or a wheelchair. Sometimes, such equipment is low to floor, enabling children who are sitting on the floor to use it. In selecting the equipment, you should consider the height of the chair or wheelchair that is used and the length of the child's arms. In this way, you can determine the optimum height of the working space for a particular child. Consider purchasing tables with adjustable heights. If children are crawling in body casts or leg braces, they need comfortable floor surfaces. Wheeled equipment such as a sturdy wagon or a special buggy with seat belts will make it possible for all children to enjoy tours around the program's neighborhood.

Some children may require the use of assistive technologies to be successful in the classroom. For example, children may need an augmentative communication system so they can interact with staff and other children. A child with cerebral palsy who has reduced fine motor control may benefit from an adapted computer keyboard or mouse. Others may find that a touch screen enables them to be more successful. Children with hearing loss may need ample visual cues such as pictures attached to storage

Growth Mindset Moment

Think about your previous experiences with individuals with disabilities. Have you had enough experience to be aware of their special needs? If you have a friend or relative with a lifelong disability, imagine what his or her special needs might have been during preschool. Now consider yourself responsible for equipping an environment that is suitable for that child along with a group of typically developing children. What special provisions would have to be made for your friend or relative with special needs to provide a suitable learning environment?

areas so they can tell where equipment belongs, even though they cannot hear the educator's directions. Children with visual impairments may need some toys that vary in terms of weight, texture, and sound. Balls with a bell inside and storage containers covered with different materials (e.g., velvet on a container of beads or corduroy on a box holding small blocks) are especially appropriate for these children. When children who do not have disabilities use these same materials, they may develop greater insights into the experience of children with disabilities.

In purchasing equipment for a program, the director will need to know in general the lifestyles of the families and what the learning styles and interests of individual children are. Children must be provided with enough ordinary, simple equipment so that they need not be bombarded 9 hours a day with novelty. This is particularly true for children who have sensory issues such as those with attention deficit hyperactivity disorder, autism, visual impairments, or hearing loss. A balance of the familiar with the novel creates a learning environment that is neither overstimulating nor boring; the proper balance may be different in full-day child care programs than in half-day programs.

Watson and McCathren (2009) provide an excellent Preschool and Kindergarten Inclusion Readiness Checklist, based on UD principles, for program administrators and educators to use as they plan for children with disabilities. Numerous companies now sell adaptive equipment that can meet the differing needs of most children as well. For example, Rifton Equipment, an offshoot of Community Playthings, provides high-quality equipment for children and adults with disabilities. Some directors purchase packaged kits or curricula for their programs, particularly when the staff members have had little early childhood educational background. In such cases, it is essential that the materials are appropriate because they may be used with the belief that they must be good just because they were included in a curriculum package. The director has a major responsibility for ensuring that the components meet the needs of children and educators. (Similar materials often can be purchased separately at lower cost.) The director must also provide training to ensure that educators are using a curriculum plan to meet the needs of children rather than following a page-by-page or random plan. Not every component must be implemented. Such a preplanned curriculum can be viewed as a framework rather than a mandate. It is the director's responsibility to determine who prepared the curriculum and what premises about teaching and learning are supported through its use. Keep in mind that it is unlikely that someone who does not know the children in your program could develop a day-to-day curriculum that would meet their needs and interests. You will read more about providing appropriate curriculum in Chapter 11.

7-2h • Ease of Maintenance

Ease of maintenance also should be considered when choosing equipment. Sinks, toilets, and drinking fountains that must be cleaned daily and tabletops that must be washed several times each day should be extremely simple to clean. The surfaces should be smooth, and all areas must be easy to reach. Small pieces that are hard to clean around may cause problems and harbor dirt and dangerous microorganisms. Equipment parts that are cleaned separately, such as feeding table trays, should be easy to remove and replace. Some plastic chairs have surfaces that are slightly roughened or ridged. And although the surface feels relatively smooth to the hand, there are actually shallow indentations that attract and hold dirt. It is almost impossible to wipe or even scrub these chairs so that they look clean. This type of furniture may be slightly less expensive than other furniture, but maintenance problems outweigh the possible savings. A clean, well-maintained environment is important for all children and staff, but it may be critical for

children and staff who have allergies or asthma. In those cases, it may be helpful to have curtains, drapes, and carpeting cleaned frequently, or they may have to be eliminated.

Outdoor equipment that must be repainted frequently should be designed so that it can be sanded and painted easily. Places that are difficult to reach are a nuisance, and surfaces that catch and hold rain increase the need for maintenance. Equipment that will rust or rot easily should not be purchased for outdoor use.

7-2i • Aesthetics

Child care program equipment should be well designed and aesthetically attractive. Most parents and educators would like their children to appreciate beauty, and one of the best ways to help children acquire this appreciation is to surround them with beauty. An attractive environment also carries the subtle message that children, families, and staff who enter the setting are much appreciated and that great care is taken to make their environment beautiful. A material that is aesthetically appealing need not be expensive. In fact, it often is the ability of the director or educator to find beauty in nature that provides the most attractive places for children. For example, a colorful tablecloth on the housekeeping area table with a small vase of wildflowers in the center makes that classroom area attractive and inviting. A large square of interesting gift-wrapping paper, neatly trimmed, or a square yard of fabric serves as an attractive and inexpensive wall hanging and can be changed or cleaned often.

Be aware of the wide variety of art forms and styles developed by each culture. Displaying these introduces children and families to beauty they may not have had the opportunity to experience and provides an interesting and appropriate way to begin discussions and explorations of other cultures.

When equipment is made for the classroom, it should be prepared with special attention to its visual appeal. A math game, for example, can be made using well-designed stickers or beautiful pictures cut from duplicate copies of magazines instead of cartoonlike gimmicky stickers or drawings. The cardboard should be cut evenly and laminated or covered with a plastic coating instead of being presented to children with rough, crooked edges. Preparing beautiful materials takes a little longer and may require initial costs that are somewhat higher, but the product is worth the investment. One of the director's roles is to help staff and children value quality rather than quantity and to appreciate and care for the beauty in the objects around them.

7-2j • User Preference

The classroom is a place in which the early childhood educator can express her personality. By including some items that represent her interests, she communicates to children and families that she has preferences just as they do. It's reasonable to expect that sometimes educator preference determines the type of equipment ordered. One educator may choose to buy many books while another depends heavily on the library, or one sees an autoharp as a necessity but another finds this instrument encumbering. One educator may choose a guinea pig as the ideal classroom pet, another prefers fish, and still another considers all pets to require an inordinate amount of the educator's time. As long as these educator preferences are not contrary to appropriate classroom practice, they are legitimate and should be honored if at all possible. When budgeting constraints or other equipment needs make it impossible to fill all educators' requests, the director must notify educators that their preferences are under consideration and that plans are being made to fill all requests as soon as possible. The educator who wants an autoharp may have to wait until next year's budget provides it; meanwhile, the director can support that educator by informing the staff of planned equipment purchases. Each educator's preference deserves careful consideration because

each educator will ultimately set the stage for learning through the use of the program's equipment. Of course, the director will have to intervene if an educator chooses to order inappropriate items such as toys and games with tiny pieces for toddlers or flash cards for preschoolers.

7-3 • Working within a Budget

As you bring together information about purchases to be made, notice how various components of your program's systems come into play. You are addressing finances, staff, and equipment simultaneously, and you will follow the policies and procedures established around the program's equipment. With that perspective in mind, you will be ready to relate the choices that you and the staff have made, the needs of the children, and a component of the budget.

Major considerations when working with an equipment budget are durability and economy, which often go hand in hand. The climbing apparatus that costs three times as much as a competitor's product is worth the original investment if it lasts three times as long or is safer and sturdier. When more durable items are purchased, the program is not faced with the problem of replacement so often, and considerable shipping costs are saved, particularly with large pieces of equipment. Price and durability are not always perfectly correlated, but it is safe to say that inexpensive tricycles, which may be appropriate for home use, are inappropriate for group use. When used at a program, the standard equipment that is used at home will be in the repair shop far sooner and more frequently than will the sturdier, more expensive equipment that is designed for school use. Keep this fact in mind when well-meaning board members want to donate items their children have outgrown instead of including sufficient dollars in the equipment budget.

In child care program kitchens, many adults (and occasionally children) use the equipment. This heavy usage (and perhaps misuse), coupled with lack of care, may lead to the need for earlier replacement. Refrigerator and freezer doors are opened frequently and often are left standing open while children, accompanied by a educator, of course, take out ice cubes or put in trays of sloshing Jell-O.

Dishwashers may be improperly loaded or overloaded, and sinks are sometimes scoured with rough scouring pads or abrasive powders. It is important to provide heavy-duty kitchen equipment because equipment made for home use will require costly service calls when it is subjected to the hard use it inevitably will get in a program. A prepaid maintenance agreement may be a cost-effective way to manage equipment repairs. Checking the total cost of the maintenance agreement against the record of repairs typically needed over time for a particular type of equipment is a smart practice. Two possible sources of such information are consumer guides, usually available at libraries, and discussion with other directors. Furthermore, instructions on how to use equipment may be posted on each item, and a short in-service session may be helpful.

In setting up a new program, the director can expect to spend $20,000 to $40,000 per classroom on equipment. The variance results from the number of children in each classroom and the quality of the items purchased. A typical budget for manipulatives (puzzles, table toys, and small blocks) for a program of some 75 children is around $6,000, assuming that the items are centrally stored so that educators can share them. Although the costs should be increased by 20 percent to reflect the increased cost of items in the year 2020, Morgan and Emanuel (2010) suggest allocating $60 ($72 at 2020 costs) per child for classroom supplies and $60 ($72 at 2020 costs) per child for kitchen and office supplies as part of the start-up budget. They also suggest you will need $700 to $1,000 ($840 to $1,200 at 2020 costs) per child for all equipment, including kitchen and office, with $50,000

Children enjoy working with found materials collected on the playground.

Order furniture based on the children's age, size, and ability.

to $98,000 ($60,000 to $117,600 at 2020 costs) for playground equipment. They offer many examples to help you with all aspects of managing your program's money. Directors often search for free materials and supplies to reduce these costs. However, the director then may have to pick up the items or enlist a volunteer for this service. Recognize that free items are not necessarily worthwhile, and expensive items are not always better.

Preschoolers and their teachers lunch together using child-sized tables and chairs.

7-4 • Ordering Equipment

Decisions about what, when, and where to buy equipment are usually **naeyc** left to the director. In any case, directors are consulted, and they have considerable control over what is bought with the money that is budgeted for equipment and supplies.

7-4a • Equipment Requisition

Directors usually develop an equipment request procedure. Staff members notify the director in writing of the type of equipment needed or desired, providing additional information such as the rationale to support the need, a possible vendor, and an estimated purchase price. All of these data are helpful when final purchase decisions are made. Some programs use purchase order or requisition forms, which are nothing more than request forms that can be sent to vendors with a duplicate retained for program records (see **Director's Resource 7-1**). Even though this request procedure is formal and perhaps cumbersome, it puts the purchase of equipment on a businesslike basis and gives each staff member an equal opportunity to bid for the equipment dollars in the budget.

In corporate systems, requisitions are processed through a central purchasing agent, and shipments are made directly to the program from the manufacturer. The central office handles all the orders and saves money through collective quantity buying and careful selection of suppliers. This approach cuts costs but limits the options for those staff members selecting equipment. Public school programs usually have specific purchasing procedures to follow, with supplies requisitioned through the principal or through a supervisor responsible for the preschool or after-school programs. However, if a nonschool organization is implementing the program within a school building, that group may have wisely negotiated an agreement that will allow them to provide and own their own equipment. The program director will then be able to maintain the philosophy that the program espouses. If the school system no longer has room for the program or prefers to run its own program, the organization maintains its equipment.

In programs where directors are fully responsible for receiving staff requests and placing orders, they check requests against the established selection criteria and the budget allowance before completing order forms. All order forms should include quantity, price, catalog order number (if available), and name or description of each item. When making final decisions on purchases, make certain to carefully consider possible savings through bulk buying. For example, newsprint for painting can be bought from some vendors for much less per ream when bought in 48-ream packages. Economies realized through bulk

Director's Corner

When I think about ordering equipment for our program, I recall a five-generation Community Playthings block family. About 40 years ago, a great-grandmother and her daughter ordered blocks for a little boy on several occasions, providing him with quite a collection that he used daily. This year, the boy's mother ordered more blocks to be added to his collection and given to his two sons. The boys are still too young to understand that this tradition of block giving was started years ago by their great-great grandmother, but they (and their father) are maintaining the tradition of playing with their blocks daily.

—*Director of a nonprofit early childhood program*

Growth Mindset Moment

Assume that your classroom, which is stocked with basic equipment for your 15 four-year-old children, has been allocated $400 from petty cash. Think about how you might spend it.

buying are practical only if adequate storage space is available for the unused materials.

Equipment costs also can be reduced in nonprofit programs by applying for tax-exempt status. When orders are sent to suppliers, the program will not be charged sales tax if the order includes the program's tax-exempt number. Some programs have provisions for educators to purchase specified dollar amounts without permission and within a given time period. For example, an educator may receive $400 to spend for the classroom each year (in addition to the program-wide purchases that the director makes). In most cases, the purchase is made, and the educator is reimbursed after presenting the receipts to the director or fiscal manager. Giving educators some freedom to provide for special program needs helps them meet children's interests without having to wait for more formal procedures.

7-4b • Purchase Time Line

Equipment purchasing occurs in three different time frames: (1) start-up, (2) supplementary, and (3) replacement.

First, there must be a major start-up equipment purchase when a program is opened so that all the basic aspects of the program can function with appropriate equipment. This phase obviously is the most expensive of the three, but extensive purchases at this point are absolutely essential because it is unfair to children and staff to operate a program without basic equipment. To save money, some secondhand, borrowed, or homemade equipment can be used, keeping in mind the criteria described earlier. There is no formula that can tell a director exactly what must be provided, but the staff will need equipment of the type, quantity, and quality that will allow them to focus on the children and their needs instead of on the equipment or the lack thereof. Children in a classroom with inappropriate

or inadequate equipment will be quite likely to engage in inappropriate behavior as they seek to create something interesting to do.

Providing enough appropriate storage is also essential. In the classroom, educators need storage for supplies for use later in the day or week. Major classroom storage space should be available to the children so they can independently choose and put away materials. Crowded shelves and cluttered spaces make it difficult for children to find the materials they want to use. Children are also more likely to leave materials strewn about the classroom when it is not clear where they belong.

The second phase of equipment purchasing is the supplementary phase that provides for additional equipment purchases throughout each year. When supplementary equipment purchases are spaced throughout a program year, both children and staff members enjoy greater variety and a change of pace. Furthermore, educators can adjust equipment requests to meet the needs of particular children such as a child with special needs who enrolls midyear and requires a chair with particular supports, a prone board, or a walker. Although outside funding may be available for some of these larger items for an individual child's use, educators still need to consider books with large print, puzzles with large knobs, or writing tools that have been adapted for easier handling.

Lastly, the replacement phase helps maintain a constant supply of equipment that is in good repair and allows for adjustments in available equipment and materials as program needs change or as new items come on the market. For example, a few years ago, all African American dolls had Caucasian hairstyles and facial features, but newer dolls have features that more closely match the ethnic group being represented. Nontoxic, washable markers have replaced the old malodorous markers. Similarly, filmstrips have been replaced by videos and DVDs. At the same time, much-loved children's books such as *Goodnight Moon* (Brown, 1947) remind us that new is not always better.

The budget also should include enough money for emergency replacements. Although careful usage, combined with a fund for maintenance, minimizes the need for emergency replacements, unexpected breakage or loss is sure to occur. When a copier repair is too costly, it is sometimes more economical to buy or lease a new model than to repair the old one.

When ordering cots, consider where and how they will be stored, as well as ease of setting them up daily and keeping them clean.

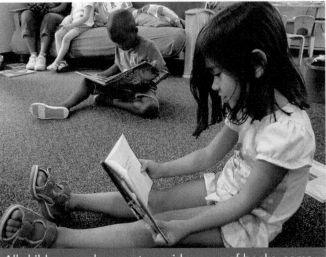

All children need access to a wide range of books, some of which may come from the public library.

As for buying a maintenance plan, consider what the warranty covers and for how long before paying for a plan.

7-4c • Sources of Equipment

Much of the equipment for early childhood education programs is purchased from catalogs. If the dealers are reliable, this arrangement is satisfactory. It is wise to check with other directors, professional organizations, or the Better Business Bureau to determine the suitability of making purchases from a particular company. Among the advantages of purchasing by catalog are the wide variety of merchandise that is available and lowering costs through bypassing the retailer. On the other hand, shipping costs may be charged, and returning unsatisfactory merchandise may be cumbersome. It is helpful to have a supply of catalogs offering good-quality merchandise available to the staff. Catalogs from companies that sell easily breakable toys, items that are always only in especially bright colors, cars and trucks with faces, and so on should be discarded. Most companies will be pleased to put your program on their mailing list. Refer to the list in **Appendix F**.

When you are placing a large order, request a discount. Another opportunity for price reduction is prompt payment. Vendors who establish a relationship with your program are more likely to inform you

of upcoming special prices. Then it is up to you to purchase items because the program needs them instead of because they are on sale. Many companies charge about 30 percent of the cost of items that have been returned unless they arrived damaged. In addition, the program pays the return shipping. Impulse buying is irresponsible when you are in charge of purchasing equipment.

Equipment purchased from local retail outlets can be seen and tried out, which has obvious advantages. But most retail outlets cater to home users and carry a limited stock of classroom equipment. If a local outlet has access to a manufacturer of school equipment, then it may be possible to order from a catalog through a local retailer. A buying co-op is another equipment source worth investigating because group buying can be especially economical. In this system, the co-op group buys in quantity at a wholesale price and sells items to co-op members at just enough above cost to pay the co-op's operating expenses.

Exhibit areas at state or national early childhood conferences provide great opportunities to view a huge range of products for early childhood classrooms and to talk with the vendors. Keep in mind that their goal is to sell their products, but a careful shopper can garner a wealth of information and sometimes a special price. Particularly at the end of the exhibit hours, vendors would just as soon give you a discount as ship materials back to their home base. Remember also that conference sponsors rarely endorse products being displayed. Conferees are responsible for using their own good judgment because what is available is not always appropriate for early childhood education.

Toy libraries are popular equipment sources in some areas. A program director or educator may borrow anything from a puzzle to a complete set of housekeeping equipment, just as one borrows library books. Sometimes, a group of program directors finds it worthwhile to help establish a toy library for their mutual benefit, and it is especially helpful to have toy-lending programs that furnish materials for special-needs children. Occasionally, toy-lending or toy-sharing systems are set up by community organizations to make equipment available to programs and parents.

Secondhand shops, discount stores, antique shops, and garage or yard sales frequently are excellent sources of equipment or raw materials for pieces needed by the program. The buyer may discover a garlic press that can provide an interesting physical knowledge experience for children when they are working with Play-Doh. Using imagination and effort, directors can turn large ice cream cans into storage places for musical instruments or some other equipment that demands many relatively small, easily accessible spaces. Perhaps a used desk or file cabinet for the program office can be located. When such discoveries need to be put into finished, usable, and attractive form, it sometimes is possible to enlist the help of the parent group, a high school vocational class, or a senior citizens' organization whose members enjoy repairing and painting. In some regions, high school woodworking or metalworking classes make new equipment and sell it to programs at reasonable prices.

Another way to obtain equipment is to solicit the help of parents, educators, board members, or residents of the community in equipment-making parties. This activity enhances the feeling of community in the program. Early child care program staff members often take advantage of the children's nap time to make classroom materials. Encouraging staff members to make some materials is important because few programs have unlimited resources, and commercial equipment cannot always be suitably adapted to meet individual children's needs.

Gifts of equipment are usually welcome, but their suitability must be measured against the same criteria employed for equipment purchases. A gift such as a toy gun in a program where pretend gunplay is discouraged or the gift of an animal that induces allergic reactions in some children must be refused graciously.

7-5 • Managing Equipment

Even before equipment is delivered to the program, the director must consider how it will be managed. All equipment must be checked and inventoried on delivery, and a maintenance plan should be set up to minimize repair and replacement needs before the equipment is stored or put into use.

7-5a • Checking and Inventorying Equipment

When equipment is received, it must be checked against the order to ascertain that it corresponds to the quantity, size, color, and so forth ordered. It also is important to make certain that only the items actually received are listed on both the order and the packing slip and that prices are correct. If discrepancies are found, the vendor must be notified immediately. Keep original packing materials in case any equipment needs to be returned.

Most program directors keep a record of at least the major items purchased, and some directors keep a running account of all small items and consumables as well. An inventory of purchases can be recorded as items are unpacked by listing each item on the computer or a file card, noting the description, supplier, price, date of purchase, and location in which the item is to be used. Some directors mark equipment with the name of the program, with an inventory number, or with an identifying number so that if a program owns four identical computers, each is individually identifiable. In public schools, the usual practice is to put the room number on each piece of equipment. The labeling practice is helpful when pieces are sent out for repair, when school buildings are cleaned during vacation periods, or when items are stolen. Of course, valuable equipment should be insured. When equipment is added or removed from the program, the inventory must be updated.

An accurate record of equipment will always be available when the inventory is updated regularly. **Director's Resource 7-2** shows a suggested inventory form. A backup disc of the inventory should be kept in a safe place—a fire-resistant file cabinet or other storage unit if possible—so that losses can be reported accurately in the event of fire or theft. Furthermore, an ongoing, updated inventory minimizes the work of taking an annual inventory (usually necessary for insurance purposes) for annual reporting to the board or the sponsoring or funding agency or for reporting to a corporate central office that must have an accurate annual inventory to determine the assets of the corporation. Updated inventories also give directors a clear picture of what is available in the program and help pinpoint areas or types of equipment that are incurring heavy damage. This information is useful in determining how much and when to reorder and in making decisions about changing vendors or brands of equipment ordered. Information about persistent damage in certain areas should lead to a careful examination of the storage and maintenance system.

After the equipment is checked in and inventoried, the director must notify the staff that the new equipment is available for use. No doubt, everyone will know when a new climbing tower arrives or when a new microwave oven is available, but if a dozen new puzzles are placed on the shelves or a fresh supply of felt markers is stored, it could be weeks before every educator in a large program discovers the new materials.

7-5b • Maintaining and Storing Equipment

As soon as equipment is placed in the program, the job of maintenance begins. In the very act of placing equipment, maintenance decisions are made. For example, an untreated wooden climber that is placed outdoors in a rainy area is doomed to rot. It will need immediate treatment, followed by periodic coatings of a penetrating, nontoxic stain if it is to withstand weathering. Large tempera paint containers that are left open will dry out quickly, as will clay that is not properly stored.

Equipment used by the children must be checked daily and removed if in need of repair, even if immediate replacement is impossible. Children need attractive, usable equipment and should not be frustrated when trying to make sense of broken or incomplete classroom materials. Puzzles with missing pieces, tricycles with broken pedals, or books with torn or defaced pages should not be left in the classroom.

Equipment storage also is directly related to its maintenance. It is easy to return equipment after it has been used when each piece has a specific, clearly delineated storage space. Whether in a storage room or on a classroom shelf, the space must be large enough that the object does not have to be jammed into place and perhaps damaged. The space must be accessible to staff members (and to children in many cases) to ensure that it will be used for storage purposes. When storage is far from a classroom or the educators have to go through another area such as the director's office to get to the storage room, it is more likely that the equipment and materials will be shoved out of the way in the classroom rather than returned to the storage room. Each program must work out a method for storing certain equipment and supplies that are used daily and must remain in the classroom. Other supplies should be designated for return to

Most program directors keep a record of at least the major items purchased, and some directors keep a running account of all small items and consumables as well.

a central area. Storage also must be provided for items such as tricycles that are used daily but must be protected from weather and theft. Additional storage is needed for items that are purchased in quantity for long-range use such as paper towels and paint.

When a large number of people have access to the central supply storage areas, there is some tendency for each person to assume that someone else will maintain order and cleanliness in the area. Therefore, many of the users feel little or no responsibility for maintaining the area. When this happens, some users return materials in a haphazard way, fail to place them on the correct shelves, or return them in poor condition. Other staff members become irritated when they try to find what they need and have to cope with a messy storage area. These frustrations lead to conflict and a breakdown in positive staff relationships. Sometimes, this problem can be avoided by assigning each educator the responsibility for maintaining a specific storage area, such as the area for art materials, outdoor equipment, or books and records, for a given length of time. In other programs, periodic work sessions are scheduled to involve the entire staff in cleaning and straightening central storage areas. Some programs institute a system for checking equipment in and out of the storage room that is similar to how libraries operate; an example is shown in **Table 7-1**. In a large program, putting the checkout list on a computer may be helpful, but posting a clipboard with a checkout

Table 7-1 Sample checkout sheet for equipment and materials

Date	Item	Teacher	Date Returned
10/7/20	Large Legos	Denyce	10/28/20
10/7/20	Magnetic Letters	Sam	
10/10/20	CD: Ella Jenkins	Maria	10/31/20
	CD: Elgar violin		

sheet is more likely to be convenient for educators in most programs. A few programs keep all the equipment in classrooms on shelves available to the children or in closed cabinets available to the educator, but this practice is expensive because it requires so much duplication.

In whatever way equipment is stored, its placement should be neat and easy to find so that children and educators alike will be encouraged to maintain some degree of order in their attractive environment. The director's job is to establish and follow routines that lead to the easy accessibility of all equipment to everyone. These routines make putting things away far less burdensome for both educators and children. Orderliness does not have to be an obsession; rather, it is an appropriate way to manage a large variety of equipment that is used in a number of ways by a wide range of people. (See **Table 7-1**.)

Summary

Appropriate equipment allows the staff to focus on the essentials of their work as they provide an excellent early childhood program. Directors must be able to do the following:

- select appropriate equipment that meets the needs of children, staff members, and families;

- understand criteria that should be used to select equipment and reliable vendors;

- work within a budget to purchase the most useful, durable, economic, easily maintained, attractive, and safe equipment possible; and

- revise a plan for the use and regular care of equipment.

TRY IT OUT!

1. Obtain the prekindergarten learning standards for your state. In a small group, review the standards and discuss the implications of what children should know and be able to do on the equipment purchases you would need to make for a new program.

2. Work with fellow students on the following role-play situations. Have several students role-play using different approaches to each problem. Discuss the strengths and weaknesses of each group's approach.
   a. You are a preschool director. Mrs. Jane Jones has just given you 24 coloring books with an advertising message for her husband's business on the cover. You never use coloring books at the program because you believe they are not developmentally appropriate and would not meet NAEYC guidelines. How might you handle this situation?
   b. Suppose that the same situation in problem (a) occurred but that the donor is Mrs. Thomas Vanderbilt. Last year, she gave your program $10,000 for equipment. What might you say to Mrs. Vanderbilt? How might you try to prevent this situation from occurring in the future?

3. Your public preschool class is in the planning stages and will be held in a public school building. Discuss with your principal the needs of your 4-year-olds and ways in which their equipment will be different from that of older children. Use a role-play format, working in pairs, or perhaps volunteering to role-play for the class.

Director's Resource 7-1

PURCHASE ORDER FORM

REQUISITION/PURCHASE ORDER

THE CHILDREN'S CENTER

To: _____

Catalog No.	Description	Quantity	Price	Total

Ship to: The Children's Center 1099 Main Street Centerville, CA 00000–0000

Account charged: _____

Approved by: _____

Date ordered: _____

Date received: _____

Director's Resource 7-2

SAMPLE INVENTORY FORM

		INVENTORY FORM			
Date Purchased	Description	Identifying Number	Source	Price	Location in Center

REFERENCES

American Academy of Pediatrics, American Public Health Association, & National Resource Center for Health and Safety in Child Care and Early Education. (2013). *Stepping stones to caring for our children* (3rd ed.). Elk Grove Village, IL: American Academy of Pediatrics, Washington, DC: American Public Health Association; Aurora, CO: National Resource Center for Health and Safety in Child Care and Early Education. https://nrckids.org/CFOC/Stepping_Stones

American Academy of Pediatrics, American Public Health Association, & National Resource Center (NRC) for Health and Safety in Child Care and Early Education. (2013). *Stepping stones to caring for our children* (3rd ed.). https://nrckids.org/CFOC/Stepping_Stones

Aronson, S. (2012). *Healthy young children: A manual for programs* (5th ed.). Washington, DC: National Association for the Education of Young Children.

Brown, M. W. (1947). *Goodnight moon*. New York, NY: Harper.

Chalufour, I., & Worth, K. (2004). *Building structures with young children*. St. Paul, MN: Redleaf Press.

Child Care Aware of America. (2018). Indoor environments. https://www.childcareaware.org/wp-content/uploads/2018/11/Child-Care-Center_R21_IndoorEnvironment.pdf

Child Care Aware of North Dakota. (2013). Child care facility development guide. http://www.ndchildcare.org/file_download/ebdd4563-1748-47b6-bddb-f463c6ae48d7

Dodge, D. T., Colker, L. J., & Heroman, C. (2016). *The creative curriculum for pre-school* (6th ed.). Washington, DC: Teaching Strategies.

Morgan, G., & Emanuel, B. (2010). *The bottom line for children's programs: What you need to know to manage the money* (5th ed.). Watertown, MA: Steam Press.

NAEYC & the Fred Rogers Center for Early Learning and Children's Media. (2012). Technology and interactive media as tools in early childhood programs serving children from birth through age 8: A joint position statement issued by the National Association for the Education of Young Children and the Fred Rogers Center for Early Learning and Children's Media at Saint Vincent College. http://www.naeyc.org/positionstatements

Stoecklin, V. (2005, July). Creating environments that sustain children, staff, and our planet. *Child Care Information Exchange, 164*, 39–48.

U.S. Consumer Product Safety Commission. (2015). *Public playground safety handbook*. https://www.cpsc.gov/s3fs-public/325.pdf

U.S. Consumer Product Safety Commission. (2019). Injuries and deaths associated with nursery products among children younger than five. https://www.cpsc.gov/s3fs-public/Nursery%20Products%20Annual%20Report%20Dec2019_2.pdf?TkU_cVyVv69sq6Lpx0aSRjoLomqXWxRq

Utah Department of Workforce Services, Office of Child Care. (2012). Opening a quality child care center. https://careaboutchildcare.utah.gov/pub/qualityCenter.pdf

Wardle, F. (1999). The story of a playground. *Child Care Information Exchange, 128*, 28–30.

Watson, A., & McCathren, R. (2009). Including children with special needs: Are you and your early childhood program ready? *Beyond the Journal: Young Children on the Web*. http://www.naeyc.org/files/yc/file/200903/BTJWatson.pdf

White Hutchinson Leisure & Learning Group. (2007, May–August). Illinois becomes second state to require green cleaning, reducing chemical exposure for children. *Children's Learning Environments eNewsletter, VI*(2), 1.

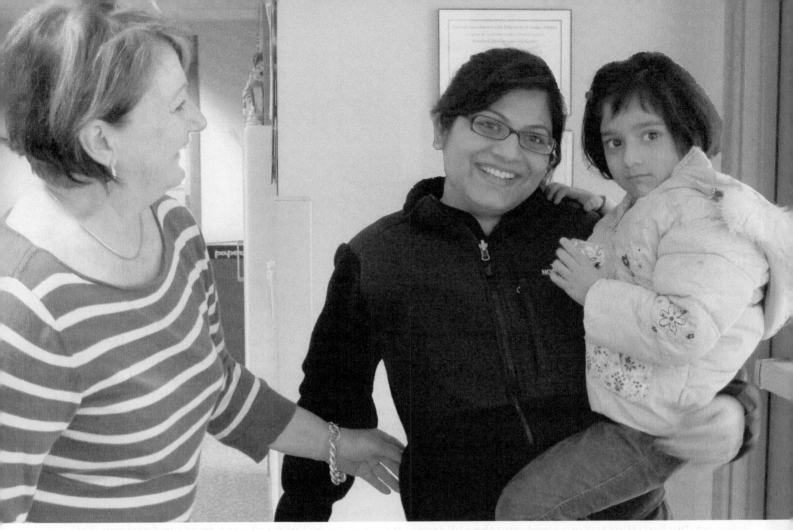

The center director sets the emotional tone for the program.

Chapter 8

Staffing the Program

naeyc

Standards and Recommendations Addressed in This Chapter

ADVANCING EQUITY RECOMMENDATION 2 Take proactive steps with measurable goals to recruit and retain educators and leaders who reflect the diversity of children and families served and who meet professional expectations.

ADVANCING EQUITY RECOMMENDATION 3 Employ staff who speak the languages of the children and families served.

PROGRAM STANDARD 6 Staff Competencies, Preparation, and Support

PROGRAM STANDARD 10 Leadership and Management

PROFESSIONAL STANDARDS AND COMPETENCIES: STANDARD 6 Professionalism as an Early Childhood Educator

LEARNING OBJECTIVES

After reading this chapter, you should be able to:

8-1 Discuss ways to create a positive climate and motivate staff.

8-2 Describe the major sections of an employment policy.

8-3 Explain the steps in the hiring process.

8-4 Identify strategies that facilitate staff retention.

This chapter focuses on the importance of developing good leadership skills and then using these skills—with good communication skills—to be an effective administrator of an early childhood program. Obviously, the person in charge must know how to develop and oversee a budget, write policy and job descriptions, and determine the program's facility and equipment needs. However, writing policy, hiring staff, developing budgets, and ordering equipment all will be wasted efforts unless the manager has the interpersonal and communication skills necessary to hire and motivate the staff. After the policies have been established, the staff are hired, and the children enrolled, the function of the director is to develop structures that motivate staff and create a climate that inspires adults and children alike.

8-1 • Creating a Positive Climate and Motivating Staff

Clearly, the interpersonal issues and **naeyc** the time it takes to resolve them are at the core of being an effective administrator. Much of what is discussed in this text deals with budgets, boards, licensing, and record keeping, but the real task of the director as a manager is to work effectively with and support those who will implement the program. The terms *manager, director, administrator,* and *leader* used throughout this book, all refer to the person in charge of and responsible for the program. The manager must relate to the staff and motivate them to do the tasks delegated to them. Members of the staff implement the program, but the director acts in the capacity of leader and motivator and ensures that

all the components work together. "Strong, positive relationships are always important to your child care center's success, especially when crises hit. Developing relationships now will buoy your center later by generating support and flexibility from staff and families amid change, and through more revenue-driving benefits like referrals and long-term loyalty" (Kintzel, 2020, p. 27).

8-1a • Creating a Positive Climate

As a leader, the director has the major responsibility for creating a climate of care, trust, and respect. This climate can be achieved best by demonstrating caring behavior, taking steps to build a feeling of community or partnership, and creating a climate for good communication among and between all members of the program community. The goal is to optimize the developmental potential of children, families,

Director's Corner

In most cases, to be successful as a director of an early childhood program, you have to be a people person. You have to realize that this job goes far beyond administrative policy and doing paperwork—that being the boss here is not really being a boss in the traditional sense. Being the boss here has to do with forming trusting relationships with your staff, respecting their individuality, being firm when you need to be firm and being gentle when they need a gentle hand. It's important to remember that you won't get respect if you don't show respect. Also, remember that others can do the paperwork, but you are the one who must build the relationships with your staff. Of course, you are also responsible for building and maintaining relationships with parents and the community.

—Director of a community nonprofit early childhood program

and staff in an environment that respects diversity. The director not only sets the emotional tone of a program but also works with staff to develop structures that empower, organize, and build a sense of community.

8-1b • Modeling

The director creates a climate of warmth, caring, and acceptance by relating to staff members, parents, and children with honesty and openness. Mutual trust will grow in an environment in which respect is earned, and the best way to earn respect is to show respect for others. When respect for difference is modeled, the tone is set for the entire program.

Maturity and self-awareness are the basic characteristics of a leader who can maintain professional interaction in even the most intense situation. Self-awareness is being able to identify one's own emotions and link those emotions to one's actions. Leaders who are self-aware and attuned to their emotions and actions are better equipped to understand the emotions of others (Bloom, 2007). These leadership attributes create a climate that, in turn, motivates others to be understanding, accepting, and warm. Most of you have read about and observed "modeling" in young children. One child who is perceived as the leader displays a pattern of behavior, and others imitate it. One child might say, "Yuck! Spinach!" and soon everyone at the table is saying "Yuck, spinach!" However, if the child were to say, "Yummm, spinach!" then other children are more likely to respond positively to the vegetable being served. Although this example is clearly an oversimplification of what typically happens in a group, behavior is contagious, and there is evidence that a leader who serves as the model indeed drives the behavioral climate of the setting.

Modeling begins with the initial encounter the director has with new staff members as they come into the program for interviews or when a newly hired director is introduced to the staff for the first time. The trust and mutual respect that are communicated during these initial meetings are the building blocks for the relationships that will develop over time. During the first meeting of a new year, at a new program, or with a new director, there is a unique opportunity to establish procedures and practices that will set the stage for future respectful interactions. In addition, the director who shows intellectual curiosity and is always seeking more information to do a better job can inspire others to do the same. A leader who does not serve as a model of professional commitment and enthusiasm for learning more about children, families, human relationships, and trends and issues in early childhood cannot expect staff members to invest energy in these areas. The leader's responsibility is to show interest and enthusiasm for what is going on in the program and in the profession and to serve as a resource for staff members and parents.

8-1c • Community Building

The director is responsible for developing and maintaining a sense of community among staff, parents, and children. Morale will be higher and the environment more conducive to growth for all involved if there is a "we" feeling of belonging. As the feeling of belonging increases, feelings of anxiety, self-doubt, hostility, and rejection decrease.

Staff members who feel a sense of ownership about the program will be more self-assured and enthusiastic about assuming responsibility. They not only will perform the tasks they were hired to perform but also will be more likely to invest energy into learning more so they can extend their area of responsibility. The total task of serving children and families becomes our task, and we provide the richest and best service we can.

The "we" feeling radiates beyond staff to families and children. It becomes "our" program and children begin to talk about "my" school. The feeling of community permeates the entire environment; all who participate in the many aspects of the center program feel they play an important part in the total program. All participants feel that they own a piece of the program and contribute to its success or failure. Parents and children alike recognize that they, their cultures, and their languages are valued; that diversity is at the core of the program; and that their contribution to the program is important. They come to understand that they are the reason for the program's existence. There would be no reason for the program to continue if there were no families and children to serve.

Director's Corner

I often think back on my own experiences in the classroom when I was there eight hours a day. I remember that I was expected to be nurturing and giving of myself all day long—it helps me remember how much I, in turn, needed to be nurtured. That's why I have an "open door" policy for my staff—I take time to actively listen, to problem-solve with them, to encourage them. I often have to put my paperwork aside because I know that a staff person sometimes needs to talk right now! This job goes beyond, "I'm the boss, and you're the staff person" relationship. The other side of this is knowing when and where to set the boundaries. When and how do I set limits on my availability to staff members or family members so that I can focus on what will be best for others and for me, as well as what is best for the program?

—Director, for-profit corporate program

8-1d • Communication

Every director will engage in written communication. When there is a need to communicate in writing, the first question to ask is, "Who needs to know?" Interpersonal relationships are often damaged inadvertently because some members of the group do not receive information they feel should have been relayed to them. For example, although a change in next week's menu may, on the surface, affect only the cook in an early childhood program, an educator who has planned a special science activity around one of the foods to be served on a given day may be annoyed to learn about the change in menu on the day of the lesson. The

Growth Mindset Moment

Take a moment to reflect on your own experiences. Think about whether there was a sense of community in the program in which you gained experience. Consider whether you were made to feel you were an important member of the community. If you recall feeling positive about the experience, who was most instrumental in creating that accepting environment for you? Did you sense the children also felt this was their place? Who was responsible for creating the "we" feeling in the classroom?

message itself, including the exact wording, can be more easily drafted when the audience for the message has been determined. Therefore, the audience that will receive the message will determine both the content and the wording.

Although some communication will be in writing, much of it will be face-to-face verbal or nonverbal. To be an effective leader, the director must be a competent communicator and take responsibility for helping the entire staff develop communication skills.

Verbal communication skills can be learned. The director can learn to send effective messages, become a good listener, and engage in effective problem solving. It is possible to define specific behaviors, both verbal and nonverbal, that block communication. It is possible to improve communication skills and, as a result, enhance interpersonal relationships. Note that we have said this is possible, not that it is easy. Unless directors believe wholeheartedly in the importance of open communication for good interpersonal relationships, they are unlikely to invest the energy necessary to develop the skills and practice them until they become totally integrated into a personal communication style. However, after this integration has come about, the director's communication style inevitably will serve as a model for others. The model will set the pattern for all the other people in the program and create an atmosphere more conducive to open communication.

Verbal and nonverbal messages must be congruent. Sensitive leaders will take care to convey the real message with both their words and body postures. Words that convey approval or acceptance but are accompanied by a frown and a closed body posture conveying rejection and hostility send a mixed message that is confusing to the receiver. Supportive, positive words and actions will help build trusting relationships among the people in the program. In a trusting relationship, criticism or negative reactions can be handled without destroying the relationship, provided they are given discreetly and are carefully timed. For the director to criticize an educator in front of the receptionist when the educator is on the way to the classroom to help a crying child is the epitome of poor communication skills and will negatively impact future attempts at open communication. Other, more subtle blocks to communication that will set the stage for a defensive response, hostility, or feelings of inadequacy include the following:

- demanding and controlling messages,
- put-downs,
- use of sarcasm or threats, and
- flip, humorous responses to serious concerns.

It is important to consider what needs to be said, how to say it, and when to say it, while always being aware of the cultural nuances of language.

A sensitive leader is well advised to consider carefully whether a situation calls for telling or listening. Telling often comes more easily than listening but must always be done with full awareness of the cultural nuance of language. However, in many situations, listening is a better vehicle for maintaining open communication and strengthening a relationship. Dealing with the personal problems of families or professional issues of staff members often requires listening instead of telling. The benefit of listening is not only to gain information but also to validate the message of the sender. Such communication can be energy draining and time-consuming but has a powerful and positive influence on the network of interpersonal relationships when done well. Listening is time and energy well spent.

Despite all the care and planning that go into creating a supportive atmosphere, conflict will arise. This is human nature and does not necessarily mean poor management, nor does it imply weakness in the network. It does, however, require attention. The director and the staff can learn specific communication skills to facilitate conflict resolution. Recognizing that conflict will exist is the first step in developing a system for dealing with it. Because many people find conflict to be uncomfortable, they commonly try to avoid it. Effective leaders overcome the natural tendency to overreact or to avoid, blame, or punish those who are involved in the conflict. They maintain a calm, rational style of interaction. Being proactive is an effective tool to deal with conflict as it arises. It includes developing a conflict-resolution policy and communicating it to both teachers and families as part of the orientation process. Addressing expectations for dealing with conflict before the emotions of an actual tense situation arise is an important strategy to implement. Consider the conflict-resolution policy shown in **Figure 8-1**.

8-1e • Motivating the Staff

Although the director does the orchestrating, programs are implemented through the efforts of staff members. A program's staff must be motivated to plan and implement the total program. Just as communication skills can be learned, the skills for guiding mental and physical energies toward defined goals can also be learned. Without training in how to guide and motivate human energy toward shared goals, the director will follow some rules of thumb that may leave the role of director as motivator to chance. This practice may be compared to designing a program for young children based on knowledge gained from having been a child, having parented a child, or having been through a public school system. Although these experiences may be useful, they cannot substitute for theoretical knowledge and a sound educational background in the field.

As directors begin to think about ways to motivate employees, they usually think about salary increases, a better building, new equipment, more help in the program, and several other issues are related to money and budget. Certainly, low salaries and poor working conditions can lead to dissatisfaction, but the promise of more money—or the threat of less—probably will not have far-reaching or long-lasting effects on individual or group performance levels. However, if a leader is using dollars to control and motivate performance, then it becomes increasingly more difficult to find the necessary supply to meet the demand. In addition, extrinsic incentives motivate employees to get the rewards but rarely alter the emotional or intellectual commitments that underlie behaviors.

What, then, is a director to do? Several useful strategies are available for motivating people to commit themselves to a task and actualize their potential.

Director's Corner

As a director, I want my staff to know that it is good to have different opinions about any number of things, and when I hear about these differences, I want to provide an opportunity for discussion rather than have concerns turn into bad feelings, unproductive activity, and gossip.

—*Director, church-based not-for-profit program*

Sample conflict-resolution policy

Conflict-Resolution Policy

We provide a safe, secure environment where children learn to respectfully resolve conflicts that naturally occur in an early childhood program:

- Adults help children develop vocabulary that expresses not only their wants and needs but also other's feelings as well as their own.

- Adults model respectful interactions with others, using their own words and actions to develop an understanding of how to deal with conflict.

- Adults affirm everyone's right to be safe emotionally as well as physically by setting standards for behavior and implementing caring, consistent consequences aligned with developmentally appropriate expectations according to the children's age levels.

- Adults facilitate resolution between preschool children by asking guided questions but resist solving the children's problems for them, thus providing children the opportunity to make decisions and practice self-regulation of socially responsible behavior.

Conflict between Adults

While every effort is made to meet the needs of children, parents, and staff, we realize that from time to time a conflict may occur between parents, staff, and administrators. The following process is followed should a conflict occur:

- Step One—A respectful discussion is held between the persons directly involved at a time and place that assures privacy and sufficient time for a thorough resolution to take place.

- Step Two—If resolution is not found at the first meeting, a second meeting is held with the director for the purpose of creating a plan for resolution and a timeline for expected success.

- Step Three—If the conflict is not resolved according to the timeline, adjustments may be made to the plan, and an additional timeline be established, or:

- Step Four—If at any time the director determines that resolution is not possible, s/he will consider one of the following for immediate action:

  - Removal of the child from the classroom

  - Withdrawal of services from the center

  - Suspension of the staff member until disciplinary steps can be taken

  - Involvement of the Assistant Dean of the School of Education and Allied Professions

Grounds for determining that a resolution is not possible include but are not exclusive of the following:

1 any person involved displays inappropriate behavior such as shouting, accusing, name-calling, swearing, or physical assault.

2 any person involved refuses to follow the prescribed process.

3 any person involved jeopardizes the process by spreading information concerning the conflict to those outside the immediate conflict or those involved in the resolution of the process.

FIGURE 8-1

Source: Reprinted with permission from the Bombeck Family Learning Center of the University of Dayton.

Two strategies that seem particularly applicable to the early childhood setting are the use of encouragement and the provision of job enrichment.

8-1f • Use of Encouragement

Rewards or reinforcements may motivate the staff; as with teaching, however, they tend to increase dependency on the one who controls the source of the rewards. They also heighten competition, thereby defeating the overarching goal of developing a sense of a cooperative community. Encouragement, on the other hand, tends to build self-confidence and a sense of intrinsic job satisfaction.

Just as the classroom teacher makes sure that encouragement is specific, focused on process, given usually in private, and neither judgmental nor evaluative, the director also keeps these same principles in mind when working with staff. To encourage an educator who has just helped a screaming toddler, you might say, "I noticed how calm you managed to be with Tommy while he was having such a hard time

The director needs to recognize when teachers design quality experiences and communicate that recognition regularly.

them develop. If you view your staff as people with problems, only noticing their lack of skills and knowledge to manage behavior or plan lessons for learning, you will most likely approach your coaching with quick fixes, one-size-fits-all techniques, and impatience rather than engage them in the dynamics of the teaching and learning process. In contrast, if you acknowledge the complexities of working with children and regard your teachers as competent human beings with rich life experiences, important perspectives, and the potential to rise to their best selves, you will invest the time, resources, and enthusiasm to engage with them in their work. (p. 131)

Job enrichment is a management strategy that enhances job satisfaction and honors the strengths of staff by presenting more challenges and increasing responsibility; in turn, these produce a sense of personal achievement and on-the-job satisfaction. It is possible to design a job-enrichment program for an early childhood program so that staff members are motivated to higher levels of commitment. As a result, they will experience greater intrinsic rewards. The job-enrichment principles particularly applicable to early childhood programs are listed here:

1. Give new and added responsibilities to staff members so they are constantly challenged and empowered to control aspects of their work setting.
2. Provide opportunities for ongoing training and college-based education that will contribute to quality of performance and to personal and professional growth.
3. Give staff members special assignments by occasionally delegating coworkers' or supervisors' jobs to broaden each person's understanding of the organization's total operation. This is recognition but has no monetary reward. This procedure can bring more recognition from other staff members and open up greater opportunities for advancement.

in the bathroom. It worked out well." These words of encouragement are more specific and process oriented than, "I like the way you work with toddlers." Telling the teacher of 4-year-olds, "You must have done some detailed planning for the science experience you did today to make it go so smoothly. It's surely fun for you to watch how engaged the children were in inflating their model lungs" is more specific and less evaluative than, "That was a nice science activity."

8-1g • Job Enrichment

Carter and Curtis (2010) encourage leaders to view teachers as competent thinkers and learners:

> How you (the director) see teachers and the scope of their work is critical to your success in helping

Obviously, there is some overlap among the three stated principles, both in terms of the method used and the outcome expected. There also are other ways to enrich staff members' jobs that will broaden their experience and bring them both intrinsic and extrinsic rewards. The many possibilities are limited solely by the creativity and imagination of the person in charge.

Director's Corner

Encouraging staff is so important. The little words of praise, "good job" or "how nice" do not mean the same as when you take ten minutes of conversation with a staff person to say, "Look at the changes in your room! What happened that made you think about changing the dramatic play area to a doctor's office? The design of the area and the detailed thought you've given to the choice of props are surely a delight for the children."

—*Director, independent not-for-profit program*

At first glance, it may seem that added responsibility will lead to dissatisfaction and demands for more money or other material rewards. However, there is evidence to suggest that, more often than not, the person who is challenged and who "stretches" to assume more responsibility will feel a sense of pride and achievement. For example, the classroom aide who, at midyear, is given the added responsibility of meeting and greeting parents and children at arrival time probably will find that job intrinsically satisfying. The aide will develop better skills for helping children make that first daily break from a trusted caregiver and acquire new skills for accomplishing the added responsibility. Assigning added duties can be accomplished best in an atmosphere of mutual trust, and it must be done through the use of positive communication skills.

The training needed to develop the skills necessary for managing a new task effectively often can be offered informally by other staff members and by exposure to resources such as books, pamphlets, videos, PowerPoint presentations, or opportunities to observe. Ongoing training can be expanded to include more formalized in-service sessions on curriculum, child abuse, communication skills, working with children with special needs and their families, or other topics selected to serve a specific need within the program. Use of release time or financial support for workshops and seminars, online resources, and additional course work are still other ways to provide job-enrichment opportunities for staff members' personal and professional growth.

Delegating special assignments to staff members usually evokes a sense of achievement and recognition, even though it means extra work. A cook who is consulted about menu planning and buying and is later asked to help evaluate the total food service program when the program is undergoing a self-study for accreditation not only gains an understanding of what is involved in the total food planning and preparation program but also develops a greater potential for advancement, whether in the current job or in another work setting.

8-2 • Designing Employment Policies

Directors of new programs are faced with the daunting task of developing new employment policies while directors of existing programs must deal with the recurring task of reviewing and revising these policies. Employment policies are required documents for National Association for the Education of Young Children (NAEYC) accreditation in the Leadership and Management Standard. The Program Administration Scale (PAS) has employment policies as part of the human resources development system. When writing or revising employment policies, it is important to consider the purpose served by the policies, the best interests of all parties covered and affected by the policies, and what is to be included in the policies.

8-2a • Purpose

Personnel needs for security and confidence in job performance should be balanced with the program's need to function effectively in the establishment of carefully conceived employment policies. When staff members are unsure of their rights and responsibilities, some may tend to probe and test to determine where the limits lie. Dissension among staff members drains energy from early childhood. Staff members who know what is expected can recognize how their assigned roles fit into the overall organization and can function more comfortably in those roles. Administrators also can function more effectively when there is little doubt about policies.

Inclusive employment policies tailored to a specific early childhood operation, whether staffed by a few or by many, serve two purposes.

1. They reduce procedural errors and free administrators from unnecessary involvement in resolution.

2. They reduce anxiety by helping each staff member to understand expectations and move, independently and as part of the team, toward efficient operation of the program.

A written statement of the employment policies and procedures should be given to each employee at the beginning of the term of employment. These policies set the parameters within which the staff will function. Of course, the administrator should periodically check with employees to ascertain whether the policies are understood. Although these policies must be tailored to the needs of each program, the samples in **Director's Resource 8-2** can serve as a guideline for their preparation.

Good employment policies need to be revisited with staff in order to be fair and current.

Director's Corner

During my new staff orientation program, I sit down with each new employee and read through the employment policies, leaving time for questions and discussion. I give special attention to the section on holidays, sick days, personal days, and vacation time. It helps me feel comfortable that this new staff person has at least looked at the employment policies once and not just put the document in a file or on her night table to read later when she has more time.

—*Director, private not-for-profit program*

8-2b • Source

The task of writing employment policies is complex, and the sphere of their influence is extensive. They must not only be precise, well written, and inclusive but also consider the best interests of staff, children, and families. The interest of the sponsoring group, whether it be to make a profit or not, deserves consideration as well. Those who are responsible for writing the policies must have both an understanding of the scope of the program and insight into the vested interests of all involved.

Employment policies might be prepared by such persons as the hired director of a community-sponsored program, an owner of a proprietary program, a human resources department for a program sponsored by a corporation or institution, or the human resources director of a national early childhood chain. Existing public school employment policies for teachers or, in some cases, for civil service employees often will be applicable in programs sponsored by public schools or on military bases. When the program staff is part of a labor union,

the union contract will likely impact how policies and procedures are written to reflect agreements that were made during the contract negotiations.

It is somewhat common practice for early childhood settings to have policies drawn up by a subcommittee or a standing human resources committee of the policy-making board. As drawn up by the policy board, the bylaws should contain the mechanism for creating a human resources committee and should detail the manner in which the membership of that committee will be selected. The program director serves on the committee and represents the staff's interest. Other members of the committee might be parents, people from the community, and representatives of licensing or certifying groups who would, in each case, represent the interests and diversity of special-interest groups.

8-2c • Inclusions

Employment policies cover all matters relating to employment and include job responsibilities, organizational charts, schedules of reimbursement for services, evaluation and grievance procedures, and description of the steps necessary to change the policies themselves. They must conform to union requirements where applicable and to all regulations that apply to employment practices. For example, as of July 1994, employers with 15 or more employees must comply with the Americans with Disabilities Act (ADA), which covers nondiscrimination practices related to recruitment, advertising, tenure, layoffs, leave, fringe benefits, and all other employment-related activities (ADA National Network, n.d.). Since its inception, the ADA has been revised, so it is important for directors to stay current with any new mandates or nuances in the interpretation of the law. Because many of these elements are included in the employment policies, it is important to understand the implications of the ADA for you and your staff to both ensure compliance with these regulations and to protect your program. Employment policies specifically spell out the rights of employees and what they may expect from the employer, and they should include the items described in the following sections.

8-2d • Job Descriptions

The job description is a detailed outline of what is expected from the person who fills a specific position. Position descriptions must be developed holistically, making note of how positions support each other, where they overlap, and where there are duties that are specific to a position. The job descriptions should

- reflect the program's mission and philosophy,
- reflect the designations as presented in the Power to the Profession's Unifying Framework (**Figure 8-2**),

ECE I
Certificate/
Credential
(at least 120 hours)
- Support birth–age 8

ECE II
Associate Degree
- Lead birth–age 5*
- Support K–Grade 3
- Guide the Practice of ECE I

ECE III
Bachelor's Degree or Master's Degree
(initial prep)
- Lead birth–age 8
- Guide the Practice of ECE I and ECE II

*Because we support progression and not regression in state- and district-funded programs, where "state-funded" is defined by NIEER, provided in mixed-delivery settings and explicitly aligned with the K–12 public school system, ECE II graduates can serve only in the support educator role. ECE III graduates must serve in the lead educator role.

Additional and innovative guidance, support, and supervisory models will need to be explored, developed, and evaluated, particularly for early childhood educators operating and/or working in family-based child care homes. Roles will continue to shift as public financing significantly increases to support all families with children in all settings and sectors.

Individuals serving in ECE I, II, and III roles may work as part of teaching teams and be prepared through programs of study in early childhood education that are aligned to the appropriate depth and breadth of the *Professional Standards and Competencies*. ECE I individuals must earn an industry-recognized national credential like the Child Development Associate® (CDA) national credential and other portable credentials. ECE II individuals must earn an early childhood education associate degree, and ECE III individuals must earn an early childhood education bachelor's degree or initial master's degree.

Compensation (including benefits) will increase with greater responsibility and deeper preparation. Compensation will be aligned with comparable roles in public K–12 settings. The deep need for increased investment (for compensation and more) cannot come on the backs of parents or educators. Additional state investment is necessary, but not sufficient. Increased federal support is essential.

FIGURE 8-2
One profession, three designations.
Source: Reprinted with permission from the Power to the Profession Taskforce (2020, p. 25).

- accurately represent the job as it currently exists,
- be shared with all members of the teaching teams so that roles are clear, and
- align with staff-evaluation tools.

8-2e • Career Lattice

Developing a career lattice or opportunity for progression is a challenge to the director, the board, or both. Each program must develop a career lattice after reviewing the roles and responsibilities of each staff position, budget limitations, and the professional goals of the program. The career lattice clearly defines education, experience, and corresponding salaries and benefits for every step in the hierarchy (Bloom, Sheerer, & Britz, 2005). Fortunately, Power to the Profession's Unifying Framework (2020) has addressed this hierarchy (**Figure 8-2**).

8-2f • Contract

The contract usually is a bilateral agreement signed by both parties that mutually binds the employee and the employer to agree on certain rights from each other. In this case, the employee agrees to provide a service (as defined by the appropriate job description), and the employer agrees to reimburse the employee for the service at a given rate for a specific length of time. Of course, those employers who have an at-will policy do not use employment contracts.

8-2g • Salary Ranges

Salary ranges for each position on the career lattice should be indicated clearly. Salary ranges should be based on the training, experience, and years of service required for each position. If salary increases are performance based, the plan for those increases is stated in the employment policies.

Each state may have its own laws regulating minimum wage and overtime pay, but all state regulations must be compatible with the federal Fair Labor Standards Act (FLSA). In that act, employees classified as *exempt* from the FLSA are professional,

salaried staff; those who earn an hourly wage and are entitled to overtime pay are considered *nonexempt* and are covered by the FLSA. (The federal government has instituted new rules that clarify employee rights and employer obligations relative to overtime pay.) Because these definitions and rules are scrutinized and revised regularly, consult an attorney with expertise in labor law when making decisions about questions related to compliance with government regulations. The Child Care Law Center can provide information on the current status of the issues involving how the FLSA affects employees in different states.

8-2h • Staff and Fringe Benefits

Fringe benefits available to employees must be stated clearly in the employment policies. Retirement plans, health insurance, educational opportunities, and other policies that impact the lives of employees should be reviewed in detail during orientation and should also be available for reference when questions arise. Changes in benefits must be communicated with staff in writing, and updates must be maintained in benefits documents.

8-2i • Employment at Will

Employment at will is common in most states and refers to an employment status in which the employee does not have an annual or ongoing contract and can be terminated without reason. "Even in states which allow for 'at will' employment (as opposed to states [that] require 'good cause' for termination), an employer may still be found liable if the employer violates its own employment policies" (Cohen, 1998, p. 86). The sample employment policies in **Director's Resource 8-2** provide exact wording for those who choose to use the at-will employment provision. That being the case, it is important to use caution when developing the staff handbook to avoid wording that can be viewed by the court as a contract. Employment law varies from state to state and changes frequently. One rule of thumb is to be fair and adhere to clearly stated policies that avoid discrimination. Have your policies reviewed regularly by an attorney.

8-2j • Health and Safety Measures

A health examination for all staff members is required upon hire in most states. In many localities, the law requires the health examination of program administrators who are viewed as being ultimately responsible for the health and safety of the children in the program. Those who work with children should be free of any infectious disease, whether or not there is a local certifying or licensing group responsible for monitoring health regulations. In addition, all staff are required in most states to have training in universal precautions (blood-borne pathogens) and hazardous materials. It also is recommended that early childhood staff be advised to update their immunizations because close contact with children puts them at risk for contracting a variety of infectious diseases. Furthermore, because the work is often physically demanding, the examination protects members of the staff by exploring their health limitations and reminding them to follow basic practices such as getting adequate rest and proper nutrition.

Child abuse and other child safety issues are a major concern among early childhood professionals. Therefore, most states mandate that staff have background checks, and many seek ways to certify that employees do not use drugs. Employers with more than 15 employees must comply with the ADA when dealing with employment issues.

Most states require that applicants for positions working with children complete a form declaring that they have not been convicted of a crime involving children. It is also common to require background checks. Many states have required forms for this important information, which can be used to glean information that is not permitted to be asked directly in an interview. The sample form in **Figure 8-3** that covers the criminal record issue will serve as a guide for obtaining information from staff members as well as job candidates about some sensitive areas of inquiry. If there are questions about the legality of making inquiries of this nature, contact the Equal Employment Opportunity Commission (EEOC) or seek legal counsel.

Employment policies should state clearly that professional staff must submit certified copies of credentials and that personal and professional references furnished by all new employees will be contacted before job offers are made.

8-2k • Daily Hours and Employment Period

Careful scheduling of personnel is critical for effective and efficient operation of all programs. This schedule should be stated in the employment policies and should be reiterated in each contract or letter of employment if these are used. Daily hours will not be the same for each staff member. Some staff members must arrive before children to prepare the learning environment. A large early childhood program will need extra staff to cover peak hours. For example, if school-age children come to the program before and after school or for lunch, the staffing needs will be increased during those hours. A key staff member must be present late in the day to chat with people who pick up the children near closing time. When all children have gone, the program must be in order for the early arrivals the following day; therefore, some of the staff must stay beyond the time that all children have left.

The complexity of the staffing schedule and the format used to lay out the schedule in an understandable way will vary. It should be set up to provide sufficient coverage to meet the licensing requirements where applicable and to guarantee safety of children and adequate staff to maintain high standards of quality throughout each day. In planning the staffing patterns, directors should keep in mind the concerns about child abuse in early childhood programs and take preventive measures. Schedule at least two caregivers to be present at all times, particularly early and late in the day and during nap and toileting routines. This will help protect children and staff if someone is unjustly accused of abuse (Cohen, 1998; Copeland & Bruno, 2012). **Director's Resources 8-2** and **8-3** will serve as guidelines for setting up staffing schedules and staffing plans. Use of graphing, listing by staff member, listing by room, or listing by program are a few ways to record a staffing schedule so it is clear to those who are interested in it, including staff, board members, licensing agents, and especially parents.

Ohio Department of Job and Family Services
STATEMENT OF NONCONVICTION
FOR CHILD CARE CENTERS AND TYPE A HOMES

This statement must be signed by every individual owner, administrator and employee of a child care center, Type A Home and all persons eighteen years of age and older who reside in a Type A Home. This statement must be kept on file at the center or Type A Home. Please note that owners and administrators must also attach the JFS 01314 which is a supplement to this form.

Employee Name (please print or type)

☐ I hereby attest that I have never been convicted of or pleaded guilty to child abuse or other crimes of violence set forth in section 5104.09 of the Revised Code and that no child has been removed from my home as described in section 2151.353 of the Revised Code.

Employee Signature	Date

Street Address

City	State	Zip Code	Telephone Number

☐ I am unable to sign the statement above because I have been convicted of a crime included in section 5104.09 of the Revised Code. However, after reviewing the rehabilitation requirements of rule 5101:2-13-26 or 5101:2-12-26 of the Administrative Code with the administrator, it has been determined I meet the rehabilitation requirements. Please see attached verifications that the requirements for rehabilitation have been met.

Note: Anyone who withholds information from, or falsifies information on this statement is guilty of falsification, a misdemeanor of the first degree. If the offender is an owner of a center or a licensee of a Type A Home, the conviction constitutes grounds for denial, revocation, or refusal to renew a child day care license application. If the offender is an employee of a center or Type A Home, or is a person eighteen years of age or older who reside in a Type A Home, and if the owner or licensee had knowledge of, and acquiesced in the commission of the offense, the conviction constitutes grounds for denial, revocation, or refusal to renew a child day care license application.

Please note: effective June 1, 2006 all civilian background checks must be submitted electronically through use of WebCheck or other approved methods. More information can be accessed at: www.webcheck.ag.state.oh.us.

The administrator is required to sign and date below verifying that fingerprints have been electronically submitted to the Ohio Bureau of Criminal Identification and Investigation (BCII), or mailed if electronic processing exemption criteria are met.

A criminal records check for the above named individual was requested on (date) _____

☐ Ohio records check ☐ FBI records check (please check)

Signature of Administrator	Date

TYPE A HOMES ONLY

In addition to the above, the licensee of a Type A Home must sign the following statement.
I hereby attest that no one who resides in my home and who is under eighteen years of age has been adjudicated a delinquent child for committing a violation of any offense listed in section 5104.09 of the Ohio Revised Code.

Signature	Date

This is a prescribed form which must be used to meet the requirements of section 5104.09 of the Revised Code. Failure to complete the form shall preclude issuance of the child care license or certificate.
JFS 01313 (Rev. 9/2006)

Page 1 of 2

FIGURE 8-3
Sample statement of nonconviction form for prospective employees.
Source: Ohio Department of Job and Family Services.

Section 5104.09 Prohibitions Against Employment

Homicide
1. R.C. 2903.01 – Aggravated murder
2. R.C. 2903.02 – Murder
3. R.C. 2903.03 – Voluntary manslaughter
4. R.C. 2903.04 – Involuntary manslaughter

Assault
5. R.C. 2903.11 – Felonious assault
6. R.C. 2903.12 – Aggravated assault
7. R.C. 2903.13 – Assault
8. R.C. 2903.16 – Failing to provide for a functionally impaired person

Menacing
9. R.C. 2903.21 – Aggravated menacing
10. R.C. 2903.22 - Menacing

Patient abuse and neglect
11. R.C. 2903.34 – Patient abuse, neglect

Kidnapping and related issues
12. R.C. 2905.01 – Kidnapping
13. R.C. 2905.02 – Abduction
14. R.C. 2905.04 – Child stealing (as this law existed prior to July 1, 1996)
15. R.C. 2905.05 – Criminal child enticement

Sex offenses
16. R.C. 2907.02 - Rape
17. R.C. 2907.03 – Sexual battery
18. R.C. 2907.04 – Corruption of a minor
19. R.C. 2907.05 – Gross sexual imposition
20. R.C. 2907.06 – Sexual imposition
21. R.C. 2907.07 – Importuning
22. R.C. 2907.08 – Voyeurism
23. R.C. 2907.09 – Public indecency
24. R.C. 2907.12 - Felonious sexual penetration (as this former section of law existed)
25. R.C. 2907.21 – Compelling prostitution
26. R.C. 2907.22 – Promoting prostitution
27. R.C. 2907.23 – Procuring
28. R.C. 2907.25 – Prostitution
29. R.C. 2907.31 – Disseminating matter harmful to juveniles
30. R.C. 2907.32 – Pandering obscenity
31. R.C. 2907.321 – Pandering obscenity involving a minor
32. R.C. 2907.322 – Pandering sexually oriented matter involving a minor
33. R.C. 2907.323 – Illegal use of a minor in nudity-oriented material or performance

Arson
34. R.C. 2909.02 - Aggravated arson
35. R.C. 2909.03 - Arson

Robbery and Burglary
36. R.C. 2911.01 – Aggravated robbery
37. R.C. 2911.02 – Robbery
38. R.C. 2911.11 – Aggravated burglary
39. R.C. 2911.12 – Burglary

Offenses against the family
40. R.C. 2919.12 – Unlawful abortion
41. R.C. 2919.22 – Endangering children
42. R.C. 2919.24 – Contributing to unruliness or delinquency of a child
43. R.C. 2919.25 – Domestic violence

Weapons control
44. R.C. 2923.12 – Carrying a concealed weapon
45. R.C. 2923.13 – Having a weapon while under disability
46. R.C. 2923.161 – Improperly discharging a firearm at or into a habitation or school

Drug offenses
47. R.C. 2925.02 – Corrupting another with drugs
48. R.C. 2925.03 – Trafficking in drugs
49. R.C. 2925.04 – Illegal manufacture of drugs or cultivation of marijuana
50. R.C. 2925.05 – Funding of drug or marijuana trafficking
51. R.C. 2925.06 – Illegal administration or distribution of anabolic steroids
52. R.C. 2925.11 – Possession of drugs or marijuana that is not a minor drug possession offense in section R.C. 2925.01

Other
53. R.C.2905.11 - Extortion
54. R.C. 3716.11 – Placing harmful objects in food or confection
55. R.C. 2909.04 - Disrupting public services
56. R.C. 2909.05 - Vandalism
57. R.C. 2917.01 - Inciting to violence
58. R.C. 2917.02 - Aggravated riot
59. R.C. 2917.03 - Riot
60. R.C. 2917..31 - Inducing panic
61. R.C. 2921.03 - Intimidation
62. R.C. 2921. 34 - Escape
63. R.C. 2921.35 - Aiding escape or resistance to authority
64. Or an existing or former offense of any municipal corporation, this state, any other state, or the United States that is substantially equivalent to any of these offenses.

FIGURE 8-3
(continued)

8-2l • Relief Periods

A planned system of daily relief periods or breaks should be stated. The policy on rest periods may be highly flexible or carefully scheduled. In either case, the policy should clearly state and include the designated space where staff may take breaks. In half-day programs, it is rare to find a set policy on rest periods because of the short time span of concentrated effort required by staff members. On the other hand, in early childhood programs in which an educator may work an 8- or 9-hour day that includes having lunch with children, it is essential to provide time to rest and be away from the children. Some programs prefer to have some staff members work a split shift to provide time for rest, shopping, or study at midday. This serves to reduce costs at a time of low need.

8-2m • Vacations, Holidays, and Sick Leave

A statement on vacations and holidays should appear in the employment policies. Specific details about lead time for vacation applications and the length and timing of vacations is advisable for larger, year-round programs, but smaller programs in session only during the typical school year may not require that level of specificity in their policies. However, both large and small programs observe certain holidays. These holidays will vary, depending on the religious and ethnic orientation of the staff or the children served, the agency with which the school is affiliated (church or public school), and the community standards. All employees should know exactly which holidays will be observed by the program.

Sick days, personal days, maternity leave, newborn parental leave for either parent, and special leave days for jury duty should be included in the employment policies. Directors can check the Family and Medical Leave Act regulations when dealing with these requests. It also is wise to cover details such as the use of unused leave days, the necessity for documenting illness, and policies about closings because of bad weather. The program's plan for hiring substitutes for each staff position during vacation periods, for special holidays, and for sick days must be spelled out clearly. The policy should state that all health, safety, and training qualifications for staff also apply to substitutes. Maintaining a substitute file that includes the necessary employment information and payroll paperwork on available people will make it easier to find substitutes on short notice. A plan for hiring substitutes prevents confusion when emergencies occur and also facilitates budget planning for these special needs.

8-2n • Probationary Periods

Many programs include probationary periods after initial employment to allow an adjustment period for both adults and children in the program. A director may be appointed on an "acting" basis for as long as a year. The time period must be long enough for the new employee to demonstrate competency in a given position but not so long that valuable aspects of the program can be undermined by an incompetent individual.

Educator competency can be validated in a 3- to 6-month probationary period by an experienced director who operates under a clearly defined philosophy of education and evaluates with an experienced eye. Because the educator works directly with the children and any incompetence could have direct detrimental effects on him or her, the probationary period for all educators should be delineated carefully and understood clearly at the time of employment. This practice not only protects the welfare of the children but also becomes more equitable for the educators in the long run because they come into a new role with a clear understanding of the time allowed for initial review and evaluation. Precise and thorough evaluation and documentation throughout the probationary period is essential because this trial period could lead to an employee's termination.

8-2o • Staff Evaluation and Grievance Procedures

Performance evaluations should be scheduled on a regular basis. Evaluation and grievance procedures are included in the employment policies (**Figure 8-4**). These procedures should be made available to all program personnel. Ideally, they will include details about the following:

- who evaluates whom,
- when the periodic evaluation will take place,
- what techniques or instruments will be used in the evaluation,
- who makes the decision on whether or not the criteria are met, and
- what the consequences are for not meeting the stated criteria.

Not meeting stated criteria could mean no recommendation for a raise, no opportunity for advancing to a higher-level position, or termination. When there are other actions that could cause dismissal, such as use of corporal punishment, these should be in writing. In some situations, there may be no recourse after a decision has been made to deny a raise or to terminate an employee. Although that may seem unfair, it is better to state it at the outset than to deal with all the negative feelings generated by the decision when an employee is unaware that there is no way to appeal it.

8-2p • Performance Evaluations

Staff members are entitled to know evaluation procedures as well as evaluation criteria. There-

---

Townville child-development center (a United Way agency) evaluation and grievance procedures

Evaluation and Grievance Procedures

1 Frequency of Evaluation
Performance evaluations will be made twice during the probationary period for every new staff member—at the midpoint and the end of the probationary period—and annually thereafter. It is the responsibility of the personnel committee to evaluate the work of the director and the responsibility of the director to evaluate all members of the staff. All evaluations will be shared with the employee and then become part of the employee's file.

2 Purpose of Evaluation
The primary purpose of the annual evaluation is to create a mutual understanding between the director and each member of the staff of what is expected and how they both view the best way to move toward fulfilling those expectations.
Annual evaluations will be used as a basis for continued employment, horizontal or vertical movement on the career lattice, salary increments in cases where the job description allows for merit raises, and demotion or dismissal.

3 Basis for the Evaluation
Staff members will be evaluated on knowledge of the job as described in the job description, quality

of skill demonstrated in fulfilling the job, interest and initiative, dependability, personal and professional growth, attendance and punctuality, and ability to work effectively in cooperation with other staff members.
Evaluation forms for each staff position in the center are included in these personnel policies.

4 Evaluation Procedure
Each staff member will be notified as to when his or her evaluation will take place. The evaluation will be discussed with the staff member, at which time the staff member will be given the opportunity to express his or her agreement or disagreement with the evaluation. The outcome of this discussion will become part of the staff member's record.

5 Review of Grievances
The staff member who wishes to present a grievance must present it first to the director. Failing to reach settlement with the director, the staff member may submit to the chairperson of the personnel committee a written statement of the situation, requesting that the grievance be reviewed by the personnel committee. The personnel committee will review the grievance and report with recommendations to the board of directors for action.

FIGURE 8-4

fore, performance evaluations for all staff positions should be part of employment policies or the orientation materials and discussed during staff orientation. Teaching staff are usually evaluated by the director who, in turn, may be evaluated by the human resources committee of the board or by the human resources director in cases where programs are part of a larger organization. Other support staff may be reviewed and evaluated by the director or by other designated staff. The sample performance evaluation (**Director's Resource 8-4**) might be used as a prototype for performance evaluation tools. Although there may be some overlap in areas covered by the evaluation forms, such as physical and mental health, ability to work well with other adults, and personal attributes such as enthusiasm or sense of humor, some are unique to a given position. For example, the cook must be able to manage time well in order to have meals ready for serving at a given hour, whereas an educator must adjust the daily schedule based on the changing needs of children. Performance evaluation forms usually are based on job descriptions. Knowledge of evaluation criteria helps build a sense of trust and partnership between the staff to be evaluated and the evaluator, who is either the director or another staff member.

8-2q • Organizational Chart

An organizational chart that is sometimes part of the employment policies and is made available to all members of the staff can clarify lines of communication and responsibility for everyone in the program. For a newcomer, even the simplest organizational pattern may be difficult to see unless it is presented in a diagram or flowchart (**Figure 8-5**). An organizational chart enables an employee to determine how each position meshes with other positions in the program. This information, coupled with complete job descriptions, performance evaluation procedures and forms, and open staff communication, leaves little doubt about expectations, areas of responsibility, and who will be the evaluator for each position. In a sense, it defines reporting relationships as well as limits of authority.

8-2r • Amending and Changing the Policies

The employment policies should contain a section that details the procedure for amending the policies. The amending procedure presumably parallels the one that was used initially for developing the policies and that is stated in the bylaws, but the policy-making body now may be expanded to include staff members or parents who were not available during the initial stages of development. As the program undergoes its regular evaluation period, the employment policies also should be checked to determine whether changes are needed. Then the board or the policy-making staff can follow the amendment procedures when making changes becomes necessary. After a change has been adopted, it is important to inform all personnel of the changes, and the director is charged with implementing the new policy.

Clearly, small, private programs will not use all the preceding items in their employment policies. However, large, complex organizations undoubtedly will include all of these and more. Policies are drawn and shaped to the unique needs of each program and are constantly evaluated and modified to meet the ever-changing and growing needs of the program for which they are written.

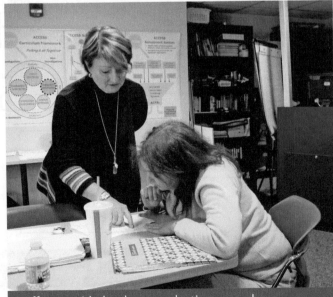

Staff are entitled to know evaluation procedures and criteria.

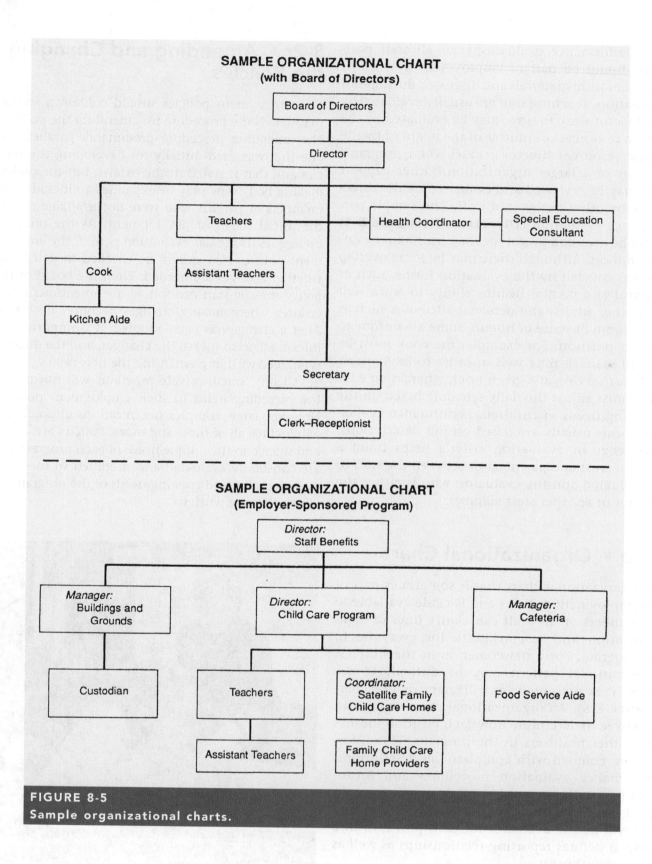

SAMPLE ORGANIZATIONAL CHART
(with Board of Directors)

Board of Directors

Director

Teachers

Health Coordinator

Special Education Consultant

Cook

Assistant Teachers

Kitchen Aide

Secretary

Clerk–Receptionist

SAMPLE ORGANIZATIONAL CHART
(Employer-Sponsored Program)

Director:
Staff Benefits

Manager:
Buildings and Grounds

Director:
Child Care Program

Manager:
Cafeteria

Custodian

Teachers

Coordinator:
Satellite Family Child Care Homes

Food Service Aide

Assistant Teachers

Family Child Care Home Providers

FIGURE 8-5
Sample organizational charts.

8-3 • The Hiring Process

The basic tools used in developing plans **naeyc** and procedures for hiring early child-hood program staff members are written employment policies and job descriptions. On the surface, these documents and procedures appear to be easily drawn and delineated; at a more subtle level, they reflect the philosophy of the overall program as it focuses on individuals and their worth as human beings. As policies and procedures are adjusted and changed, they will reflect the ability of responsible administrators in the organization to make optimum use of available human resources.

An analysis of each program's purposes and manner of operating will determine the broad policy areas to be covered in the employment policies. The program that employs large numbers of professional and ancillary staff may have policies with separate sections for each category of employee and other employment, including substitutes, resource educators, and other support staff. In all cases, every policy statement should contain an affirmative action section that verifies the program's intent to adhere strictly to acceptance of all personnel regardless of race, age, sex, creed, national origin, sexual preference, or disability. (For information regarding employment discrimination and affirmative action issues, contact the U.S. Equal Employment Opportunity Commission, 800-669-3362 or call 800-669-4000, to be connected to your state EEOC office.)

8-3a • Developing Job Descriptions

One mechanism for reducing conflict and uncertainty for staff members is to provide a clear definition of the role of each member on staff. Each role requires a thorough description so that the same basic job will be done no matter who fills the role. The description can be written to clarify expectations yet retain the personal freedom of all staff members to follow through in the performance of their roles according to their own unique style. Well-written job descriptions provide a framework within which an individual can function creatively while performing the tasks required for the program. Detailed descriptions of required knowledge, skills, and physical abilities are important because subsequent performance evaluations are based on the job description. For teaching staff job descriptions, include the idea that staff will be able to supervise children within sight and sound and have the ability to physically attend to the children. For infant and toddler educators, also add that the staff person must be able to lift at least 40 pounds regularly during an 8-hour period. The applicants then are asked if they can perform the duties as described in the job description.

A sample job description (**Director's Resource 8-5**) provides a prototype for writing descriptions for various staff positions, including full-time and part-time professional and support staff for both agency-sponsored and proprietary early childhood programs, as well as public school preschools. Job descriptions may cover some of the following, plus other items as needed:

- job title,
- person to whom responsible,
- people for whom responsible,
- qualifications (education, experience, personal health, physical abilities, etc.),
- duties and responsibilities, and
- salary schedule and work schedule.

Job descriptions should be reviewed on a regular basis to determine whether changes are necessary. Such periodic review is useful because the director or governing body can deal with changing rules or regulations governing practices, adjust the policies as role expectations at different levels shift, and change job descriptions when new personnel bring changing talents and skills to a staff. For example, menu planning and shopping may be part of a director's job description, but a new cook who has been trained to plan meals may take over that function. Job descriptions for both the director and the cook can be adjusted accordingly, allowing staff members to perform at their highest creative level.

The initial writing of job descriptions is only the first step in an ongoing process. This process requires expertise in using information from the program evaluation and an ability to adjust to changing and growing strengths of personnel to make efficient use of available talent for a more effective program.

8-3b • Recruiting

After the job descriptions have been written, the major hiring procedure begins. In fact, in many large programs or in programs with a board, the first task assigned to a new director is to initiate staff-recruitment procedures. Each program establishes and follows some general procedures regarding advertising, interviewing, and selecting employees to use during initial hiring in a new program and in filling vacant staff positions for an ongoing program.

Advertising for new staff is usually the director's responsibility. However, in some public schools and in corporate settings, the human resources office may set up school district or company advertisements that cover available positions throughout the organization. If the program is ongoing, the director first should notify current staff members, board members, and parents about job openings as they become available. People in the organization may choose to apply for the new job, or they may know qualified individuals who would like to apply. For employees to learn of openings in their own program from an outside source is disconcerting, and it exemplifies poor communication within the program.

Affirmative action statements must be included when advertising for program

personnel. These statements are always included in advertising for staff, not only because that has been the usual practice but also and more importantly because it is essential that programs strive to maintain and enhance staff diversity. It is helpful to have advertising appear in a range of publications to make the information available to diverse segments of the population. **Figure 8-6** shows examples of some advertisements. Local professional organizations that publish classified ads in their newsletters are good places to advertise for classroom staff, as are high schools, colleges, or universities that have early

Sample advertisements

Sample LinkedIn Job Posting

Are you a creative and caring person with a desire to make a difference in the lives of children? Do you have a strong understanding of child development and teaching and want to join an organization that values your skills? Are you interested in a career with opportunities for advancement? Our NAEYC-accredited program is seeking dedicated teachers who wish to become part of our preschool team.

Position Summary

Works as part of an educational team to plan and implement a high-quality preschool program. Maintains strong communication with families and administration. Works with the team to maintain a clean, safe, and effective learning environment.

Essential Functions

Provides care and education to children.

Works as part of an education team to develop and implement curriculum.

Engages with current and prospective parents and family members and is responsive to their needs.

Is aware of and complies with all licensing standards.

Completes timely and accurate assessment and documentation of children's learning and development.

Attends and participates in all staff meetings, center events, and parent or customer meetings as requested.

Requirements: Skills, education and knowledge, experience.

Education

Bachelor's degree in early childhood education
Experience
2+ years of early childhood education experience desirable.
1+ years of experience working with assigned age group desirable.

You are applying to an Equal Opportunity Employer. All qualified applicants will receive consideration for employment without regard to race, national origin, age, sex, religion, disability, sexual orientation, marital status, military or veteran status, gender identity or expression, or any other basis protected by local, state, or federal law.

Click to submit application.

Sample Notice on the Local Early Childhood Leadership Online Group

Director wanted for the Community Head Start Center. Responsibilities include hiring and supervision of entire staff for a program serving 75 children, record keeping, proposal writing, and working with center staff, community action agency, parents, and other community agencies. Applicant must have a master's degree in early childhood education with some training in at least one of the following: social work, special education, administration. Three years' administration experience required—Head Start teaching experience preferred. Send resume to Community Head Start Center, 352 Ninth St., Sioux City, Iowa. Deadline for applications, July 1. We are an Equal Opportunity Employer.

Sample Classified Advertisement for the *New York Times*

Preschool teacher wanted for suburban church-affiliated preschool. Responsibilities include planning and implementing an age-appropriate developmental type early education program for a group of 15 three- and four-year-old children. Bachelor's degree required—early childhood education teacher experience preferred. Write for application to Ms. D. L. Jones, Director, Upper Plains Christian Church, 130 Meadows Place, Upper Plains, New York 11112, or call (713) 431-6037 Monday through Thursday from 1:00 to 3:00 p.m., or email upperplains@ hotmail.com. We are an Equal Opportunity Employer.

Sample Classified Advertisement for the *Parkville Times*

Cook wanted for child care center at outskirts of town. Responsibilities include preparing snacks and lunch for 65 preschool children, cleaning kitchen appliances and cupboards, and making weekly shopping list. Experience preferred. Please send resume to P. O. Box 932, Parkville, VA 23221. Equal Opportunity Employer.

FIGURE 8-6

childhood training programs. Ads also may be placed in national professional journals or put on their websites if there is sufficient time to meet publication deadlines. Some colleges and vocational high schools maintain placement services, and some hold placement conferences so that employers can interview applicants. Notices of job openings also can be posted on community bulletin boards and in community papers that reach special segments of the population, such as the African American or Native American community and non–English-speaking groups, and on various appropriate websites.

The classified section of newspapers is frequently used for advertising, but the result may be large numbers of unqualified applicants who then must be screened before interviewing can begin. Nonetheless, when a position must be filled quickly, advertising in both small community weekly newspapers and large city daily newspapers is helpful because information is quickly disseminated to large numbers of people.

Personnel ads should include enough information to minimize the number of applications from completely unqualified people but should not be so narrowly written that qualified people fail to apply. If you are expected to write the advertising copy, you must be completely familiar with all the qualifications that are essential for performance of the job. Careful review of the job description is a good way to become familiar with the desired qualifications for potential candidates. Each advertisement should include the following:

- job title,
- brief job description,
- essential qualifications,
- method of applying (telephone, letter, application form), and
- name of the person to contact with a telephone number, street address, or email address.

Starting date, working hours, starting pay, fringe benefits, and goals of the organization also may be included.

Advertisements that clearly state all nonnegotiable items will eliminate practically all unqualified applicants. On the other hand, negotiable items stated equivocally tend to attract a more diverse pool of candidates from which to choose. For example, "experience necessary" is much more restrictive than "experience preferred." If experience is a nonnegotiable

qualification, then say, "experience necessary." However, if the position could be filled by a person with good training and a variety of life experiences that may or may not have been with children, then say "experience preferred." The latter phrase appeals to a broader population and will not only increase the number of applicants but also have appeal to a more diverse group.

The director should be cautious about luring people into the field by presenting a glowing picture of life in an early childhood program. Hiring staff members under false pretenses can lead to job dissatisfaction quickly. Rapid staff turnover disrupts program continuity and is hard on the families and children who must constantly establish new relationships. During the past decade, the staffing crisis in the early childhood field has increased the challenge for directors who prefer to wait until they find qualified candidates to fill vacancies but are unable to meet required teacher-to-child ratios because of staff shortages. Many well-qualified early childhood educators are choosing to move into public school or Head Start programs where pay and benefits often are better than those in other early childhood settings. The availability of qualified staff is limited, and the competition for their services is keen. But dealing with the consequences of hiring staff members who are unable or unwilling to do a good job inevitably leads to more turnover, which is hard on other staff members, families, and children. Therefore, a job opening notice that lists the required job qualifications in specific and realistic terms and careful hiring increase the probability of getting the best match between applicants and available positions and reduces turnover.

Careful consideration must be given to the best method for receiving applications. If the need is urgent and immediate, it may be necessary to accept applications by telephone. This option means that a new employee can be found quickly because an interview can be scheduled moments after a notice is seen. But it also means that current staff members may have to spend hours on the telephone, which detracts from their work with the children and puts them in the position of answering questions from people who are not seriously interested in the job.

Listing a post office box number in an ad places fewer demands on the director and the staff because potential candidates do not know the identity of the program and are unable to call. On the other hand, qualified people may decide not to apply if they are unsure of the source of the ad. Others may feel that they could be applying to the program in which they work, another reason for notifying all employees of every opening. In fact, occasionally ads read, "Our employees know about this advertisement."

Allowing applicants to apply in person can be inconvenient as well as inappropriate for some positions. Unless the program has its own human resources director or is affiliated with a sponsoring agency such as a public school, having applicants appear at the door during the hours in which children are present is awkward. However, this problem can be handled by setting specific hours during which interviews may be scheduled. In neighborhoods where many people do not have telephones and where writing letters is difficult for some adults, it may be appropriate to have people apply in person. If the job does not entail making written reports, such as the case of a cook or a housekeeper, the ability to communicate effectively in writing may not be a criterion for selection, and there is no need to see a résumé or written application. On the other hand, in the case of an educator, teacher assistant, or special education resource teacher, writing skills are important. For these positions, a written response offers helpful data for initial screening of applicants and should be mandatory before an interview is scheduled.

The advertiser also will have to decide whether to have the candidates request an application form or send a résumé. If a secretary is available to answer requests for application blanks, the process can be speeded up. If the director will be distracted from work by recording the name and address of applicants and mailing out applications, it is wiser to have candidates mail in résumés and fill in a formal application when they are interviewed. Sample application forms (**Figures 8-7** and **8-8**) show how applications are adjusted, depending on the availability of a résumé from the applicant.

When all the applications have been collected, they must be screened to eliminate obviously unsuitable candidates. If no suitable candidates have applied, and attempts to recruit staff from other programs have failed, the advertising and application process is reopened. The director or the chairperson of the human resources committee usually screens the applications for those who meet the job requirements, particularly in the areas of education, health, or experience. Then interviews can be arranged. Interviewers should not be burdened with candidates who have no qualifications for the job. Therefore, the careful writing of job opening notices to interested qualified candidates and the initial screening process to eliminate totally unqualified candidates are both important steps in the recruiting process.

Applications that are received from people who are not subsequently called for an interview should be retained so that affirmative action procedures can be completed where that is a requirement. A record must be kept listing the reasons why any applicant was not interviewed, and they should receive written notification that they will not be interviewed. Applicants who are called for an interview should be advised to bring identification to prove citizenship. A candidate who is not a U.S. citizen will be required to prove eligibility to work in this country. To be in compliance with the Immigration Reform and Control Act of 1986, every person hired must complete Form I-9, which is available from the Immigration and Naturalization Service.

8-3c • Interviewing

Interviewing is essential and should not be eliminated no matter how urgent the need for obtaining a staff member may seem. Even though a candidate can make an excellent impression during an interview and then turn out to be an ineffective staff member, interviewing will provide insights that cannot be gleaned from written applications or résumés and will facilitate judicious hiring decisions in the majority of cases. The relative amount of time spent interviewing can be extremely profitable when compared with the amount of time that might otherwise be spent solving personnel problems and higher staff turnover because a poor candidate was hastily selected. "Although not a magic solution to cure all turnover woes, effective interviewing is a step in the right direction" (Hamrick, 2000). The person or group responsible for staffing the program must decide who will review applications and interview the candidates and then must develop the plan for the interview.

Sample Application Form
(Suggested for use when no resume is on file)

Application for Employment

Jewish Community Child Care Center—Fairmount, Pennsylvania

Name of Applicant _____

                       Last   First   Middle or Maiden

Address _____

State _____ ZIP _____

Telephone _____ Social Security No. _____

Citizenship: USA _____ Other _____

Record of Education

School	Name and Address of School	Check Last Year Completed	List Diploma or Degree
High		1 2 3 4	
College		1 2 3 4	
Other (Specify)		1 2 3 4	

FIGURE 8-7
Sample application form (no résumé).

8-3d • Reviewing Applications

Reviewing applications is the first step in the total interviewing process. The director or group in charge of staffing the program first must make sure that the job description for the position being filled is up to date. It also is helpful to think about what type of person who will best fit the position. Consider not only what the job description defines as required for the position but also the program's culture, the match with other staff members, and the comfort level for working with the program's families. These considerations will keep the focus on finding a good match with the existing program "family" as well as enhance and

List below all present and past employment, beginning with your most recent

Name and Address of Employer	From Mo./Yr.	To Mo./Yr.	Describe in detail the work you did	Weekly Starting Salary	Weekly Last Salary	Reason for Leaving	Name of Supervisor

List all professional and community organizations with which you are affiliated. *(Indicate if you hold office in the organization.)*

Write your educational philosophy.

What do you feel most qualifies you for this position?

What are your professional goals?

List names and addresses of three references.

_____

_____

_____

I give permission to contact references _____
　　　　　　　　　　　　　　　　　　　　　　　　　　　(signature)

FIGURE 8-7
(continued)

TeachSource Digital Download

support the program's interest in diversity. Using a systematic approach for application screening makes the job easier and will cover you later if anyone questions your hiring decision.

Begin the application review process by developing a form that covers the required qualifications for the job, including education, experience, and specialized training. Add qualifications that may not be required for the position but are preferred and could contribute to the candidate's ability to do the job. For example, experience working with diverse populations may be a requirement, but special experience on a Native American reservation or student teaching in Latin America could be a plus, depending on the location of your program and the population served. Include items on the form that would cover

Sample Application Form
(Suggested for use when a resume is on file)

Application for Position

University Day Care Center—Ogden University, Ogden City, Michigan

Name of Applicant _____
                          Last   First   Middle or Maiden

Address _____

State _____ ZIP _____

Telephone _____

Title of position for which you are applying. _____

What do you feel best qualifies you for this position? _____

_____

_____

Would you be willing to continue your education by taking college courses or in-service training if
recommended to do that? _____

_____

_____

What satisfaction do you expect to receive from this position? _____

_____

_____

List three references (preferably one former employer, one former teacher, and one community person).

        1. _____

        2. _____

        3. _____

I give permission to contact references _____
                                                            (signature)

FIGURE 8-8
Sample application form (résumé on file).

TeachSource Digital Download

those special experiences by having a place to check whether or not the candidate has had experience with diverse groups and a place to note which ethnic, cultural, and socioeconomic groups were part of that experience. The changing demographic profile in our society calls attention to the importance of adjusting staff hiring practices so they will be responsive to the diversity among families, children, and program staff. The screening form should include all the items that are on the application and also cover the job description.

Develop a rating scale for the items on the screening form so each reviewer can arrive at a total score for each applicant (Hamrick, 2000). A three-point scale can be used for this purpose. It is helpful to provide reviewers with some definitions for the three levels on the scale. If the candidate does not meet the requirement at all, then the score on that item would be 0. Ratings might be defined as follows:

1 = barely meets requirement,
2 = meets requirement, and
3 = exceeds requirement.

Definitions of ratings will vary, depending on exactly how the requirements or criteria for the job are stated. In any case, a rating scale gives those who screen the applications a way to evaluate the qualifications of the candidates and provides a score for each one. There should be places on the screening form for comments and recommendations of reviewers and a place where they can note that the candidate does not have the qualifications to fill the position that is open. All applications are kept on file should there be any question about the hiring procedures.

When the reviewers meet to discuss the next step in this process, they can eliminate those candidates who do not have the qualifications for the job as described in the job description and use their scores on the screening forms to rank the remaining candidates. The next steps are to decide who will be interviewed and who will do the interviewing.

8-3e • Interviewers

While applications are being collected and screened, decisions are made about who will interview the viable candidates. In a small program, the director may take full responsibility for all interviewing or may do it with the help of one or more of the following:

- staff person,
- member of the board,
- community person,
- other professional (social worker, special educator, physician, school principal),
- person responsible to the new employee, and
- parent representative.

In some programs, the interviews are conducted by committees, often by the human resources committee.

The composition of the interview committee may be established by the board beforehand, as in the case of the human resources committee; the committee can also be set up by the director to pertain specifically to the job being filled. For example, when there is an opening for an educator, the committee might include the director, an educator, and a parent. The expertise of an educator on the interviewing team is valuable. Including educators also makes them feel valued and appreciated. Community people could be included as well as people from other professions, such as community health or special education. There might be more than one person from a given category, but if the committee is too large, its effectiveness will diminish. It can be difficult for large numbers of people to interview a given candidate at one time, and the procedure can be highly threatening for the candidate. Nonetheless, it is best if the committee is diverse and representative of the program staff with whom the person will work, the families who use the program, and the people who represent the sponsoring agency.

Although the committee makeup may vary depending on the type of program and on the position to be filled, both the committee members and the candidates must be aware that the organizational structure of the program takes precedence in making hiring decisions. For example, if a janitor is being hired, it may be appropriate to have the educators express a preference for the candidate who would be most able to meet their needs for classroom maintenance. However, if the person who becomes janitor is going to be responsible to the program director, then the director's opinion must weigh heavily in the final hiring decision.

A major exception to this hiring and interviewing procedure is in programs sponsored by public schools, where hiring is based on established school district policies. Public school union contracts often dictate hiring policies and procedures. Sometimes, the human resources office will handle advertising, interviewing, and hiring. Involving educators or parents in the process is unlikely. This could result in a team that will have to spend time building a partnership and working through possible philosophical differences.

8-3f • Preparation for the Interview

Just as candidates should come to the interview prepared to express their strengths, weaknesses, goals, expectations, and past experiences, so the interviewers should be prepared for each interview. Their questions should reflect a thorough knowledge of the program, its program, its staff, and the clients served by the program. Interviewers should be familiar with the information in the candidate's résumé, application form, and reference letters, and they should look for evidence of warmth, good-natured calmness, and ease of relating to others. An interview is conducted most productively when all parties are well prepared and when the environment has been set up for a meaningful dialogue between interviewers and interviewee.

8-3g • Interviewer Information

Each interviewer should be totally familiar with the job description for the vacant position and should have copies of the candidate's application and references. When contacting references, the process should be consistent so that references will provide comparable data for all candidates. It has become more common for responses to be collected using electronic questionnaires that are sent via email. The most popular method of collecting feedback from references is by phone. **Figure 8-9** shows a sample questionnaire that is administered by phone.

Telephone reference check list

University of Dayton Telephone Reference Check List

This list includes suggested questions for telephone reference checks. Please select questions you wish to uniformly and consistently use for each candidate. If you wish to ask other questions, please contact the Office of Human Resources Staffing Department at 229-2722 for guidance on whether questions are legally permissible.

My name is (___), and I work at the (name of center/program). We are filling a position within our department and would like to verify employment information on (applicant's name), who was employed by you from (beginning date) until (ending date).

1 What was the nature of his/her job?
2 What did you think of his/her work?
3 What are his/her strong points?
4 What are his/her weak points?
5 How did he/she get along with other coworkers?
6 Would you comment on his/her

- attendance:
- dependability:
- ability to take on responsibility:
- ability to follow instructions:
- degree of supervision needed:
- overall attitude:
- quality of work:

7 Why did he/she leave the position? Would you rehire the person? Yes or no? If no, why not?

8 Is there anything else you would like to comment on regarding (applicant's name) employment or job performance?

FIGURE 8-9
Source: From the University of Dayton, Office of Human Resources.

8-3h • Interview Plan

Interviewers plan the type of interview they will conduct. Sometimes, a predetermined list of questions is developed so that all candidates will respond to the same questions. This procedure provides uniform data but is somewhat inflexible and may not elicit the most useful data from each candidate. Sometimes, questions are developed as the interview progresses. This spontaneous procedure is more likely to give rise to potentially constructive data but requires more skill on the part of the interviewers.

The person who develops the questions should keep in mind the parameters of the job description and should understand the requirements of Title VII of the 1964 Civil Rights Act, the EEOC, and the ADA. There must be a "business necessity" for all questions asked during the interview. Consider the list shown in **Figure 8-10** when determining what questions to ask and avoid during an interview.

The first question of the interview should be open ended and require more than a simple yes or no answer. Furthermore, it should focus on previous jobs, education, hobbies, or any other subject matter with which the candidate is familiar. This technique puts the candidate at ease and creates an environment for more focused probing later in the interview. For example, the interviewer might say, "I see in your resume that you have worked for Head Start in California and that the committee was made up of Mexican and Asian parents. What were the aspects of that job that you liked best?" or "I see you studied at Wheelock in Boston. Tell us about that program." From these questions, it is possible to cull material that can be examined at greater depth. "You said you enjoyed working with the Parent Policy Committee in California. What did you do with that group that you think is applicable to this job?"

Interviewers can learn a great deal about the ways in which an educator candidate would fit into their program's program by posing hypothetical situations and asking questions such as, "What would you do if a child kicked you?" or "How would you work with a toddler who is not yet talking?" This type of question can produce ideas about curriculum, classroom management, parent involvement, staff relations, and understanding of the development of young children. Of course, the questions should relate to the job for which the person is applying. For example, a prospective cook might be asked, "What would you do if sandwiches were on today's menu, and the bread delivery had not been made by 10:00 a.m.?" A list of sample questions in **Director's Resource 8-6** can give you some ideas for questioning both degreed and nondegreed job candidates.

8-3i • Interview Setting

Before the interview, give careful thought to the setting:

- Will the candidate be as comfortable as possible?
- Will everyone be able to see and hear everyone else?
- Is the seating arrangement comfortable and planned so that desks or large tables do not separate the candidate from the interviewers?
- Is the interviewing room free from distractions?

Working Smart with Technology

Infants and Toddlers and Optimal Learning

In the video titled *Infants and Toddlers: Creating an Optimal Learning Environment*, a program director has moved the interview process from her office to a classroom. Watch as the candidate for a position in the program reveals her philosophy of children and knowledge of developmentally appropriate practice.

1. By extending the interview to the classroom, what is the director able to learn about the candidate that might not be evident in an interview confined to an office or conference room?

2. As the program director, now that you have heard the candidate's responses, what have you learned that can inform your decision as whether or not to hire this person? What do you still want to know?

Benefits for Infants and Toddlers

What not to ask when interviewing candidates

Subject	Questions Permissible to Ask in an Interview	Question to Avoid in an Interview
Name	Inquiry into whether an applicant's work records are under another name, for purposes of access to these records: "Have you worked for the university under a different name?"	A. Inquiry into any title that indicates race, color, religion, sex, national origin, handicap, age, or ancestry. B. To ask if a woman is a Miss, Mrs., or Ms.
National origin and citizenship	A. To indicate that the institution is an equal opportunity employer B. "What languages do you read, speak, or write fluently?" (This question is fine, as long as this ability is relevant to performance of the job.)	A. If native born or naturalized. B. Proof of citizenship before hiring. C. Whether parents or spouse are native-born or naturalized.
Age	Any inquiry limited to establishing that applicant meets any minimum age requirement that may be established by law.	A. Requiring birth certificate or baptismal record before hiring. B. Any inquiry that may reveal the date of high school graduation. C. Any other inquiry which may reveal whether applicant is at least 40 years of age.
Sex, gender, and sexual orientation	None	A. Any inquiry that would indicate sex. B. Any inquiry made of members of one sex but not the other.
Marital, parental, and family status	A. Whether an applicant can meet specified work schedules or has activities, commitments, and responsibilities that may hinder the meeting or work attendance requirements. "This job requires overtime occasionally; would you be able and willing to work overtime as necessary?" (This question is fine as long as all applicants for the job are asked consistently.) B. "Would you be willing to relocate as necessary?"	A. Before hiring to ask marital status: "What's your marital status (married, single, divorced, engaged)?" B. To ask the number or age of children, who cares for them, and applicant's plans to have more children. C. "Whom do you live with?" D. "Do you plan to have a family? When?" E. "How many kids do you have?" F. "What are your child care arrangements?"
Education	A. Inquiry into nature and extent of academic, professional, or vocational training. B. Inquiry into language skills, such as reading and writing of foreign languages if job related.	A. To ask the racial or religious affiliation of schools attended. B. Inquiry as to what mother tongue is or how foreign language ability was acquired.

FIGURE 8-10

Source: Reprinted with permission from the University of Dayton, Office of Human Resources.

Subject	Lawful	Unlawful
Work schedule	Inquiry into willingness or ability to work required work schedule.	Any inquiry into willingness or ability to work any religious holidays.
Religion or creed	Questions pertaining to the applicant's familiarity or interest in coming to work for a Catholic or Marianist institution.	A. Any inquiry that would indicate or identify religious denomination or custom of the applicant. B. Request pastor's recommendation or reference.
Organizations and affiliations	Inquiry into membership in professional organizations and offices held, excluding any organization, the name or character of which indicates the race, color, religion, sex, national origin, handicap, age, or ancestry of its members.	Inquiry into every club and organization where membership is held.
Personal and physical	Inquiries as to ability to perform actual job requirements.	Being a certain height or weight will not be considered a job requirement unless the employer can show that no employee with the ineligible height or weight could do the work.
Disabilities	To ask whether the applicant is capable of performing the essential functions of the job with reasonable accommodation. Note: This question may be asked after the interviewer thoroughly described the job and if all applicants are going to be asked in a consistent manner whether they are able to carry out all the necessary job assignments and perform them in a safe way.	A. Before hiring: to initiate questions regarding the specific accommodation needed. B. Inquire if job applicant is handicapped or ask about nature and severity of handicap: "Do you have any disability." C. "Have you had any operation or recent or past illnesses?"
Criminal record	Inquiries into conviction of specific crimes related to qualifications for the job applied for.	Any inquiry relating to arrests if not substantially related to functions and responsibilities of the particular job in question. "Have you ever been arrested?"
Military service	A. Inquiry into service in U.S. armed forces when such service is a qualification for the job. B. Require military discharge certificate after being hired.	A. Inquiry about the type of discharge. B. To request military service records. C. To ask about military service in armed service of another country.
References	To request general and work references not relating to race, color, religion, sex, or national or ethnic origin, age, disability, or marital status.	To request references specifically from clergy or any other person who might reflect race, color, religion, sex, or national origin, age, disability, or marital status.

FIGURE 8-10
(continued)

- Has the time of the interview been chosen appropriately so that everyone can focus on the interview instead of on the next appointment, and are all cell phones turned off?
- Is adequate time available for developing rapport and exploring details of the answers to the questions?
- Has provision been made to offer water or some refreshments to the candidate?

When the goal is to make applicants feel welcome and at ease, the interview setting becomes a matter of central concern. The interviewers are revealing to the candidate a major part of the program's culture and philosophy as they create an accepting environment for an interview and are more likely to obtain an accurate picture when the candidate is at ease.

The director sets the nonverbal tone for the interview by being relaxed and friendly. It is important to sit back, smile, and maintain an open posture with arms down in the lap and body facing the candidate.

8-3j • The Interview

At the beginning, candidates should be given some idea about the length of the interview and informed that there will be a time at the end of the interview to ask questions. Interviewers should be prepared to present information about the program's philosophy, the job, and the program, and they should clearly and honestly answer the applicant's questions. The interviewers should maintain eye contact and let the applicant do most of the talking. They can refer to

Growth Mindset Moment

Can you recall your first job interview? If so, you may be able to remember some of your reactions during that interview. Were you put at ease when you entered the room? Were you introduced to everyone before the questioning began? Did you feel the interviewers had prepared for the session by reviewing your résumé and credentials? Were you given time to ask questions? How did the interviewers close the interview? As you think about being interviewed and recall the stress you experienced, you will increase your sensitivity to an applicant's feelings.

the employment policies and clarify thoroughly the expectations regarding performance standards for the position.

The interviewers will look for an applicant who plans to stay with the program for many years because staff stability provides continuity for children and nurtures a sense of community at the program. Nonetheless, caution should be used about requesting any information in sensitive areas mentioned earlier. It is recommended that employment records be limited to that information relevant to employment decisions, and disclosures of that information to third parties should be strictly limited when not authorized by the candidate or employee. It is advisable that early childhood programs develop written policies and procedures concerning this issue. Also, because federal law provides only a portion of the employment discrimination picture, and many states have their own discrimination laws, it is wise to consult an attorney regarding applicable state laws for your program and to clear up uncertainties about the content of interview questions.

Interviewers should obtain as much information as possible during the interview, but note-taking or discussing the candidate's qualifications should be done after the interview. Some discussion about the candidate is useful, and reaching a group consensus serves a worthwhile purpose. Discussion provides the opportunity for interviewers to share their impression of the candidate as they draw on each other's perceptions. Confidentiality is a critical issue, and all committee members must understand that information on candidates and any committee discussion must be kept confidential.

8-3k • Teaching Interview

Observing an educator candidate in a classroom setting provides the committee with additional data on classroom presence and skills with children. Some candidates are able to give interviewers all they want to hear in an interview, but it becomes obvious they are not comfortable with children when observed in a classroom. It is unfair to have the regular classroom educator leave a new person alone in the classroom because of the anxiety that would be produced in both the candidate and the children, but a great deal can be learned by observing a prospective educator

Observing the candidate in a classroom setting provides the committee with data on rapport with children and classroom presence.

read a story to a few children or join a small group for snacks. Asking to see sample lesson plans, resource files, or picture files also provides useful information to the interview committee. Some programs select candidates from the substitute list or from among a pool of student teachers whom they know. In this case, the program staff will have worked with the candidate before the interview.

8-3l • Second Interview

A second interview for prospective candidates after the teaching interview can be helpful when there are several candidates with comparable training and credentials or when more information is needed before making the final hiring decision. Having a second interview also offers opportunities to discuss the teaching interview and to answer questions the candidate may have at this point in the interview hiring procedure. Additional questions that focus on the candidate's opinions and personal style also can be discussed at a second interview. **Director's Resource 8-6** gives sample interview questions for first and second interviews.

8-3m • Selecting the Employee

When interviewing is completed, the person or committee responsible for selecting the

employee uses material such as the employment policies and the job description, combined with all the information from the interview and the observation, to reach a final decision. All data are weighed and balanced until the best match among job description, current staff composition, and candidate qualifications is obtained. It also is important to review the nondiscrimination prohibitions in this decision-making process, especially if an applicant is disabled. An employer is not required to give preference to a qualified applicant with a disability over other applicants; however, the employer may not consider the candidate with disabilities unqualified if that person can perform the essential functions of the job. It may be helpful to have a second interview with selected candidates from the pool who seem best qualified for the position to further narrow down the choice. The procedure for making a decision should be clear to all interviewers. Will the director ultimately choose the employee? Will the director present two or three names to the board and have the board make the decision? If there is a board, will that group make the decision, or will the committee rule by majority vote? Generally, the director will make the decision, taking into account the recommendations of the interviewing committee. Final approval from the board sometimes is part of the hiring policy.

The selected candidate should be notified of the job offer by the director or the chairperson of the committee. On acceptance, the new employee may be asked to sign a contract stating the salary and the length of time covered by the contract, provided the employment policies do not state that all employees are employees at will. Immediately after the new employee has been informed of the job and accepted it, all other interviewees are informed of the selection, thanked for their interest, and told that their résumés will be kept on file in case another vacancy occurs.

8-4 • Retaining Staff

Hiring the staff is only part of the work **naeyc** to be done. Directors can put substantial effort into hiring a qualified staff, and efforts must be made to support new employees and maintain a positive work environment in order to retain an effective staff.

8-4a • Employee Orientation

The director is responsible for introducing the new employee to the work environment. The new person will need to know where to find work space, what storage facilities and materials are available, and what schedule is to be followed. A tour of the building and introductions to all other staff members, either during the tour or at a staff meeting shortly thereafter, are essential to the orientation procedure. The person who conducts the tour and makes the introductions sets the tone for the employee's future interpersonal relationships with other staff members. Each staff member has an obligation to become involved with making the new employee's transition to the staff position as smooth and satisfying as possible.

The new employee also should be introduced to parents at the earliest possible time. Some directors notify parents of staff additions or changes by mail; others use their bulletin boards, email, website, or newsletters; and still others introduce the new member informally as the occasion arises or at a regularly scheduled meeting.

During the initial weeks of employment, it is important for the director to check with the new staff member to answer any questions and make a conscious effort to build a positive relationship. At the same time, the director can continue to reiterate expectations and expand on ways to follow and implement the program philosophy. A carefully planned staff orientation program can promote better staff relationships and reduce staff turnover. A written staff orientation plan document is required as part of the human resource development system for the PAS.

Sometimes, it is difficult for the director to be available to the new educator often enough. It can be helpful to establish a mentor program or assign a staff member to watch over the new staff person. Mentors can help new staff with basic orientation questions such as where to find and file various forms and introduce them to all staff and support people such as the van driver and custodian. Mentors also can provide new staff with information about special talents of other educators, such as planning effective group times, planning and carrying out smooth transitions, or making challenging math games. A mentoring system assists the director with orientation of new staff and enriches and enhances the self-esteem of the mentor (Turner, 2020).

It also helps for the director to leave a note in the educator's box asking questions such as, "What went well today?" or "What did I miss today in your room that you would like to share with me?" The director also might leave a message about being available the next day at nap time or a plan to stop in before lunch to see how things are going. These steps help make the new educator feel that the director really is available to give support and help.

Some programs have handbooks for each employee. In corporate programs, the parent firm may prepare a handbook for use in all programs, whether franchised or run by the corporation. Guidelines in this handbook may detail how many children should be permitted in blocks or dramatic play at any given time, or exactly how the daily cleaning is to be done by the classroom educators. However,

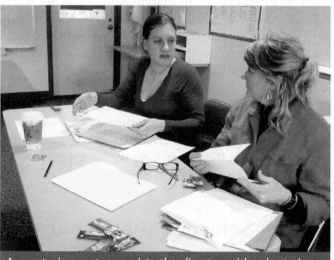

A mentoring system assists the director with orientation of new staff.

handbooks are rarely that detailed and usually do not include expectations for educators to clean the premises. More often, they include items such as the following:

- philosophy of the program,
- bylaws of the board (if applicable),
- employment policies,
- policies and procedures for the children's program,
- copies of forms used by the program,
- information about the community the program serves,
- information about the staff (job titles, home addresses, telephone numbers, etc.), and
- NAEYC Code of Ethical Conduct (see **Appendix A**).

A handbook is useful because it gives everyone a common reference point and provides new employees with materials that familiarize them with the program.

8-4b • Handling Turnover

Each year, approximately 30 percent of the early childhood workforce changes jobs or leaves the field altogether. Such instability in the early childhood workforce has a negative impact on quality (Gable, Rothrauff, Thornburg, & Mauzy, 2007). It is estimated that staff turnover has a minimum cost of $3,000 for each lost employee. Programs cannot afford the high cost of staff turnover, especially when turnover results not only in financial costs but also damage to employee morale, customer satisfaction, and program image (Hamrick, 2000).

Growth Mindset Moment

Perhaps you can recall your first day as a new student or employee in an early childhood program. How did you feel on that first day? What else do you wish you had known about the program? Do you recall what it was like not to know where the extra paper towels were kept or how awkward it was when you could not find the easel paper? As you recall those feelings, consider what you would tell a new educator in your program if you were responsible for orienting the new employees.

Although some people would say low wages and poor benefits are the major causes, it is important to recognize that there are many different ways to think about turnover. As Hamrick (2000) points out, poor hiring decisions are a major factor, along with compensation concerns.

In making hiring decisions, take time to reflect on what type of person would best fit the position. What are you looking for in this person in terms of the fit?

- the program culture?
- the parent group?
- the support staff?
- the teaching staff?
- the administrative staff?

The first step in reducing turnover is to hire the right people. Collins (2005) emphasizes how important it is to "get the right people on the bus." He goes on to point out that it is often difficult to "get the wrong people off the bus," thus making it doubly important to get the right ones on in the first place.

Although compensation and careful hiring have an impact on turnover, they are not the only factors affecting staff stability. Evidence suggests that highly trained educators are more likely to remain at their jobs. It follows that these educators are usually compensated at a higher level and work with other highly trained staff who are also inclined to stay with a job. These qualified staff people are also more often in accredited programs, and there is evidence that accredited programs have a more stable workforce and less turnover.

Finding dollars to offer the kind of wages and benefits to keep qualified staff is difficult. Although some staff turnover is inevitable, and some may even allow for positive changes, much of the time the loss of a staff member is disappointing and traumatic for the families, children, and staff who remain.

The director's task is to try to reduce staff turnover by attending to variables that can be adjusted and changed. A few inexpensive perks might compensate staff and help them feel good about their job. Consider the following:

- flex time,
- treats in the staff lounge for break times,

- occasional personal use of the office copier (limits are necessary here),
- token gifts for birthdays and other special days, and
- opportunities to attend conferences as well as take additional education courses.

This last item does involve some cost to the program, but there may be tax breaks for this benefit (check with your tax adviser or attorney).

Striving to give staff higher wages and more benefits is worthy, but stabilizing the workforce by refining hiring practices, improving the work environment, and making sure a thorough orientation plan is in place for all new hires can all be done without great cost. Because there are no magic solutions to solving the problem of staff retention, directors are almost always involved at some level in looking for and hiring new staff.

8-4c • Work Environment

Work environment is an inclusive term that covers the physical space and, more important for our purposes, the interpersonal climate—that is, relationships with coworkers. An involved director constantly evaluates the quality of the work environment and makes adjustments when possible. (See Chapter 15 for more discussion on evaluating work environment.) Sometimes, alterations in the physical environment are costly and can happen only if the budget allows. However, adjustments can be made to alter other aspects of the work environment with little or no added expense. For example, it is vital that every staff member feels respected and valued. Offering staff opportunities to write for the newsletter, help with the design and equipment choices for the new playground, join an advocacy group, or serve on the committee to plan the program's tenth anniversary celebration are but a few ways staff can feel a sense of ownership in the program's total program. Pride, commitment, and collegiality abound among those who share ownership in a successful enterprise.

"In early childhood we tend to spend very little time on adult development. We are often more democratic and participatory in spirit with children than we are among ourselves" (Whitebrook & Bellm, 1999). Although classroom educators are encouraged to help children solve problems, resolve conflicts, and make decisions, in some programs major decisions are made by administrators with minimal input from staff, even though they are much affected by those decisions. Adults who are accustomed to top-down management may initially need a lot of support and encouragement from the director, who really wants active participation in writing articles, planning program events, leading staff meetings, or joining focus groups. When staff are invited to help plan meeting agendas and submit their questions and concerns for group meetings, they feel valued and important to the organization. When directors seek staff participation in decision-making and help educators feel valued,

Making the Case for *Growing Your Own Leaders*

Many leaders in the field of early childhood started out as educators. Characteristics that allow educators to guide the behavior of young children and manage a classroom often do not translate to the supervision of adults and management of an early childhood program. Likewise, bringing in administrators who have developed their management skills outside of the field of early childhood can result in leadership that does not grasp the nuances of a developmentally appropriate practice in an early childhood setting. Many have found that understanding the distinctive complexities of early care and education is critical to being a successful director, and developing leadership skills within existing staff is the most effective approach (Childcare Exchange, 2016). This notion of being intentional and growing your own leaders can lead to job satisfaction in the staff as new skills are developed and opportunities for career advancement are made available.

they are nurturing loyalty and commitment in the work environment.

Issues of race, class, and culture are aspects of the work environment that impact interpersonal relationships and can affect staff turnover. Directors like to describe their programs as color blind, but on careful analysis of the reasons for turnover, they may find that issues of class, color, or culture contributed to friction that led to resignations. Constant attention to open communication with a focus on understanding and acceptance of diversity is essential because diversity can never be taken for granted.

8-4d • Exit Interview Questionnaire

It is important for the director to try to understand the cause of turnover. One approach to collect this information is the exit survey or interview. Some turnover situations result in strained relationships

> ### Growth Mindset Moment
>
> Think about the best and worst jobs you ever had. What made you stay with the best one? What made it appealing? What was bad about the worst job? How much were your feelings about the best and worst jobs affected by the relationships you had with other adults in the setting?

in which the exiting staff member is unlikely to participate in an open and sincere exit interview or complete and return a survey. However, many exiting staff members leave the program on good terms and are willing to provide feedback about the factors that led to their decision. It is important to try to get information from both disgruntled former employees and those who left the program on good terms. Whether using an exit interview or survey, careful thought needs to be given to the types of questions to be asked.

Summary

The importance of good interpersonal relationships and trust within a program cannot be overstated. Only through a feeling of community and a spirit of cooperation can a director create a supportive environment in which both adults and children can grow to their fullest potential. There must be a strong element of acceptance and positive regard in the surrounding climate to establish a mutually helping relationship for staff, families, and children. It is the responsibility of the director as a leader to serve as a model of caring and respect for others in order to build a strong sense of community among all the diverse people involved in the program. Effective interpersonal communication among the staff members, children, and families also is an important

basic element in creating a supportive, comfortable environment at a program, and it is up to the director to be the model of good communication to create an atmosphere of openness, warmth, and acceptance. To successfully staff an early childhood program, directors must do the following:

- discuss ways to create a positive climate and motivate staff,
- describe the major sections of an employment policy,
- explain the steps in the hiring process, and
- identify and implement strategies that facilitate staff retention.

TRY IT OUT!

1. In small groups, discuss how you can motivate your staff.
   a. List five effective motivating factors directors can control.
   b. Compare the lists produced by the small groups, and develop a final list of strategies (that do not cost money) to encourage staff and enrich jobs.

2. Think about yourself as the director of a program where you have observed or taught. Based on your understanding of the use of encouragement as a motivator, write an appropriately phrased positive acknowledgment for
   a. the administrative assistant,
   b. the nutrition specialist,
   c. the custodian, and
   d. a volunteer.

3. **Directors Resources 8-2** and **8-3** provide information about staffing schedules and costs. The Power to the Profession's Unifying Framework (2020) states that employees who work in the field of early childhood education need a living wage. Looking at these staffing tables, how might a director cut staffing costs while maintaining a quality program?

Examine the Bombeck Center Handbook in **Director's Resource 8-1** and use the information to create an outline for an orientation or onboarding program for new employees.

4. **Director's Resource 8-4** includes a performance evaluation that is tied to a position description. What are the advantages of this evaluation format? What are the disadvantages?

5. Review the job description for the Early Childhood Educator III in **Director's Resource 8-5** and develop a list of questions that would be appropriate to ask candidates applying for the job.
   a. Select three class members to serve as interviewers of applicants for the ECE III. Select one class member as a candidate for the position.
   b. After the three interviewers review the candidate's application for the position, have them role-play an interview with the candidate using the questions that the team developed.
   c. After the interview, have all class members participate in summarizing the candidate's qualifications for the job.

Director's Resource 8-1

BOMBECK FAMILY LEARNING CENTER HANDBOOK

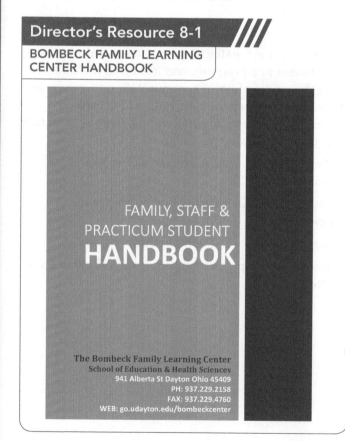

FAMILY, STAFF & PRACTICUM STUDENT
HANDBOOK

The Bombeck Family Learning Center
School of Education & Health Sciences
941 Alberta St Dayton Ohio 45409
PH: 937.229.2158
FAX: 937.229.4760
WEB: go.udayton.edu/bombeckcenter

Director's Resource 8-1 (continued)

Table of Contents

Director's Resource 8-1 (continued)

What We Believe

The Characteristics of a Marianist University

Marianist Universities Educate for Service, Justice and Peace

The Marianist approach to higher education is deeply committed to the common good. The intellectual life itself is undertaken as a form of service in the interest of justice and peace, and the university curriculum is designed to connect the classroom with the wider world. In addition, Marianist universities extend a special concern for the poor and marginalized and promote the dignity, rights, and responsibilities of all peoples (2006, p. 27).

As part of a Catholic, Marianist university, we readily adapt and change with the times. We build communities of faith and educate in what we call a "family spirit." We provide an integral, high-quality education on a campus that's known for its hospitality and inclusiveness.

The Bombeck Center Commitment to Community

Three foundational elements represent who we are and define how we interact.

- **Respect**—We are a community of learners in an environment of respect for children, families, staff, early childhood faculty, and students.
- **Reflective Practice**—Quality care and education requires conscious reflection of the people, policies, and practice that takes place.
- **Research**—We base our practice on a sound understanding of the rich historical research in early childhood that has determined best practices for working with children.

Director's Resource 8-1 (continued)

Mission Statement

Provide high-quality early care and education for young children while demonstrating assessment-supported, child-centered, emergent, science-focused, and integrated curriculum.

Vision Statement

Work together as reflective decision makers who seek to improve the quality of care and education for young children by mentoring early childhood graduate and undergraduate students and sharing research-supported practice with the larger early childhood community.

Goal 1 – Promote the optimum social, emotional, physical motor and health, cognitive development, and approaches to learning of the children at the center.

Goal 2 – Promote the professional development of early childhood students in the University of Dayton's School of Education and Health Sciences.

Goal 3 – Provide professional development opportunities for the Bombeck Family Learning Center staff and the greater early care and education community.

Goal 4 – Advocate for children, their families, and the profession in community and society.

Goal 5 – Model the Catholic Marianist tradition of faith formation, service, adaptation, and change by providing, in the family spirit, a quality education for children, teacher candidates, and staff.

Director's Resource 8-1 (continued)

Philosophy Statement

We are dedicated to giving our full attention to the needs of all the children for whom we provide care and educate. We believe that positive experiences for infants, toddlers, and young children are critical to healthy development and that these experiences serve as the foundation for future development and learning. Our philosophy is based on the work as such classic early childhood theorists as Ainsworth, Bandura, Bowlby, Bronfenbrenner, Erikson, Gerber, Honig, Montessori, Partens, Piaget, and Vygotski. We have learned from prominent early childhood approaches such as the Project Approach (Katz and Chard) and the programs of Reggio Emilia, Italy. We believe that children benefit from practices that are well grounded in research. We also strive to maintain a program where diverse children and families are welcome and engaged. We believe in the following developmental principles:

1. Each child's uniqueness is the result of interplay between genetic and environmental factors. Child development involves interrelated physical, cognitive, emotional, and social changes. Rates of development vary from one child to another, but the sequential progression of growth does not.
2. With these principles in mind, we believe that infants, toddlers, and young children are individuals in their own right and must receive the same respect and consideration afforded to older children and adults.

Director's Resource 8-1 (continued)

3. We believe that it is our responsibility to provide responsive care and responsible guidance where strong social and emotional development is promoted and modeled. Furthermore, we are committed to providing a developmentally appropriate environment in order to nurture growth in all areas of development, while treating each child as a whole person.
4. We believe that it is the job of adults to provide children with enticing and accurate learning experiences that are based on sound content knowledge and developmentally appropriate practices. Our science-focused curriculum is intentional, integrated, inclusive, inquiry- based, and innovative.

Director's Resource 8-2

STAFFING SCHEDULES

Classroom	Full-Time Staff Arrive			Lunch and Nap					Staff Depart		
				Children Eat 11:45 – 12:30 Staff Lunch			Children Nap 12:30–3:00 Plan				
	7:30	8:30	10:00	11:00	12:00	1:00	2:00	3:30	4:30	5:00	6:00
Young Infants	A	B	C	A	B	C	ABC	A	B		C
	Part-time teacher D arrives at 11:00 and departs at 5:00										
Older Infants	A	B	C	A	B	C	ABC	A	B		C
	Part-time teacher D arrives at 11:00 and departs at 5:00										
Toddlers	A	B	C	A	B	C	ABC	A	B		C
	Part-time teacher D arrives at 11:00 and departs at 5:00										
Preschool 1	A	B	C	A	B	C	ABC	A	B		C
	Part-time teacher D arrives at 11:00 and departs at 5:00										
Preschool 2	A	B	C	A	B	C	ABC	A	B		C
	Part-time teacher D arrives at 11:00 and departs at 5:00										

A = Teacher A
B = Teacher B
C = Teacher C
D = Part-time teacher arrives at 11:00 a.m. to help with lunch and cover nap time so that teacher can plan and attend meetings. He or she departs around 5:00 p.m. when ratios allow.

TeachSource Digital Download

Director's Resource 8-3 (continued)

Staff Plan by Classroom

Classroom	No. of Children	Staff–Child Ratio
Infants	8	Required: 4:1 Maximum: 8:3
Rm: 101 Toddlers	11	Minimum: 8:2 Required: 7:1 Maximum: 11:3
Rm: 201 2- and 3-year-olds	17	Minimum: 11:2 Required: 12:1 Maximum: 17:3
Rm: 202 3- and 4-year-olds	17	Minimum: 17:2 Required: 12:1 Maximum: 17:3
Rm: 203 4-year-olds	17	Minimum: 17:2 Required: 14:1 Maximum: 14:3
Rm: 204		Minimum: 14:2

ECE Educator III	7:30 a.m.–3:00 p.m.
ECE Educator I	11:00 a.m.–7:00 p.m.
ECE Educator I	7:30 a.m.–12:30 p.m.
ECE Educator I	12:30–7:00 p.m.

This flexible schedule allows ample time for classroom planning in the morning and evening when the ratios will be

TeachSource Digital Download

Director's Resource 8-3

SAMPLE STAFFING PLAN— MULTIPLE PROGRAM B

Staff Plan by Staff Member

Title	How Many	Schedule	Recommended Salary	Total Yearly
Director or Administrator	1	MWF 7:30 a.m.– TTH 12:00 p.m.	$50.000/yr	$50,000
ECE Educator IIIs	5	7:30–3:00 p.m. 30-min. break between 12:00 p.m. and 1:30 p.m.	$17/hr $30,940/yr	$154,700
ECE Educator IIs	5	11:00–7:00 p.m. 30-min. break between 1:00 p.m. and 2:30 p.m.	$ 16.00/hr $29,120/yr	$145,600
Morning ECE Educator I	5	7:30–12:30 p.m. 15-min. break between 11:00 a.m. and 12:00 p.m.	$15.00/hr $18,750/yr	$93,750
Afternoon ECE Educator I	5	12:30–7:00 p.m. 15-min. break between 2:30 p.m. and 3:00 p.m.	$15.00/hr $18,750/yr	$93,750
Secretary/ Bookkeeper	1	9:00 a.m.–5:00 p.m. 1-hr. lunch	$16.00/hr $29,120/yr	$29,120
Custodian	1	6:00 p.m.–9:00 p.m. Mon.–Thur. 5 hrs. on Sat. 15-min. break	$15.00/hr $12,750/yr	$12,750
Nutrition Specialist	1	7:00 a.m.–3:00 p.m. 1-hr. lunch	$16.00/hr $29,120/yr	$29,120
Total Yearly Salaries:				$288,210

TeachSource Digital Download

Director's Resource 8-3 (continued)

low because most children arrive at the center between 8:00 and 9:00 a.m. and leave between 5:00 and 6:00 p.m. Nap time is when team planning and communication takes place.

Additional Comments about Staffing

- Breaks must maintain staff-to-child ratio at all times.
- Flexibility in scheduling breaks is necessary to meet the immediate needs of the classrooms.
- Short restroom breaks or emergency phone calls could be arranged as needed, as long as the ratio is maintained.
- Staff schedules are designed for enhancing staff communications and for meeting the needs of the children.
- Swing scheduling for directors is designed to encourage and maintain communication with all staff members, family members, board, and community contacts.
- It is the teacher's responsibility to take care of housekeeping emergencies during the day.
- The cook is solely responsible for cleaning the kitchen, other than the cleanup after the afternoon snack, which is the teacher's responsibility.
- One morning snack, one afternoon snack, and one full meal will be provided each day.

TeachSource Digital Download

Director's Resource 8-3 *(continued)*

- Encourage male applicants for all positions to balance male–female models.
- Parents or surrogates provide transportation.
- Tuition is $205/week for infants and $185/week for all others.
- Eighty percent of tuition income goes for salaries.

Director's Resource 8-4

UNIVERSITY OF DAYTON

ECE II Name:		Eval completed by:							Date:
Bombeck Center Early Childhood Educator IIs will	**Expectations Not Met**		**Expectations Partially Met**		**Meets Expectations**		**Exceeds Expectations**		
	ECE II	Director	ECE II	Director	ECE II	Director	ECE II	Director	
1. Adhere to the NAEYC Code of Professional Conduct									
Comments:									
2. Learn **5% of time**									
a. Attend professional development sessions that address the needs and/or interest of the teacher, teaching team and that satisfy the requirements for accreditation, licensure, and QIRS/SUTQ rating.									
b. Actively and positively participate in center-sponsored meetings and professional development.									
c. Complete a personal professional development plan and monitor progress to completion.									
d. Engage in reflective supervision as a means to learn about and reflect on their practice, the practice of their peers, and the practice of the ECE students who they mentor.									
e. Accept constructive feedback and implement strategies for professional growth.									
f. Keep teaching team informed of new information from professional development, and collaborate with team to infuse current information throughout classroom practice.									
Comments:									

Director's Resource 8-4 *(continued)*

Bombeck Center Early Childhood Educator IIs will	Expectations Not Met		Expectations Partially Met		Meets Expectations		Exceeds Expectations	
	ECE II	Director	ECE II	Director	ECE II	ECE II	Director	Director
3. Collaborate 5% of time								
a. Demonstrate a value for collaboration by consistently engaging in team decision-making and problem solving.								
b. Disagree respectfully and utilize effective conflict resolution strategies to address differences of opinion.								
c. Demonstrate a growth mindset and adjust to change.								
d. Maintain positive center climate that fosters job satisfaction of individuals and a strong educational team.								
Comments:								
4. Plan 5% of time								
a. Plan collaboratively with others in the teaching team to create a cohesive, play-based, child-centered, emergent, and age-appropriate curriculum.								
b. Observe children to identify their interests and base instructional decisions, in part, on those interests.								
c. Use the *ACCESS* assessment system to document leaning and inform instruction.								
d. Integrate the *Ohio Early Learning and Development Standards* throughout the day using authentic materials and experiences.								
e. Use the *ACCESS Science Concept Planner* to plan science-focused investigations or mini-investigations and share with administration before an investigation begins.								
f. Collaborate with the educational team to construct intentional learning opportunities during daily routines.								
Comments:								

Director's Resource 8-4 *(continued)*

Bombeck Center Early Childhood Educator IIs will	Expectations Not Met		Expectations Partially Met		Meets Expectations		Exceeds Expectations	
	ECE II	Director	ECE II	Director	ECE II	Director	ECE II	Director
5. Implement: 66% of time								
a. Maintain a clean, safe, organized, and engaging classroom environment throughout each day.								
b. Work with the teaching team to implement the ACCESS Curriculum.								
c. Work with the teaching team to support emotional development, self-regulation, and mental health of children through such techniques as Conscious Discipline.								
d. Work with the teaching team to make decisions about daily routines, room arrangement, and select appropriate and safe materials that align with the curriculum.								
Comments:								
6. Assess/Document 2% of time								
a. Use a deep understanding of child development to observe children and identify what they know and are able to do.								
b. Take pictures, write anecdotal notes, and collect work samples to document learning and development.								
c. Compile documentation using check sheets, portfolio forms and/or the whole class tracking system as appropriate for the age.								
d. Maintain portfolios for each child by adding two entries each month for each child.								
Comments:								

Director's Resource 8-4 *(continued)* /////

Bombeck Center Early Childhood Educator IIs will	Expectations Not Met		Expectations Partially Met		Meets Expectations		Exceeds Expectations	
	ECE II	Director	ECE II	Director	ECE II	Director	ECE II	Director
7. Communicate 2% of time								
a. Maintain open and ongoing communication with the teaching team to ensure that the program is cohesive and								
b. intentional so that all members of the teaching team understanding what is being done and why.								
c. Maintain responsive, friendly and respectful communication with families during drop off and pick up times and as needed throughout the day.								
d. Use MomentPath daily to keep track of teacher-child ratios, document learning and to communicate with families.								
e. Engage families in routine, scheduled conferences with the families of children in their group.								
Comments:								
8. Mentor 5% of time								
a. Model and explain classroom routines and the *ACCESS Curriculum* to ECE students.								
b. Answer questions about classroom practice and support ECE students to develop as teachers and to complete their course assignments effectively in the classroom.								
c. Participate in midterm and end of term performance evaluations with each of their assigned ECE students.								
d. Inform the EDT 211 and 212 lab coordinator when students are not meeting expectations and support intervention plans as needed.								
Comments:								

Director's Resource 8-4 *(continued)*

Bombeck Center Early Childhood Educator IIs will	Expectations Not Met		Expectations Partially Met		Meets Expectations		Exceeds Expectations	
	ECE II	Director	ECE II	Director	ECE II	Director	ECE II	Director
9. Demonstrate 2% of time								
a. Explain classroom practice to visitors to the classroom/center.								
Comment:								
10. Other duties 3% of time								
a. As assigned by the director, executive director, and/or school or University leadership.								
Comment:								
Growth Mindset Goals:								

Signatures: _____   _____   Date: _____

         EC Educator II   Director

Director's Resource 8-5

JOB DESCRIPTION

Working Title: Early Childhood Educator III-a

Full time, 12 months, 1,820 hours, 7 hours per day, one of the following shifts: 7:30 to 3:00; 8:30 to 4:30, or 10:00 to 6:00

Position Summary

The purpose of this position is to coordinate an educational team to plan, implement, and evaluate a high-quality curriculum for infants, toddlers, or preschoolers. All members of the team are responsible for creating and maintaining a high-quality learning and environment that adheres to the NAEYC Statement of Developmentally Appropriate Practice and the NAEYC Code of Ethical Conduct.

Early childhood educators work with their educational team to provide high-quality early care and education for infants, toddlers, and preschoolers. They will demonstrate an understanding of the code of ethical conduct for early childhood and incorporate ethical conduct throughout their practice. Teachers will engage in collaborative planning and critical reflection to maintain classrooms where the environment, curriculum, and responsive interactions are intentional and based on the most current research of the field. They will provide a positive climate for children, families, early childhood students, and team members where differences are valued and a growth mindset is required. All members of the teaching team will actively engage children and maintain classroom organization and routines using play-based and child-centered pedagogies. They will work together to support social and emotional development that fosters positive behavior and grows children's brains. Teachers will provide responsive care and with quality feedback so that children understand concepts deeply, engage in inquiry, and establish a love of learning. All members of the teaching team will mentor and evaluate early childhood students and provide them with the feedback needed to grow in their development as early childhood professionals.

The Early Childhood Educator level V is required to have advanced skills in collaboration, team decision-making, mentoring, and role release to foster a creative and caring environment for children, early childhood students, families, and their colleagues. At a university-affiliated demonstration school, the Early Childhood Educator V will use professional writing and technology skills to document exemplary practice and share it with center families and the university community as well as early childhood professionals locally, regionally, nationally, and internationally.

This position requires an understanding of the current research that informs best practice and work with the teaching team to collaboratively adjust practice as warranted. Also required are the skills to work with the program leadership to support the development of team members as they grow as early childhood professionals.

Minimum Qualifications

Holds a master's degree in early childhood education, early childhood leadership and advocacy, or a related field focusing on young children.

Has at least 2 years of teaching experience with infants, toddlers, or preschoolers.

Demonstrates understanding of child care licensing requirements and safety protocols.

Demonstrates understanding of developmentally appropriate practice that is child centered and play based.

Demonstrates understanding of Quality Rating and Improvement Systems such as Step up to Quality.

Respects individual differences in children, families, and peers.

Demonstrates understanding of the collaboration skills needed to work effectively as part of an educational team.

Demonstrates understanding of culturally responsive practice with children, families, and peers.

Demonstrates the ability to communicate effectively orally and in writing.

Demonstrates a high level of professionalism.

Is proficient in Microsoft Office Suite, Google Mail, docs, and forms.

Can conduct database searches to find research that informs practice.

Is familiar with computer-based learning management systems and social media tools.

Preferred Qualifications

Has more than 2 years teaching experience with infants, toddlers, and preschoolers.
Has experience teaching an integrated, project-based, emergent, and science, technology, engineering, and math curriculum.
Has experience with reflective supervision or other mentoring or coaching models.

Duties and Responsibilities by Position with Percentage of Time by Position

ECE III-a   Master's degree in early childhood or related field
ECE III-b   Bachelor's degree in early childhood or related field
ECE II   Associate's degree in early childhood
ECE I   Child Development Associate (CDA) in either preschool or infant and toddler, high school diploma, or equivalent
Part-time substitute   High school diploma
Full-time floater   High school diploma

Director's Resource 8-5 (continued)

Bombeck Center Early Childhood Educators will	Percent of Time by Rank					
	ECE III-a	ECE III-b	ECII	ECI	PT Sub	FT Floater
1. Adhere to the NAEYC Code of Professional Conduct	X	X	X	X	X	X
2. Learn: % of time	10	10	10	10	5	5
a. Attend professional development sessions that address the needs or interest of the teacher and teaching team and that satisfy the requirements for accreditation, licensure, and Quality Rating and Improvement System or Step Up to Quality rating.	X	X	X	X	X	X
b. Actively and positively participate in center-sponsored meetings and professional development.	X	X	X	X	X	X
c. Complete a personal professional development plan and monitor progress to completion.	X	X	X	X	X	X
d. Engage in reflective supervision as a means to learn about and reflect on their practice, the practice of their peers, and the practice of the ECE students who they mentor.	X	X	X	X		
e. Accept constructive feedback and implement strategies for professional growth.	X	X	X	X	X	X
f. Keep teaching team informed of new information from professional development, and collaborate with team to infuse current information throughout classroom practice.	X	X	X	X		
3. Collaborate: % of time	15	15	15	15	15	15
a. Demonstrate a value for collaboration by consistently engaging in team decision-making and problem-solving.	X	X	X	X	X	X
b. Disagree respectfully and utilize effective conflict-resolution strategies to address differences of opinion.	X	X	X	X	X	X
c. Demonstrate a growth mindset and adjust to change.	X	X	X	X	X	X
d. Maintain positive center climate that fosters job satisfaction of individuals and a strong educational team.	X	X	X	X	X	X
4. Plan: % of time	10	10	10	10	0	0
a. Plan collaboratively with others in the teaching team to create a cohesive, play-based, child-centered, emergent, and age-appropriate curriculum.	X	X	X	X		
b. Observe children to identify their interests and base instructional decisions, in part, on those interests.	X	X	X	X		
c. Use the ACCESS assessment system to document leaning and inform instruction.	X	X	X	X		
d. Integrate the Ohio Early Learning and Development Standards throughout the day using authentic materials and experiences.	X	X	X	X		
e. Use the ACCESS Science Concept Planner to plan science-focused investigations or mini-investigations and share with administration before an investigation begins.	X	X	X	X		

Director's Resource 8-5 (continued) ///

f. Collaborate with the educational team to construct intentional learning opportunities during daily routines.	X	X	X	X		
5. Implement: % of time	15	25	30	40	72	72
a. Maintain a clean, safe, organized, and engaging classroom environment throughout each day.	X	X	X	X	X	X
b. Work with the teaching team to implement the ACCESS curriculum.	X	X	X	X	X	X
c. Work with the teaching team to support emotional development, self-regulation, and mental health of children through such techniques as conscious discipline.	X	X	X	X	X	X
d. Work with the teaching team to make decisions about daily routines and room arrangement and select appropriate and safe materials that align with the curriculum.	X	X	X	X		
e. Ensure that all members of the teaching team understand their roles and responsibilities in engaging with children and implementing the curriculum.	X	X				
6. Assess and document: % of time	10	10	8	5	0	0
a. Use a deep understanding of child development to observe children and identify what they know and are able to do.	X	X	X	X		
b. Take pictures, write anecdotal notes, and collect work samples to document learning and development.	X	X	X	X		
c. Compile documentation using check sheets, portfolio forms, or the whole class tracking system as appropriate for the age.	X	X				
d. Maintain portfolios for each child by adding two entries each month for each child.	X	X				
e. Maintain the classroom documentation board to share children's work and teachers' intentionality in planning.	X	X				
7. Communicate: % of time	10	10	7	5	3	3
a. Maintain open and ongoing communication with the teaching team to ensure that the program is cohesive and intentional so that all members of the teaching team understand what is being done and why.	X	X	X	X	X	X
b. Maintain responsive, friendly, and respectful communication with families during drop-off and pick-up times and as needed throughout the day.	X	X	X	X	X	X
c. Use Moment Path daily to keep track of teacher–child ratios and to communicate with families.	X	X	X	X	X	X
d. Engage families in routine, scheduled conferences with the families of children in their group.	X	X	X	X		
e. Create a classroom communication system that meets the needs of families and provides opportunities for two-way communication and family engagement.	X	X				

Director's Resource 8-5 (continued)

f. Compile data, work with administration and the teaching team to handle challenging situations, design interventions, make referrals, and handle difficult conversations with families when needed.	X	X				
8. Mentor: % of time	10	10	10	10	1	1
a. Model and explain classroom routines and the ACCESS curriculum to ECE students.	X	X	X	X	X	X
b. Answer questions about classroom practice and support ECE students to develop as teachers and to complete their course assignments effectively in the classroom.	X	X	X	X		
c. Participate in midterm and end-of-term performance evaluations with each of their assigned ECE students.	X	X	X	X		
d. Inform the EDT 211 and 212 lab coordinators when students are not meeting expectations and support intervention plans as needed.	X	X	X	X		
9. Demonstrate: % of time	15	10	5	1	0	0
a. Explain classroom practice to visitors to the classroom or center.	X	X	X	X		
b. Compile examples of Bombeck Center practice that can be used to demonstrate the curriculum and articulate the practices of the Bombeck Center Family Learning Center as a demonstration school.	X	X	X			
c. Explore the current research of the field, state, and national trends and share new information with the teaching teams, ECE students, and broader early childhood communication.	X	X				
d. Create Ohio-approved professional development programs, both face-to-face and online in order to share the practice of the Bombeck Center.	X					
e. Support the initiatives of the Center for Early Learning, including but not limited to sponsored projects, contracts, and initiatives.	X					
10. Other duties: % of time	5	5	5	4	4	4
a. As assigned by the director, executive director, or school or university leadership.	X	X	X	X	X	X

Physical Demands

Balancing:	Frequently
Carrying:	Frequently
Climbing:	Occasionally
Crawling:	Frequently
Crouching:	Occasionally
Handling:	Constantly
Hearing:	Constantly
Kneeling:	Occasionally
Lifting:	Frequently
Pulling:	Frequently
Pushing:	Frequently
Sitting:	Constantly
Standing:	Constantly
Talking:	Constantly
Vision:	Distinguish color, depth, close vision: Frequently
Walking:	Constantly

Work in noisy areas (above 85 decibels): Rarely
Sedentary work—exerting 10 pounds: Constantly
Light work—exerting up to 20 pounds: Frequently
Medium work—exerting 20–50 pounds: Frequently
Heavy work—exerting 50–100 pounds: Rarely
Very heavy work—exerting in excess of 100 pounds: N/A

Equipment

Machines, tools, equipment, electronic devices, communication devices, software: Copy machine, computer, surface pro, laminator, security monitors, LCD projector, IPAD, camera

Other Knowledge

Is the ability to read and understand simple instructions required to perform the essential duties of the position? Yes
Is the ability to write a simple sentence or a series of numbers, names, and addresses required to perform the essential duties of the position? Yes
Is a driver's license or other type of license required to perform the essential duties of this position? No
Does this position require a National Agency Check? Yes
Does this position require a security clearance? No
Does this position require use of a university vehicle, rental car, golf cart, or forklift on a regular basis? No

Director's Resource 8-6

INTERVIEW QUESTIONS

Be intentional in choosing interview questions. Identify the attributes that you are seeking. Remember that candidates' priorities and beliefs are typically part of who they are and will be difficult to change after hiring. Consider starting with a "Grand Tour" statement that can give insight into what is most important to the applicant. It can also put the applicant at ease and give the interviewer ideas for good follow-up questions.

What applicants believe about early care and education will likely drive their actions. Consider asking questions that uncover what the applicants believe about themselves, children, families, their role in a team, and the field of early care and education.

It is common to ask applicants about their education and experience. Also try to access their level of commitment to the profession. One way to find out more about this is to see how well prepared they were for the interview. Commitment can often be predicted by how well applicants can answer questions about their future in the field of early care and education.

The following are examples of questions or statement prompts that are designed to gain different types of information.

Sample "Grand Tour" Prompts

Tell me about yourself.

Describe your experience with children.

Belief Questions

What do you wish the public knew about early care and education?

How do you think children learn best?

What do you believe is important for a teaching team to be effective?

Describe the ideal relationship between families and educators in an early care and education setting.

How do you think children at the various age groups should be disciplined?

What would you see as your role in staging and maintaining a classroom environment?

How important do you believe play is in the daily curriculum?

To Learn about the Applicant's Experience

What is your experience in working with young children?

What are your greatest strengths?

What are your greatest challenges and how have you worked to address them?

Describe yourself as a member of a teaching team.

Describe strategies that you have used to establish relationships with families and maintain open communication.

To Learn about How the Applicant Might Contribute

What can you bring to our center that would be an asset?

Why do you want to work here?

What can we (the center's administration) do to help you be successful?

To Learn about What the Applicant Knows

What types of activities would you do with the children as infants, toddlers, preschoolers, and schoolagers?

What do you think is most important in taking care of infants?

If two children were disagreeing over something and became physical, what would you do and how would you deal with the situation?

How would you address a situation in which non-nappers are preventing nappers from sleeping?

How would you address early learning and development standards in the classroom?

Describe a high-quality curriculum.

How would you help new parents of infants feel that you are providing the best care to their baby?

How do you feel that you communicate with parents?

Describe how you would handle a behavior-challenged child.

Commitment Questions

What do you know about our program, and what attracted you enough to apply for this position?

What are your long-term career goals?

REFERENCES

ADA National Network. (n.d.). *Americans with Disabilities Act: Frequently asked questions*. Washington, DC: ADA Author. https://adata.org/top-ada-frequently-asked-questions

Bloom, P. J. (2007). *From the inside out: The power of reflection and self-awareness*. Lake Forest, IL: New Horizons.

Bloom, P. J., Sheerer, M., & Britz, J. (2005). *Blueprint for action: Achieving center-based change through staff development*. Lake Forest, IL: New Horizon.

Carter, M., & Curtis, D. (2010). *The visionary director* (2nd ed.). St. Paul, MN: Redleaf Press.

Childcare Exchange. (2016). *The art of leadership—3 Developing people in early childhood organizations*. Lincoln, NE: Exchange Press.

Cohen, A. J. (1998). Bettering your odds of not getting sued. In R. Neugebauer & B. Neugebauer (Eds.), *The art of leadership: Managing early childhood organizations*. Redmond, WA: CCIE.

Collins, J. (2005). *Good to great and the social sectors*. New York, NY: Harper Collins.

Copeland, T., & Bruno, H. E. (2012). *Managing legal risks in early childhood programs: How to prevent flare-ups from becoming lawsuits*. New York, NY: Teachers College Press.

Gable, S., Rothrauff, T. C., Thornburg, K. R., & Mauzy, D. (2007). Cash incentives and turnover in center-based child care staff. *Early Childhood Research Quarterly, 22*, 363–378.

Hamrick, J. (2000). Reduce staff turnover through effective interviewing. *Child Care Information Exchange, 134*, 26–28.

Julius, G. D. (2020). Advancing preschool teachers through evaluation and coaching. *Child Care Information Exchange, 251*, 8–11. http://www.childcareexchange.com/article/advancing-preschool-teachers-through-evaluation-and-coaching/5025108/

Kintzel, J. (2020). Five indisputable child care management principles that stand the test of time (and a global pandemic). *Child Care Information Exchange, 256*, 26–28. http://www.childcareexchange.com/article/five-indisputable-child-care-management-principles-that-stand-the-test-of-time-and-a-global-pandemic/5025626/

Power to the Profession Taskforce. (2020). Unifying framework for the early childhood profession. Washington, DC: NAEYC. https://www.naeyc.org/resources/pubs/yc/mar2020/unifying-framework-early-childhood-education

Turner, M. (2020). Onboarding (and occasionally off-boarding) staff. *Child Care Information Exchange, 256*, 58–60. http://www.childcareexchange.com/article/onboarding-and-occasionally-offboarding-staff/5025658/

Whitebrook, M., & Bellm, D. (1999). *Taking on turnover: An action plan for child care teachers and directors*. Washington, DC: Center for Child Care Workforce.

Families are more likely to choose a program where they feel they belong.

Chapter 9 Recruiting Children

naeyc

Standards and Recommendations Addressed in This Chapter

ADVANCING EQUITY RECOMMENDATION 5 Recognize the value of serving a diverse group of children and strive to increase the range of diversity among those served.

PROGRAM STANDARD 4 Assessment of Child Progress

PROGRAM STANDARD 6 Staff Competencies, Preparation, and Support

PROFESSIONAL STANDARDS AND COMPETENCIES: STANDARD 2 Family-Teacher Partnerships and Community Connections

PROFESSIONAL STANDARDS AND COMPETENCIES: STANDARD 6 Professionalism as an Early Childhood Educator

LEARNING OBJECTIVES

After reading this chapter, you should be able to:

9-1 Identify how early care and education meets the needs of all children, including those with special learning and developmental needs.

9-2 Demonstrate how to make informed decisions about grouping children in programs.

9-3 Identify effective practices for enrolling children.

Effective directors are informed decision makers who consider multiple and sometimes competing factors before coming to conclusions. Decisions related to enrolling and grouping children are complex because many factors related to the needs of children and families as well as the quality of the program must be considered. Of course, there are pressures to admit all applicants when enrollment is not full. However, it is important for the director to exercise good professional judgment and base admission decisions on what is in the best interests of children and families.

Ultimately, the director is responsible for the decisions about how children will be admitted to the program and how they will be grouped. The educators may be called on to assist in these decisions, and sometimes a standing committee authorized by the board is asked to make policy or give advice. An admissions and recruitment committee might be charged with policy-making decisions about the population the program is designed to serve as well as the procedures to be followed when enrolling children. Decisions must also be made about how children will be grouped and how the program can support children with disabilities.

9-1 • Meeting the Needs of All Children and Families

Quality programs are inclusive and strive to meet the needs of all children and families admitted to the program. This means that directors must have a realistic understanding of the strengths and limitations of the program and the unique needs of the children and families to be served. Developing this understanding requires that the director and staff engage in ongoing program evaluation to understand what the program can do, where improvement or support is needed, and what the realistic limits are to the types of services a program can offer.

In a research policy brief produced by the Equity and Early Childhood Education Task Force of the National Council of Teachers of English (2016), the role of quality early childhood education in achieving a more equitable society cannot be overstated.

> Research shows that even very young children can adopt, enact, and interrupt racism and other forms of institutionalized discrimination. Young children are capable of examining and confronting racist ideologies and should have opportunities to do so. Cultivating these racial literacies from very early on in a child's life is a responsibility we all have to our nation's youngest children. (p. 3)

To demonstrate a commitment to overcoming racism and promote equity, a program may want to increase enrollment by serving a larger number of subsidized children, but an economic downturn at the state level has led to severe cuts in the reimbursement rates. The program must now look elsewhere to increase enrollment or end up with a budget shortfall. In addition, many of the families that are eligible for a county subsidy are also eligible for Head Start, where children have access to additional program options such as dental and medical evaluations and, in some instances, mental health services. Directors need to make an honest assessment of what their program can provide for children and families and if services can be enhanced by partnering with other agencies while also working to advance equity.

A program director may understand the need to include children with special learning or developmental needs. Noting an increase in the number of children with autism spectrum disorders, a director might recognize a limitation in the expertise of his or her staff and determine that special training is needed so that educators understand and can implement strategies that support children with autism. The director might also note that many children with autism require early intervention services to best meet their needs. Directors need to maintain an ethical balance of striving to be inclusive, working with families to find services that best meet the needs of children, and recognizing the strengths and limitations of their program.

Professionals at the program must decide if the available staff and the particular program offerings at the program can provide the most enriching experience for a particular child. In other words, can this program provide what this child needs to develop to his or her fullest potential? If there is any doubt in the minds of either the members of the family or the director, careful consideration should be given to three specific questions.

- Can the program be adjusted to accommodate this child?
- Is there another program with a different focus that would provide a better match for this child and family?
- Are there programs to partner with that would enhance what can be offered in order to meet the needs of children and families?

Partnering with the local school district or the county early intervention program can provide access to itinerant special educators who will work with children with special needs in early childhood program and home settings. Likewise, many Head Start grantees have developed partnerships with early childhood programs, allowing children and families to reap the benefits of Head Start services in an early childhood program.

Inclusive directors see that their program can be one option on a continuum of program options for children and families. Progressive directors need to be realistic while also understanding the need to grow and change to meet the needs of children and

Making the *Case* for *Inclusion* naeyc

The inclusion of children with special learning and developmental needs can be challenging and also richly rewarding for the child, his or her peers, and the teaching staff. The fear of the unknown and a lack of understanding of special education law can prevent programs from accepting children with special needs. For programs that are inclusive, the benefits for the program children and staff frequently outweigh the disadvantages.

In an inclusive program, developing children typically learn about diversity and compassion while also learning that children with disabilities are more like them than not. Staff members learn to differentiate and support learning throughout the day. Including children with special needs often helps educators be more intentional in their planning and assessment. They become better collaborators and are often more ready to view families as partners. Children with special needs are often eligible for itinerate services that bring new expertise to the classroom, broadening the educators' skill base, which benefits all children. To support inclusion, directors need to do the following:

- Be aware of the services that are available to children with special needs in early childhood programs. Visit the special education resource program in your region to learn how to access support services.
- Become familiar with the special education intake team in the schools where the children in the program tend to go to kindergarten. Inquire about the processes they use to handle referrals from early childhood programs. When you have a question about the development of one of the children in your care, work with the family to connect with the school district. If the referral pertains to an infant or toddler, learn about the early intervention services that are available for the youngest children in your county.

families facing the demands of the 21st century. One particular challenge is to understand the myriad of federal laws, mandates, and procedures that govern how children with special needs are to be served in inclusive settings.

9-1a • Admission of Children with Disabilities

A federal law that directors must be familiar with is the Americans with Disabilities Act (ADA), which was enacted in 1990 and amended in 2008. Knowledge of the ADA is important as directors review requests for admission of children with disabilities. Programs are prohibited from denying admission to a child simply because of a disability unless such admission would "fundamentally alter the nature of the program" (ADA Amendments Act, 2008). Likewise, children who pose a direct threat or "a substantial risk of serious harm to the health and safety of others" do not have to be admitted into a program. The determination that "a child poses a direct threat may not be based on generalizations or stereotypes about the effects of a particular disability; it must be based on an individualized assessment that considers the particular activity and the actual abilities and disabilities of the individual" (U.S. Department of Justice, n.d.).

Directors in early childhood education programs must be prepared to address the challenge of providing quality inclusive environments for increasing numbers of young children with disabilities. They are obligated to understand that a child may not be excluded simply because he or she has a disability. It is important for them to know how the law applies to infants, toddlers, and preschoolers and to understand how early childhood programs are likely to fit into the scheme of services for children with disabilities. They also should know what roles they and their staff can play as part of the interdisciplinary, interagency team effort to give these children the benefit of quality early childhood education experiences. The well-being of the child is best served when families are a part of the team.

Another important law that was enacted by Congress is Public Law 99-457, which amended the Education of Handicapped Act (PL 94-142). This 1986 amendment mandated services for children 3 to 5 years of age. The reauthorization of both PL 94-142 and PL 99-457 came in 1990 with the passage of PL 91-476, Individuals with Disabilities Education Act (IDEA). It was further amended in 1997 as PL 95-17. The law requires that states provide a free, appropriate public education to everyone with a disability between ages 3 and 21. In the past, IDEA was specific to public-school–based programs for preschoolers and older

Effective directors support teachers as they make intentional decisions about how to include children with special learning and developmental needs in their classroom.

children with special needs. However, states are now applying the early childhood itinerant model, which brings early intervention services to community-based early childhood programs (Dinnebeil, 2011). This means that children with disabilities can now receive inclusive intervention services in early childhood and other community-based programs, which opens a wide variety of options for families.

9-1b • Provisions of the IDEA

IDEA, as amended by PL 95-17, the Individuals with Disabilities Act Amendments of 1997, extends all rights and due process protection to children with disabilities ages 3 to 5. Therefore, preschool children with disabilities are ensured free public education in a least-restrictive environment based on an individualized education plan (IEP) developed by a team that includes the child's parents. The programs are to be administered through state or local education agencies that may contract with other service providers to offer a range of service models. The designated state agency ultimately is responsible for monitoring overall services and use of the federal funds. Other sources of funding such as Medicaid or maternal and child health also must be used when the children are eligible, and the new funds are to supplement, not supplant, these existing sources. Therefore, the new funds may be used in addition to but not instead of existing sources of funding.

According to Allen and Cowdery (2014), IDEA also establishes a state grant program to provide financial assistance to states to maintain and implement a comprehensive, multidisciplinary system of services for infants and toddlers with disabilities. Part C of IDEA, known as *discretionary legislation*, says that states may serve this age group but are not required to do so. The exception is for those states that serve nondisabled infants and toddlers: They must serve those children in that age group who are disabled. The governor of each state designates a lead agency in the state to administer the program. That agency develops eligibility criteria, and the law allows but does not require extension of services to those babies viewed as at risk for developmental delay based on medical or environmental factors, in addition to identified infants with disabilities. A case manager, sometimes called a *service coordinator*, must be designated for each child. That person, the liaison between agencies and services needed, also is responsible for the development of the individualized family service plan (IFGCRP), which must have evidence of multidisciplinary input and include information about the child's level of development, the family's strengths and needs as they relate to the child, the specific intervention services planned, and the projected outcomes for the child and the family. Therefore, the IFGCRP is somewhat comparable to the IEP required for children ages 3 to 5 and brings the focus to the importance of the family in each young child's life.

9-1c • Role of Early Childhood Programs

IDEA allows for variation in length of day, as well as range and variety of programs. This means that services to be used may be part-time or full-time and home-based or program-based. This is likely to lead to more inclusion models as state and local agencies contract with half-day and full-day early childhood programs to expand the continuum of services to include more center-based care in integrated settings. Now that the values of early childhood education programs are sufficiently high and demand public notice, state education agencies that have discretion to choose program models see that these programs offer viable alternatives to the current typical public school categorical model. In addition to integrated early childhood program options that are now available through itinerant services, Head Start is an option for many low-income families because 10 percent of Head Start's classroom slots must be reserved for children with disabilities.

The vast majority of unserved children with disabilities who come into programs under the new law are identified as needing mild to moderate intervention. Most children who require intensive intervention already receive services and may or may not be included in preschools or early childhood programs, depending on how well their needs can be met in an inclusive environment. However, based on the ADA, each applicant must be considered on a case-by-case basis and may not be excluded merely because of a disabling condition. If the program can include the child by making reasonable accommodations in the environment, then it is expected to do so (U.S. Department of Justice, n.d.).

IDEA requires that children with disabilities have access to the *least-restrictive environment* (LRE). Legally, this means that every effort must be made to integrate children with their peers in a regular educational setting. In practice, the LRE facilitates opportunities to function and grow optimally in all areas of development. Directors of programs are responsible for providing such an environment for children with disabilities, who must share the pedagogical and social environment; educators are expected to be specifically trained to facilitate interaction among and between typically developing children and those who have special needs. They should also have an understanding

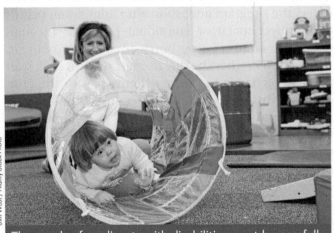

Jim West / Alamy Stock Photo

The needs of applicants with disabilities must be carefully assessed to determine how best to serve them.

of the implications of developmental differences and be able to adapt the learning environment to enhance the development of children with diverse abilities.

Although evidence suggests that significant benefits accrue to children with special needs who participate in groups with typical peers, these benefits are not the result of merely being in the same classroom. The factors that determine how well children with special needs do in an inclusive environment depends on the quality of the program and the presence of an educator who has developed specific intervention plans to support interaction between and among the children with disabilities and their typically developing peers (Allen & Cowdery, 2014).

When available staff struggle to find sufficient time or lack the background to provide the special support for children with special needs in the classroom, it may be possible to reach out into the community for additional help. In addition to reaching out to school districts and early intervention providers, volunteers from parent groups, senior citizens, service organizations, or students from university early childhood or special education programs can help in the classroom. Special training for the volunteers and the staff can be arranged through special educators at the local school or university or from other community agencies (Allen & Cowdery, 2014).

Including children who have been identified with special needs can be both inspiring and challenging for the teaching staff and the director. However, because so many resources are available to children with special needs and their families, inclusive can work out to benefit everyone involved. The more vexing challenges are those faced when a new child enters the program and, soon after admission, begins to manifest social or emotional problems through disruptive emotional outbursts in the classroom. In these cases, neither the director nor the teaching staff has had a chance to prepare themselves or the children for this new student. It becomes stressful and time-consuming to work with this new family and to provide the necessary support for the troubled child and the classroom educator. In these situations, directors are pulled in many directions, sometimes struggling with a screaming, angry child; sometimes talking with hostile, defensive, or bewildered parents; and sometimes taking time after hours to give support to an exhausted educator. These are the times when directors must call on all their professional skills to help the child, the family, and the educator cope and eventually move forward toward resolution.

In the past decade, the challenge of working with troubled, angry children has created a great deal of interest among early childhood educators as they consider preventive measures as well as explanations for the phenomenon and any remedies that might help children, their families, and their educators. One sample of such a remedy focuses on refining and adjusting classroom practice to promote the emotional well-being and resilience of all children in the classroom, not just those who are seen as "troublesome." This type of refined and modified approach to children and families requires training and coaching for all staff, including administrators, with a director who participates and serves as a model for other staff. It is essential that everyone who sees, greets, or talks with children and families reflects the same focus of respect and caring. Everyone must engage in what the program views as best practice. The adjusted attitude and practice focuses on strengths of children and families and provides highly predictable, safe, and supportive experiences throughout the program. The classroom is a place where children come to know and trust that they are respected, protected, and heard by trusted adults. When this modified approach is implemented throughout a program, it seems to minimize the need for the more traditional procedure of identification, referral, and intervention for troubled children. That traditional routine is reserved for those children and families who require

Director's Corner

When a child with a disability becomes part of a classroom in our program, the educators meet with me to identify the resources that the teaching team has to offer this child and family and to identify areas where the team might need assistance. I see my role as facilitating the conversation and also as helping educators see how their areas of strength can support the child. I also realize that my role is to act as a sounding board when needed and to identify community resources available to the teaching team so that they can better meet the needs of the child. I know I need to provide opportunities for the team to talk. There are times when educators need to vent, and there are times when educators are asking for help. My job is to know the difference.

—*Director, university-affiliated early childhood program*

specialized support in addition to the support provided by the uniquely trained and qualified staff that understands the importance of the emotional well-being of children, families, and colleagues.

9-1d • Role of the Director in an Interdisciplinary or Interagency Effort

Cooperation among education agencies, social service agencies, medical groups, and early childhood education providers is **naeyc** essential if young children with special needs and their families are to be well served. Directors conversant in the law and its implications for early childhood programs will be able to respond more knowledgeably to professionals from related agencies who make inquiries about placements for children with special needs. These directors may be called on to make decisions about whether their programs can meet the needs of the selected special needs children, serve on interdisciplinary teams where IEPs are developed and referral decisions are made, and support their educators who will be working with special educators, therapists, and the children's families. If the children are to benefit from what early childhood educators have to offer, "turf guarding" must be set aside; yet directors must assertively advocate developmentally appropriate practice, which is the area of expertise they bring to the interdisciplinary and interagency team.

To facilitate communication between and among members of interdisciplinary teams and to support their work, directors must understand how and why inclusivity works and what prevents it from working. That often means directors must learn more about children with special needs through additional training and reading to prepare themselves for coaching classroom staff and for working with an interdisciplinary team. When members of the interdisciplinary team view each other as colleagues, all of whom bring special skills and training to the situation, and when they keep in mind that their common goal is to provide the best environment for the children and their families, they can work together to that end.

9-2 • Grouping the Children

As part of the process of meeting the **naeyc** diverse needs of children and families, directors need to make informed decisions about how the structures of the program impact a variety of stakeholders, including children, families, and staff. Decisions about how children are grouped create structures that affect how staff are called upon to work together, how children and families interact at the program, and how much such care costs. Decisions about grouping also reflect a program's philosophy of education and the approach that the program has adopted. These decisions need to be carefully considered because they are more than logistical and will have a long-term impact on the children, families, staff, and budget of the program.

Decisions about grouping the children—group size, ages of children, and composition of the groups—must be reached before making the group assignments and pursuing all the subsequent steps in the enrollment procedure. After assignments have been made, educators can contact families and initiate the enrollment process. Although the degree of flexibility around grouping in ongoing early childhood education programs is sometimes more limited than in half-day programs, even there the cyclical nature of demand usually follows the public school year, thus giving rise to numerous grouping decisions for newcomers in the fall.

Many factors are considered in dealing with the complex question of how children should be grouped appropriately. The size of groups is determined by a variety of factors, including the physical space available, the licensing requirements, the number of staff members, and the program philosophy. Appropriate group size has a positive influence on both children and educators (Freeman, Decker, & Decker, 2017). Other factors that relate to the grouping of children are the needs and skills of the staff, the needs of the children, the question of chronological age grouping versus vertical grouping (sometimes called *family* or *multiage grouping*), the number of children with special needs to be enrolled, and the nature of their disabilities.

9-2a • Total Number of Children

To a large extent, the number of children available and the size of the physical space determine the total number of children in a program. For a new program, after the needs assessment in the community has been completed (Chapter 2) and the facility has been selected (Chapter 6), the final decision about the total number of children in the program must be made. Often this decision is simply to take all available children. However, when the requests for service are overwhelming or when the available space cannot accommodate large numbers of children, the director or the board (or both) may want to limit the enrollment. Accreditation standards and many state licensing regulations limit total group size as well as adult-to-child ratios, both of which affect program quality. (See Chapter 3 for further details.)

Programs for young children must radiate a feeling of intimacy and warmth. Little children often feel frightened and uncomfortable about entering a large, forbidding building. The noise, the inevitable confusion, and the motion created by many people concentrated in one area can provoke anxiety in young children. It is difficult to maintain an inviting, comfortable atmosphere for small children when buildings are large and when children are moved through crowded play yards, hallways, or receiving areas before they reach their room and their educator.

Because the atmosphere in large public school buildings can be overwhelming for the youngest children, it is important for early childhood professionals and public school educators to give special attention to the selection of the classroom and play yard space for the preschool children. Partnerships between early childhood educators and public school personnel can result in site selection for public-school–sponsored programs that may be in a separate wing of the building or in a facility completely separate from the school building. Some of the advantages of funneling preschool and full-day child care services into public school sponsorship include greater stability, insulation from political attack, and protection from sudden economic shifts.

9-2b • Space and Group Size

Group size varies according to the licensing regulations and how the available space is organized. Licensing regulations often limit the number of children in a room and usually dictate the adult-to-child ratio for children of different ages. Because space requirements and adult-to-child ratio standards in the licensing regulations are not always based on the knowledge of experienced professionals, it is wise to follow a standard of small groups with low educator-to-child ratios, meeting standards of the National Association for the Education of Young Children or achieving even lower ratios under special circumstances (National Association for the Education of Young Children, 2013).

The organization or plan of the available space affects the size of the groups that can be accommodated. When bathrooms are two floors down or outside areas are not directly adjacent to the classroom, groups must be smaller to be manageable during the transition periods when children move from one place to another. If fenced-in play areas outside can be reached directly from the classroom, the total space can be supervised more easily, and a larger group could be assigned to the space.

When space is adequate to accommodate large numbers of young children, some directors and educators find creative ways to use dividers, draperies, or movable partitions to break the space into smaller units. Even where available space would accommodate larger groups, smaller groups are viewed as optimal.

9-2c • Skills of Staff and Group Size

In deciding on the size of groups, the director considers the skill level **naeyc** of the staff and factors that led to the decision about how many children should be assigned to each classroom. The staff for each group must be available to provide frequent personal contact; promote age-appropriate, meaningful learning experiences; create a nurturing environment using effective classroom management strategies; and respond immediately to all emergencies.

9-2d • Needs of Children and Group Size

Discussing the policy of making group size or placement decisions on the basis of differing individual family and child needs or ages of children is beyond the scope of this book, even though every director must consider such needs carefully. However, some basic considerations apply to all children, whether infant, toddler, preschool, or school age.

The needs of children will vary depending on their experiences, their level of development in all areas, and their ages. However, it is generally agreed that the youngest children in their first group experience find it most satisfying to relate to a constant adult. After the initial shift in attachment from the primary caregiver (usually the mother) to a constant adult at the program, the child begins to branch out and relate to other adults and other children in the group. This developmental progression suggests that the child's first experience should be in a small, intimate group with a consistent adult. The children in this group may be the same chronological age or range over a year or two in age. Volunteers, student educators, or parent helpers may rotate through the classroom, but the one primary constant caregiver becomes the trusted adult figure to whom children can turn when they need caring and attention. Continuity of care is especially important for infants and toddlers, who should have an assigned primary caregiver who works closely with the parents. When change is carefully planned and minimized, infants and toddlers begin to be able to predict what will happen, thus feeling less powerless or uneasy and more secure (Gonzalez-Mena & Widmeyer Eyer, 2017).

For young children spending the full day in a program, it is wise to consider small, intimate grouping patterns. Because children in full-day programs spend practically all of their waking hours in the program, it becomes a surrogate home for them. Young children who are dealing with all the stimulation and interpersonal relationships of a large group for an extended period of time may be exhausted by the end of their long day. Small groups in a carefully planned space provide both time and space for the child to be alone, to establish close relationships with just one or two children, or to spend time alone with just one adult. Quiet and intimacy in a comfortable setting with a few people more closely resembles the home environment and can soften the institutional atmosphere that prevails in many large programs.

Careful planning and adequate staffing enable directors to maintain consistency in caregivers and to avoid having to regroup children to maintain required staff-to-child ratios throughout each day. In fact, some programs take significant steps to maintain continuity of care by grouping children in broader age ranges such as 3 months to 3 years or by implementing a practice called *looping* in which educators follow a group of children from infancy through preschool. Both of these grouping practices offer the children the benefits of consistency throughout these formative years. Moving children to different spaces for the critical and sometimes fragile times of separation and reunion creates tension for everyone involved. If at all possible, directors should plan staffing so that children stay in the same familiar space with their caregivers from the time they see that special parent disappear behind that closed door in the morning to the time they see that familiar face reappear for pickup at day's end. It is recommended that children of all ages have an assigned primary caregiver.

9-2e • Chronological versus Vertical Age Grouping

There is no consensus on the best grouping practice. Although there has been some movement toward greater homogeneity in classrooms for young children, which usually results from chronological age

---

Growth Mindset Moment

Think about your first practicum experience in a classroom. Think about how many children you were able to manage at one time. Could you comfortably work with five children? If you were asked to work with 9 children without a second person to help, did you still feel that you could practice effective management skills? What adult-to-child ratio and total group size is most comfortable for you, keeping in mind your philosophy of early childhood education?

---

grouping, there is a resurgence of interest in multiage or vertical grouping (Freeman et al., 2017). Program philosophy may dictate the preferred approach to grouping the children. However, unless licensing regulates how children should be grouped, the way classrooms are organized within the program is left to the discretion of the director and the professional staff.

Directors are faced with the challenge of maintaining full enrollment while keeping groups balanced and exercising caution when decisions are made about moving children among established program groupings. When infant–toddler groups are at capacity, but there are openings in the preschool, it is tempting to move some of the older toddlers to the preschool to make space for families on the waiting list. It is important to balance the need for full enrollment to meet budget requirements against the social-emotional readiness of these youngest children and their ability to manage a more complex environment with older children and new adults.

Too often, children are moved based solely on their chronological age or in response to pressure to make room for new children rather than on a careful analysis of the readiness of the children involved in the move. The first step is to give careful consideration to a child's readiness to thrive and grow with the older children. Then take note of the challenges to the family and educators involved in supporting the child through this critical adjustment to many unknowns such as different spaces with new adults and few familiar faces. The transition process for any child to a new group in the program can be eased by setting up a transition plan that parallels the phasing-in process described in the "Intake Procedures" section further

The younger the child, the more important it is that experiences should be in a small, intimate group with a consistent and responsive adult.

on in this chapter. The family and the educators from both rooms will be involved in the transition process, just as a parent and the educator are involved when a new child enters the program.

Parents may need a special conference with the director to clarify the importance of the parental role in the transition process, not only when the child enters the program but also for all subsequent transitions from one group to another and the final one when the child leaves the program. Meeting with the child's parents as these transition times approach offers the director the opportunity to help them understand how their presence in the new room can help reduce stress for their child because both are adjusting to the families and staff. It is helpful to parents if they understand that taking time for their child during potentially stressful changes will contribute to the emotional well-being of their child.

9-2f • Chronological Grouping

Grouping by age traditionally has been a more common practice in early childhood programs than vertical grouping. It involves grouping based solely on the basis of age: 3- and 4-year-olds are in different groups, and toddlers are separated from infants. When children are grouped chronologically, there is little discussion about which group a given child will join. The director's task is simplified because in

accepting the program, parents understand that their 3-year-old will be in Group 1 and their 4-year-old will be in Group 2. Of course, there will be ranges of ability and behavior within an age group from individual differences, but the child's exposure to differences is inevitably lessened when chronological grouping is used. Therefore, the child's opportunity to develop a broad appreciation for diversity is diminished. On the other hand, there are advantages to age grouping such as simplifying the planning of the learning environment and making classroom management less troublesome. The less experienced educator may find this type of grouping more comfortable.

Chronological age grouping is based on the assumption that children of the same age are within the same range in ability and level of development. Because children of the same age are not homogeneous, many programs go to multiage grouping in which children advance at their own rate through individualized or differentiated programming. Multiage

▶ TeachSource Video Vignette

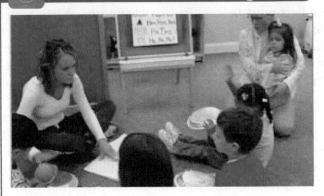

Preschool: IEP and Transition Planning

View the video vignette titled, *Preschool: IEP and Transition Planning for a Young Child with Special Needs.*

Transition meetings are common when children move from public school preschool programs to kindergartens that are part of the same school system. Early childhood providers who work with children and families but who are not part of the school system are often not included in the transition planning meeting. As director, how might you facilitate avenues to support children and families to be more involved in this transition process?

grouping allows for children's uneven development and provides an environment in which younger children engage in more interactive and complex types of play with older children, who are easily accessible. There is also compelling evidence that children will do well when they are in a mixed-age group where children differ not only in age but also in ethnic and socioeconomic backgrounds. With the guidance of a well-trained educator, children will engage in projects that match their interests and move toward more cooperative play (Katz & Chard, 2014).

9-2g • More on Multiage Grouping

Multiage grouping, or *vertical grouping* **naeyc** as it is sometimes called, involves placing children of different ages in the same group; the children in any one group may range in age as much as 2 to 3 years. This multiage grouping more closely resembles one that would occur in a family and is sometimes referred to as *family grouping*. Depending on licensing requirements, infants and sometimes even toddlers must be kept in separate groups. When vertical grouping is the pattern, decisions about the size and the composition of each group, as well as the number of adults needed for each one, become more complex. The broad age range also complicates managing the children and planning their learning environment.

Sometimes, parents object to having their 2-year-old with older children who may be viewed by the toddler's parents as being loud and rough. These parents often are concerned about the safety of their toddler and sometimes fear that their young child will be unable to cope in a group covering a wide age range. However, many of these parents can be helped to see that a young child in a multiage group has more opportunity to learn from older children in the group and that every child has a chance to teach the other group members. Peer teaching and learning have intrinsic value because they not only enhance a child's sense of mastery and worth but also facilitate cooperation and appreciation of others. For example, 2-year-olds may not be as efficient as 5-year-olds about putting equipment back on the shelf, but the total concentration they give to an activity such as water play and the curiosity they show in exploring this material may help their more controlled 3- or 5-year-old counterparts to try splashing in the water.

Parents who are familiar with programs that have chronological age grouping are usually aware of differences in tuition as children move up from infant to toddler to preschool in these programs. Costs are lower because of more generous ratios in classrooms for older children, which is a financial benefit for families as children move up from one level to the next. This cost differential and its inevitable result are a reality that program sponsors and directors must deal with when they choose to do vertical age grouping. Fees per child in vertical grouping are usually the same, regardless of the child's age.

The director must cope with the skeptical parents and with the educators who are reaching out for support as they work with a broad age range. However, sometimes the advantages of multiage grouping, such as peer modeling and peer tutoring, are outweighed by the challenges of planning for the age span and equipping and managing the classroom. Helping families understand that it is typical for the development of 3- to 5-year-olds to vary across developmental domains comes from educators who also understand this concept and can communicate it in clear and consistent ways. Consider using graphics that show how the profiles of individual children might intersect with the skill levels of older or younger children. As children mature into the primary grades, this variation in developmental rate tends to even out. However, typical 3- to 5-year-olds are sporadic in their rate of development, and many children have peaks and valleys that make the opportunities to connect with older and younger children in a multiage group configuration highly appropriate (see **Figure 9-1**).

Directors become coaches and sources of support for staff as they try to meet challenges. Educators who are able to individualize planning for a multiage group also will be better qualified to create culturally responsive programs for children from diverse backgrounds and inclusive programs for children with special needs. These educators develop a keen

Growth Mindset Moment

How might you, as a director, use **Figure 9-1** to equip your staff so they can convey a clear explanation of multiage grouping to families?

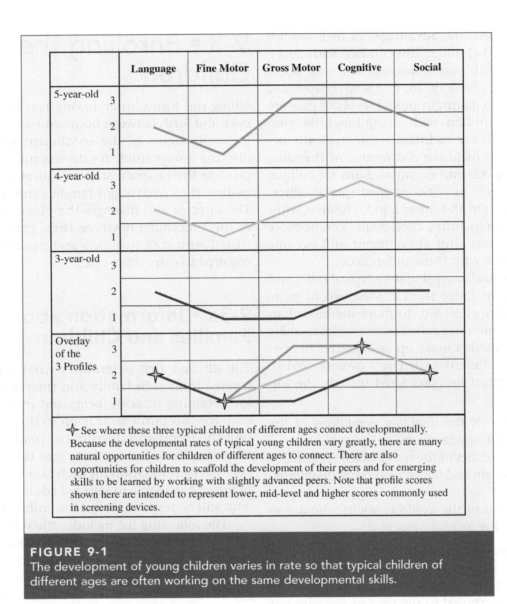

	Language	Fine Motor	Gross Motor	Cognitive	Social
5-year-old 3 2 1					
4-year-old 3 2 1					
3-year-old 3 2 1					
Overlay of the 3 Profiles 3 2 1					

 See where these three typical children of different ages connect developmentally. Because the developmental rates of typical young children vary greatly, there are many natural opportunities for children of different ages to connect. There are also opportunities for children to scaffold the development of their peers and for emerging skills to be learned by working with slightly advanced peers. Note that profile scores shown here are intended to represent lower, mid-level and higher scores commonly used in screening devices.

FIGURE 9-1
The development of young children varies in rate so that typical children of different ages are often working on the same developmental skills.

awareness of the fact that "one size does not fit all." Directors can help educators both develop these skills and also become proficient in communicating what they do and why to families.

9-2h • Impact of Children with Exceptionalities on Group Size

When children with exceptionalities are included in the group, the size and composition of the group may need to be adjusted accordingly to ensure that enough adults will be available to respond to the children's needs. Consider which group can best meet the needs of the child with the disability, as well as how that child can offer something to the group. Unless the child is truly integrated into the group, which will likely require scaffolding from the educators, there is a risk that the child with the disability will be ignored and will not reap the benefits of being included with typical peers. The least-restrictive ruling is not necessarily a mandate to enroll all children with a disability into regular programs; however, the advantages of inclusive for both nondisabled children and children with developmental disabilities are numerous and well documented (Allen & Cowdery, 2014). Social competence and the ability to maintain higher levels of play are enhanced for children with exceptionalities who have the opportunity to interact with typically developing peers in inclusive classrooms. At the same time, their language and cognitive gains are comparable to their peers in self-contained special education classrooms. On the other hand, children without disabilities in inclusive classrooms become more accepting of others who are different and become more comfortable with those differences.

There is no ideal exceptional-to-typical ratio, and recommendations range from at least two or more to an even balance (50:50), to more disabled than nondisabled, sometimes called *reverse mainstreaming* in which nondisabled make up one-quarter to one-half of the enrollment (Allen & Cowdery, 2014). Variables that must be considered include the following:

- the severity of the disabling conditions of the children with special needs,
- the characteristics of the nondisabled children,
- how to explain and understand peers' disabilities, and
- the expertise of the available adults who are to work with the inclusive group.

Multiage groups are advantageous for children with special needs because they provide peer models who have a broad range of skills and abilities. The atypical child is exposed to the peer model who has higher-level skills or abilities and also will have a chance to develop friendships with younger children who may be more compatible developmentally.

Decisions about group size or group patterns will affect program planning, child and educator behaviors, group atmosphere, and ultimately the experiences of both educator and child in the learning environment. An inclusive program must consider the uniqueness of every child and family in the classroom and how each child's strengths and needs will be addressed (Allen & Cowdery, 2014). Therefore, grouping the children is a complex issue that has far-reaching results.

9-3 • Enrolling the Children

Filling out forms, interviewing parents, and visiting back and forth between home and school are the major components of the enrollment procedure. The director is responsible for developing forms that will provide the program staff members with the information they need about families and their children. The director also manages the planning and timing of this procedure; however, these plans must be discussed with staff members and parents who will be required to carry them out.

9-3a • Information about Families and Children

The director first determines what information is needed from each family and then develops a plan for obtaining it. Both forms and interviews can be used for this purpose. It is up to the director to design the forms and develop the plan for interviews or conferences. The ultimate goal is to assemble the necessary information for each child and family and to make it available to selected adults at the program who will be responsible for the child and the family.

The following list includes the type of preenrollment information that is typically obtained from the family. Note that all the information is important to efficient business operation of the program, the health and safety of the children, and the better understanding of the child and the family:

- name of the child (including nickname);
- names of family members and ages of siblings;
- names of other members of the household and their relationship to the child;
- home address and telephone number;
- name, address, telephone number (home, work, cell), and email addresses of parents' employers;
- arrangement for payment of fees;
- transportation plans for the child (including how the child will be transported and by whom);
- medical history and record of a recent physical examination of the child by a physician;
- social-emotional history of the child;

- name, address, and telephone number of the child's physician or clinic;
- emergency medical treatment authorization;
- name, address, and telephone number of a person (outside the family) to contact in an emergency if a member of the family cannot be reached; and
- permission to participate in the total school program (field trips, photos, videotaping, research, etc.).

To ensure that you have all the information and signed releases required to satisfy licensing and to cover liability questions, contact your local licensing agent and consult an attorney.

9-3b • Forms

Many sample forms included in the **Director's Resources 9-1**, **9-2**, and **9-3** demonstrate various ways in which the information just listed can be recorded. These are only sample forms and cannot be used in the exact format presented, but they can provide a basis for developing appropriate forms to meet the specific needs of each program. For example, the director of a small cooperative preschool does not need all the data on family income required by Head Start or publicly funded programs but does need details on family schedules to plan for parent participation.

Programs sponsored by public schools may or may not require family income information but will require a Medicaid number for those children entitled to the benefits of that program and also may need a birth certificate to validate the age of the child.

Because programs vary so much concerning the information required on children and families, directors must develop forms that meet the specific needs of the program.

In the case of early childhood education programs and preschools, applications for admission are often included on the program's website, which allows families to print out the forms that are relevant to them. In some instances, the forms are automated so they can be submitted to the program electronically. If selection and grouping of the children require more subjective data than can be gleaned from the application form or any other written information that has been collected before admission, the director can arrange to talk with the parents.

After most of the children have been admitted and assigned to groups, those who have not yet been

Working Smart with Technology

Developing an Effective Website

Developing an effective website can facilitate communication with parents and also provide access to the forms needed for a wide variety of program needs. The development of the website should reflect collaboration with staff and families to determine how the website will be used as well as the kinds of materials that will be included on the site. Some programs choose to use a password-protected section of the site that includes the handbook and forms for families and staff as well as pictures of children and their work. Having a password-protected section of the website is especially important if your program serves children with special needs because special education laws are especially clear about maintaining confidentiality. It is also important to have an open-access section of the program website, which is designed to market the program and include application and enrollment information. The website developer must understand the intended use and audience for the website as well as the need to protect children and their identity from public view. After the website is developed, it must be maintained, which can involve ongoing costs. Consider using a free or inexpensive user-friendly website development tool such as Weebly.com to create a website. It is not only possible to develop a free or inexpensive website using drag-and-drop technology but also exceptionally easy to keep the website up to date without incurring additional costs.

A well-developed website is essential for today's early childhood education program. Website development should be a collaborative effort between staff and families in order to design a website that meets the needs of all involved.

placed are held for deferred enrollment or, in the case of ongoing programs, put on a waiting list. If a child is rejected for reasons other than full enrollment, the reasons should be discussed with the family to avoid any misunderstandings that could quickly undermine the public relations efforts of the program staff and impair communication between the staff and potential clients from the community.

9-3c • Confidentiality

Information about families and children that is recorded on forms or ob-tained by staff members during interviews or home visits is confidential and must not be released to unauthorized people without parental consent. Furthermore, the Family Educational Rights and Privacy Act of 1974 (FERPA) provides that any public or private educational institution that is the recipient of federal funds made available under any federal program administered by the U.S. Department of Education must give parents access to their children's educational records. Because all information in the files must remain available to parents, staff members must be discreet when recording information to be placed in a child's permanent record. Parents should be informed of what information will be kept confidential and what will be available to teaching staff, office staff, and other support staff. Parents decide how much detail they are willing to release. They realize that emergency telephone numbers and names of people authorized to pick up the child will be needed by all teaching and office staff, but they may choose to make medical histories and income information available only to the director and the lead.

Records and other confidential information should not be disclosed to anyone other than program personnel without written consent of the parent or guardian, unless its disclosure is necessary to protect the child's health or safety. Written parental consent is required to pass information on to the public school by any preschool or Head Start program. As a general rule, parental consent should be obtained except in emergency cases or when it appears that the parent is a threat to the child (Family Educational Rights and Privacy Act, 1974). Programs that receive funds from government sources should be familiar with any regulations or guidelines on confidentiality and privacy that are tied to the funding source.

Program directors in collaboration with staff, parents, and board members can develop written policies for the protection of confidentiality and the disclosure of children's records. These policies should be made available to all program personnel and families (Feeney & Freeman, n.d.). The trust that develops between staff and families will be damaged if there is a breach of confidentiality. Setting aside one staff meeting each year to review the confidentiality policies is one way to encourage the staff to reaffirm their pledge to maintain confidentiality.

9-3d • Intake Procedures

The director decides which staff members will be involved in each step of the intake procedure, but it is imperative that the child's educator be actively involved throughout. The adult who will work directly with the child must interact with the child and family to begin to establish feelings of mutual trust among the child, the family, and the educator.

Parents often feel apprehensive about placing children in an early childhood program. A carefully planned intake process that provides frequent opportunities to talk with the educator, the director, and the social services staff (if available) can help parents cope with their feelings. At the same time, young children are often upset when they are first separated from their parents and family. Children worry about who will take care of them or how they will get home. Some children display regressive behaviors. Both educators and parents need help to understand that children are uneasy about this new experience and must have special attention and care during this initial transition. Because children feel frightened and lonely, their transition to a new physical and social environment is done gradually and must be accompanied by continuous support from family members. For the mental health of both the parents and children, the sequences followed in the intake process should be arranged so that everyone involved will be able to cope successfully with the separation experience. Four steps are commonly employed in introducing the family and the child to the program and to the educator. They are discussed here because it is the director's responsibility to ensure that this careful intake procedure is implemented.

9-3e • Initial Interview with Parents

The purpose of an initial interview is **naeyc** to get acquainted with the parents, answer their questions about the program, communicate what will be expected of them, take them on a tour of the program, and familiarize them with the forms that must be filled out before their child can be admitted. During the interview, it may be useful to go over the family information, the child's social history, the medical history, the emergency information record, and the various release and permission forms to answer questions about any confusing items. The sample forms in the **Director's Resources 9-1**, **9-2**, and **9-3** give some idea of the way these forms may look. The informality and friendliness of this first personal contact will set the tone for all future contacts. This is precisely the time to establish the foundation for mutual trust among director, educator, parent, and child, so it is important that these interviews be conducted in a nonthreatening manner.

Scheduling the interview is usually done at the convenience of the family. Even though the educator or the office staff may do the interview scheduling, it is essential that the director monitor it to ensure that families are not unduly inconvenienced. Careful consideration of family needs indicates that the program staff is sensitive to individual lifestyles and family preferences. For working parents, evenings or weekends may be best for interviews. Program staff members also must consider the transportation problems for some families, the availability of babysitters, and the schedules of other children in the family.

9-3f • Home Visit with the Family

A home visit may be the next **naeyc** step in the intake procedure. The director first describes the purpose of home visits to the staff and goes over a home visit report with them before family appointments are made (see **Director's Resource 9-4**). The purpose is not to evaluate the home but to gather information that will enable the staff to better understand the child. Trust between parents and staff will be destroyed and communication impaired if the family interprets the purpose of these home visits as evaluative. Observing a family at home will help the

Director's Corner

We make it clear at the outset and are fairly firm with parents about spending some time here with their child because we know, from experience, that even a child who comes in with apparent ease may have a problem two months hence, which harks back to skipping the gradual transition into the group. Even if a parent can spend only 15 minutes in the morning with a child for a week or two, we accept that and make it clear we expect it. My staff is sold on the importance of gradual separation and will even come in 15 or 30 minutes early—before we open—to give a new child time in the classroom with both the parent and the educator present.

—*Director, corporate-sponsored program*

educator understand the family lifestyle, culture, and attitudes about childrearing.

9-3g • Initial Visit to the Program

The scheduling of the initial visits to the program is arranged by the director and the staff before home visits begin so that information about visiting the program can be given to parents during the home visit.

This initial visit to the classroom is planned to help the child make that first big step from home and the trusted caregiver to the program and a new caring adult. For preschool children, the visit can last from 30 to 45 minutes and should terminate before the child is tired or bored. This entire orientation process is longer and more complex for infants and toddlers. Although the educator is clearly responsible for working with the child and the accompanying adult during preliminary visits, it is important for the director to be available to greet the newcomers and answer any questions that might arise. It provides a perfect opportunity for the director and parents to get to know each other better and is a good time to give them a copy of the parent handbook. (A sample parent handbook is available as a TeachSource Digital Download.)

9-3h • Phasing in the Children

The first three intake steps for pre- **naeyc** school children described here can be implemented in all types of program-based programs.

The scheduling of each step should be adjusted to individual family needs and obviously is much more difficult for working parents. In fact, the scheduling of these steps may seem to be somewhat unrealistic for full-day early childhood programs but can be done through creative planning. Implementing the intake procedures for all ages of children in early childhood programs could involve evenings, early mornings, or weekends. The director, therefore, must work out the scheduling with the staff and may give comp time to professional staff or overtime for hourly employees.

The phasing in (or *staggered entrance*) is the fourth and last step in the intake procedure and will, of necessity, be quite different in ongoing early childhood programs than in programs that are just starting or in those based on the typical school calendar. Arranging for the staggered entrance of a group of 12 to 15 preschool children at the beginning of the year poses a complex scheduling problem, but it is an essential step in the orientation process. Because scheduling is completely involved, it is important for the director and staff to consult with parents about convenient times for them to come and stay with their child. Successful implementation of the plan depends on staff and family commitment to it. Extended intake procedures for younger children can require special planning.

In public-school–sponsored programs, which usually have no precedent for gradual intake of new children, early childhood staff will have to meet with administrators and building principals to explain the importance of this procedure for the well-being of children and families. Because some early childhood programs in public schools are considered part of the elementary school and are accredited with the elementary school in the local school district, they usually are expected to provide a given number of instructional days to maximize the amount of state funds they receive. Often the developmentally appropriate practice of phasing in children is one of the first issues that creates conflict between developmental early childhood educators and the more academic and readiness-focused elementary educators.

The major problem in full-day early childhood program is to find a trusted adult to stay with the child until all people involved feel comfortable about the child being at the program every day for the full day. When a family needs a full early childhood program for a child, both parents usually are working, or the child may be a member of a one-parent family or in foster care. In these special cases, a grandparent or other member of the extended family may be the best person to provide the emotional support necessary for the child during the phasing-in period.

If there is any question among staff members about the importance of the gradual orientation program for the child, the family, and the success of the total program, it is up to the director to help everyone understand that this process represents the next logical step in developing mutual trust within the educator–child–family unit. Orienting children is usually exciting and productive for the educator, but it is also time-consuming and energy draining. The process can be successful only if the entire staff understands its relevance to the total program and recognizes it as being consistent with developmentally appropriate practice.

Summary

Most of the decisions about grouping children appropriately are made by the director, who must consider the unique needs of the children, available space, and licensing regulations about ratios and group size. Policy decisions about chronological or multiage grouping must be made before children are assigned to groups. Skills and experience of staff, ages of children, and the numbers and types of children with special needs selected for admission are all factors that will affect where children will be assigned.

Enrolling children involves filling out forms, interviewing parents, making home visits, and gradually phasing in the children. Although the staggered enrollment procedure is complex and time-consuming, it is a critical step in the process of building trust among the school, the child, and the family. To effectively recruit and enroll children, directors must do the following:

- Identify how early care and education meets the needs of all children, including those with special learning needs, and their families.

- Demonstrate how to make informed decisions about grouping children in programs.

- Identify effective practices for enrolling children.

TRY IT OUT!

1. Using **Director's Resource 9-1**, work out a staggered enrollment schedule for 12 children, then reflect on your personal reactions to the information in this chapter under the heading "Intake Procedures" (page 260).

2. In small groups, discuss how you can motivate your staff.
   a. Did you think about how parents might feel about the procedures described in the various steps of the intake procedures?
   b. Were you having any particular negative (or positive) feelings about the intake procedures?
   c. Did you identify with this material as a
      - student?
      - classroom educator?
      - prospective parent?
      - director?
      - other?

3. Working with another student, role-play an initial interview with a young mother who is sending an only child who is 3 years old to your program. The Sample Personal History (**Director's Resource 9-2**) and the Policy Summary Form (**Director's Resource 9-3**) are to be explained during this interview. At the close of the interview, discuss reactions to this role-play with the entire group.

4. In groups of four, role-play a home visit with a mother, father, and their 3-year-old daughter. When you arrive, you see no evidence of toys in the home, and you find the child dressed and sitting in a chair with her hands folded, apparently having been told to "be good and sit quietly while we talk to your educator." The purpose of the visit is to explain the initial visit to the program and the staggered enrollment plan for the child.

5. After the role-play, stay in groups of four and evaluate your reaction to the child and to the family. Evaluate your reactions as you played educator, mother, father, or child. Consider how successful the educator was at developing a relationship with the child. Fill in the Home Visit Report (**Director's Resource 9-4**) in sufficient detail so the director will have a clear picture of what transpired during the visit.

Director's Resource 9-1

DEVELOPING A STAGGERED ENROLLMENT PLAN

(for use with Try It Out! 9-1)

Enroll 12 children over a period of 8 days.
The plan is for a half-day preschool that meets from 9:00 a.m. to 11:30 a.m. daily.
Remember to have children come for shorter hours, in small groups, and gradually move toward having all children together for the full 2½ hours on the ninth day of school.
Fill in the time slots with the child's number—1, 2, 3, . . . , 12.
Time slots can be adjusted to suit your plan.

Week 1	Monday—1	Tuesday—2	Wednesday—3	Thursday—4	Friday—5
9:00					
9:30					
10:00					
10:30					
11:00					
11:30					
Week 2	**Monday—6**	**Tuesday—7**	**Wednesday—8**	**Thursday—9**	**Friday—10**
9:00				Children 1–12	Children 1–12
9:30					
10:00					
10:30					
11:00					
11:30					

Director's Resource 9-2 ////

SAMPLE PERSONAL HISTORY—YOUR CHILD'S DEVELOPMENT

(for use with Try It Out! 9-3)

Date _____

Child's Name _____ Nickname _____
Address _____ ZIP _____ Phone _____
Date of Birth _____ Place of Birth _____
Sex _____

I. The Child's Family
   Parents or Guardians
A. Name _____ Birth Date _____
   Education (include highest grade completed or degrees)
   _____
   _____
   Occupation _____ Usual working hours _____
                         Work phone _____
B. Name _____ Birth Date _____
   Education (include highest grade completed or degrees)
   _____
   Occupation _____ Usual working hours _____
                         Work phone _____
Status of Parents (Check) Living together _____
Living apart _____
Child lives with _____
If parents work or are students, who keeps the child in their absence?
Circle one   Grandparent   Other Relative   Friend   Paid Sitter   Other

Director's Resource 9-2 (continued) ////

Other children in the family (list in order of birth)

Name	Sex	Birth Date	What grade if in school

Additional members of household (give number)
Friends _____   Others _____
Boarders _____   Relatives _____

(Indicate relationships)

What part do these other persons have in the care of your child? _____

Has your child been separated from his/her parents for long periods of time, and if so, why? _____

Have you moved frequently? _____
What language is usually spoken at home? _____
(If more than one, what other language(s) are spoken?)
_____

Director's Resource 9-2 (continued) ////

C. Income _____ (per month) _____
   (per year) _____
D. Medical card number _____ (parent)
   Child's number _____
II. Development in Early Childhood
   Comment on the health of the mother during pregnancy
   _____
   Comment on the health of your child during delivery and infancy _____
   When did your child walk? _____
   When did your child talk? _____
   Is your child adopted? _____
   Does he/she know it? _____
   Does your child have bladder control? _____
   Child's terminology _____
   Does your child have bowel control? _____
   Child's terminology _____
   Does your child need help when going to the bathroom?
   _____
   Does your child need reminding about going to the bathroom? _____
   Does your child usually take a nap? _____
   At what time? _____
   Describe any special needs, handicaps, or health problems.
   _____
   _____

Director's Resource 9-2 (continued) ////

Does your child have any difficulty saying what he/she wants or do you have any trouble understanding his/her speech? _____
III. Eating Habits
   What is your child's general attitude toward eating? _____
   What foods does your child especially like? _____
   For which meal is your child most hungry? _____
   Does the child feed himself/herself entirely? _____
   Does your child dislike any food in particular? _____
   Is your child on a special diet? _____
   Does your child take a bottle? _____
   Does your child eat or chew things that are not food? Explain. _____
   Do you have any concerns about your child's eating habits? Explain. _____
   Is there any food your child should not eat for medical, religious, or personal reasons? _____
IV. Play and Social Experiences
   Has your child participated in any group experiences?
   _____
   Where? _____
   Did your child enjoy it? _____
   Do other playmates visit the child? _____
   Does your child visit other playmates in their homes?
   _____
   How does your child relate to other children? _____
   Does your child prefer to play alone? _____ With other children? _____

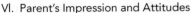

Director's Resource 9-2 (continued)

Does your child worry a lot or is he/she very afraid of anything?
_____

What causes worry or fear? _____
Does your child have any imaginary playmates? _____
Explain._____
Does your child have any pets? _____
_____
What are your child's favorite toys and/or activities?
_____
_____
What is your child's favorite TV program? _____
How long does your child watch TV each day? _____
What are your child's favorite books? _____
How many times a week is your child read to?_____
Is there anything else about your child's play or playmates that
the school should know? _____
_____
_____

V. Discipline
In most circumstances, do you consider your child easily
managed, fairly easy to manage, or difficult to manage?
_____
What concerns do you presently have about your child?
_____
_____
How are these concerns dealt with? _____
_____

Director's Resource 9-2 (continued)

VI. Parent's Impression and Attitudes
From your point of view, what were the events which seemed
to have had the greatest impact on your child (moving,
births, deaths, severe illness of family members, divorce)?
_____
_____

How would you describe your child at the present time?
What changes have you seen in your child during the past
year? _____
_____

Does your child have any behavior characteristics which
you hope will change? Please describe. _____
_____

In what ways would you like to see your child develop during
the school year? _____
_____
_____
_____
_____
_____
_____

_____
Signature(s) of person(s) filling out this questionnaire

Director's Resource 9-3

SAMPLE POLICY SUMMARY FORM

(for use with Try It Out! 9-3)

**BOMBECK FAMILY LEARNING PROGRAM SUMMARY
OF POLICIES**

PLEASE SIGN AND RETURN THAT YOU HAVE RECEIVED
AND READ THIS NOTICE. THANK YOU!!!!
_____
I have received and read the summary of Bombeck Family
Learning Program policies.
Child(ren)'s name: _____
Parent Signature: _____
Date: _____
The following is a summary of some of the policies that impact
daily life at the program. Complete information can be found
in the Parent Handbook which we encourage you to read
and keep on hand for reference. Please address questions or
concerns to the director.

Attendance

A parent should notify the Program by 9:00 a.m. when a child
will not be attending on a scheduled day. This procedure also
applies to those children who attend half-day kindergarten.

Director's Resource 9-3 (continued)

Drop Off–Pick Up

Children must be brought to and picked up inside the child's
classroom. A Child Release Form must be on file in the office
for anyone other than a parent or guardian to pick up a child.
Picture ID is required. Children may be dropped off at any
time during the day except lunch and naptime.

Illness/Sick Policy

As a Program licensed by the State of Ohio, we are required to
strictly follow procedures concerning communicable diseases
to protect the children and staff at the Program. The parent
will be expected to pick up the child immediately if a child
exhibits the following symptoms:

Temperature of at least 100 degrees Fahrenheit—or less if
accompanied by another symptom of illness
Two or more bouts of diarrhea
Severe coughing
Difficult or rapid breathing
Yellowish skin or eyes
Redness, discharge, burning, itching of the eye
Infected skin patches, spots or rashes
Dark urine or gray or white stool
Stiff neck with elevated temperature
Lice, scabies or other parasitic infestation
Vomiting one or more times, or if accompanied by another
symptom of illness

Director's Resource 9-3 (continued)

The child or staff member will not be readmitted to the program until s/he is symptom free for a period of 24 hours, or until a physician's written permission verifies that there is no risk of contagion.

Medications

"Administration of Medication by the Program Personnel" form must accompany any medication, prescription or over-the-counter drugs to be administered to a child. The child's name and specific times and dosage must be written on the form provided in the classroom each day. "As needed" is insufficient information.

Administration of medication by a person other than a program staff member and other than the parent, requires written permission signed by the parent. Name of the person, date, time and dosage should be included.

Payment of Tuition

Tuition payments are to be paid one full week in advance. If payment is not received on time a $25.00 late charge will be added to the balance.

Tuition payments and late charges not paid by the following week are cause for withdrawal of service by the program.

Late Pick Up Fees

A late fee will be charged for children left at the Program after 6:00 p.m. Late fees are charged as follows: (program clock used as basis). Calls ahead do not negate late charges.

Director's Resource 9-3 (continued)

6:01–6:30—one dollar per minute later than 6:31 is five dollars per minute

Back-Up Plan

Please have a back-up plan in place for medical exclusions or emergency closings.

Parent Participation, Visitors and Custody

Any custodial parent, custodian, or guardian of a child enrolled at the Program is welcome to visit at any time.

Visitors to the program are required to sign in and out of the building at the front desk.

When custody rights or visitation of a child has been determined by a court or other legal entity, a copy of the order must be provided to the Program.

Medical Emergencies

The program's staff is trained in First Aid procedures. If a serious medical emergency should arise, a call to the University Public Safety Department would summon an emergency vehicle staffed with EMTs who would evaluate the situation and transport to an area hospital if necessary. Parents will be notified immediately and a staff member will stay with the child until parents arrive. The child's emergency transport, health and medical records will accompany them. A child safety seat is available if needed.

Director's Resource 9-3 (continued)

Accidents

In case of accidents, a staff member will complete an incident report that is given to the parent on the day of the occurrence, which must be signed and returned to the educator.

Child Abuse

If any abuse or neglect is seen or suspected involving a child enrolled at the Bombeck Program, the situation must be reported to the Children's Services Board in the county in which the child resides.

Discipline

Discipline is not punishment. If conflicts occur, staff members strive to help children find alternative modes of behavior and explain why inappropriate behavior is not acceptable. The Program strictly adheres to the discipline guidelines set forth by the Ohio Child Care Licensing Code.

Emergency Closings

The Bombeck Program will make every effort to remain open in the event of inclement weather. However, if weather conditions warrant closing, the program will follow the University's directions for the closure. Please check your local television broadcast of school closing. Closing will also be posted on the Bombeck Program Facebook page.

Director's Resource 9-3 (continued)

Vacations

Families are entitled to five vacation days annually. Two-week advance notice is requested. Vacation request forms may be picked up at the front desk.

Grievance Procedures

In the event that a problem or complain should arise, the following are suggested procedures for resolution:

It is strongly encouraged that the issue be resolved with the staff member involved. If the issue is not resolved at that level, the issue should be brought to the attention of the director, who will counsel with all individuals involved in order to resolve the issue in a positive way.

Use of Videotapes and Photographs

The parent of every child enrolled at the Program must sign a "Permission to Videotape and Photograph Form." University students may be required to periodically videotape or photograph the children as they participate in classroom activities. The university photographer also takes photographs at the Bombeck Program.

Source: Reprinted by permission of the Bombeck Family Learning Program of the University of Dayton.

Director's Resource 9-4 ////

SAMPLE HOME VISIT/PARENT CONTACT REPORT

(for use with Try It Out! 9-5)

Program _____
Type of Program _____

1. Name of visitor _____ Title _____
2. Child's name _____
3. Parent or guardian _____
4. Address _____
5. Date and time of visit or meeting _____
6. Purpose of visit or meeting _____
   _____
   _____

7. Specific action taken as result of visit or meeting _____
   _____
   _____
   _____
   _____
   _____
   _____
   _____

Director's Resource 9-4 *(continued)* ////

8. Observations and comments _____
   _____
   _____
   _____
   _____
   _____
   _____
   _____
   _____

Director's Resource 9-5 ////

SAMPLE PERMISSION FORM

While your child is enrolled in this program, he/she will be involved in a number of special activities for which we need your permission. Please read the following information carefully. You are encouraged to ask questions about anything that is unclear to you. You, of course, have the option of withdrawing permission at any time.

_____

(CHILD'S NAME)
(PLEASE CIRCLE YOUR CHOICE)
A. I DO DO NOT give my permission for my child to go on walks with the classroom educator and class in the nearby neighborhood.
B. I DO DO NOT give my permission for my child to be screened for speech and language.
C. I DO DO NOT give my permission for my child to be screened for hearing.
D. I DO DO NOT give my permission for my child to be screened for specific educational needs.
E. From time to time photographs of our preschool program will be made for educational and publicity purposes. These pictures will be representative of the enriching experiences offered your child during the year.

I DO DO NOT give my permission for my child to be photographed for use in educational, nonprofit publications/presentations intended to further the cause of public education. This permission is applicable for current as well as future project use.

Director's Resource 9-5 *(continued)* ////

As part of this program, your child's records may be included in research that evaluates the value of the program. In all cases, the confidentiality of individual children's records is maintained.

_____

Parent's Signature

_____

Date

Director's Resource 9-6

SAMPLE EARLY CHILDHOOD PROGRAM APPLICATION (REQUESTING INCOME INFORMATION)

For office use only
District Status: _____
Income Status: _____
Priority Status: _____
Date Application Received: _____
Date Eligible for Entrance: _____
Enrollment Age: _____
Child's Name: _____ Date of Birth: _____
Sex: _____
Race, Nationality, or Ethnic Group: _____
Address: _____ Phone: _____
Mother's Name: _____ Date of Birth: _____
SS # _____
Father's Name: _____ Date of Birth: _____
SS # _____
Child lives with _____
Children attend the program-based program four (4) half days per week; they eat lunch and snack at the program. Transportation is provided for handicapped or special needs children.
Do you wish to apply for the program-based program? Yes _____ No _____
Session preferred A.M. _____ 8:45–11:45
  P.M. _____ 12:45–3:45
Children and families in the home-based program are visited once per week in the home and are transported to the program on

Director's Resource 9-6 *(continued)*

Friday for a group experience. The home-based educator will assist parents in creating a home environment to promote children's growth and development. This program is in the morning only.
Do you wish to apply for the home-based program? Yes _____ No _____
* *

Family Size: _____
Family Income:
$ _____ per week $ _____ per month $ _____ per year
Source of Reimbursement or Services (Circle "Yes" or "No" for each source)

YES	NO	EPSDT/Medicaid (Latest certification #):	___
YES	NO	Federal, State, or Local Agency:	___
YES	NO	In-Kind Provider:	___
YES	NO	Insurance:	___
		I.D. #:	___
YES	NO	WIC	
YES	NO	Food Stamps	

Does this child or any of your family members have a disability or special need?
Describe: _____
How well does your child speak and understand English?
_____
How did you obtain information about this program?
_____

Director's Resource 9-7

SAMPLE APPLICATION (NO INCOME INFORMATION REQUESTED)

Walnut Corner Children's Program Preregistration Form
CHILD'S FAMILY INFORMATION
Child's Name _____ Name Used _____
Date of Birth, or Expected Date of Birth _____
Child's Address _____
Father/Guardian Name _____ Mother/Guardian Name _____
Home Address _____ Home Address _____
Employer _____ Employer _____
Address _____ Address _____
Business Phone _____ Business Phone _____

REQUESTED DAYS OF ATTENDANCE
Days: M T W TH F Hours: _____ AM _____ PM
Requested Start Date: _____

HOW DID YOU LEARN ABOUT WALNUT CORNER CHILDREN'S PROGRAM?
Personal Referral/If so, who? _____
Newspaper _____ Radio _____ Website
_____ Other _____
Thank you for this information

Director's Resource 9-7 *(continued)*

PLEASE INCLUDE THE NONREFUNDABLE $25 REGISTRATION FEE WITH THIS FORM.
THIS FEE WILL SECURE YOUR CHILD'S NAME ON OUR WAITING LIST.

Director's Resource 9-8 ///

SAMPLE STUDENT ENROLLMENT FORM

(Public School–Sponsored Program) STUDENT ENROLLMENT FORM

(MUST BE RETAINED IN STUDENT'S CUMULATIVE RECORD)

Assigned to: Gr _____ Hr _____
SDF sent to Census _____
Type a new CR _____
CR in office file _____
CR requested _____
Health Record Yes _____
No _____
Rec'd. 4-part SDF _____

Name of school student is entering _____ Grade Enter
_____ Special Ed _____
Name _____

Student's Legal Name (as listed on birth certificate)

Circle
Sex: Male Female
Address _____ Apt. No. _____ ZIP Code _____
Phone No. _____
Place of birth _____ Date of birth _____
City State Country

Circle
Race: Black White Other

Mo Day Yr

Director's Resource 9-8 (continued) ///

Check one of the birth verifications listed below:
☐ Birth Certificate No. _____ ☐ Baptismal Certificate
_____
☐ Physician's Record ☐ Passport

	DPT	Polio	Measles	Rubella	Mumps
IMMUNIZATION DATA					

SOCIAL RECORD

Name	Place of birth		Deceased (Date)
	State	Country	
Father: _____			
Mother: _____			
Step-Parent: _____			
Guardian: _____			

If family is supported by another source indicate: _____

	Occupation	Place of Employment	Business Phone No.
Father's occupation			
Mother's occupation			

Director's Resource 9-8 (continued) ///

Name of Brothers and Sisters: School Attendance	Still in School:	
	School or Preschool	

Circle one:
Family Status: Married Single Divorced Separated
Remarried
Of parent: Student is living with _____ Relationship _____
LANGUAGE OTHER THAN ENGLISH SPOKEN IN HOME: _____
Did student attend this school last year?
☐ Yes
☐ No Name of school _____ Address _____
☐ Yes—Privacy Requested: If this box is checked, no information pertaining to this student will be released to any person or institution (including colleges or universities) without your written approval.
☐ No—Privacy is not requested
Parent/Guardian's Signature _____ Date: _____
In case of emergency, call _____
Name Relationship Phone No

Director's Resource 9-9A ///

PREENROLLMENT FORM OF CHILD DEVELOPMENT LEVELS

Demonstration School for
the School of Education
and Allied Professions
941 Alberta St., Dayton,
Ohio 45409 / (937) 229-2158 /
http://www.udayton.edu/education/Bombeckprogram

Child's Name: _____ Today's Date: _____
Child's Date of Birth: _____ Current Age: _____
yrs. _____ mos. _____
Parent/Guardian filling out form: _____
Birth to 9 months: Security Stage

Sensory Preferences: My child enjoys learning about his/her world most by: _____ seeing _____ hearing _____ tasting _____ smelling _____ touching
Relationships:
My child responds to others by:
_____ gazing _____ making faces _____ smiling _____ making sounds _____ other: _____

My child gets my attention by:

Director's Resource 9-9A (continued)

_____ crying _____ gesturing _____ holding on tight _____ squealing _____ other: _____

Language: My child's language development is shown by:
_____ smiling/gurgling when spoken to
_____ using different cries/sounds for different needs
_____ imitating sounds, rhythms, tones of adult talk
_____ playing games like peekaboo, pat-a-cake, etc.

Movement: My child's physical development is evidenced by:
_____ moving his/her arms, legs, and other body parts
_____ enjoying touching and being touched
_____ rolling over _____ holding up his/her head _____ scooting/crawling _____ other: _____

Emotions: My child is generally:
_____ calm _____ agitated _____ fussy
_____ sensitive _____ alert _____ happy
_____ demanding

Health: My child has _____ no health issues _____ colds _____ allergies _____ fevers _____ other: _____

Director's Resource 9-9B

PREENROLLMENT FORM OF CHILD DEVELOPMENT LEVELS

Demonstration School for the School of Education and Allied Professions, 941 Alberta St., Dayton, Ohio 45409 / (937) 229-2158 / http://www.udayton.edu/education/Bombeckprogram

Child's Name: _____ Today's Date: _____
Child's Date of Birth: _____ Current Age: _____
yrs. _____ mos. _____
Parent/Guardian filling out form: _____

8-18 months: Exploration Stage

Sensory Preferences: My child enjoys learning about his/her world most by:
_____ seeing _____ hearing _____ tasting _____ smelling _____ touching

Relationships: My child responds to others by:
_____ making sounds _____ physically approaching /touching _____ watching _____ imitating
_____ other: _____
    My child gets attention by:
_____ squealing/crying _____ touching/hitting
_____ pinching/biting _____ watching/waiting
_____ other: _____

Director's Resource 9-9B (continued)

Language: My child's language development is demonstrated by:

_____ responding to his/her name, to directions, or to questions
_____ expressing emotions through verbalizing
_____ demonstrating an awareness of concepts of cause/ effect, more/less
_____ adding words to his/her vocabulary, imitating the tone and rhythm of adult speech
_____ recognizing people and objects by name
_____ demonstrating an interest in books and pictures

Movement: My child's physical development is evidenced by: becoming mobile by _____ scooting _____ bouncing _____ crawling _____ cruising _____ walking _____ other: _____
_____ standing or sitting _____ going up or down ramps/steps _____ bending over without falling
_____ holding objects _____ pushing toys
_____ opening/closing items _____ using tools
_____ gesturing

Emotions: My child displays his/her emotion by:
_____ smiling/laughing _____ cuddling
_____ crying _____ tensing/screaming when angry _____ other: _____

Health: My child generally has:
_____ no health issues _____ colds _____ earaches _____ allergies _____ breathing problems _____ fevers _____ other: _____

Director's Resource 9-9C

PREENROLLMENT FORM OF CHILD DEVELOPMENT LEVELS

Demonstration School for the School of Education and Allied Professions, 941 Alberta St., Dayton, Ohio 45409 / (937) 229-2158 / http://www.udayton.edu/education/Bombeckprogram

Child's Name: _____ Today's Date: _____
Child's Date of Birth: _____ Current Age: _____
yrs. _____ mos. _____
Parent/Guardian filling out form: _____
16 to 36 months: Toddlers—Independent Stage

Sensory Preferences: My child enjoys learning about his/her world most by:

_____ seeing _____ hearing _____ tasting _____ smelling _____ touching

Relationships: My child responds to others by: _____ communicating wants/needs _____ asserting himself/ herself _____ displaying empathy other: _____
My child gets attention by:

Director's Resource 9-9C (continued) ///

_____ asking questions _____ demanding
_____ cooperating _____ physical interaction
_____ other: _____

Language: My child's language development is demonstrated by:
_____ initiating conversations, back and forth discourse, conflict over "mine" or "no"
_____ repeating after others or reenacting series of events or daily adult tasks
_____ saying single words _____ phrases
_____ sentences _____
_____ following directions, asking questions, naming objects, people, places
_____ demonstrating understanding of concepts of shape, size, color, type, other cognitive skills
_____ "telling" stories through play—with or without words

Movement: My child's physical development is evidenced by:
_____ walking _____ running _____ climbing
_____ jumping _____ stepping "over" _____ up and down stairs
_____ using small objects _____ using writing and art materials _____ pouring/serving food _____ other: _____

Emotions: My child displays emotional responses such as:
_____ empathy _____ pride in accomplishment
_____ generosity _____ comforting _____
demanding _____ other: _____

Director's Resource 9-9C (continued) ///

Health: My child generally has:
_____ no health issues _____ cold/flu _____
earaches _____ allergies _____ asthma _____
fevers _____ other: _____

Director's Resource 9-9D ///

PREENROLLMENT FORM OF CHILD DEVELOPMENT LEVELS

Demonstration School for the School of Education and Allied Professions, 941 Alberta St., Dayton, Ohio 45409 / (937) 229-2158 / http://www.udayton.edu/education/Bombeckprogram

Child's Name: _____ Today's Date: _____
Child's Date of Birth: _____ Current Age: _____ yrs.
_____ mos. _____
Parent/Guardian filling out form: _____
3-5 years—Preschooler

Physical Development: My child's physical activity includes:
_____ running _____ jumping _____ climbing _____ skipping _____ galloping _____ creative movement such as dancing
_____ coordinated movements _____ small muscle control _____ large muscle control _____ other: _____

Social/Emotional Development: My child displays the following behaviors:
_____ enjoys learning _____ develops friends
_____ follows directions/rules _____ relates well to adults/peers _____ emotional awareness

Director's Resource 9-9D (continued) ///

_____ shares easily _____ takes turns _____ resolve conflicts without aggression
_____ develops conscience _____ copes with stress
_____ shows resilience to adversity _____ exhibits self-control

Cognitive Development: My child has the ability to:
_____ think about past/present/future
_____ reenact storylines accurately following sequence of events
_____ coordinate and assume roles during dramatic play
_____ organize thoughts into explanations, questions, and other categories
_____ use symbols to represent reality—i.e., pictures, words, numbers
_____ understand "pretend" and the difference between imaginary and real in most instances
_____ predict what will happen next with some accuracy
_____ solve problems through thoughtful reasoning with guidance
_____ express thoughts and feeling several ways (verbalizes, draws, sings, moves creatively)

Health: My child generally has:
_____ no health issues _____ cold/flu _____
earaches _____ allergies _____ asthma/breathing difficulty _____ fever
_____ within normal range of physical growth
_____ has regular check-ups _____ has received immunizations

Developed by Diana Smith, Director of Program Development, University of Dayton, Bombeck Family Learning Program, November 4, 2011.

Source: Reprinted by permission of the Bombeck Family Learning Program of the University of Dayton.

Director's Resource 9-10 ///

SAMPLE CHILD'S MEDICAL STATEMENT

Enrollment Date _____
Early childhood program _____
Preschool Certificate of Medical Examination to Be Completed by Family Physician or Clinic
This is to certify that _____
Child's Name _____ Birth Date _____
Mother _____ Address _____ Phone _____
Father _____ Address _____ Phone _____
was examined by me on _____, and based on his/her medical history Date of Examination _____ and physical condition at the time of this examination, is free from apparent communicable disease, and is in suitable condition for enrollment in a child early childhood program facility; and has had the immunizations required by Section 3313.671 of the Revised Code for admission to school, or has had the immunizations required by the State Department of Health for infants and toddlers, or is to be exempted from these requirements for medical reasons. Tuberculin test (within last year for new enrollee) Date _____
Type of test _____ Results _____
DPT Series and booster dates 1st _____ 2nd _____
3rd _____ 4th _____ 5th _____
Oral Polio
Series dates 1st _____ 2nd _____ 3rd _____
4th _____
The 5th DPT and 4th polio are normally administered just prior to kindergarten.

Director's Resource 9-10 (continued) ///

Measles (Rubella, 9-day)	Date _____	
Rubella (3-day)	Date _____	
Mumps	Date _____	
Haemophilus B polysaccharide (HIB)	Date _____	(HIB vaccine is required for children ages 2 years through 4 years)

Is able to participate in all regular activities except _____
Remarks _____
Physician's Signature _____ Date _____
Clinic Name _____ Phone _____
Office Location _____
City, State, ZIP _____
Parent should retain this sheet when child withdraws from program.

Director's Resource 9-11 ///

SAMPLE EMERGENCY INFORMATION RECORD

Child's Name _____
Home Address _____
Father's name/Husband Place of Employment _____
Bus. Phone _____
(or guardian) _____
Mother's name/Wife Place of Employment _____ Bus.
Phone _____
(or guardian) _____
Please fill in information below so that the school may act more effectively in event of illness or injury to the child.
EMERGENCY: Person to be called if parent (husband or wife) cannot be reached:
Name _____ Address _____ Phone _____
Date _____ Parent's Signature (or guardian) _____

Director's Resource 9-12 ///

CHILD RELEASE FORM

To maintain the safety and protection of your child, please provide us with a complete list of persons who may pick up your child or children from the program. Anyone other than the parent should sign in at the front desk. The staff will ask for picture identification before releasing the child(ren).

Child's name: _____ classroom: _____
Child's name: _____ classroom: _____
Child's name: _____ classroom: _____
Child's name: _____ classroom: _____

The following individuals have my permission to pick up the child(ren) listed above from the Bombeck Family Learning program:

Name: _____ relationship: _____
Name: _____ relationship: _____
Name: _____ relationship: _____
Name: _____ relationship: _____

I have instructed these individuals to sign in at the front desk and be prepared to present picture identification when requesting release of the child(ren). Questions or concerns should be directed to me at the following phone numbers:

Work: _____ Home: _____ Cell: _____

If efforts to reach me should fail, please call the following person to verify permission to pick up my child(ren):
Name: _____ Relationship: _____
Parent Signature: _____ Date: _____

REFERENCES

Allen, K. E., & Cowdery, G. E. (2014). *The exceptional child: Inclusion in early childhood education* (8th ed.). Clifton Park, NY: Thomson Delmar Learning.

ADA Amendments Act of 2008, Public Law 19–325, 122 Stat. 3553 (2008).

Equity and Early Childhood Education Task Force. (2016). *Equity and early childhood education: Reclaiming the child—a policy research brief.* Urbana, IL: National Council of Teachers of English. https://cdn.ncte.org/nctefiles/equityearlyedbrief.pdf

Freeman, N. K., Decker, C. A., & Decker, J. R. (2017). *Planning and administering early childhood programs* (11th ed.). Upper Saddle River, NJ: Prentice Hall.

Dinnebeil, L. A. (2011). *A guide to itinerant early childhood special education services.* Baltimore, MD: Brookes.

Family Educational Rights and Privacy Act (Buckley Amendment). (1974). The 1974 Education Amendments, 20 U.S.C.A., Sec 1232g. (Supp. 1975).

Feeney, S., & Freeman, N. (n.d.). *Ethics and the early childhood educator: Using the NAEYC Code of Ethics,* Section II. Washington, DC: NAEYC.

Gonzalez-Mena, J., & Widmeyer Eyer, D. (2017). *Infants, toddlers and caregivers: A curriculum of respectful, responsive, relationship-based care and education* (11th ed.). New York, NY: McGraw-Hill.

Katz, L. G., & Chard, S. C. (2014). *Engaging children's minds: The project approach* (3rd ed.). Stamford, CT: Ablex.

National Association for the Education of Young Children. (2013). *NAEYC early childhood program standards and accreditation criteria & guidance for assessment.* Washington, DC: Author.

U.S. Department of Justice. (n.d.). Commonly asked questions about child care programs and the Americans with Disabilities Act. Retrieved from http://www.ada.gov/childq%26a.htm.

Program administrators support curriculum so that enriching experiences are woven throughout every child's day.

Chapter 10
Supporting Quality Curriculum

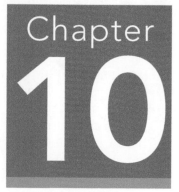

naeyc

Standards and Recommendations Addressed in This Chapter

ADVANCING EQUITY RECOMMENDATION 1 Provide high-quality early learning services that demonstrate a commitment to equitable outcomes for all children.

PROGRAM STANDARD 2 Curriculum

PROGRAM STANDARD 3 Teaching

PROGRAM STANDARD 4 Assessment of Child Progress

PROGRAM STANDARD 9 Physical Environment

PROFESSIONAL STANDARDS AND COMPETENCIES: STANDARD 1 Child Development and Learning in Context

PROFESSIONAL STANDARDS AND COMPETENCIES: STANDARD 3 Child Observation, Documentation, and Assessment

PROFESSIONAL STANDARDS AND COMPETENCIES: STANDARD 4 Developmentally, Culturally, and Linguistically Appropriate Teaching Practices

PROFESSIONAL STANDARDS AND COMPETENCIES: STANDARD 5 Knowledge, Application, and Integration of Academic Content in the Early Childhood Curriculum

PROFESSIONAL STANDARDS AND COMPETENCIES: STANDARD 6 Professionalism as an Early Childhood Educator

---

LEARNING OBJECTIVES

After reading this chapter, you should be able to:

10-1   Describe quality early childhood curriculum.

10-2   Explain the importance of feedback, support, and intervention.

10-3   Describe how to support intentional teaching.

10-4   Identify strategies that support a seamless birth to age 8 early childhood system.

In its long-awaited revision to the position statement on developmentally appropriate practices, the National Association for the Education of Young Children (NAEYC) states,

Each and every child, birth through age 8, has the right to equitable learning opportunities—in centers, family child care homes, or schools—that fully support their optimal development and learning across all domains and content areas. Children are born eager to learn; they take delight exploring their world and making connections. The degree to which early learning programs support children's delight and wonder in learning reflects the quality of that setting. Educators who engage in developmentally appropriate practice foster young children's joyful learning and maximize the opportunities for each and every child to achieve their full potential. (2020, p. 1)

For the director and educational leader of an early childhood program, decisions about curriculum are among the most difficult to make. The increasing national focus on the importance of the early years for brain development, school readiness, and sound emotional development provides both opportunities for the field and pressure to make informed decisions for the director and staff (Dickinson & Porche, 2011; Education Commission of the States, 2009; Yoshikawa et al., 2013). Public awareness of the importance of quality early care and education is growing. Understanding the many factors that constitute quality and impact today's curriculum decisions is a monumental task for the director, who must understand developmentally appropriate practices, early learning content and development standards, equity and access, accountability, appropriate assessment, school readiness, achievement gaps, and teaching children in poverty, children with disabilities, and children who are English-language learners. Not only do young children require an experience-rich environment, but it is now apparent that children who lack key experiences are more likely to start kindergarten without the fundamental knowledge and skills necessary for school success (Preschool Curriculum Evaluation Research Consortium, 2008). The director must be the "curriculum leader and mentor" who embraces the challenge of leading a program that meets the needs of the whole child while also sorting through societal pressures that challenge the traditional notions of early childhood curriculum. (In some larger programs, the director may share the role of curriculum mentor with a curriculum specialist.)

As the educational leader of an early childhood program, the director needs to be aware of curriculum requirements that constitute a quality program and that support the program's mission. The director must monitor the richness and appropriateness of the curriculum and serve as a curriculum mentor for educators who need a

forum for critical reflection and feedback as well as support and resources. The director is responsible for ensuring that all educators in the program know that everyone is accountable for offering a high-quality program each and every day. The curriculum should be part of the program's culture, which means that it reflects the culture of the children and families who use the program and is also informed by the culture of the professionals who design and implement it. By being part of the program's culture, high-quality curriculum should be apparent to all who enter the program and see children's work samples and documentation on the walls. In programs with a philosophy that limits what goes on the walls as is common in Montessori programs, alternate methods of sharing the emphasis on curriculum must be implemented.

Evidence of the importance placed on curriculum should be apparent when educators talk in the break room, during staff meetings, and most definitely during dedicated planning time. Parents should see evidence of curriculum in the parent handbook and should hear about it informally during drop-off and pick-up transition times and more formally during the programs' open house events and parent conferences. The importance placed on curriculum should also be evident on the program's website and Facebook page, where parents and other stakeholders can get daily updates, including the curriculum in action.

By meeting regularly with teaching teams to discuss the curriculum that is evolving in each classroom, the director and the curriculum specialist, if applicable, clearly articulate the importance placed on curriculum quality. These meetings help to establish a climate in which staff reflect critically on their practice, and program leaders come to understand the decisions that educators make and the resources and support that they need. As a curriculum mentor, the director works with staff to establish curricular expectations and to ensure that educators feel valued for their quality curriculum contributions. The director also needs to be aware of opportunities for growth or lack of follow-through so that teaching teams in need of curriculum intervention are given the support and oversight needed to improve. Failure to validate good curriculum practice or hold people accountable when their curriculum efforts do not meet the program's standards, sends the message that it is not important.

Quality Benchmarks from the National Institute for Early Education Research (NIEER)

The program:

- incorporates early learning and development standards;
- has teachers with bachelor's degrees with specialized training in pre-K;
- has an assistant teacher with a child development associate's degree or its equivalent;
- has staff professional development;
- has maximum class sizes of no more than 20 preschoolers (12 toddlers, 8 infants);
- has a staff–child ratio of 1:10 preschoolers (1:6 toddlers, 2:8 infants);
- has vision, hearing, health screening, and referral; and
- has curriculum supports.

Source: National Institute for Early Education Research. (2020). New report on pre-K in cities shows 33 of nation's largest cities now have public pre-K program. NIEER Re-search Report. New Brunswick, NJ: Rutgers, The State University of New Jersey. https://nieer.org/wp-content/uploads/2020/12/CityHealth-Pre-K-Summary-Benchmarks-and-Enrollment-2020.pdf

Director's Corner

We are an NAEYC-accredited program and have earned the highest level on our state's quality rating system. Of all of the indicators of quality that parents and visitors see when they enter our building, our curriculum which reflects our mission is what they comment on most. Part of our mission is to demonstrate high-quality science and inquiry experiences with young children. This emphasis on science transforms our environment and is obvious to all who enter the building.

—*Director of a university-affiliated demonstration school*

▶ TeachSource Video Vignette

Signs Of Good Child Care

▶ A Caring Relationship

▶ Discipline That Teaches

▶ Good Adult-Child Ratio

earlyShow   CBS

Early Childhood Program Quality

In the video titled *The Quality of Early Childhood Education*, Ellen Galinsky, from the Families and Work Institute, describes the findings of three research studies related to early childhood education. She discusses the characteristics of high-quality early childhood programs and the warning signs parents should look out for when a program is lacking in quality.

View the video vignette titled, *The Quality of Early Childhood Education*. Reflect on the following questions:

1. As a director, what factors should you consider to ensure quality programming for the young children in your care?

2. How might you use this information to communicate the benefits of a quality program for the children?

10-1 • Quality Early Childhood Curriculum

The focus on "quality" early childhood programs includes a curriculum that reflects a strong understanding of the philosophical underpinnings of the field, a comprehensive definition of curriculum, and a well-grounded understanding of developmentally appropriate practices.

10-1a • Philosophical Underpinnings

Although some people may see selecting a curriculum as the purchase of commercially prepared activities and assessment, quality programs see curriculum as an extension of the theory base that represents beliefs about children and families. Time needs to be taken to discuss how beliefs about curriculum represent the theory base for the field and also align with the mission, vision, and purpose of the program. Taking the time to establish a shared understanding of the program's educational philosophy means that practice will be consistent and intentional.

Teachers come to the classroom with varied educational backgrounds and prior experiences with children and education. They also come with varied dispositions and internally held beliefs and values about children, parenting, and teaching. These beliefs have an obvious impact on their practice (Seplocha, 2018, p. 5).

This common understanding should not be left to chance, and the failure to take the time to have these conversations will likely result in a curriculum that reflects the beliefs and practices of individual educators and not a cohesive reflection of the program's mission and vision.

10-1b • Defining Curriculum

To establish a culture that embraces high-quality curriculum, communicates curriculum to others, and participates in curriculum reflection and mentoring, there must be a common understanding of what is meant

Growth Mindset Moment

Consider the following example from Seplocha:

A teacher may believe that children learn best when the teacher is in front of the class teaching. In that classroom, children spend a large portion of the day in whole group doing the same thing, often responding to rote and repetition. Free play is seen as a time for the children to play while the teacher catches up on paperwork, handles discipline and prepares for the next lessons.

Another teacher may believe that children learn best through active exploration with teachers who scaffold children's learning through listening, observing, asking questions, and interaction. In this classroom, whole group time is short and purposeful in building community and introducing ideas and concepts. Free play is valued as an important time for learning, and the teacher's role is to trust children, follow their interests, and engage with individuals to follow the child's lead to support learning and differentiate interactions. (Seplocha, 2018, p. 6)

As a director and curriculum coach, how will you bring this team to a common understanding of best practice. What resources will you rely on to help communicate this message? Some might identify *compromise* as the best approach. Is that really the strategy that will result in quality programming for children?

by *curriculum*. In its new position statement on developmentally appropriate practices, the NAEYC states:

The curriculum consists of the plans for the learning experiences through which children acquire knowledge, skills, abilities, and understanding. Implementing a curriculum always yields outcomes of some kind—but which outcomes those are and how a program achieves them are critical. In developmentally appropriate practice, the curriculum helps young children achieve goals that are meaningful because they are culturally and linguistically responsive and developmentally and educationally significant. The curriculum does this through learning experiences that reflect what is known about young children in general and about each child in particular. (NAEYC, 2020, p. 25)

The importance of a quality and developmentally appropriate curriculum is evident; however, the reality is that for many, the term *curriculum* refers to a commercially produced book that is adopted by the program to satisfy a regulation or mandate. Moving the curriculum from a book on the shelf to an integral and visible component of the program's culture requires staff buy-in and strong educational leadership. As curriculum leaders, program administrators are responsible for ensuring that a comprehensive quality curriculum is being implemented consistently throughout the program. A quality comprehensive curriculum:

- is planned intentionally to include learning experiences that are meaningful to and developmentally appropriate for the children being served;
- focuses on the whole day and the whole child;
- is child centered and reflects the belief that play is how young children learn;
- reflects the children's strengths, needs, and interests;
- is informed by ongoing authentic assessment conducted by trained observers;
- involves collaborative decision-making by teaching teams who have a shared understanding of research-based practice, quality early childhood education, and the routines and philosophy of the classroom and the program;
- reflects a strengths-based and respectful partnerships with families and is culturally responsive;
- incorporates knowledge from children's homes and communities;
- maintains nurturing relationships with children, colleagues, and families;
- creates inside and outside environments that support learning and development;
- provides authentic materials that inspire curiosity and fosters inquiry; and
- provides professional development to enhance understanding of children and families, pedagogy, and content knowledge.

10-1c • Developmentally Appropriate Curriculum

For a program to maintain a developmentally appropriate curriculum, the director needs to be aware of, understand, and be able to articulate the positions established by early childhood professional organizations. Keeping up to date with position statements and standards provides evidence of a commitment to the profession. This is especially critical now with NAEYC recently developing or revising four foundational documents:

1. Advancing Equity Recommendations for Early Childhood (2019)
2. Early Learning Program Accreditation Standards (2018)
3. Position Statement on Developmentally Appropriate Practice (2020)
4. Power to the Profession Unifying Framework for the Early Childhood Profession (2020)

In addition, Child Care Aware of America completed the Licensing Benchmark Project and release revised licensing standards.

10-1d • Components of an Effective Curriculum

Head Start has developed the Early Learning Outcome Framework (2015) and has identified 13 components that need to be present in an effective curriculum:

- grounding in child-development principles,
- evidence based,
- shows effects on child outcomes,
- comprehensive across learning domains,
- depth for each covered learning domain,
- specific learning goals,
- well-designed learning activities,
- responsive teaching,
- supports for individualized instruction,
- culturally and linguistically responsive,
- ongoing assessments,
- professional development opportunities, and
- family involvement materials (Early Childhood Learning & Knowledge Center, n.d.).

Another important document that the informed early childhood director should be well versed in is the NAEYC program accreditation standards (NAEYC, 2018). This set of standards demonstrates the evolving priority that the field places on curriculum and is the standard that directors should strive to achieve (see **Figures 10-1** and **10-2**).

This standard is effective in negating the *either–or* perspectives on curriculum that many in the field have practiced as the call for more accountability has become more prominent. The standard moves the conversation from, "Should curriculum for young children be child-programmed and play-based *or* should it focus on content standards?" to "How can children be exposed to early learning content standards within the context of a child-centered and play-based curriculum?" This standard encourages a *both–and* dialog such as, "It is possible to be intentional in our planning and also rely on an emergent curriculum that follows the child's lead." The role of the director is to facilitate ongoing both–and conversations about how this standard can be implemented

---

Essential findings in child-development research

In its Summary of Essential Findings, the Center for the Developing Child at Harvard University found the following:

- Early experiences determine whether a child's developing brain architecture provides a strong or weak foundation for all future learning, behavior, and health.

- Young children who grow up in homes with high incomes and high parental education levels have more than twice the expressive vocabulary at age 3 compared to children raised in homes characterized by low socioeconomic status.

- The basic principles of neuroscience tell us that providing the right conditions for healthy development in early childhood is likely to be more effective than treating problems at a later age.

- It is possible to improve a wide range of outcomes for vulnerable children well into the adult years as well as generate benefits to society far in excess of program costs.

FIGURE 10-1

Source: National Forum on Early Childhood Program Evaluation & National Scientific Council on the Developing Child (2007).

Evidence of an effective curriculum

Program standard: The program implements a curriculum that is consistent with its goals for children and promotes learning and development in each of the following areas: social, emotional, physical, language, and cognitive.

Rationale: A curriculum that draws on research assists teachers in identifying important concepts and skills as well as effective methods for fostering children's learning and development. When informed by teachers' knowledge of individual children, a well-articulated curriculum guides teachers so they can plan learning experiences that promote children's growth across a broad range of developmental and content areas. A curriculum also helps ensure that the teacher is intentional in planning a daily schedule that (a) maximizes children's acquisition of desired knowledge and skills through the effective use of time and materials and (b) offers opportunities for children to learn through play and through structured activities, individually and in groups, according to their developmental needs and interests.

FIGURE 10-2
Source: NAEYC Early Learning Program Standards, 2018.

practice for young children looks like. Some directors rely on formal tools such as the Early Child Environment Rating Scale-Revised (ECERS-R) (Harms, Clifford, & Cryer, 2014) and the *Infant/Toddler Environment Rating Scale*, revised updated edition (ITERS-R) (Harms, Cryer, Clifford, & Yazejian, 2017), which can evaluate the quality of such aspects of the classroom as space and furnishings, personal care routines, and support for language and reasoning, as well as the quality of activities, interactions, and more (Harms, Clifford, & Cryer, 2014). Another tool that is well regarded for assessing high-quality teacher–child interactions is the Classroom Assessment Scoring System (CLASS) (Pianta, La Paro, & Hamre, 2008). CLASS assesses emotional support, classroom organization, and instructional support, and it offers insight into important but sometimes difficult-to-measure qualities of teaching such as active and engaged learning and concept development. Results from ECERS-R, ITERS-R, and the CLASS can serve as impartial data that can inform teaching goals. In addition to relying on formal tools, directors also need to consider the following as clues to quality as they are observing their staff and providing feedback.

This child-centered classroom is investigating how bridges are built. Although all of the children are investigating the topic, they are encouraged to explore an aspect of the topic that most interests them. This child is interested in how much load different types of supports can hold and is stacking blocks on a variety of columns. The children in the background have chosen to work together to explore different types of bridge-building materials.

in each and every classroom. Each classroom will demonstrate this standard in its own unique way just as the curriculum must reflect the individual children in the room, the culture of their families, and the personalities and teaching styles of the teaching staff. This means that the director must provide opportunities for discussion of and reflection on classroom curriculum.

10-2 • Establishing Opportunities for Feedback, Support, and Intervention

As the educational leader of an early childhood program, the director must be able to provide valuable and informed feedback that reflects an understanding of what developmentally appropriate and quality

10-2a • Is the Classroom Curriculum Child Centered?

Child-centered practice has been synonymous with quality for many early childhood professionals. However, the meaning of the phrase is not conclusive; more than 40 definitions have appeared in the literature, starting with Froebel in 1778 (Tzuo, 2007). In one of its simplest interpretations, the term encourages a curriculum that focuses on the child's interests. It is often contrasted with teacher-directed approaches that give the control for content and selection of materials and activities to the educator. In reality, the notion of child centeredness is complex but should "attempt to balance the requirements of building a secure, socially responsive environment in which all individual and group interests are respected, and attention to progress in the acquisition of academic skills" (Tzuo, 2007, p. 34).

In a child-centered classroom, the director should note the classroom's emotional climate; children whose needs are not being met often become disengaged, emotionally distraught, or disruptive. A child-centered classroom can include some large group and even educator-directed activities, but it also needs to include opportunities for children to make choices, play and learn in small groups or individually, and be active in experiences that support developmental skills across all domains (motor, social, emotional, cognitive, language, and aesthetic) and academic content. When mentoring an educator, the director should always look for evidence that all of the developmental domains are being addressed. The children must be given opportunities for large-motor activity every day, preferably outdoors whenever weather permits, and for artistic expression as part of a comprehensive program that supports all developmental domains and academic content areas.

10-2b • What Is the Role of the Adult in the Classroom?

If a child-centered approach is favored in your curriculum, the director's approach may be to encourage staff to let children solve their own problems and be responsible for their own achievements.

However, Honig (2010) suggests there are times when a bit of staff intervention may be just the right thing to do:

> Children can accomplish some tasks on their own after trying hard. Others are too easy or too difficult. Children get restless and bored when toys or tasks are too easy. They feel frustrated when tasks are too challenging. The Russian child-development theorist Vygotsky taught that teachers are priceless in supporting child learning and accomplishment when a task is just a bit too difficult at the child's present level of development. Then a teaching adult provides just that bit of help that will result in further child learning and satisfaction. Vygotsky used the term "zone of proximal development" for the difference between what a child can do on his or her own compared with what the child can do with adult help. With the assistance of an adult, a child will be able to succeed at a cognitive or social learning task beyond what he or she could have accomplished alone. (p. 47)

10-2c • How Does the Educator Communicate the Use of Play to Support Learning and Development?

Early childhood educators typically understand the importance of play as a vehicle for learning in young children. People outside the field, including many parents, often miss the connection between play and learning and may question its value unless its importance is proactively and consistently explained. One role of the director can be to help educators be proactive and explain and document what children are learning. Directors should find ways to help educators articulate their practice so that the information flow becomes an automatic part of what educators do, allowing others to understand the learning that is occurring in their classroom.

One reason why some educators have difficulty explaining what children learn during play is that many use free play as a time to do other things; many are not involved in children's play. Although play is an ideal time for children to practice evolving skills

Young Children's Stages of Play

The video titled *Young Children's Stages of Play: An Illustrated Guide* provides a description of play as the medium through which young children learn. An overview of the stages of play is presented with examples of real children engaging in play at each stage.

View the video vignette and reflect on the following questions:

1. As director, what will you look for in a toddler classroom that suggests play is being adequately supported? What kinds of materials and equipment should be available? How should the adults in the room be supporting play?

2. Now consider an observation of a preschool classroom. What will you look for in a toddler classroom that suggests play is being adequately supported? What kinds of materials and equipment should be available? How should the adults in the room be supporting play?

Taking the time to listen to children is the basis for high-quality teacher–child interaction. Children can read the listener's face to see if they are being heard.

how to become participant observers who support language, concept development, and social development through play. They can also learn to use play as a vehicle for assessing and documenting learning and development.

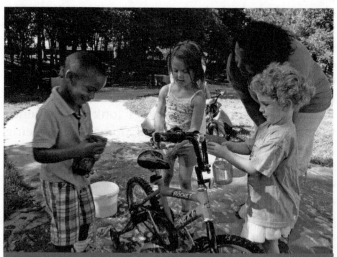

The children in this picture are engaged in dramatic play around a bike-washing service on the center's playground. They are developing oral communication skills while also learning the purpose of money when providing their service to other children who brought their bikes to school for the day. The teacher is enhancing their play by asking them how they might attract more customers. She will chart each child's response in order to document their ability to answer questions and solve problems.

that can be enhanced with the support of an adult, many educators use free choice or play time to attend to housekeeping, paperwork, or other classroom organization duties. In addition, some educators are not accomplished in supporting play and do not understand how to augment play without dominating it. Directors can help educators understand

10-2d • Is the Curriculum Emergent?

An emergent curriculum has been considered a hallmark of quality in early childhood programs. For many educators, it is a difficult concept to understand, and it frequently challenges the educator who is inclined to plan well in advance to meet his or her need for control. To facilitate instruction that follows the children's lead and incorporates their interests, the director can ask educators how the children and their interests were included in instructional decisions. Some educators cite the need to focus on content standards as a reason not to use an emergent curriculum framework.

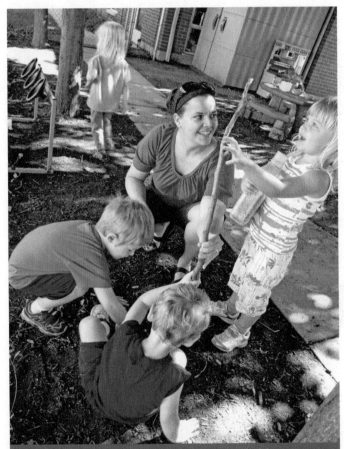

This teacher is taking advantage of a teachable moment in which children showed an interest in the difference between a stick, a branch, and a tree. Because this teacher has collected data on what the children know and are able to do related to content standards, she knows that she can easily incorporate the standards into an extended investigation of trees.

The director needs to facilitate a both–and paradigm shift and point out that it is possible to create a child-directed and emergent curriculum that addresses content standards. Specifics about how this can be done are explained in more detail in the following section.

10-2e • How Does the Educator Plan and Integrate Curriculum?

Although the NAEYC identifies an integrated curriculum as a preferred practice, many early childhood professionals struggle with how to plan connected and meaningful experiences for young children. The new NAEYC (2020) position statement identifies as good practice that "[t]eachers make meaningful connections a priority in the learning experiences they provide children, to reflect that all learners, and certainly young children, learn best when the concepts, language, and skills they encounter are related to something they know and care about, and when the new learnings are themselves interconnected in meaningful, coherent ways." This standard includes the following element: "Educators plan curriculum experiences that integrate children's learning *within* and *across* the domains (physical, social, emotional, cognitive) and the disciplines (including language, literacy, mathematics, social studies, science, art, music, physical education, and health)" (NAEYC, 2020, p. 21). Clearly, an integrated curriculum is identified as good practice, but how can the director support educators who are uncomfortable with this process?

The director can be instrumental in supporting educators in the planning process by establishing expectations for connected curriculum and by working with educators to develop a planning system that supports integration. One easy strategy that can have a huge impact on the types of curriculum created is the lesson planning form that is adopted by a program. Consider the form that is currently used: Does it support the notion of interconnected and meaningful curriculum? Or does it represent a perceived need to keep children busy? Consider the lesson planning format shown in **Figure 10-3**.

		Monday	Tuesday	Wednesday	Thursday	Friday
Morning Meeting/ Circle Time						
Free Play/Center Time	Art					
	Blocks					
	Housekeeping/ Dramatic Play					
	Science					
	Math/ Manipulatives					
	Writing					
	Computer					
Snack						
Gross Motor/ Play Ground						
Closing						

FIGURE 10-3
Fill the week lesson planning format—blank.

This form represents the type of planning that is common in many early childhood classrooms. Directors will frequently collect such lesson plans weekly and review them. For some educators, the lesson-planning process is perfunctory, with the goal being to fill the boxes communicating that the children in their classroom will be busy and, perhaps, even engaged. The director often tends to review these plans at a cursory level, looking to see that all of the boxes are filled. Now take a closer look at the types of experiences that a child might encounter in a given day by examining **Figure 10-4**. Note that the items with an asterisk are strategies or programs listed on the Institute of Education Science's *Early Childhood Education Abstract* (n.d.) list of programs that have been shown to improve reading or math skills in young children. Imagine that you are a child in this program, and consider your experience for each of the days as planned.

		Monday	Tuesday	Wednesday	Thursday	Friday
Morning Meeting/ Circle Time		Dialogic picture book reading*	Dialogic picture book reading*	Dialogic picture book reading*	Dialogic picture book reading*	Dialogic picture book reading*
Free Play/Center Time	Art	Finger painting	Found object collage	Watercolor markers	Pudding painting	Tempera at the easel
	Blocks	Add farm animals to the blocks this week				
	Housekeeping/ Dramatic Play	Kitchen with pretend food this week				
	Science	Aquarium observations	Sensory table	Plant seeds	Water the seeds	Water the seeds
	Math/ Manipulatives	SRA real math activity*	Geoshapes	SRA real math activity*	Puzzles	SRA real math activity*
	Writing	Phonemic awareness* the letter g	Phonemic awareness* the letter h	Phonemic awareness* the letter i	Phonemic awareness* the letter j	Phonemic awareness* the letter k
	Computer	Headsprout early reading*	SRA real math*	Headsprout early reading*	SRA real math*	Headsprout early reading*
Snack		Goldfish and juice or milk	Apple chunks and juice or milk	Pretzel sticks and juice or milk	Mini muffins and juice or milk	Cheese chunks and juice or milk
Gross Motor/ Play Ground		Outside play or obstacle course in the gym	Outside play or trikes in the gym	Outside play or balls in the gym	Outside play or parachute in the gym	Outside play or trikes in the gym
Closing		Sing goodbye song	Sing goodbye song	Sing goodbye song	Sing goodbye song	Sing goodbye song

*Included in the USDE *What Works Clearinghouse* list of programs that have been shown to improve reading or math skills.

FIGURE 10-4
Fill the week lesson planning format—completed.

Even though you, as the child, are able to experience these research-based strategies, what are your thoughts on the continuity of the day? Do you see any connection between one activity and the next? Do you understand why you are engaged in the activity? Are you asked to engage in inquiry or study a topic in depth?

As director, it is imperative that you understand the complexity of planning curriculum for young children. Your role is to push planning beyond the surface level—a mere clerical activity. Effective directors guide educators into reflective and intentional planning that connects learning in deep and meaningful ways. As our society continues to be invested in research-based, research-supported, and evidence-based practice, it is important to understand the curriculum as a whole and maintain your vision for the complete program.

Growth Mindset Moment

Think about yourself as a director and curriculum mentor to the educator who created the plans in **Figure 10-4**. How would you support this educator to create more connected and inquiry-based experiences for young children?

Planning webs are a way to assist educators in integrated planning. It has become common for educators to identify a curriculum goal as the basis for integration. In **Figure 10-5**, note how the curriculum goal "To become familiar with shapes" has been used to connect the experiences throughout the day. This planning strategy places great value on having children learn a discrete skill. The children experiencing

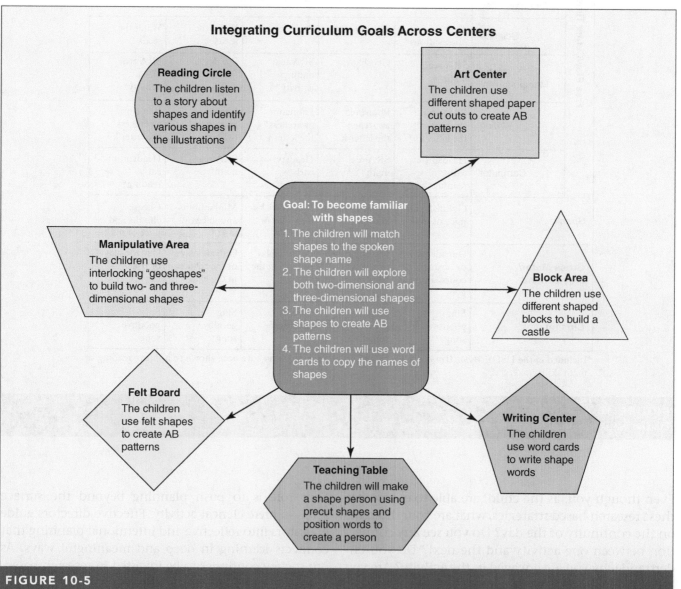

Integrating Curriculum Goals Across Centers

Reading Circle
The children listen to a story about shapes and identify various shapes in the illustrations

Art Center
The children use different shaped paper cut outs to create AB patterns

Manipulative Area
The children use interlocking "geoshapes" to build two- and three-dimensional shapes

Goal: To become familiar with shapes
1. The children will match shapes to the spoken shape name
2. The children will explore both two-dimensional and three-dimensional shapes
3. The children will use shapes to create AB patterns
4. The children will use word cards to copy the names of shapes

Block Area
The children use different shaped blocks to build a castle

Felt Board
The children use felt shapes to create AB patterns

Teaching Table
The children will make a shape person using precut shapes and position words to create a person

Writing Center
The children use word cards to write shape words

FIGURE 10-5
Integrating curriculum goals across learning centers.

this plan are likely to have a more cohesive and meaningful day and are likely to learn the skill, depending on the quality of the experiences.

Another planning process shifts away from skill-centered planning and toward planning focused around in-depth investigations of topics worthy of children's time and energy (Katz, Chard, & Kogan, 2014). Eliason and Jenkins (2016) describe a variety of planning webs that focus on themes, units, concepts, projects, or extended investigations, and they identify the following as helpful steps for web-based planning:

1. identify a theme and related subtopics,
2. brainstorm,
3. identify desired learning outcomes, and
4. prepare for teaching.

Extended investigations are the basis of such early childhood approaches as the Reggio Emilia approach developed by Loris Malaguzzi and the Project approach created by Lilian Katz and Sylvia Chard. Inspired by the work of Malaguzzi, Katz, and Chard, the *ACCESS to Science Concept Planner* (**Figure 10-6**) was developed to facilitate in-depth concept development through the investigation of science topics (Adams, Baldwin, Comingore, & Kelly, 2013; Baldwin, Adams, & Kelly, 2009). In contrast to many web-based planning strategies that focus on a theme, unit, or topic and culminate in a topic-related literacy lesson, a math lesson, an art activity, or another discipline specific lesson, the *ACCESS to Science Concept Planner* generates experiences that lead to deep understanding of concepts related to the science topic. Content-area skills are incorporated into the experiences in authentic ways that give the skills a purposeful context. When children see how discrete skills can help them understand or document an investigation, they tend to be more motivated to learn new skills.

To complete the planning process using the *ACCESS to Science Concept Planner,* teachers identify a science topic that is worthy of study and that reflects the children's interests. The quality of the investigation partly depends on the teacher's content knowledge related to the investigation. This is not to say that teachers should only teach what they know; rather, teachers need to be lifelong learners who seek out new information about the topics to be investigated. One goal of the *ACCESS to Science Concept Planner* is for teachers to develop in-depth understanding of science content related to the topic of study so

they can plan experiences that lead to a deeper understanding by the children. In contrast to the planning web in **Figure 10-5**, in which the activities are focused on a discrete skill, the *ACCESS to Science Concept Planner* provides opportunities for inquiry, depth of understanding, and a context for the discrete skills that children are learning. Connected and meaningful learning is also a goal of the planning method,

▶ **TeachSource Video Vignette**

Exploring Math in Early Childhood

The video titled *Exploring Math Concepts through Creative Activities: Integrated Curriculum in Early Childhood* shows how a series of lessons were integrated around the curriculum goal "The children will become familiar with shapes." The lessons included whole group direct instruction and center-based, small-group experiences designed to teach discrete skills related to shapes. View the video vignette and reflect on the following questions:

1. The teacher tells us there is a language of spatial relations that children learn best "if there is a visual attached to the word." This educator is intentional in her planning and can articulate her purpose well. As a curriculum mentor, what processes can you put into place so that other educators can be intentional planners who can explain why they do what they do?

2. How well did the lessons that this educator planned teach the curriculum goal and lesson objectives? Explain why.

3. How well did the lessons make the material connected and meaningful? Explain your answer.

4. How well did the lessons support inquiry?

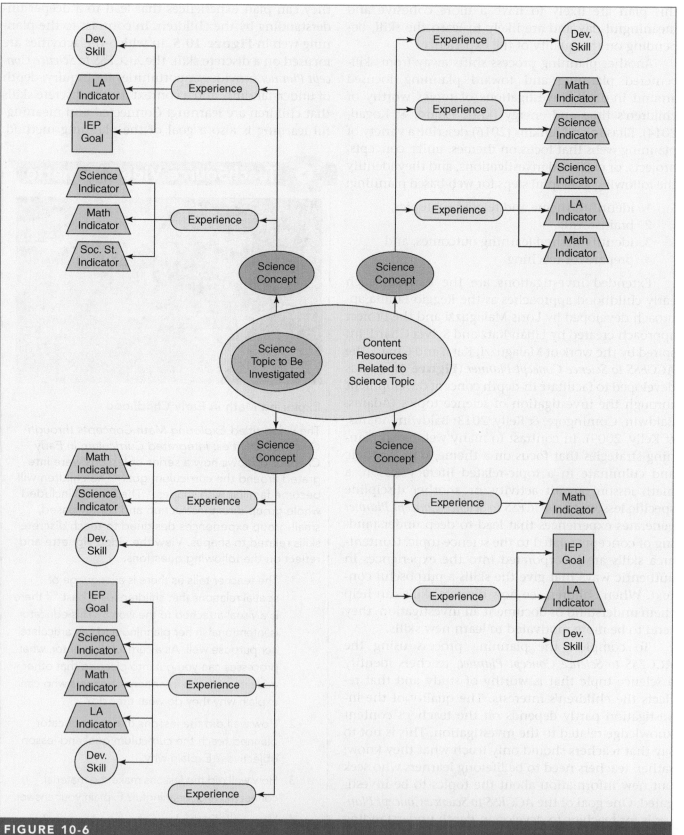

FIGURE 10-6

Access to science concept planner.

Source: Reprinted with permission from Adams et al. (2013).

Integration that is centered on an important topic can bring meaning to content areas while supporting developmental domains. This investigation of ants grew out of the children's fascination with an anthill on the playground. The investigation inspired children to count, problem solve, and re-create the ants' habitat. This group of children asked the teacher to include ant-related words in the habitat so that they could write them when they recorded their observations in their science journals.

which illustrates for educators how it is possible to accomplish the following:

- Focus on interesting topics.
- Identify the important concepts needed to understand the science topic.
- Design experiences that allow children to explore, investigate, and understand the concepts deeply.
- Identify how those experiences support developmental skills, and address early learning content standards (indicators) and individualized education plan (IEP) goals in meaningful and connected ways.

Examine the planning progression in **Figure 10-6** from the central science topic outward to the concepts and then the experiences. Notice how the experiences are designed to support the science concepts but also support meaningful and connected integration because math and science indicators might be emphasized in one experience and art, science, and language arts in another. Now consider **Figure 10-7**, in which the central unifying science topic is obscured; with the Fill the Week planning method, it is possible to address academic content standards, developmental skills, and IEP goals without a unifying

topic of study. The result is a series of unrelated or disconnected experiences in which children are left to determine the relevance of what they are learning. Directors may find these figures to be useful training tools as they guide their staff toward deeper and more meaningful curriculum development.

10-2f • How Are Early Learning and Development Standards Implemented?

As of 2019, all states have developed early learning and

TeachSource Video Vignette

Reggio Emilia and Early Childhood Education

This video describes the Italian approach to early childhood education known as Reggio Emilia, which focuses on the organization of the physical environment, child-directed activities, opportunities for creative thinking, and collaborative problem-solving. View the video vignette titled *The Reggio Emilia Approach* and reflect on the following questions:

1. How does the Reggio Emilia approach facilitate integrated curriculum and inquiry?

2. What is the role of the physical environment in the Reggio Emilia approach?

3. How well does this approach translate to programs outside of Italy?

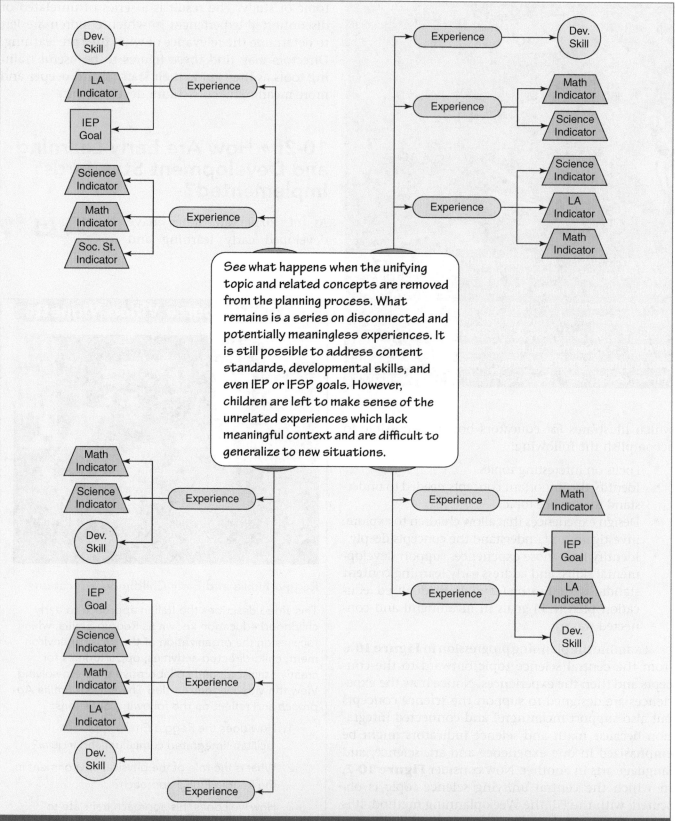

See what happens when the unifying topic and related concepts are removed from the planning process. What remains is a series on disconnected and potentially meaningless experiences. It is still possible to address content standards, developmental skills, and even IEP or IFSP goals. However, children are left to make sense of the unrelated experiences which lack meaningful context and are difficult to generalize to new situations.

FIGURE 10-7

Access to science concept planner with topic covered.

Source: Reprinted with permission from Adams et al. (2013).

development standards (also known as *early learning guidelines*) for preschool children, and all but two states (Oregon and Texas) have adopted guidelines for infants and toddlers (National Center on Early Childhood Quality Assurance, 2019). Early learning content standards are new to some early childhood educators and may appear to contradict the child-centered practice and emergent curriculum model that has been preferred practice in the field. Many early childhood educators struggle with the notion of how to blend systematic instruction of content with NAEYC's Principles of Learning and Teaching (NAEYC, 2020).

One common concern about content standards for young children is the potential for academic content to be taught inappropriately. Working together to address this concern and clarify the purpose of content standards for young children, the NAEYC and the National Association of Early Childhood Specialists in State Departments of Education (NAECS–SDE) developed a joint position statement stating that early learning content standards must align with K–12 standards in a "careful" manner. This means that early learning standards are to be developed in an age-appropriate manner, giving emphasis to all domains of early development and learning. Likewise, content standards are to be "meaningful and important to children's current well-being and later learning" (NAEYC & NAECS–SDE, 2002, p. 2).

The role of the director in addressing content standards in the curriculum is to work with educators to establish a planning process that includes standards but does not allow standards to be taught as a series of disconnected activities. Content standards should not drive the curriculum, but they must be addressed in connected, accurate, and meaningful ways. It is also important for educators to understand the content represented in content standards. Directors need to provide opportunities for the staff to gain current professional knowledge in literacy, mathematics, science, and social studies in addition to development and appropriate teaching strategies. It is no longer acceptable for children to learn inaccurate content because educators only know the myths associated with Thanksgiving or still think Pluto is a planet because they haven't had any exposure to science content since high school.

Directors need to have a big-picture view of curriculum and understand that developmentally appropriate content standards can be taught within the context of a wide variety of projects, units, or themes. This reality allows for emergent curriculum. It is also important to note that within an emergent curriculum model, it is common for educators to gravitate to projects, units, or themes that interest them. Because of this, some project topics, units, or themes are often overused. For example, many educators include the study of butterflies, dinosaurs, apples, leaves, and pumpkins in their curriculum. It is quite possible for young children to study these topics every year from the age of 2 through the primary grades. Educators are less likely to focus on topics related to earth or physical science, in part, because they are unfamiliar with or intimidated by the content. The director needs to encourage a more comprehensive curriculum that pushes educators to learn new content so that they can provide enriching experiences for children (see **Figure 10-8**).

Investigating Ramps

Several children were engaged in an investigation of race cars and the physics that makes them go faster or go farther down an inclined plane. The teacher provided the children with ramp-making materials, small toy race cars, and a variety of measuring tools. Up until this point, the children had shown little interest in learning about measurement using blocks, cubes, and other nonstandard units of measurement considered to be appropriate for preschoolers. After racing their cars down the ramps for a while, the children decided that they wanted to keep track of the distance that the cars traveled. They constructed a long measuring tool and sought out a pencil and paper so that they could record the distances after each race. This experience provided a context and purpose for measurement and a reason to learn to write numbers.

FIGURE 10-8

10-2g • How Does the Program Facilitate the Development of Language and Emergent Literacy Skills?

The role of the early childhood program as a vehicle to reform education in the United States has altered the way that language development and emergent literacy is viewed for children from birth through age 5. Research-based literacy instruction has been identified as a means of reducing the achievement gap between children from the middle and upper socioeconomic classes and those who are raised in poverty. After the National Early Literacy Panel (NELP) reported that "conventional reading and writing skills that are developed in the years from birth to age 5 have a clear and consistently strong relationship with later conventional literacy skills" (2008, p. vii), national reform dialogue focused on literacy instruction for young children. What does this mean for the director who must advocate for appropriate practice for young children, address the concerns of worried parents, and deal with the forces from outside the field that are pushing for more accountability related to systematic literacy instruction? Today's director must address the needs of multiple stakeholders while still keeping the needs of the children front and center. The research review conducted by NELP has impacted what is considered to be best practice for young children, and educators must be aware of the panel's findings. Directors should ensure that educators are aware of the research on emergent literacy and also provide their staff with a forum to discuss how best to infuse research-supported practice into a developmentally appropriate curriculum.

The National Early Literacy Panel has identified several core competencies as having a consistently strong relationship with later conventional literacy skills: Many early childhood professionals who are well grounded in developmentally appropriate, child-programmed, and play-based curriculum may review these competencies with intense reservation (see **Figure 10-9**). There is a strong possibility that inappropriate and potentially harmful practice could be developed to address these skills. Children face long-term harm when they lack experiences that support the development of these skills. The role of the director is to make sure the staff is well grounded

---

Early literacy skills with a strong relationship to later literacy skills

- Alphabet knowledge (AK): knowledge of the names and sounds associated with printed letters

- Phonological awareness (PA): the ability to detect, manipulate, or analyze the auditory aspects of spoken language (including the ability to distinguish or segment words, syllables, or phonemes), independent of meaning

- Rapid automatic naming (RAN) of letters or digits: the ability to rapidly name a sequence of random letters or digits

- RAN of objects or colors: the ability to rapidly name a sequence of repeating random sets of pictures of objects (e.g., car, tree, house, man) or colors

- Writing or writing name: the ability to write letters in isolation on request or to write one's own name

- Phonological memory: the ability to remember spoken information for a short period of time

FIGURE 10-9
Source: National Early Literacy Panel (2008, p. vii).

---

in both the early literacy research and developmentally appropriate practice so that curriculum can be developed that infuses these skills in age-appropriate, meaningful, and connected ways. Directors should also be watchful for educators who see these skills as typical for older children and who might thus be inclined to use instructional strategies that are common in the primary grades. Set the expectation that curriculum in the program will honor the age of the child and support a system that encourages critical reflection and problem-solving so that the skills identified in **Figure 10-9** are included in the curriculum in developmentally appropriate ways.

The NELP's list of competencies that have a moderate relationship to long-term literacy acquisition includes skills that may be more comfortable for teachers of young children (see **Figure 10-10**). These broader skills are common in print-rich early childhood environments, which tend to emphasize oral language, including vocabulary development, matching, and book-handling skills. A comprehensive language and emergent literacy component of a complete early childhood curriculum establishes a purpose for literacy. When observing in a classroom, the director can note how print is used. For example, is there a purpose for print when the educator has decided to label and name everything in the room? Children begin to understand that there is a purpose for print when they use a picture label on a shelf to decide where to put a toy. When everything in the room is labeled (e.g., door, table, chair), however, it communicates that the purpose of print is to label. Are the environment and experiences set up so that children understand how writing can help them to record, remember, track, and communicate? The teaching staff needs to be aware of the literacy research but also needs feedback and support so that they have a purposeful print-rich environment in which literacy has context and meaning.

10-2h • How Do Educators Support Math, Science, and Inquiry in the Classroom?

Science, technology, engineering, and math (STEM) has emerged as an important concept and acronym in the educational reform movement. Although STEM may be relatively new, theorists such as Jean Piaget and Constance Kamii have a long history of exploring mathematical concepts with young children. The importance

and appropriateness of mathematics for young children was further validated in the National Mathematics Advisory Panel (NMP) report, which found that

> most children acquire considerable knowledge of numbers and other aspects of mathematics before they enter kindergarten. This is important because the mathematical knowledge that kindergartners bring to school is related to their mathematics learning for years thereafter—in elementary school, middle school, and even high school. Unfortunately, most children from low—income backgrounds enter school with far less knowledge than peers from middle-income backgrounds, and the achievement gap in mathematical knowledge progressively widens throughout their PreK–12 years. (2008, p. xviii)

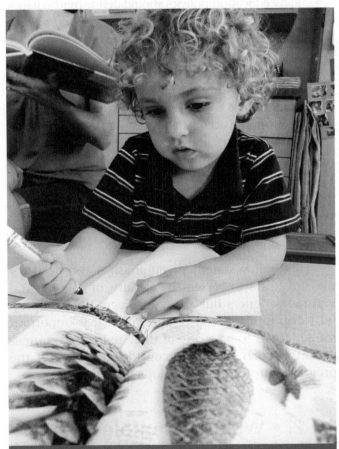

Children are more likely to choose to write when the purpose is clear. This child is fascinated by the investigation of seeds in which his class is engaged. Using attractive nonfiction books has inspired him to keep track of his own seed collection by locating the seed and "writing" its name in his science journal.

Like the NELP report, the NMP report highlights the importance of experience with academic competencies as an important factor in later learning and in reducing the achievement gap.

The release of national reports such as the NMP report has impacted policy recommendations for both math and science. The National Institute for Early Education Research Preschool Policy Brief on Math and Science made the following policy recommendations:

- Mathematics and science should be treated as essential components of a comprehensive, high-quality preschool program, not as extras.
- Policy makers must be certain that curricula, learning standards, and teaching expectations for early mathematics and science are research based and must outline expectations that are attainable and appropriate for preschool learners.
- Early education policies should define mathematics as more than counting and numbers, and science should be treated as more than learning lists of facts.
- Preservice and in-service educators need improved preparation to understand math and science content and to provide experiences integrating this content into their teaching practice.
- Appropriate accountability systems that focus on the classroom, educator, and child must be built to support high-quality early mathematics and science education.
- Mathematics and science learning should be integrated with each other and with other content domains (Brenneman, Stevenson-Boyd, & Frede, 2009).

This policy statement emphasizes the need for the director to oversee the quality of science and math experiences but also encourages the meaningful integration of science and math. It is important for educators to be aware of these policy recommendations, which should be considered as part of the program's professional development plan.

10-2i • What Is the Role of Technology in This Classroom?

"The push to integrate technology into early childhood settings can lead to inappropriate use of technology" (Cruickshank, 2010). Although there are appropriate ways to include the use of technology in developmentally appropriate programs for young children, there has been a reluctance on the part of many who fear that the passive use of technology will replace active play and high-quality, play-based interactions between children and adults. The revised position statement on developmentally appropriate practices (NAEYC, 2020) includes a new standard on technology that states, "Used responsibly and intentionally, technology and interactive media can be valuable tools for supporting children's development and learning" (p. 13).

Educators who are grounded in child-development theory and developmentally appropriate practices and are technologically and media literate have the knowledge, skills, and experience to select and use technology and digital media that are appropriate for the ages and developmental levels of the children in their care, and they know when and how to integrate technology into the program effectively. Educators who lack technological and media literacy are at risk of making inappropriate choices and using technology with young children in inappropriate ways that can negatively impact children's learning and development (National Association for the Education of Young Children & Fred Rogers Center for Early Learning and Children's Media at Saint Vincent College, 2012). Because of the impact of what is being called the *digital divide* on children in poverty, it is no longer an option for early childhood professionals to be uninformed about the use of developmentally appropriate technology with young children (see **Figure 10-11**). Children who have access to technology tools and the Internet at home are more likely to have highly developed technology skills at an early age. Children who lack these experiences, commonly because of limited financial resources, start school behind their peers (Calvert, Rideout, Woolard, Barr, & Strouse, 2005). Directors should remind educators about the important role they play in ensuring equity by providing access to developmentally appropriate technology for all children. The director also needs to find opportunities for educators to develop technology skills and reflect on how technology might be incorporated in meaningful ways.

Technology recommendations for classroom practice

Infants and Toddlers

During the earliest years, infants and toddlers need interactions primarily with human beings. They need to freely explore, manipulate, and test everything in the environment. Increasingly in today's world, this includes the exploration of digital technology and interactive media. Children of this age are drawn to buttons and cause-and-effect toys. Technology tools that infants and toddlers might use must be safe, sturdy, and not easily damaged. Just as toddlers tend to chew on their books, children under 2 are especially likely to chew on technology tools.

- Allow children to explore digital materials in the context of human interactions, with an adult as mediator and coplayer. As with shared book reading, use shared technology time as an opportunity to talk with children, use new vocabulary, and model appropriate use.

- Avoid passive screen time. Although many parents claim that baby videos calm an otherwise fussy child, little research suggests that infants and toddlers learn from watching videos. If they are distressed, they need the comfort of a caring adult, not an electronic toy.

- Provide children with toy representations of digital objects to encourage toddlers to begin pretending about the ways in which others use technology: cell phones, cameras, laptops, CD players, and so on.

Preschool and Kindergarten

During the preschool years, young children are developing a sense of initiative and creativity. They are curious about the world around them and curious about learning. They are exploring their ability to create and communicate using a variety of media (crayons, felt-tipped markers, paints and other art materials, blocks, dramatic play materials, miniature life figures) and creative movement, singing, dancing, and using their bodies to represent ideas and experiences. Digital technologies provide one more outlet for demonstrating their creativity and learning.

- Freely explore touch screens loaded with a wide variety of developmentally appropriate interactive media experiences that are well designed and enhance feelings of success.

- Begin to explore and feel comfortable using "traditional" mouse and keyboard computers for using Flash-based websites or looking up answers with a search engine.

- Capture photos of block buildings or artwork that children have created; videotape dramatic play and replay for children to view.

- Celebrate children's accomplishments with digital media displayed on a digital projector or on a classroom website.

- Record children's stories about their drawings or their play; make digital audio files for documentation of progress.

FIGURE 10-11

Source: From NAEYC & the Fred Rogers Center for Early Learning and Children's Media (2012).

10-3 • Supporting Intentional Teaching

The director can be informed by the policies, position statements, and research reports that have been highlighted thus far in this chapter, but creating an environment in which educators use this information to inform their practice requires structures that support intentional teaching. "Intentional teaching means educators act with specific outcomes or goals in mind for children's development and learning. Educators must know when to use a given strategy to accommodate the different ways that individual children learn and the specific content they are learning" (Epstein, 2007, p. 1). Intentional teaching requires that teaching teams have time for reflection and planning and that assessment is an integral part of instructional decision-making. Directors can establish ground rules that support a climate where it is safe to express opinions in respectful ways. They will need to be creative in how they develop a program schedule so time exists for educators to plan as a team. The program should have an established assessment system with the expectation that documentation will be collected, recorded, and used

Working Smart with Technology

Effective Use of Technology with Young Children

When supporting educators to consider how best to use technology, encourage them to rely on the same decision-making process used when identifying developmentally appropriate practices. They should use knowledge of children's interests, what engages them, and also what they need to know and be able to do. The learning and development standards need to be considered along with family culture. Using the developmentally appropriate practice decision-making framework helps educators use technology to enhance existing curriculum.

Although not every experience can be enhanced with technology, educators should think critically about the goals they have for the students or the experiences to decide what will work best and whether technology can enrich the experience and deepen the children's understanding.

Help educators understand that when they are planning to include technology devices in the classroom, they should be intentional in their planning. Ask them about their purpose for technology use. Too often, educators provide access to technology without an intended purpose. The computer station becomes a way to fill the children's time but may not be used intentionally to enhance the curriculum. The director's role as educational leader and curriculum mentor can help educators use technology effectively.

Although the time at a computer should be limited and the software carefully selected, the computer can support focused collaboration and inquiry.

to make instructional decisions; track the progress of individual children; and inform program evaluation.

10-3a • Time for Planning and Critical Reflection

> ▶ **TeachSource Video Vignette**

Curriculum Planning in an Early Childhood Setting

This video case reveals how excellent curriculum planning must be based on developmentally appropriate practice, be inclusive and integrated, highlight play, and take cues from the children. You'll see all these principles implemented in an early childhood program, as Ke Nguyen and her colleagues plan activities and interact with the children. You'll also see the children engage in teacher-initiated and child-initiated activities, and learn together in small and large groups.

View the video vignette titled *Curriculum Planning: Implementing Developmentally Appropriate Practice in an Early Childhood Setting* and reflect on the following questions:

1. How does the program director define developmentally appropriate practice?

2. Ke, the lead teacher, tells us that her teaching team meets regularly to discuss developmentally appropriate practices and related curriculum development. Describe the dialogue that takes place during Ke's team meeting that suggests the team is responding to the developmental needs of at least one child.

could sign in while their parents signed in. This practice not only eased transition time strife but also provided a purposeful opportunity for children to write their name at least once every day. Periodically, educators collected and documented work samples, which showed the progression of skills that started with mark making and advanced over time until all children were able to print their name using uppercase and lowercase letters. As director, be on the lookout for examples such as the one just described and find a place to showcase examples that demonstrate intentional teaching.

10-3c • Time for Planning, Sharing, and Critical Reflection

Consider a profession in which teams of adults are expected to work together to implement a complex and coordinated program with a highly unpredictable client group whose education, health, and safety depend on team members' ability to know what each

Peer observation is a valuable practice for both the teacher being observed and the peers who are observing. Ideas can be shared between classrooms, and teachers have an opportunity to articulate their practice.

10-3b • Intentional Teaching in the Daily Routine

Planning is an important component of intentional teaching. Educators are often much more enthusiastic about planning big projects and special celebrations than they are establishing daily routines that constitute a significant portion of the program. Daily routines can serve as excellent vehicles for teaching with a purpose. Consider something as ordinary and mundane as the daily sign-in procedure. One teaching team noted that upheaval occurred each morning when parents were trying to sign in with children clinging to their legs. Several children expressed an interest in being able to "sign in" on the same chart as the parents. The educators met to reflect on this situation. They referred to the early learning content standards and related assessment data and determined that even though the children were at various stages on the emergent writing continuum, most if not all of the children could benefit from a station where they

Making the Case for *Curriculum Mentors*

With all that a director has to do to manage the operations of the program, it may be tempting to view the curriculum as the responsibility of the teaching staff. The importance of a rich and engaging curriculum cannot be overstated, and quality experiences require educators to be intentional in their planning. The curriculum mentor can serve as a support to teaching teams who benefit from reflecting on their practice. This role can be served by the director or by another person whose leadership is acknowledged by the staff. Each teaching team should meet with the curriculum mentor at least monthly to share their planning process, reflect on how the curriculum is being implemented, and identify where they are going next. Teaching teams work better when they have a shared understanding of what is happening in the classroom. By establishing the routine of meeting with a curriculum mentor regularly, teaching teams come to understand that intentional decision-making about curriculum is valued (Frede & Ackerman, 2007). In addition, the curriculum mentor can come to understand the strengths and needs of the teaching teams so that support, resources, and professional development can be provided as needed.

other is thinking from across the room. Now consider that the team has little or no time to plan together to develop a common understanding of the goals of a lesson or educational philosophy for the classroom. This scenario is all too common in early childhood classrooms, where the budget is so tight that paying two or three educators to plan is incredibly difficult to manage. An early childhood teaching team without planning time is like an orchestra without practice time. It does not matter how talented the musicians are: Notes will be missed, the timing will be off, and the audience will be left unimpressed. Teams that plan together are able to brainstorm and plan in a way that allows the talents of their individuals to emerge. Classroom tasks can be chosen by team members who have the skill and enjoy the task in contrast to being assigned based on some institutional hierarchy. Directors must find and support team planning time and, in order to encourage the best use of this time, must help teams establish models for respectful interaction and critical reflection as well as a team decision-making process that encourages open communication.

10-3d • Assessment Supported versus Assessment Driven

Assessment data constitute an important tool for educators who are engaged in intentional teaching and is considered to be an essential component of a quality curriculum. Although the NAEYC and NAECS–SDE recommendations state that quality curriculum depends on appropriate assessment to support instructional decisions, assessment of content and development in early childhood settings is an emerging practice for the field (Meisels, 2004; Meisels et al., 2002). Assessment techniques that are used with older students are not valid or reliable for preschoolers. In addition, many experienced early childhood educators are unfamiliar with assessment strategies that are appropriate for young children. An important role of the director is to help educators make sense of assessment and how it can be used and managed in their classroom. It is not enough to require that educators collect assessment data and documentation for their children; a system must be in place that helps educators collect meaningful data and organize them in way that is useful and that informs instruction. Many educators are committed to data collection and have found ways to observe

children and note their progress. The challenge becomes what to do with all of the work samples, anecdotal records, Post-it notes, and portfolios that accumulate in piles around the classroom. Many educators struggle with how to pull data together in a way that allows them to make instructional decisions for a class or track the progress of an individual child.

Methods for collecting data often represent a combination of program requirements and educator preference. If educators are given the freedom to design a method of collecting data that works for them, they are more likely to follow through and make the system work. The director needs to make educators aware of the required components of the program's assessment system while also communicating where educators have freedom to design their own strategies. The director also needs to make sure that intentional planning informed by ongoing assessment is part of the curriculum culture of the program. The expectation for data collection needs to be clear, and educators need to know that their assessment efforts will be discussed during curriculum mentoring sessions.

Figure 10-12 represents the assessment system developed by the Bombeck Family Learning Center of the University of Dayton. The teachers and leadership

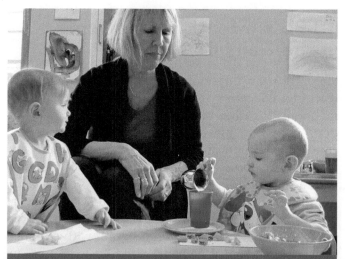

Meals and snacks can be planned with intentionality. This teacher knows that toddlers need opportunities to develop independence. The teacher has provided a small pitcher partially filled with milk and a much larger cup in order to increase the child's ability to pour his own milk with success. Staging the environment in this manner involves reflective, insightful, and intentional planning as well as a sound understanding of what the child is able to do.

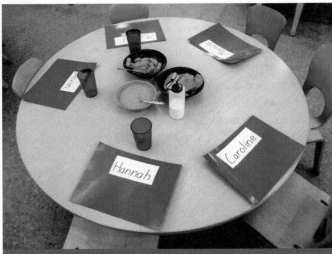

This preschool teacher worked with her team to plan naturally occurring and meaningful ways for children to recognize their names and the names of the other children in the class. After a while, the placemats will be moved, motivating children to identify who they get to sit next to at the next meal.

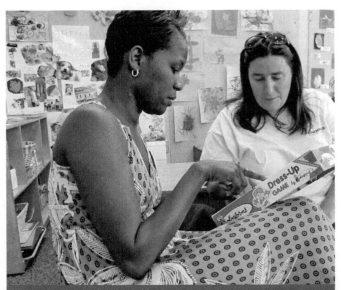

Team planning time is essential for teachers to brainstorm ideas, develop a planning web, share resources, and establish a common understanding of the children and the curriculum.

FIGURE 10-12
ACCESS assessment funnel.
Source: Reprinted with permission from Adams et al. (2013).

at this program worked with early childhood faculty to develop a tracking system that allows educators to record the data collected through a variety of teacher-determined assessment strategies. The curriculum mentor works with educators to ensure they understand appropriate and unbiased ways of documenting what children know and are able to do. After the educators understand sound assessment practices and are aware of a wide array of tools and strategies they can use to collect data, they are allowed to develop an assessment plan that works for their teaching team. The educators determine who will collect data, when the data will be collected, and what tools will be used, thus realizing that a variety of tools will be necessary. Each teaching team shares its assessment plan and is held accountable for follow-through. It is important for the director to understand how educators have chosen to assess children so that he or she can ensure that assessment is completed in an ongoing and sufficient fashion. By expecting educators to compile their assessment data onto the ACCESS Classroom Tracking Sheet (ACTS) and to bring an up-to-date ACTS to all curriculum planning sessions, educators are held accountable for implementing the assessment system and for using data to make instructional decisions. Although there is a program-wide assessment system in place, educators determine the data-collection methods that work best for them.

10-3e • Developing an Assessment System

One of the director's responsibilities is to work with staff to develop and oversee an assessment system that provides strategies to support educators as they make decisions about children's learning in order to meet their current developmental needs and, in turn, to lay the foundation for their success in K–12 schools while maintaining developmentally appropriate classrooms that rely on play and other child-directed instructional techniques (Meisels et al., 2001). In addition, assessment is to be an integral component of the curriculum, with results used to guide teaching, identify concerns for individual children, and provide information to improve and guide interventions if needed. Assessment methods to be used are those that are "developmentally appropriate, culturally and linguistically responsive, tied to children's daily activities, supported by professional development, and inclusive

of families" (NAEYC, 2020). Indicators of effectiveness for assessment systems include the following:

- Ethical principles guide assessment practices.
- Assessment instruments are used for their intended purposes.
- Assessments are appropriate for ages and other characteristics of children being assessed.
- Assessment instruments comply with professional criteria for quality.
- What is assessed is developmentally and educationally significant.
- Assessments use multiple sources of evidence gathered over time.
- Use of individually administered, norm-referenced tests is limited.
- Assessment evidence is used to understand and improve learning.
- Assessment evidence is gathered from realistic settings and situations that reflect children's actual performance.
- Screening is always linked to follow-up.
- Staff and families are knowledgeable about assessment.

10-4 • Supporting a Seamless Birth through Age 8 System

Early childhood educators agree that an emergent, play-based, child- directed, and constructivist approach is preferred practice (NAEYC, 2020). However, the recent results of a multistate study of prekindergarten classrooms make it clear that 48 percent of children experience moderate to serious problems in making a successful transition into kindergarten (Clifford et al., 2005; Pianta et al., 2008). There is often a poor fit between the skills of incoming kindergarteners and the expectations of their teachers. In addition, there has been no common definition of kindergarten readiness, meaning that preschool teachers are often preparing children to meet standards that vary greatly from school district to school district, school to school, and teacher to teacher in some instances. In the past, it was common for early care and education to exist in a separate

Monitoring Progress in an Early Childhood Classroom

The teacher in this video demonstrates how intentional planning can lead her to collect data to document the progress of the children in her class. View the video vignette titled *Progress Monitoring: Using Transitional Time in an Early Childhood Classroom.* Watch how the teacher engages the children as they prepare to transition to the next experience in the day, and reflect on the following questions:

1. Click on the *artifacts* button and examine the "Progress Monitoring Form." List the three curriculum goals on which the teacher is gathering data. How many children met their goals and how many did not? How might the data that she has collected inform her instructional decisions?

2. Note that this teacher is using the form a little differently than it was intended. How was the form supposed to be used, and how did the teacher adapt it? Was this appropriate? Why or why not?

silo from K–12 schooling. This separation leads to misperceptions and a lack of understanding of what programs for younger children accomplish and what kindergarten and primary grades programs expect.

Pianta and Kraft-Sayre (2003) note the importance of effective kindergarten transition practices that are enhanced by a seamless system of early childhood programs for children ages birth through third grade. Directors of programs for young children need to understand their role in this system and act accordingly. Looking for opportunities to reach out to the kindergarten teachers and principals of the schools that receive your children is important.

Director's Corner

Like many other communities, our county's children and families face a disconnect of communication between preschool and kindergarten. There is no common understanding of kindergarten readiness, and the methods used to screen readiness are varied and inconsistent. My teachers dread the time of year when local school districts start screening children for kindergarten entry because parents want answers to the ongoing question, "Is my child ready for kindergarten?" We believe that the readiness process starts before birth and is enhanced through rich and engaging experiences that grow the brain. We also hold firm to the idea that all children are ready to start school when they are chronologically eligible and that it is the responsibility of the kindergarten teacher and receiving school to meet the needs of all of the children who come to them. What we believe, however, can be irrelevant when a family has their child screened by three different schools only to have one school report that the child is ready, a second identifies the child as advanced, and a third says that the child should be held out for a year because he has a summer birthday and cannot write his name. No wonder parents are confused and doubt our stance on readiness even though it is supported by NAEYC.

—*Director of a university-affiliated early childhood program*

Summary

In this chapter, the importance of the role of the director as the educational leader and curriculum mentor in the program was described. One important component of this role includes a sound knowledge of the research that informs quality curriculum.

The chapter was organized around a series of considerations that directors may find helpful when preparing staff feedback. It also described how directors can support intentional teaching and enhance a seamless system for children ages birth through grade three. To be able to support quality curriculum, a director must do the following:

- identify quality curriculum;
- establish opportunities for feedback, support, and intervention;

- support intentional teaching; and
- support a seamless birth through age 8 system.

TRY IT OUT!

Work in a team to integrate curriculum using the *ACCESS to Science Concept Planner* shown in **Director's Resource 10-1**. Assign one member of the team to be the curriculum mentor and the others to be members of the teaching team.

Director's Resource 10-1

ACCESS TO SCIENCE CONCEPT PLANNER: A STUDY OF ANTS

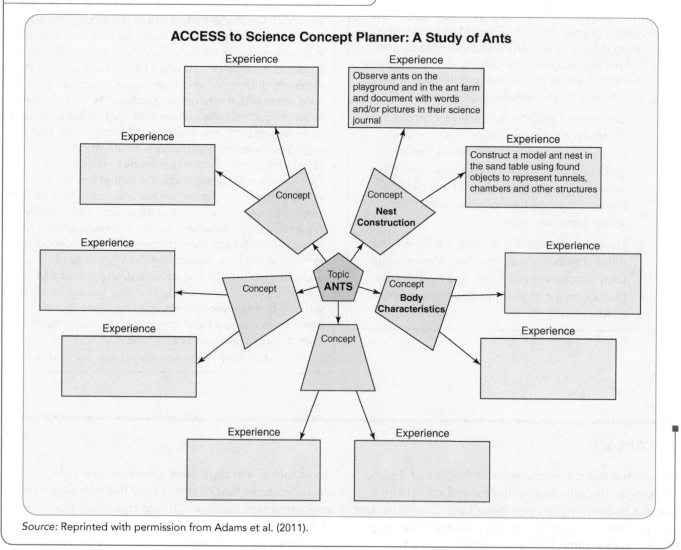

ACCESS to Science Concept Planner: A Study of Ants

Experience

Experience: Observe ants on the playground and in the ant farm and document with words and/or pictures in their science journal

Experience

Experience: Construct a model ant nest in the sand table using found objects to represent tunnels, chambers and other structures

Concept

Concept — **Nest Construction**

Experience

Experience

Concept

Topic **ANTS**

Concept — **Body Characteristics**

Concept

Experience

Experience

Experience

Experience

Source: Reprinted with permission from Adams et al. (2011).

Director's Resource 10-1 (continued) ////

Background Information: The teachers determined that ants would be a worthy topic of investigation after the preschoolers found an anthill on the playground. The children became fascinated watching the ants enter and exit the nest and were amazed at the strength of three ants that were able to carry a potato chip across the sidewalk. The teachers followed the children's interest but were also aware that there was a need to address an area of life science sometime during the year.

1 The curriculum mentor should begin by facilitating a brainstorming session to generate the concepts about ants that children can learn more about. Avoid introducing activities at this stage, and redirect team members who start with activities, materials, or experiences. Focus on the science concepts that support an understanding of ants. Use **Director's Resource 10-1** to record your concepts. Note that several concepts have been done for you. If the Internet is available, look up ants to add to the team's content knowledge; if not, take time after class to do some

Director's Resource 10-1 (continued) ////

research. What new information did you learn that would have made your concept planner more complete?

2 Now that you know what is possible for children to know about an interesting topic, consider the experiences that you facilitate so that children can investigate the topic. How will the teachers find out what questions the children have about ants? What authentic materials would support their inquiry?

3 After the team has completed the concepts and experiences, consider language and literacy, math, science, social studies, art, music, social-emotional, or movement goals that children can learn through the experience. Try to identify two main goals from two different content areas and developmental domains that can also be supported through the experience.

4 How did this planning process support inquiry and connected learning? What were the pros and cons with planning in this manner?

REFERENCES

Adams, S. M., Baldwin, J. B., Comingore, J. L., & Kelly, M. K. (2013). *The ACCESS curriculum: Intentional, integrated and inquiry-based for infants through grade 5.* Bloomington, IN: Xlibris.

Baldwin, J. L., Adams, S. M., & Kelly, M. K. (2009). Science at the center: An emergent, standards-based, child-centered framework for early learners. *Early Childhood Education Journal, 37,* 71–77. DOI 10.1007/s10643-009-0318-z

Brenneman, K., Stevenson-Boyd, J. S., & Frede, E. (2009). Math and science in preschool: Policies and practice. *Preschool Policy Matters,* Issue 19. New Brunswick, NJ: National Institute for Early Education Research. https://nieer.org/policy-issue/policy-brief-math-and-science-in-preschool-policies-and-practice

Calvert, S. L., Rideout, V. J., Woolard, J. L., Barr, R. F., & Strouse, G. A. (2005). Age, ethnicity and socioeconomic patterns in early computer use: A national survey. *American Behavioral Scientist, 48*(5), 590–607.

Clifford, R. M., Barbarin, O., Chang, F., Early, D., Bryant, D., Howes, C., et al. (2005). What is prekindergarten? Characteristics of public prekindergarten programs. *Applied Developmental Science, 9*(3), 126–143.

Cruickshank, A. (2010, September–October). Empowering images: Using photography as a medium to develop visual literacy. *Exchange for Early Childhood Leaders.* http://stage.childcareexchange.com/article/empowering-images-using-photography-as-a-medium-to-develop-visual-literacy/5019553/

Dickinson, D. K., & Porche, M. V. (2011). Relation between language experiences in preschool classrooms and children's kindergarten and fourth-grade language and reading abilities. *Child Development, 82*(3), 870–886.

Early Childhood Learning & Knowledge Center. (n.d.). Curriculum. Washington, DC: U.S. Department of Health & Human Services. https://eclkc.ohs.acf.hhs.gov/curriculum/consumer-report

Education Commission of the States. (2009). *Linking ready kids to ready schools: A report on policy insights from the governors' forum series.* Denver, CO: Author. https://files.eric.ed.gov/fulltext/ED507714.pdf

Eliason, C., & Jenkins, L. (2016). *A practical guide to early childhood curriculum* (10th ed.). Columbus, OH: Merrill/ Prentice Hall.

Epstein, A. S. (2007). *The intentional teacher: Choosing the best strategies for young children's learning.* Washington, DC: National Association for the Education of Young Children.

Frede, E., & Ackerman, D. (2007, March). Preschool curriculum decision-making: Dimensions to consider. *NIEER Policy Brief* (Issue 12). New Brunswick, NJ: National Institute for Early Education Research. https://nieer.org/policy-issue/policy-brief-preschool-curriculum-decision-making-dimensions-to-consider

Harms, T., Clifford, R. M., & Cryer, D. (2014). *Early childhood environment rating scale* (3rd ed.) (ECERS-3). New York, NY: Teachers College Press.

Harms, T., Cryer, D., Clifford, R. M., & Yazejian, N. (2017). *Infant/toddler environment rating scale* (3rd ed.). New York, NY: Teachers College Press.

Honig, A. S. (2010). *Little kids, big worries: Stress-busting tips for early childhood classrooms*. Baltimore, MD: Brookes.

Institute of Education Sciences. (n.d.). *Early childhood education abstract*. What Works Clearinghouse. Washington, DC: https://ies.ed.gov/ncee/wwc/

Katz, L., Chard, S., & Kogan, Y. (2014). Issues in selecting topics for projects. In L. Katz, S. Chard, & Y. Kogan (Eds.), *Engaging children's minds: The project approach* (3rd ed.). Santa Barbara, CA: ABC-CLIO.

Meisels, S. J. (2004). Should we test 4-year-olds? *Pediatrics, 113*, 1401–1402.

Meisels, S. J., Harrington, H. L., McMahon, P., Dichtelmiller, M. D., & Jablon, J. R. (2002). *Thinking like a teacher: Using observational assessment to improve teaching and learning*. Boston, MA: Allyn & Bacon.

National Association for the Education of Young Children (NAEYC) and the Fred Rogers Center for Early Learning and Children's Media. (2012, January). Technology and Interactive Media as Tools in Early Childhood Programs. https://www.naeyc.org/resources/topics/technology-and-media/resources

National Association for the Education of Young Children (NAEYC). (2018). Early childhood program accreditation standards. Washington, DC: Author. https://www.naeyc.org/sites/default/files/globally-shared/downloads/PDFs/accreditation/early-learning/overview_of_the_standards.pdf

National Association for the Education of Young Children (NAEYC). (2020). Statement of the position. Washington, DC: Author. https://www.naeyc.org/resources/position-statements/dap/statement-position

National Association for the Education of Young Children & the National Association of Early Childhood Specialist in State Departments of Education. (2002). Early learning standards: Creating the conditions for success. Washington, DC: NAEYC. https://www.naeyc.org/sites/default/files/globally-shared/downloads/PDFs/resources/position-statements/position_statement.pdf

National Center on Early Childhood Quality Assurance. (2019). *Early learning and development standards*. Fairfax, VA: U.S. Department of Health and Human Services. https://childcareta.acf.hhs.gov/sites/default/files/public/075_1907_state_eldgs_web_final508.pdf

National Early Literacy Panel. (2008). *Developing early literacy: Report of the national early literacy panel*. Jessup, MD: National Institute for Literacy at ED Pubs. https://lincs.ed.gov/earlychildhood/NELP/NELP09.html

National Forum on Early Childhood Program Evaluation & National Scientific Council on the Developing Child. (2007). A science-based framework of early childhood policy. Cambridge, MA: Harvard Center for the Developing Child. https://46y5eh11fhgw3ve3ytpwxt9r-wpengine.netdna-ssl.com/wp-content/uploads/2016/02/Policy_Framework.pdf

National Institute for Early Education Research. (2020). New report on pre-K in cities shows 33 of nation's largest cities now have public pre-K program. NIEER Research Report. New Brunswick, NJ: Rutgers, The State University of New Jersey. https://nieer.org/wp-content/uploads/2020/12/CityHealth-Pre-K-Summary-Benchmarks-and-Enrollment-2020.pdf

National Mathematics Advisory Panel (NMP). (2008). Final report of the National Math Advisory Panel. Washington, DC: U.S. Department of Education. https://www2.ed.gov/about/bdscomm/list/mathpanel/report/final-report.pdf

Pianta, R., & Kraft-Sayre, M. (2003). *Successful kindergarten transition: Your guide to connecting children, families, & schools*. Baltimore, MD: Paul H. Brookes.

Pianta, R., La Paro, K., & Hamre, B. (2008). *Classroom assessment scoring system*. Baltimore, MD: Brookes.

Preschool Curriculum Evaluation Research Consortium. (2008). *Effects of preschool curriculum programs on school readiness* (NCER 2008–2009). Washington, DC: National Center for Education Research, Institute of Education Sciences, U.S. Department of Education. Washington, DC: U.S. Government Printing Office. https://ies.ed.gov/ncer/pubs/20082009/pdf/20082009_rev.pdf

Seplocha, H. (2018). *Coaching with ECERS: Strategies to improve quality in pre-K and & K classrooms*. New York, NY: Teachers College Press.

Tzuo, P. W. (2007). The tension between teacher control and children's freedom in a child-centered classroom: Resolving the practical dilemma through a closer look at the related theories. *Early Childhood Education Journal, 35*(1), 33–39. https://eric.ed.gov/?id=EJ769675

Yoshikawa, H., Weiland, C., Brooks-Gunn, J., Burchinal, M. R., Espinosa, L. M., Gormley, W. T., . . . , Zaslow, M. J. (2013). *Investing in our future: The evidence base on preschool education*. Ann Arbor, MI: Society for Research in Child Development.

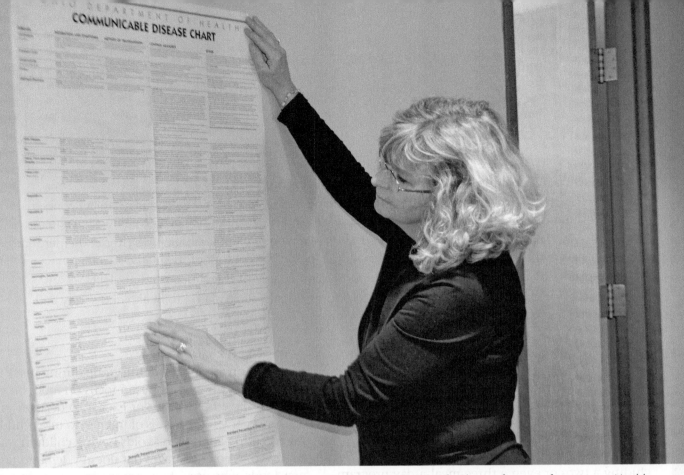

Where we are going: Our audacious vision for the profession of tomorrow. Health and safety information should be posted where both parents and teachers can see it.

Managing the Food and the Health and Safety Programs

naeyc

Standards and Recommendations Addressed in This Chapter

ADVANCING EQUITY RECOMMENDATION 1 Provide high-quality early learning services that demonstrate a commitment to equitable outcomes for all children.

PROGRAM STANDARD 1 Relationships

PROGRAM STANDARD 5 Health

PROGRAM STANDARD 7 Families

PROGRAM STANDARD 8 Community Relationships

PROGRAM STANDARD 9 Physical Environment

PROGRAM STANDARD 10 Leadership and Management

PROFESSIONAL STANDARDS AND COMPETENCIES: STANDARD 1 Child Development and Learning in Context

PROFESSIONAL STANDARDS AND COMPETENCIES: STANDARD 3 Child Observation, Documentation, and Assessment

PROFESSIONAL STANDARDS AND COMPETENCIES: STANDARD 6 Professionalism as an Early Childhood Educator

LEARNING OBJECTIVES

After reading this chapter, you should be able to:

11-1   Describe the components of a complete food service program.

11-2   Explain staff responsibilities related to maintaining health and safety regulations, liability concerns, preventing and managing communicable disease, and providing a sick early childhood program.

11-3   Describe factors that must be considered when planning and implementing disaster and emergency policies and explain the importance of staff training on the content of the plans.

11-4   Explain the need for staff training and reporting in the area of child abuse and neglect.

11-5   Discuss strategies that directors can use to address legal issues related to health and safety and strategies that may help avert potential lawsuits.

11-1 • Food Service Programs

The total food service program—whether **naeyc** limited to a midmorning snack or including a two- or even a three-meal-a-day program—is important, not only because nutrition affects the mental functioning and physical well-being of the child but also because nutritional habits and attitudes toward eating are established during children's early years. Establishing an appropriate emotional atmosphere and providing variety in food choices and the style of serving the food are foremost considerations, whether the children's meals and snacks are catered, served from frozen prepackaged microwave dinners, come from public school or company cafeterias, or are prepared completely from start to finish in the program's kitchen.

In some programs, children bring brown-bag lunches, a practice that can be a boon to your budget and provide an opportunity to help parents learn more about good nutrition. All brown-bag lunches must be dated and properly labeled. They must be refrigerated, and all leftover foods must be discarded and not sent home in the child's lunch box. It is also important to make certain that children do not trade food with their friends. Nutritious foods should be offered daily and use a variety of serving styles such as self-help and group snacks, family-style and cafeteria-style meals, picnics, bag lunches, and more casual food service for special occasions.

Adults in the classroom sit down with the children when food is served, eat the same food that is served to the children, and take charge of creating pleasant conversation among the entire group during snack time or mealtime. Conversation can focus on food, on what children have been doing or expect to do later in the day, or on any topic that is of interest to most children. An accepting adult who avoids having children wait to be served, who encourages but doesn't demand tasting new foods, who uses utensils appropriately and suggests that children try to manipulate their own small forks or spoons, and who avoids associating unpleasantness or punishment with food is demonstrating healthy habits and attitudes toward eating.

For the young infant, a caring, familiar adult who is unrushed is important during feeding time. Infants should be held while taking a bottle but encouraged to begin to hold it for self-feeding as voluntary control progresses. Staff must be reminded *not* to prop bottles for infants because of the dangers of choking and of falling asleep with milk or juice in the mouth, which is detrimental to healthy gums and teeth and

Director's Corner

During COVID an important part of mealtimes was no longer allowed. Educators were required to plate each child's meal to avoid having multiple children using the same serving utensils. Family-style meals are an important part of mealtime, so although children were no longer serving themselves, the educators needed to continue focusing on the communal moment and use the time as an opportunity to create a relaxing environment while encouraging healthy eating and discussions.

Due to mask requirements, teachers could not eat with the children but continued to encourage the children to try new foods.

—Director of an urban early childhood program

Adults should sit with children during meals and encourage pleasant interaction.

could lead to a possible increase in ear infections. In addition, for their emotional and social well-being, it is critical that babies be held and cuddled while being fed.

Older infants benefit from sitting in adapted chairs near the table with older toddlers and preschoolers, whenever that is possible. They often can enjoy finger foods with the toddlers and participate in the pleasant atmosphere of eating time. Choking may be a problem for babies who are beginning to feed themselves, so a caregiver must be close by at all times. Foods should be cut in bite-sized pieces, be of proper consistency, and initially offered one piece at a time. Make sure the cook and the caregivers in the program know that there are high-risk foods that are likely to cause choking in young children. Ninety percent of all fatal chokings occur in children under age 4. In addition, the American Academy of Pediatrics' Council on Injury, Violence, and Poison Prevention (2019) reports that approximately one child dies every 5 days in the United States from choking on food.

Foods that may cause choking include the following (American Academy of Pediatrics et al., 2019):

- hot dogs,
- nuts and seeds,
- popcorn,
- raw carrots,
- chunks of meat,
- marshmallows,
- chips,
- peanut butter (spoonfuls),
- pretzels,
- whole grapes,
- hard candy,
- raw peas, and
- rice cakes.

Candy is the leading cause of nonfatal choking incidents (Chapin et al., 2013). Nonetheless, it is essential for children to sit down and to be supervised while eating or drinking any food item to avoid the dangers of choking.

Directors are responsible for all aspects of the food service program, so they must monitor and supervise the atmosphere, health, and safety features of mealtimes. They also must oversee the planning, buying, and preparation of food and provide opportunities for in-service training to the food service staff members and other adults who work with the children during snack time and mealtime.

Making the Case for *Using Food Thoughtfully*

As a director, you understand that making conscientious decisions regarding your food program is critical. Your menu can provide children with clear messages about what constitutes healthy eating. But have you considered that other uses of food in the program may send messages you did not intend? One area of debate concerns the use of food as a learning material. For example, does "playing with food" send the message to younger children that play items can be eaten? Or does the use of food as an art or sensory table material demonstrate a lack of respect for a vital resource that is valued by some cultures? How might adults who have come from impoverished areas perceive the "wasting" of food? There is no clear-cut solution to this debate. Nonetheless, as a director, you must make decisions regarding your stance and that of your program on this important issue. For an expanded discussion of this topic, see Swim and Freeman (2004).

11-1a • Menu Planning

The proportion of the total daily food requirement provided by the program depends on the total number of hours the child spends in the program. Licensing regulations vary, but general guidelines state the following:

- Children in care for 8 hours or less should be offered at least one meal and two snacks, or two meals and one snack.
- Children in care for more than 8 hours should be offered at least two meals and two snacks, or one meal and three snacks.
- A nutritious midmorning and midafternoon snack should be offered to all children.
- Children should be offered food at intervals of not less than 2 hours and not more than 3 hours apart unless the child is asleep (American Academy of Pediatrics et al., 2019).

Of course, infants in group care have different needs and require individualized eating schedules with carefully prepared formulas and special diets.

The MyPlate food guidance system (**Figure 11-1**) has been developed by the U.S. Department of Agriculture (USDA) to provide guidelines for daily food intake. Portion sizes and food selections for young children are presented in the *Dietary Guidelines for Americans, 2020* publication available on the USDA website.

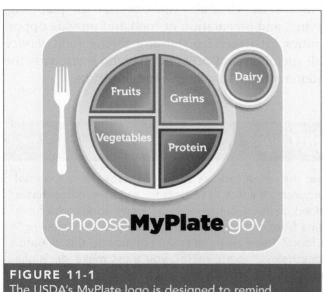

FIGURE 11-1
The USDA's MyPlate logo is designed to remind individuals to eat healthfully.
Source: https://www.myplate.gov

Nutritious meals and snacks can be selected from among the following food groups:

- bread, rice, cereal, and pasta;
- vegetables;
- fruits;
- milk, yogurt, and cheese;
- meat, poultry, fish, dry beans, eggs, and nuts; and
- fats, oils, and sweets.

Careful planning includes ample choices of fruits and vegetables along with dairy products; some meat, fish, and poultry; and some selected items from the bread and pasta group. It is important to check local licensing standards for additional details on nutrition requirements. For programs involved in the USDA Child and Adult Care Food Program (CACFP), nutritional standards for meal and snack serving sizes for children birth through age 12 can be found on the USDA website (Food and Nutrition Service, 2017).

Every precaution must be taken to ensure that children with food allergies or other conditions requiring a special diet, such as cultural or religious customs or family food practices (e.g., vegetarianism), are served only those foods on their prescribed diets. Both the cook and all classroom staff must be alerted to these special dietary requirements, and both the director and the staff must know the emergency procedures to follow in the event a particular child has an allergic reaction. According to the U.S. Food and Drug Administration (n.d.), the most common foods that cause allergies are milk, eggs, fish, shellfish, tree nuts (e.g., almonds, walnuts, pecans), peanuts, wheat, and soybeans. With the increasing

Growth Mindset Moment

Think about your earliest recollections of eating with the family or with an educator. Do you recall being pressured about table manners, finishing your main course before dessert, and tasting foods that you disliked? Can you recall how you felt at those times? What emotions did you feel? How did you feel about the adults who made demands on you? How did you feel about eating and mealtime when you were under pressure to eat too much or eat foods you disliked? What are your current attitudes about eating and about unfamiliar foods? Can you relate these current attitudes to your earlier experiences with eating and sampling new foods?

incidence of peanut allergies among young children, some programs choose to eliminate all peanut products, including peanut butter, from their menus. For some special diet cases, parents may choose to send food for the child. These packed lunches must be properly refrigerated until served and must *not* be shared with other children. Any food from home also must be labeled, showing the child's name and date.

Nutritional considerations in meal planning for young children are necessary but not enough to guarantee that children will be adequately nourished (U.S. Department of Agriculture & U.S. Department of Health and Human Services, 2020). Children's appetites and food preferences also must be considered when meals are planned. Children 3 and 4 years old tend to have small, unpredictable appetites, and they are prone to food sprees. Their foods must not be too hot nor too cold, not too spicy or gluey, and cut into bite-sized and manageable portions. Variation in texture, color, and flavor also are important considerations in planning children's meals. Every effort should be made to limit the use of salt and sugar as well as foods high in fat. Serving certain ethnic foods will provide wider variation for all the children and make available familiar foods to the children from specific ethnic groups represented in the classroom. It is always a good idea to introduce a new food along with old familiar favorites.

Further considerations that affect menu planning are the availability of equipment and utensils and the preparation time for each menu item when all foods are prepared in the program's kitchen. It is virtually impossible to prepare hot breads, an oven-cooked main dish, and a baked dessert for one meal if only one oven is available. Also, the number and sizes of pots and pans must be checked when menus are planned to ensure an adequate supply of equipment of an appropriate size to prepare the foods for a particular meal. Preparation time is another factor that influences meal planning. Meals that require too much last-minute preparation create problems for the cook and potentially delay the serving time. Hungry children who are forced to wait for their food become impatient and restless, and educators then must find ways to help them cope with these unnecessary delays.

Meal and menu planning can be systematized and simplified by using meal-planning guides, standardized recipes, and sample menus. Many government booklets and other menu-planning guides are useful in planning 4 to 6 weeks of basic menus. Menu changes based on the availability of seasonal or plentiful foods can be made on a weekly basis. But beyond those minor changes, basic menu patterns can be repeated every 4 to 6 weeks.

Educators and parents often have helpful suggestions about changes in the basic menu patterns, so a process for collecting feedback should be established. Some lunches include too many items that are difficult for children to manage or are too time-consuming to serve. For example, banana sections that have to be peeled and packaged crackers that have to be opened are both difficult to serve and problems for children to manage.

To demonstrate respect and support for diversity, programs will want to consider families' cultural and religious needs during menu planning. In addition, some parents may be interested in organic or locally grown foods. Inviting the cook to lunch with the children provides an

TeachSource Video Vignette

Food Allergies: Children

Food allergies in children have risen dramatically in the past 20 years, and these allergies can result in mild to potentially deadly reactions. View the video vignette titled *Children and Food Allergies*. Reflect on the following questions:

1. Why has the number of food allergies risen so dramatically?

2. As a director, what strategies would you use to make sure that your program is addressing the needs of children with food allergies?

opportunity for the cook to hear comments from the children about the food and to observe how well they manage the foods served. A "cook's mailbox" not only invites children to write requests for favorite foods and send thank-you notes to the cook but also serves as an excellent meaningful literacy experience. The mailbox and lunch with the children also give the cook a chance to feel more a part of the total program rather than one who spends all day in the kitchen and away from the children.

Parents often are interested in what children have been served for snacks and breakfast and lunch, so it is helpful to post weekly menus or publish them regularly in the parent newsletter. Posting menus not only helps the parents plan for a child's meals at home but also serves as a model for parents who may be inexperienced with planning balanced family meals.

TeachSource Video Vignette

Early Childhood Nutrition

Nutritious meals and snacks are an important component of early childhood programming. Young children also can learn about making healthy food choices—behaviors that can guide them throughout their lives. View the video vignette titled *Promoting Children's Health: A Focus on Nutrition in an Early Childhood Program*. Reflect on the following questions:

1. What strategies does the educator use to teach children about healthy snacking?

2. As a director, how could you support educators' integration of appropriate nutrition information into the curriculum?

An interesting feature to add to the menu-posting area is a pictorial menu for the children. The cook, another staff member, or an interested parent may be willing to collect food pictures and post each day's snack and lunch on an eye-level bulletin board for children to "read." It creates interest among the children, who can look forward to a dish they especially enjoy, and it becomes part of the program's nutrition program.

11-1b • Food Buying

Careful menu planning reduces cost and waste and provides a clear-cut basis for setting up shopping lists for daily, weekly, and monthly food buying. Whether meals are catered, partially prepared from prepackaged meals especially designed for children, or fully prepared in the program kitchen, the food budget will affect both meal planning and food purchasing. Quantity buying and cooperative buying arrangements among a group of programs sometimes results in lower prices but also might limit choices, increase the pressure to purchase foods of lesser quality, and create storage problems when quantity purchases exceed the available storage space. Therefore, although price is an important consideration, quality, available storage space, and, of course, food preferences of the children must be taken into consideration when food-purchasing decisions are made.

Catered meal services require practically no shopping time, no storage space, and little time selecting foods and developing shopping lists. They also eliminate the need for a complete meal-preparation space and a full-time cook, but the services may be more expensive than meals prepared at the program. In addition, the food could turn out to be less satisfying to the children, and the number of food choices available may be limited.

The prepackaged frozen meals that are prepared in convection or microwave ovens are expensive conveniences. This type of food service requires large freezers and special ovens yet require neither a full-time cook nor complete meal-preparation space. The director must select carefully so the choices are appropriate for young children and there is variety in the menu. Fresh foods and beverages must be bought daily or weekly as needed to supplement prepackaged meals.

The Farm to School (F2S) Network (F2SN) "envisions a nation in which Farm to School programs are an essential component of strong and just local and regional food systems, ensuring the health of all school children, farms, the environment, economy and communities" (Farm to School Network, n.d.). F2SN links food service programs in schools across the country with local farms that are able to provide locally grown food for meals and snacks. You can find additional information about F2SN and its programs in all 50 states on the F2SN website (http://www.farmtoschool.org/).

Using company or public school cafeterias requires planning with the cafeteria manager and staff. Foods brought from cafeterias serving adults or older children are sometimes served in containers or in portions difficult for young children to manage. A whole hamburger, a large wedge of dill pickle, catsup in a sealed foil container, and milk in a sealed carton are all difficult for young children to handle. Because that is standard public school cafeteria fare, however, you may find no other choices for your children. Also, cafeteria service customarily means self-help and carrying trays. That is out of the question for young children. It is important to develop clear-cut guidelines for portion sizes, family-style service, and alternative menus so you can work with the cafeteria food service staff to find ways to make appropriate adjustments for young children.

Meals prepared at the program mean that the program must have a complete meal-preparation space that meets all licensing requirements and must employ a full-time cook if it is a full-day early childhood program. Preferably, the cook will have planning and buying skills. If not, a staff person (sometimes the director) plans and purchases the foods in consultation with the cook. Planning purchases, doing the shopping, and checking deliveries are all time-consuming; however, total meal preparation at the program allows for greater variation in foods served and more involvement of the children in shopping, preparing, and serving. It also guarantees that items on the menu will be prepared and served with young children in mind.

11-1c • USDA Child and Adult Care Food Program

Some programs serve children who are eligible for free or reduced-price meals from the USDA's Child and Adult Care Food Program. Although the CACFP

is federally funded, individual states are responsible for managing the program. Determining a family's eligibility is based on income, and early childhood program (not-for-profit or for-profit), home-based programs, and after-school care programs may participate. For-profit programs may participate when 25 percent of the program's enrollment or licensed capacity receives either Title XX assistance or is eligible for free or reduced meals. Providers who may not qualify under the Title XX criteria may meet other qualification expectations. The National Child Care Association is a helpful resource for for-profit programs. Although some programs may have a designated staff person or cook do some of the paperwork to receive the USDA reimbursement, in most cases, the director does the necessary paperwork or at least is responsible for making sure it is done correctly.

Eligibility of children for free or reduced-price meals is based on family income. Income levels for family eligibility and reimbursement rates for providers are adjusted annually effective July 1 each year. To obtain the most recent information regarding eligibility and management of the food program, view the *income eligibility guidelines* on the U.S. Department of Agriculture & U.S. Department of Health and Human Services (2020) website. Other helpful sources of information include your state licensing agent or your state agency that administers the CACFP. A meal benefit form must be on file for every child who receives meals under the USDA food program. These forms must be kept on file for at least 3 years to ensure they will be available at the time your agency undergoes monitoring reviews. It is essential that the information on the forms is complete and accurate to avoid the possibility of penalties if errors are discovered during a periodic review. USDA forms vary from state to state, so the federal form may not match those required by your state. Also, new forms are issued yearly with updated income guidelines.

To obtain forms from your state, contact your state agency that administers the CACFP. In most cases, this will be the state department of education. The state agency will provide updated application forms, worksheets that can be used to determine eligibility of your clients, and worksheets for record keeping and applying for reimbursement. Most states require programs to submit the final information and requests for reimbursement online.

Working Smart with Technology

Data-Management Systems for Early Childhood Programs

Today's directors have many resources at their fingertips thanks to the continuing growth of technology. One advancement that provides numerous benefits has been the development of data-management systems for early childhood programs. One key advantage of these software programs is the reduction in time that must be spent developing weekly menus. For example, directors might be able to plan 1 or 2 months of menus at one time using a management system and then be able to reuse them over time. If changes are desired to the menu, adjustments can be made quite easily. In addition, many programs enable you to print out food shopping lists based on the number of meals to be served. Another significant benefit is that data-management systems can help directors purchase and prepare only what is needed. In this way, food is not wasted, which saves money. For more information on the use of early childhood program data-management systems, see Ho, Schoenberg, Richards, and Morath (2009) and Simon (2012).

Many data-management systems are now available for directors to facilitate their work.

Director's Corner

One of the things I learned quickly when I started to work with this program in the public school was to become friendly with the cafeteria manager. Now she cuts the hamburgers in quarters, sends pickle slices instead of those huge strips of dill pickles, and includes a sharp knife for my use when there are apples to be cored and sliced or oranges to be quartered.

—*Director, public school Head Start program*

Providers who fit into one of the following categories may receive USDA reimbursement for eligible children enrolled:

- nonresidential public or private not-for-profit early childhood programs and Aid to Dependent Children (ADC) programs (some forms or documents replace ADC with Temporary Assistance for Needy Families),
- profit-making early childhood programs that receive Title XX compensation for at least 25 percent of the children attending,
- Head Start programs,
- settlement houses and recreation programs, and
- family early childhood program homes (only if they participate in the CACFP under a sponsoring organization that has tax-exempt status).

All participating agencies must serve foods that follow the USDA's CACFP meal patterns that are updated regularly and published on the USDA's food and nutrition website. You may also find updated meal pattern information on the website of your state agency that oversees CACFP.

The patterns provide information about the types and portions of foods that must be served to each child for meals and snacks so programs can receive reimbursement. Following USDA guidelines ensures well-balanced meals; however, some recommended serving sizes may be overwhelming for young children if put on the plate all at one time.

Directors of programs enrolled in the USDA food program must complete extensive paperwork on a regular basis. Reimbursement claims and financial reports must be filed monthly, reporting data on the following:

- attendance;
- number of meals served;
- cost of food, which is calculated on the basis of information obtained from a monthly food inventory;
- labor and purchased service costs; and
- income from reduced lunch fees and other sources.

To complete these claim forms, you must have accurate attendance records, invoices or cash tapes and receipts for all food and some nonfood purchases, canceled checks, and financial records on all cash received from those families who pay full or reduced lunch costs. The reimbursement form helps with record keeping. Some states provide worksheets to assist with record keeping. Directors may also develop their own worksheets.

Even when there is an extra person on staff to do the USDA paperwork, data collection for the reports and preparation for reviews involve the director, the cook, and the teaching staff. Some states require regular training for all staff involved in the food program. Items such as point-of-service meal counts, safe and sanitary food handling, record-keeping procedures, and size of servings are appropriate topics for these mandatory staff training sessions. Although the sessions are time-consuming and costly, all staff members must understand the details of the requirements to qualify for reimbursement from the CACFP because it is the program's primary source of revenue to finance the food program for eligible families. Federal regulations require that programs taking part in CACFP must be reviewed periodically. The purpose of these reviews is to ensure that all CACFP regulations are being addressed. Documents that will be examined during reviews include the following:

- income eligibility forms,
- attendance records, and
- enrollment forms (to confirm that children listed as eligible for reimbursement are enrolled).

In addition to reviewing records on children, the food program official will examine the following administrative records:

- record of meal counts,
- menus,
- monthly food inventories,
- documentation of food and supply costs,
- documentation of labor costs, and
- documentation of Title XX enrollments if it is a proprietary program.

As a director, it is essential that you understand the USDA program so you can do the paperwork if it is part of your job description, or delegate the responsibility and then coach those who are doing the detailed record keeping and reporting.

11-1d • Food Storage

Food storage requires careful planning so that sufficient quantities of food items are conveniently accessible to the preparation area and that storage areas and containers are sanitary and chilled. The available shelf space and containers must be appropriate to accommodate the packaged size of the food items as they are delivered from the supplier. All food items should be stored separately from nonfood items, and food storage rooms should be dry, relatively cool (60 °F to 70 °F), and free from insect or rodent infestation. Commodities should be stored in tightly covered, labeled metal or heavy plastic containers that are at least 6 inches above the floor level to permit air circulation and to protect them from dirt. Dating containers ensures food supplies will be used in the order received.

Perishable foods must be stored at temperatures that prevent spoilage. Refrigerator temperatures must be 41 °F or lower; freezer temperatures should be 0 °F or lower (American Academy of Pediatrics et al., 2019). Shelf space must allow for air circulation around the refrigerated foods, and thermometers in the warmest sections of refrigerators and freezers should be checked daily.

11-1e • Food Preparation

Cooks must be instructed to follow recipes in meal preparation and are expected to adhere to directions about cooking times and temperatures, proper techniques, temperatures for holding prepared foods, and proper methods for storing and using leftovers. Sanitation in the food-preparation area is of utmost importance. The food service staff must follow sanitary food-handling practices and maintain good personal hygiene while handling foods and cleaning food-preparation equipment and utensils. Even though a nutritionist or other staff member may be responsible for the total food service program in the program, it is advisable that you as director periodically check the food-preparation techniques and sanitation practices of the cook as food is prepared and served to the children. It often becomes the director's responsibility to coach the cook when correct preparation procedures are not being followed.

Sanitation guidelines are available from your local health department or your state or local licensing agent. The licensing regulations at all levels include clearly stated sanitation requirements related to food preparation in early childhood programs. A local health department staff member or your program licensing agent is an excellent resource for helping interpret and implement the sanitation regulations applicable in your area.

It is advisable for you as the director to make periodic checks on food preparation and service.

11-1f • Resources

Every state has a child nutrition agency. These agencies can supply copies of laws, regulations, and guidelines in response to questions about nutrition and health. The following list includes additional places to go for printed material and for consultation on the program's nutrition component:

- public health nutritionists in your state or local health department or the county extension agency,
- nutritionists in local dairy councils or comprehensive health programs,
- USDA extension home economists,
- dietitians in nearby high schools or universities, and
- dietitians in local hospitals.

11-2 • Health and Safety Program

The program's staff members are responsible for the health and safety of the children while they are at the program; therefore, directors must be knowledgeable about health and safety regulations as stipulated in the licensing regulations, about staff liability in cases of accidents at school, and about procedures for protection from and reporting of communicable disease and child abuse and neglect. Although some large programs may have a health consultant on staff, in most places the director is the designated individual responsible for the health program.

The health services provided through the early childhood program may range from no service at all to comprehensive service, including regular physicals, dental checkups and treatment, vision screening, hearing screening, and mental health services. The scope of the health services program depends on the program's health policies set by the funding agent, the socioeconomic status of the families, the family expectations, and the licensing regulations. All programs should maintain up-to-date health and immunization records on the children, whether or not direct health services are provided.

11-2a • Health Records for Children and Staff

Children's health records cover information up to the time of registration and any new health or medical information received while the child is in the program. Formats for these records vary and may be set by local health departments. The information provided (in addition to the basic demographics such as name, birth date, parents' names, and the like) should include medical and developmental information and must be completed and signed by the child's health care provider. The medical report on the child should include the following:

- results from the child's most recent well-care visit with physician's signature;
- health history, including records of the child's immunizations;
- description of any disability or special need and a care plan for how these needs will be accommodated;
- assessment of the child's growth based on height, weight, and head circumference (percentile for these if the child is younger than 24 months);
- results of developmental screenings as well as those for vision, hearing, dental health, nutrition, tuberculosis, hemoglobin, urine, lead, and so on;
- dates of significant communicable diseases;
- prescribed medications, including information on recognizing and reporting potential side effects;

- description of current acute or chronic health problems under care or needing treatment;
- description of serious injuries sustained by the child in the past;
- special instructions for the caregiver; and
- emergency medical and dental care authorization form (American Academy of Pediatrics et al., 2019).

It is advisable to have the child's medical report on file before or at admission, but it is imperative that it be completed within 6 weeks after admission or as required by licensing laws. These records should be updated every 6 months for children younger than 2 and every year for children ages 2 to 6.

A dental screening should be included in the medical report. An authorized health care provider often does the dental screening on children under age 3, at which time the child should visit a dentist. If the earlier dental screenings reveal special oral or dental problems, the child should see a dentist immediately.

Staff medical records that follow the licensing requirements must be on file at the program. Even when not required by licensing, there should be a medical record on every adult who has regular contact with the children, including substitutes, volunteers, practicum students, cooks, and van drivers. The staff records should include not only a physical assessment but also an evaluation of the emotional fitness of those who are to care for the children. The staff health appraisal should include the following:

- health history;
- physical and dental exams;
- vision and hearing screening;
- tuberculosis (TB) screening with the tuberculin skin test or the interferon gamma release assay;
- review of immunizations (measles, mumps, rubella, diphtheria, tetanus, polio);
- review of occupational health concerns;
- assessment of need for immunizations against influenza, pneumococcus, and hepatitis B (and those required by individual states); and
- assessment of any other condition that may impair a staff member's ability to perform the job (American Academy of Pediatrics et al., 2019).

Unless licensing regulations require more frequent updating of staff health records, it is recommended this be done every 2 years. After many years of decreasing numbers of cases, tuberculosis seems to be on the rise again, so it is wise to consult your local health authorities to determine the frequency of repeat TB testing.

Currently, there are no screening or self-appraisal tools to identify specific health conditions that may seriously impair a caregiver's ability to provide safe and healthy experiences for children. However, there are some obvious things that a director can assess, including the ability or willingness to do the following:

- move quickly to supervise and assist the children;
- lift children, equipment, and supplies;
- sit on the floor and on child-sized chairs;
- respond quickly in case of an emergency;
- practice frequent handwashing;
- eat the same food served to the children;
- hear and see at a distance for playground supervision; and

▶ TeachSource Video Vignette

Communicating with Parents about Health Issues

Informing parents about the health-related policies and procedures of an early childhood program is an important responsibility of administrators and educators. View the video vignette titled *Communicating with Parents about Health in Early Childhood: A Parent-Educator Meeting*. Reflect on the following questions:

1. What types of information should be shared with parents related to health-related issues?

2. What are the benefits of meeting face-to-face with the parent to discuss health policies and procedures?

3. What advice is given to parents regarding a child's return to the classroom following an illness?

- not be absent from work because of illness more frequently than the typical adult in order to provide continuity of care for young children (American Academy of Pediatrics et al., 2019).

11-2b • Communicable Disease

Cases of communicable diseases at the early childhood program must be reported to all program families and to the local health authorities. The usual children's diseases, as well as cases of meningitis, scarlet fever, infectious hepatitis, and head lice, must be reported so that necessary precautions can be taken immediately. It is important that pregnant staff members consult their physician about precautions related to exposure to communicable diseases at the workplace.

Directors and some of the teaching staff should have training in communicable diseases to enable them to recognize symptoms and make decisions about excluding children from the group. Communicable disease training is available in most communities through the Red Cross or the local health department. Licensing usually requires updated communicable disease training for classroom staff. Every program should provide easy access to a communicable disease chart to help staff recognize symptoms and make exclusion decisions. In addition, communicable disease apps (applications) are now available for mobile devices. Many states require that educators conduct a daily health check as each child arrives so that potential health issues can be quickly identified.

The most important measure in preventing the spread of disease in early childhood programs is handwashing, not only after toileting and diapering but also after nose blowing or helping a child with a runny nose or cough and before handling dishes or serving food (**Figure 11-2**). There are other occasions when handwashing should be considered. For example, some states mandate handwashing following outdoor play. You may also want to encourage the practice before and after water play or following the handling of class pets. Sanitizing surfaces after diapering or on tables before eating also will help cut down on the spread of disease. Cleanliness is the major contributing factor to effective disease control in early childhood program environments.

Staff members responsible for giving first aid to children and those likely to come in contact with

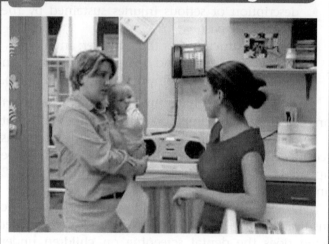

▶ TeachSource Video Vignette

The Daily Health Check

The daily evaluation of a child's health status takes little time but can yield numerous benefits. View the video vignette titled *Infants & Toddlers: Daily Health Checks*. Reflect on the following questions:

1. You are the director of an early childhood program who has just hired a new toddler educator. What information would you provide to this new employee regarding the benefits of the daily health check in your program?

2. What information should be included in a form that educators might use as they conduct daily health checks?

blood or body fluids should have special training in dealing with blood-borne pathogens such as hepatitis B or HIV (a viral infection that can lead to AIDS). Early childhood programs are required to offer free hepatitis B immunizations to employees when hired or within 24 hours following exposure to blood or body fluids containing blood (Marotz, 2015).

The spread of disease also is minimized through precautionary measures for handling situations when children become ill during the day and when children are ill on arrival. A written policy regarding management of sick children must be conveyed to parents when children are enrolled. Few programs have the facilities to care for a sick child who must be separated from the other children, so the usual practice is to call the parent or a designated adult to come for the child. In the meantime, the child usually is removed from the classroom and rests or plays

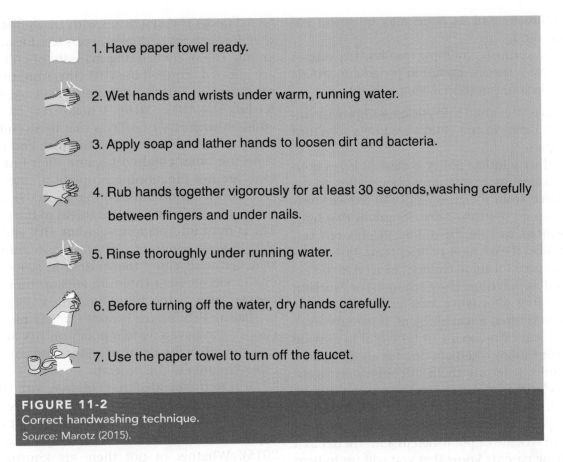

1. Have paper towel ready.

2. Wet hands and wrists under warm, running water.

3. Apply soap and lather hands to loosen dirt and bacteria.

4. Rub hands together vigorously for at least 30 seconds, washing carefully between fingers and under nails.

5. Rinse thoroughly under running water.

6. Before turning off the water, dry hands carefully.

7. Use the paper towel to turn off the faucet.

FIGURE 11-2
Correct handwashing technique.
Source: Marotz (2015).

quietly under adult supervision. Often the director is the only staff person who has a schedule flexible enough to allow for time to stay with the sick child. An extra cot and a few toys for use while children are waiting to be picked up by a parent is standard equipment in many directors' offices.

11-2c • Exclusion Policy

Exclusion policies must be made clear to parents and to the early childhood program staff. If the purpose of excluding an ill child is to prevent the spread of infection to others in the group, it is important to specify which types of illnesses require exclusion and under what circumstances children will be sent home. This list may include conditions such as the following:

- diarrhea,
- vomiting three or more times within the 24-hour period before attending the program, and
- fever above 101 °F (oral), 102 °F (rectal), or 100 °F (axillary) with changes in behavior or other

symptoms such as lethargy, sore throat, vomiting, or rash.

Note that a rise in body temperature is common in young children and may or may not be a symptom of a contagious or serious illness. Nonetheless, most programs have strict policies about excluding children with a fever. Infants younger than 4 months should be evaluated by medical personnel if they have an unexplained temperature above 100 °F (axillary) or 101 °F (rectal).

- abdominal discomfort present for more than 2 hours or intermittent pain accompanied by other symptoms such as fever;
- rash accompanied by fever or behavior changes;
- mouth sores accompanied by drooling;
- chicken pox (until lesions have crusted);
- head lice (until after the first treatment has been received);
- scabies (until after first treatment has been received);
- impetigo (until 24 hours after treatment has begun);

- strep throat (until 24 hours after treatment has begun); and
- rubella, pertussis, mumps, measles, hepatitis A (each has a specific exclusion period and criteria for exclusion) (Aronson & Shope, 2019).

In many cases, the child's physician will provide information relative to the child's readiness to return to the program.

When the exclusion policy is clear, it helps both parents and staff make decisions about when to exclude children from the group and can reduce stress for all concerned (Button, 2008). Programs that have staffed facilities to care for mildly ill children can have more liberal exclusion policies than those without staff or space for these children to receive the extra rest and supervision they require. For working parents, finding alternative care arrangements for sick children is often a real problem. If parents don't have family leave time to use, it is helpful to provide resources for finding alternate care for an ill or recuperating child. Referring them to community agencies such as "sitters on call" or nanny services may be an answer for some families. If you locate alternative services in your community, they could be posted on the program website or published in a newsletter as a way of letting parents know that you will try to help as much as possible when their sick children are temporarily excluded from the classroom.

Although there is an ever-increasing amount of information on the risks posed by children infected with HIV attending early childhood programs, evidence is inconclusive at this time. Because new information about HIV and AIDS is being generated constantly, stay in touch with local health authorities or the Centers for Disease Control and Prevention (CDC) for updated information and guidance. If a child infected with HIV applies for admission, the public health department and the child's physician can help determine if it is safe for the child to be in a group situation. They also will provide help in determining whether the presence of this child exposes other children and adults to undue risk. Note that it is illegal to ask about a child's HIV or AIDS status at admission.

The number of children in group care infected with HIV may increase because newer medications and treatments make it possible for infected children to live longer. These HIV-positive children are pro-tected under the Americans with Disabilities Act and therefore cannot be denied access to educational programs. The overwhelming majority of children who are infected acquired the HIV virus from their mothers during pregnancy, labor and delivery, or breastfeeding (UNAIDS, 2016). A major risk of admitting children with HIV or AIDS is that these children run a greater risk of contracting illnesses and infections from the other children because their immune systems are not functioning properly (Centers for Disease Control and Prevention et al., 2009), and these infections can pose a serious threat to the child's life. The current information regarding HIV and the hepatitis B virus (similar to HIV but more infectious) is that neither is easily transmitted in school or early childhood program environments or through casual contact such as touching, hugging, eating together, or sharing bathrooms. However, many programs are choosing to have a written policy on HIV and hepatitis B to protect the rights of an infected child and the other children in the program.

It is recommended that children with HIV be excluded from the group *only* if they have open sores or bleeding that would put other children at risk from exposure to the infected child's body fluids (Marotz, 2015). Whether or not there are known cases of HIV or AIDS among enrolled children, it is essential that staff follow standard precautions to prevent transmission of disease through bodily fluids such as blood, saliva, vomit, nasal or eye discharges, and

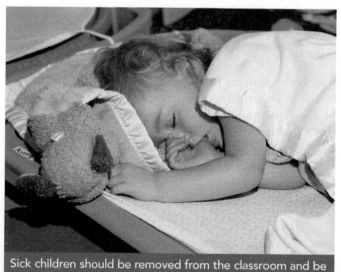

Sick children should be removed from the classroom and be made comfortable under adult supervision.

human waste (urine, feces). Specific recommendations include the following:

- Use single-use disposable gloves when handling or cleaning up bodily fluids and human waste and when staff members have cuts or breaks in their skin. Utility gloves can be used, but they must be sanitized with soap and water and then dipped in a disinfectant solution up to the wrist and then air-dried. Disposable gloves should be discarded without being handled.
- Sanitize diaper-changing surfaces, toys, floors, walls, bathrooms, tables, and other surfaces that come into contact with bodily fluids, including human milk and human waste.
- Wash hands after coming into contact with infected surfaces or materials even if gloves are worn.
- Place contaminated materials in a plastic bag that is then securely tied and disposed of away from the children (American Academy of Pediatrics et al., 2019).

To obtain updated information on this question or others involving infectious diseases, contact your local health department or the CDC.

11-2d • Sick Child Care

As more children under age 5 require some type of care outside the home, there is a consequent increase in the need for sick child care. The first alternative is to have the child at home with a caring parent whose employer allows time off for that purpose. Being at home may be the best alternative, but it is not always the most realistic. That means early childhood professionals, with the help of health professionals, are beginning to develop alternative sick early childhood program models. For example, sick children might be

Director's Corner

I'm very interested in sick early childhood program because of my background in nursing, and I know how much kids need Mom or Dad when they are sick! I also know there is a critical need for sick early childhood program for those cases in which job pressures force parents to get to work, even when their baby is sick. My dream is to develop a satellite family early childhood program home system that will use our program as a base.

—*Director, proprietary for-profit program*

accommodated in the following ways:

- in a sick bay at the program (a "get well" room),
- a program in a separate building that might be the cooperative venture of several early childhood programs,
- a program in a wing of a hospital or on hospital grounds that is available to the general public,
- a "satellite" system of family early childhood program homes linked to an early childhood program, and
- the child's own home under the supervision of a trained person sent from the program or local health agency.

Because children with AIDS are extremely vulnerable to infection from other children, it may be unwise to have them in a sick early childhood program facility where they would be exposed to other sick children.

11-3 • Planning for Disasters and Emergencies

One of the most critical responsibilities **naeyc** of directors is to consider how potential disasters and emergencies might affect the lives of program staff, children, and families. Written policies should be developed that specify how such events are to be managed, and these should be shared regularly with all those associated with the program.

11-3a • Disaster Planning

Although licensing regulations may not always require disaster plans, it is important to plan for building evacuation in the event of fire and to detail additional measures to be taken during tornadoes, earthquakes, smog alerts, floods, sudden loss of heat or air conditioning, or any other major emergency or national disaster. The director must instruct all staff members on the best ways to evacuate the premises and the safe places to shelter children in weather or other emergencies. It is important to practice all emergency procedures with staff so they are conditioned to respond and be less likely to panic. An evacuation plan should be posted in every classroom (**Figure 11-3**). Fire

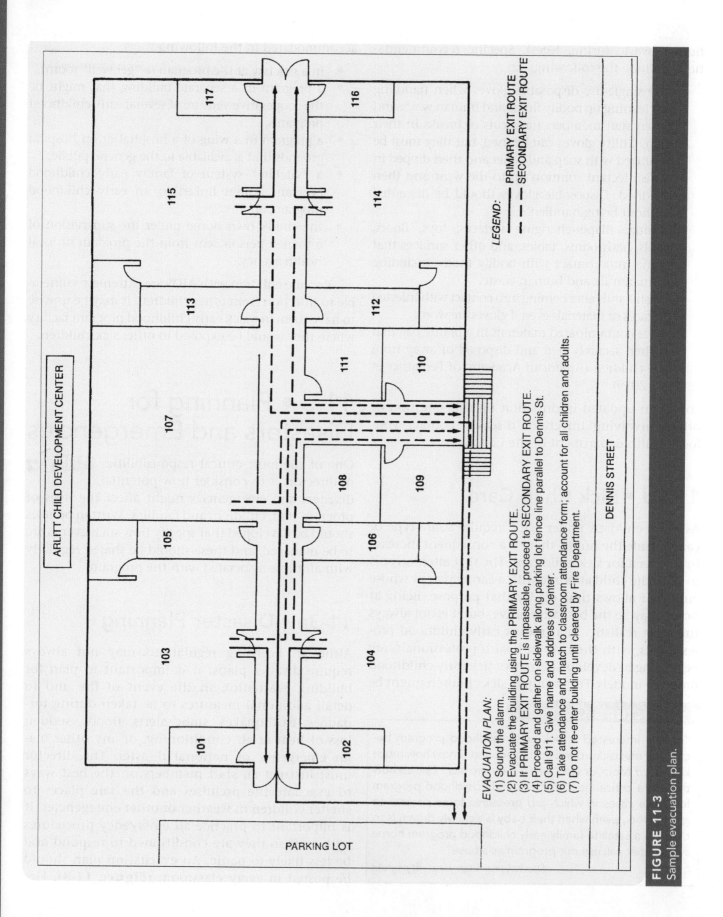

FIGURE 11-3
Sample evacuation plan.

emergency plans should show alternative exit routes, and evacuation drills should be held regularly so children become familiar with this routine. Parents must be informed in advance about alternative shelters so they know the whereabouts of their children during emergencies.

Daily attendance records and information needed to reach parents must be maintained in a convenient location and removed from the building by the designated adults as part of the evacuation procedure. The chain of command regarding who will call for emergency fire or police help, who will secure the building and make a final check that everyone is out, how the building will be secured, and who will contact the parents all must be arranged in advance and communicated to staff by the director. Fire alarms, fire extinguishers, and emergency exit lights should be checked regularly to ensure they are in working order. Charged cell phones should be available as well.

Supplies stored in emergency evacuation areas and to be taken to the alternative shelter include the following:

- first aid kit,
- blankets,
- food and water,
- battery-operated radio,
- flashlight, and
- children's books, crayons, paper, and so on.

Fire, earthquake, tornado, and national emergency plans and drills are important, but keep in mind that there many other disasters can impact the early childhood program in addition to those that require building evacuation. Rehearsals for building evacuation are a necessity, but how will the staff respond when a sleeping child stops breathing, when an angry noncustodial parent appears with a gun, or when an inebriated person harasses departing parents and children? How will the staff deal with a warning of a terrorist threat? There are resources in most communities to call on for help as you develop emergency plans for a vast array of possible emergencies and as you train the staff to deal with unexpected events. Invite local law enforcement personnel, health professionals, Red Cross experts, legal aid, and social service people to help you develop procedures and doing staff training. In addition, Child Care Aware of America (2021) provides several resources to assist early childhood programs in preparing for disasters as does Ready.gov (2021).

Directors' responsibilities do not end with plan development, training and rehearsing staff on procedures, and carrying out the plan when a real disaster strikes. They also must handle the follow-up for parents and children and deal with the news media. After a crisis such as a fire, a shooting, the death of a child at the program, an allegation of child abuse or neglect, or a national disaster, it is critical that accurate information be presented to families and to the public through the media. Although this responsibility usually falls to the director, it is wise to consider who else might serve as a spokesperson. A carefully selected, knowledgeable

▶ TeachSource Video Vignette

Creating Safety for Toddlers

The video titled *Creating a Safe Physical Environment for Toddlers* provides an overview of the considerations in maintaining a space that is safe for young children. As you view the video, reflect on the following questions:

1. What safety factors must be considered when planning the physical space for young children?

2. Review the *Monitoring the Classroom for Safety Issues* video clip that appears on the same page as the previously cited video. What strategies can be used to ensure that staff members are using procedures to ensure children's safety?

spokesperson who is savvy about handling the press can help protect the program and its families when serious emergencies or damaging allegations such as those related to child abuse or injury arise. Choices for spokesperson may be the program's administrator or director or the program's lawyer (Bruno & Copeland, 2012). In cases where the program is an employer-sponsored program, the director of public relations or other designated individual may be selected as spokesperson. No matter who is chosen, your program's confidentiality policy precludes discussion of program staff and families. All staff must be trained to deflect media questions to the spokesperson or director and to answer informal questions from parents and others by quoting program written policy or by referring these inquiries to the director.

To obtain more information on the best methods to provide protection in particular areas, directors can contact local health and fire department and national security officials, building inspectors, the Environmental Protection Agency, or the Occupational Safety and Health Administration. Also, make sure *all foreseeable issues* are covered by various insurance policies.

11-3b • Emergency Safety, Health, and Accident Planning

The 21st century presents those who care for children new challenges relative to planning not only for children's health, injuries, accidents, and natural disasters but also for the possibility of terrorist attacks. All of these plans are usually developed by the director with input from parents, staff, the board, and community groups responsible for homeland security.

Some programs may have disaster plans that are in place in case of hurricanes, tornadoes, or other weather-related events. In some cases, they will suffice for possible national security alerts as well. However, these plans need to be reviewed to make sure they are broad enough to cover bomb threats, exposure to hazardous material, and various potentially violent situations. Many states and licensing agencies prescribe forms that must be used for emergency plans (**Figure 11-4**).

An emergency health plan is also developed by the director. It includes the step-by-step procedures to be followed when a child is injured at the program. The purpose of this plan is to provide the program staff with a detailed set of instructions to follow when giving an injured or sick child the best and quickest treatment, notifying the family, and filling out the necessary papers for maximum liability and insurance protection for both staff and family. Many states require that programs have a medical treatment consent or authorization form on file for every child in the program (**Figure 11-5**). When properly completed, this form will give the program authority to obtain medical treatment in an emergency situation. It usually contains specific information related to the child, such as the child's name, date of birth, address, known allergies, the child's physician, and medical insurance information. Often, there is a requirement to have this form notarized. A good resource for information on what is required for this form is your early childhood program licensing agency.

If the child must be taken away from the program for emergency care, the caregiver must stay with that child until the parent arrives or accompanies the child to the hospital. A signed consent form from parents that gives detailed information on where the child should be taken for emergency treatment and permission to transport the child for emergency treatment should be in each child's folder (**Figure 11-5**). Because the parent cannot give informed consent in advance for emergency treatment (the nature of the injury being unknown), it is essential that parents understand that the program must know their whereabouts or that of another responsible adult at all times. It is suggested that the telephone numbers on the child's emergency record, including those for the child's usual source of health care, be updated several times a year.

The director, as well as some members of the teaching staff, must be trained in administering first aid, including cardiopulmonary resuscitation, so preliminary emergency treatment can begin before professional help arrives and so minor injuries will be handled correctly. An injury report must be filled out any time a child is hurt, and it should be filed in a central location with a copy in the child's file

Ohio Department of Job and Family Services

MEDICAL, DENTAL AND GENERAL EMERGENCY PLAN
For Type A Homes and Child Care Centers

Center Name	Center Address
Campus Children's Learning Center	555 Any Street
Center Telephone Number (XXX)XXX-XXXX	

EMERGENCY TELEPHONE NUMBERS
Including 7-digit back up number as well as area code if area code must be dialed to complete the call.

Emergency Squad 911 or (XXX)XXX-XXXX	Hospital 911 or (XXX)XXX-XXXX
Police Department 911 or (XXX)XXX-XXXX	**Fire Department** 911 or (XXX)XXX-XXXX
Poison Control (XXX)XXX-XXXX)	**Public Childrens' Service Agency** (XXX)XXX-XXXX

LOCATION OF:

First Aid Kit(s)
Each classroom, gyms, and closet located in main hallway

Fire Extinguishers
Each classroom and hallways

Fire Alarm System/Main Panel
Mechanical room west wing

Fire Alarm Pull Stations
Located throughout the building.

Electrical Circuit Box
Hallway next to kitchen and mechanical rooms

Children's Records
Front office

Child Safety Seat (Or a statement that the center will use the emergency squad for emergency transportation of children.)
Storage closet/teacher's work room

In case of a **Dental Emergency**, stay with the child and summon help. When an additional staff member is present to assume responsibility for the rest of the group, consult the Dental First Aid Chart which should be posted in each room. Follow instructions indicated, notify the parents, and write an incident report. Remember if blood is involved, use vinyl or non-latex gloves and sanitize afterwards following standard precautions.

Names of staff with current training in First Aid/Communicable Disease:
Identify staff members by name.

Names of staff with current training in CPR:
Identify staff members by name.

In case of an environmental emergency such as fire or tornado/weather alert, consult the posted evacuation plan/diagram or route to your classroom's "safe place". (Your local fire department or Emergency Management service should be able to help you determine this "safe" location ahead of time.) **Fire:** Take attendance roster, secure the classroom, and exit the building with the children to the designated meeting place, which is <u>Southwest corner of PS Playground/West side of Parking Lot</u>. Account for all children and notify administrator or staff in charge whether all children are present or if any are missing. Do not return to classroom until the all clear is sounded. The administrator or designee should be responsible

---

FIGURE 11-4

Medical, dental, and general emergency plan for a child care center.

Source: Ohio Department of Job and Family Services.

for contacting the fire department or 911 if system is not automatic.

Weather Alert: Take attendance roster, secure the classroom, and lead children to the designated "safe place," which is classroom bathrooms and coat rooms. Account for all children and have them assume the safe position, covering head and neck. If blankets or protective covering are available, cover children. Notify administrator or staff in charge if all children are present or if any are missing. Stay in designated "safe place" until the all clear is sounded.

Emergency Evacuation (bomb threat, gas leak, etc.): Take attendance roster, first aid kit, and emergency contact information for children. Account for all children and exit building to the primary evacuation spot, which is southwest corner of PS playground/west side of parking lot. Account for all children with a name to face check off. Follow instructions from emergency personnel as to whether to stay in that spot or to proceed to your secondary evacuation location (which should be further away from your center in case the area around your facility also must be evacuated). The secondary location is Frericks Center on Campus. Always follow instructions of the emergency personnel on site. Parents should be notified as soon as possible. Continue to complete name to face attendance check offs on a regular basis to assure children are not lost. Complete an incident report and provide to the parents as soon as possible. ODJFS must be notified within 24 hours.

Threat of Violence: Secure children in the safest location in the building or outside. Take attendance roster and contact 911/Police. Follow instructions from authorities, account for all children with name to face attendance, notify parents as soon as possible, and complete an incident report for parents.

Loss of Power, Water, Heat: Contact utilities company to notify of outage and assess expected time of outage. Evaluate factors, including safety, temperature, daylight, refrigeration requirements, and ability to follow sanitary hygiene practices. Administrator or designee will make the determination whether the center needs to be closed or not. If in doubt contact your licensing specialist or your local health department for assistance in determining whether you can continue to provide child care services and meet rule requirements.

In the event of a **Serious Injury or Illness:** Stay with injured/ill child at all times and summon additional help if needed to supervise rest of children. Quickly complete an assessment: Appearance, Breathing, Circulation. Summon a staff member trained in First Aid/Communicable Disease if you are not trained, and determine whether EMS needs to be contacted. Check child's health information to determine if a Medical/Physical Health Care Plan has been completed for the child and contact parents. Provide basic first aid until EMS or parent arrives. Complete an incident report for parents. If child is ill, isolate away from other children; reference the ODH Communicable Disease Chart and follow instructions. Determine whether illness needs to be reported to ODH. Post exposure sign or written notice for parents. Complete an incident report for child's parent and sanitize cot/blanket if used. If blood or bodily fluids are involved, remember to wear vinyl or non-latex gloves and follow standard precautions for cleanup.

If situation requires medical attention, ODJFS must be notified within 24 hours of the incident and report submitted within three days.

Supervision: Children must be supervised at all times. Children in the group must be kept within sight and hearing until additional staff are available to take control of children. Staff shall stay with children until the parent arrives.

This plan should be posted in every room used by children and by every telephone. Every room should also have posted: written instructions for fire and weather alert, diagrams showing evacuation route and "safe place", and a Dental First Aid Chart.

Additional instructions for this facility:

FIGURE 11-4
(continued)

EMERGENCY CONTACT INFORMATION

Child's Name _____ Date of Birth _____

Address _____ Home Phone _____

Mother's Name _____ Business Phone _____

Father's Name _____ Business Phone _____

Name of other person to be contacted in case of an emergency:

1. _____ Address _____

   Relationship (sitter, relative, friend, etc.) _____ Phone _____

2. _____ Address _____

   Relationship (sitter, relative, friend, etc.) _____ Phone _____

Authorization is hereby given for the Child Development Center Staff to release the above named child to the following persons, provided proper identification is first established (list all names of authorized persons, including immediate family):

1. _____ Relation: _____
2. _____ Relation: _____
3. _____ Relation: _____

Physician to be called in an emergency:

1. _____ Phone _____ or _____
2. _____ Phone _____ or _____

Dentist to be called in an emergency:

1. _____ Phone _____ or _____

I, the undersigned, authorize the staff of the Child Development Center to take what emergency medical measures are deemed necessary for the care and protection of my child enrolled in the Child Development Center program.

_____
(Signature of Parent or Guardian/date)

               Signature witnessed by:
               (Notary)

_____
(Signature of Parent or Guardian/date)

The above statement sworn before me on:

_____

_____

FIGURE 11-5
Sample emergency contact information form.
Source: Marotz (2015).

(**Figure 11-6**). It is essential to follow the accident plans, have staff properly trained to deal with injuries, and fill out injury reports, both for the safety and well-being of children and for the protection of staff. Directors and board members must understand that taking all these precautions may not protect the staff from liability completely. Therefore, the program should carry accident insurance on the children and have liability coverage for the staff as additional precautionary measures. It is wise to consult both an attorney and an insurance agent about what constitutes adequate coverage.

Injury Report Form

Name of Child _____   Birth Date _____

Parent Name _____

Address _____   Phone Number _____

Usual Source of Health Care _____

Date of Injury _____ Time _____ Age _____ Sex _____

Type of Injury (circle)   Bite   Broken Bone   Bruise   Burn   Choking   Cut   Eye Injury   Foreign
Body   Head Injury   Poisoning   Scrape   Sliver   Sprain   Sting
Other _____

Location Where Injury Occurred _____
e.g., child care room, bathroom, hall, playground, large-muscle
room, bus, car, walk

Type of Equipment Involved _____

How Injury Happened (details of who, what, when, how): _____

_____

_____

_____

_____

Type of Treatment Required _____
e.g., first aid only in day care, visit to doctor's office or clinic,
emergency room, hospitalized, sutures, cast, bandage, medication
given

Signature of Person Filling Out the Report _____

Signatures of Witnesses _____

Name of Medical Professional Consulted _____

Date _____ Time _____ Advice _____

FIGURE 11-6
Sample injury report form.

11-4 • Child Abuse and Neglect

Directors must be vigilant and take **naeyc** steps to prevent the possibility of abuse on the premises, recognize signs of abuse on children who come to the program, and make certain that suspected cases of abuse are properly reported.

11-4a • Prevention on the Premises

Precautions must be taken to prevent both physical and sexual abuse on the premises. Physical abuse occurs most often when adults are stressed; further, the abusive act is unplanned and explosive and usually occurs when other adults are not around. Sexual abuse, on the other hand, is frequently planned ahead (although it also occurs when other adults are not around). Pedophiles may seek employment in early childhood programs to gain access to children. In the latter case, careful preemployment screening and use of criminal record checks and fingerprinting may provide helpful information.

Because abuse of all types usually occurs when other adults are not around, the preventive measures mentioned in connection with staffing patterns (Chapter 9) and developing the facility (Chapter 7) and making it clear to everyone that parents may visit at any time should help eliminate the possibility of abuse occurring in your program.

11-4b • Recognizing and Reporting Abuse and Neglect

All directors and members of the teaching staff in early childhood programs should have some training in recognizing the physical and behavioral signs of abuse and neglect, whether or not licensing requires it. A good resource for programs is the U.S. Department of Health and Human Services document *The Role of Professional Early Childhood Program Providers in Preventing and Responding to Child Abuse and Neglect* (Child Welfare Information Gateway, 2008). In most states, professionals involved with children are required to report suspected cases of abuse. When mandated to report suspicion of abuse or neglect, those reporting are not required to prove their allegations. Nonetheless, reports should be made carefully because much harm can come to children and families when the accusations are unfounded. The director should be notified of all suspected cases of abuse and review the case with the staff member who has found evidence of abuse before the case is reported to the authorities. In most states, information is given to law enforcement agencies or child protective agencies. Familiarity with state laws and local rules for reporting is essential for all early childhood program directors.

11-5 • Legal Issues: Health and Safety

Lawsuits by parents resulting from injury to a child in playground accidents, **naeyc**

exposure to serious illnesses such as HIV or AIDS, injuries inflicted by other children, or alleged child abuse are major concerns for all program staff, administrators, and board members. Lawsuits are to be avoided, not only for reasons of wanting children in our care to be kept safe and healthy but also because the suits can be won by plaintiffs even when the program staff is right. These unfortunate results can occur as a consequence of the sympathies engendered in the courts and in news media. Programs risk losing insurance coverage and suffering irreparable damage to their reputations.

The possibility of being sued for any reason, whether for an accident, a suspicion of child abuse, or alleged wrongful exclusion of a child, can be minimized by building preventive steps into your day-to-day practices.

1. Promote open, trusting communication with parents from the time they walk in the door. When parents trust program staff, they are less likely to sue when things go wrong. The positive regard they hold for the staff encourages them to talk it through and make more rational decisions before calling in their lawyers.

2. Honor the civil rights of all people with whom you work and those whom you serve. The Civil Rights Act of 1964 forbids discrimination based on sex, color, religion, race, disability, and national origin. In addition, the Americans with Disabilities Act of 1990 prohibits discrimination against children and adults with disabilities. Beyond the legal requirements are the ethical principles that promote acceptance of diversity (NAEYC, 2011a).

3. Maintain a well-trained staff in adequate numbers to ensure proper supervision and appropriate health and safety procedures throughout each day. Make sure that staff members are aware of adults who are approved to pick up children from the program. Train staff to inspect all toys and equipment for safety hazards, report all problems in writing, and carefully fill out detailed accident reports.

4. Purchase adequate liability insurance and accident insurance on all the children, even when parents have health insurance. It

promotes goodwill and means some parents will not have to cover a deductible or co-pay requirement. You will also want to work closely with insurance agents to promote principles of risk management at the program.

5. Check all applicants' references carefully and question any gaps in their employment history. Document that references have been checked under the applicant's current name as well as all previous names.

6. Keep records of all board meetings, staff meetings, licensing monitoring reports, and staff training sessions. A plaintiff's attorney can subpoena copies of any or all of these documents, in addition to other related materials such as personnel files, memos, and appointment books.

7. Have your lawyer review all promotional and marketing materials for information that might be viewed as "deceptive" under your state's consumer-protection legislation.

8. Choose an attorney who is thoroughly familiar with both liability and early childhood program laws in your state, and periodically check with your legal advisers. Make sure you discuss the idea of "due diligence" with your attorney regarding the health and safety of children and adults in your program. It is also essential to ensure that all members of your staff understand the behaviors that constitute due diligence and that they are expected to practice those behaviors.

Keep in mind that individual staff members are rarely held personally responsible for claims against the program. It is the employer who is held responsible, provided the act in question occurred within the scope of employment. Staff members may be held individually responsible only when they cause harm outside their legitimate scope of authority.

Programs are especially vulnerable to legal actions over issues of playground equipment safety and supervision and of performance of specialized health procedures to children with special needs. In addition, programs are also vulnerable over issues related to transportation safety.

Although the information in this section provides you with guidelines regarding appropriate practice, it should not be viewed as legal advice. As stated previously, administrators or directors should obtain an experienced attorney who can provide regular counsel related to owning and operating a successful, high-quality early childhood program.

Material in this section is taken from Bruno and Copeland (2012); Cohen (1998); Early Childhood Program Law Program (2012).

Summary

Directors are responsible for overseeing the food service and the health and safety programs in the early childhood program. This significant responsibility includes the following:

- understanding how to plan menus and prepare meals with safe, nutritious food while at the same time considering cost and waste factors;

- being aware of the responsibilities related to maintaining health and safety regulations, addressing liability issues, preventing and managing communicable disease, and providing sick early childhood program;

- ensuring that disaster and emergency plans are written and implemented and that staff understand the plans;

- being familiar with child abuse and neglect laws and reporting procedures and making sure that staff members have received training; and

- recognizing that important legal issues exist related to health and safety in a program for young children and that professional legal guidance may help forestall potential lawsuits.

TRY IT OUT!

1. Before class, obtain the current reimbursement rates for both free and reduced-rate meals for eligible children on the USDA Child and Adult Food Program website (http://www.fns.usda.gov /cacfp/reimbursement-rates). In class, follow these steps:
   a. Using **Director's Resource 11-1**, record reimbursement allowances in the spaces provided.
   b. Using information from **Director's Resource 11-1** and the information given in the chart "Number of Meals Served" (**Director's Resource 11-2**), complete the Director's Resource by calculating the amount to be reimbursed for meals served during the month.
   c. Share your results with a classmate. If your results differ, review your calculations together. If you are unable to resolve the discrepancy, share your results with another student pair.
   d. Discuss the potential administrative challenges in maintaining accurate records related to the food program.
   e. Discuss how the use of technology would facilitate the process of determining reimbursement rates for your program.
2. Work with another student and role-play a conference between a director and a cook, assuming the two roles as follows.

Director: As a director, you are responsible for monitoring food-preparation and serving methods. You have read numerous government publications on the best way to prepare vegetables to retain nutrients. You know that cooking time should be short, that the amount of water used should be small, and that the vegetables should be prepared only minutes before eating. Furthermore, you know that children's foods should be cut in bite-sized portions—that is, stew meat in half-inch cubes, bread slices in quarters, fish sticks halved, and so forth. Your cook prepares all vegetables early in the day and keeps them over low heat until serving time. Even though the recipes indicate that meat should be served in bite-sized pieces and portions should be small, the meat comes from the kitchen in the same sizes in which it was delivered from the meat market.

Cook: You were hired for this job in the early childhood program after being an assistant cook in a restaurant for 5 years. You have looked forward to having your own kitchen, and you are proud of your previous experience and what you know about preparation of food in quantity.

As director, you must call the conference and deal with the problem. Keep in mind that you are committed to maintaining open communication and to promoting the personal and professional growth of your staff.

3. You are a new director who is interested in purchasing locally grown foods for your program. Visit the Farm to School Network website (http://www.farmtoschool.org/about) and check to see if your state has a Farm to School program. (If your state does not have resources available, you may want to view the materials provided for California, Massachusetts, or Ohio.) What types of programming are available in your state related to F2S? How might you go about planning to use the resources that are available in your state? What strategies would you use to convince the owner of your program, as well as the families, of the benefits provided by an F2S program?
4. As a group, discuss the evacuation plan for the room in which you are now having class. Do you see exit signs or evacuation directions in this room or in the adjacent hallways?
   a. If you were responsible for this building, what steps would you take to develop a building evacuation plan and inform the staff about it?
   b. If you had to use this room for a children's classroom, how would you evacuate the children, and how would you prepare the children for an emergency evacuation procedure without creating anxiety and fear?
   c. What issues would you need to consider in order to evacuate children or staff with medical or mobility concerns?
5. Your local chapter of the NAEYC has asked you to give a presentation to its new director discussion group regarding the development of an emergency preparedness plan. Discuss what needs to be included in such a plan and develop an outline for your presentation. What resources would you share with the group?
6. A new family has requested that the program provide their child with a milk substitute. Review the form in **Director's Resource 11-3**. What will your answer be and provide your rationale?
7. You are the parent of a preschooler with a severe peanut allergy. How would you fill out the form in **Director's Resource 11-4**?

Director's Resource 11-1

FOOD REIMBURSEMENT ALLOWANCES

(for use with Try It Out! 11-1a)

	Free	Reduced
Breakfast	_____ per child	_____ per child
Lunch/dinner	_____ per child	_____ per child
Snack (supplements)	_____ per child	_____ per child

Fill in this chart with information from the USDA Child and Adult Food Program website (https://www.fns.usda.gov/cacfp). Use this information to complete the assignment on Director's Resource 11-2.

Director's Resource 11-2

NUMBER OF MEALS SERVED

(for use with Try It Out! 11-1b)

Date	Breakfast Free	Breakfast Reduced	Lunch/Dinner Free	Lunch/Dinner Reduced	Snack Free	Snack Reduced
3	12	2	21	3	21	3
4	13	2	20	3	20	3
5	11	1	18	2	19	2
6	15	1	18	2	19	2
7	15	2	18	1	18	1
10	12	1	17	1	18	1
11	14	2	21	1	20	1
12	15	1	20	2	20	2
13	15	2	18	3	18	3
14	13	2	18	3	18	3
17	12	2	19	2	19	2
18	11	2	19	1	19	2
19	13	1	18	3	19	3
20	13	1	17	3	19	3
21	14	2	19	3	18	3
24	13	2	19	2	19	2
25	14	1	18	3	18	3
26	15	1	18	2	18	2
27	16	0	19	3	19	3
28	14	2	18	3	18	3
31	14	2	20	3	20	2
TOTAL						

Director's Resource 11-2 *(continued)*

Using the information from Director's Resource 11-1 on reimbursement amounts for free and reduced-rate meals and the information from the chart "Number of Meals Served," fill in the following table:

Breakfast	Number of free meals × Free rate =	
	Number of reduced meals × Reduced rate =	
Lunch/dinner	Number of free meals × Free rate =	
	Number of reduced meals × Reduced rate =	
Snack (supplement)	Number of free meals × Free rate =	
	Number of reduced meals × Reduced rate =	
	Total claim for reimbursement	

PARENT/GUARDIAN REQUEST FOR FLUID MILK
SUBSTITUTION

PARENT/GUARDIAN REQUEST FOR FLUID MILK SUBSTITUTION

Parents or guardians may now request in writing that non-dairy beverages be substituted for fluid milk for their children with special dietary needs without providing statement from a recognized medical authority. However, fluid milk substitutions requested are at the **option** and expense of the facility/center.

The non-dairy beverage provided must be nutritionally equivalent to fluid milk and meet the nutritional standards set by the U.S. Department of Agriculture (USDA) for Child Nutrition Programs in order for the facility/center to claim reimbursement for the meal through the Child and Adult Care Food Program (CACFP).

A non-dairy beverage product must at a minimum contain the following nutrient levels per cup to qualify as an acceptable milk substitution:		
a. Calcium 276 mg	d. Vitamin D 2.5 mcg	g. Potassium 349 mg
b. Protein 8 g	e. Magnesium 24 mg	h. Riboflavin .44 mg
c. Vitamin A 150 mcg	f. Phosphorus 222 mg	i. Vitamin B-12 1.1 mcg

To be completed by Child Care Center/Provider prior to distribution of form	
Name of Child Care Center/Provider:	
	This child care center/provider will provide the following non-dairy beverage which meets the USDA-approved nutrient standards for a milk substitute: (list substitute(s))
	This child care center/provider has chosen not to provide non-dairy beverages for the substitution of fluid milk.

To be completed by Parent/Guardian	
Child's Full Name:	
Identify the medical or other special dietary need that restricts the diet of your child (why your child needs a non-dairy beverage as a milk substitute):	
	I request that my child is served the non-dairy beverage which meets the USDA-approved nutrient standards for a milk substitute that is provided by the center/provider as indicated above.
	I am aware that the center is not providing a non-dairy beverage for the substitution of fluid milk. I will provide a non-dairy beverage for my child that meets the USDA-approved nutrient standards for a milk substitute as stated above.
	I will provide a non-dairy beverage for my child that does **not** meet the USDA-approved nutrient standards for the substitution of fluid milk. I understand that the center cannot claim meals that require milk unless I get written statement from a recognized medical authority.
Signature of Parent/Guardian:	Date:

Director's Resource 11-4

SPECIAL DIET FORM

SPECIAL DIET FORM

This center/facility participates in the Child and Adult Care Food Program (CACFP) and any meals, snacks, or milk claimed for reimbursement must meet program requirements. Food accommodations must be made when the food accommodation is due to a disability (a physical or mental impairment which substantially limits one or more major life activities, has a record of such impairment, or is regarded as having such impairment). Reasonable food accommodations may be made for children/participants without disabilities who may have special medical or dietary needs. Food accommodations are to be supported by a statement signed by a recognized state medical authority which is defined as a state licensed health care professional who is authorized to write medical prescriptions under state law.

To be completed by parent, guardian or authorized representative		
Child/Participant Name:		Birth Date:
Parent/Guardian/Authorized Representative Name:		
Email:		
Home Phone:	Work Phone:	Cell Phone:
Address:		
City:	State:	Zip:

To be completed by recognized state medical authority
Check and complete appropriate information. For the safety of the child, please be as specific as possible.

	Yes, this child/participant has a disability that requires food accommodation?

Describe disability:

What major life activity is affected?

How does the disability restrict the diet?

	Child/Participant has no disability but requires a special diet

Describe the medical or other special dietary need that restricts diet.

List food/type of food to be omitted.

List food/type of food to be substituted for omitted food(s). Please be specific regarding any needed food texture changes or detailed menu to be followed.

Signature of Recognized State Medical Authority:	**Date:**
Printed Name:	Phone:

This is an equal opportunity provider and employer.

Rev. 9/18/2019

REFERENCES

American Academy of Pediatrics, American Public Health Association, & National Resource Center for Health and Safety in Child Care and Early Education. (2019). *Caring for our children: National health and safety performance standards: Guidelines for out-of-home child care programs* (4th ed.). Elk Grove Village, IL: American Academy of Pediatrics; Washington, DC: American Public Health Association; Aurora, CO: National Resource Center for Health and Safety in Child Care and Early Education. https://nrckids.org/files/CFOC4%20pdf-%20FINAL.pdf

Aronson, S., & Shope, T. (2019). *Managing infectious diseases in child care and schools: A quick reference guide* (5th ed.). Elk Grove Village, IL: American Academy of Pediatrics.

Bruno, H. E., & Copeland, T. (2012). *Managing legal risks in early childhood programs.* New York, NY: Teachers College Press.

Button, L. (2008). When is a child too sick? Devising a "sick child" policy for your center. *Child Care Information Exchange, 183,* 88–91.

Centers for Disease Control and Prevention, National Institutes of Health, HIV Medicine Association of the Infectious Diseases Society of America, Pediatric Infectious Diseases Society, & American Academy of Pediatrics. (2009). *Guidelines for the prevention and treatment of opportunistic infections among HIV-exposed and HIV-infected children.* https://www.cdc.gov/mmwr/preview/mmwrhtml/rr5811a1.htm

Chapin, M. M., Rochette, L. M., Annest, J. L., Haileyesus, T., Conner, K. A., & Smith, G. A. (2013). *Nonfatal choking on food among children 14 years or younger in the United States.* https://pediatrics.aappublications.org/content/132/2/275

Child Care Aware of America. (2021). Emergency preparedness. Arlington, VA: Author. https://www.childcareaware.org/our-issues/crisis-and-disaster-resources/

Child Welfare Information Gateway. (2008). *The role of professional child care professionals in preventing and responding to child abuse and neglect.* Washington, DC: U.S. Department of Health and Human Services, Children's Bureau. https://www.childwelfare.gov/pubPDFs/childcare.pdf

Cohen, A. J. (1998). Bettering the odds of not getting sued. In R. Neugebauer and B. Neugebauer (Eds.), *The art of leadership: Managing early childhood organizations.* Redmond, WA: CCIE.

Council on Injury, Violence and Poison Prevention, American Academy of Pediatrics. (2019). Policy statement—prevention of choking among children. *https://pediatrics.aappublications.org/content/125/3/601*

Farm to School Network. (n.d.). *Our vision.* http://www.farmtoschool.org/about

Food and Nutrition Service. (2017). *Nutrition Standards for CACFP Meals and Snacks.* Washington, DC: U.S. Department of Agriculture. https://www.fns.usda.gov/cacfp/meals-and-snacks

Ho, S. H., Schoenberg, D., Richards, D., & Morath, M. (2009). Using technology to control costs. *Child Care Exchange, 187,* 74–77.

Marotz, L. R. (2015). *Health, safety, and nutrition for the young child* (9th ed.). Stamford, CT: Cengage Learning.

National Association for the Education of Young Children. (2011a). *Code of ethical conduct.* Washington, DC: Author. https://www.naeyc.org/resources/position-statements/ethical-conduct

National Association for the Education of Young Children. (2011b). *Playing with food by Peter John.* http://www.naeyc.org/files/naeyc/file/newsroom/TYC_Nancy_Gerber_Interview.pdf.Ready.gov. (2021). Welcome to Ready Kids! Washington, DC: Federal Emergency Management Agency. https://www.ready.gov/

Simon, F. (2012). Technology tools for the tough tasks: Plug in for great outcomes. *Child Care Exchange, 205,* 84–97.

Swim, T. J., & Freeman, R. (2004). Time to reflect: Using food in early childhood classrooms. *Young Children, 59*(6), 18–22.

UNAIDS. (2016). Closing the diagnostics gap for HIV for young infants. UNAIDS Update. https://www.unaids.org/en/resources/presscentre/featurestories/2016/october/20161025_UNITAID

U.S. Department of Agriculture & U.S. Department of Health and Human Services. (2020, December). *Dietary guidelines for Americans, 2020–2025* (9th ed.). Washington, DC: Author. http://www.dietaryguidelines.gov

U.S. Food and Drug Administration, (n.d.). Allergies and food safety. https://www.fsis.usda.gov/wps/portal/fsis/topics/food-safety-education/get-answers/food-safety-fact-sheets/food-labeling/allergies-and-food-safety/allergies-and-food-safety

Crisis brings challenge and opportunity.

Chapter
12
Leading in Times of Change and Crisis

naeyc

Standards and Recommendations Addressed in This Chapter

ADVANCING EQUITY RECOMMENDATION 1 Provide high-quality early learning services that demonstrate a commitment to equitable outcomes for all children.

PROGRAM STANDARD 2 Curriculum

PROGRAM STANDARD 3 Teaching

PROGRAM STANDARD 6 Staff Competencies, Preparation, and Support

PROGRAM STANDARD 9 Physical Environment

PROFESSIONAL STANDARDS AND COMPETENCIES: STANDARD 1 Child Development and Learning in Context

PROFESSIONAL STANDARDS AND COMPETENCIES: STANDARD 4 Developmentally, Culturally, and Linguistically Appropriate Teaching Practices

LEARNING OBJECTIVES

After reading this chapter, you should be able to:

12-1 Differentiate between the types of stress and their impact on children and adults.

12-2 Describe how leaders guide staff through the change process.

12-3 Identify strategies to support children, families, and staff during times of crisis.

12-4 Describe how nature can be used as a means of reducing stress.

In many ways, the previous chapters provide guidance for the typical days, months, and years in which a director runs a center. This chapter could be considered "the exceptions to those rules." In the past several years, communities have been faced with dynamic and complex challenges, including natural disasters, racial injustice, mass casualty events such as shootings, and an economic crisis that devastated the field and caused many programs to close. Although it is important to encourage directors to roll with the changes as much as possible, having a framework for understanding the complexities of leading in times of change, crisis, and trauma is vital for defining what success is for individual programs.

As a program director or administrator, you will see times of transition in which the challenges are many and the support seems sparse. Consider all the change that have occurred in the field just since 2018:

- New Unifying Framework for the Early Childhood Education Profession (Power to the Profession, 2020)

- Revised Licensing Benchmarks (Child Care Aware of America, 2020)
- Revised Program Accreditation Standards (NAEYC, 2018)
- Revised Position Statement on Advancing Equity in Early Childhood (NAEYC, 2019)
- Revised Position Statement on Developmentally Appropriate Practice (NAEYC, 2020)

These changes in foundational documents for the field of early childhood education will ramp up the rate of change for the foreseeable future.

This chapter will provide valuable definitions and insight into the multifaceted elements of change and crisis management. Part of the necessary balance for directors and administrators falls between leadership and management. Running a program successfully on a typical day involves making programmatic decisions as a leader of curriculum and personnel while also managing tasks such as budget, payments, and implementing health and safety measures. During a time of crisis, these elements still exist, but road maps to navigate these challenges simply cannot predict every possible scenario. These moments require those in positions of responsibility and power to serve as steadfast leaders, bearing the burden of supporting staff, children, families, and themselves along the way.

12-1 • The Mentally Healthy Person: a Refresher for Directors

To understand mental health and its disorders, it is important to have an image of a mentally healthy person. The official, clinical definition of mental health has undergone revisions over the last several years from its previous, minimizing version, which focused solely on the absence of mental illness or disability. The World Health Organization has defined mental health as a state of being wherein a person can acknowledge his or her abilities, adapt and cope with everyday stress, accomplish goals, and contribute to the community. Although this demonstrates progress toward a more inclusive, accessible definition, it minimizes the many aspects of mental health that can have physiological implications and impact our general understanding of key concepts. Mentally healthy people may be able to address challenges in their personal and professional lives, experience positive emotions, and accomplish goals, but they may not understand the impact of prolonged stress or the ability to foresee the limits placed on them by cultural or societal norms. With these factors in mind, Galderisi, Heinz, Kastrup, Beezhold, and Sartorius (2015) reviewed current definitions and research to determine that "mental health is a dynamic state of internal equilibrium which enables individuals to use their abilities in harmony with universal values of society." Within this definition are the universal values of "respect and care for oneself and other living beings; recognition of connectedness between people; respect for the environment; respect for one's own and others' freedom." Inherent in this definition, and relevant to work with young children and families, are self-regulation, resilience, and the umbrella term of *executive function skills*.

Director's Corner

Managing people is already difficult—even in the best of times. In challenging times, when you feel the responsibility to protect your staff, it can feel like staff are being micromanaged or monitored too closely; it can feel like there is a lack of trust. So how do you manage those needs fairly across the board? This extends beyond classroom staff and includes maintenance, cleaning, and kitchen staff as well. It is creating and forming habits that are healthy and protect everyone as equitably as possible. Forming those habits takes time. It involves considering everyone's mental health, including your own; being responsive to the needs of the program but also the *people* of the program. It takes the *knowing* of key mental health concepts but also the *feeling* of working with real, flawed humans.

—*Director, university-affiliated early childhood program*

12-2 • A Refresher for Directors

Research in the last several decades has yielded data supporting the conclusion that high-quality, effective early childhood programs can improve the "life outcomes for children facing adversity, produce important benefits for society, and generate positive returns on investment" (Center on the Developing Child, 2016). The foundations of three critical elements for later

Providing a safe environment for children to be curious and safe supports executive function development.

Bombeck Family Learning Center

success are established in early childhood: self-regulation, resilience, and executive function. Through responsive relationships fostered in early childhood education programs, children living through times of change and crisis can continue to develop these skills both within and outside the program environment. Although it may seem like understanding these key terms is beyond the scope of our work, it is vital that directors, administrators, and early childhood professionals view themselves as brain builders, providing a framework for their own health as a means to support the growth and development of the children in their care.

12-2a • The Key Three: Self-Regulation, Resilience, and Executive Function Skills

In the critical developmental period that occurs in the first 5 years of life, skills within three key areas—self-regulation, resilience, and executive function skills—are being established to provide the foundation for higher-order thinking and later academic as well as life success (see **Figure 12-1**). Disruption in overall development can have serious consequences for children with both long-term and immediate impact. Within these early years, children develop mental models of relationships and themselves, begin to develop strategies for managing stress, and continue to grow in their ability to process information internally, making sense of the world around them.

12-2b • Self-Regulation

Self-regulation is a critical piece of internal mental processes. According to Dr. Becky Bailey, creator of Conscious Discipline, self-regulation "is a set of skills that enables children, as they mature, to direct their own behavior towards a goal, despite the unpredictability of the world and our own feelings" (Bailey, 2020). This skill involves managing sensory input and navigating emotional triggers through cognitive processes; in essence, it is tuning out noise, managing emotions, and trying to think clearly in a given situation (see **Figure 12-2**).

Self-regulation is not a skill we are born with, but one that takes roughly 24 years to develop. Within this umbrella term, we can dig further into three types of regulation:

1. **Behavior self-regulation:** This can involve impulse control, resisting the urge to react aggressively or against one's own best interest.

The Key Three Definitions

SELF-REGULATION

- can refer to one's ability to regulate emotions, control impulses, and maintain cognitive processes in response to emotional triggers and sensory input.

EXECUTIVE FUNCTION

- an umbrella term for a set of skills that support self-regulation; these skills include cognitive or mental flexibility, working memory, inhibitory control.

RESILIENCE

- refers to one's ability to thrive and rise above challenges; this is developed through responsive and supportive relationships in addition to biological components (nature AND nurture) and can continue to be strengthened over time.

FIGURE 12-1

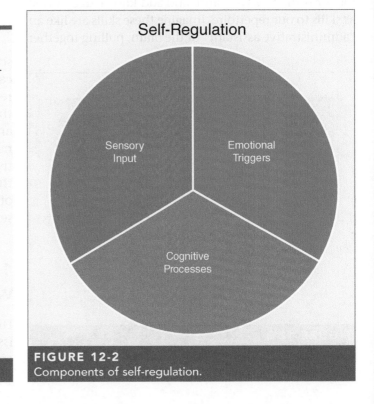

FIGURE 12-2
Components of self-regulation.

2. **Emotional self-regulation:** This refers to the ability to maintain composure when you are upset, returning to a calm state when faced with triggers and cheering yourself up.

3. **Thought regulation:** This skill involves avoiding negative self-talk, being mindful to our own thoughts and triggers, and flipping the script on disturbing or destructive thoughts that can have a negative impact on behavior and emotions.

12-2c • Executive Function

In addition to self-regulation, executive function can build the skills necessary for resilience in times of crisis. Put simply, executive function is essentially like an air traffic controller that works in our brains to manage the functions that allow us to learn, focus, and self-regulate. The skills begin to develop as soon as we are born and go through a critical period in the first 5 years of life. But why exactly are they so important in determining future academic success? (See **Figure 12-3**).

Three main skills are associated with executive function: mental or cognitive flexibility, self-regulation, and working memory. When working together, these skills allow us to look at a problem in a variety of ways, filter out distractions, control our emotional responses, focus on the tasks at hand, and add knowledge as well as skills to our repertoire. Imagine these skills are like an "administrative assistant" of the brain, pulling together

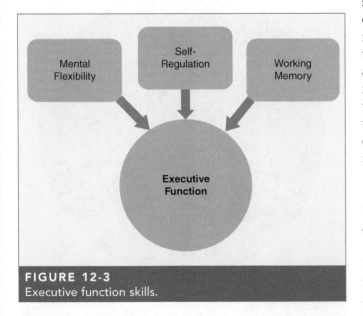

FIGURE 12-3
Executive function skills.

and sorting files, managing the influx of new information, and turning away distractions. In the developed brain, these skills allow adults to filter out distractions, attend to the task at hand, set long-term and short-term goals, and control or minimize impulses.

Executive function skills are a protective factor against toxic stress. Combined with positive and responsive relationships, these skills help build resilience to adverse factors associated with toxic stress. Environmental and biochemical factors associated with prolonged activation of the fight-or-flight response, in the absence of protective factors, have detrimental effects on the developing brain. Early learning experiences, both at home and in the classroom, have a significant long-term impact on an individual's ability to develop resilience, learn, and adapt to stimuli—both positive and negative.

12-2d • Resilience

Resilience is a big concept with significant implications, but can be a bit difficult to envision. The Center on the Developing Child at Harvard University compares resilience to a balancing scale on which positive and negative outcomes are weighed against one another. Resilience can be described as the fulcrum in the middle, determining how easy or difficult it is to counterbalance one side with the other (see **Figure 12-4**).

If we visualize every person as having a unique scale and with the fulcrum in a different place, we can begin to understand why some people are more resilient than others in times of crisis. That being said, the fulcrum is not in a permanently static position and can be moved by reducing the stressors on the negative side and increasing the weight on the positive side (especially through responsive interactions), thus helping children establish a firm foundation of executive function and self-regulatory skills that serve as the fulcrum.

12-2e • Common Issues with Mental Health

Directors need to have knowledge of mental health issues, the skills to support mental health in children and staff, and when they need help to address more

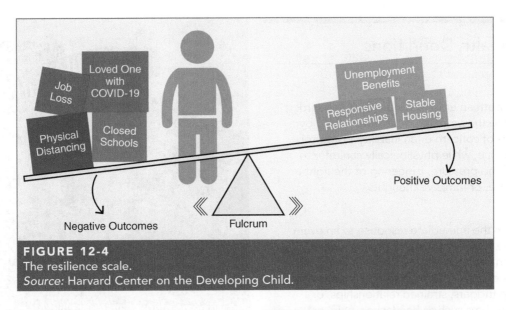

FIGURE 12-4
The resilience scale.
Source: Harvard Center on the Developing Child.

serious mental health issues. Two critical concepts that impact early childhood education programs in our society both involve one's perception of their world, how they respond to stressors, how they react when they cannot control their environment, and what violence they have experienced or witnessed. Anxiety and trauma often go hand in hand, but not necessarily. The trouble with anxiety and trauma is

Crisis As Opportunity for Positive Change

During the COVID-19 global pandemic, the ripple effects of the disease significantly shifted the fulcrums for many people. Controlling the spread of the virus, losing jobs from the economic crisis, social distancing from loved ones, and significant changes in daily routines with school closures and remote work meant that program providers had to get creative in supporting children and families. Although we may not have been able to respond to all of the negative impacts of nationwide shutdowns, programs were able to get creative in connecting with families. These responsive relationships are critical for balancing the scales of resilience; teachers created online read alouds to connect with families, directors greeted families at the door to keep staff and families safe, and the small interactions between families and programs were cherished more than ever. This served as a small reminder that connection, no matter how small it may seem, can have a strong impact on the well-being of children and families.

Director's Corner

As a director, I realize that my staff has more to focus on than time permits. With their plate so full, it is common for some tasks to be overlooked. With the increase in children in stress in our program, I needed to make sure that I was making those teacher skills associated with establishing responsive relationships with children and supporting the development of resilience and executive function skills to be a priority for our program. To this end, our staff was trained in *Conscious Discipline*, so I knew they had the knowledge needed to implement these strategies. To make sure that the staff was prioritizing relationships, resilience and executive function I implemented a two-prong strategy in which examples of good practice were identified and shared during our regular staff meetings. This allowed us to share examples of good practice and also established that supporting relationships, resilience and executive function was a priority. The second prong establishes a system of accountability and involves my daily building walk-throughs. I share a feedback tool [see **Director's Resource 12-1**] with the teaching team ahead of time so they are reminded of the program priorities. I complete the feedback tool and share it with the teaching team for them to discuss. During our next coaching session, we have a conversation about the feedback and establish goals for the classroom. Keep in mind that the conversation also leads to goals for me as a director. I need to understand the classroom context and how to best support my staff.

—*Director, university-affiliated early childhood program*

Mental Health Definitions

ANXIETY

- can refer to both an emotion and a clinical disorder; in reference to the emotion, it is characterized by both feelings of concern or an inability to control a given outcome, while physilogically can refer to increased blood pressure, triggering of the fight or flight response, or intrusive thoughts.

TRAUMA

- refers to both the immediate response to an event as well as the long-term impacts on one's life; it is an emotional response to violence, neglect, or stress; long-term effects can result in unpredictable responses to triggers, strained relationships, or physical symptoms such as headaches, pain, or general weakness.

FIGURE 12-5

Providing comfort to an upset child is key for connection, returning from chaos to calm.

that the symptoms can present in different ways, and identifying the cause of these symptoms is not a simple process (see **Figure 12-5**).

12-2f • Anxiety

Anxiety can be defined as both a natural reaction to stressors or challenging situations, but it can also be diagnosed as a disorder when it is pervasive and interferes with an individual's ability to navigate everyday life. In young children, anxiety can look different from one child to the next. Signs or symptoms may include difficulty sleeping or irregular sleep patterns; complaining about stomach pain or other physical pain with no clear source of illness or injury; resistance of certain situations such as school, leaving the home, or the playground; becoming suddenly clingy around trusted adults; or disruptive or unpredictable behavior and sudden outbursts (Child Mind Institute, n.d.a). All children experience some level of anxiety, but it is important to know what is normal development and what is abnormal. All children can sometimes exhibit separation anxiety, social anxiety, and fears of certain specific things such as spiders or storms. However, when these behaviors become difficult for adults to manage and prevent the child from engaging in typical play or routines, then professional

insight or a clinical diagnosis can provide resources and understanding of how to support children navigate their anxiety. Although separation and social anxiety can occur in normal levels, they can also be debilitating for children, preventing them from thinking of anything else and making learning difficult. Other clinical diagnoses can include selective mutism, generalized anxiety, and obsessive–compulsive disorder (Child Mind Institute, n.d.b). When early childhood professionals understand that inattention, clinginess, restlessness, difficulty focusing, and displaying disruptive or challenging behavior can be the result of anxiety in children, they can provide critical interventions and supports to help children develop coping mechanisms for long-term success.

12-2g • Trauma

Trauma is a concept that is relatively easy to define but difficult to identify, diagnose, and navigate. Trauma can be defined as both the immediate response and long-term impacts of an event perceived as threatening to one's life, physical wellness, or emotional well-being. Further, it can fall under the category of acute (experiencing an overwhelming, stressful event) or complex (chronic, ongoing physical or emotional violence or neglect), as well as firsthand (directly experienced by the child) or secondhand (indirect exposure through retelling or watching) impacts. We will talk more about secondhand, or secondary, trauma as it relates to leaders within the field later in this chapter.

To understand the dangerous impact trauma, acute or complex, can have on a child, consider the role of the adult within a child's life. Erdman, Colker, and Winter (2020) write that "young children need guidance and support to thrive emotionally, socially, cognitively, linguistically, and physically. For many children, trauma disrupts this development, making it challenging to learn until the effects are addressed. It is critical that early childhood educators be able to support children and help them develop resilience and coping strategies" (p. 1). It is also important to consider the impact of trauma on adults, and the role it plays in their ability to support young children both at home and in the early childhood education program. But first, let us dig a little deeper into the basic concepts of trauma.

Trauma can be further defined by three key components. These "Three E's of Trauma," as defined by the Substance Abuse and Mental Health Services Administration (SAMHSA), involve the event, experience of the event, and the effect.

- *Event:* As identified by the *Diagnostic and Statistical Manual of Mental Disorders*, fifth edition, this includes stressor-related disorders and trauma, the actual or threat of violence, physical abuse, psychological harm, or neglect that impacts development.
- *Experience of the event:* The perception and experience of an individual may differ from another, making it possible for an event to be traumatic for someone, but not for someone else. Factors that impact the experience of the event may include personality, the developmental stage of the person, cultural beliefs, and the availability or strength of social support.
- *Effects:* The impact of the event on an individual can be long-lasting, occurring soon after the event or with a delayed onset. These effects can be both short-term and long-term and may not be easily identified as connected to a traumatic event (Substance Abuse and Mental Health Services Administration [SAMHSA], 2014).

Within these three components, potentially traumatic events can be categorized into four broader buckets:

1. **Household and family:** This type of trauma can include physical abuse, emotional abuse, sexual abuse, neglect, family dysfunction, household instability, severe and chronic illness, family discord, financial insecurity, and poverty. Generally, these traumatic events occur within the home or other primary care setting and involve both immediate and extended family members.

2. **Loss:** This refers to the death of someone important or cared for by a child, the reaction to that death, and the resulting grief. This can be complicated by the age of the child, his or her ability to understand and cope with death, and cultural or societal norms surrounding death and dying.

3. **Family separation:** Trauma involving family separation occurs when children are physically distanced from their families as a whole or from individual members of their families through a variety of means, including refugees and migrants separated from their family, incarceration of one or more family members, and military deployment.

4. **Violence and disaster:** Violent events and natural disasters often occur suddenly and without warning and can include both human-made and natural disasters. These kinds of experiences can create both firsthand and secondary traumatic events such as gun violence; natural disasters such as tornadoes, hurricanes, earthquakes, wildfires, and floods; health crises such as viral spread and pandemics; automobile collisions or crashes; witnessing or being victim to violence, injury, or assault; and terrorism (Erdman et al., 2020).

Within each category lie further complications such as posttraumatic stress disorder (PTSD), the influence of cultural and societal factors on how children experience trauma, and how others within the child's environment cope with stress.

12-2h • Impact of Trauma and Fear on Learning and Brain Development

Stress and trauma can lead to such long-term reactions as "unpredictable emotions, flashbacks, strained relationships, and even physical symptoms like headaches or nausea. While these feelings are normal, some people have difficulty moving on with their lives" (American Psychological Association, 2020, para. 1).

Types of Stress

POSITIVE STRESS

- refers to moderate, short-lived stress responses, such as brief increases in heart rate or mild changes in the body's stress hormone levels.

TOLERABLE STRESS

- refers to stress responses that have the potential to negatively affect the architecture of the developing brain but generally occur over limited time periods that allow for the brain to recover and thereby reverse potentially harmful effects.

TOXIC STRESS

- **Toxic:** refers to strong, frequent, or long-term activation of the body's stress management system, and can have an adverse impact on brain architecture.

FIGURE 12-6

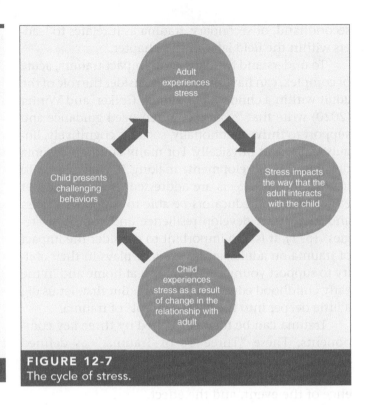

FIGURE 12-7
The cycle of stress.

Not all stress is trauma inducing or toxic. Some stress can positively influence growth (**Figure 12-6**). The spectrum of stress ranges from brief periods of physiological responses to stimuli to pervasive, persistent activation of stress hormones over an extended period of time.

Leaders must understand the difference and ensure that their staffs understand how to support children across a wide range of stressors (National Scientific Council on the Developing Child, 2005/2014). Although some stress, such as positive and tolerable stress, can help build resilience, providing teachable moments for children to learn to overcome challenges and work through complex problems, toxic stress can derail typical development for children and wire the neurological pathways to perceive threats where there are none, causing children to live in fear and anxiety. As previously discussed, toxic stress can yield a chemical response in the body that alters typical physical development, as well as these psychological developmental concerns.

12-2i • Stress Begets Stress

The role of adults in the lives of children who are in trauma cannot be overstated. Manyema, Norris, and Richter (2018) found that adults who are in stress-induced trauma are more likely to transmit that stress to the children and youth with whom they work (**Figure 12-7**). The stress of 2020 on teachers has been unrelenting as they deal with expectations to change their teaching format and interact with students while dealing with the fear of becoming sick or transmitting the COVID-19 virus to their loved ones. Addressing the impact of toxic stress on children requires that we address the toxic stress in teachers and staff. Cycles of stress can have significant, negative effects on children and adults, so intervention using self-care practices are critical for averting permanent damage to the relationships between the two.

12-2j • The Cycle of Stress

As adults become caught up in the daily grind of work and life, it can be easy to take for granted the impact our stress has on our relationships with both adults and children within the early education program. **Figure 12-7** provides a visual representation of the cycle of stress and how stress can pass from caregivers to children and back again. In Conscious Discipline, the idea of coregulation is most

Having a caring, responsive relationship with children involves breaking the cycle of stress through a variety of strategies such as shared breathing.

Bombeck Family Learning Center

clearly represented here, where the "I" impacts the "we": My emotional state dictates, is influenced by, and results from your emotional state (Bailey, 2020). This is true of adults working with one another as well as adults working with children both in the home (parents) and in early childhood education programs (teachers and administrators). Everyone has experienced stress at some point in their lives. Although some people feel they can separate work and home stress, the work–life balance is often more difficult to maintain than one expects. Even though adults may put on a "game face" to try to maintain composure in the classroom, children can still sense the stress in their caregivers. This stress can present as a shorter temper, less patience for pushing boundaries, and a colder demeanor toward otherwise normal interactions. This inability to mitigate stress with self-care or to acknowledge the impact this stress can have on daily practice with children starts a vicious cycle.

Sometimes as adults we may not even realize that stress is impacting our work within the classroom and affecting our relationships with others. Maybe you are used to having more patience than

you do now as you're dealing with a lot of stress in your life, reflecting on the way you teach. It might not be evident that you were teaching differently. Still, your co-teacher may notice it, or your administrators may see how your interactions have changed or that your body language is different. Asking yourself why you are acting in such a manner is essential for figuring out how to reduce stress and practice self-care.

Thinking again about how the "I" can impact the "we" in the classroom, it is important to understand the longer-term effects of stress on responsive relationships between children and early childhood educators. Your stressful morning at home can transfer into the children's behavior or cause a disconnect between children and adults. Think about a child entering a classroom without a greeting from the adults, no reassurance that the day will be okay, and no one to help transition away from their family. That feeling of invisibility for a child can lead to connection-seeking behavior. A child who is seeking safety and connection from adults will use any means necessary to be seen. And the cycle starts over again: The adult is stressed, the relationship with the child is negatively affected, and the child displays challenging behavior. Over time these negative interactions can lead to a disconnect between the child and the teacher. It is imperative that educators find strategies for breaking the cycle and for administrators to find ways to support teachers in meaningful self-care.

12-2k • Mitigating Stress with Self-Care Practices

Taking into consideration the nature of co-regulation, and the impact of stress on responsive relationships, the importance of breaking the cycle of stress turns from a possibility to a priority. Eliminating stress entirely is an impossibility, but providing opportunities and support to adults who need self-care—families and staff—is a necessary responsibility in caring for young children (see **Figure 12-8**). There are times when we become stressed out as adults; this stress can have many causes both within and outside of the classroom or program. Navigating differing personalities, working closely with people we may disagree with, having crucial conversations with families, or

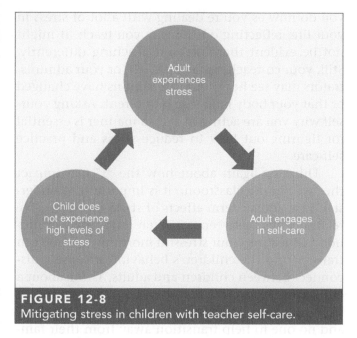

FIGURE 12-8
Mitigating stress in children with teacher self-care.

supporting everyone with the program in navigating crises takes its toll. Engaging in self-care, mindful practice, acknowledging when you need help, and stepping back to remain calm are needed to break the cycle of stress.

Later in this chapter, we will provide specific strategies and other considerations for leaders regarding self-care, as well as the dangers if the cycle of stress is not broken. In general, however, it is important to understand when your early childhood educators need to take a break even when they may not ask for help or support; in addition, it is important for leaders to know when they should ask for help or engage in self-care themselves.

By following the cycle of intention, assessment, and action, leaders can create an environment in which adults can thrive in challenging times. When leaders can think outside of the box with creativity and divergent thinking and are willing to collaborate with all staff, it will provide a strong foundation for our relationships with our school families. The idea that "schools need to become places where effective education is guaranteed to every child" is critical (Singleton, 2014, p. 50). Within that statement should also be the idea that programs are places where responsive relationships between adults and children and between adults alone provide the framework from which effective education can bloom.

12-2l • Early Childhood Administrators Play and Important Roles

Administrators in early childhood programs play an important role in the social and emotional health of the center. It is important for them to be well grounded in the literature that informs good practice in social and emotional learning, trauma, and resilience so that they can affirm and support their staffs and foster growth in practice that needs to change. The first step to support staff is to know what they need to know. This means being well informed about stress and trauma and proven strategies such as Conscious Discipline and the Pyramid Model so that administrators can support their staff. It is important to avoid allowing a lack of understanding to send mixed messages and create confusion and anxiety in staff members.

12-2m • A System's View of Emotional Health for All

Sometimes, it can be difficult to identify why a child is displaying challenging behaviors. Gartrell (2014) describes how it is more helpful to consider these behaviors to be "mistaken" instead of "challenging." This idea frames the child as working from a "calling for help" framework instead of one aimed at triggering responses from adults (Bailey, 2015). In situations where we have used our available toolkit of responsive

Even with safety measures and personal protective equipment, an early childhood program can provide responsive practices with children and families.

relationships within our supportive, high-quality environment, we must look for more intensive interventions. Ian, a teacher at an early childhood center located in the Midwest, described a situation where the program practices seemed not to be enough.

> I can think of a few instances where our standards of practice within the program didn't seem to be enough for the child. We had safe spaces for children to seek out in times of stress, with comforting items available; we utilized breathing strategies to help the child return to calm; and we had established protocols to use with all the children in times of upset. But sometimes, that just isn't going to cut it; it won't mitigate the effects of trauma or help the child navigate anxieties they cannot fully understand. We knew we needed something

more, a different perspective that was outside the realm of what we could provide exclusively in the classroom.

The Center for Social and Emotional Foundations for Early Learning and the Technical Assistance Center on Social and Emotional Interventions used federal funding to focus on supporting the development of social-emotional skills utilizing evidence-based practices. From these initiatives came the Pyramid Model Consortium, which uses a pyramid model to work toward that end, focusing on three tiers of intervention: universal promotion, secondary prevention, and tertiary intervention (see **Figure 12-9**). All of this builds on a foundation of an effective workforce established by supported staff and evidence-based policies and practices (National Center for Pyramid Model Innovations).

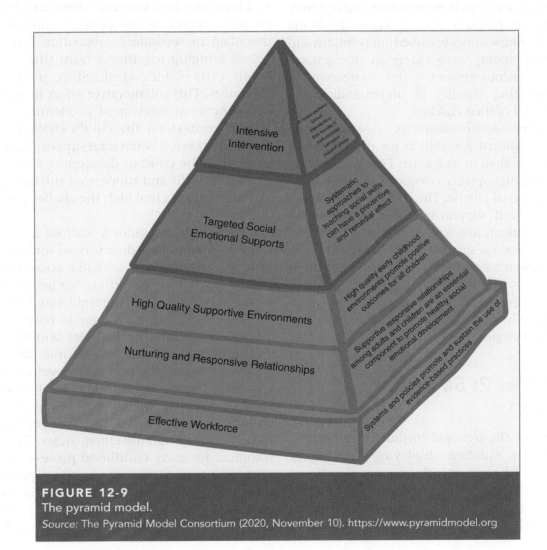

FIGURE 12-9
The pyramid model.
Source: The Pyramid Model Consortium (2020, November 10). https://www.pyramidmodel.org

12-2n • Tier 1: Universal Promotion

Within the first tier of the pyramid is universal promotion, which includes practices that are used for all children within an early childhood education program. This includes a clear description of curricular, family engagement, and culturally responsive programs. This universal promotion of social emotional skill development emphasizes the importance of high-quality learning environments and establishing nurturing, responsive relationships. These relationships include not only those between educators and children but also the relationships early childhood educators have with families and colleagues.

- *Nurturing and responsive relationships:* This includes relationships between adults and children, collaborative practices among early childhood teams, utilizing routines to embed interventions and skill development, serve-and-return interactions, positive encouragement and engagement, and supporting families in understanding the development of their children.
- *High-quality environments:* As designated by both the National Association for the Education of Young Children as well as the Division for Early Childhood, high-quality environments must meet certain universal criteria. This includes predictable, consistent, and supportive expectations within the environment; interactions that promote social interactions and a safe space for taking risks; the use of research-based curricula and assessment programs; ongoing and reflective program evaluation; the use of developmentally appropriate and culturally responsive practices; and positive guidance strategies.

12-2o • Tier 2: Secondary Prevention

The next tier of the pyramid includes target strategies to support children displaying challenging behaviors and who are at risk of more significant social-emotional delays. At the level of prevention, interventions are provided to focus on instruction for specific skill development. Although all young children need support in understanding, expressing, and naming emotions for solving interpersonal problems, this level of intervention involves supporting children who need more opportunities and feedback. These skills include identifying, naming, and expressing emotions; self-regulation and self-control; initiating and sustaining interactions with peers; responding to cooperative play situations in a positive manner; and coping with anger, frustration, and disappointment.

12-2p • Tier 3: Tertiary Intervention

As provided in the example, tertiary intervention is reserved for children who require individualized and intensive intervention. These are children who do not respond to the targeted support strategies described in secondary prevention. This level involves bringing together a team that includes the family, early childhood educators, and intervention specialists. This collaborative effort involves the use of a functional assessment to identify triggers and specific context for the child's challenging behaviors; from there, a behavioral support plan is created to support the child in developing necessary social emotional skills and supporting the family through all environments in which the challenging behavior occurs.

This model provides a scaffold for early childhood educators and directors to understand what universal practices can look like across the program as well as what interventions can be provided within the classroom. The pyramid can help reinforce the idea that it takes a village to raise and support a child—a village that includes families, children, and professionals across multiple disciplines to support the social-emotional development of *all* children. The National Center for Pyramid Model Innovations has additional resources for early childhood professionals and families for times of national disasters and emergencies. This includes resources for early childhood professionals, adults using self-care to manage stress, supporting children exhibiting challenging behavior because of increased stress, and strategies for supporting children in the home when schools are closed. More

Manage the stress of leadership: rely on other leaders; find a way to communicate what you need. Have a key word or phrase to let each other know when you need a break so the other can pick up the pieces. It's hard to know that you are taking care of so many people. It's a lot, because you want to give more. And you want everyone to have what they need. Those are the times you feel bad, or less than, because you want everyone to have what they need. You have to consider what you need to. It's hard, because you're constantly being bombarded by the needs of others. And you feel so much empathy for them. You have to stay task-oriented, one day at a time. It's such a dynamic time, you want to help everyone. The needs of the center are pounding at the door, too. You have to continue to juggle those pieces, and you don't feel like you have a choice. Some days I can handle everything, and other days you feel like you can't handle the smallest things. Relying on your team, on other leaders, is critical.

—Assistant director, university-affiliated early childhood program

Working Smart with Technology

The COVID-19 pandemic brought about an increase in the need to use technology to communicate with staff and families. Although face-to-face meetings were the most effective way to communicate, they were no longer safe. Mixed messaging was a challenge before COVID-19, and now directors had another hurdle to clear. Directors were forced to utilize email and videoconferencing as their main modes of communication. Mixed messaging occurs when messages are left unread or deleted without reading. How do you ensure the information is being read? Requesting feedback or a read receipt may be one way to confirm the information is being read. Another way is to use an early childhood communication platform. A communication platform offers a way to streamline communication by sending announcements and messages efficiently. Examples of platforms are Moment Path, Brightwheel, Tadpoles, and Procare. This dramatically reduces mixed messaging with families and staff as you are able to provide updates in real time. For example, upon reopening early childhood programs after the initial pandemic health-order closures, directors were faced with the challenge of teachers who needed emotional support. One way our leadership team could plan to keep spirits up was to surprise our teachers with small tokens of appreciation and emails full of self-care resources. Reminding them how important it is to have gratitude even during challenging times. Our program followed COVID ratios which put teachers with a lower number of children. It was one positive that COVID gave us and our hope was the teachers would take advantage of this opportunity to provide increased one on one responsive care for each child. We held meetings with individuals and teams to find out how to support them when they were having a difficult time balancing all of the demands, changes and stressors. We made sure they knew where to turn if they needed more support than we were able to provide.

—Assistant director, university-affiliated early childhood program

information about this resource can be found at the end of this chapter.

12-2q • Social and Emotional Learning Is for Staff, Too

Social and emotional learning (SEL) enhances students' capacity to integrate skills, attitudes, and behaviors to deal effectively and ethically with daily tasks and challenges. It is also critical for educators who need to demonstrate these skills and take care of themselves. One framework that is designed for older students can also be used with adults. The Collaborative for Academic, Social, and Emotional Learning (CASEL) developed a framework that promotes intrapersonal, interpersonal, and cognitive competence. "There are five core competencies that can be taught in many ways across many settings. Many educators and researchers are also exploring how best to assess these competencies" (Collaborative for Academic, Social, and Emotional Learning, [CASEL] 2017, para 1).

CASEL's SEL strategies align with trauma-informed practices. Social and emotional learning competencies are organized in five categories: self-awareness, self-management, social awareness, relationship skills, and responsible decision-making. The purpose is to give students skills and coping strategies to be successful. The SEL framework is used for teachers as well.

12-2r • Enhancing Systems with Policy and Procedural Protocols

Perhaps one of the biggest challenges for leaders during times of transition, disaster, or crises involves policy and protocols. Anticipating the needs of a program without knowing the details or circumstances of a potential crisis can feel like looking into a crystal ball and trying to plan for the unknown. In general, a key for success is having three tiers of policies and procedures for programs to operate within. In addition, it is helpful to consider examples for each of these types of responses in considering planning for future crises. The COVID-19 pandemic is a useful time to help plan for future circumstances within existing and new programs. Some considerations involve guidance from health departments and the CDC, such as how long and under which conditions a family should quarantine; as well as protocols that align with program expectations,

such as whether families should be required to pay tuition if they are required to self-quarantine and not participate in the program. (See **Table 12-1**.)

Working within this tiered system for policy development can provide a framework for protocols that can be adapted as needed for shifting situations. Although the program has a policy handbook for typical daily practice, addendums are often needed during times of change and crisis.

12-2s • Establishing and Adapting Protocols

The COVID-19 pandemic put a spotlight on how challenging it can be for leaders to navigate policy changes and plan protocols to support families. It is difficult to plan programmed responses when health departments or government guidelines are constantly evolving and changing. **Table 12-2** provides some

Table 12-1 Types of policy responses

Type of Response	Definition	COVID Example
Programmed	These types of responses are considered "the rule" without exception; within programmed responses, there are many clear, specific details for what to do in certain situations. Zero-tolerance policies are considered to be programmed responses, with a specific plan of action following given guidelines from licensing organizations, existing program policies, and field standards of practice.	If you have a positive test, you must follow CDC guidelines, quarantine for 10–14 days from onset of symptoms, and only return to school when medically cleared; you have to make some sort of policy about whether the family will still be required to pay tuition while they are prohibited from coming.
Semiprogrammed	Response based on your core principles and underlying values/mission of your organization or program. There is some flexibility to adapt to given circumstances or contexts. Decisions that are semiprogrammed involve a judgment call of a director, taking into account what the program values and how they aim to support families.	If families have an exposure and have to quarantine per health department guidelines, the child cannot attend the program. This provides some gray area that requires a judgment call—if it happens frequently, do families still need to pay? You have to decide under what circumstances a family (1) cannot bring their child to the program and (2) does not have to pay for tuition if they are unable to attend because of health codes.
Unprogrammed	These are the unforeseeable exceptions to the rule; there are some guidelines related to the other two tiers of policy, but this is mostly based on teacher or administrative intuition, assessment of the situation, sociocultural aspects and perspectives, and individual judgment.	This involves making decisions such as what to do if the child was exposed to COVID within the program setting, how many classrooms will be closed because of exposure, how long the classroom will be closed, which children will be asked to quarantine, etc.

Table 12-2 Navigating policy changes

Strategy	Key Players	Purpose	Outcomes
Drafting health and safety procedures	Centers for Disease Control and Prevention (CDC); state or local health departments; licensing agencies; departments of juvenile and family services; key stakeholders or board members; medical professionals	Create programmed and semiprogrammed responses to make decisions which keep families, staff, and children safe and healthy	Creating policies for families based on changing or updating information; communicating with families via handbook addendums; separate policies sent via email
Establishing task forces	Task force members depend on the goal of the committee; types of task forces may include budget, health, safety, and risk management	Creating task forces can provide guidance for making decisions, including budgets, health codes, keeping the program open, mitigating or minimizing risks, and creating long-term and short-term plans	Creating policies that have direct input from people who have expertise in the specific area of the program
Communicating programming changes	Owners, directors, educators	To ensure families and staff are aware of any program changes	Clear communication with consistent messaging through multiple formats, including texts, newsletters, handbook addendums, and email
Supporting staff	Families, directors, educators, licensing or departments of health and human services	To consider how to support staff within the program logistically and personally. From staffing ratios to caps on how many children can be in a space to mental health considerations, it's important to consult staff about their needs.	The staff will feel supported and heard; connecting to staff in challenging times and prioritizing self-care yields deeper, more responsive relationships between adults within the program.
Connecting families to resources and support	Local organizations or agencies, counselors, staff from resource and referral agencies, directors, educators	To provide assistance when families need it, including therapy, financial support, housing, food, and resources to meet basic needs	Children and families have the resources they need for daily life, as well as the support needed for coping with trauma, homelessness, hunger, and poverty.
Connecting and supporting families	Directors, educators, families	To survey the needs of families and findings ways to have accountability or commitment to the program	Continuing to support families in their times of need and maintaining open lines of communication in a variety of formats

guidelines for organization leaders to work with in times of crises and practical strategies for navigating uncharted waters.

12-2t • Common Challenges for Staff That Administrators Can Support

In the midst of challenging times, crises, and disasters, concerns arise for the well-being of early childhood educators, support staff, and leaders. We previously described the mentally healthy person, as well as the key three components of self-regulation, executive function, and resilience. Despite

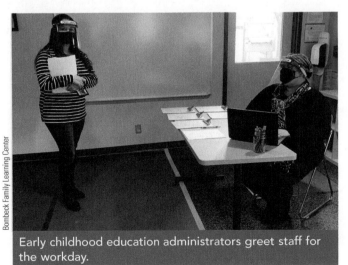

Bombeck Family Learning Center

Early childhood education administrators greet staff for the workday.

Crisis: As Opportunity for Positive Change

We had an incident at the center, where our director called a lockdown of the center. There has been a reported active shooter in the area—we had been practicing drills for lockdowns for as long as I could remember, but this was the first time it wasn't a drill. During our drills, we had practiced with the children moving into a safe space; in our case, this was the bathroom, which did not have windows and had solid brick walls. Our staff had practiced gathering a first aid kit, a list of children's names and family contact information, and accounted for the children and staff as we entered the space, closing and locking the door behind us.

We had practiced what to do physically to keep everyone safe, but I hadn't thought about what to say to children in this type of situation. We program our physical response to keep children safe, but we don't often think about what we will say to children, or what we will do to keep children occupied. The children do not understand the gravity of the situation, or the severity of the threat, and we were in lockdown for 45 minutes. We had prepared for the quick movement and logistics of getting everyone into a safe space but never really thought about what would happen once we were in the bathroom or how long we might actually be in the space in an actual emergency. This was eye opening—I didn't anticipate how to entertain 15 three- to five-year-old children, or the disruption to the daily routine. This happened during nap time, so we had to wake children up from nap, meaning some children did not have on shoes and were upset from being awakened.

After the lockdown ended, we were glad that everyone was safe and there was thankfully no real threat to us or the children. But it got us thinking about the bigger picture. How can we prepare for keeping children calm and quiet in the event that the threat is real without causing a panic? What sort of activities can we have for the children to do to keep them calm for an extended period of time? What do we need, as adults, to protect the children in the case of a violent attack?

We created a potential list of things to keep in our safe space to protect children in the event of an emergency that would likely already be in the classroom—a hammer, hairspray, bug spray—things that could provide some sort of protection. But it begged the question—what could our program do as a whole to prepare staff for an assault? This differed from preparing for lockdown for weather conditions, which is sort of how we treated it before this incident. What physical or psychological training did we need to program our responses in the event of a real, violent threat?

For me, the main thing I was worried about was that I was telling the children the right thing. I was aware that what I was saying would be the dialog that sticks with them after the moment has passed. Honestly, I couldn't imagine that it was a real threat with a shooter coming into the classroom. I trusted my instincts, but at the time I got a text from my director that we needed to take cover. I felt that I should have prepared for a script or some sort of consistent language to reassure the children, and something that, if it stuck with them for a long time, would be reassuring instead of retraumatizing.

—*early childhood educator, urban early childhood program*

these developed skills in adults, concerns still exist about the lasting effects of stress on those working within the program. Understanding the signs and symptoms of these challenges can help directors and administrators plan for support and engage in self-care as well.

12-2u • Compassion Fatigue

Compassion fatigue is a significant concern for those working with children and families, both in the classroom and in the role as director or administrator. This refers to an inability to regain energy or drive as the result of the physical and emotional labor in caring for others. Signs or symptoms of compassion fatigue can involve feelings or behaviors similar to those of depression and may include feeling as though everyone *needs* something from you *all the time*, the sense that you could be doing more and feelings of guilt that you cannot, mental fatigue and physical exhaustion, decreased attention span or difficulty concentrating on tasks, not taking the same pleasure from hobbies or caring for others, and changes in sleep patterns or insomnia (Lemoine et al., 2020). Although each person experiences the effects of compassion fatigue differently, the symptoms can be similar to those with PTSD. This can include anxiety, fear, apathy, an increase in dangerous or compulsive behaviors, and self-medicating with drugs or alcohol.

12-2v • Secondary Traumatic Stress

Similar to compassion fatigue is the phenomenon known as *secondhand trauma*. "Secondary traumatic stress (STS) is the term most commonly found in the literature to describe the phenomenon brought on by helping someone exposed to trauma" (Erdman et al., 2020). This is sometimes referred to as *vicarious traumatization*, and it is the result of indirect exposure to traumatic events such as violence, difficult or disturbing stories or images, or stories of others' suffering (Lemoine et al., 2020). Some of the literature separates STS from *vicarious trauma*, which can lead to a deep shift in one's personal values or beliefs and changes in someone's view of the world because of trauma experienced through others. In addition, part of the danger of STS is that it can be a trigger, causing one to relieve previously experienced trauma and signs or symptoms that one might not understand or easily identify. Signs and symptoms of STS can cover a wide range, but they potentially lead to burnout. These symptoms cover physical, behavioral, and emotional and psychological realms, and they include changes to perception or difficulty with memory, an altered sense of self-worth or efficacy, feeling drained of emotional or physical energy, and a change in feeling of trust, safety, or security (NCTSN, 2011).

12-2w • Burnout

Left unresolved or untreated, the previously described issues can lead to burnout. This is perhaps one of the most common reasons why early childhood educators and professionals leave the field and do not return. Burnout may be one of the most common phenomena associated with fields of care and education, and it has real psychological, relational,

physiological, and cognitive impacts (Erdman et al., 2020). Burnout is directly related to the pervasive, unrelenting stress caused by the conditions of one's work and the environment in which someone lives every day. Further, "Burnout often includes feelings of diminished personal accomplishment, a sense of lowered competence, and a lack of successful achievement in work with families and colleagues. Both compassion fatigue and vicarious traumatization can contribute to burnout. However, burnout can occur from other factors such as intensity and concentration of workload with little support" (Lemoine et al., 2020). The role of the director in this situation is to provide a supportive environment in which teachers can feel supported despite the workload. In times of challenge and crisis, directors cannot control the strain of the workload, the reach of the trauma, or how others perceive or cope with stress; however, they *can* provide a supportive environment, thoughtful strategies, and safe spaces through responsive relationships as well as positive interactions to ease the burden.

12-2x • Addressing the Relationship between Race and Trauma

Note here that underlying each category is the issue of racism and systemic inequalities that make trauma much worse for Black and minority families, especially those living in poverty. Arguably, race-based trauma and posttraumatic stress can fall into their own categories (Carter, Kirkinis, & Johnson, 2020). The emotional impact race-based violence and systemic racism has on its victims is comparable to PTSD but unique in the way that the symptoms manifest within the body and mind. It is imperative to consider these concerns when working with and developing policies for minority children and families of color.

To fully address trauma and operate as trauma-responsive programs, schools and early childhood education programs need to address racism (Simmons, 2020). The increased focus on race-based violence, including the media coverage of the deaths of Black men in particular, can cause both primary and secondary trauma. When we avoid talking about violence and racism with young children, we become silent figures when our children and families need reassuring voices to talk openly and frankly about antiracism, addressing the inherent toxic stress within racism, and adverse effects, especially on people of color.

Issues of systemic racism and race-based violence can be found in each of these categories of trauma; however, it is important to separate this issue out to highlight the severity of these experiences for Black and minority families. As educators, we must be aware of our actions and understand the dangers of seemingly harmless claims of being color-blind and potential microaggressions (Sehgal, Jeffries, & Rappaport, 2017). Our goal within a trauma-responsive program is twofold: to help children heal from the effects of trauma and to avoid retraumatization through our actions. The least directors can do is to seek out professional development opportunities staff that educate staff about racial issues, multicultural approaches to curriculum, thoughtful development of family engagement programs, and having crucial conversations with both children and their families.

As part of our role in addressing racism and moving toward antiracist communities, our actions must move beyond learning and thinking toward living and doing. Gorski (2020) suggests that we must make three commitments toward this end:

1. addressing policies and practices within our programs to ensure a culture that supports all children and families, limiting the traumatization of children within schools;
2. understanding the role of systemic oppression and weaving trauma-responsive practices together with culturally responsive ones; and
3. consider the role of punitive practices within all education programs and how they disproportionately affect boys and children of color.

These commitments present a springboard for developing culturally responsive and antiracist policies to support all children and families.

Adapting to times of change and crisis means embracing the small moments.

and staff can make for an uphill battle for directors in both policy and practice. But there is hope: For each challenge, there are chances for positive change, and for each dark day there is a new opportunity to work toward brighter futures. There are strategies and skills leaders can grow and foster within themselves and their educators to become resilient guideposts for slow and steady progress.

Armed with an understanding of the nuances of mental health, trauma, toxic stress, and the science behind all three, there are implications for the daily management and practices of early childhood educators and administrators. These implications start with taking a trauma-informed approach and continue with making policies that are adaptive, flexible, but clear. Being an early childhood program administrator involves the careful balance between manager and leader, creating policies and also educating about and enforcing them. Leading a program also requires care for educators and auxiliary staff in addition to the children and families—all which factor into the creation of policies and practices that can provide guidance through challenging times.

12-2y • Strategies and Skills for Leaders

Understanding the complex and concerning dangers that threaten the mental health of children, families,

12-2z • Trauma-Informed Practice at the Program Level

Understanding the nature and complexity of trauma is half the battle for early childhood education program administrators and directors. Establishing an environment that is responsive to trauma is referred to as trauma-informed practice. SAMHSA defines the following four R's within a trauma-informed approach, outlining critical assumptions for effective support within an organization or program.

1. **Realization:** Those involved with the program understand the nature of trauma, how wide it reaches, and how it impacts groups, families, communities, and individuals.

2. **Recognition:** People within the program are able to identify the signs, symptoms, and reactions to a traumatic experience.

3. **Responsiveness:** Program staff reach out to families, children, and each other, using the principles of trauma-informed practice and all available knowledge and resources.

4. **Resist retraumatization:** Organization staff actively works to establish programs, practices, and policies that support the recovery and well-being of both adults and children and seek to avoid accidentally creating additional stress (SAMHSA, 2014).

Embedded within trauma-informed and responsive care are two promises: to respond to behaviors and needs in an emotionally neutral manner and to consider the nature of co-regulation (Keels, 2020). Working with and caring for young children and families involves a high level of empathy and care; understanding our own triggers and helping children develop strategies for coping with their own are critical for ensuring children's growth and success.

12-2aa • Resilient Teachers

Building a resilient staff is a necessary step toward supporting children and families in ordinary times, let alone extraordinary circumstances. Lamoine and colleagues (2020) state that as early childhood education professionals, "How we are is as important as what we do." In their webinar and subsequent resource created for the Zero to Three organization, the authors explore the importance of self-preservation in a time of crisis when our vocation of helping others becomes hazardous to our own health and well-being. During the COVID-19 pandemic, the early childhood field was considered *essential* for the first time, with those working in the field falling under the classification of *essential workers*. This meant that early childhood education professionals showed up for families, continued to provide services, and navigated the constantly changing tides of policy and health orders to keep children and families safe—often at the risk of getting the novel coronavirus themselves. Those working within the field of early childhood education know that this work with young children involves a level of empathy and dedication that can be difficult on any given day; adding in the emotional weight, stress, and uncertainty of a global pandemic can take its toll.

Establishing and supporting a strong network of early childhood educators involves being an intuitive and perceptive leader. The National Child Traumatic Stress Network (2011) described the essential elements in establishing a resilient workforce within trauma-informed systems. These elements serve as preventative measures as well as intervention strategies for avoiding secondary traumatic stress for those who work with children and families in trauma. It is recommended that in times of change and crisis, a task force is established to focus on risk-management

Bombeck Family Learning Center

Adapting to new policies and procedures.

strategies for the conditions of staff working directly with children in traumatic situations. The recommendations for this system include:

- acknowledging and addressing the impact of secondary traumatic stress on those in direct contact with children and families;
- understanding the risk inherent in working with traumatized children and families;
- recognizing that the fundamental shape and culture of organizations can be permanently altered by trauma;
- accepting that an organization that has survived community trauma, or has individuals within that have or are experiencing trauma, is less effective in supporting those experiencing trauma; and
- developing an ability to take knowledge of trauma-based reform and responsiveness and turn it into meaningful policy development, action, and practices.

These concepts ought to be considered in developing policies and procedures that support staff directly, understanding the challenges of working with children and families while attempting to mitigate the effects on adults working with the program.

12-2ab • Reframing: Looking for Opportunities in Crisis

During times of crisis and change, it can be difficult to find silver linings. Especially when there are so many uncertainties, it can be a struggle to look for positive outcomes—it's hard to see the forest through the trees. As directors, engaging in reflective practice can help find opportunities within these moments, realizing our strength and will during times when we feel we cannot keep going, and continuing to grow through these challenges. Though hindsight may be 2020, it is important to focus on small victories, minor changes that help us in the long run, and adapting to make things better.

A key example of this occurred during the COVID-19 pandemic, with restrictions on families allowed to enter facilities, strain on staff, reduced ratios, and the constantly changing policies set out by federal, state, and local governments. Administrators were thrust into changing roles and responsibilities. To assist the program in running smoothly, direc-

tors and administrators took on the role of greeting families, escorting children into the building, and overseeing movement of children into, throughout, and out of the building. This meant that administrators were in the classroom more frequently, engaging more directly with families on a daily basis as well as communicating directly with teachers throughout the day. Although this shifted communication between teachers and families to a virtual or digital format, it meant that directors had a better idea of the needs of teachers and supported the role release from manager of operations to pedagogical, instructional, emotional, and logistical support.

In this process, the perspectives of both educators and directors shifted in a sort of role release. With directors out of the office more and helping with the logistics of minimizing movement of adults through the building and keeping children safe from unnecessary potential exposure to others, they could see the needs within the classroom more clearly. Similarly, with the understanding that administrators were out of their office more frequently, educators had to be more discerning about when they needed administrative help and what they could do on their own. This increased educator's confidence and autonomy, increasing the efficacy of making decisions for themselves that they otherwise would have shifted to someone else of higher authority.

One assistant director from a child development program in the Midwest reflected on this process with a positive outlook:

> Prior to these changes in procedures for COVID, teachers would call us into the classroom for a variety of reasons that probably did not require our input or help; through the early phases of this role release, our administrators had better understanding and insight into what was happening in the classroom. We could see what the teachers did and did not know how to do, which was not always positive. But it helped us to meet them where they are at, what we needed to delegate to others, and what decisions we needed to make directly. For our teachers, they were able to decide where they needed to ask for help and where they could meet with each other for support instead.

This mutual understanding of one another's roles and responsibilities, as well as the give and take of role release between administrators and educators, paves the way for strengthening teams throughout the program and establishing a climate of trust.

12-2ac • Team Building and Climate

As demonstrated by the Pyramid Model, a strong, reliable workforce is the foundation of all early childhood education program. This means that at the heart of what we do within programs is just that—*heart*. This means having responsive relationships not only with children and families but also with other adults working in the building.

Establishing a climate that supports differing viewpoints, personalities, and cultural backgrounds involves a level of trust and understanding beyond icebreakers and the occasional professional development day. This means working thoughtfully through difficult and crucial conversations, as well as checking in on a personal and professional level. An early childhood director balances the role of leader and manager but must also have enough trust with colleagues to be vulnerable enough to know when to ask for and provide support. Disagreements, disappointments, and frustrations will come up; it is imperative that a director does not avoid these difficult conversations and creates an environment of trust where others can share their concerns, feelings, and thoughts without judgment or penalty. This process takes time—building trust and being vulnerable happen authentically over time through thoughtful, intentional, and reflective communication.

12-2ad • Mindful Practice

One strategy for mitigating stress within education programs is the idea of *mindfulness*. This practice of mindfulness has been gaining popularity, although research that supports claims of effectiveness is just starting to emerge. This practice of grounding oneself in the present moment and using deep-breathing techniques to return to a calm composure has shown positive impacts for teachers and children. The key, explains Gerwertz (2020), is to help teachers remain in control of their thoughts, preventing the negative impacts that short tempers and stress can have on

Director's Corner

After the Memorial Day tornadoes, I was extremely concerned about who the tornadoes impacted. First, I needed to deal with the immediate needs of the program. I was informed there was a boil advisory for our program location. I went to pick up bottled water for the staff and children the morning after and knew quick communication was essential. I sent an email letting everyone know about the boil advisory and how there were ways they could help and gave resources for those who needed help. The biggest concern for most was providing a place for people to stay, electricity, food and water. I worked with our families to put together a disaster relief program. We collected essential items and delivered them to vans on campus which drove the donated items directly to the most impacted areas. We also organized a collection for 3 staff members who were dealing with not having electricity or water. Our goal was to decrease the worry the teachers may have had about meals. During the upcoming days, it would be important to make sure teachers felt support as they work with children who may have experienced trauma. Tornado drills may trigger fear. It would be crucial for the teachers to provide a comfortable environment for children to express those fears and have discussions surrounding the tornadoes and hopefully ease any stress they are experiencing. What we didn't realize at the time was how these efforts would bring the staff together which had a positive impact on the climate and in turn the mental health of staff.

—Director, urban-located public early childhood program

relationships with children. In a growing research program called Cultivating Awareness and Resilience in Education (CARE), the aim of targeted training for educators is to help adults identify the physical and emotional signs of stress, including pain in the neck, shoulders, and head; increased heart rate; and feeling flushed. From there, participants learn how and when to use deep-breathing exercises, counting steps, and tracing shapes with their finger to decompress and diffuse tension. The idea is to help adults understand their triggers, identify the symptoms of stress in the moment, and see challenging behaviors from children as calls for help instead of an intentional act to upset adults.

In thinking about the importance of self-regulation as previously discussed—emotional, behavioral, and thought—it's important to understand the role

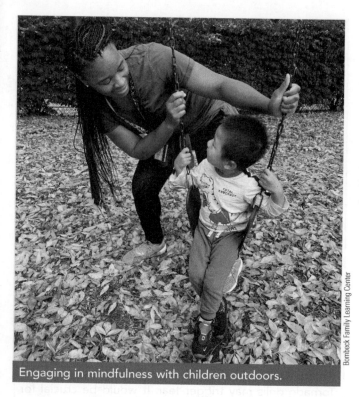

Engaging in mindfulness with children outdoors.

mindful practices can have on developing self-regulation skills even as adults. Providing training on mindfulness-based interventions, which are similar to those outlined in the CARE program, has demonstrated long-term positive outcomes, even a year after the professional development occurred. At the end of this chapter is a list of resources for administrators and educators, including websites and programs to practice mindfulness through apps such as Headspace and Calm, as well as information about the CARE training program (Jennings, Doyle, Oh, Rasheed, Frank, & Brown, 2019).

12-2ae • Self-Care Strategies

As educators, we often place the needs of others before our own, where our skills of empathy and compassion drive our decisions. Understanding the importance of nurturing and caring for children is what drives us to the field, knowing that for some children the school building is a place of refuge, consistently warm care, and safety. The weight of this responsibility is also a significant stressor for teachers and can negatively affect the children they are trying to help grow and protect. It is essential to make sure that we

are making time for self-care and providing the space for staff to do the same. As previously mentioned, the cycle of stress can be a constantly turning merry-go-round. Using self-care is an essential step to stop from spinning out of control.

Erdman, Colker, and Winter (2020) provide a robust list of recommendations to help early childhood educators begin self-care practices to overcome stress and secondary trauma. This includes adults nurturing their physical, social, mental health, emotional, and spiritual needs. Strategies for self-care include:

- treating yourself like someone you love;
- trying to improve the "balancing game" by emphasizing a life–work balance;
- improving time management;
- learning to use an assertive voice effectively;
- practicing mindfulness;
- integrating nature-based experiences into daily life;
- utilizing an attitude of gratitude;
- engaging in activities that feel good such as reading, volunteering, and engaging in social activities;
- journaling as a way of processing complex thoughts or transforming negative self-talk;
- finding hobbies that are fulfilling;
- establishing a supportive network of peers;
- providing reflective supervision;
- seeking professional support as needed; and
- making a self-care action plan.

Table 12-3 provides specific actions early childhood educators can take to engage in these self-care practices. Here we highlight in more detail the strategies of mindfulness and nature-based interventions.

12-2af • Using Nature to Reduce Stress

During the COVID-19 pandemic, especially in the early days, there seemed to be a phenomenon emerging: People sought refuge outdoors as much as possible. With schools closed and families working from home when possible, the outdoors provided relief from the anxieties associated with constant news cycles, the feeling of being trapped inside instead of feeling safe at home, and looking for new hobbies that were safe for the whole family. This phenomenon sparked

Table 12-3 Examples of self-care strategies

Self-Care Categories	Specific Practices
Life–work balance	Taking a lunch break instead of working through it
	Starting each day by doing something for yourself, your family, or your home before beginning the workday
	Saying no to additional work commitments to prioritize self-care
Reframing negative thoughts	Utilizing a journaling practice to process complex or complicated thoughts
	Creating a gratitude journal, writing three things to be grateful for each day
	Engaging in hobbies that provide an outlet for disengaging stress and offer a sense of accomplishment
Creating a peer network	Volunteering in the community
	Establishing a coffee hour with work colleagues to just listen to struggles as well as solve problems
	Utilizing a critical friends group in which an individual can present challenges and colleagues can offer solutions in a judgment-free way
Providing reflective supervision	Providing a safe space for staff to engage with peers in a positive, healthy way
	Engaging with individual educators, listening to their needs and concerns
	Engage in the practice of role release, acknowledging where tension exists between directors and teachers and where direct support can be provided
Making a self-care plan	Taking care of a pet or plants
	Making a to-do list and acknowledging accomplishments
	Prioritizing self-care practices on a to-do list
	Time blocking to achieve work tasks as well as including time for self-care

conversations that many early childhood educators already knew—meaningful, thoughtful engagement with nature can have overwhelmingly positive effects on mental health.

Richard Louv, author of *Last Child in the Woods: Saving Our Children from Nature-Deficit Disorder* (2006), described the danger of creating a culture in which nature is observed passively instead of experienced actively. He stated that this alienation from the great outdoors can lead to larger behavioral shifts, including reduced use of the five senses, difficulty paying attention, and increased risk of physical and social-emotional strain. He also argued that withdrawing from natural spaces can increase rates of depression in addition to other issues with mental health. Louv and his colleagues have stated that he had not intended for the term *nature deficit disorder* to be considered a diagnosis with medical or clinical implications, but its reception among educators, families, and physicians demonstrated how deeply it resonated within those working with children.

As a result of Louv's work regarding nature-deficit disorder, the organization named Children and Nature Network (https://www.childrenandnature .org/) has been established, connecting educators and parents to resources supporting engagement with nature. This includes monthly research digests

Growth Mindset Moment

Advice to others: Know that everything is going to change, and it will be OK. Take it one day at a time. Try not to allow yourself to be overwhelmed by the whole problem because it can be enormous. It's going to change, and that's OK. Desmond Tutu once wisely said, "There is only one way to eat an elephant: a bite at a time." What he meant by this is that everything in life that seems daunting, overwhelming, and even impossible can be accomplished gradually by taking on just a little at a time. Break it into smaller pieces you can manage; try not to control or resist it.

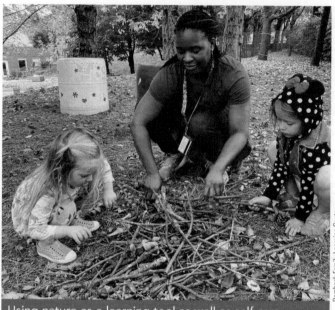

Using nature as a learning tool as well as self-care.

Bombeck Family Learning Center

focusing on different topics, a resource library where you can search for specific topics, and a space for those working with children to find ways to connect with nature.

One easy strategy that directors can use to reduce their own stress or encourage their staff to use is simply to sit outside for as little as 5 minutes. As a sort of grounding exercise, find a place to sit comfortably outside and plant your feet firmly on the ground. Take time to just sit and listen to the outside world, noticing the sounds of birds, the feel of the wind, and the movement of nature around you. Although this process of mindfulness and grounding oneself in nature can be done alone, you can also have teachers practice it with the children. By engaging with and modeling these practices for children, the benefits of nature—and the pull to engage with it more—become apparent.

Summary

The responsibilities of leaders during disasters, emergencies, and difficult times are great. The complex nature of helping others through trauma while being sensitive to your own needs is a difficult balancing act. However, each day provides a new opportunity to grow, learn, and adapt to surf the changing tides. Focusing on connecting with others, engaging in self-care, and providing space for others to do the same are critical tasks for adults. In doing so, adults are better prepared to support children as they navigate stress and develop skills as well as strategies that will serve them throughout their lives.

TRY IT OUT!

1. Look at **Director's Resource 12-1**. As a director, imagine how you could use this form. The form is intended to provide a framework that supports critical conversations regarding teacher's self-care and is aimed at having thoughtful, reflective conversations. Discuss the following with a classmate:

   a. How would you use this form to frame conversations?

   b. How often would you use this tool or something similar?

   c. Explain the steps you would take in using this form.

2. Take a look through the websites for the organizations listed in the **Director's Resource 12-2**. Answer the following questions:

   a. Who are the intended audiences for these organizations—children, families, educators, or other professionals?

   b. Describe how these organizations can help their intended audiences.

   c. Write an example of when you might refer to each organization.

3. Consider the mindfulness toolkit section of the **Director's Resource 12-2**. Try out the strategies recommended by each organization on your own. Discuss with a classmate which of the strategies you tried and how you felt when you were done. Create a list of how you could use this toolkit in your own program.

4. Explore the website for the National Center for Pyramid Model Innovations found at www.challengingbehavior.org.

a. List who is involved at each tier of the pyramid. Include families, specific professionals, and people working within early childhood programs.

b. Describe what practices or policies come into play at each level.

c. Practice with a partner having a difficult conversation with a team about the need for targeted interventions described at the top of the pyramid. How can you use strengths-based language and growth mindset to communicate the need for additional support?

Director's Resource 12-1

NAVIGATING CRITICAL CONVERSATIONS COACHING FORM

The authors of the book *Crucial Conversations: Tools for Talking When the Stakes Are High* focus on a few key questions and strategies to navigate conversations with others that are uncomfortable and challenging and can have serious repercussions. Use the following form to guide you in crucial conversations with others with the following concerns.

Concern	Things to Remember	Key Questions
Friction between director and educator or staff	Focus on me, then we; think about what in a situation is upsetting you and how you can respond, not just focus on changing the educator or how they feel or act.	How can you change your reactions to the situation? What do I really *want* out of the situation? How can I ask what my educator wants? What is my role in the situation?
Concerns with educator behavior, attitude, actions, observed by director	Refuse the false dichotomy of either–or; either you change your behavior or there will be consequences	How do I go about finding a resolution that supports both myself and the educator? What can you do to ensure clear messaging and connect with the educator in a positive way? STATE: Share your facts, Tell your story, Ask for other's facts, Talk tentatively, Encourage sharing
Concerns with educator behavior, attitude, actions, observed by colleague	Dialog is always an option; encourage and support crucial conversations between colleagues	What can I do to rebuild trust between colleagues? Are we actively exploring other's views?
Observed symptoms of trauma ■ Confusion ■ Difficulty concentrating or completing work ■ Withdrawing from others ■ Talk of guilt, shame, or self-blame ■ Irritability, mood swings ■ Withdrawing from colleagues	Make it safe: apologize when appropriate, commit to finding a common goal in processing trauma, and recognize the need for connection	ABC: Agree, Build, Compare Am I avoiding necessary concerns or creating unnecessary conflict? AMPP: Ask, Mirror, Paraphrase, Prime Does my team know that I respect them, and do they believe my goals in this situation are to help?
Observed symptoms of anxiety ■ Trouble concentrating or completing work ■ Increased use of sick days ■ Reported sleeping issues ■ Avoidance of responsibilities or colleagues ■ Increased restlessness ■ Shortened temper/rage	Emotions don't just happen; others don't make you feel a certain way, and you are more than your emotions. Help others process their emotions in a safe space through active, responsive listening	How do I continue to support an ongoing dialog to reduce the strain and provide some control in this situation? Are my questions and actions focusing on the facts? Is our conversation supporting the processing of emotions? How can I help my educators take control of their stories instead of falling into the role of helplessness or victim?
Observed symptoms of burnout ■ Reports of exhaustion ■ Changes in mood or personality ■ Difficulty with memory ■ Reported sense of lowered competence ■ Observed sense of defeat or lack of success or achievement in tasks	Focus on the person, not just the behavior; why would a rational, reasonable professional be acting in this manner?	Am I confidently expressing my concerns in a supportive, nonjudgmental manner? Am I going to silence or violence in this situation (withdrawing from concerns or becoming judgmental)? How can I guide us toward mutual purpose, focusing on what needs to be done and how we can get there?

Source: Patterson, K., Grenny, J., McMillan, R., Switzler, A. (2012). Crucial conversations: Tools for talking when stakes are high. (2nd ed.) McGraw Hill.

Director's Resource 12-2

RESOURCES AND ORGANIZATIONS SUPPORTING MENTAL HEALTH

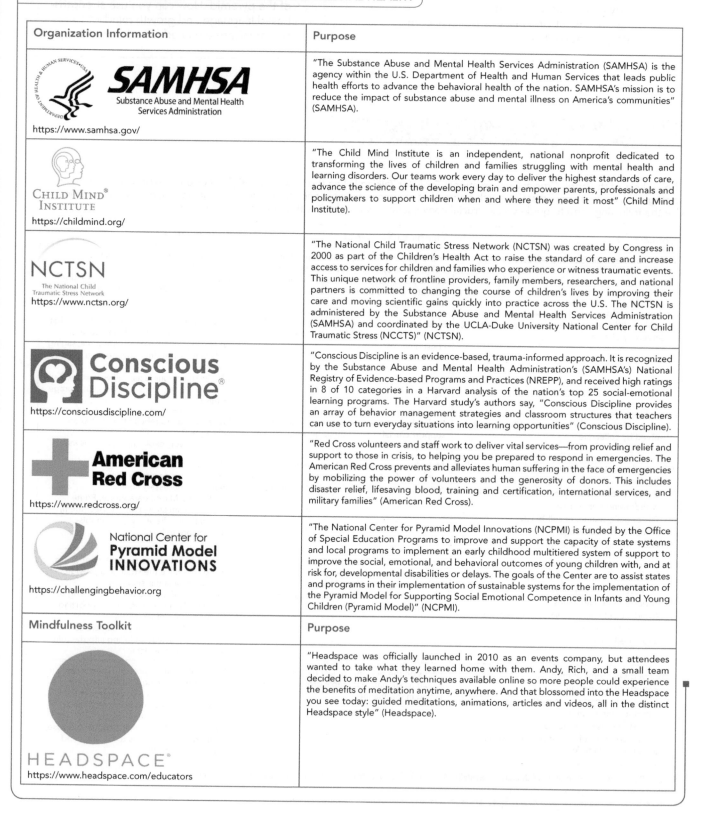

Organization Information	Purpose
SAMHSA Substance Abuse and Mental Health Services Administration https://www.samhsa.gov/	"The Substance Abuse and Mental Health Services Administration (SAMHSA) is the agency within the U.S. Department of Health and Human Services that leads public health efforts to advance the behavioral health of the nation. SAMHSA's mission is to reduce the impact of substance abuse and mental illness on America's communities" (SAMHSA).
CHILD MIND® INSTITUTE https://childmind.org/	"The Child Mind Institute is an independent, national nonprofit dedicated to transforming the lives of children and families struggling with mental health and learning disorders. Our teams work every day to deliver the highest standards of care, advance the science of the developing brain and empower parents, professionals and policymakers to support children when and where they need it most" (Child Mind Institute).
NCTSN The National Child Traumatic Stress Network https://www.nctsn.org/	"The National Child Traumatic Stress Network (NCTSN) was created by Congress in 2000 as part of the Children's Health Act to raise the standard of care and increase access to services for children and families who experience or witness traumatic events. This unique network of frontline providers, family members, researchers, and national partners is committed to changing the course of children's lives by improving their care and moving scientific gains quickly into practice across the U.S. The NCTSN is administered by the Substance Abuse and Mental Health Services Administration (SAMHSA) and coordinated by the UCLA-Duke University National Center for Child Traumatic Stress (NCCTS)" (NCTSN).
Conscious Discipline® https://consciousdiscipline.com/	"Conscious Discipline is an evidence-based, trauma-informed approach. It is recognized by the Substance Abuse and Mental Health Administration's (SAMHSA's) National Registry of Evidence-based Programs and Practices (NREPP), and received high ratings in 8 of 10 categories in a Harvard analysis of the nation's top 25 social-emotional learning programs. The Harvard study's authors say, "Conscious Discipline provides an array of behavior management strategies and classroom structures that teachers can use to turn everyday situations into learning opportunities" (Conscious Discipline).
American Red Cross https://www.redcross.org/	"Red Cross volunteers and staff work to deliver vital services—from providing relief and support to those in crisis, to helping you be prepared to respond in emergencies. The American Red Cross prevents and alleviates human suffering in the face of emergencies by mobilizing the power of volunteers and the generosity of donors. This includes disaster relief, lifesaving blood, training and certification, international services, and military families" (American Red Cross).
National Center for **Pyramid Model** INNOVATIONS https://challengingbehavior.org	"The National Center for Pyramid Model Innovations (NCPMI) is funded by the Office of Special Education Programs to improve and support the capacity of state systems and local programs to implement an early childhood multitiered system of support to improve the social, emotional, and behavioral outcomes of young children with, and at risk for, developmental disabilities or delays. The goals of the Center are to assist states and programs in their implementation of sustainable systems for the implementation of the Pyramid Model for Supporting Social Emotional Competence in Infants and Young Children (Pyramid Model)" (NCPMI).
Mindfulness Toolkit	**Purpose**
HEADSPACE® https://www.headspace.com/educators	"Headspace was officially launched in 2010 as an events company, but attendees wanted to take what they learned home with them. Andy, Rich, and a small team decided to make Andy's techniques available online so more people could experience the benefits of meditation anytime, anywhere. And that blossomed into the Headspace you see today: guided meditations, animations, articles and videos, all in the distinct Headspace style" (Headspace).

Director's Resource 12-2 *(continued)* ///

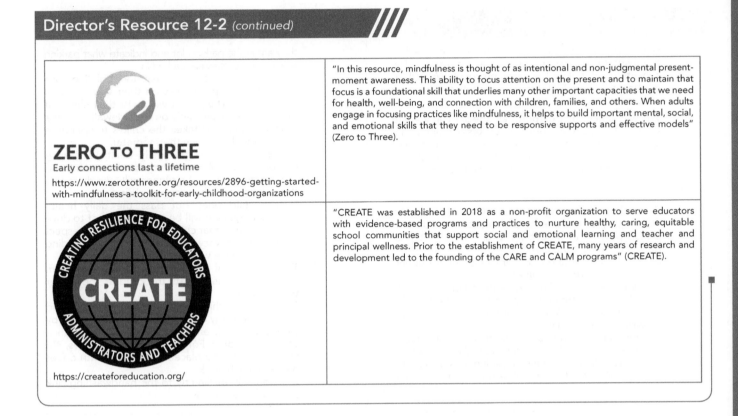

	"In this resource, mindfulness is thought of as intentional and non-judgmental present-moment awareness. This ability to focus attention on the present and to maintain that focus is a foundational skill that underlies many other important capacities that we need for health, well-being, and connection with children, families, and others. When adults engage in focusing practices like mindfulness, it helps to build important mental, social, and emotional skills that they need to be responsive supports and effective models" (Zero to Three).
ZERO TO THREE Early connections last a lifetime https://www.zerotothree.org/resources/2896-getting-started-with-mindfulness-a-toolkit-for-early-childhood-organizations	
CREATING RESILIENCE FOR EDUCATORS **CREATE** ADMINISTRATORS AND TEACHERS https://createforeducation.org/	"CREATE was established in 2018 as a non-profit organization to serve educators with evidence-based programs and practices to nurture healthy, caring, equitable school communities that support social and emotional learning and teacher and principal wellness. Prior to the establishment of CREATE, many years of research and development led to the founding of the CARE and CALM programs" (CREATE).

Director's Resource 12-3 ///

SAMPLE COVID-19 PROTOCOLS

It is difficult to maintain a safe social distance between children in early education and child care settings. For optimal development, it is important for young children to explore their environments and interact with friends. Understanding the challenges social distancing presents for children in the way we think about it for adults, it is not required for children to remain 6 feet apart. However, the following practices will be implemented.

Social Distancing

1. **Group size and ratios.** We will adhere to reduced staff to child ratios and maximum group size limitations, following those set by the State of Ohio at all times.
   a. One child care staff member per four infants (1:4) with no more than six children in the room. Allowing up to two teachers with six infants.
   b. One child care staff member per six toddlers (1:6) with no more than six children in the room. Allowing up to one teacher with six toddlers.
   c. One child care staff member per nine preschool children (1:9) with no more than nine children in the room. Allowing up to one teacher with nine preschool children.

Director's Resource 12-3 *(continued)* ///

2. **Classroom groups do not mix.** We have established classrooms with set precautions in place to ensure that groups do not mix between classrooms, when entering and exiting the center, when using the restroom or when on the playground.
   a. Each group of children will have their own classroom that is exclusively used by the staff and children assigned to that room.
   b. Each group of children will have their own entrance and exit to the classroom and teachers will use sanitizing wipes to disinfect interior door handles upon entry and exit to the classroom.
   c. All classrooms will have egress to the outside.
   d. Each group of children/classroom will have exclusive use to sinks for toileting or diapering that are separate from handwashing and food prep.
   e. Each classroom [or] group will have exclusive use of bathrooms. Bathrooms will be disinfected with bleach spray after every use with a 1-minute wait before the next child can use it.

3. **Consistent teachers and children.** Classroom rosters will be created so that the same group of children are together every day and the same two teachers will remain with that group of children each day to help minimize the spread of an infection. Teachers

Director's Resource 12-3 (continued)

will need days off. Only at that time will we schedule a substitute teacher to be in the classroom. The substitute will follow the same protocol. We will do our best to schedule the same substitute for the same classroom.

4. **We will cancel or postpone all special classes and events.** This includes field trips, excursions, and large-group events, festivals, holiday events, and special performances. It also means that Webby Dance, Soccer Shots, and Faith Formation cannot occur.

Upon Arrival

1. **Curbside and parking lot drop-off and pickup.** We will employ a curbside or parking lot drop-off and pickup process to reduce the virus spread potential between families and staff.
   a. Parents are required to wear face coverings during pickup and drop-off times!
   b. Right before families leave their home, parents will use Moment Path to complete the daily health check and check their child in using "Informed Arrival" for the day.
   c. Upon arrival, families will use their smartphone to access Moment Path, the center's digital communication tool, to message the drop-off or pickup account. This will notify the front office staff and runners that

Director's Resource 12-3 (continued)

they are in the parking lot and indicate what parking space number they are parked in.
   d. Designated runners will exit the building, use hand sanitizer, put gloves on their way out, and wear a mask. The parent will assist their child out of the car and wait safely on the sidewalk until the runner comes and takes the child's temperature with a digital no-touch thermometer.
   e. If the child passes the daily health screening completed via Moment Path by the parent and temperature check, the runner will take them into the building and then to their classroom.
      ▪ If a child does not pass the daily health screening, care will be taken so as not to draw attention to that child or vehicle out of respect for their privacy. Also, information regarding their absence will be stored securely.
   f. The runner will remain outside the classroom while the teacher greets the child as they enter the classroom.
   g. On cold days, children will remove their coat and hang it in a cubby or on a hook. Every other cubby will be blocked, ensuring an adequate distance between children. For rooms without cubbies, 3M coat hooks will be placed on the wall with 6 feet between each hook.
   h. Children will go directly to the handwashing sink and wash their hands.

Director's Resource 12-3 (continued)

2. **Staff entry to the building**
   a. Upon entering the vestibule, staff will take their temperature using a no-touch digital thermometer. Individuals with a fever of 100.0 degrees or higher may not enter the facility. They will use hand sanitizer before and after touching the thermometer.
   b. Staff will stop at the reception desk, use hand sanitizer, and complete the daily health check using the electronic check-in. When finished, they will wipe the screen with a sanitizing wipe. They will again use hand sanitizer.
   c. If they pass the health check and temperature test, staff can proceed to their work location continuing to wear a mask.
      ▪ Staff who do not pass the health check will not proceed to where the children are; their supervisor will be notified, and they will leave the center immediately.
   d. Staff will take a disinfectant wipe with them to their work space door where they will use it to open the door handle and turn on the lights.
   e. Staff will have a designated spot for their personal belongings, including their coat, which is separate from and out of reach of children.
   f. Upon entering their workspace (classroom, kitchen, etc.) staff will wash their hands again.

Director's Resource 12-3 (continued)

During the Day

1. **Handwashing.** Staff and children must follow rigorous handwashing procedures. All classrooms have permanent sinks that are separate from sinks used for toileting and food preparation. Staff will wash their hands at the following times:
   a. Upon arrival for the day, after breaks, and upon returning from outside.
   b. After toileting or assisting a child with toileting.
   c. After each diaper change or pull-up change.
   d. After contact with bodily fluids or cleaning up spills or objects contaminated with bodily fluids.
   e. After cleaning or sanitizing or using any chemical products.
   f. After handling pets, pet cages or other pet objects that have come in contact with the pet.
   g. Before eating, serving or preparing food or bottles, or feeding a child.
   h. Before and after completing a medical procedure or administering medication.
   i. When visibly soiled (must use soap and water).
   j. After returning inside after outdoor play.
   k. Prior to departure.

2. **Protective equipment**
   a. **Protective face coverings**—Bombeck staff are required to wear face coverings properly, even

Director's Resource 12-3 *(continued)*

during outdoor times. Face coverings may be removed in order to eat or drink; care must be taken not to touch the outside surface where contamination may exist. The University will provide two cloth reusable face masks and one reusable face shield for each staff member. Because it is still possible to spread germs while wearing protective equipment, staff will be trained in the proper use required to help prevent the spread. Staff members may use their own face coverings if they:

- fit snugly but comfortably against the side of the face, covering the mouth and nose;
- are secured with ties or ear loops;
- include multiple layers of fabric;
- allow for breathing without restriction; and
- can be laundered and machine dried without damage or change in shape.

Staff members are responsible for the cleaning and care of reusable masks provided by the program or face coverings they secure on their own. Disposable face masks are to be replaced daily and whenever they become wet or soiled.

Face coverings may be removed in order to eat or drink; care must be taken not to touch the outside surface where contamination may exist.

Director's Resource 12-3 *(continued)*

Cloth face coverings should not be worn if the person has trouble breathing, is unconscious or incapacitated, or is unable to remove the mask without assistance. We will direct any questions about a staff member's ability to wear a mask to the administrator or to human resources, if available.

b. Gloves: Disposable gloves are no substitute for handwashing. Disposable gloves are not required for working unless running children to the classroom, serving food, preparing bottles, or changing diapers. Gloves should be changed between each new bottle feeding or diapering. Hand hygiene as described above must be practiced with gloved or bare hands. If worn, gloves must be removed without touching the outside of the glove. Staff will be trained in the appropriate use of gloves.

3. **Toys and materials.** Staff will provide materials that are single-use, child-specific or can be sanitized.
   a. Children can play with toys and when they are finished, the children will place them in the dirty bin (black) located in the hallway outside their door.
   b. The toys will be disinfected throughout the day by the daytime cleaner from Alpha-Omega.
   c. Once cleaned, the toys will be returned using the clean bin (clear), which will be placed outside the

Director's Resource 12-3 *(continued)*

classroom. A knock at the door will signal teachers that the toy bin (clear) is there and toys are ready to be returned to the shelves. The dirty toy bin (black) will be left outside the classroom door.
   d. Materials that are single use will be discarded in the trash (paper cups, paper, leaves, sticks, and flowers) or put in a folder to be sent home at a later date.
   e. Materials that are reused but not easily cleaned like crayons, markers, journals, etc. will be placed in containers that are designated for each child's sole use.
   f. Books will be rotated daily so that the class has a bin of books for each day of the week. This will allow 7 days to pass before books will be used again.

4. **Nap time.** Preschoolers and older toddlers will use cots that are disinfected each night. We allow one lightweight blanket from home that is laundered by the Alpha-Omega cleaner weekly. If a pillow is necessary, we will allow one no larger than a travel pillow. Large oversized blankets or pillows will not be allowed due to the amount of laundry the center is responsible for on a daily basis, and the teachers will work with you to bring in the appropriate size.
   a. Children who are sleeping on cots will have at least 6 feet between cots. Children sleeping in cribs will have at least 2 feet between cribs. We will place children head to toe in order to expand

Director's Resource 12-3 *(continued)*

the space between children and further reduce the potential for viral spread.
   b. The Bombeck Center will provide sheets for children in cribs, which will be laundered weekly by the Alpha-Omega cleaner.
   c. Toddlers and preschoolers will be able to keep a washable lovie on their cot for nap time. This item must remain at the Bombeck Center. It will be washed weekly with bedding.

5. **Playground.** To restrict the use of the playground to only one group of children at a time, the preschool playgrounds will be separated into three areas, which are cordoned off. Double barriers will be used to provide a 6-foot space between barriers in order to maintain social distance between groups.
   a. The three playground areas include (1) swings on the hill (classes will access this playground from their back classroom exits), (2) a large play structure with the bathroom to the east of the other bathroom (classes will access this playground through the door at the end of the preschool hallway), and (3) the preschool courtyard. Children would use their classroom bathrooms when using the courtyard. Classes will enter the courtyard through the doors that open onto the courtyard.
   b. Playground restrooms will be disinfected with bleach spray after every use with a 1-minute wait before the next use.

Director's Resource 12-3 (continued) ////

c. A schedule for which playground is used by which classroom and when will be created and adhered to.
d. Water fountains will be disabled and covered so that children cannot access them. Children will have their own distinctive water bottle for use when they are on the playground. Water bottles will be kept in a designated location with adequate distance between bottles.
e. Each classroom will have a bin of its own outside toys, including sand toys, bubbles, trucks, etc., which they will take with them and gather up and place in the bin when they leave the playground. This bin of toys to be disinfected by the daytime cleaner will be left outside the classroom door.
f. Water bottles will be put in a labeled bin to be taken to the kitchen by the PM teacher on their way out of the building at the end of the day. Water bottles will be sanitized in the kitchen by the nutrition aid and returned to the classroom for use the following day.

6. **Common areas.** Only teachers, children, and staff will be allowed in the Bombeck Center. We will limit the use of any communal indoor space. An Alpha-Omega daytime cleaner will disinfect common areas every two hours from 9:00 a.m. to 6:00 p.m. This includes the hallways, two adult restrooms in the front hallway, the staff restroom in the work room, the staff

Director's Resource 12-3 (continued) ////

lounge, the reception counter, door handles, light switches, and other frequently touched surfaces.

Disinfection and Cleaning

Note: Only cleaning and disinfecting products provided by the program and approved by state and local licensing and compliance entities are to be used. For more information, see link to Rule 5101:2-12-13.

1. **Cleaning procedures.** Adapted from the CDC's "How to Clean and Disinfect" resource page.
   a. Wear disposable gloves to clean and disinfect.
   b. Clean surfaces using soap and water, then use disinfectant.
   c. Cleaning with soap and water reduces the number of germs, dirt and impurities on the surface. Disinfecting kills germs on surfaces.
   d. Wash the surface or item with a detergent solution or other appropriate commercial product used for cleaning purposes.
   e. Questions about products must be directed to the manufacturer of the product. Follow the manufacturer's instructions exactly.
   f. Practice routine cleaning of frequently touched surfaces including but not limited to tables, doorknobs, light switches, countertops, handles, desks, phones, keyboards, toilets, faucets, and sinks.

Director's Resource 12-3 (continued) ////

2. **Common areas.** An Alpha-Omega daytime cleaner will be hired for the Bombeck Center from 9:00 a.m. to 6:00 p.m. daily. To reduce the risk of spread, this needs to be the same person all day every day. They would be responsible for disinfecting the frequently touched surfaces in all common areas, including hallways, entrances, the reception desk, living room, the staff workroom and break room, the laundry area and three public restrooms every 2 hours. They will also pick up dirty toys from outside classroom doors, sanitize them, and return them to outside the same classroom door. The cleaner would be responsible for doing laundry, including tot cot mats, smocks, crib sheets, and sleep sacks. Laundry procedures include:
   a. Launder items according to the manufacturer's instructions.
   b. Use the warmest appropriate water setting and dry items completely.
   c. Wear disposable gloves when handling dirty laundry.
   d. Do not shake dirty laundry.
   e. Clean and disinfect clothes hampers according to guidance for surfaces.
   f. Remove gloves and wash hands right away.
   Administrative staff members are responsible for frequently cleaning and disinfecting areas in which they work and that are commonly touched. Examples of these commonly touched

Director's Resource 12-3 (continued) ////

areas include desks and workstation surfaces, keyboards, phones, printers, and copiers. This is not an all-inclusive list.

The nutrition aide is responsible for cleaning and sanitizing surfaces in the kitchen regularly and the carts before and after use for laundering towels and washcloths used in the kitchen using the procedures above.

3. **Classrooms.** Teachers are responsible for frequently cleaning and disinfecting children's work areas throughout the day and providing a thorough disinfecting before dropoff and after pick-up. Teachers should remove toys from their classroom after each use and place them in a tub to be sanitized outside of their room. Toys made of fabric or cloth and dress-up materials will be removed from the classroom permanently. Books will be rotated out of the classroom each day and kept in a container out of reach of the children for 7 days before being rotated back into the classroom. Teachers are also responsible for cleaning all classroom electronics with disinfectant wipes after use.

4. **Nighttime cleaning.** A nighttime Alpha-Omega cleaning crew cleans and disinfects the Bombeck Center each night and will use a commercial product registered by the United States Environmental Protection Agency (US EPA) as a sanitizer that has

Director's Resource 12-3 *(continued)* ////

directions for use that are appropriate for the surface or item being sanitized.

Alpha-Omega is responsible for ensuring that cleaning crews are trained on appropriate use of cleaning and disinfection chemicals. They are also required to wear disposable gloves for all tasks in the cleaning process, including handling trash. Gloves should be removed carefully to avoid contamination of the wearer and the surrounding area.

Note: Only cleaning and disinfecting products provided by the program and approved by state and local licensing and compliance entities will be used. For more information, see Appendix A to Rule 5101:2-12-13.

a. Soft surfaces such as carpeted floors, rugs, cushions, and drapes will be cleaned and sanitized using an ionizing disinfectant sprayer. After being disinfected, carpet will be vacuumed.
b. Tiled floors will be mopped with soap and water and disinfected.
c. Hard surfaces will be disinfected with both soap and water and bleach spray or using the ionizing disinfectant sprayer.

5. **Cleaning and disinfecting outdoor areas and playgrounds.** Outdoor areas like playgrounds generally require normal routine cleaning but do not require disinfection. We will follow these procedures:

Director's Resource 12-3 *(continued)* ////

a. We will not spray disinfectant on outdoor playgrounds as it is not an efficient use of supplies and is not proven to reduce risk of COVID-19 to the public.
b. Teachers will use disinfecting wipes to clean commonly touched surfaces made of plastic or metal such as grab bars and railings after each group of children has left the playground.
c. We will not clean and disinfect wooden surfaces (play structures, benches, tables) or ground covers (mulch, sand), sidewalks, or roads.

Confirmed Cases

Programs are required to take several steps when a staff member or child enrolled in the program has tested positive for COVID-19. Programs must:

1. **Isolate.** We will immediately isolate and seek medical care for any individual who develops symptoms while at the Bombeck Center. The Launch Pad has been designated as a space for children who are sick.
2. **Shutdown and sanitize.** We will follow all procedures established by the Department of Public Health for Dayton and Montgomery County. Typically, this requires us to shut down classrooms for 48 hours for deep sanitation and use the infant toddler gym as a temporary space until the classroom is ready. The Bombeck Center will employ the following cleaning and disinfecting procedures if someone is sick.

Director's Resource 12-3 *(continued)* ////

a. We will close off areas used by the person who is sick.
b. We will pen outside doors and windows to increase air circulation in the area. If possible, use fans to vent air outside of the room.
c. We will wait 24 hours before we clean or disinfect. If 24 hours is not feasible, we will wait as long as possible.
d. We will clean and disinfect all areas used by the person who is sick, such as offices, bathrooms, common areas, shared electronic equipment like tablets, touch screens, keyboards, and remote controls.
e. We will vacuum the space using a vacuum equipped with a high-efficiency particulate air (HEPA) filter.
f. We will not vacuum a room or space that has people in it. We will wait until the room or space is empty to vacuum, such as at night for common spaces, or during the day for private rooms.
g. We will temporarily turn off room fans and the central HVAC system that services the room or space so that particles that escape from vacuuming will not circulate throughout the facility.
h. Once an area has been appropriately disinfected, it can be opened for use.
i. If more than 7 days have elapsed since the person who is sick visited or used the facility, additional cleaning and disinfection is not necessary.

3. **Notify ODJFGCR.** We will notify the Ohio Department of Job and Family Services (ODJFGCR) by the next

Director's Resource 12-3 *(continued)* ////

business day in the Ohio Child Licensing and Quality System (OCLQS) as a serious incident.

4. **Notify UD and the Local Health Department.** We will notify Robin Oldfield in UD Risk Management and Dr. Mary Buchwalder, Medical Director of the UD Health Center. Dr. Buchwalder will notify Public Health—Dayton & Montgomery County about the positive case, which will initiate the contact tracing process. Contact tracing facilitates the identification of potentially infected or exposed individuals and helps ensure that the person completes isolation or quarantine procedures for COVID-19 in coordination with the local health department.
5. **Notify families.** We will send notification via email with an alert via Moment Path to all families in the center as soon as we have an identified case. Care will be taken not to release the identity of the positive case (for privacy purposes).
6. **Communication.** The Center Director will share that a positive case exists with the Executive Director of the Center for Early Learning and the Dean of the SEHS as well as the University PR department, which communicate with the University community and the media.

The Bombeck Center Director will communicate with Bombeck Center staff and will send an email to families.

REFERENCES

American Psychological Association (2020, October 6). *Trauma*. https://www.apa.org/topics/trauma

Bailey, B. (2015). *Conscious discipline: Building resilient classrooms*. Oviedo, FL: Loving Guidance. https://consciousdiscipline.com/product/the-new-conscious-discipline-book-expanded-updated/

Bailey, B. (2020). Start strong: SEL foundations and resiliency in infants and toddlers. *Loving Guidance*. https://consciousdiscipline.com/e-learning/start-strong/

Carter, R. T., Kirkinis, K., & Johnson, V. E. (2020). Relationships between trauma symptoms and race-based traumatic stress. *American Psychological Association, 26*(1), 11–18. https://psycnet.apa.org/doi/10.1037/trm0000217

Center on the Developing Child. (2016). *From best practices to breakthrough impacts: A science-based approach to building a more promising future for young children and families*. Cambridge, MA: Harvard University. https://developingchild.harvard.edu/resources/from-best-practices-to-breakthrough-impacts/

Child Mind Institute. (n.d.a). *Anxiety basics*. https://childmind.org/guide/anxiety-basics/

Child Mind Institute. (n.d.b). *Teachers guide to anxiety in the classroom*. https://childmind.org/guide/a-teachers-guide-to-anxiety-in-the-classroom/

Collaborative for Academic, Social, and Emotional Learning (CASEL). (2017). *What is SEL?* https://casel.org/what-is-sel/

Erdman, S., Colker, L. J., & Winter, E. C. (2020). *Trauma and young children: Teaching strategies to support & empower*. Washington, DC: NAEYC. https://www.naeyc.org/resources/pubs/books/trauma-and-young-children

Galderisi, S., Heinz, A., Kastrup, M., Beezhold, J., & Sartorius, N. (2015). Toward a new definition of mental health. *World Psychiatry, 14*(2). https://www.ncbi.nlm.nih.gov/pmc/articles/PMC4471980/

Gartrell, D. (2014). *A guidance approach to the encouraging classroom* (6th ed.). Boston, MA: Cengage Learning.

Gewertz, C. (2020, July 21). Mindfulness for teachers: A program with proof. *Education Week*. https://www.edweek.org/teaching-learning/mindfulness-for-teachers-a-program-with-proof/2020/07

Gorski, P. (2020). How trauma-informed are we, really? *Educational Leadership, 78*(2), 14–19. http://www.ascd.org/publications/educational_leadership/oct20/vol78/num02/How_Trauma-Informed_Are_We,_Really%C2%A2.aspx

Jennings, P. A., Doyle, S., Oh, Y., Rasheed, D., Frank, J. L., & Brown, J. L. (2019, October). Long-term impacts of the CARE program on teachers' self-reported social and emotional competence and well-being. *Journal of School Psychology, 76*, 186–202. https://doi.org/10.1016/j.jsp.2019.07.009

Keels, M. (2020). Building racial equity through trauma-responsive discipline. *Educational Leadership, 78*(2), 40–45. http://www.ascd.org/publications/educational_leadership/oct20/vol78/num02/Building_Racial_Equity_Through_Trauma-Responsive_Discipline.aspx

Lemoine, S., Green, K., Mulrooney, K., & Macasaet, K. (2020). You matter: Promoting professional resilience during collective crisis. Zero to Three. https://www.zerotothree.org/resources/3653-you-matter-promoting-professional-resilience-during-collective-crisis

Louv, R. (2006). *Last child in the woods: Saving our children from nature-deficit disorder*. Chapel Hill, NC: Algonquin Books.

Manyema, M., Norris, S. A., & Richter, L. M. (2018). Stress begets stress: The association of adverse childhood experiences with psychological distress in the presence of adult life stress. *BMC Public Health, 18*, 835. https://doi.org/10.1186/s12889-018-5767-0

National Child Traumatic Stress Network, Secondary Traumatic Stress Committee. (2011). Secondary traumatic stress: A fact sheet for child-serving professionals. Los Angeles, CA, & Durham, NC: National Center for Child Traumatic Stress. https://www.nctsn.org/sites/default/files/resources/fact-sheet/secondary_traumatic_stress_child_serving_professionals.pdf

National Child Traumatic Stress Network. (2020, October 6). Understanding child trauma. https://www.samhsa.gov/sites/default/files/programs_campaigns/nctsi/nctsi-infographic-full.pdf

National Scientific Council on the Developing Child (2005/2014). *Excessive stress disrupts the architecture of the developing brain*. Working Paper no. 3, updated edition. www.developingchild.harvard.edu

Patterson, K., Grenny, J., McMillan, R., & Switzler, A. (2012). *Crucial conversations: Tools for talking when stakes are high* (2nd ed.). New York, NY: McGraw Hill

Sehgal, P., Jeffries, J., & Rappaport, N. (2017). Combatting race-related stress in the classroom. *Educational Leadership, 75*(4), 51–55. http://www.ascd.org/publications/educational_leadership/dec17/vol75/num04/Combatting_Race-Related_Stress_in_the_Classroom.aspx

Simmons, D. (2020). Confronting inequity/Healing Black students' pain. *Educational Leadership*, *78*(2), 80–81. http://www.ascd.org/publications/educational -leadership/oct20/vol78/num02/Healing-Black -Students%27-Pain.aspx

Singleton, G. E. (2014). *Courageous conversations about race: A field guide for achieving equity in schools* (2nd ed.). Thousand Oaks, CA: Corwin Press.

Substance Abuse and Mental Health Services Administration (SAMHSA). (2014). *SAMHSA's concept of a trauma-informed approach.* HHS publication no. (SMA) 14-4884. Washington, DC: Author. https:// store.samhsa.gov/product/SAMHSA-s-Concept -of-Trauma-and-Guidance-for-a-Trauma-Informed -Approach/SMA14-4884

Family and community partnerships can enrich the curriculum, making learning more meaningful for children.

Working with Families, Volunteers, and the Community

naeyc

Standards and Recommendations Addressed in This Chapter

ADVANCING EQUITY RECOMMENDATION 3 Employ staff who speak the languages of the children and families served.

ADVANCING EQUITY RECOMMENDATION 6 Provide regular time and space to foster a learning community among administrators and staff regarding equity issues.

PROGRAM STANDARD 7 Families

PROGRAM STANDARD 8 Community Relationships

PROFESSIONAL STANDARDS AND COMPETENCIES: STANDARD 2 Family–Teacher Partnerships and Community Connections

LEARNING OBJECTIVES

After reading this chapter, you should be able to:

13-1 Identify strategies that support and engage families.

13-2 List items to be included in written communication for families.

13-3 Describe the components of an effective volunteer program.

13-4 Identify local, state, and national professional organizations that can support professional growth.

13-5 Explain why community involvement is important to early childhood programs.

The focus of this chapter is on the importance of establishing reciprocal relationships with families. In its newly released position statement, the National Association for the Education of Young Children (NAEYC) (2020) states that "Developmentally appropriate practice requires deep knowledge about each child, including the context within which each child is living. Educators acquire much of this knowledge through respectful, reciprocal relationships with children's families. Across all ages, families' expertise about their own children is sought out and valued" (p. 1). These trusting relationships require staff to be inclusive and nonjudgmental. Staff members also should have the knowledge and skills to value and work with all types of families. This includes but is not limited to nuclear, single-parent, blended, adopted, foster, grandparental, and same-sex parents families. Staff must be culturally responsive.

In her classic 1984 article "How to Work with Working Parents," Ellen Galinsky describes the job of early childhood program directors as

one that calls for enormous skill, particularly in working with parents. It is being a professional who simultaneously creates a friendly atmosphere yet retains an appropriate distance; an expert who builds competence in others, who

is understanding, empathetic, yet at times firm. Most important is the role of the model—whose words or way of handling a sad, tired, or exuberant child are inspiring to parents. (p. 4)

Developing a first-class program for children is the goal of the early childhood program administrator, and having a high-quality program cannot happen without involving families and tending to their needs. Working with volunteers and community organizations or agencies also is an integral part of the total program that falls within the director's purview. Creating a positive climate based on good communication and demonstrating cross-cultural competence is essential for the success of this part of the program.

13-1 • Supporting and Engaging Families

Program directors have a unique role in helping to establish a program that is respectful of families while also meeting the needs of children and staff. The needs of these stakeholder groups are sometimes in conflict, and the director needs to be intentional about creating a system of policies and procedures as well as opportunities for relationship building that promote positive outcomes for all. Although classroom staff members or someone designated as a family coordinator may assume some responsibility for family involvement strategies, directors are ultimately responsible for monitoring these efforts, providing an effective role model, and serving as a resource for both staff and families.

With the recent revision of the NAEYC position statement on developmentally appropriate practices (2020), expectations regarding family support and involvement have increased and are clearly stated in the second guideline *Engaging in Reciprocal Partnerships with Families and Fostering Community Connections*. Educators who engage in developmentally appropriate practice take responsibility for forming and maintaining strong relationships with families and communities. They recognize that the traditional models of "parent involvement" or "parent education" are one-sided approaches that fail to give educators the knowledge or insights they need to provide learning experiences that are fully responsive to each child's needs and experiences. The following descriptions of educators' behavior indicate the kinds of relationships that are developmentally appropriate for children from birth through the primary grades, in which family members and educators work together as members of the learning community.

13-1a • Reciprocal Relationships with Families from Diverse Backgrounds

The director must demonstrate a positive attitude toward families and what they can contribute to the program. As is stated in the NAEYC position statement (2020), the success of these efforts depends on a reciprocal relationship with families based on mutual respect. Establishing and maintaining this kind of relationship with families is challenging because of the different cultures that make up today's society and the resulting diverse views on parenting and education. A 2019 U.S. census reports that 22.5 percent of families use a language other than English at home (U.S. Census Bureau, 2019). This diversification of the U.S. population is impacted not only by language differences but also by varied values, beliefs, traditions, and customs related to childrearing, parenting, education, health, and a myriad of other topics that can lead to miscommunication, mistrust, and discord. Recognize that differing opinions will always exist, conflicts will arise, and an open exchange of ideas, goals, and needs is required among families, staff, and the director.

Interactions between program staff and families must be respectful; staff members must demonstrate intercultural competence. With the significant alterations in the American family, the changing complexion of program families requires a multicultural mindset that values diversity (Gordon & Browne, 2010). As U.S. society becomes more heterogeneous, intercultural competence is an essential skill set for all service providers who work with young children and their families. The need to be interculturally competent is critical for all who work with young children and their families (Hanson, 2011). As Gonzallez-Mena (2016) states,

> Some child care directors and staff are experts at handling two children squabbling; but when

▶ **TeachSource Video Vignette**

Infants and Toddlers

View the video vignette titled *Infants and Toddlers: Family Interactions, School, and Community.*

As part of the newly revised guidelines for developmentally appropriate practice, the NAEYC explains the importance of establishing reciprocal relationships with families (NAEYC, 2020). Consider how well the educators in this video met these guidelines. How did the educators in this video strive to involve families as partners in the care and education of the toddlers?

tensions arise between themselves and parents, it can be a different story. Conflicts may come up around program policies or maybe it's just a small practical matter like bibs on toddlers. Behind the conflict may be differing notions of what's best for children, or a particular child. When professionals find themselves in such a conflict with a parent, it's a good idea to ask if this is a cultural conflict. (p. 113)

Language differences can be addressed with a translator. Cultural differences often lie below the surface and, unless there is a trusting reciprocal relationship with families, the conversations needed to understand these differences may not be surfaced. Notions of parenting and values for independence or interdependence in parent–child relationships would appear at the bottom of the iceberg. These cultural differences can lead to intercultural conflicts if they are not discussed preferably before a conflict arises.

Because of changes in laws nationally and at the state level, it is more common for children to have parents who fit on the LBGTQ+ spectrum. The common situation is having same-sex parents, but it is possible for parents to be on a continuum of gender identity (Burt & Lesser, 2016). The gender identity continuum may be a new concept for staff that can lead to situations in which staff lack the understanding that can impact the quality of the relationship. Professional development in serving parents who are LBGTQ+ is essential for staff members to understand what may be a new family dynamic to them.

TeachSource Video Vignette

Supporting LGBT Families' Preschool Planning for Young Children with Special Needs

View the video vignette titled *Preschool: IEP and Transition Planning for a Young Child with Special Needs.*

Communicating with families can be a challenging part of the job for many early childhood educators and directors. When working with families who have a special-needs child, the communication demands become even more complex. This video shows a preschool IEP and transition planning meeting. As you watch the video, jot down the different strategies that the educator uses to welcome the family and help it be part of the meeting.

13-1b • Challenges to Communicating with Parents

In addition to language and cultural differences, parents may be hesitant about communicating with the program director or staff for many reasons. Parenting is a challenging endeavor in even optimal circumstances. Parents who are successful in other areas of their lives may have great difficulty dealing with the unpredictability of or lack of control associated with having young children. Many parents are amazed by the skill that early childhood practitioners demonstrate in getting young children to cooperate. These same parents often report feeling incompetent when they struggle to transition their crying or uncooperative children into the classroom. Add factors such as poverty or a lack of school success, and many parents feel inhibited in their ability to communicate their needs to program staff (Freeman, Decker, &

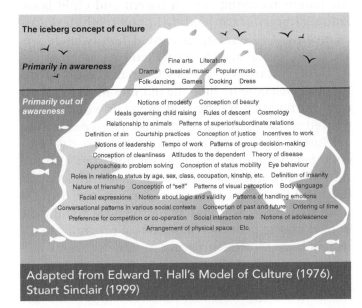

Adapted from Edward T. Hall's Model of Culture (1976), Stuart Sinclair (1999)

Decker, 2012). Feeling fully included in the program's community may also be difficult for parents who face challenges such as being a single parent, having a child with a disability, being a victim of domestic violence, having limited competence in English, or struggling with literacy.

Teachers tend to interface most easily with families who are most like their own families of origin. It is important to recognize this tendency and to strive to create environments that are welcoming to all families.

> A critical element in such an environment is an educator who has taken the time to identify personal biases and has the courage to go beyond bias to reach for real understanding and appreciation of differences. Biases are mostly the result of fear, ignorance, and misinformation. It is vital that educators make the effort to become comfortable and informed about the kinds of life experiences, values, and behaviors of diverse cultural groups and develop nonjudgmental

▶ TeachSource Video Vignette

Best Practices When Communicating with Families

After watching *Communicating with Families: Best Practices in an Early Childhood Setting*, reflect on the following questions:

1. What strategies did the teacher implement that made families feel welcome in her classroom?

2. What communication strategies could be applied to other early childhood settings?

dispositions toward working with the diversity of individual families. (Gestwicki, 2013, p. 11)

The actions of staff and the program's atmosphere must communicate to family members that each one is valued as an individual and that each is highly regarded as the child's first teachers and as those who know a great deal about the child. All parents should be aware that they are welcome to come as frequently (or as infrequently) as they wish.

Many things can communicate a feeling of acceptance and trust to family members, although some are more tangible than others. A parent receiving area is the place where parents establish their first impressions of the program. Take time to look at this transition space from the perspective of a rushed parent who is late for work or a tired grandmother or uncle who enters the building to drop off or pick up a child. Is it welcoming and aesthetically pleasing, softly lit, freshly painted, carpeted, and clean? It can be made to feel "homey" and more pleasant if there is comfortable adult seating with a collection of items for children to handle and explore. A fish tank or collection of musical instruments can draw both parents and children into the program, helping to facilitate more calm and pleasant transitions.

Parental information holders in this space sometimes contain information about the program, highlight interesting articles, and display a calendar of coming events. Pamphlets and journals on parenting, child development, toy selection, nutrition, and other resources for families can be made available in the parent receiving area. A parent and child book lending library or toy lending library might be located nearby. Sometimes, interested family members are asked to manage the entire lending program.

The less tangible things that make family members feel welcome include the manner in which their calls are handled by the staff member who answers the telephone or the greeting they receive from the van driver who picks up their child each day. Parents' feelings about the program and staff also are substantially influenced by their first contact with their child's teacher or the program director. It is difficult to perceive what is having the most significant impact on the parents' reactions to a program, so directors have to be alert to any number of subtle factors that may be influencing parental attitudes and feelings.

You are a director who is coaching a new EC Educator II in a preschool classroom. The other members of the teaching team and several parents have come to you with concerns about this new staff member's conversations with family members who pick up their children minutes before the program closes. The concerning conversations often include criticisms for leaving children at school for too long and encouragement for family members to spend more time with their children. Apparently, this new staff member was able to be a stay-at-home mom and believes that this parenting model is best for children. The other members of the teaching team share that programs' philosophy that honors families' decision without judgment. They would only intervene if there was an obvious and ongoing negative impact on the child. How would you handle this situation?

The building of reciprocal relationships with families depends on the feelings of trust that are established among the program staff, the children, and the families who use the program. Such trust begins to develop at the first contact and will continue to grow as it is nurtured by program staff.

The family program can be divided into three major categories: (1) family interactions, (2) family support, and (3) family involvement. Clearly, these three aspects of the program overlap; however, they are separated here for the purpose of discussion.

13-1c • Family Interactions

Family interactions range from the most informal arrival or departure greetings, phone calls, email, and Facebook postings to formal interviews, regularly scheduled conferences, and special meetings when problems are encountered. Whatever the occasion, interactions with family members can be the basis for establishing trusting relationships. Through these contacts, program staff members communicate to parents that they have important information to share with one another and that they have a special mutual concern for a child they both value. Information that is not shared during enrollment or orientation will often be shared when trust has been established, so it is important to provide ongoing opportunities to talk. Viewing parents as part-

Web-Based Portfolio Systems

The parents of young children are often digital natives who grew up using technology as an important communication tool. Web-based portfolio systems appeal to many parents and offer educators many new options for communicating with families. Early childhood programs can now provide families with access to secure web-based portfolios that include photographs, video streams, and educator notes. Educators can share assessment data and documentation as well as daily records that include daily routines such as diaper changes, feeding, and naps while also highlighting the rich and engaging curriculum that children experience throughout the day. Web-based portfolios can be accessed anywhere and anytime, making it possible to maintain an ongoing dialogue with family members. In contrast to the classroom cameras that parents can access in real time, web-based portfolios can provide meaning to what the parent is seeing. Because the educator chooses what to add to the portfolio and also provides an explanation, parents are better able to understand what they are seeing. Another benefit to a web-based portfolio over a video stream is that what parents only see their own child; this maintains confidentiality for all children in the program.

Family members can enjoy seeing what their children are doing in school by logging onto a web-based portfolio system that can share photographs, video, and teachers' notes using a password-protected website.

ners rather than as "us" versus "them" enhances the family–program staff relationship. Chapter 9 discusses details of initial interviews and intake procedures. When staff members are not fully prepared to handle

Growth Mindset Moment

Think about a common situation in a toddler classroom when one child bites another. The fact that biting is developmentally typical for toddlers does not calm the parent who is watching a live video stream as another children takes a bite out of their son or daughter's arm. The parent of the victim is aware of who bit their child. This knowledge can lead to altercations between parents. Many see web-based portfolios as a means of sharing up-to-date information about what is happening at school while being intentional about what is shared. Confidentiality can be better maintained, and misconceptions can be avoided.

Director's Corner

I make it clear at my very first meeting with a prospective family that we are open to parents visiting at any time. Our parents understand that even before admission to the program, they can come by to observe in our classrooms as they are weighing the pros and cons of sending their child to this program. It's the first step on the road to building a trusting relationship between the staff at the program and the families that we serve.

—*Director and owner, for-profit program*

initial contacts with families, in-service training time should be devoted to discussion or role-play of parent interviews and intake procedures. (See Chapter 14 for the discussion of in-service training.)

Contacts with families range from the daily drop-off and separation in the early morning and occasional phone calls and exchange of information during the day to the late-day reunion that can be emotional and rushed. In addition to these daily casual contacts, have a system in place for daily written communication to parents through a report form or a parent journaling plan so educators can share something special each day about each child. All of these occasions provide opportunities to greet, welcome, and exchange information with parents but are inappropriate times to address a child's progress

or to bring up more substantial problems or issues that require focused attention and discussion. It is best for educators, families, and, ultimately, the child if these discussions are left for a planned phone conference or a scheduled parent conference.

Regularly scheduled parent conferences provide an opportunity for parents and educators to meet at a mutually agreed-upon time and place to discuss the child. It may take several scheduled conferences and unscheduled calls or casual contacts before an educator is successful in creating a totally relaxed environment in which both parent and educator can discuss the child comfortably. When a good relationship exists, the scheduled conference is a time when parents and educators can discuss the child's progress, present their concerns and their satisfaction about the child's progress, and develop a plan to follow both at home and at school that will help the child grow to full potential. In the interval between scheduled conferences, casual telephone calls and informal contacts at the program

Web-based portfolios allow families to review the child's day from the comfort of home using a variety of technology devices, including smartphones and tablets in addition to computers.

Photograph by Nicholas Dworsack

Transition times can provide a unique opportunity for informal but important conversations.

Making the Case for a *Comprehensive Communication System*

Highly effective directors understand the importance of a comprehensive system of communication. Communication strategies vary greatly from traditional paper fliers placed in children's mailboxes to Facebook notices and electronic portfolios. Families are often bombarded with information, so directors should be selective in what they send out and should be prepared to communicate *important* messages several times using different formats. Meeting the communication needs of families requires that directors are aware of the technologies available and the preferences of the families being served. Directors who are effective communicators develop a communication system that represents the formats preferred by families and often includes a combination of paper and digital platforms. It is important to ask families about their communication preferences and not make assumptions. Directors who assume that older parents will not use social media or that families in poverty will not have a computer so a digital portfolio is not an option will quickly learn that their assumptions are not accurate. For example, many families in poverty rely on smartphones as both phones and means of accessing the Internet. For them, text messages and digital portfolios may be the best means of communication, so always ask. In addition, communication should be both two-way and ongoing. Too often we talk "at" rather than "with" families. If families are valued as partners, then the time spent communicating "with" them needs to be more common, and one-way communication should be used sparingly.

are both ways to quickly comment and update how the plan for the child and the family is working.

Preconference planning sheets can be a useful tool in planning some parent conferences. Depending on the parent population being served, you as a director may have both the parents and the educators complete a preconference planning sheet (**Figure 13-1**). Those parents who may have limited writing or reading skills may feel uncomfortable filling out a form with open-ended questions like those in the sample. In cases like this, educators can call or chat with the parents when children are brought to the classroom. When dates and times are set in these casual conversations, it probably is wise for the educator to remind families when their scheduled conference time draws near. Experienced educators can plan the conference based on information from their notes and observations of the child, the information supplied by the family, and their knowledge of the characteristics of an effective parent conference. The director can model and provide some coaching for inexperienced staff before they conference with parents. Role-playing works well when coaching educators.

After the preconference planning sheet has been developed, it can be used as a basis for outlining the conference itself. Items on the conference outline might include the following:

- greeting and stating the plan for this conference;
- sharing a positive experience the child had within the past couple of days;

- asking parents how things are at home and actively listening to their responses;

Sample preconference planning sheet

Child's Name: _____

Parent(s) Name: _____

Date and Time of Conference: _____

Thank you for completing the Parent-Teacher conference survey. We have used the information that you provided to schedule your conference for the date and time shown above. Please call the office and reschedule if the assigned time is not convenient.

We look forward to talking with you about your child. Some of the things we will share with you are:

We are specifically interested in finding out about the areas of interest or concern that you would like to discuss with us. Please use the space below to list the topics that you would like us to be prepared to discuss.

Please return this to my box in the office at least a week before the scheduled conference.

Thank you very much.

FIGURE 13-1

TeachSource Digital Download

- showing work samples from the child's portfolio and discussing developmental expectations in various areas represented in the samples (e.g., art, writing);
- sharing anecdotes that will focus discussion on the child's strengths as well as on those areas for potential growth (e.g., math concepts, social interactions, self-help and independence, self-control);
- asking the parents to share what they would like to see happening for their child in the classroom during the ensuing months;
- developing a plan that will facilitate the child's progress toward the agreed-upon goals and expectations discussed during this conference; and
- closing with consensus on when the next conference should be held while making sure the door is left open for ongoing dialogue.

Parent conferences should always start and end on a positive note, and incidents or samples of work should be used to make specific points about the child's progress. Parents must be given time to express concerns while educators practice their best listening skills. During the conference, attention to differences in communication skills, beliefs, values, and childrearing practices, all of which reflect growing up in a particular region or culture, will shape the tone and direction of the conversation. Just as early childhood professionals build trust with children by listening to concerns and reflecting those feelings, so they build trust with parents by practicing those same listening skills. Putting parents at ease and avoiding arousing anxiety enhances the quality of the relationship during the conference and carries over to the daily interactions with parents as well.

Special conferences sometimes are necessary when either parents or educators have a need to discuss particular concerns about a child or the program. The special conferences are likely to produce anxiety for everyone because they are called most often when a problem arises. Sometimes, the director is asked to sit in on a special conference to give support to both teacher and the family and to help clarify what is being said and heard. The teacher may have a conference with the director prior to a particularly difficult parent conference so that they both clearly understand the problem to be discussed. The teacher also may ask the director to recommend the best way to present a problem and offer some suggestions on how to handle parents' questions and reactions during the conference. Sometimes, these special conferences include other specialists or consultants from other agencies, such as a mental health specialist or a speech and hearing professional. Both the teacher and the director should be well prepared for special conferences because they will be expected to make a knowledgeable contribution to the discussion about the child. In some cases, when outside specialists are called in, they will have to provide support for the parent, who may feel tense and threatened.

Uninterrupted time and a comfortable space are essential for successful parent conferences. Timing is important; the time of day or evening that is chosen must suit both the staff members and the family so that no one feels pressured or rushed. The time allotted must be long enough to discuss matters thoroughly, but not so long that the discussion becomes tedious. Consider allowing at least 30 minutes of uninterrupted conversation time for a conference. Usually, both parents are encouraged to attend conferences, but in cases of divorce or separation, teachers may be expected to arrange a separate conference with each parent. Both teachers and family members leave a successful conference feeling they have accomplished their goals. In addition, parents should go away with the awareness that their child is valued and appreciated. Finally, it is *critical* that parents have complete confidence that confidentiality will be maintained. The parent–teacher trust relationship will be seriously damaged if a parent learns from some outside source that shared information about the family or the child was not kept confidential.

A postconference review will help teachers evaluate the quality of their participation. It is especially important for the director to meet with inexperienced teachers after they have had a conference with a center family, even if the director participated in the conference planning or the conference itself. It is an excellent way to support new teachers and provides a time to encourage them to reflect on how they are feeling about the conference as well as what may help them in their subsequent interactions with the family. The following checklist will help them focus on their responses during the conference. Directors may want to review the following questions with their teachers after their encounters with parents:

- Did you give the parents plenty of time to talk about their concerns?

- Did you remain an accepting listener?
- Were you able to restrain yourself from giving advice? Did you ask rather than tell?
- Did you remember that suggestions usually are nothing more than advice under a different guise?
- Did the parents do most of the talking?
- Were you able to restate to the parent the feelings just expressed, always using your best active listening skills?
- Do you feel comfortable that the parent left feeling that you really cared?

13-1d • Family Support

In recent years, the field has moved away from the parent education model that tends to focus on deficits and toward a family support approach designed to build on their strengths and foster resiliency. One such effort is the *Strengthening Families* program developed by the Center for the Study of Social Policy (CSSP). This open-access program is research based and incorporates an approach to build five protective factors in families. Originally, the program was designed to "reduce the incidence of child abuse and neglect by providing parents with what they need to parent effectively, even under stress" (CSSP, n.d.). Note, however, that many of the strategies in this program have been useful for families who have not been identified as at risk. *Strengthening Families* has been adopted by many states as the framework for state-sponsored family support programs for young children and families.

One popular strategy from the Strengthening Families program is the Parent Café, which is an approach that has been used in many programs for young children nationally. The Parent Café concept brings families together to discuss topics they feel are important. This program capitalizes on the skills and strengths of families through a series of informal but structured small group conversations that are facilitated by trained parent leaders. The goal is to directly engage parents in building the protective factors needed to prevent maltreatment and promote healthy outcomes for their children.

The Center for the Study of Social Policy has learned that this approach is especially effective in engaging parents because of the following:

- The intimacy of the conversation and parent leadership help to create a level of candor that might not be achieved in a standard focus group or other feedback or input process.
- The careful structuring of the questions helps synthesize knowledge across a range of individual experience.
- Parents trained as cafe hosts feel that they have an area of expertise and skill base for other leadership roles (CSSP, n.d.).

Directors who seek to strengthen families look for opportunities to meet needs that are specific to the population they serve. For example, a program that serves many immigrant families may consider offering a program for English-language learners. Some programs provide vocational education programs or special remedial classes to help parents complete high school or take the general education development (GED) test. (A successful score on the GED leads to a high school equivalency certificate.) One program that served many busy professional families offered parent-support resources online and chose to moderate an ongoing blog in which parents could ask questions and participate in conversations from their home or office computer. Regardless of the format and content of the parent-support program, it must be built on mutual trust and strive to foster a reciprocal relationship with families.

Planning parent-support programs is the responsibility of the director, but the planning group should include parent and staff representatives. Format and content must reflect the needs and interests of the

Director's Corner

A group of parents came to me with a request for a workshop on parenting skills. We had held workshops like this in the past that were not very well attended and one that ended with several parents arguing about an approach that was recommended by one of our staff members. I have to say I was a little gun-shy about offering a workshop. We then learned about the "Parent Café" through our local child care resource and referral agency. Because the "Parent Café" was sponsored and facilitated by families, it was well attended. Parents talked about topics important to them, and a support network was created.

—*Director, suburban for-profit program*

parents and be adjusted to the level of education and previous training of the parent population. Programs that serve families from diverse educational, cultural, and socioeconomic backgrounds should present a wide variety of choices from which the parents can select programs that are best suited to their needs.

Activities in the parent-support program may be as informal as casual classroom observations followed by one-to-one or small-group discussions with a staff member or as formal as a planned lecture, workshop, panel discussion, or seminar. The planned activities should meet the parents' needs in terms of timing, content, and presentation strategy. Casual classroom observations are particularly helpful to parents who are curious about how their child's behavior compares with that of peers. For example, a mother who feels great concern about the explosive yelling and unacceptable language of her preschool son may feel reassured when she observes other 4-year-olds who also are noisy and explosive. It is then helpful for that mother to discuss these erratic outbursts with the director or a staff member who can interpret the behavior in terms of expected behaviors at this developmental stage. Group discussions, lectures, films, videotapes, DVDs, or workshops that are offered by program staff members or by outside consultants can be useful tools for providing parents with information on parenting, child development, or topics related to parental problems and concerns. Including a social time along with information sharing creates a nonthreatening and relaxed learning atmosphere.

Topics of interest and concern to parents range from specific questions like, "What do I do about my child who awakens at 4:30 a.m. every day and wants to get up?" to broader issues facing employed parents who struggle with the stresses of job, home, and family. Programs should build on family strengths that increase parents' sense of expertise. In planning parent-support programs, consider emphasis on empowering parents to explore ways to cope with their concerns and issues around parenting.

Directors are responsible for ensuring that parent-support programs and parent meetings are both timely and responsive to the parents' interests and concerns.

Parent meetings usually are considered part of the total parent-support program. The frequency of scheduled parent meetings varies widely from program to program. Some programs offer monthly meetings, whereas others have as few as one or two meetings a year. The first meeting of the year for a preschool on the typical public school calendar often is devoted to introducing the staff and taking parents through a typical day at school by using slides, videos, DVDs, or classroom visits. The format for all parent meetings should include time for questions and informal socialization. Regular parent meetings are a good way to create a parent-support group that can be mobilized to act as a strong political force when threats to early childhood programs arise in your community.

Low parent turnout is a chronic issue and is often discouraging for program directors and staff who plan for parent visits to the classroom, prepare refreshments, and look forward to meeting and sharing with parents. It requires creative planning, taking time to determine the best timing for meetings, and exploring what might interest this particular population of parents. Maybe they want to learn about using the Internet or have a tasting party of Thai foods. Shifting from an exclusive focus on parenting sometimes can encourage more families to attend program functions. As program gatherings become popular, parents may begin to ask for more meetings that focus on parenting issues or child development.

13-1e • Engaging Parents

Parent conferences and parent-support programs are, indeed, parent engagement, but the parent involvement concept implies a more extensive parental commitment than participation in parent conferences or in selected parts of the parent education program. Although parents should be encouraged to become involved, they also should have the option to remain uninvolved. It is an imposition on the parents' right to choose if they are made to feel that they must become involved in the program. Of course, if the program is a co-op, then by definition it requires full parent participation.

The NAEYC has incorporated family and community culture as an important influence in designing quality and developmentally appropriate practice for young children (National Association for the Education of Young Children, 2020). One purpose of parent involvement is to get parents active in planning, implementing, and evaluating the total program. In some comprehensive early childhood programs such as Head Start, parents may serve on advisory and policy boards, participate in all aspects of program planning and classroom activity, take part in the evaluation of staff and program, participate in budget and personnel decisions, and come to understand their role as advocates for their children.

Parents sometimes enjoy working regularly in the classroom or helping with children's parties or field trips, and some programs depend on the help that parents can provide. Before parents participate in any aspect of the children's program, they should know something about classroom ground rules, routines, and what to expect of the children. The mother who comes to read to the children may need help on how to include children other than her own in a small, informal, shared reading experience. The father who takes a morning off to come and read to the children may be disappointed when only three or four children are interested enough to stay for more than one book. He must be helped to understand that children have choices and that they are free to choose not to participate. It also is helpful if he knows the ground rules about deciding who chooses books to be read and techniques for helping children wait to have their choice read. Parents who work in the classroom on a regular basis should be expected to participate in a more extensive orientation program before being assigned specific tasks when they come to the program. Both parents and volunteers can attend the same orientation sessions.

There are innumerable ways for parents to be involved in the program other than direct classroom participation. They can do clerical work, repair or make equipment, take responsibility for the lending library, babysit during conference periods or committee meetings, drive carpools, and participate in advocacy endeavors with help from staff. If they have special talents or interests in fundraising, they can serve as a resource for the program board or the director. If they have special language skills, they can provide priceless service in bilingual programs. There also are many opportunities for parents to serve in a variety of ways on the board, on advisory committees, or on any number of standing or ad hoc committees. (See Chapter 4 for the discussion of the composition of the program board and of the committee structure.)

Clearly, when the director is committed to parent involvement and that attitude prevails throughout the program, it is possible to find a special place for every parent to participate, provided the parent has the time

Parent volunteers can inspire children to look at an existing activity as new and novel.

and interest to become involved. However, the director must be sensitive to individual family situations. Employed parents who are unable to be involved with program activities must be reassured that they are free to choose not to participate. Successful parent involvement does require some management; therefore, the program staff must make a commitment to give that program the time and attention it requires.

13-1f • Working with Demanding Parents

The best programs work to empower parents. Administrators and educators develop partnerships over time with parents who gradually come to feel they are valued participants in their child's care at the program. There always will be angry parents and some so-called high-maintenance parents who will challenge the staff. Staff members will have to remember and practice their best communication, conflict-resolution, and problem-solving skills when faced with these parents.

There are situations in which staff feelings and perceptions work against forming partnerships with parents. Parents can become "they" when these staff members get together for staff meetings. "They don't tell us what is happening at home." "They don't follow through at home." "They don't set any limits at home." Or "They are too restrictive at home." Staff might comment, "They don't care" when referring to a parent who seems to have no interest in discussing child-related issues. On the other side of that coin, a staff member may comment, "She will not leave me alone—she questions me about everything he did or said while he was here at school and wants to know exactly what I did in response to his actions." Helping staff value diversity in family lifestyles and attitudes, as well as how various parents choose to communicate or not communicate with staff about their concerns, is something directors can discuss at staff meetings and staff retreats and model in their interactions with families (adapted from Greenman, 2003). It is helpful if staff can manage to view parents as partners and find ways to see situations from the parents' point of view.

Sooner or later, every program will have to deal with angry or high-maintenance and demanding parents. Directors can encourage all staff to make encounters and exchanges with these and other parents as customer friendly as possible. Early childhood program staff may not view families and children as customers, but a review of what customers are may clarify for everyone that the program's clients are its customers.

- Customers are people who buy products or services from you.
- Customers are not dependent on you; you are dependent on them.
- Customers are not interruptions to your work; they are the purpose of your work.
- Customers are not people you argue with; they are people you value and serve. (Adapted from Phipps, 2003)

Directors and all program staff are obliged to work on building positive relationships with children and program families (customers). When confronted with the angry parent's tirade or the needy high-maintenance parent's demands on their time, it is an opportunity for program staff to make effective

conflict resolution part of their customer service plan strategies (see **Figure 13-2**). Customer interests and needs must be dealt with in a helpful and respectful manner, even when they are extreme and unrealistic in terms of program policy or developmentally best practices or violate privacy and confidentiality rights of the director, educators, or families.

Responses to parent demands will depend on the nature of the concern and availability of resources to meet those demands. Many demands will be best served by talking with the parents, inviting them to observe or encouraging them to attend parent meetings that focus on topics such as child development, early childhood practice, or program policies regarding transitions, fees and admissions, referrals, and so forth. Parents who demand that toddler educators use whatever procedures necessary to toilet train their child or insist the "biter" in the classroom be removed from the program may respond to reading materials about toddler development or a discussion group with other toddler families after discussing the issue with the director. Preschool parents who insist that their child be taught the alphabet through drill and practice or finish all the food on the plate before leaving the table may need to better understand program curriculum and be willing to look over a copy of the program's curriculum framework and discuss it with the director or attend a meeting with other preschool parents to hear the staff talk about best practices for this age group. When there are issues regarding meals, a parent might be interested in observing mealtime in one of the preschool classrooms followed by a conversation with the director and the educator about developmental expectations that relate to eating and appetite for this age group. Working with demanding parents is time-consuming and difficult but essential for program morale, program community building, and letting families know that their needs and concerns are taken seriously and will be heard.

13-1g • Parent Feedback

Parents' viewpoints and suggestions can be solicited with rating scales or questionnaires. Some method of gathering evidence about family satisfaction with the parent program or with parental involvement opportunities should be done annually. The information gathered is then summarized and evaluated

Sample conflict-resolution policy in a parent handbook

Conflict Resolution Policy: Conflict between Adults

While every effort is made to meet the needs of children, parents, and staff, we realize that from time to time a conflict may occur between parents, staff, and administrators. The following process is followed should a conflict occur:

- Step One—A respectful discussion is held between the persons directly involved at a time and place that ensures privacy and sufficient time for a thorough resolution to take place.

- Step Two—If resolution is not found at the first meeting, a second meeting is held with the director for the purpose of creating a plan for resolution and a timeline for expected success.

- Step Three—If the conflict is not resolved according to the timeline, adjustments may be made to the plan, and an additional timeline be established, or:

- Step Four—If at any time the director determines that resolution is not possible, she or he will consider one of the following for immediate action:

1. Removal of the child from the classroom
2. Withdrawal of services from the program
3. Suspension of the staff member until disciplinary steps can be taken
4. Involvement of the Assistant Dean of the School of Education and Health Science

- Grounds for determining that a resolution is not possible include but are not exclusive of the following:

1. Any person involved displays inappropriate behavior such as shouting, accusing, name-calling, swearing, or physical assault.
2. Any person involved refuses to follow the prescribed process.
3. Any person involved jeopardizes the process by spreading information concerning the conflict to those outside the immediate conflict or those involved in the resolution of the process.

FIGURE 13-2

Source: Reprinted with permission from the Bombeck Family Learning Center of the University of Dayton.

so adjustments can be made to best meet parents' needs. Much information can also be gleaned from parent–educator conferences when educators can make family-specific inquiries such as "Are your needs for information on Alley's daily experiences and interests being met?" or "How would you prefer we communicate during your maternity leave about how Ben is handling the arrival of the new baby?" However, written evaluations or rating scales that draw attention to particular features of the total parent program, like the daily reports that are prepared for parents or the specialists brought in to discuss issues relevant to kindergarten readiness or infant "tummy time," offer respondents time to ponder and reflect on the attention given to the program. As families have time to consider what is offered, they will not only realize the breadth and depth of the parent program but also may choose to communicate ideas about how it might be improved. Directors must continue to let parents know that they are eager to hear from them and to partner with them to provide the best possible experiences for all members of the program community.

Director's Corner

I realize now that I really have to keep in touch with what parents are thinking about our program and how they see us. Last year we had two or three families leave our program, and I wasn't really sure why they were making a move. When I contacted several of them, I realized they were feeling that the quality of our program was not what they had come to expect from us. Of course, I acted on that immediately, but I also developed a rating scale for parents to complete so they could let us know how we're doing.

—*Director, suburban for-profit program*

13-2 • Written Communication Materials for Families

A handbook for families is a convenient way to communicate basic program information and should be distributed to all families at some point in the enrollment procedure. The contents may change from year to year and vary from program to program, so directors will have to use some general guidelines for developing a handbook and then adapt those to their specific program. Some items, such as program philosophy or grouping children, may or may not be part of the marketing brochure but could be repeated in the handbook. As a director, you will have to decide what information parents need to know and the best way to convey it to them. If a handbook seems too overwhelming for the particular parent population in your program, consider putting an item or two on colorful single sheets to be handed out over a period of several weeks after admission to the program.

The suggested list of items that follows is not exhaustive but provides broad guidelines for developing a parent handbook (see sample handbook for families in **Director's Resource 13-1**). Directors often choose to avoid including items likely to change such as names of staff and fees. One option is to have a pocket in the back cover where single pages can be added and removed as updates are needed.

Suggested items for a parent handbook include the following:

- brief statement of the program philosophy;
- outline of the daily program and an explanation of how it fits into the program philosophy;
- fees and arrangements for payment, including details about reimbursement possibilities and credit for absences;
- car pool or transportation arrangements; if transportation is not provided, indicate that fact and state what information you need to have about the family's transportation arrangements for the child;
- expected arrival and pickup times and procedures;
- program policy on health and safety precautions to be taken by the family and the program staff to ensure the health and safety of children; state your policy about bringing medication to the program and children coming to the program when symptoms of illness are apparent, cover the procedures used by the program staff when a child becomes ill at school, and so on;
- explanation of liability and medical insurance carried by or available through the program;
- sample menus for snacks or meals and any expectations the staff may have about eating;

- services the program staff will offer to children and families, such as opportunities for having conferences, special medical or psychological services or referrals, discussion groups, group meetings, and so on;
- program discipline policy;
- requests for help from parents such as for time spent in the classroom, help on field trips, clerical help, making materials for the classroom, and so on;
- summary of scheduled events at the program and what families may do at the program to celebrate holidays and birthdays; make the policies in this regard reflect the program philosophy by including what to send, what to expect the child to bring home, which holidays will be celebrated, and so on;
- expectations about the child's use of transition objects while getting adjusted to the program and policies about bringing other items or food from home, making clear how these policies are developed to meet the needs of children and to reflect the program philosophy; and
- a description of the legal obligations of program staff to report any evidence of child abuse.

This list provides guidelines for developing a handbook that ultimately must be fashioned to fit your program and your parent population. In writing material for a handbook, consider content, format, length, and, most important, style of writing. Should the style be scholarly or chatty, formal or informal, general or detailed? Answers to these questions can be found by giving careful consideration to the families being served by the program.

The family handbook is a useful tool to acquaint parents with the program initially and to help them understand what to expect. However, it must be supplemented with other written and verbal communications to keep them abreast of program events and the progress of their children. Other details concerning your program can be listed on your website. In some communities, it will be necessary to publish not only the handbook but also all written materials in another language in addition to English.

Some directors send parents a newsletter describing special events that are being planned for children or families. Although the traditional paper newsletter is still used by some directors, many have moved newsletter content to closed Facebook groups, a password-protected section of the program or classroom website or email blasts. Using digital tools allows directors to send smaller bits of information in a manner that today's digital native families are most likely to read.

The culture of the program must be considered. To what degree do families view themselves as part of the classroom community? Although children are often aware of the important life events of their classmates, efforts to make connections between home and school are encouraged. Ask families about their preference for information that is shared about them and also what they want to receive. It may be important for most families to know that one family brought its new baby to visit the classroom or that a musician from a symphony orchestra came to show the children a slide trombone, but others may have limits on the information they wish to share. Make sure families know that information about what is happening at school will help them understand a child's questions and any ideas that are expressed at home. Social media, website updates, email blasts, and newsletters can keep parents informed about the program's progress, program philosophy, special programs, and future plans. They can include a monthly calendar, information about fundraisers, updates on staff changes, and activities. Including a profile of a staff person, another parent, or a program volunteer is a sure way to generate readership and enthusiasm about your communications. Other ways to communicate with families include meetings, regularly scheduled parent conferences, and telephone calls to tell parents about happy experiences their children had at school. Program staff must take advantage of every opportunity to communicate with the family to learn more about them and their child, to share ideas about the child, and to strengthen the basic trust in the relationship.

13-3 • Volunteer Program

Volunteers are welcomed in most early childhood education programs, and the volunteer program usually is managed by the program director. Occasionally, someone else—a member of the program staff other than the director or a volunteer who is willing to undertake the coordinating responsibilities—will manage the volunteer activities. The coordinating function includes recruiting, orienting, and scheduling the volunteers. Other aspects of the volunteer program such as planning activities for the volunteers and handling the supervision and record-keeping responsibilities connected with a volunteer program, either must be delegated or performed by the director. Volunteers are often interested in ways to advocate for children.

13-3a • Volunteer Recruitment

Recruiting volunteers is time-consuming, but there are individuals in every community who are potential volunteers. Finding those people who have both the time and the interest in serving an early childhood program may present a problem at the outset; however, a program that provides both challenge and appropriate incentives soon will build up a roster of available volunteers who come regularly.

Available sources for recruiting volunteers will vary, depending on the size of the community and the demands of other agencies in the community. Larger cities have organized volunteer bureaus, Junior Leagues, universities with student volunteer programs, child advocacy groups, and any number of philanthropic groups that can supply volunteers. Church groups, high schools, senior citizen groups, and business groups are other sources that can be found and approached in both large urban communities and small rural areas. The volunteers must feel that they are welcome and needed; in addition, they must feel a sense of personal regard for their efforts.

After volunteers are recruited, screening them is essential to the success of the program. Meeting with each one personally will enable the director or volunteer coordinator to find a good fit between the volunteer's interests and abilities and program needs. Volunteers must understand that they will be supervised by the volunteer coordinator, who will apply essentially the same principles of supervision that are used for regular staff.

13-3b • Volunteer Orientation

Participation in the volunteer orientation program should be a requirement for every person who chooses to give time to the program. Although it may seem presumptuous to insist that volunteers participate in an orientation, it is essential that they become

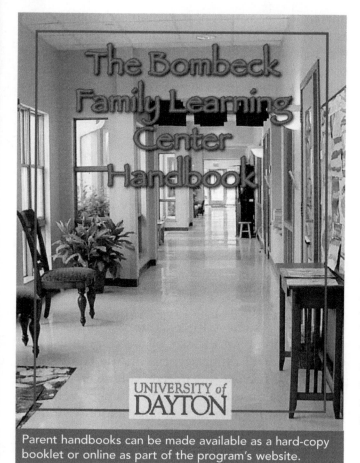

Parent handbooks can be made available as a hard-copy booklet or online as part of the program's website.

surance requirements. When the rationale for that ruling is understood, volunteers are less likely to be offended when told they may not take the children on a walk or drive them the few blocks to the park.

Confidentiality is an issue for everyone at the program, including the volunteers. It is wonderful to have volunteers who become ambassadors for the program in the community, but it is essential that they adhere to a strict policy of absolute confidentiality. Volunteers who share their general enthusiasm about working with the children or doing other work for the program can be a great asset, but talking about specific children, families, or educators can be extremely damaging to your program.

Other details that should be covered at the orientation meeting include sign-in and sign-out procedures for volunteers, and where they should call if they expect to be absent. Record keeping is necessary because many publicly funded programs must report volunteer hours, and some private agencies often choose to keep records and reward volunteers based on their hours of service. Evidence of a strong commitment to a program by volunteers is useful when applying for grant money.

completely familiar with the operation of the program and clearly understand how their services fit into the total service offered by the program. Furthermore, the volunteers usually recognize that a program staff person who will take the time to plan and carry through a meaningful and helpful orientation program for them also will value their involvement in the program.

Orientation meetings should provide volunteers with a staff directory and introduction to as many staff members as possible. The director should talk about the agency's organizational structure, the program's goals and objectives, and volunteers' importance in meeting those goals and objectives. Further, licensing standards and health requirements for volunteers must be explained. That will clarify what is expected of them regarding immunizations, health examination, and classroom health and safety procedures, as well as help them understand the rationale for restrictions on their participation. For example, in most places, a volunteer may not be alone at any time with a group of children because of licensing and in-

13-3c • Volunteer Activities

Volunteers can do most things that family members do in a program, and they often have more free time than working parents or parents with

Volunteers are sometimes asked to participate in setting up classroom activities.

Appendix F). Through these memberships, directors can accomplish several goals.

First, directors can obtain information and make contacts that may be personally and professionally helpful. Therefore, they may select organizations that focus on development of administrative skills, presentation of research data, and provision of information about legislation and funding. Through contacts at group meetings, the director may meet potential staff members, although "pirating" staff from other programs certainly should be avoided. Directors also may see professional organizations as providing a forum for their ideas, a place where they can speak before a group and discuss their concerns with other professionals. They may volunteer to hold meetings at their programs, thereby providing opportunities for others in the field to see different early childhood education facilities.

When directors join a professional organization, the organization is enhanced because the directors have had several years of education and experience and carry some influence in the community. As a result of their having belonged to these organizations or similar groups for a time, they have expertise that can help move the group forward, and they can give guidance to newer, less experienced members.

Directors may join professional organizations to become part of a group that effects change. The professional groups offer many advocacy opportunities. Legislators who will not listen to an individual's recommendations on educator-to-child ratios or low-wage issues may be persuaded by an organization's stand, and directors can have input through their membership in the organization.

In some communities, directors form support groups because they need a forum to discuss problems unique to their particular positions. They can share information and ideas and work out cooperative plans for staff training. With the increased widespread focus on early childhood program, national support groups are forming to provide hotlines, websites, consultation services, and management retreats.

When they join organizations, directors serve as models for staff members. In some cases, the staff profits more directly from the organization than the director, but staff members put off joining or may even be hesitant about attending meetings if they do not know other members. Directors can provide an incentive by offering to accompany educators to the

---

Growth Mindset Moment

Think about your own volunteer activities. Perhaps you tutor younger students or work in a program for children with disabilities. What motivates you to be there at the scheduled time? Do you look for excuses not to go? If not, why not? How do you feel about yourself after you spend time volunteering? What rewards do you receive?

---

young families. Like parents, volunteers must be made to feel welcome; also like parents, they must leave with a sense of satisfaction and a feeling that their services are needed and appreciated. Because they do not have the reward of seeing the joy their own children experience by having them participate in the program, it is doubly important for the program staff to make them feel welcome, define their tasks for them, and let them know how highly their services are regarded. Volunteers will continue to serve only in situations in which they feel needed.

13-4 • Organizations and Agencies

In addition to working with parents and volunteers, the director is responsible for involvement with professional organizations, referral agencies, and the community in which the program is located. In each case, the amount of time and degree of involvement vary according to the type of program and the director's individual style. Involvement in professional organizations and community outreach are both addressed in NAEYC Accreditation Standards and the Program Assessment Scale.

13-4a • Professional Organizations

Directors frequently join one or more local, regional, and national professional organizations. Sometimes, the board encourages and assists them by paying their dues (a list of professional organizations is presented in first meeting and by notifying staff members of up-coming meetings. Directors may work out a plan for released time from program duties that staff members can use to participate in the work of professional organizations. They also may provide staff meeting time for members who have attended sessions to share their information.

For similar reasons, directors should attend (and facilitate staff members' attending) lectures, courses, and conferences that are related to early childhood education. Directors also have the responsibility for reading current books, periodicals, and resources on the Internet and passing relevant materials on to staff members. Most staff members will respond positively to an article from the director that is marked to indicate a personal application such as, "This article addresses an interest of yours, new ways of teaching math concepts." Or, "Have you seen the reviews of these new multicultural books? Which ones should we order?" This personal touch encourages the staff member to read the article and perhaps discuss it further with the director. When the director has provided a model of this behavior, staff members may begin to circulate articles or books that they have found to be worthwhile.

13-4b • Referral Agencies

Directors contact referral agencies and advise staff members to use special services when that is appropriate. Directors also help staff members delineate the boundaries of their own professional expertise and recognize those circumstances under which an opinion obtained from another type of professional could be useful.

The job of relating to referral agencies begins with the collection of a list of services that are available in the surrounding community. In some areas, a booklet is published that contains the names of all the social service agencies, their addresses, telephone numbers, fax numbers, websites, hours, charges, what services are provided and to whom, and whether a referral from a physician or case worker is required. Some communities add other kinds of information, such as lists of recreation programs, churches, schools, and government agencies and officials. If this type of directory is not available, a program director can develop a referral list. Writing the data on file cards or

putting the information into a computer file provides a convenient reference that can be updated easily.

After determining which agencies provide services related to the clients' needs, directors should attempt to make personal contact with as many of these agencies as possible. This contact can be accomplished by visiting the agency, attending programs sponsored by the agency, and meeting its staff members at professional meetings. Later, when the need arises for services from such an organization, it will be easier for the director to make contacts with the people whom he already knows. The director also is in a good position to explain the nature of the services provided by these agencies to the program staff and to parents when necessary.

In addition to working with the staff in referring children and families for care and treatment, directors use agencies in other ways. For example, agencies usually have personnel and material resources available for in-service training or parent meetings. Some agencies in the community, such as community coordinated early childhood programs or early childhood program resource and referral agencies, provide consultation and technical assistance. A range of services may be available from other types of agencies such as the public library, which usually offers storytellers, films, and educators' collections of books.

If the program includes the provision of medical, dental, and mental health services to children, the director may be able to provide these services at low cost and with convenient scheduling through agency

Director's Corner

When I first became a director, one of the things I learned about was the whole referral. You have to know the agencies, how they work, and the particular people to contact before you can help your teachers or your families with referrals. I always feel better when I can call a specific person whom I have already met. In addition to growing my network over time, I started with two key resources available in most counties—our referral hotline that could direct me to services across a variety of needs and our Child Care Resource and Referral agency, which was a one-stop shop for information related to young children, families, and early childhood program services.

—*Director, YMCA-sponsored center*

contacts. For example, arrangements can be made for a physician to come to the program to do routine physical checkups so that children do not have to endure long trips, boring waiting rooms, and strange, frightening buildings. The director, who is well acquainted with physicians, psychologists, speech therapists, and social workers, is able to depend on their services but is sensitive to the needs and limitations under which they operate. It is important that directors establish reciprocal relationships with these professionals by being open to accepting children referred to the program by them and their agencies.

13-5 • Community Involvement

The director explains the program to the community and the community to the staff. This function requires familiarity with the community in which the program is located. If some or all of the children who attend the program live in other communities, then the director should become informed about those areas as well.

In marketing and publicizing the program to the community, the director uses public relations and communications techniques that were covered in Chapter 10, including news releases, open houses, and tours of the program. The effective use of the interpersonal skills that were discussed in Chapter 8 is particularly appropriate when working with the community. The appearance and maintenance of the program's building and grounds also can have an influence on the relationship with the community.

Sometimes, individual members of the community become interested in the program and its work through the director's efforts. For example, the owner of a lumberyard may agree to provide scrap lumber for the children's woodworking projects, or a printer will offer to save all the paper ends from print jobs for the children's use. If the director and staff have met the local grocer and other shopkeepers, these businesspeople may be far more responsive to the children when they visit on field trips or when they walk by as they explore the area with classmates. A university in the area may be interested in sending architecture or product design students or they may come to do research. In addition, child advocacy groups in the community may offer information and support to program staff and families.

Directors help their staff members understand the community by encouraging involvement in community activity and by providing information about life in the community. Having knowledge of the historical background of the area and the cultural or ethnic groups that live there will increase staff awareness of the needs of families who come to the program. The director is responsible for making program staff members sensitive to the customs, language, and values of the people they serve. Frequently, staff members live in other communities and represent different cultural or ethnic groups. It is impossible for staff members to work effectively with children and parents from a culture about which they have no knowledge.

When the director has done a good job of understanding the community and when all the pertinent information is conveyed to the staff, everyone at the program gains a greater appreciation of the community, and a strong working relationship can emerge. The program's team of staff, parents, and children working together can be expanded to incorporate community members as well.

Summary

The director works with or is accountable for establishing a reciprocal relationship with families. A major aspect of this role is helping staff members establish effective relationships with parents. Attention needs to be paid to family interactions, family support, and family involvement. The director needs to emphasize the participation of individual parents to the degree that is appropriate and comfortable for them. Directors also are involved in recruiting and orienting volunteers and in providing recognition for their services. In addition, they work closely with professional organizations, referral agencies, and members of the community. Part of their role involves setting an example of an appropriate amount of professional involvement for staff members and training them in the techniques of working with a variety of resources. Directors also provide information to staff members and give them opportunities to make use of the services that professional organizations, referral agencies, and the community have to offer. To be able to collaborate with families, volunteers, and the community, directors must do the following:

- identify strategies that support and engage families,

- list items to be included in written communication for families,

- describe the components of an effective volunteer program,

- identify local, state, and national professional organizations that can support professional growth, and

- explain why community involvement is important to early childhood programs

TRY IT OUT!

1. Consider an early childhood program where you work or had a practicum experience. Use **Director's Resource 13-1** to evaluate the components of the communication system being used in this program. Start the evaluation by reading the principles and strategies listed in column II and evaluate the current level of performance using the following ratings:

   N = not yet addressed,
   E = emerging, or
   P = proficient.

   From the list of principles and strategies that were rated "not yet addressed" or "emerging," select a target for improvement, and complete the action plan.

2. Divide into groups of three for the purpose of role-playing a parent conference. In this situation, a young mother has requested a conference about her 3-year-old son who spends a great deal of time in the housekeeping area in the classroom. He also plays with dolls, washes dishes, and dresses up in a skirt and high heels at home. The father is extremely upset and annoyed by this behavior and has pressured the mother into calling for a conference. The father is unable to attend the conference. The roles are as follows:

   - male teacher,
   - mother, and
   - female director.

   Using the checklist shown in **Director's Resource 13-2**, discuss each item listed. If you were the director or the mother in the role-play, give your perception of how well the educator handled the questions asked.

3. Using the Volunteer Tasks Form in **Director's Resource 13-3**, develop a list of specific tasks a volunteer could do in the specified classroom areas.

Director's Resource 13-1

FAMILY ENGAGEMENT SYSTEM SELF-EVALUATION

Person/s completing this form: _____ Date: _____

Strong family engagement emerges from an intentionally developed system that engages families in meaningful ways. While a system may include activities, experiences and programs, effective family engagement is broader and more inclusive than models that view family engagement as an event. This tool is designed to assist professionals as they develop and facilitate family engagement systems and strive to reflect research based practice. This tool can be used to communicate these practices to others who may not be familiar with the research on family engagement. The process of self-evaluation starts by asking the user to read the principles and strategies listed in column II and evaluate the current level of performance using the rankings provided below (N = not yet addressed. E = emerging. P = proficient). Then, from the list of selected principles and strategies, users select a target for improvement and complete the Action Plan. Those interested in learning more about effective family engagement systems should visit the Family Engagement Collaborative of the Miami Valley at www.familyengagementcollaborative.com.

NOTES

1. For the purposes in this document, "culture" is broadly defined and refers to family characteristics related to ethnicity, heritage or history, race. religion, socio economic status, education level, sexual orientation, region of origin, language and communication style, family configuration, and other factors that comprise aspects of the family's identity.

2. SOA refers to school, organization, or agency

Program **Current Level** Rankings N = not yet addressed. E = emerging. P = proficient

1. Program Current Level	II. Principles and Strategies	III. Examples of Practice That Support the Principles and Strategies	Priorities
	A. Effective family engagement programs build relationships between the school, organization, or agency (SOA) and families.		
	1. **Establish and maintain partnerships** between the family, educators, and SOAs that reflect the belief that families, educators, administrators, and community members jointly share responsibility for school readiness and success.	▪ Programs are generally interactive with opportunities for all parties to contribute to the agenda and participate in programming. ▪ Information is communicated respectfully in a manner that shows regard for the contributions of both families and SOAs to support children as they learn and develop.	
	2. **Establish a family engagement** team that includes families and representative members of SOAs to design, implement, and monitor the family engagement plan.	▪ SOAs include families from the very beginning of the design process. ▪ SOAs include families in the design, implementation, and evaluation of the family engagement plan in meaningful ways.	
	3. **Conduct a family survey** to learn about how the family engagement system can meet the needs of families.	▪ SOAs get family input in the design of the survey. ▪ The survey utilizes family friendly language. ▪ The survey garners valuable information without being intrusive.	
	4. **Use data about families** to plan, implement, and reevaluate a comprehensive family engagement program.	▪ The program reflects the data collected from families through the survey. ▪ Data is collected from families and reevaluated on an ongoing basis.	
	5. **Incorporate many roles** for the SOAs including but not limited to that of facilitator, co-trainer, learner, advisor, host, cook, convener, advocate, business broker, cultural interpreter, instructional leader and others as appropriate.	▪ SOAs are not limited by the traditional view of professional roles. ▪ SOAs acquire new knowledge, develop new skills, and expand their roles to meet the needs of families.	

Director's Resource 13-1 *(continued)* ////

1. Program Current Level	II. Principles and Strategies	III. Examples of Practice That Support the Principles and Strategies	Priorities
	B. Effective family engagement programs appropriately meet the needs of families and children.		
	1. **Empower families by focusing on strengths** and avoiding a deficit model.	▪ SOAs demonstrate a broad understanding of the complexities of family life and seek out and support areas of strength. ▪ SOAs avoid assigning blame and seek out strategies to support families toward success. ▪ SOAs avoid expert–novice role assignments in which the role of the SOA is that of expert while families are uninformed novices. Instead, use information-sharing models that value strengths.	
	2. **Address children and families' basic needs** before higher learning skills.	▪ Programs attend to physical needs such as food and comfort. Efforts are made to make children and families feel welcome and safe.	
	3. **Recognize that many factors act together** to influence the development of a child.	▪ Programs balance the needs of SOAs to communicate information, policies, and procedures with the needs of families to be engaged in meaningful ways. ▪ Programs are both relationship and task oriented.	
	4. **Provide information about community resources** available to support families and educators.	▪ Community resources are shared through a variety of mediums (print, web-based, verbally). ▪ Where and how to find resources is communicated effectively overtime. ▪ The resources provided are up-to-date with working links and accurate contact information.	

	5. **Incorporate the six protective factors** associated with strengthening families as described by the Child Welfare Information Gateway (U.S. Department of Health & Human Services) https://www.childwelfare.gov/	▪ The program fosters and addresses the importance of the following factors:
		  1. nurturing and attachment
		  2. knowledge of parenting and child development
		  3. parental resilience
		  4. social connections
		  5. concrete supports for parents
		  6. social and emotional competence of children.	

	C. Effective family engagement programs establish a comprehensive system of communication.		
	1. **Work with families to create a clear mission statement** for family engagement systems in order to establish, communicate, and accomplish goals.	▪ Families are actively engaged in creating a clear mission statement. ▪ The goals for the family engagement program are clearly stated and regularly communicated.	
	2. **Include a two-way home and SOA's communication system** consisting of multiple opportunities for families to receive and provide information orally, in writing, or through the use of technology.	▪ Information is communicated multiple times using a variety of communication vehicles both formal and informal. ▪ Vehicles for communication utilize new media (Facebook, Pinterest, Tumblr) when appropriate and reflect how families access information.	

1. Program Current Level	II. Principles and Strategies	III. Examples of Practice That Support the Principles and Strategies	Priorities
	3. **Include both formal and informal meetings or home visits** with families in which both SOAs and families can contribute to the agenda.	▪ SOAs plan opportunities for informal interaction with families. ▪ SOAs schedule formal meetings or conferences during which families can participate and contribute to the agenda.	
	D. Effective family engagement programs embrace and respect the cultural background of all families.		
	1. **Include activities that have a clear cultural connection** to the community and the participants.	▪ Family engagement activities respect and, when appropriate, celebrate the traditions and culture of families.	
	2. **Involve SOA facilitators who are familiar with the culture** of the school and community.	▪ In addition to obvious cultural traditions, the family engagement system reflects an understanding of subtle cultural tendencies. ▪ SOA facilitators make use of culture guides who interpret and provide access to culture understandings of the families.	

Family Engagement System Continuous Improvement

Action Plan

Select a strategy or strategies from column II (principles and strategies) as a target goal or goals for improvement. Develop a plan of action including the activities, timeline, and persons responsible for completing all aspects of the plan. Activities should be observable and measurable and evaluated regularly.

Targets for Improvement	Activities	Timeline	Persons Responsible	Check When Complete
State in observable, measurable terms	Observable and measurable tasks that relate directly to target goals	Start and end dates		
Principle or strategy: Goal(s):				
Principle or strategy: Goal(s):				

Source: Reprinted with permission from Adams (2014).

Director's Resource 13-2 ////

ROLE-PLAY CHECKLIST

(for use with Try It Out! 13-2)

After the role-play is completed, discuss the items in this checklist. If your role was that of a director or parent, respond to the questions in terms of your perception of how well the educator handled the conference. You are expected to give more than yes or no answers. Document your answers with examples from the conference.

Did you give the parent time to talk about her concerns?

Were you a receptive listener?

When you made comments, did you talk in terms of the parent's feelings?

Were you able to restrain yourself from giving advice?

Did the parent do most of the talking?

What was accomplished during the conference?

Director's Resource 13-3 ////

VOLUNTEER TASKS FORM

(for use with Try It Out! 13-3)

List specific tasks a volunteer could be assigned to do in each of the classroom areas or activities listed below. Think beyond supervising children. Consider care and development of materials, enriching the area, or making it more aesthetically pleasing.

Dramatic play (expand beyond house-type play)

Carpentry

Literature or library area

Writing center

Lunchtime

Nap time

REFERENCES

Adams, S. M. (2014). *Family engagement system self-evaluation.* Dayton, OH: Family Engagement Collaborative of the Miami Valley. http://www.familyengagementcollaborative.com/family-engagement-system-self-evaluation.html

Burt, T., & Lesser, L. K. (2016). Lesbian, gay, bisexual, transgender (LGBT) families: Tools for directors in supporting staff discussion dealing with fears. In *The art of leadership: Engaging families in early childhood organizations.* Redmond, WA: Exchange Press.

Center for the Study of Social Policy (CSSP). (n.d.). *Strengthening families: A protection factors framework.* New York, NY: Author. http://www.cssp.org/reform/strengthening-families

Freeman, N. K., Decker, C. A., & Decker, J. R. (2012). *Planning and administering early childhood programs* (10th ed.). Upper Saddle River, NJ: Prentice Hall.

Galinsky, E. (1984, July). How to work with working parents. *Child Care Information Exchange,* 1–4.

Gestwicki, C. (2013). *Home, school & community relations* (7th ed.). Belmont, CA: Cengage Wadsworth.

Gonzallez-Mena, J. (2016). Dialogue to understanding across cultures. In *The art of leadership: Engaging families in early childhood organizations.* Redmond, WA: Exchange Press.

Gordon, A. M., & Browne, K. W. (2010). *Beginnings and beyond: Foundations in early education* (6th ed.). Clifton Park, NY: Thomson Delmar Learning.

Greenman, J. (2003). Places for childhood includes parents, too. In R. Neugebauer & B. Neugebauer (Eds.), *The art of leadership: Managing early childhood organizations* (rev. ed.). Redmond, WA: Child Care Information Exchange.

Hall, E. T. (1976). *Beyond culture.* New York, NY: Knopf Doubleday.

Hanson, M. J. (2011). Diversity in service settings. In E. W. Lynch & M. J. Hanson (Eds.), *Developing cross-cultural competence: A guide for working with children and their families* (4th ed.). Baltimore, MD: Brookes.

National Association for the Education of Young Children. (2020). *Developmentally appropriate practice in early childhood programs serving children from birth through age 8.* Washington, DC: Author.

Phipps, P. A. (2003). Working with angry parents: Taking the customer service approach. In R. Neugebauer & B. Neugebauer (Eds.), *The art of leadership: Managing early childhood organizations* (rev. ed.). Redmond, WA: Child Care Information Exchange.

U.S. Census Bureau. (2019). *Languages other than English spoken at home in United States.* American Community Survey 1-Year Estimates. Washington, DC: Author. http://www.census.gov/programs-surveys/acs/

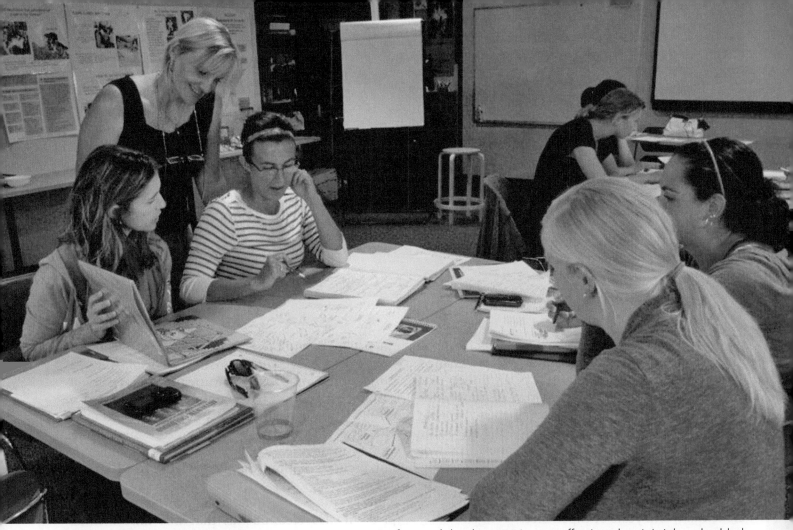

Professional development is most effective when it is job embedded
and interactive, and follow-through is expected.

Providing for Personal and Professional Staff Development

Standards and Recommendations Addressed in This Chapter

ADVANCING EQUITY RECOMMENDATION 6 Provide regular time and space to foster a learning community among administrators and staff regarding equity issues.

PROGRAM STANDARD 10 Leadership and Management

LEARNING OBJECTIVES

After reading this chapter, you should be able to:

14-1 Explain why understanding equity is essential to creating a culture of collaborative inquiry.

14-2 Describe the role of staff meetings as an important professional development tool.

14-3 Identify the elements of an effective staff-development system.

14-4 Describe effective supervision and coaching strategies.

At a time when the field of early childhood education is in the midst of rapid change, the profession must "both honor and include our existing field of those working across learning settings, recognizing their diversity, dedication, and experience" (Power to the Profession Taskforce, 2020). Administrators must provide comprehensive professional development, coaching, and mentoring that are differentiated to meet the needs of staff with a wide range of educational levels, credentials, and years of experience.

Leaning Forward (2020), a professional learning association, emphasizes that professional learning is the best means for educators to develop the new knowledge, skills, and practices needed to improve program quality and meet the needs of children. This organization seeks to transform education and emphasizes the importance of educators taking an active role in their development as professionals. The basic assumptions underlying staff-development programs are that learning is a lifelong process and that adults have the capacity to change and grow. In a sense, this capacity is analogous to that manifested by children in their growth processes. The director's responsibility as it relates to the staff is to create a favorable environment for optimal growth and development of all the people in the environment. When the director serves as a model of professionalism in handling staff meetings, staff training, coaching programs, and staff supervision, as well as assessing staff problems, the personal and professional development of the program staff is facilitated and enhanced.

Leaning Forward has developed a bold new model (see **Figure 14-1**) of professional learning that permeates a program's culture to transform practice by providing rigorous and inclusive content designed to create conditions for success. Equity is foundational and is woven throughout professional learning experiences. The emphasis on equity is also reflected in Advancing Equity in Early Childhood Education (National Association for the Education of Young Children [NAEYC], 2019) which recommends that program administrators "provide regular time and space to foster a learning community among administrators and staff regarding equity issues" (p. 9). It also recommends that this time include

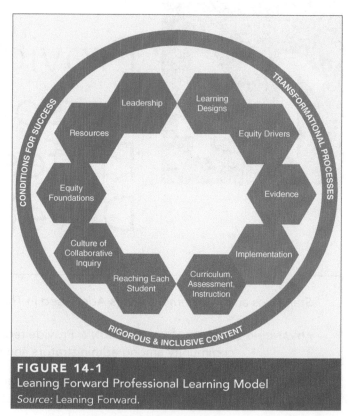

FIGURE 14-1

Leaning Forward Professional Learning Model

Source: Leaning Forward.

"opportunities for all individuals to reflect about their own cultural attitudes and behaviors as well as to uncover and change actions that reflect implicit bias and microaggressions toward children, families, school staff, and administrators" (NAEYC, 2019, p. 9). These conversations are difficult but necessary to advance equity for staff, children, and their families.

14-1 • Creating a Culture of Collaborative Inquiry

One important but challenging component to include in quality professional development is creating a culture of collaborative inquiry where staff members feel secure enough to reflect on and share their practice. This should include what they see as strengths and opportunities for growth. To reach this level of trust, leaders need to examine how they build trust. Lencioni (2002) identifies trust as "the confidence among team members that their peers' intentions are good, and that there is no reason to be protective or careful around the group . . . teammates must feel vulnerable with one another" (p. 165).

The core of high-quality professional learning is that educators are expected to commit to continuous improvement, engage in collaborative learning, and assume responsibility for their own development (Leaning Forward, 2020).

The specific content or strategy employed in any aspect of the staff-development program depends on group composition. In the same way that classroom teachers assess the needs of children in planning appropriate learning environments, directors evaluate staff needs and plan staff-development programs accordingly.

In place of the "career ladder" common to many professions, the field of early care and education has adopted the metaphor of the *career lattice*. It represents the multiple entry points for and the expertise of those in our field who have years of experience and job-embedded professional development but may be pursuing a degree by stacking credentials and degrees incrementally. Others in our field may have relatively new degrees in early childhood but lack the experience of the veteran teacher. To meet the needs of both groups of teachers, the field must provide multiple opportunities for growth and development. Early childhood professionals often need to advance their careers lattice horizontally, vertically, and even diagonally to meet their goals. (See **Figure 14-2**.)

14-2 • Planning Meetings to Support Development

One vehicle for providing ongoing and job-embedded professional development is the staff meeting. The director is responsible for planning and conducting meaningful and relevant staff meetings. Bloom (2002) states that meetings are critically important. In fact, she says meetings are "the glue that holds the organization together" (p. 1). Although conducting a staff meeting may seem to be a routine and relatively easy task, holding meetings that are satisfying and worthwhile for both the director and the staff requires careful planning and preparation. Effective implementation of the planned agenda largely depends on the director's ability to maintain open communication among those attending the meeting.

14-2a • Purpose of Staff Meetings

Communication is the main purpose of staff meetings. Although much can be communicated through email, newsletters, posted bulletin board notices, and information exchanged casually on a one-to-one basis, many issues and problems are resolved most effectively in a meeting. Communication should be two-way, with opportunities for staff to solve problems, share ideas, engage in team discussion, and complete important tasks.

Two-way communication in a meeting permits an interchange of ideas and feelings and provides a forum for thoughtful discussion and clarification of problems and issues. The final outcome for each individual should be a better understanding of problems and issues and of self and others. When staff members are involved in discussing program issues or

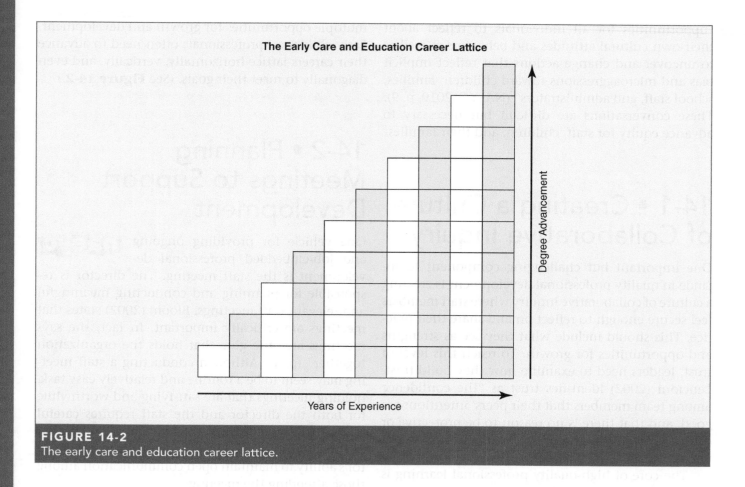

FIGURE 14-2
The early care and education career lattice.

problems, when their opinions have been heard, and when they have had some voice in decision-making, they feel a greater sense of self-worth and consider themselves a more integral part of the total program community. To be comfortable for everyone, staff meetings must provide a safe environment where staff members can ask questions, challenge others by presenting alternative ideas, and share feelings with the group.

To prevent the meeting from deteriorating into a "gripe session," the director can take an active role in channeling the complaints and concerns toward improvement strategies. Open communication during staff meetings is one way to develop cooperation and harmony and to encourage the "we" feeling among staff members. This is further advanced when staff members are encouraged to suggest staff meeting agenda items. A sense of community is fundamental

for the creation of a favorable environment for the personal growth of staff members, children, and families who participate in the program.

When the director becomes aware that there is an undercurrent of discontent among the staff, a staff meeting discussion focused on concerns and issues may be useful but only after talking informally with several staff to see if the problem can be remedied, thereby leaving staff meeting time for other agenda items. If staff unrest persists, then it may be necessary to assess staff morale through the use of a *climate survey*. A well-designed survey tool that includes items related to motivation, commitment, satisfaction or dissatisfaction, and other concerns can yield useful information that directors can use to provide a framework for a staff meeting discussion. The climate survey becomes a means to an end because it helps staff members focus on

Staff meetings can be good times for training if the amount of time needed is short and the task at hand would benefit from peer or director support.

their most urgent issues, and it helps the director bring the staff meeting discussion toward problem resolution. Bloom, Sheerer, and Britz (2005) suggest that the climate of the organization is akin to the personality of the program. Both the director and staff can have input into the design of the survey tool, which can be developed easily through such online tools as Survey Monkey, a platform for surveys that can be completed anonymously and compiles the data into easy-to-read charts. It may be appropriate to share the results of the survey at the next staff meeting, presenting new action items as appropriate.

Staff meeting discussions may involve specific questions, such as which piece of outdoor equipment to buy, or whether to buy tricycles or books with the equipment money available at the end of the year. Sometimes, discussions focus on the use of available

building or outdoor space, or on the appropriateness of timing the meal service or the monthly fire drill. The director may decide to use staff meeting time to discuss more general philosophical or educational program issues such as, "What changes should we consider in our program planning to focus more attention on emerging literacy?" A question that logically follows is, "How do we, as a staff, learn more about the application of a balanced and interactive early literacy approach?" Discussions about both educational program and general program philosophies often lead to group decisions about the focus and content of future in-service training sessions. If the group makes decisions about the training needs of the teaching staff, there undoubtedly will be a greater commitment to the training program than if the director makes those decisions without group input.

Nonetheless, when staff meeting discussions are not of particular relevance to those in attendance, boredom and restlessness become apparent, and members feel that the time is wasted. To maintain interest and open communication, try to select agenda items that are of concern to most of the staff members who are expected to attend the regular staff meetings. Remember to use icebreakers and various problem-solving strategies that will help maintain interest and keep staff focused. Make certain that the purpose of the meeting, whatever it may be, is clearly stated and understood by everyone at the meeting (Bloom, 2002). The agenda items that pertain only to the work of a few can be reserved for special meetings or assigned to small committees for discussion and subsequent decision-making.

14-2b • Timing of Staff Meetings

The frequency and timing of staff meetings vary, depending on the amount of business typically transacted and the amount of time devoted to each meeting. Weekly or biweekly meetings that are well planned and brief may be more productive than long sessions that are held less frequently. Although staff members usually prefer daytime meetings because they need evenings and weekends to rest and take care of personal matters, evenings may be the only time everyone can meet together.

In half-day programs, staff meetings can be scheduled after the children leave at noon or in programs with double sessions, either early in the morning or late in the afternoon. However, full-day programs present special problems because the programs are open from early morning until late in the afternoon, and the program staff usually works a staggered schedule. Nap time is often the time set aside for meetings because most staff members are present in the middle of the day; however, sleeping children must be supervised. Use of volunteers or parents for nap time supervision is an alternative but one that licensing disallows in some places. In smaller programs, hiring substitutes to cover nap rooms may be a better solution.

The program staff and the director decide which staff members, in addition to classroom staff, should be encouraged to attend staff meetings. It may be beneficial to have the bus driver, the cook, or the receptionist at staff meetings because the kind of contact these staff members have with the children and families enables them to make unique contributions to staff meeting discussions. Directors also may find it useful to ask the consulting psychologist, the special education resource teacher, or other professionals who are involved in the program to attend staff meetings. Anyone who can profit from or contribute to the discussions should be encouraged to come to the meetings.

14-2c • Preparation for Staff Meetings

Both the director and the staff members must prepare for a staff meeting so that the meeting will be productive for everyone. The director is responsible for obtaining staff input on agenda items, preparing and posting the agenda, and distributing any material that should be read by the staff before the meeting. Even though the director holds final responsibility for planning the agenda, all staff members should be invited to suggest agenda items before or after the agenda is posted. The posted agenda might include a brief description of each item and the action to be taken. (See **Figure 14-3**.)

For example, if the agenda item about the use of outdoor space is to cover the timing for its use, then the responsibility for setting up and cleaning up and meeting equipment needs would list all of these these subjects for discussion. The agenda also should state clearly which items are open for discussion *and* group decision and which items are open only for discussion. In the latter case, the director hears the discussion, considers the ideas and feelings of the staff, and subsequently makes the decision. In the case of the outdoor space questions, the classroom staff probably should decide about the timing for the use of outdoor space; the total staff, including the janitor or housekeeper, should be involved in the discussion and decision about setting up and cleaning up the space; and the final decision about equipment purchase is made by the director after hearing the preferences of the entire staff. When all these expectations are spelled out clearly on the posted agenda, there is little room for confusion or misunderstanding about what will occur during the meeting.

Each item on the posted agenda includes the name of the person responsible for presenting the item and leading the discussion and a rough time estimate for adequate coverage of the item (see **Figure 14-3**). This procedure notifies staff members about their responsibility during the meeting and ensures coverage of the entire agenda within

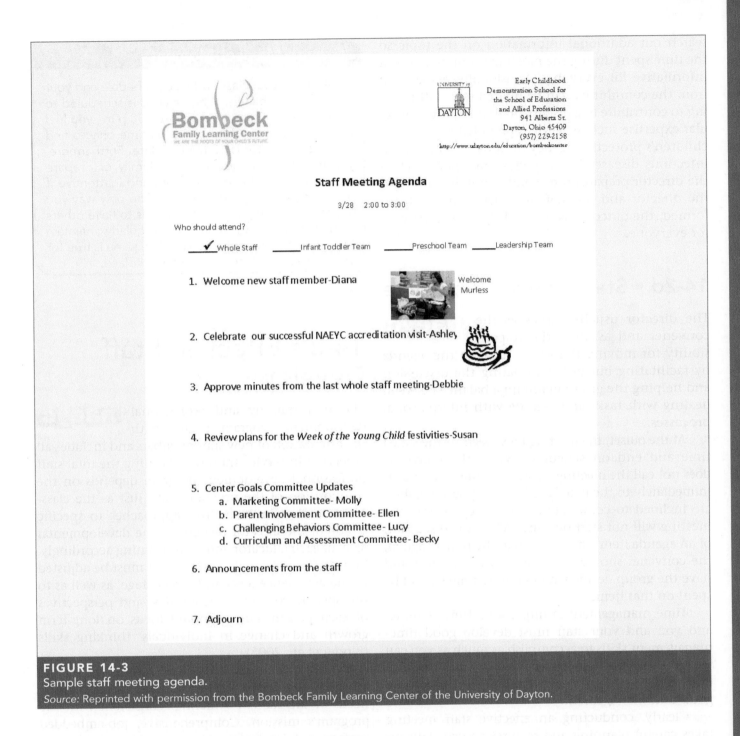

FIGURE 14-3
Sample staff meeting agenda.
Source: Reprinted with permission from the Bombeck Family Learning Center of the University of Dayton.

a specified meeting time. Giving staff members responsibility for selected agenda items is an excellent way to encourage interest in program operations. Reserving part of each meeting to have a staff member present on a topic of interest also contributes to the feeling of collegiality.

The director should distribute copies of readings, minutes from previous staff or board meetings, and any other information that will provide a common basis for discussion to enhance the quality of the dialogue during the meeting. For example, if curriculum planning will be discussed as it relates to authentic assessment, research studies and program ideas on this topic could be duplicated and given to staff members several days before the meeting. Individual staff members can also be encouraged to search out additional information on the topic so the time spent during the meeting is productive and informative for everyone. Occasionally, a specialist from the community can be invited to a staff meeting to contribute to a discussion that requires particular expertise such as services provided by the local children's protective agency or new information on infectious diseases in early child programs. When the director prepares the agenda carefully and both the director and the staff members come well informed, the outcome is more likely to be satisfying for everyone.

14-2d • Staff Meeting Procedure

The director usually serves as the convener and assumes the responsibility for moving the group through the agenda by facilitating but not dominating the discussion and helping the group maintain a balance between dealing with tasks and dealing with interpersonal processes.

At the outset, the meeting must begin at the stated time and end on schedule. When the convener does not call the meeting to order on time and moves immediately to the first agenda item, group members are inclined to come late because they assume the meeting will not start on time. When the discussion of an agenda item extends beyond the time assigned, the convener should call attention to that fact and have the group decide whether more time should be spent on that item.

Time management is important. Time is finite, and you and your staff must develop good time-management skills to accomplish as much as you can within a specified time frame. The staff meeting is an excellent place for you as a director to demonstrate good time management.

Clearly, conducting an effective staff meeting takes careful planning and requires special skills on the part of the director. However, when meetings are satisfying and productive for the staff, they serve as a vehicle for communication and promote cooperation and good feelings among staff. Furthermore, staff meetings give the director a chance to model interpersonal communication skills that serve as the basis for all interactions with children, parents, and other staff members.

Growth Mindset Moment

Think about your class and study schedule and your other responsibilities. When a class is scheduled to convene at 4:00 p.m. and end at 5:30 p.m., you feel frustrated if you rush to arrive on time only to find that the instructor is 15 minutes late. Furthermore, you may have to get home to family or prepare dinner, and you become restless and inattentive if the class goes beyond 5:30 p.m. The only way you are able to manage your time well is to have others with whom you must interact regularly maintain their time commitments to you. The same is true for you and your colleagues at the workplace.

14-3 • Effective Staff Development

The staff training and professional development program begins with the orientation of new staff members and includes all aspects of in-service training. Planning the total staff professional development program depends on the composition of the program staff. Just as the classroom teacher individualizes approaches to specific children, the director recognizes the developmental level of each educator and plans training accordingly. The staff professional development must be adjusted to the experience level and career stage, as well as to the specific concerns, capabilities, and perspectives of each person, and it should focus on long-term growth and change in individuals' thinking skills (Bloom et al., 2005).

The director's job is to work with staff to construct a professional development program that meets the needs of the staff in a manner consistent with the program's mission. Comprehensive, job-embedded professional development is required for educators to advance through what Tanner and Tanner (2007) describe as the three levels of educator competency. In a field where many educators have limited training, it is common to find early childhood programs with teachers who are at Tanner and Tanner's *first level* in which teachers rely on materials made by others (e.g., kits, worksheets, and prepackaged curricula) and do not critically evaluate materials or instructional activities. Frequently, teachers at level I implement a series of disconnected activities that fill the day but do not reflect what children know and are able to do in order to design curriculum that incorporates the children's interest and meets the children's individual needs. Teachers in this stage require professional development that recognizes where the teachers are and supports their progress to the next level.

As teachers receive higher levels of professional development and support, they develop competencies at Tanner and Tanner's *second level*, which requires them to recognize that instruction should reflect the emerging issues of the classroom and should also integrate content areas and developmental skills. A teacher at this level may understand that effective classrooms respond to individual needs but may be unsuccessful in knowing how to put their understanding into action. For example, Tanner and Tanner (2007) describe one level II teacher who tried to focus on a letter of the week and connect it with each new theme because she knew that good programs support emergent literacy and connected learning. Her lack of understanding of how to implement this understanding led to simplistic connections, such as choosing the letter "d" for the farm unit, singing "Bingo" (because it was about a dog), and also singing the "Farmer in the Dell" (because dell begins with "d") (p. 10). Level II teachers may be more aware of what young children should know and be able to do, but they often lack the skills to design instructional environments that fully integrate curriculum content into learning experiences that challenge and inspire young children. Directors who have a lot of teachers at level II will need to be highly intentional in providing professional development that moves the staff from where they are to level III.

Teachers at level III are able to exercise independent judgment and adapt curriculum to meet children's individual needs (Tanner & Tanner, 2007). Tanner and Tanner describe a level III teacher's ability to make curricular decisions in an example where the teacher had planned to teach a theme about living things and began the theme with a class visit to a pet store. Although the teacher had planned to focus on pets in general, she adapted her curriculum when she saw the children's excitement about the snake that was fed a live mouse, which led to a more specific focus on snakes and their prey. In this example, the teacher had

a sound understanding of what children should know and be able to do and had sufficient understanding of related content knowledge. The teacher also demonstrated a sense of efficacy in that she had confidence in her skill to design a learning environment that capitalized on the interest of the children and facilitated an extended investigation of a topic worthy of study.

According to Tanner and Tanner (2007), no matter what a teacher's background, he or she cannot implement a curriculum well without initial training and ongoing professional development. To be effective, such training should be provided by individuals who are familiar not only with adult learning principles but also with the realities of teachers' classrooms. Tanner and Tanner (2007) advocate the use of comprehensive professional development plans.

▶ TeachSource Video Vignette

The Responsibilities and Development of an Early Childhood Teacher

View the video vignette titled *Teaching as a Profession: An Early Childhood Teacher's Responsibilities and Development*.

In this video, you will see Samantha, an early childhood teacher who is skilled at articulating her practice. Being able to talk about what she is doing and why makes her an excellent mentor for other teachers. In the video, Samantha talks about her experience as a mentor. She also describes her own professional development, which includes examples of job-embedded professional development. Listen carefully and list all of the types of professional development that Samantha mentions. Be sure to include both formal and informal examples.

14-3a • Professional Development Plans

Professional development plans should be comprehensive in terms of both the staff's professional level and the length of time that the staff member has been at the program. Fully trained and qualified classroom teaching staff members should have basic child-development information and should be able to plan curriculum and classroom-management strategies with minimal additional training. However, they may be ready for some help on working with the special education resource teacher who comes to consult with them about the children with disabilities in the program. Because special classroom strategies must be employed to truly include children with disabilities into a noncategorical classroom, training in techniques and strategies to accomplish that integration also will be helpful to the experienced teacher. The interdisciplinary classroom team of early childhood and special educators must work together to provide quality programming for all children in an inclusive environment. An interdisciplinary team building and staff-development approach for both the special educators and the early childhood staff is to provide mutual training so these professionals together develop their own professional skills as well as come to appreciate more fully the knowledge and skills of other members of the team. As team members come to accept and extend the skills and knowledge of fellow professionals, mutual respect and camaraderie are reinforced.

Teachers at Tanner and Tanner's (2007) first level, assistants, aides, and other paraprofessional classroom staff may need coaching in preparing classroom materials in understanding growth and development or in developing basic management skills. The classroom teacher is responsible for ensuring that all adults working or volunteering in the classroom understand the program's philosophy as well as the curriculum being implemented. Those who work in the field of early care and education are commonly more comfortable working with young children than supervising adults. The program director needs to ensure that staff members have the knowledge, skills, and time to collaborate with the other adults working in the classroom. Likewise, the custodians, food service staff, and clerical staff will need different levels and types of assistance.

When planning a staff training program, the director will have to assess the training needs of everyone, and then make decisions about time, content, and training methods for the sessions. An experienced director can assess training needs by observing staff as they carry out their job responsibilities and by having conferences with them to discover more about their own analysis of needs and their interest in professional advancement. Assessment of staff training needs and professional development should flow from staff self-evaluation as well as from directors' formal evaluation procedures and discussions from staff meetings. As directors glean insights into individual staff needs and interests, they can search for appropriate and challenging staff training and educational opportunities.

14-3b • Time for Training

Finding a suitable time for training meetings is even more difficult than finding a suitable time for staff meetings. In the case of regularly scheduled staff meetings, the staff can plan ahead for the full year and schedule their other duties and commitments around the meeting times. However, training sessions that usually occur with less regularity often require a larger block of time than a staff meeting and have to be planned to coincide with the schedules of consultants or outside experts whose services are needed. If the director and program staff members are the only people involved in the training, then scheduling difficulties are alleviated somewhat. Nonetheless, the issues of late afternoon or evening fatigue and the inability of the staff to leave the classroom during the day, create special problems for training early child staff, unless the sessions can be planned for nap time or incorporated into staff meetings. Because most training requires larger time blocks, it may be necessary to discuss the possibility of a Saturday meeting or a weekend retreat. Half-day preschool programs that usually meet during the public school academic year often have training meetings in the early autumn before school begins or in the spring after school closes. In any case, if in-service training attendance is mandatory, then this point must be included in the employee's job description and spelled out during new employees' orientations.

14-3c • Mandatory Training

Decisions about whether attendance at training sessions should be mandatory or optional used to be decided by the director at the program level. Now licensing, state quality rating systems, and reimbursement policies often require a given number of hours of training each year. Individual teachers may be responsible for keeping track of and completing required training to maintain their teaching credential or eligibility. Because the stakes are so high (i.e., programs can lose funding, a quality rating, or accreditation if staff lack required training), the director needs to establish a process for tracking mandatory training and a vehicle for staff to be able to go to training during work hours when possible.

Training may be required by the program to maintain consistent programming or to address new challenges, opportunities, and program goals. This kind of training can be exciting to plan because it reflects what makes the program unique. Directors and interested staff can work together to create professional development opportunities that reflect the program's unique culture and goals. This training is important and requires whole staff involvement to gain buy-in.

Growth Mindset Moment

Think about your personal feelings when you were told that you had to attend some function such as a meeting, a party, or a class, as opposed to the times when you were given a choice. When it was a matter of choice, what were the factors that motivated you to attend? Was it curiosity about who would be there or what would take place? Was it your interest in the topics or activity? Was it to please the person who requested you attend or who told you about the event? Can you analyze your feelings and reactions when you went someplace to please someone else as opposed to the times when you went because you were intrinsically motivated?

14-3d • Place for Training

When there is a comfortable lounge or conference room at the program, the staff may prefer to stay in the building for the training sessions. The comfort and familiarity of the program will help create a feeling of openness, which could be important if the success of the training depends on dialogue and exchanging ideas among staff members. If the training is a cooperative effort involving several programs, then a space in a centrally located community building may be more convenient for the trainees. Sometimes, getting away from the program can be helpful. Regardless of the venue, the space should be comfortable, with adult-sized furniture, including tables that provide a writing surface, and an opportunity for interacting with colleagues.

14-3e • Training Methods and Resources

The methods or strategies employed in the in-service training program will depend on the amount of time provided, the resources available, and the nature of the content selected. For example, if 1 hour of a staff meeting is set aside for a refresher course in first aid,

Making the Case for *Job-Embedded Professional Development* naeyc

The paradigm for professional development has shifted from one-shot inspirational training to a model in which professional development is job embedded and follow-up is included. Teaching teams need to feel accountable for implementing what they have learned, and they also need to have support and feedback. Research shows that effective professional development is job embedded and integrated into the workday. Professional development that is most likely to impact change focuses on improving classroom practice and consists of teachers finding solutions for authentic and immediate problems (Leaning Forward, 2020). Directors who want to get the biggest impact invest in job-embedded professional development.

then the best way to present that information may be in a lecture given by an approved trainer from the health department. On the other hand, if there is more time to spend on the topic of first aid, then it may be desirable to plan a full-day session with a Red Cross specialist. Another alternative is to enroll some staff members who do not have first aid certificates in a Red Cross course that extends over several weeks and is available evenings or on Saturdays. First aid training can be expanded to include health, nutrition, and safety. The expansion of the program creates new training strategy possibilities. Group discussion led by the director is an appropriate method to use in making the staff more aware of safety issues in the program. The program could include discussions about safety when using outdoor equipment, when planning cooking experiences, or when organizing field trips. The health or nutrition questions might be handled best by a nurse, physician, or dietitian who would come for a seminar. A special educator might come to discuss health and safety issues as these relate to special-needs children. When outside consultants are brought in, the director's role is to sit in on the training to be able to do follow-up with the staff, thereby extending the new information to specific situations that each teacher encounters in the classroom. Directors can choose from many possible methods, each one requiring different amounts of time and different resources and all of them individualized to meet the needs of the trainee. A list of training resources in the community as well as national opportunities should be available in the director's library at the program.

On-site workshops are useful mechanisms for encouraging direct involvement of the staff in a special content area. Implicit in the workshop concept is the idea that those who attend participate actively in the program. Frequently, workshops are planned for a staff that expresses a need to know more about curriculum areas such as writing programs, math or science experiences for young children, or music in the classroom. Other areas, such as building skills for more effective conferences with parents or ways to interact with volunteers, also can be handled in a workshop format that involves participants in a series of role-plays or simulation games. Workshops require active involvement from the participants and are more suitable for some training needs than are lectures, films, or seminars.

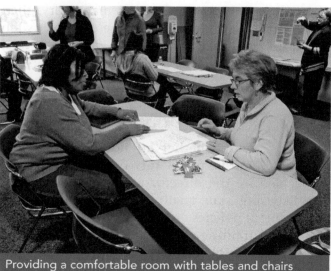

Providing a comfortable room with tables and chairs facilitates collaboration between colleagues.

Planned follow-up should be provided for all types of training. Behavioral change is not likely to follow a one-shot session or even a series of meetings unless there is follow-up by the director or supervisor at the program. Teachers need feedback and support to integrate new information into their day-to-day practice. It is helpful to follow up by periodically revisiting the ideas and information teachers have received to discuss progress and problems they have had when attempting to implement new procedures or ideas and to reaffirm each teacher's commitment to dealing with the challenges of change.

Visits to other programs are encouraged by some directors and can be a helpful piece of the total staff-training program. Watching other teachers and children is refreshing and interesting for some staff members. After such visits, they bring back program ideas, new and different ways to set up the physical environment, and sometimes a renewed interest in developing classroom materials such as math games or interactive charts. Some teachers who are able to move beyond the more obvious things such as equipment or curriculum ideas may begin to compare and contrast classroom environments and teaching strategies, relating these differences to the differences in the stated philosophies of the programs. Follow-up group discussions will help teachers refine their understanding of how theory relates to practice. Why are the children in one program encouraged to negotiate with one another about dividing the Play-Doh, whereas the teacher in another program controls the amounts each child receives? The two strategies clearly reflect different program goals. Group discussions also may encourage teachers to reexamine the theoretical basis for the program in which they work and reevaluate the curriculum to ascertain how closely it reflects the stated philosophy of the program, as well as their own philosophy of early childhood education.

Professional conferences and workshops provide excellent training opportunities for staff. Directors who commit to a personal program of professional development by attending professional meetings set a standard of excellence for their teachers to emulate. It is important to encourage staff to take advantage of these opportunities and facilitate their attending conferences by allowing time off from work and subsidizing their travel and registration expenses whenever possible. Some early child programs not only subsidize conference attendance but also pay for teachers' memberships in professional organizations such as the NAEYC, which includes membership in state and local affiliates, the Council for Exceptional Children, the Association for Childhood Education International, the National Association of Child Care Professionals, and the National Child Care Association.

Staff members who express an interest in professional advancement are to be commended for their ambitious goals and encouraged to take courses toward a college degree in child development or early childhood education or toward the Child Development Associate (CDA) or certified Child Care Professional certificate in communities where these types of training programs are available. The availability of online courses offers easy access to educational opportunities for many staff

members. Some programs will help pay tuition for relevant courses as well as adjust work schedules to allow staff to attend daytime classes. Directors can lend further support to these part-time students by showing interest in what they are learning and guiding them to helpful resources available at the program.

More and more professional development training is expected to be credit based. In addition to not-for-credit or credit-based CDA programs, teachers are being encouraged to take course work that could lead to an associate or bachelor's degree in early childhood education or a closely related field. Some federally funded early childhood education programs, including Head Start, as well as many state licensing systems and NAEYC accreditation teachers standards, have established criteria that require a certain minimum number of degreed staff before a program is approved. Therefore, more program directors are encouraging staff to take college credit courses, and colleges and universities across the country are trying to meet that demand. At this time, there are also many opportunities for professional development training on the Internet. In some places, students are permitted to enroll in individual classes without matriculating in a degree program. Staff-development course work for continuing education credit is also available online. Committing to any type of credit-based staff-development work is intimidating for some staff members. They have had little or no experience with any type of college-level work, and they resist even the thought of taking courses because they are uneasy about their ability to do the work or have serious concerns about how time-consuming it will be. Directors can help them by being available to talk through what they are experiencing and what they feel may help them succeed. When they are taking classes, it may be useful to suggest that they meet with other staff at break time to share concerns and seek help with assignments or study skills.

To provide on-site materials to support and enhance all aspects of the staff-development program, the director's job is to establish a professional library and a teachers' resource center. The library books should cover information on child development, curriculum, classroom management, special-needs children, diversity, and working with other professionals and families. Books on specific curriculum areas such as literacy, math, science, cooking, or music will help the staff plan for the children. Recent

Director's Corner

One of the most helpful things we did in my administration class at college was role-playing. I especially remember role-playing a parent conference. Now I use that technique all the time with my staff. In staff training sessions, when we are discussing an issue like dealing with a difficult parent, I ask for a specific example and immediately turn it into a role-play. "OK—now I'm the parent and here is my concern—you are the teacher," and we play it out. Then we often reverse roles so I take the role of the teacher. It works very well for me as a director.

—Director, YMCA-sponsored center

copies of professional journals and newsletters should be available in the teachers' library, along with a collection of audiovisual materials, including tapes, slides, videotapes, DVDs, and computers, to provide a rich source of information on curriculum development and classroom management.

The teachers' resource center should be a space where teachers can make math games, charts, big books, and other teacher-made classroom materials. Supplies such as paper, tagboard, paper cutter, scissors, glue, tape, a single plain die, marking pens, and so forth must be available in addition to a large working surface. It is a luxury to have things like a laminating machine or an Ellison machine for stamping out letters and shapes for charts. When teachers have materials and space to work, they are more likely to develop individualized teacher-made classroom materials that will enrich the program for the children.

14-3f • Training Content

Many ideas for the professional development training program for staff already have been mentioned in the previous discussions on methods of training. Training needs will vary according to the previous training and experience of the program staff. Many teachers constantly seek new curriculum ideas and resource materials for the classroom; consequently, training in curriculum areas is usually welcomed. There is always interest in strategies for dealing with the difficult, challenging, disruptive, or withdrawn child. Furthermore, most teachers are interested in learning more about community resources where they can get advice about how to handle children with special needs or about where to refer children and families for additional help. Although staff will rarely request it, directors are obligated to hold at least one staff meeting per year or set aside a time at a regularly scheduled staff retreat to review the NAEYC Code of Ethical Conduct and Statement of Commitment and the Code of Ethical Conduct Supplement for Early Childhood Program Administrators (see **Appendix A**). Although the orientation of new employees includes mention of the NAEYC Code of Ethics, yearly review of this important document will renew staff members' awareness of their professional commitment to ethical practice.

The director should determine whether staff members need special coaching in conducting home visits or parental conferences. These duties are taxing, produce anxiety, and require specialized and culturally sensitive communication skills that are suitable for the particular parent population being served. It is important to know that some families may be slow to accept a stranger and will draw back from someone they perceive as too intrusive. Attitudes about accepting newcomers, education, and childrearing vary among cultural, ethnic, and socioeconomic groups, and it is essential for staff to know what those differences are when they work with children and families. Staff members also find it helpful to have special guidance from the director in effective interpersonal communications.

There is a pressing need to assist staff in dealing with diversity in the classroom. Including children with disabilities and children from diverse cultural and ethnic groups into early childhood education programs means there must be training programs that focus on providing information about ways to meet the individual needs of children and families from these groups. Teachers may also need help handling issues regarding children of divorce, single-parent families, hospitalization of a parent or sibling, children who have been abused, and so forth.

When the staff is experienced and fully capable of coping with the day-to-day, here-and-now events in the classroom, staff-development efforts can move on to the questions that challenge us in the 21st century. What do children need to know to survive in this new century? How will life change in the next 50 years, and what personality characteristics and thinking dispositions will be essential to function competently during those 50 years? The job of staff training is never complete because there are always new challenges.

Director's Corner

When the central office in Dallas called to offer me the director's position at our center in Topeka, I accepted. I knew I was a good teacher—that is one of the things that qualified me for the promotion. But I was not prepared for the challenge of supervising the adults at the center. Without a doubt, supervising the staff was the hardest thing for me to handle when I stepped into the director's position.

—*Director, large corporate for-profit center*

Working Smart with Technology

Online Professional Development

It can be difficult not only to find the time for everyone to attend training but also to find training that meets the needs of individual staff members. Online professional development is becoming more common and offers unique advantages. Because online training is not limited to a specific locality, state, or national region, the offerings can provide your staff with a wide range of topics. Many workshops are *asynchronous*, meaning staff can log on and participate at times that work best for them and for the program. Staff members can take the training as individuals or with a teaching partner or team. They can take it during assigned times at work or in the comfort of their own homes. As directors consider adding online training to their professional development offerings, they need to consider the following in the selection process.

1. Choose online training that is facilitated. Facilitated training typically includes opportunities for interaction with an instructor and also is more likely to include moderated peer discussions. The level of accountability and the quality of the work produced tends to increase dramatically when training is facilitated.

2. Look for training that asks participants to apply what they have learned to their work environment. Some online training provides new information and then asks participants to try out what they have learned and bring their experiences back to the online discussion for feedback and reflection. Job-embedded professional development has been shown to have better long-term outcomes.

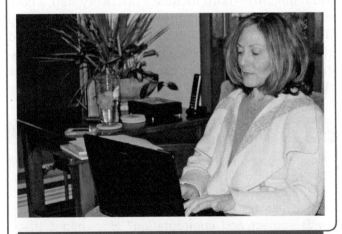

Online professional development allows participants to train in the comfort of their own home.

14-4 • Staff Supervision and Coaching

The director—or the educational director in the case of large programs or some corporate chains—is responsible for supervising classroom staff. (The director will be referred to as *supervisor* for the purposes of this discussion.) By observing, doing one-to-one mentoring and coaching, plus working in the classroom with the children and the staff, the supervisor gives support and guidance to each staff member and establishes a trusting relationship with each one. As a coach, the supervisor's job is to "encourage and provide opportunities for defining and solving problems and for self-reflection and collaboration. It is important that you (the director) model the kind of behavior you want staff to use with children—providing for self-initiated learning, risk taking, and exploration" (Carter & Curtis, 2010, p. 122). The trust and mutual respect that develop between coach and teacher provide the basis for building a teaching–learning relationship that parallels the relationship between adult and child. Then the supervisor is able to create a favorable environment in which each staff member can gain new understandings of children, self, and the supervisor's expectations.

An experienced supervisor knows that sometimes growth and change take place slowly. Working, talking, and planning together will promote personal and professional competence on the part of classroom staff members, provided the supervisor is supportive and encouraging and is not perceived as being critical or threatening.

14-4a • Principles of Supervision

Keep in mind several basic principles or assumptions as you think about the director as staff supervisor. The same principles apply to the supervisory role, whether you are working with a new, inexperienced staff member or a mature, qualified, and experienced educator or are a new director moving into a fully staffed program.

- Supervision is a dynamic, evolutionary process that is based on trust.
- Supervision is individualized and adapted to the personality and teaching style of each staff member.

- Supervision provides a support system for each staff member.
- Supervision provides a framework within which the supervisor demonstrates professional skills for the entire staff.

However, an individualized model of staff development means you must use a developmental approach to supervision, and educators who are at different stages in their careers will require qualitatively different supervisory strategies.

14-4b • Supervisory Process

As classroom staff members grow and change, the thrust and focus of the supervisory process shift accordingly. The process begins by providing support and guidance for a new staff member, who is integrating past learning experiences into a personal teaching style that is compatible with the program philosophy. The process changes as the staff member adjusts and develops into an accomplished educator, who will in turn supervise assistants, aides, and student teachers or be paired with a new teacher and become a mentor. If you think of this supervisory process on a continuum, it moves from a highly directive approach for new teachers in which control is in the hands of the supervisor to a collaborative model where an accomplished educator and the supervisor share control of the process.

One-to-one coaching is the essential ingredient of the supervisory process, whether working with the beginning teacher or the accomplished professional who, in turn, will coach others in the program. Coaching includes encouraging, modeling, observing, and giving specific feedback. A coach is a cheerleader who watches, listens, and shares skills, resources, and experience. Communicating with staff after an observation usually is handled in a conference, but when time is short, a brief note with some specific feedback may have to suffice.

The director must ensure that staff members engage in high-quality practices at all times. When there are questions and concerns about educator performance, it is always a challenge to communicate those concerns in a way that addresses the issues but maintains program quality and does not compromise staff morale. Depending on the level of training and experience of the staff, you as director will have to deal with questions and concerns about classroom practices on a regular basis. There may be issues about curriculum, classroom management, staff relationships, or interactions with parents. On any given day, you will see and hear things that must be addressed. The following are examples:

- How should I approach Estella, who continues to call across the room to set limits for children who are not doing what she thinks they should be doing?
- I must talk with Consuelo about using positive redirection instead of the constant, "Stop running in the room" or "Don't spill your milk."
- Colin's group times are not rich or challenging these days. I must call him in and talk about that.
- What is the best way to tell Betsy that she and her assistant should be sitting with the children at lunch and eating what children eat? I also will have to tell them that they must wait until they are on break to have coffee or a Coke.

Dealing with questionable practices is especially distasteful for directors who prefer to avoid conflict and confrontations, but it is an important part of the supervisory process and goes to the core of what it takes to maintain the integrity of the program. Keep in mind that when you are responsible for supervision of staff, you will inevitably have to spend time and energy dealing with conflict (Sciarra & Dorsey, 2002).

14-4c • Supervisory Cycle

The two pieces of the supervisory cycle—*formative* and *summative*—both include a discovery step, a conference step, and a planning and goal-setting step (**Table 14-1**). Ideally, the director or supervisor and the teacher and supervisee begin to build a relationship based on trust and mutual respect during the initial orientation sessions because that provides the

---

Growth Mindset Moment

How do you feel about confrontation and conflict? Do you withdraw and avoid it like a turtle? Do you approach and attack like a shark? Do you wait and watch like an owl? What is your style of dealing with conflict and confrontation? How might that affect your performance as a supervisor? (Sciarra & Dorsey, 2002, p. 147)

Table 14-1 Supervisory process

Summative Supervisory Cycle	Formative Supervisory Cycle
Discovery Step	

Supervisor observes supervisee.
 	
  Evaluation tool
 	
  Performance appraisal
	Supervisor observes supervisee.
	
	  Anecdotal records
	
	  Narrative records
	
	  Checklists
	
	  Casual notes and comments

Conference Step	
Supervisor reviews previously set goals. Supervisor presents findings based on the performance appraisal. Supervisor and supervisee discuss results of the performance appraisal.	Supervisor empowers supervisee. Nurturing and coaching Sharing information and concerns
Planning and Goal-Setting Step	
Supervisor states the decisions based on the performance appraisal. • Raise • Promotion • No change in status • Probation • Dismissal Develop the action plan and put it in writing. • Training • Course work • Reading • Conditions of the probationary period • Steps to finalize dismissal Set the time for the next summative conference.	Supervisor and supervisee set mutually agreed-upon goals. Develop the action plan and put it in writing. • Readings • Training or course work • Observing peers or teachers in other programs Set the time for the next formative conference.

Source: Sciarra & Dorsey (2002). Reproduced by permission. www.cengage.com/permissions.

foundation for a collaborative, ongoing supervisor–supervisee relationship.

The first step in the supervisory cycle is the discovery step for both the formative and summative segments of the cycle. The discovery step begins with a scheduled classroom observation that is followed by a scheduled conference with the educator. Although making time and covering classrooms for regularly scheduled observations and conferences is not easy, it contributes significantly to the success of the educator assessment or evaluation process. During the formative time period of the cycle, the emphasis for the observation and conference is reflection, discussion, and sharing of information and concerns about classroom events and practice. At the conference following the observation, the director and the educator review and discuss events and actions observed. The formative conference is helpful for both participants if the director listens carefully and encourages the educator to reflect, analyze, vent if needed, and evaluate events or issues that arose during the observation. A checklist for classroom observations is sometimes used to help supervisors focus on specific aspects of an educator's performance. Sometimes asking open-ended questions will generate discussion that will be helpful for both the educator and the director. For example, the director may ask the following:

- What was on your mind as you asked Tully what she was thinking about when she was repeatedly stabbing the play dough with the tongue blade?
- Did you have a sense of what Farah was upset about in the bathroom before his "meltdown"?
- Did you realize that Perot had grabbed Lissa's doll baby away from her earlier in that dramatic play sequence—and that later she took his cowboy hat away from him and that is when you intervened?

The coaching and mentoring segment of the conference might include references to the program curriculum framework and books that are useful to support that framework, the NAEYC Program Accreditation Standards, the Program Assessment Scale, Quality Rating and Improvement System (QRIS), or licensing expectations. There may be times when sections of the job description or the performance appraisal can be used to support both the positive notations in the observation notes as well as those items that may require special attention. The conference always ends with agreed-upon goals and plans to think about and act on before the next scheduled observation. If it is time for the educator to be evaluated, then the planning time can be used to describe the summative steps in the process. It is an ideal time for the educator and the director to review the performance-appraisal tool so the educator understands that the next steps will be related to performance appraisal, and both the educator and the director will be prepared for that step in the cycle. With this planning in place, the supervisory cycle continues.

The pattern of observation and conferencing for the summative segment of the supervisory cycle is also a scheduled observation followed by a scheduled conference. Programs differ in how and when summative evaluations are done. They may be done annually or semiannually or scheduled individually based on hiring date. For the summative observation, the director uses the performance-appraisal tool, summarizes the findings, and prepares to present these to the educator at the conference. At this conference, the director takes the lead and presents the observation findings, which were based on the performance appraisal. Remember that this meeting comes after many casual contacts, several scheduled observations and conferences, and frequent communication between the director and educator. Therefore, there are usually no surprises for the teacher at this time. If the information shared is critical or negative, the teacher may object or argue, but that has to be expected. However, if the director has coached, offered help, provided opportunities for training, and been up front about expectations during previous conferences, and if that has all been carefully documented with notes from conferences and previous encounters, then the educator should see that the results of the performance appraisal are fairly accurate. After discussion and clearly stated decisions based on the appraisal have been communicated, the conference ends with plans for the next step in the cycle, which is scheduling the coming series of formative observations and conferences to repeat the cycle (Sciarra & Dorsey, 2002).

Supervising new teachers New teachers need daily or even hourly support; therefore, the director or supervisor must plan to spend time each day observing and teaching with the new teacher. If a new teacher is recently trained, that teacher will be developing a personal teaching style and will profit from the example set by an experienced supervisor. It is critically important for a supervisor to work beside a new teacher with the children in the classroom. This supervisory procedure creates a rich learning environment for the new teacher and often provides a more favorable transition for the children and families who know the supervisor but are not yet well acquainted with the new teacher. As a supervisor, you must make sure to remove yourself gradually so that the new teacher can build a relationship with the children and families and begin to manage the classroom without your constant support. What you are doing in effect is providing hourly or daily support during the initial trust-building period but stepping back when the new teacher can function independently. You are scaffolding the experience for the teacher just as you would for a child in the classroom, gradually increasing the challenge as you stay nearby because your ongoing support is still important when things do not go well.

Director's Corner

Since I am new here, I haven't developed a schedule for regular observations as yet, but I make the rounds at least twice a day, if only to let my teachers know I am available. Of course, I have a chance to catch things going on in each room—maybe a new chart or a teacher reading a book to a sleepy child. I make sure I leave a short note in each teacher's box, mentioning some little thing I noticed when I came by. If I see an activity or a procedure that concerns me, I mention it. "I noticed you had the toddlers finger painting with chocolate pudding today. Drop by when you have a chance—I have some ideas about that that I would like to share with you." It seems to work well for me.

—*Director, community agency center*

Staff members are used to informal drop-in visits where they are more likely to hear something good about what they are doing than they will in a complaint. Having established a trusting relationship between staff and director is important when there is a need for constructive criticism.

Supervising experienced teachers As educators develop their skills and become more competent, they continue to profit from the supervisor's support. Positive reinforcement and constructive criticism from supervisors are excellent motivating factors. But experienced educators also are ready for expansion and growth in new directions. They still are integrating and reorganizing what they have learned in the past, but they can now reach out for new learning opportunities. These educators have become comfortable with their teaching style and can direct more attention to curriculum development. They are ready for the intellectual stimulation they can draw from taking course work, reading new publications, and attending professional meetings. Therefore, although the supervisor continues to observe these educators and have conferences with them on a regular basis, emphasis now is placed on the supervisor as a resource person. The supervisor can supply new program ideas, new theoretical information, articles from professional journals and websites, research materials, and as many opportunities as possible for educators to participate actively in professional organizations and conferences.

Although experienced educators are perfecting their teaching skills under the guidance of the supervisor, they also should be developing self-evaluation skills. With encouragement and help from a supervisor, experienced educators feel secure enough to step back and evaluate their teaching. They can begin to ask themselves some of the questions a supervisor has been asking them and engage in some self-searching about their methodology. For example, one teacher might make the inquiry, "How could I have better handled the situation between those two children who had a conflict over the sand bucket? What I did was really not productive. I must find alternative ways of handling those two children." Another teacher might ask, "How can I adjust my questioning techniques for all the children to help them become better problem solvers? I heard you mention Rheta deVries. Maybe you could give me something she has written on that topic that will help me."

Supervising the accomplished educator The accomplished, long-term educator still is perfecting teaching and self-evaluation skills and revising curriculum. However, having reached a new level of mastery, this educator is ready to develop supervisory skills. While working with the educators, the director or supervisor not only has exemplified teaching and self-evaluation skills but also supervisory skills. In working with accomplished educators, the director or supervisor now turns to coaching them in supervisory skills. This educator is preparing to assume responsibility for supervising assistants, aides, and, in some situations, student educators. To serve in this capacity, the educator will need instruction and support to develop the necessary skills for fulfilling supervisory responsibilities. The director or supervisor still is observing and having conferences on a regular basis, giving attention to teaching strategies and self-evaluation. However, the new thrust is directed to this educator's interaction with and supervision of other adults in the classroom.

Involving accomplished educators with novice educators in a mentoring program is an ideal way to offer the benefit of job enrichment for both. The director's role becomes one of modeling for the mentor by engaging in reflective practices and helping this educator, who is skilled at working with young children, learn more about the characteristics of the adult learner. The director models ways to use many of the same skills that educators use when caring for young children and now explores ways to "care for a fellow caregiver." Pairing mentors with novices is a challenge for the director who must observe, reflect, and confer with staff to ensure a "good fit" in each pairing. A successful peer-mentoring program contributes to the well-being of staff and children alike. It is connected to both staff development and supervision while still being separate. It provides unique opportunities for both mentors and novices to learn from each other and grow professionally.

Supervision is one of the most difficult and anxiety-producing aspects of the director's job. It draws on every bit of professional skill the director has because it demands expertise in interpersonal communication, children's programming, teaching strategies, and self-evaluation. It also helps the director focus on the importance of being a model for the staff by making positive suggestions to coach and motivate and by using supportive caring gestures and voice tone. This sets the tone for staff, who, in turn, are more likely to follow a similar pattern in their interactions with children and families.

Accomplished practitioners, like successful CEOs, give thoughtful attention to grooming their successors. Through ongoing encouragement and coaching that is fashioned to the talents and abilities of each accomplished educator, the director guides them toward optimal professional growth. This prepares them to take on more responsibility and advance their own professional careers. It is the talented and visionary center directors who can best bring along and groom the future leaders in the field.

> **Growth Mindset Moment**
>
> Think about the cooperating teacher who supervised your practicum. Did you receive support and constructive criticism? Did that person serve as a model of good supervisory skills for you? Think about how your cooperating teacher might have been more helpful. What do you feel you need before you can become a supervisor of a program classroom staff?

14-4d • Identifying Topics for Supervision and Coaching

Staff members' areas of strength and need can provide the basis for designing the staff-development program and focusing individualized supervision activities. Teacher input is essential, and after you have identified what educators believe their needs to be, you can take the first steps toward helping them solve those problems (Bloom et al., 2005). The expressed needs of staff can be addressed directly. If an educator has problems handling the aggressive behaviors of a child, the director can respond in a variety of ways, including offering relevant readings, observing or participating in the classroom, discussing various management strategies, calling in a consultant to observe and conference with the classroom staff, or discussing the general problem of dealing with aggression in a staff meeting. This direct response to an expressed need may motivate the staff member to become involved in a training plan offered by the director.

On the other hand, when the selection of staff-development activities is based on those issues the director views as problems, motivating staff interest will be more difficult. For example, if a new director finds the long-term staff using punitive and age-inappropriate techniques in response to unacceptable classroom behaviors but the educators are comfortable with their management methods, then those educators will resist committing to any training designed to encourage them to use more positive management strategies. The new director will have to spend time establishing a trusting working relationship with the professional staff before training related to the classroom-management question will be accepted. Because the use of punitive management techniques can be hard on children, the new director may choose to bring in a consultant to work with individual staff members or may even consider making staff changes. A new director is well advised to design the initial staff-development activities in response to the educators' expressed needs.

Selection of staff-development activities is often based on expressed needs of staff or is in response to new requirements that come down from funders, licensing agencies, or government agencies, but it also emerges from the interests and goals of a visionary director. The staff-development program is often designed to guide the staff to make changes in what they think and in what they do. Response to change differs from one person to another—some are exhilarated and motivated by the opportunity to work with change, whereas others are anxious and immobilized. As individuals on the staff begin to respond to expectations or requirements presented to them, they need the director's support and encouragement. It is now critical that responsible directors keep a watchful eye on those who fail to progress. Documentation and regular observing and conferencing throughout the process are helpful to all staff but are essential for those whose failure to progress could be a problem that will require action on the part of the director in the future.

14-4e • Expressed Teacher Concerns

Expressed teacher concerns often cluster around several problem areas (Bloom et al., 2005). The director's task is to identify and then respond to these concerns. The areas of greatest concern include those points discussed in the following paragraphs.

Supporting teaching teams A teaching team may have problems getting all team members to follow through on assigned responsibilities and to work as members of a cooperative team. In response to this problem, team decision-making, communication strategies, and giving feedback are appropriate areas to address in the staff training program for the teams. The best way for the director to help educators with this problem is to model exemplary supervisory and communication skills.

Trauma informed classrooms The COVID-19 pandemic changed our way of life and introduced fear and anxiety to children and families who struggled with demands of work, home schooling, financial insecurity, isolation, anxiety, and more. Trauma and toxic stress are common consequences of the extended disruption associated with the pandemic. The need to support children in trauma and social and emotional learning is a common request for professional learning topics.

Managing the classroom Teachers report problems with managing children's challenging behaviors. Behaviors on their list include aggression and violence, not picking up, not sharing, and not cooperating. In addressing the problem of working with these children, the director first might focus on developmental expectations for the specific age group in question, followed by ways to encourage prosocial behaviors. This is a sensitive problem area because the perceived problem sometimes results from educators' unrealistic expectations. Directors must model developmentally appropriate responses to children's behaviors whenever they have encounters with children in the program. Managing children who present extremely oppositional or violent behaviors often requires the help of a mental health specialist.

Helping children with special needs and their families Educators report that they do not know enough about how to deal appropriately with children with special needs. This becomes a serious problem when children with previously unidentified social-emotional problems join the group. Educators suddenly realize that this child is indeed disturbed and needs special help, but they are not prepared for the disruption and management challenges this new child presents. They want help on how to provide rich environments for these children as well as ways to work effectively with their families. Providing reading materials and planning special meetings on this topic will be helpful to educators who are searching for better ways to help these special children. Directors also must watch for upcoming conferences and meetings on the topic and encourage staff to attend.

Because educators and directors are seeing an increase in the number of children who exhibit challenging behaviors, some program directors are seeking funding for more mental health services or for a mental health specialist on the staff.

The role of the mental health specialist on staff is to plan regularly scheduled classroom observations, usually taking place in the morning and lasting from 2 to 3 hours. The conference to discuss the observation, with the director and the educators in that room, should be on the same day, if possible, so the events of the day are still clear and fresh. Conferences can often be arranged for nap time. It is essential that directors attend these meetings because they must assume responsibility for curriculum and monitor all classrooms regarding curriculum matters. The conference time is devoted to discussing events of the day and highlighting those that precipitated anxiety and tension for the children. These notable events were often those that tended to pose problems for the more fragile children.

The role of the mental health specialist in the conference is to support staff members as well as coach them as they all talk about the reactions of the children, what the children may have been trying to accomplish, or what they may have been thinking. With new insights into the effects of experiences on children and their reactions to those experiences, educators begin to feel more competent about their ability to plan, evaluate, and work with them. The major thrust of the mental health specialist is to help program staff saturate the classroom and eventually the entire program with refined practices that will enhance the emotional well-being of all children in the program, not just those who have been called "challenging."

For the children who continue to require additional help, the mental health specialist can arrange to meet and work with them and their families for as long as needed. Clearly, this approach is a departure from the more typical procedure in which the mental health specialist is called on to observe a specific child. In this case, the expectation is that the specialist will observe the child, identify the problem, and then offer help to the child, the child's educators, and members of the family. This surely benefits all who participate and work with

the specialist. The plan described previously puts the focus on all children in the classroom, knowing that everyone in the classroom is entitled to have the benefit of ongoing daily practice that has at its core the emotional well-being of young children.

Relating to supervisors Staff members often clash with directors. Educators complain about not being treated fairly and not being respected as professionals. The response to this problem is clearly in the director's hands. Directors must work on their own professional development to enable them to become better staff managers.

Maintaining parent cooperation Educators have problems with parents who send a sick child to school, who are not prompt about picking their child up after school, and who do not cooperate with the educators' efforts, such as when educators encourage the use of messy materials. Here the director can reinforce program policies by reviewing the parent handbook material with the parent, as well as participate in parent conferences when necessary, to mediate and give support to both the educator and the parent. In-service training focused on working with parents and becoming sensitive to their needs may help educators feel more secure about handling difficult situations with parents.

Managing time Time to deal with nonteaching tasks such as cleaning, planning, making materials, or doing other paperwork is a problem for educators. Because time management is also a major problem for directors, directors and educators have this issue in common. Time-management seminars under the guidance of an experienced trainer can be part of the staff-development program. It is especially important for the director to be a part of this training and to model good time management.

Although staff concerns always are situation specific, a common core of recurring problems fall into the categories just listed. It can be reassuring to you as a director to know that your educators' expressed needs are much like those of most teaching staffs.

Summary

The staff-development program contributes to both the personal and professional growth of the program staff. Through the planning and implementation of effective staff meetings, staff training programs, and staff supervision, the director creates an enriched learning environment for the staff. Given the benefits of an enriched environment and a director who demonstrates good interpersonal and professional skills, the staff members have the opportunity to enjoy the inevitable personal satisfaction and excitement that result from positive, individualized, professional growth experiences. To plan and implement an effective professional development system, directors must do the following:

- describe the role of staff meetings as an important professional development tool,
- identify the elements of an effective staff-development system, and
- describe effective supervision and coaching strategies.

TRY IT OUT!

Role-play an early child program staff meeting and discuss one agenda item: timing for weekly staff meetings. The director has decided that the entire staff (including the cook, the janitor, and the secretary) must meet every week. The questions open for discussion are the day of the week on which the staff should meet and when and how long the meetings should be. Assign the following roles to class members:

a. Director: works Monday through Friday 9:00 a.m. to 5:00 p.m.
b. Teacher A: works Monday through Friday 9:00 a.m. to 5:00 p.m.
c. Teacher B: works Monday through Friday 6:00 a.m. to 2:00 p.m.
d. Assistant teacher C: works Monday through Friday 10:00 a.m. to 6:00 p.m.
e. Assistant teacher D: works Monday through Friday 6:00 a.m. to 2:00 p.m.
f. Part-time teacher E: works Monday through Friday 10:00 a.m. to 2:00 p.m.
g. Cook: works Monday through Friday 9:00 a.m. to 3:00 p.m.
h. Janitor: works Monday through Friday 3:00 p.m. to 8:00 p.m.

Thirty-five children in the program arrive on a staggered schedule between 6:15 a.m. and 9:30 a.m. and leave between 2:30 p.m. and 5:30 p.m. The children occupy two classrooms and two sleeping rooms. Sleeping rooms are adjacent to one another and to the outdoor area.

The staff meeting discussion is to be led by the director, and the group is to come to some decision about when the regular staff meeting will be held. Use the blackboard or newsprint for note-taking if you need it. Practice good listening skills; make sure that everyone participates.

Role-play a special staff meeting that has been called by the director to discuss and reach a decision about allocating classroom space in the early child program. One additional classroom will be available beginning in September, and new teacher Mark will be employed. The new classroom is larger than the others and opens directly to the playground.

Sandra currently has the best classroom, which has its own bathroom. The other four rooms share a bathroom down the hall. Jean will be working with a new pilot program and will have many parents participating in her classroom. She was responsible for getting the pilot program funded, which is a real asset for the program. Bob's classroom is far from the outside play area and from the storage room. Bob feels that this location is inconvenient. Sheila would like to keep her current classroom because she recently made curtains and painted the walls. Barbara feels that her 10 years of teaching qualify her for the new classroom.

Name	Years at Center	Degree	Current Classroom
Sandra	6	MS	Excellent
Barbara	10	BS	Very good
Sheila	4	BS	Very good
Bob	6	AS	Good
Jean	1	AS	Poor
Mark	0	BS	

The staff has allocated 30 minutes for making this decision. After the group has arrived at a decision, individually rate your level of satisfaction with the decision from 1 (low) to 5 (high). Also, rate your level of participation from 1 to 5. Tally the results on the chalkboard. As a group, discuss the factors that contributed to the level of satisfaction or dissatisfaction. Was the level of participation a factor?

Think about a time when you were called in by a teacher or a boss for an appraisal of your performance (athletic performance, singing or dancing event, your work in a store or restaurant, etc.). Reflect on how the teacher or boss handled the situation—how you felt about what she or he said, how you felt about yourself during the conference, how you feel about yourself now as you recall the incident, and so forth. Write a few paragraphs about why you think you had the feelings about yourself then as you experienced the conference as compared with how you feel about yourself now as you remember it, and why you think those feelings differ, if they do.

REFERENCES

Bloom, P. J. (2002). *Making the most of meetings: A practical guide.* Lake Forest, IL: New Horizons.

Bloom, P. J., Sheerer, M., & Britz, J. (2005). *Blueprint for action: Achieving center-based change through staff development.* Lake Forest, IL: New Horizons.

Carter, M., & Curtis, D. (2010). *The visionary director: A handbook for dreaming, organizing and improving.* St. Paul, MN: Redleaf Press.

Leaning Forward. (2020). Revised standards for professional learning: Discussion draft. Oxford, OH: Author. https://learningforward.org/wp-content/uploads/2021/01/standards-dec5-draft.pdf

Lencioni, P. (2002). *The five dysfunctions of a team: A leadership fable.* San Francisco, CA: Jossey-Bass.

National Association for the Education of Young Children (NAEYC). (2019). Advancing equity in early childhood education position statement. Washington, DC: Author. https://www.naeyc.org/resources/position-statements/equity

Power to the Profession Taskforce. (2020, March). Unifying framework for the early childhood profession. Washington, DC: NAEYC. http://powertotheprofession.org/wp-content/uploads/2020/03/Power-to-Profession-Framework-03312020-web.pdf

Sciarra, D. J., & Dorsey, A. G. (2002). *Leaders and supervisors in child care programs.* Clifton Park, NY: Thomson Delmar Learning.

Tanner, D., & Tanner, L. (Eds.). (2007). *Curriculum development: Theory into practice* (4th ed.). New York, NY: Pearson.

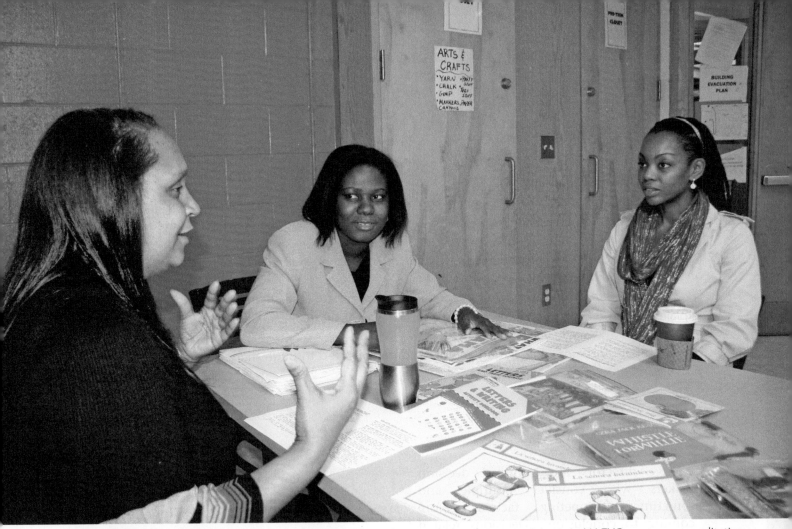

The director and staff members work together to participate in NAEYC program accreditation by becoming familiar with accreditation materials before they begin their self-study.

Chapter 15

Evaluating Program Components

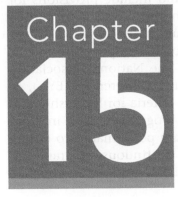

naeyc

Standards and Recommendations Addressed in This Chapter

ADVANCING EQUITY RECOMMENDATION 2 Take proactive steps with measurable goals to recruit and retain educators and leaders who reflect the diversity of children and families served and who meet professional standards.

ADVANCING EQUITY RECOMMENDATION 4 Ensure that any formal assessment tools are designed and validated for use with the children being assessed.

PROGRAM STANDARD 10 Leadership and Management

LEARNING OBJECTIVES

After reading this chapter, you should be able to:

15-1 Explain the purpose of evaluation.

15-2 Describe the importance of developing an evaluation plan and identify what should be included.

15-3 Become familiar with the Child Care Licensing Benchmark Project and the Benchmark Category Language.

15-4 Discuss the processes and procedures associated with evaluating staff members, including the director, and the director's role in professional evaluation.

15-5 Describe the methods and strategies for conducting appropriate assessment of children's progress.

15-6 Explain the purpose of program evaluation as it relates to licensing, accreditation, and Quality Rating and Improvement Systems in ensuring quality.

15-7 Explain the importance of analyzing and using data collected through the program evaluation process.

Effective directors are informed decision makers who consider multiple and sometimes competing factors before coming to conclusions. Decisions related to enrolling and grouping children are complex because many factors related to the needs of children and families as well as the quality of the program must be considered. Of course, there are pressures to admit all applicants when enrollment is not full. However, it is important for the director to exercise good professional judgment and base admission decisions on what is in the best interests of children and families.

Evaluations can be tailored to address the components of an individual program to identify its strengths, needs, and challenges. They can also measure the performance staff, progress assessment of children, and effectiveness inventories of administrative policies or procedures or of some other component of an early childhood education program. Periodically, long-range planning should occur, and the mission should be examined. Such an examination should provide data about usefulness or worth. After an early childhood education program has been planned, its evaluation should be designed immediately as part of the program's operational system.

15-1 • Establishing an Evaluation Plan

The evaluation plan should include provisions for everyone connected with the program to participate. Staff members should be encouraged to participate in discussions about the program and its policies and procedures. The National Association for the Education of Young Children (NAEYC), in its program accreditation criteria for leadership and management, states that programs engage in "routine monitoring of program performance to ensure program accountability, continuous program improvement, and enhanced outcomes for children are addressed" (2019, p. 121).

Ideally, evaluation that is planned during the early stages of program development facilitates the process and notifies everyone from the start how the evaluation process will be conducted. The evaluator uses the mission statement or goals that were prepared before the opening of the program as the basis for making judgments about what is valuable in the program (see Chapter 2). These documents provide guidelines for assessing the program and the performance of individuals affiliated with the program.

Regular evaluation can indicate how successful the director and staff have been in adhering to their mission and in meeting their goals. Evaluation can help the director, board, and staff revise their goals as changes occur in the community and the world. This process also enables the director to make needed changes quickly before current practices have a negative effect on the program. Continuation of an ineffective aspect of the program is fruitless and frequently expensive. Inappropriate staff behavior may be detrimental to children's development or to staff relations and can be identified as part of the performance evaluation process (see **Director's Resource 15-1**). Desirable behavior, on the other hand, should be recognized, encouraged, and supported as a result of the evaluation process. The performance evaluation process should be closely aligned with the employee's job description and employees should be acutely aware of their duties as stated in the job description as well as the job description of those roles which impact them directly such as those of their teaching team which may be different depending on their rank as an early childhood educator I, II, or III.

Assuming that the director has worked to create a "we" feeling rather than a "boss" approach, evaluation also will take on a collaborative tone. Rather than being threatening or punitive, evaluation will be a way to note and celebrate progress and to plan for the next stages. Some directors choose to have staff rate themselves using the evaluation form before coming to the performance evaluation meeting. This facilitates a fruitful conversation about areas of strength, opportunities for growth and the development of a continuous improvement plan.

15-2 • Purpose of Evaluation

Early childhood program evaluation has often focused on classroom prac- tices. However, current understandings of program effectiveness indicate that the overall administrative procedures and policies and the ways in which these are implemented ultimately relate to the educational quality that children receive at the program. The overriding purpose of evaluation of the program's administration is to ensure good-quality early childhood education. Talan and Bloom (2011) have developed a tool, the Program Administration Scale (PAS), that is designed to evaluate leadership and management. The results of the PAS can inform leaders and facilitate an examination of goals and supporting policies and procedures.

Because a major purpose of evaluation is to determine whether the program's goals are being met and whether they or the program needs to be modified, the evaluators need to know what these goals are before gathering data. In effect, the evaluators must know who the clients are, what their needs are, and which of these needs the program is attempting to meet. For example, in a community where the local high school is expressing concern about the high number of dropouts from pregnancy, a program director may decide to work with the school system to assess how many students could return to school if care were provided for their infants and toddlers. Together, the program and the school may be able to obtain funding to provide this service. In such a situation, particularly if tax dollars are to be used, community education would be important because many taxpayers may believe that the program would encourage teen pregnancy rather than prevent school dropouts.

Another purpose of evaluation is determining how effective the program is in meeting the needs of clients and how efficient it is in terms of cost, time, and energy. Are needs met to the satisfaction of the program and the clients? Are they partially met or not met at all? More important, in our example, are significantly more teen parents returning to and staying in school when their babies receive child care? Even if needs are met, could the same job have been done for less money or with less time or energy? Funding agencies, board members, and clients expect documentation that the program is doing what it has agreed to do. An evaluation provides the data for such documentation and possibly the basis for further funding.

The director uses the data from the current evaluation to determine the strengths and needs of the program and to adapt the plan for the following year to correct any deficiencies or to respond to newly perceived needs. For example, if one of the goals of the program is to provide a parent education program for all parents and the data show that only 10 percent of the parents participated, then the director must determine whether the goal is inappropriate or whether the method of achieving it is not meeting the needs of the clients. If a thorough evaluation has been done, the director will have information from parents regarding how they felt about the parent program and why they did or did not attend. The information then can be used to plan changes in next year's program or to ascertain that this community does not need parent education from this particular program.

It would be easy to arrive at the conclusion that parents in the preceding example do not want or need parent education. But directors have to consider other factors and perhaps ask themselves the following questions:

- Have parents been involved in the planning so that they feel as though they are part of the program?
- Is there another parent education program already established in the community that is meeting these parents' needs?
- Is the timing, format, or content inappropriate for these parents?
- Has there been a breakdown in communication so that parents do not feel welcome or comfortable about coming?
- Are there other, more pressing matters confronting the parents?
- Are there ancillary problems such as babysitting or transportation?

Because one or more of these factors may have had a major effect on parent participation, the director should certainly address them to make sure that the evaluation is accurate.

15-2a • Evaluation Principles

Evaluation plans should be based on certain principles that reduce anxiety and increase cooperation among the individuals being evaluated.

1. The evaluation process is open; that is, the people or groups being evaluated know about the evaluation process in advance and have access to their own evaluation data. Furthermore, the people being evaluated have an opportunity to give input into their own evaluation.

2. Evaluation relates directly to program goals and objectives.

3. Each person being evaluated knows why, when, where, how, and by whom the evaluation is to be done.

4. Evaluation is conducted on an individual basis. However, for reporting purposes, the results are compiled and group data rather than individual data are presented.

5. The individual's evaluation is a confidential matter and is accessible only to those who need to know, such as an employee's supervisor or a child's teacher.

6. Evaluation is built into the program so that it occurs on a regular basis.

15-3 • Evaluation System

As the director and staff work together to create an evaluation system, they consider what will be evaluated and why. They determine the intended audience for the evaluation plan. Will all or part of it be available to families, all staff members, board members, funders, and the general public—or will it be available "in house" only? What does each of these groups need to know? What are they entitled to know? How will the information be used? Issues of confidentiality must be considered and specifically mandated in the program's policy

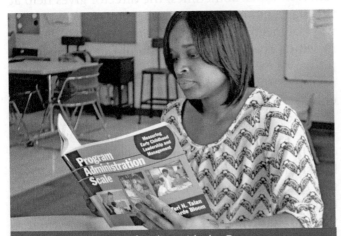

The director must be familiar with the Program Administration Scale as well as NAEYC Program Accreditation Standards.

manual. All who have access to information must agree to this overarching policy. Moreover, adopting the NAEYC's Code of Ethical Conduct, its supplements, and Statement of Commitment will provide guidance when ethical dilemmas are encountered (see **Appendix A**).

Planners must give serious consideration to the appropriate amount of data to be collected. Keep in mind that someone has to prepare or select the evaluation tools. Someone has to see that the data are gathered and analyzed. And someone has to determine how the information will be used. Who will be responsible? Where will the information be kept and for how long? Specifying procedures to be used, including time lines, will facilitate the process and help determine the optimum amount and type of information to be gathered.

An early childhood education evaluation plan involves three components: staff, children, and total program evaluation. A plan for each component includes delineating who will evaluate, how and when the evaluation will be conducted, and for what purposes a particular evaluation is being done.

15-4 • Staff Evaluation

Performance evaluations of staff were previously introduced because of their impact on the overall climate of the program. This section will dive more deeply into the details of a performance evaluation system as a natural outgrowth of supervision and one of the basic duties of the director. Every staff member should be evaluated on a regular basis according to the procedure included

Director's Corner

The steering committee conducts an annual parent survey. One parent gathers all the information and then gives each classroom a printout of what the parents in their room specifically said. The parents' names aren't included, though. Parents seem willing to write things that they might not take time to say in person, and it's been real helpful to the staff to get this kind of feedback.

—*Director, agency-sponsored early childhood program*

in the policies and procedures manual. Performance evaluation is also tied to a clearly stated position description as discussed in Chapter 8.

Performance evaluation (see **Directors' Resource 15-1**) is conducted to enable the director and the staff member to analyze what the staff member is doing well and in what areas growth and change are desirable or required. This type of evaluation provides information to the funding agency and the board about how employees spend their time; it also validates the work of the employees and is often a requirement of licensing, QRIS, and accreditation.

In assessing an applicant's ability to work well with other employees, the director must be cautious and avoid selecting only those people who fit a mold. A successful choice is based on a careful evaluation of credentials and behavior rather than on an overgeneralization of positive or negative traits. For example, the candidate who answers an early question to the interviewer's liking then may be regarded as being highly qualified, although he actually may be poorly skilled in working with young children. On the other hand, the candidate with an unusual style of clothing may be considered initially as incompetent when, in reality, that person might work quite well with young children. The director should avoid hiring only those applicants who are most similar to current employees and still consider whether or not the qualifications of a particular candidate will combine well with those of current employees to provide the total staff strength needed to meet program goals. In any case, the most important criterion is, "Is this the best person available to do the job?" Of course, the director will check applicants' references and will require documented background checks. Keeping these implicit biases in check also facilitates a program's ability to advance equity in the field as it is recommended that administrators take "proactive steps with measurable goals to recruit and retain educators and leaders who reflect the diversity of children and families served and who meet professional expectations" (NAEYC, 2020, p. 9).

15-4a • Process and Procedures

Ongoing evaluation of staff members begins when they accept their positions. The director and new staff member go over the job description together carefully and make adjustments as needed to fit the circumstances, writing any changes into the job description. A comprehensive evaluation is based on this job description. The director makes it clear to employees from the beginning that they will be evaluated. However, another important component to be discussed with employees is the support that will be provided to assist new staff members as they become acclimated to new roles. This support is particularly helpful for first-year educators.

The director informs each employee why, when, where, and by whom the evaluation will be done; outlines the basis for the evaluation; and describes the method to be used. Often, a new employee is evaluated after a 2- or 3-month probationary period. If the employee's work is found to be satisfactory at this time, the employee and director then plan together for further growth by writing out what the employee expects to accomplish before the next evaluation. In this initial step in the evaluation cycle, the employee writes out goals and brings them to a meeting with the director, at which time both must agree on their importance and reasonableness. The goals must relate to the job description, and the subsequent evaluation is based on the mutually agreed-upon objectives.

For example, if one of the educator's goals is to maintain a more orderly classroom, that educator's procedural plan may include teaching the children to return things to the proper shelf, rearranging the classroom, or working with the classroom aide to develop a mutually agreeable plan for keeping materials in order. Sometimes, the director gives help at this stage, either by assisting the employee in finding ways of meeting an objective or by designating areas in which specific objectives should be defined. The primary goal at this step is to draw up a workable plan that the staff member can follow and that will enhance the overall program.

Next, the director and employee decide how data will be gathered. Will the director observe? Will parents be asked for their opinions? Will the educator be asked to engage in a self-evaluation process? Will the educators observe each other? Will children's behavior be used as a criterion? Again, both director and staff member reach agreement on what is the best plan to use. Some programs use checklists or rating scales. These tools are most useful in large programs in which many staff members are working on comparable skills such as fostering a comfortable classroom atmosphere or preparing appropriate classroom materials.

The objectives and evaluation format are called a *work plan*, which is the formative component of staff evaluation. After the plan has been written, the director and the staff member each receive a copy for reference as they work to achieve the objectives and evaluate the progress that is made. They plan a specific time period for the next meeting—in a month, at the end of the semester, or whatever length of time fits their needs.

When a staff member is already doing an outstanding job, the director can support the employee in finding a new related interest and area for growth and development. Possibilities include offering to reschedule hours so that the employee can participate in training on technology for children, or granting additional responsibilities for working with educators new to the program and possibly even new to the field. If the employee is interested in administration, then you may begin to involve her or him in work that would introduce that component of the early childhood field and would, at the same time, begin to prepare a successor for your role. Obviously, you will have to be able to replace the employee in the classroom during the time he or she is spending on these new endeavors, and, of course, additional funds would be needed. However, when an educator feels that she has outgrown her job, it is likely that she will search for new opportunities with other programs.

15-4b • The Director's Role

The director's role in staff evaluation is to observe and analyze the work of a staff member, encourage the development of her or his strengths, and look for ways to promote growth in weaker areas. If the weak areas considerably outweigh the strong, then the director must terminate that individual's employment because the director's role (except in special cases) is to promote growth rather than provide total on-the-job training. The staff member's role is to work out the details of meeting the agreed-upon goals and to implement these plans.

In some programs, a standard form is used to evaluate each educator. Although this may be seen as

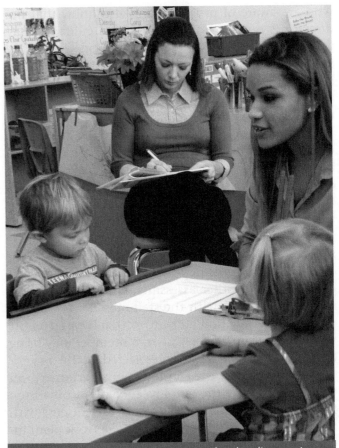

Teachers are aware that observation by the director is a regular component of the evaluation process.

more equitable, it sets the same expectations for both beginners and experienced educators. An alternative method is to evaluate all educators with a standard form that addresses basic requirements. In addition, the director should provide individualized planning and evaluation for each educator's rank and job description. Goals can be individualized according to the results.

Some directors observe each educator weekly, biweekly, or monthly and have a conference informally after making the observation. The director may take notes during the observation or write notes afterward, but any notes should be shared with the staff member because they are useful in helping to fulfill the specific objectives that have been set. It sometimes is easy to pick out and focus on the weak spots in an educator's style, which leaves the educator feeling incompetent. Other directors concentrate only on the positive aspects and are unable to address problem areas. In most instances, staff members who are aware of problems and also know that the director is not providing appropriate guidance may feel they receive an unofficial sanction when they see the director ignore the behavior. In either case, some of the program's objectives are not met, and the observation and informal conference times are nonproductive.

Some directors make video or voice recordings of educators and review them with those educators afterward. The advantage is that both view the same situation during the conference. The disadvantage is that taping is intimidating to some staff. Of course, the tapes are confidential information, and the subject's permission must be obtained if they are to be shown to others.

When the agreed-upon observations have been completed and other assessments have been made, the director meets with the staff member for a comprehensive evaluation of the work that is based on the work plan set up earlier. The staff member may bring a self-evaluation in a form preselected by the director to be completed by the employee, in a narrative form that is written by the employee, or in an unwritten form that the employee has planned to discuss with the director. During the conference, a work plan, including the objectives and an evaluation format, is drawn up again for the next evaluation cycle. This plan should also include opportunities for growth.

The director summarizes the staff person's evaluation for the previous cycle in a written and dated form. The staff member may add written comments if desired. Together they agree on a development plan based on the staff member's needs and interests and the program needs. Then both the staff member and the director sign the evaluation form and the new work plan. Although this process is somewhat formal, the director's evaluation role becomes not only businesslike but also personal if it is followed.

15-4c • Professional Approach

In all staff evaluation situations, a professional approach must be taken. Such an approach conveys to each staff member the importance of the role and of the staff member's performance. Because this may seem difficult in the rather informal child care setting, the director may want to discuss with the staff the importance of professional responsibility evaluation and planning.

Arranging unhurried, uninterrupted time and space for evaluation sessions is essential. Such procedures may seem superfluous in the majority of situations. However, establishing the pattern sets the stage for the occasional extremely difficult evaluation conference and should make it easier to proceed in a professional manner in

When teachers interact with individual children, their observations become important sources of data about each child's development.

those instances. Careful and thoughtful evaluation also sends a message to all staff members that their work is indeed serious and can leave them feeling quite positive about what they have accomplished and ready to work toward continued development.

A similar evaluation process is followed for the director, and the board is usually responsible for its implementation. In a multisite corporate system, a regional representative may conduct the director's evaluation. Because the staff members in a well-run program may feel especially close to one another and may consider the director a personal friend, it is wise to maintain structure in the evaluation process to allow everyone to be as objective as possible. Parents' perspectives on the director's performance are also significant and may be gathered by means of a survey.

Because the director is responsible for the overall quality of the program, evaluation logically focuses on reaching quality indicators. These include low staff turnover and equitable staff salaries, low rates of staff absenteeism, adequate time for staff planning and development, and sufficient classroom equipment and supplies.

Beyond that, however, managing the ever-changing needs of children, families, and staff requires tremendous organizational ability on the part of the director. Programs for children are complex, as evidenced by the fact that the director's day may involve developing new enrollment policies, assisting a struggling educator in the classroom, and meeting with funders from a national organization. The complexity of the director's role reflects the unpredictable interconnectedness described by complexity theory. As director credentialing becomes more available, the board may want to require obtaining the credential as part of the evaluation. Currently, the credential is gaining in popularity as a way to improve program quality and to market the program to families. Many states offer director credentials, and some universities provide office certificate or degree programs in early childhood leadership.

15-5 • Child Assessment

The new position statement of developmentally appropriate practice (NAEYC, 2020) includes a section related to child assessment that states:

Observing, documenting, and assessing each child's development and learning are essential processes for educators and programs to plan, implement, and evaluate the effectiveness of the experiences they provide to children. Assessment includes both formal and informal measures as tools for monitoring children's progress toward a program's desired goals. Educators can be intentional about helping children to progress when they know where each child is with respect to learning goals. Formative assessment (measuring progress toward goals) and summative assessment (measuring achievement at the end of a defined period or experience) are important. Both need to be conducted in ways that are developmentally, culturally, and linguistically responsive to authentically assess children's learning. This means that not only must the methods of assessment, both formal and informal, be developmentally, culturally, and linguistically sensitive, but also the assessor must be aware of and work against the possibility of implicit and explicit bias, for example through training, reflection, and regular reviews of collected data. (p. 19)

As mentioned in Chapter 1, the curriculum plan is determined by the director in consultation with the teaching staff. The assessment plan is also the ultimate responsibility of the director. This plan should be designed to relate to the curriculum with emphasis on the needs and interests of each child. Because the major goals of an early childhood education program revolve around expectations about the development of children, the evaluation most commonly thought of as demonstrating a program's efficacy is child outcomes. Note that assessing young children's development has always been part of the responsibility of early childhood programs. Those assessments focus on all aspects of development.

In some cases, child assessment has been haphazard or overlooked. When directors do not take responsibility for ensuring that assessment is a regular part of the program, it may not occur or be inappropriately done.

Child assessment may involve an individual child, all the children enrolled in an early childhood program, or all the children funded by a particular organization or agency. The director must be sure

Directors help teachers understand the importance of writing notes about each child's strengths and needs.

Poppy's teacher is aware that she needs time to get comfortable at school each morning.

there is a valid reason for the assessment, that the assessment process will not be detrimental to the child or children, and that parents have given consent.

15-5a • Professional Recommendations

Although policy makers often empha-size "school readiness" as a bench-mark to justify program funding, it is difficult for such benchmarks to meet the NAEYC recommendations.

naeyc

After a few minutes, Poppy peeks out.

> Effective assessment of young children is challenging. The complexity of children's development and learning—including the uneven nature of development and the likelihood of children fully demonstrating their knowledge and skills in different contexts— makes accurate and comprehensive assessment difficult. For example, authentic assessment takes into consideration such factors as a child's facility in each language they speak and uses assessors and settings that are familiar and comfortable for the child. When standardized assessments are used for screening or evaluative purposes, the measures should meet standards of reliability and validity based on the characteristics of the child being assessed. When these standards are not met, these limitations must be carefully considered before using the results (NAEYC, 2020, p. 19).

She's beginning to feel safe now. Her teacher makes a note to talk with the director about how to make Poppy feel more comfortable.

The Early Childhood Integrated Data Systems (ECDS) School Readiness Reporting Workgroup (2018) developed a comprehensive School Readiness Reporting Guide that uses a multidimensional view of school readiness and focuses on the need for ready schools and ready communities, the assessment of school readiness is largely left to the states. This often means that state legislators mandate school readiness assessment practices which often do not reflect the NAEYC recommendations. This disconnect between what is known about the limitations in assessment of young children and what is required in state mandates make it clear that assessment is a significant responsibility. The director's role is to ensure that the responsibility is met.

Center directors working with staff can help families, community members, and funders understand how the early childhood curriculum is designed to help each child learn. They can help dispel the myth that children are "just playing" by demonstrating how play contributes to broader cognitive development as well as to learning in the content areas (literacy, mathematics, science, and social studies). Directors and educators can also focus on children's need to develop socially and emotionally. Certainly they should be aware of each child's progress in relating to one another in the classroom and beyond, and in continuing to develop as a socially, physically, and emotionally healthy human being.

To help others understand the benefits and challenges of assessing young children, it is important to first spend time determining what both you and your staff believe regarding appropriate assessment. Moreover, because there is more and more pressure today to measure children's learning, it is wise to develop an assessment policy that can be included in your family and staff handbooks. In this way, you can inform new staff and families about your philosophy and maximize the potential for general agreement about your goals and methods for assessing children. See **Figure 15-1** for an example of an assessment policy.

Young children develop rapidly, so it is important that the progress they make in their normal development is not attributed solely to the center's program. Many other conditions affect the child's development, including parental behavior, cultural background, nutrition, and general health. Any one of these variables or combinations of them can affect

Assessment Policy for the Bombeck Family Learning Center

The purpose of assessment is to inform instruction in order to support the development and learning of infants, toddlers, and preschoolers. Assessment is also used to document development and learning, including progress in the Ohio Early Learning and Development Standards.

The teachers at the Bombeck Family Center implement the *ACCESS Assessment System*, which includes intentional and authentic data collection using such tools as work samples, observational checklists, photographs and videotape with anecdotal notes, and electronic portfolios. Infant and toddler teachers focus on individual child data sets. In preschool classrooms, data is aggregated or compiled using the *ACCESS Classroom Tracking System* (ACHTS), which allows teachers to see up-to-date information about the strengths and needs of individual children as well as a whole class view that can inform classroom instruction. In preschool classrooms, we use assessment to plan and implement curriculum, determine individual and whole-class progress, and to inform and initiate interventions.

Children are evaluated authentically in the naturally occurring classroom environment. Assessment is intentional, ongoing, and completed by familiar adults. Formal assessments and screenings are done as required by the State and as needed to gather diagnostic information. All assessment is completed with the consent of families and by trained, experienced professionals—i.e., teacher or consultant. Parent permission is required prior to formal testing, and results are discussed during conferences.

Assessment information is shared with families quarterly during scheduled progress report conferences. Families can request additional conferences as needed.

We follow ethical standards for maintaining confidentiality of assessments. Families may ask to view any assessment information at any time. State-required forms with confidential information and evaluation results are kept in the children's files in the office area. Daily assessments and behavioral observations are kept in confidential files within the classroom. They are used to help teachers plan both individual and whole-class activities. Electronic portfolios are updated regularly and are shared with families.

Families may contribute to assessment data in several ways. Families are consistently asked for information about children during daily discussions at drop-off and pick-up times, or during conferences and intervention team meetings.

FIGURE 15-1
Source: Bombeck Family Learning Center.

the child's development positively or negatively, just as the program's program may have a positive or negative influence. The child's total development is a result of the interaction of many factors, which makes it difficult to evaluate the influence of one variable such as a specific child care or preschool experience.

15-5b • Methods for Assessing Child Progress

Assessment of child progress is ongoing and is expected to inform the day-to-day curriculum, including educator–child interactions. Professional recommendations delineate *criteria* for choosing and using assessment tools. For example, the tool must be valid and reliable, and the assessor must be using the tool in a specified manner. The recommendations call for *appropriate methods* of assessing children. Therefore, directors must know which methods are appropriate and must ensure that only appropriate methods are employed.

Because educators gather assessment information in their day-to-day teaching, directors must evaluate the methods based on the following criteria set forth in the new position statement on developmentally appropriate practice (NAEYC, 2020):

1. Observation, documentation, and assessment of young children's progress and achievements is ongoing, strategic, reflective, and purposeful. Educators embed assessment-related activities in the curriculum and in daily routines to facilitate authentic assessment and to make assessment an integral part of professional practice.

2. Assessment focuses on children's progress toward developmental and educational goals. Such goals should reflect families' input as well as children's background knowledge and experiences. They should be informed by developmental milestones including use of state early learning standards.

3. A system is in place to collect, make sense of, and use observations, documentation, and assessment information to guide what goes on in the early learning setting. Educators use this information in planning curriculum and learning experiences and in moment-to-moment interactions with children—that is, educators continually engage in assessment for the purpose of improving teaching and learning. Educators also encourage children to use observation and, beginning in the preschool years, documentation to reflect on their experiences and what they have learned.

4. The methods of assessment are responsive to the current developmental accomplishments, language(s), and experiences of young children. They recognize individual variation in learners and allow children to demonstrate their competencies in different ways. Methods appropriate to educators' assessment of young children, therefore, include results of their observations of children, clinical interviews, collections of children's work samples, and children's performance on authentic activities. For children who speak a language the educators do not know, native speakers of the child's language such as family or community members may need to be recruited to assist with the assessment process. A plan should be in place for employing volunteer and paid interpreters and translators as needed and providing them with information about appropriate interactions with young children and ethics and confidentiality, as well as about the features and purposes of the screening or assessment tool. Once collected, the results are explained to families and children (as appropriate) in order to extend the conversations around what is collected, analyzed, and reflected upon.

5. Assessments are used only for the populations and purposes for which they have been demonstrated to produce reliable, valid information. If required to use an assessment tool that has not been established as reliable or valid for the characteristics of a given child or for the intended use, educators recognize the limitations of the findings, strive to make sure they are not used in high-stakes decisions, and advocate for a different measure.

6. Decisions that have a major impact on children, such as enrollment or placement, are made in consultation with families. Such decisions should be based on multiple sources of relevant information, including that obtained from observations of and interactions with children by educators, family members, and specialists as needed.

7. When a screening assessment identifies a child who may have a disability or individualized learning or developmental needs, there is appropriate follow-up, evaluation, and, if needed, referral. Screening is used to identify issues needing more thorough examination by those qualified to do so; it is not used to diagnose or label children. Families are involved as essential sources of information. (pp. 19–20)

15-5c • Tools for Assessing Child Progress

In consultation with the teaching staff, the director decides on the tools to be used to document each child's progress. She or he discusses goals, time lines, and process. The assessment should also lead to planning to meet each child's needs. In cases involving researchers or funders who want or need to collect data, the director should consider whether this data collection presents an ethical dilemma. If so, the director must determine what course of action to take.

The first question to ask regarding any child assessment tool is, "Is it ethical to use this procedure?" Early childhood educators must be aware of and follow the Code of Ethical Conduct. The principle "We shall do no harm to children" supersedes all other principles in the code and can be used as a first consideration. (The code can be found in **Appendix A**, is on the NAEYC website, and can be purchased inexpensively from the NAEYC in brochure form. Providing a copy for each staff member and family helps everyone understand what is expected. The Code of Ethical Conduct addresses a breadth of principles related to early care and education and makes an excellent starting point for staff discussions of appropriate assessment.)

Important issues include the following:

- Will children be put in a stressful situation?
- Will individual children be evaluated unfairly because the test was normed on a specific population?
- Will children have had the opportunity to learn the material being assessed?
- Will the results of the assessment help the child by enabling families, educators, and other professionals to plan for the child's continued progress?
- Will the use of the testing program or other assessment detract significantly from other important opportunities for the children (such as physical activity, arts, and opportunity to explore a wide range of materials)?

Preschool children may be assessed with screening instruments. These relatively brief tools identify children who need additional assessment because they *may* have a disability or a learning problem. Determining whether there actually is a concern and whether there is need for remediation then leads to a plan for the child and provision of an appropriate program and support. Input from parents is important. Children often behave differently at home than in a screening situation even when a parent is encouraged to be in the screening area. Children who have the advantage of early screening benefit from access to early program modifications to meet their needs whether in a preschool classroom or in a different setting. This is particularly important for children with disabilities.

Keep in mind that screening instruments are intended to provide information about an individual child's possible need for more thorough assessment and support. They are *not* intended to be administered twice to all children in a class to demonstrate the progress that a group has made by participating in that early childhood program.

Evaluating children's knowledge and skills can be accomplished appropriately as they are engaged in ongoing play.

Many other tools are available to be used by educators. These include teacher observations, checklists, rating scales, portfolios, reports from other professionals, and standardized tests. The following sections take a brief look at each of these tools. Keep in mind the relationship between appropriate curriculum and appropriate assessment but remember that assessment should not drive curriculum.

15-5d • Anecdotal Records and Observations

Throughout the year, the educator may keep anecdotal and running records about each child. These notes, whether recorded on Post-it notes, written in a notebook, or entered into a tablet or computer, are periodically summarized by the educator. Cohen, Stern, Balaban, and Gropper (2015) describe general guidelines for observing children. The educator notes the changes in developmental level and the specific objectives that the child has met or is working to develop. Using this method, the educator is able to make statements about each child individually, emphasizing what the child's needs were based on initial observations and how the needs were met. She may modify her approach to working with the child, develop alternate play and learning opportunities, and use her developing understanding of each child to help each child continue to develop in a range of ways. This method uses subjective data provided by the educator and is valuable only if the educator is a skilled observer and collects data regularly. In a program that is minimally staffed, use of this method may be difficult. Nonetheless, development of observational skills is critical. Professional educators must know what to look for and how to recognize it.

naeyc

Growth Mindset Moment

Think about your own feelings about being evaluated. Are your feelings positive? Negative? Mixed? How does the evaluator influence these feelings? What is the behavior of an evaluator who helps you feel positive? Can you recall the behavior of an evaluator who left you feeling incompetent? Describe an evaluation that helped you in some way.

15-5e • Checklists

The director may find or create a checklist that names the behaviors toward which some of the program's objectives are aimed. Then educators merely check whether or not the child exhibits the listed behavior based on their observations of that child. A

Working Smart with Technology

Technology That Supports Evaluation

The ability to record and interpret observations of young children's behavior is considered one of the most important skills an educator can possess. For many educators, notes have traditionally been written on paper and later filed away in folders or binders. Today, technology provides alternative strategies for collecting and using this important information. For example, numerous note-taking apps for mobile devices (smartphones, laptops, tablets) can facilitate the process. Directors or educators can type notes in the classroom and immediately file the observations in children's or staff members' digital folders. Speech-to-text apps such as Dragon Dictation and Speech Notes can also be used to record notes without having to type. In addition, digital photos or audio recordings can be gathered to support the written observations. The SoundNote app allows you to take notes at the same time you are recording audio. As you might guess, these tools can be invaluable to data collection and are particularly useful when documenting children's progress toward meeting individualized education plan (IEP) goals. See Riggleman (2020) and Simon and Nemeth (2012) for additional information.

Many note-taking applications exist that can facilitate director observations of teachers and children.

question arises when the child sometimes does the task and sometimes does not, either because the task is just being learned, because the child chooses not to do it, or because no opportunity is made available. For example, an item might be "Buttons own coat." The child who does this occasionally may be in the process of learning and may not be ready to struggle with buttons on some days, or the child may be asking the educator for help because he needs attention rather than help. Checklists generally focus on easily identifiable items, so additional assessments must also be used.

15-5f • Rating Scales

The director may create or locate a rating scale that lists the behaviors closely paralleling the program's objectives. The rating scale alleviates the problem created by a checklist by providing a way for educators to qualify their answers. The educator rates each child at least at the beginning and the end of the school year and perhaps more frequently. (See **Figure 15-2** for an example of a rating scale.)

The problems with rating scales are that each educator may interpret the categories differently, and most educators are reluctant to use the two ends of the scales (1 and 5, or never and always). Such scales, however, can be useful in pointing out general strengths and weaknesses in any child's development and in the functioning of the group. Rating scales are relatively quick to complete, and educators can do them when the children are not present if they have been observing carefully.

Both checklists and rating scales are suitable for use if they are viewed as a particular educator's assessment of an individual child instead of as a comparison of one child or class with another. In reporting data from checklists and rating scales, the educator may comment on how many children recognize their names in print or play cooperatively in a group of two or more children. But this information must be placed in proper context by pointing out the children's ages and other factors that may influence the data. When space is provided on the form, the child's ratings at two or more widely spread times during a year can be included to show progress and areas in which additional support is needed.

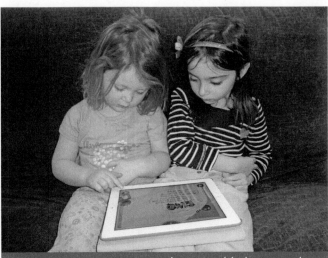

Directors may encourage teachers to add photos to the children's portfolios. This photo represents two children's beginning ability to work cooperatively.

15-5g • Portfolios

One type of assessment that can provide valuable information about each child is the portfolio. According to Lynch (2007):

> A portfolio is a tool that can be used to collect documentation of a child's growth and development over time. However, portfolio assessment is more than a compilation of unrelated writing samples, photographs, and drawings.
>
> As educators implement this approach to assessment, they systematically observe and document children's behavior and activities, collect work samples, reflect on the significance of what has been observed, and complete the assessment cycle by using the data for curricular adaptation and/or demonstrating achievement of specified goals. (p. 2)

Some educators use a two-part system with one folder in a locked cabinet and a second folder in the classroom readily accessible to the child. The first folder contains forms and information from families, the educator's written observations such as anecdotal records, notes on plans for that child, progress reports, medical reports, and reports from previous educators, agencies, or consultants who have worked with the child. This information is confidential and should be available only to those who have a legitimate right

UNIVERSITY *of* DAYTON

Child: _____

Classroom: _____

Teacher(s) completing this report: _____

Bombeck Family Learning Center
Preschool Progress Report

Explanation of Ratings

The evaluation of your child's progress is based on individual patterns of development

Y - Yes   N - No   S - Sometimes

	Rating	Teacher Comments
Emotional Development		
Identifies own feelings		
Shows concern for others' feelings		
Demonstrates self-control		
Displays self-confidence		
Emotional responses are appropriate for the situation		
Transitions to new activities with ease		
Separates from parents/guardians with ease		
Social Development		
Works and plays cooperatively (i.e., turn taking, sharing)		
Respects the rights of others		
Responds to teacher requests		
Social Studies		
Begins to use the language of time (day/night, before/after)		
Identifies similarities and differences among people		
Identifies and describes familiar places		
Identifies familiar signs and symbols		
Responsibility for Work Habits		
Knows and follows daily routine		
Takes care of materials and tools		
Completes task		
Works independently		
Finds and returns materials to proper places		
Cognitive Development		
Identifies and describes similarities and differences		
Makes predictions		
Sorts, orders, and classifies objects by one attribute		
Science		
Demonstrates curiosity about the world around them		
Exhibits respect for living things		
Participates in scientific explorations		

FIGURE 15-2

Sample preschool rating scale.

Source: Reprinted with permission from S. Adams, Bombeck Family Learning Center.

	Rating	Teacher Comments
Math		
Rote counts to 10		
Demonstrates one to one correspondence to 5		
Identifies and names numerals 0–9		
Sequences numbers up to 5		
Identifies common shapes		
Demonstrates an understanding of positional words		
Names pennies, nickels, dimes, and quarters		
Motor Development		
Fine Motor		
Shows hands preference—left or right		
Turns knobs, lids, etc. with ease		
Pours liquid into cup without spilling		
Fastens and unfastens zippers, buttons, and Velcro		
Can ___ dress ___ undress ___put on own shoes		
Uses scissors with control		
Uses appropriate pencil grasp		
Large Motor		
Walks down stairs with alternating feet		
Runs with control using opposite arms/feet-crossing midline		
Jumps ___ with feet together ___ on one foot		
Can ___ throw ___ catch ___ kick ball		
Pedals tricycle		
Language Development		
Spoken Language		
Speaks clearly to express ideas, feelings, and needs		
Uses words to solve problems and/or negotiate with friends		
Initiates and sustains conversations		
Asks and answers questions		
Listening		
Listens attentively to speakers, stories, songs, and poems		
Follows simple oral directions		
Emergent Reading		
Identifies and reads own first name		
Identifies environmental print and/or symbols		
Identifies and/or names letters		
Knows differences between illustrations and print		
Retells stories		
Emergent Writing		
Pretends to write from top to bottom, left to right, in rows		
Prints letters of own name and other meaningful words using mock or real letters		
Dictates or produces "writing" to express thoughts		
The Arts		
Demonstrates creativity through drawing, painting, clay, and a variety of art and construction materials		
Participates in singing activities, including finger plays and dance		
Demonstrates ability to move to a beat (clap, tap, etc.)		

FIGURE 15-2
(continued)

to it. The second folder provides the child with an opportunity to save products that she or he has created. The educator may add photos, videos, notes, and audiotapes, although the availability of these records depends on the program's budget and the time available to educators to prepare these records. Periodically, the records must be sorted and decisions made about what is to be retained because the record is intended to follow the child throughout her or his school years. The child should participate in deciding what is to be retained, and the family, too, may want to be involved. Some records, however, must be retained by school policy or by law. See Gronlund and James (2013) for other ideas about portfolios.

15-5h • Other Observers

The director may observe a particular child when an educator has concerns about that child. Sometimes, an outside observer such as the director or a consultant brings a more objective analysis or may see factors in the environment or even in the educator's behavior that appear to be influencing the child's behavior. After collecting data, the observer confers with the educator, and together they design a plan for working with the child. When an individual child is being evaluated to an extent that is beyond the program's regularly scheduled observation plan, parental permission must be obtained. Parental participation in planning is preferable and sometimes required by law.

When a child with identified special needs is enrolled, the director, with written parental permission, contacts agencies familiar with the child to obtain previous evaluations. The director, parent, and representatives of other agencies also may meet to share information that would be useful in working with the child and family.

Reporting a child's behavior to parents usually is handled in a conference. Written information may be provided, but the use of checklists and rating scales for this purpose often is misleading. Parents may misunderstand the significance of this type of written report and categorize their child as a success or a failure. A more appropriate written evaluation for parents may be a narrative that describes the child's strengths and progress at school and discusses areas in which the child has challenges. Sharing a child's

Making the Case for *Using Electronic Portfolios as Assessment Tools*

Portfolio assessment has long been recognized as a powerful strategy for documenting children's development. Essentially, the electronic portfolio is much like the traditional version; the major difference is that the portfolio is presented in digital format. Electronic portfolios have the benefit of being shared more readily with families and including richer documentation of children's behaviors and verbal productions. Deciding on the format of the portfolio is an important first step. One challenge in using portfolios has been the amount of time required to develop portfolios for each child. Fortunately, technology can be used to facilitate the process. For example, as mentioned in this chapter's "Working Smart with Technology" feature, many tools have been developed to help educators take notes, photos, and recordings, and these can be included as digital evidence of growth and development in the e-portfolio. For additional information about portfolio assessment and digital documentation, see Brunette (2013), Gronlund and James (2013), and Parnell and Bartlett (2012).

portfolio with parents can also help them see how their child is developing. The educator also may confer with parents about ways to help the child continue progressing toward future educational goals. For additional information about sharing assessment information with parents, see National Center on Parent, Family, and Community Engagement (2011).

Parents have the right to review information from their child's folder at any time. In some cases, they feel that having certain information passed along to the next educator is damaging to the child. In other cases, they are eager for the new educator to understand as much as possible about their child immediately so that the child does not have to endure a time period in which the educator is discovering a hearing loss or some other condition for which an instructional plan should be designed. In any case, the educator and parent discuss available information about the child and together determine which data should be sent forward to the next educator. When

The director positions herself at the child's eye level so that she can talk with both child and parent.

a child has an individualized family service plan or an individualized education plan, the new educator should have access to that plan and participate with the IEP team in updating the plan on a regular basis. Keep in mind that the family is an essential and required part of the team.

15-5i • Standardized Tests

For the last decade there has been a political push to use standardized tests with young children in an effort to collect data for accountability to be used to justify funding. Although practices vary greatly across states, the tide appears to be changing as more decision makers are coming to understand that validity and reliability when using standardized tests with children younger than third grade is questionable at best. First, young children can't be tested in a group because they can write only in a limited way, if at all. In a group situation, they have trouble attending to the type of test form typically used in such standardized tests. Even if their task is to draw a circle around one of three pictures for each question, they may be focused on an aspect of the question or the pictures that is not related to the presumed correct answer.

For example, one kindergartner was asked to circle the picture of two characters from a story. The three choices were a picture of Jack and Jill falling down the hill, a picture of the three bears, and a picture of Little Red Riding Hood. After the test, the educator talked with a child whom she was certain had

well-developed concepts of "twoness" and "threeness." She asked why he had circled the three bears. He replied, "Well, you see, there's two bears and one left over." She asked what he thought about circling Jack and Jill, and he quickly responded, "Jack and Jill is not a story; it's a poem." Although that thinking may not be typical, we have no way of knowing why young children respond the way they do in a standardized testing situation. The example demonstrates one of the reasons standardized tests, if used at all with young children, must be used only for an intended purpose, which is often to identify eligibility for intervention services.

When tests are administered to young children individually, results are often unreliable. The answer a young child gives today may differ from the answer he provides a few days later. Children do not learn in small, isolated bits. As they examine their world, they form relationships with what they already know. Those relationships initially are not always accurate from an adult perspective but are meaningful to the child. As the child encounters additional situations, he creates new relationships, which may or may not be more realistic from an adult perspective. The information that a child learns by rote may be lost relatively quickly if it is meaningless to the child. This kind of information is often assessed on standardized tests.

Even though directors must be sure the tests used in their programs are appropriate, funders may require inappropriate assessments. Such a situation presents an ethical dilemma: Administering the test and the potential use of the results may be seen as inappropriate, but refusing to allow the testing may result in lost funds and programs for children who are most in need of early education. In a critique of the Head Start National Reporting System (NRS), Meisels and Atkins-Burnett (2004) described this high-stakes achievement test for 4- and 5-year-olds as containing "items that are rife with class prejudice and are developmentally inappropriate." The authors presented several examples of NRS test items, explaining, in each case, their inadequacies. The authors concluded, "This test is not good early education practice. It is not good psychometric practice. It is not good public policy. And it is certainly not good for young children." Raver and Zigler (2004) argued that "the application of a strictly cognitive focus to assessments of school readiness runs counter to what the best developmental research tells us and what past policy experience has shown." After numerous discussions about the assessment among various constituents, the National Head Start Association reported that the NRS had been terminated and that programs were no longer required to use the NRS tests.

The director's role is to understand and use an appropriate assessment program and to work to modify or eliminate high-stakes testing. In some cases, the director's ethical decision may be to refuse to allow such testing in his program. Such a decision may involve issues such as cessation of funding based on the refusal, thus impacting many children, families, and staff. A concerted effort over time, however, with supportive position statements by professional organizations and reasoned discussions with legislators, educators, funders, and other interested parties may prove more beneficial to children in the long run.

If tests are to be administered, the director is professionally responsible for determining whether the test in question is appropriate for the children to be assessed. The director should understand what the test measures, how it is to be administered, by whom, and for what purpose. What effect will it have on the curriculum and, more important, on the children? What provisions will be made for assessing children for whom the test is culturally inappropriate based on language, other aspects of culture, or special needs? The director is expected to know or learn about terms related to testing, such as what the scores mean, what different types of tests are designed to measure, what the results mean, and how they will be used. The director is also responsible for ensuring that staff members understand these topics. A key component of the director's role is ensuring that the results from any standardized tests are not misused. A clear description of topics related to testing appears in Snow (2011).

If we find that a particular test meets the criteria described earlier in this section, the next questions include the test's reliability and validity.

- Would the results obtained by a particular data collector be similar enough to those of another trained data collector?
- If educators are expected to test their own classes, what preparation will they receive (ECDS, 2018)?
- Who will teach the class while the educator tests one child at a time?
- Does the test measure what it purports to measure?
- How will the results be reported?
- What do the results mean to educators? To families?
- Will the people who receive the results know how to interpret them?
- What will be done with the results? Will they be used for the purpose for which the test was designed? Are the results beneficial to the children? If not, will the benefits to someone else outweigh the impact on the children and the program?

Some misuses of standardized tests of young children include the following:

- keeping a child from entering kindergarten when he is chronologically eligible,
- rating a program,
- evaluating educators,
- making curricular decisions based solely on specific test content,
- giving several tests two or more times per year, and
- teaching to the test.

Although a wide range of opportunities for assessment of children's progress has been mentioned, the more observant preschool teachers are, the more they will learn about each child. In combining brief

Growth Mindset Moment

Think about report card day when you were in elementary school. Can you recall any of your feelings about receiving a report card? If the experience was not always a good one for you, what might have made the experience better?

- Your own attitude or performance?
- Your classmates' behavior after report cards were distributed?
- Your parents' response when they saw your report card?
- Your educator's comments on your report card?
- The grading system?

When you consider what you will include in a child's folder, try to remember your own grade school days. Think about the effects that the inclusion of data about your behavior may have had on your relationships with educators and your parents.

educator notes, parental comments, photos of the child engaged in the classroom, and anecdotal records, the educator has a good understanding of a child. Bringing these observations together enables educators to create a description of the child's development over the preschool enrollment period.

The director's knowledge and ability to support staff in implementing an appropriate child assessment plan is a major factor in its success. Using the results to meet children's needs is a significant part of the program's operational system. Such a plan demonstrates that laying out a detailed curriculum for the year is not appropriate because it does not address children's particular needs and interests.

15-6 • Total Program Evaluation

The goals of the program itself are designed to fulfill the particular needs that the program was established to meet. Consequently, at evaluation time, the needs—the goals—are evaluated as part of the program's overall evaluation system.

At regular intervals, the community's needs must be assessed so that the program can plan for current and future populations. Because goals are closely tied to the philosophy of the program, they change slowly. Nonetheless, they should be examined periodically,

▶ **TeachSource Video Vignette**

Setting Goals in an Early Childhood Center

The video titled *Goal Setting: A Center Director Sets Goals for an Early Childhood Center* provides an overview of issues related to evaluation of early care and education programs. As you view the video, reflect on the following questions:

1. What factors contribute to developing effective goals for directors? For educators?

2. What is the value in considering a person's strengths first?

perhaps every few years, to determine whether they still are applicable. The objectives are more directly related to the individuals served at a given time. Therefore, they may change more rapidly than the goals. The objectives should be examined annually before the start of a new school or fiscal year.

In addition, the director or the board may prepare checklists or rating scales for the evaluation of the program. They can be distributed to staff members, parents, and community representatives; or these people may be asked to provide their evaluations in written or oral forms. Board members and funding agency representatives may contribute to the evaluation by reviewing aspects of the overall program such as the physical environment, curriculum, parent program, ancillary services, and board operations. They also may evaluate the staff performance in general rather than individual terms. Periodically, perhaps every few years, the policies and procedures manual, the job descriptions, and the board bylaws are reviewed. Even the evaluation plans and procedures are evaluated!

A widely used program evaluation tool is the Early Childhood Environment Rating Scale (Harms,

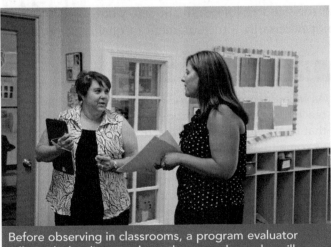

Before observing in classrooms, a program evaluator talks with the director about the procedures she will use.

Clifford, & Cryer, 2014). Seven areas are covered in separate subscales: (1) personal care routines, (2) furnishings and displays for children, (3) language-reasoning experiences, (4) fine and gross motor activities, (5) creative activities, (6) social development, and (7) adult needs. After observing, the rater circles the appropriate category from 1 (inadequate) to 7 (excellent). Each subscale total rating is plotted on a profile sheet. Program staff then can decide in which areas they want to make improvements. Profiles produced at different points in time can be used to determine changes in the program during that time period. Similar scales have been produced for rating infant–toddler programs, school age, and family child care (Harms, Cryer, Clifford, & Yasejian, 2017). Instructional guides for observers are available in print and on DVD.

Perhaps the most important evaluation a director can conduct is to look at quality of work life. Bloom (2010) points out that low morale, stress, and burnout soon affect commitment to the profession. When staff members experience these tensions, it becomes especially difficult for directors to maintain high-quality programs. Bloom recommends, therefore, that the director examine 10 dimensions necessary to create a professional climate. Among these are supervisor support, opportunities for professional growth, and the amount of staff autonomy in decision-making. She further recommends surveying the staff and then using the resulting data to plan changes.

Staff surveys usually are anonymous, although in large programs, individuals may be asked to indicate age, job type, level of education completed, or any other category that will provide productive information. The purpose is to use the data for revising administrative practices and planning realistic changes in the program. Items that are obviously unattainable should, of course, not be included. For instance, one would not list "The program shall allow monthly unpaid mental health days" if such a policy would not be workable.

Many program directors and staff members are aware that they need to check the quality of their relations with parents, children, and staff members from a variety of cultures. The self-assessment documents from the National Center for Cultural Competence (2009), which are designed specifically for early intervention and early childhood settings, may help directors provide leadership in analyz-ing areas of strength and areas where improvement is needed. This publication includes sections titled "Physical Environment," "Materials and Resources," "Communication Styles," and "Values and Attitudes."

Talan and Bloom (2011) created a publication that provides guidance related to all aspects of early childhood program assessment, focusing on the leadership and management practices of center-based early childhood organizations. The format consists of 10 categories of items, including program operations, fiscal management, program planning and evaluation, technology, and marketing and public relations. Each category is addressed on wide two-page spreads. A list of what to look for, such as needed documents and questions to ask, appears on the left. The evaluator takes notes based on a review of the category components during the data-gathering phase. For example, when completing the section titled "Assessment in Support of Learning," evaluators would probably ask the director how curriculum is planned. They would also determine whether reliable and valid assessments are being used. Next the evaluator completes the rating scale, allowing the rater to refer back to notes made during the data-gathering phase. Using a seven-point scale for each item assessed, the evaluator can create a profile depicting the program's leadership and management strengths and areas in which improvement can be considered. When completed, these documents provide valuable planning tools for directors.

15-6a • Licensing

In the past, licensing has been viewed as the standard for health and safety but not necessarily a measurement of quality in programs.

> ### Director's Corner
>
> As we prepared for our NAEYC Accreditation Self-Study, teaching teams worked together to address each item that dealt with classroom practice. This process helped us come to a common understanding by all members of the teaching team. We took the opportunities for collaboration even further by having teaching teams from another classroom review the evidence that their peers provided. This started a process of sharing that carried over to other aspects of the work of the center.
>
> —*Director, agency-sponsored child care center*

In its 2020 Child Care Licensing Benchmark Project, Child Care Aware of America (CCAA) "marks an important step forward to help states not only gauge how well they align with federal requirements, but also guide them as they strive to increase the quality of their child care system" (Engelman, Dobbins, Veatch, & Tercha, p. 2). This important benchmarking project identified the following as important for quality programs:

1. Child care licensing benchmarks should be set for basic and advanced quality standards.
2. A benchmarking tool for states should be used to self-assess their alignment with both basic and quality standards.
3. A scoring rubric, C-A-R-E, agreed on by stakeholders, scores each state's submission and classifies the state along a continuum, with a "C" corresponding to minimal alignment and "E" corresponding to perfect alignment.
4. A state report prepared by CCAA that provides a snapshot document summarizing the state's alignment on each individual benchmark and its overall alignment with all benchmarks. Currently, CCAA has data for five pilot states and has plans to gradually expand the project to all 50 states and the District of Columbia. CCAA intends for stakeholders and advocates to use these child care licensing benchmark project assets as a compass to guide everyone to higher-quality, affordable child care environments for all children. (Engelman et al., 2020, p. 2)

For more information on the language in these benchmarks, see **Appendix F**.

A licensing evaluation is typically conducted by a specialist from the state or county jobs and family services department.

15-6b • Quality Rating and Improvement Systems (QRIS)

As described in Chapter 3, QRIS are growing as an important factor in improving early childhood program quality. At the time of this revision, 48 out of 50 states, all U.S. territories, and Washington, DC had adopted QRIS. Although many of these systems are voluntary, most are tied to funding. This means that programs relying on local, state, or federal funding must achieve a certain QRIS ranking to qualify for funding. Funding is only one factor in the decision that administrators make to become part of a QRIS. As the marketing associated with quality in early childhood education program selection impacts how families make child care choices, programs that are not ranked in the QRIS find it more difficult to compete. The number of early childhood programs that apply for a QRIS ranking has increased greatly and, outside of licensing, is the most common form of program evaluation oversight. By design, QRIS require ongoing program evaluation as administrators typically provide evidence annually, and most states require site visits by an external evaluator.

15-6c • Accreditation

Also discussed in Chapter 3, accreditation in early childhood refers to a type of program evaluation also conducted by an outside agency, usually a professional organization. The most common accrediting process for early childhood programs is overseen by NAEYC, which has adopted new program accreditation standards (see **Figure 15-3**) and descriptions of high-quality early childhood education. NAEYC's website includes information about applying for accreditation and provides materials for self-study. If the program completes the self-study and decides to continue, it prepares the documents that will be reviewed and plans for a visit from trained assessors.

The NAEYC's system for program accreditation includes lists of the values and evidence-based criteria to be used in decision-making. In this system, early childhood programs are required to be in substantial compliance with all 10 standards, all of which are considered to be reliable indicators of high quality. Under this plan, the public and staff of accredited programs will know that the programs have been assessed on criteria that lead to positive outcomes for children.

The process includes four steps:

1. **Enrollment.** Engage in self-study (what you need to know in order to study what you do, what you need to think about as you study your program, and what you need to improve).
2. **Application.** Submit application. Set time frame for completing formal self-assessment report.

NAEYC Early Learning Program Accreditation Standards and Assessment Items

STANDARD 1: Relationships The program promotes positive relationships between all children and adults to encourage each child's sense of individual worth and belonging as part of a community and to foster each child's ability to contribute as a responsible community member.

STANDARD 2: Curriculum The program implements a curriculum that is consistent with its goals for children and that promotes learning and development in each of the following areas: social, emotional, physical, language, and cognitive.

STANDARD 3: Teaching The program uses a variety of developmentally, culturally, and linguistically appropriate and effective teaching approaches that enhance each child's learning and development in the context of the program's curriculum goals.

STANDARD 4: Assessment of Child Progress The program uses a variety of formal and informal assessment approaches to provide information on children's learning and development. These assessments occur in the context of reciprocal communications between teachers and families, and with sensitivity to the cultural contexts in which children are developing. The program uses assessment results to inform decisions about the children in their care, to improve teaching practices, and to drive program improvement.

STANDARD 5: Health The program promotes the nutrition and health of children and protects children and staff from illness.

STANDARD 6: Staff Competencies, Preparation, and Support The program employs and supports a teaching and administrative staff that have the qualifications, knowledge, and professional commitment necessary to promote children's learning and development and to support families' diverse needs and interests.

STANDARD 7: Families The program establishes and maintains collaborative relationships with each child's family to foster children's development in all settings. These relationships are sensitive to family composition, language, and culture.

STANDARD 8: Community Relationships The program establishes relationships with and uses the resources of the children's communities to support the achievement of program goals.

STANDARD 9: Physical Environment The program has a safe and healthful environment that provides appropriate and well-maintained indoor and outdoor physical environments. The environment includes facilities, equipment, and materials to facilitate child and staff learning and development.

STANDARD 10: Leadership and Management The program effectively implements policies, procedures, and systems that support stable staff and strong personnel, fiscal, and program management so all children, families, and staff have high-quality experiences.

NAEYC.org

FIGURE 15-3

Growth Mindset Moment

Think about where you learned about young children, their behavior, and their interests. Maybe you have lots of older brothers and sisters, or maybe you did many hours of babysitting when you were younger. You are currently studying to be a child care administrator, so surely you must have studied child development.

Now think about parents who have not had those types of opportunities. Where might they have learned about child care and what is required in providing high-quality care for young children? Although many attempts to reach parents have been made, quite a few parents have not heard about them. They therefore choose child care based on location only or on what looks fun to adults. Many of us had no idea how important early childhood education, whether at home or away from home, is to a child's development.

3. **Enter candidacy.** Submit self-assessment. Demonstrate that licensing, staffing, and health and safety requirements have been met.

4. **On-site visit.** NAEYC assessors visit and determine whether the program meets all 10 NAEYC standards and selected components related to those standards.

The NAEYC views the self-study as an important way to begin program improvement whether or not the program decides to continue with the accreditation process. Materials for the accreditation process may be obtained from the NAEYC. Most directors find that when they take the time to read through the documents, the steps they need to take are all laid out for them, and the procedures may no longer seem as intimidating. The director's role then is to obtain the support of the board and staff by letting them know what is expected and that they will be engaging in a worthwhile team effort. Sharing the accreditation materials with confidence and being open to addressing staff members' questions and concerns will help everyone get started willingly.

Some changes will almost always be needed. Everyone involved may feel stressed as change is discussed. Here again, the director must listen to concerns and help the group decide how to address them. Making changes is less stressful when the group feels ownership. Some changes may be out of the question, often because of the finances involved. This does not necessarily mean that the program cannot become accredited, but the program report will have to describe how the staff has designed an appropriate alternate approach. In many cases, the staff will have to set priorities and create a schedule for working on various components within a certain time frame. Trying to tackle everything at once can be overwhelming and counterproductive.

Although licensing and the QRIS are mandated in most situations, accreditation is optional. The board and the director must consider the cost of accreditation and the value to the children, families, and staff. In addition, the program may profit financially by being accredited as the community begins to recognize that the new process involves demonstration of quality in all aspects of the program's operation. Current information about the NAEYC accreditation process and procedures is available on the NAEYC website and in NAEYC publications.

Some directors may feel that they do not need to bother with accreditation because they have a long waiting list of children and their programs seem to be doing well. However, directors who take a professional approach will lead their staff in a self-study periodically, whether or not they choose to participate in a particular form of accreditation.

15-7 • Summarizing Data

No matter which program evaluation process is chosen, the director is responsible for summarizing the data that are collected from all aspects of the evaluation process, showing the progress or regression since the last evaluation rather than focusing solely on the current performance level. The summary should provide a clear data picture for the reader and reflect accurately the facts, ideas, and opinions provided by those who participated. Usually a comment that occurs frequently should receive more weight in the summary than an item that seldom appears in the data, no matter how striking or impressive that item appears. Furthermore, no new information should appear in the summary.

The summary is written, dated, and signed by the summarizer and should include a listing of sources used in its compilation. Some data may appear in graph or chart form, particularly if this format makes it easier to understand or more likely to be read. Appropriate computer software makes this task much easier.

15-7a • Analyzing and Using the Data

The director or a designated committee uses the summary to cull information. For example, in analyzing enrollment records, the dropout rate of children whose transportation is provided by the school may be compared with the dropout rate of those children who get to school by some other means.

In examining this information, other factors need to be kept constant. For example, if all the children receiving transportation are from low-income families, and if some or all of the other children are from middle-income families, then the dropout rate might be more closely related to income level than to mode of transportation. To clarify the situation, additional data would be needed.

After the data have been analyzed, the director prepares a report for the funding agency, the board, and other people or groups to whom the program is responsible. This type of report usually is prepared annually, although interim reports may be compiled. The report should be expressed clearly and be easily comprehensible and professional in appearance. Current software simplifies this task and enhances the results.

Each board member receives a copy of the report, one or more copies are submitted to each funding agency that is involved, and one or more copies are filed at the program. The narrative may be enhanced and clarified by the addition of appropriate graphs, charts, or tables. A pie chart showing the use of the director's time, for example, can be more effective than a lengthy narrative that contains the same information. Graphs and charts can be computer generated and add an extra professional touch to a report. Remember that the report will be read by people from a variety of backgrounds.

Usually, by the time the report for a given year is complete and in the hands of board members, the planning process for the new year has been completed and put into operation. The report then is used primarily for future planning. The board looks at the report, which includes the director's recommendations, to determine the areas that need modification. For example, if there is a high rate of turnover among the teaching staff, then the board looks further to see if the cause can be determined from the evaluation data. Perhaps the salaries at this program are much lower than those of other programs in the community, or perhaps the physical environment is poor. Decisions for change are based on available evidence that grows out of the total evaluation process.

Summary

From the program's inception, an evaluation plan is an essential component of the total program. The director should be aware of the following:

- The purpose of the plan is to determine the value of the program's operation; to evaluate the individuals within it through an analysis of the progress and functioning of the staff, the children, and the overall program; and to provide a basis for future planning for the program.

- Planning for effective evaluation of program components must be systematic and should include identifying what will be evaluated and why.

- The processes and procedures involved with evaluating staff members include collecting, summarizing, analyzing, and using data according to a prespecified plan that lets everyone involved know how, when, where, why, and by whom an evaluation is being completed.

- Certain methods and strategies are useful for conducting appropriate assessment of children's progress.

- Program evaluation and accreditation are valuable for ensuring quality.

- Analyzing and using data collected through the program evaluation process is important.

TRY IT OUT!

1. Compare the new Child Care Aware Licensing Benchmarks 2020 (**Appendix F**) with the NAEYC Program Accreditation Standards (**Appendix D**). How are the two documents alike or different in how quality is defined and measured?

2. **Director's Resource 15-1** provides an example of an annual performance review document. Review it and discuss its contents with a classmate and answer the following questions:
   a. What type of information is to be included in the first section? How do the four sections of planning relate to each other? (Note: SMART is an acronym for goals that are specific, measurable, attainable, realistic, and time-limited. Additional information about these goals can be found easily online.) What "professional competencies" might be addressed? If this were your own evaluation, on what competencies would you focus for the next year? (Use the NAEYC Standards for Early Childhood Professional Preparation Programs Standards in **Appendix B** to identify competencies.)
   b. What type of information is to be included in the *assessing* section of the performance evaluation document?
   c. What is the value of staff members setting goals and reflecting on past performance?

d. As a future director, what challenges might you anticipate when conducting a performance evaluation with a staff member?

3. Work with a partner and role-play a conference in which an educator and a director set up a work plan for the next six months. If you are assuming the role as educator, try to use your own classroom skills and areas in which you need improvement as a basis for the objectives in your work plan. If you are playing the director, use your communication skills to find out what help this educator seems to need and where his strengths lie. After the role-play, ask your classmates for a brief evaluation of the conference. Then have two other students repeat the role-play. Is the second role-play different from the one formulated in the first role-play? Identify strategies that should be used for effective goal-setting.

4. With members of your class, discuss the role that ethics plays in the assessment of children and evaluation of staff. Refer to the NAEYC Code of Ethical Conduct in **Appendix A** and describe the way in which specific principles might apply to the evaluation and assessment process.

5. Conduct an interview with a director or administrator regarding the program's evaluation and assessment plan. Ask the following questions:

- How often are staff members evaluated? What procedures are followed?
- How are evaluations used with staff to support their development as professionals?
- How often are children assessed? What types of assessments are completed? How were the assessments chosen?
- How does the administrator feel about the appropriateness of the assessments used with children? What changes might the administrator make regarding assessment of children if permitted to do so?
- What strategies are used to ensure the confidentiality of the results?
- How often is program evaluation carried out at the program? What procedures are followed? Are changes made to the program based on the evaluation?

Director's Resource 15-1

ECE II Name: _____ Eval completed by: _____ Date: _____

Bombeck Center Early Childhood Educator IIs will	Expectations Not Met		Expectations Partially Met		Meets Expectations		Exceeds Expectations	
	ECE II	Director	ECE II	Director	ECE II	Director	ECE II	Director
1. Adhere to the NAEYC Code of Professional Conduct								
Comments:								
2. Learn **5% of time**								
a. Attend professional development sessions that address the needs or interest of the teacher or teaching team and satisfy the requirements for accreditation, licensure, and QRIS or SUTQ rating.								
b. Actively and positively participate in center-sponsored meetings and professional development.								
c. Complete a personal professional development plan and monitor progress to completion.								
d. Engage in reflective supervision as a means to learn about and reflect on their practice, the practice of their peers, and the practice of the ECE students they mentor.								
e. Accept constructive feedback and implement strategies for professional growth.								
f. Keep teaching team informed of new information from professional development and collaborate with team to infuse current information throughout classroom practice.								
Comments:								

Director's Resource 15-1 (continued)

Bombeck Center Early Childhood Educator IIs will	Expectations Not Met		Expectations Partially Met		Meets Expectations		Exceeds Expectations	
	ECE II	Director	ECE II	Director	ECE II	Director	ECE II	Director
3. Collaborate: 5% of time								
a. Demonstrate a value for collaboration by consistently engaging in team decision-making and problem-solving.								
b. Disagree respectfully and use effective conflict-resolution strategies to address differences of opinion.								
c. Demonstrate a growth mindset and adjust to change.								
d. Maintain a positive center climate that fosters job satisfaction of individuals and a strong educational team.								
Comments:								
4. Plan: 5% of time								
a. Plan collaboratively with others in the teaching team to create a cohesive, play-based, child-centered, emergent, and age-appropriate curriculum.								
b. Observe children to identify their interests and base instructional decisions, in part, on those interests.								
c. Use the ACCESS assessment system to document learning and inform instruction.								
d. Integrate the Ohio Early Learning and Development Standards throughout the day using authentic materials and experiences.								
e. Use the ACCESS Science Concept Planner to plan science-focused investigations or mini-investigations and share with administration before an investigation begins.								
f. Collaborate with the educational team to construct intentional learning opportunities during daily routines.								
Comments:								

Director's Resource 15-1 (continued)

Bombeck Center Early Childhood Educator IIs will	Expectations Not Met		Expectations Partially Met		Meets Expectations		Exceeds Expectations	
	ECE II	Director	ECE II	Director	ECE II	Director	ECE II	Director
5. Implement: 66% of time								
a. Maintain a clean, safe, organized and engaging classroom environment throughout each day.								
b. Work with the teaching team to implement the ACCESS curriculum.								
c. Work with the teaching team to support emotional development, self-regulation and mental health of children through such techniques as Conscious Discipline.								
d. Work with the teaching team to make decisions about daily routines, room arrangement, and select appropriate and safe materials that align with the curriculum.								
Comments:								
6. Assess/Document 2% of time								
a. Use a deep understanding of child development to observe children and identify what they know and are able to do.								
b. Take pictures, write anecdotal notes, and collect work samples to document learning and development.								
c. Compile documentation using check sheets, portfolio forms, or the whole class tracking system as appropriate for the age.								
d. Maintain portfolios for each child by adding two entries each month for each child.								
Comments:								

Director's Resource 15-1 *(continued)*

Bombeck Center Early Childhood Educator IIs will	Expectations Not Met		Expectations Partially Met		Meets Expectations		Exceeds Expectations	
	ECE II	Director	ECE II	Director	ECE II	Director	ECE II	Director
7. Communicate 2% of time								
a. Maintain open and ongoing communication with the teaching team to ensure that the program is cohesive and intentional so that all members of the teaching team understand what is being done and why.								
b. Maintain responsive, friendly, and respectful communication with families during drop-off and pickup times and as needed throughout the day.								
c. Use MomentPath daily to keep track of teacher–child ratios, document learning, and communicate with families.								
d. Engage families in routine, scheduled conferences with the families of children in their group.								
Comments:								
8. Mentor 5% of time								
a. Model and explain classroom routines and the ACCESS curriculum to ECE students.								
b. Answer questions about classroom practice and support ECE students to develop as teachers and to complete their course assignments effectively in the classroom.								
c. Participate in midterm and end-of-term performance evaluations with each of their assigned ECE students.								
d. Inform the EDT 211 and 212 lab coordinators when students are not meeting expectations and support intervention plans as needed.								
Comment:								

Director's Resource 15-1 (continued)

Bombeck Center Early Childhood Educator IIs will	Expectations Not Met		Expectations Partially Met		Meets Expectations		Exceeds Expectations	
	ECE II	Director	ECE II	Director	ECE II	Director	ECE II	Director
9.　Demonstrate　　2% of time								
a.　Explain classroom practice to visitors to the classroom or center.								
Comment:								
10.　Other duties　　3% of time								
a.　As assigned by the director, executive director, or school or university leadership.								
Comment:								
Growth Mindset Goals:								

Signatures: _____　_____　Date: _____

　　　　　　　EC Educator II　　　　　　　　Director

REFERENCES

Bloom, P. J. (2010). *Measuring work attitudes in the early childhood setting* (2nd edition). Wheeling, IL: McCormick Center for Early Childhood Leadership, National-Louis University.

Brunette, L. (2013). Embracing technology with e-portfolios. *Child Care Exchange, 209,* 26–29. http://stage .childcareexchange.com/article/embracing-technology -with-e-portfolios/5020926/

Cohen, D., Stern, V., Balaban, N., & Gropper, N. (2015). *Observing and recording the behavior of young children* (6th ed.). New York, NY: Teachers College Press.

Early Childhood Integrated Data Systems (ECDS). (2018). *School readiness reporting guide*. Philadelphia, PA: ECDataWorks. https://slds.ed.gov/services/PDCService .svc/GetPDCDocumentFile?fileId=33450&utm_content =&utm_medium=email&utm_name=&utm_source =govdelivery&utm_term=

Engelman, K., Dobbins, D., Veatch, & Tercha, J. (2020). *Child care licensing benchmark project*. Arlington, VA: Child Care Aware of America. https://www .childcareaware.org/our-issues/research/child-care -licensing-benchmark-project/

Gronlund, G., & James, M. (2013). *Focused observations: How to observe young children for assessment and curriculum planning*. St. Paul, MN: Redleaf Press.

Harms, T., Clifford, R. M., & Cryer, D. (2014). *Early childhood environment rating scale* (3rd ed.) (ECERS-3). New York, NY: Teachers College Press.

Harms, T., Cryer, D., Clifford, R. M., & Yazejian, N. (2017). *Infant/toddler environment rating scale* (3rd ed.). New York, NY: Teachers College Press.

Lynch, E. M. (2007). Authentic assessment in the inclusive classroom: Using portfolios to document change and modify curriculum. In M. Ostrosky & E. Horn (Eds.), *Linking curriculum to child and family outcomes* (pp. 55–70). Longmont, CO: Sopris West.

Meisels, S., & Atkins-Burnett, S. (2004). The Head Start national reporting system: A critique. *Young Children, 59*(1), 64–66. https://ectacenter.org/~pdfs/eco /meisels.pdf

National Association for the Education of Young Children (NAEYC). (2019). Advancing equity in early childhood. *A Position Statement of the National Association for the Education of Young Children*. Washington, DC: Author. https://www.naeyc.org /sites/default/files/globally-shared/downloads/PDFs/ resources/position-statements/naeycadvancingequi-typositionstatement.pdf

National Association for the Education of Young Children (NAEYC). (2020). *Developmentally appropriate practice (DAP) position statement*. Washington, DC: Author. https://www.naeyc.org/resources/position -statements/dap/contents

National Center for Cultural Competence. (2009). *Promoting cultural and linguistic competency: Self-assessment checklist for personnel providing services and supports in early intervention and early childhood settings*. Washington, DC: Georgetown University. https://nccc.georgetown.edu/documents /ChecklistEIEC.pdf

National Center on Parent, Family and Community Engagement. (2011). *Family engagement and ongoing child assessment: Responsibilities, perspectives, and strategies*. Boston, MA: Boston Children's Hospital and Harvard Family Research Project. https:// eclkc.ohs.acf.hhs.gov/sites/default/files/pdf/family -engagement-ongoing-child-assessment-eng.pdf

Parnell, W., & Bartlett, J. (2012). iDocument: How smartphones and tablets are changing documentation in preschool and primary classrooms. *Young Children, 67*(3), 50–59. https://www.learntechlib.org/p/88336/

Raver, C. C., & Zigler, E. F. (2004). Another step back? Assessing readiness in Head Start. *Young Children, 59*(1), 58–63.

Riggleman, S. (2020, July). Using data collection applications in early childhood settings to support behavior change. *Journal of Special Education Technology*. https://doi.org/10.1177/0162643420942763

Simon, F., & Nemeth, K. N. (2012). *Digital decisions: Choosing the right technology tools for early childhood education*. Lewisville, NC: Gryphon House.

Snow, K. (2011, December). *Kindergarten readiness and other large-scale assessment systems: Necessary considerations in the assessment of young children*. Washington, DC: NAEYC. https://nieer.org/wp -content/uploads/2012/03/Assessment_Systems.pdf

Talan, T. N., & Bloom, P. J. (2011). *Program administrators' scale: Measuring early childhood leadership and management* (2nd ed.) New York, NY: Teachers College Press.

Brand the program by consistently using a logo on promotional materials, both in print and on the Web.

Marketing the Program

Standards and Recommendations Addressed in This Chapter

ADVANCING EQUITY RECOMMENDATION 5   Recognize the value of serving a diverse group of children and strive to increase the range of diversity among those served.

PROGRAM STANDARD 8   Community Relationships

PROFESSIONAL STANDARDS AND COMPETENCIES: STANDARD 2   Family-Teacher Partnerships and Community Connections

PROFESSIONAL STANDARDS AND COMPETENCIES: STANDARD 6   Professionalism as an Early Childhood Educator

LEARNING OBJECTIVES

After reading this chapter, you should be able to:

16-1   Identify the components of a well-developed marketing plan.

16-2   Explain strategies that maximize public relations efforts.

16-3   Identify marketing strategies that might appeal to families from different generations.

16-4   Identify ways that new media can be used to market a program.

An important part of the director's job in both new and ongoing programs is marketing and publicizing the program. The direction that marketing takes is based on competition in the area as well as identification of families that need to be reached in order to recruit children and promote the program. Obviously, young families are the first to come to mind because most programs are set up to serve children from infancy to 5 years of age or primary school-aged children in before- and after-school programs. However, there are other considerations. If program survival depends on tuition, then the target population is clearly limited to those who can afford to pay for the service. On the other hand, if outside funding sources exist, it will be necessary to increase the scope of the publicity effort so that a greater portion of a diverse potential clientele can be reached. The marketing plan is also impacted by the program's sponsor, its location, and the geographic location in which potential families will likely live. Eligibility requirements also play a role: Sometimes program sponsors limit the population to be served to university families, families who meet poverty eligibility requirements, children of hospital personnel, children of families who are employed by a particular business, children of club or church members, and so forth.

Marketing decisions require skillful analysis of circumstances specific to the program. For example, there will be minimal gains from marketing in an area where competing programs are limited to specific populations. Similarly, marketing will have a limited effect on families who choose a preschool program offered by an exclusive private school because that guarantees the child access to this private school's elementary school. What works for one program may not for another, and the director must be knowledgeable about the factors that impact how parents make decisions about where their children will receive early care and education. Programs might promote convenience, a flexible schedule, or a prime location as selling points for potential families.

A director who is skillful with marketing his or her program must have a keen understanding of the questions, concerns, and misconceptions that parents have. Marketing efforts shouldn't focus solely on attracting new children but should also seek to retain the children who are currently enrolled. Efforts to inform potential families about the benefits of a quality program for brain development and future school success can be key selling points for certain groups of parents, but this effort can be negated if a program allows currently served families to retain misperceptions and doubts about whether a play-based curriculum can prepare young children for kindergarten. A program may be at risk of losing a family whose goal is academic readiness for school success and who has doubts about whether academic skills can be developed within an emergent and developmentally appropriate play-based program. It is the job of the director and early childhood (EC) educators to see opportunities in the day-to-day life of the program to demonstrate how it addresses the goals of the families, which often includes the goal of school readiness.

Good marketing strategies are proactive and look for opportunities to communicate a consistent, clear, and positive message. Effective directors understand the differences between *advertising, marketing,* and *public relations* (see **Figure 16-1**) and craft a message that takes advantage of all three. Programs that identify and communicate a message consistently can avoid the misconceptions that crop up when there is a void of information. In the past, many EC programs have waited until the year before kindergarten to discuss school readiness. This time line misses important marketing opportunities and often portrays the purpose of the prekindergarten year as a last-ditch effort to prepare children for a kindergarten entry "event." Programs that convey an ongoing and consistent message about how children develop and learn can help parents come to understand that school readiness is a process that starts in infancy and continues through kindergarten entry and into the primary grades.

There are many ways to market your program, but do not underestimate the value of word of mouth from parents who are enthusiastic about the quality of your program. A consistently communicated message can also positively impact word-of-mouth marketing as parents talk with other parents about their child's early learning program. Staff also must understand that every time parents are in the program, they gather and interpret information about the program that impacts the word-of-mouth marketing message. Directors and staff should take regular "tours" of the program and their classrooms to examine the message that is being communicated. Arranging both formal open house events and informal morning coffee conversations or afternoon

snack gatherings that encourage parents to meet and chat are strategies that provide time for parents to hear a clear, consistent, and accurate message and also ask questions. But in the end, nothing sells better than offering a high-quality program worthy of accreditation and led by well-trained, qualified EC educators.

16-1 • Building a Marketing Plan

The landscape for marketing an EC program has changed dramatically. Strategies that have informed marketing practices in other types of business are now being applied to EC settings. Likewise, social media and other technology-supported tools have changed how and where marketing efforts take place.

16-1a • Market Research

The first step in creating an effective marketing plan is to conduct market research. Only after the values, beliefs, and needs of your market segment are better understood, is it possible to identify strategies that are most likely to capture their attention and demonstrate how your program is well suited to address potential customers' needs.

Using the results of the needs assessment and strategic planning process described in Chapter 2, program administrators will have collected important data to inform the marketing plan and will have completed the first steps in marketing the program. Knowing the needs of the customer and having a clearly articulated mission will help target the message to an audience that will be most interested in the service being provided. Your first step is to revisit the needs assessment data and mission and values statement from Chapter 2. This information will be helpful in developing a cost-effective and targeted marketing plan. Directors will also be able to use this information to complete a *strengths, weaknesses, opportunities,* and *threats* (SWOT) analysis for the program and proposed services.

16-1b • SWOT Analysis

A SWOT analysis is a simple but powerful framework for analyzing the challenges a program faces. The origins of the SWOT analysis are unclear, with some educators identifying the 1960s work of Albert Humphrey of Stanford University and others saying that the concept emerged from Harvard. Regardless of where the concept and acronym originated, it has evolved into a framework used by marketing experts that guides the user through an evaluation of internal and external factors that can impact a business's or program's success. Environmental factors internal to the organization can usually be classified as strengths (S) or weaknesses (W), and those external to the organization can be classified as opportunities (O) or threats (T). The SWOT analysis process helps program administrators focus on strengths, minimize weaknesses and threats, and take the greatest possible advantage of opportunities (see **Table 16-1**).

Identify stakeholders The first step in conducting SWOT analysis is to identify your stakeholders and data that have already been collected. A *stakeholder* is defined as someone who is impacted by your program; the most obvious stakeholders are children, families, and staff members. Less obvious stakeholders include your competitors, who strive to keep up with you, and the community, which benefits from your program's services. Each program will have a slightly different list based on its mission.

Gather existing data Stakeholders can provide important input for a well-developed marketing plan.

Table 16-1 Sample SWOT analysis chart

Strengths	Weaknesses
Excellent staff	Staff turnover
Good facilities	Limited hours of operation
Prime location	Reduction in funding available from the county and state
Opportunities	Threats
Changing community demographics	Changing community demographics
New QRIS can lead to additional funding.	Competitors have achieved stars on the QRIS, and your program has not.

A good place to start is to use information that has already been gathered as part of the strategic planning process. If completed within the past year or two, the needs assessment can provide important information. Think about other input from stakeholders that you might already have gathered. For example, if your program has chosen to be part of your state's Quality Rating and Improvement Systems (QRIS), has NAEYC accreditation, or has gone through a Head Start federal review, you will have already collected some information from your stakeholders. Many programs collect data about the quality of their program through such devices as the Early Childhood Environment Rating Scale–Revised (Harms, Clifford, & Cryer, 2014; Harms, Cryer, & Clifford, 2017) or the Program Administration Scale (Talan & Jorde Bloom, 2011). These tools provide data that are used by supervisors, administrators, and policy makers (all of whom are stakeholders) to identify the strengths and weaknesses of aspects of a program. Child assessment data can also be used to inform your SWOT analysis.

Determine missing data After you have identified your key stakeholders and any existing data sources that you can refer to, discuss ways that you can find out more about what your stakeholders think are your program's strengths and weaknesses. What information is missing? Who do you need to hear from? How can you access that information?

Gather internal and external data Most of the data that you have collected are likely internal data from stakeholders who are part of or directly impacted by your organization. Some of you may have collected information from or about your competitors, which would be the start of a review of the external data needed to determine the threats and opportunities in the SWOT analysis. To complete a thorough external review, you need to become well grounded in the context of early care and education, especially as it relates to quality and other trends that are impacting the market.

Construct a SWOT analysis chart To construct an accurate SWOT analysis chart, include the data that you have collected from stakeholders. You will use an internal focus to determine your program's *strengths* and *weaknesses*. To determine *threats* and *opportunities*, you will look to factors that are external to your program. See **Table 16-1** for a sample SWOT analysis chart.

Interpret the SWOT analysis Once completed, a SWOT analysis chart can help identify areas where a marketing plan can have the most impact. Consider the completed sample in **Table 16-1** and note how the information in the cells might be interpreted.

- *Strengths:* Note that any of the three identified strengths can become part of a marketing message that would attract new customers and retain the ones who already use the program's services.
- *Weaknesses:* It may be difficult to see how weaknesses can inform a marketing strategy until you also consider the opportunities. For example, the new QRIS that is described as an opportunity can be used to offset the reduction in funding because programs in some states can earn additional funding while improving quality. Making the connection between these two elements is an important part of the analysis of this chart. You can also deal with the perceived weakness head on by considering such moves as increasing the hours of operation after completing a careful analysis of the financial impact.
- *Opportunities:* In addition to using opportunities to address areas of weakness, they can also stand alone. For example, changing demographics can be a true opportunity to broaden the target of your marketing strategies.
- *Threats:* Note how the same item can be both an opportunity and a threat. For example, changing demographics can provide opportunities for an expanded market. It can also force change, which can be uncomfortable. It is likely to be difficult to make decisions about how to address this factor without considering it as both an opportunity and a threat.

16-1c • Developing a Marketing Plan

After the SWOT analysis is complete and **naeyc** interpreted, it is time to craft a marketing plan that can be communicated to others and in a format that can be followed by the people responsible for implementing the plan. Kalifeh (2011) suggests making a chart that includes the following when developing a marketing plan:

- your strategies (a description of what you will do),

- a time line for when you will undertake that strategy (remembering that marketing is a year-round endeavor),
- materials and resources needed to accomplish the strategy,
- a list of who is responsible or tasked with accomplishing the work, and
- a description of the costs.
- *Optional:* You might also want to create a column for evaluating the strategy, determining how you will measure success. (p. 23)

The strategic planning process from Chapter 2 and the information from the SWOT analysis should provide key information about your program and the

▶ **TeachSource Video Vignette**

Parents and Teachers Talk: Parenting in a New Culture

To best meet the needs of children in an EC setting, parents and EC educators must work as a team. From the start, the EC educator should create a trusting and open environment with the family. The family, in turn, must feel that it has a voice in the conversation. View the video vignette titled *Parents and Teachers Talk about Parenting in a New Culture.*

Effective marketing strategies require the director to know the audience and identify the needs of the market, which, for an early childhood program, is most likely made up of parents. Watch this group of parents and EC educators talk about culture to learn more about the audience. Now imagine yourself as the director of this program and create a social media post that would be appropriate for these parents as the audience. Be sure to provide information of interest to your audience.

Director's Corner

Not everyone sees through the same eyes or hears through the same ears.

—*Wassom (2004, p. 6)*

potential market that will inform the marketing plan. This information will also help to decide where, how, and to whom to promote the program.

Who: generational factors The perceptions of families who may be interested in the program and their process for making decisions vary based on a wide range of factors, including the generation to which they belong. Wasson goes on to state that a closer examination of generational tendencies "reveals valuable insight into why old marketing approaches are no longer as effective, and what changes you need to make to appeal to the majority of today's early care and education buyers" (p. 6). Wassom also identifies four generational groups in America today—matures, baby boomers, generation Xers, and millennials—and describes how members

of each generation are linked through shared life experiences. Those shared experiences cause them to view the world in unique ways, which extends to how and when they make decisions about early care and education services. Today, the parents of young children tend to be millennials, and their buying influences are quite different from the boomers of the past (see **Table 16-2**). A new generation known as generation Z (gen Z) is coming of age to have children. Neese (2020) describes gen Zers in the following manner:

Generation Z (1996–Early 2000s)

"Generation Zers were brought up with smartphones. As you can imagine, they're incredibly tech-savvy. . . . Gen Zers prefer Snapchat and Instagram for social networks. When it comes to media, they have all but abandoned traditional television viewing, opting to watch shows, movies and other digital content on their phones, tablets and laptops," according to CHNBC. This shift has led content producers to go where Gen Z lives—YouTube. They spend more than three hours a day watching videos online.

Table 16-2 Characteristics of three generations			
	Boomers	**Generation Xers**	**Millennials**
Age	Born between 1946 and 1964	Born between 1965 and 1979	Born between 1980 and 2000
Early life experiences	Secure economic times Television The start of the Peace Corps and space exploration Assassination of John F. Kennedy Civil rights assassinations of Martin Luther King and Robert Kennedy Vietnam War	Recession and layoffs or double-digit interest and inflation Watergate and other well-publicized scandals Challenger exploded Berlin Wall fell End of the Cold War Rise of digital technology and the World Wide Web The Chernobyl nuclear disaster The Exxon Valdez oil spill	A time of economic change with the longest period of economic expansion as wealth and manufacturing moved outside of the United States Emergence of the global economy AIDS emerges The space shuttle program thrives Hubble Space Telescope 24-hour news networks 9/11 and the War on Terror
Informed by	Newspapers Magazines Radio Network news Technology tends to augment the traditional way of doing things.	Network and cable news Internet accessed through the personal computer Word of mouth	Peers Online news sources Widespread on-demand access to the Internet via new media

(continued)

Group demographics	80 million	49 million	75 million
	Married boomers tend to live in dual earner families	Many parents of young children needing child care	The up and coming group of parents with young children
	Better educated than their parents	Question authority	More optimistic and ambitious
	Trusting	Grew up with uncertainty	Are realistic about what is wrong with the world but believe they can make a difference.
	Impulsive buyers	Skeptical	
	Emotional decision makers	Resourceful	
		Well educated	
		Less trusting	
	Busy and hard working	Not easily impressed	Relationships with friends and family are highly valued
	Value convenience	Tend to plan and save until they can afford the best quality	Value parents' advice
	Grant credibility based on proven history	Take time to investigate, compare, and discuss before deciding.	Value education as a means to success
	Few have young children but may influence how their grandchildren are raised.		Less religious
			Inclusive and value diversity
			Highly active and can be stressed
Childhood technology exposure	Color television	Cable TV	Interactive TV and streaming video MP3s and iPods
	Records, eight-tracks, and cassettes	Cassettes and CDs	DVDs and TiVo
	Landlines	VCRs	Laptops, netbooks, and iPads
		Personal computers	Smartphones
		Cell phones	
Communication preference tendencies	Face-to-face	Cell phone calls	Text messages
	Phone calls	Email	Facebook
Buying influencers	Impacted by emotional benefits	Skeptical and focused on quality and value	Want to be a member of the crowd yet stand out.
	May not investigate thoroughly if they have good feelings.	Will more likely rely on evidence and talk to others before making a decision.	Hopeful about the future.
	May want more flexible payment terms.	Willing to pay top dollar but will demand the highest quality.	Want to make a difference.
	Education is important, but happy children are more important.	Likely to appreciate being able to use a credit card.	Likely to consider recommendations from their peers and their parents.
	Value feeling part of the center's community.	Want good answers to questions about curriculum, policies, and procedures.	
	Value convenience and ancillary services.		
Advertising approaches that tend to work	Use color and emotions in photos and taglines.	Third-party endorsements or testimonials	Interactive digital messages
	Include photos that they can relate to.	Use bullets to outline specifics.	Includes opportunities for peers to provide feedback.
	Use bullets to communicate a quick message.	Link to professional organizations or other unbiased sources so they can verify your claims.	Easily accessed at a time convenient to them

Source: Howell & Strauss (2001), Marston (2011), Wassom (2004), Wendover (2007).

Working Smart with Technology

Social Media and the Digital Native

Marketing efforts of the past can be time intensive and expensive. Directors who use web-based marketing strategies are often surprised that these newer methods of telling your program's story can be both cost effective and time efficient. The parents of young children tend to be digital natives who are much more likely to get their information through websites and social media than from print materials used in the past. As digital natives, most young parents grew up using technology as an important method of communication and now look to the Internet to get information about child care.

1. Websites have come a long way, and the trend now is to reduce complexity and create a concise and transparent user experience. "In the end, our goal must be to provide users with the information they want, when and where they need it. To achieve this, a compelling and straightforward design, adhering to accessibility standards and personalization are indispensable" (Farese, 2020, p. 24). With this in mind, it is important that directors do the following: Make sure their program has a presence on the Internet, which means having a website. Developing websites has become surprisingly easy, and directors often find that they have a tech-savvy EC educator or even a parent who can help with website development and maintenance. Creating a website can be accomplished using an inexpensive drag-and-drop website-building program such as Weebly .com for as little as the cost of a domain name.

2. In addition to a website, EC programs need to be able to use social media to share their stories. Facebook can be a useful tool because it capitalizes on using families to promote the program when they "Like" or "Share" a post with their friends. Keep in mind that the program can have a public Facebook page that protects the children's identity and also a private Facebook page that can be limited to program family members.

Web-based marketing strategies can be both cost effective and time efficient.

Characteristics of a quality website As mentioned in this chapter's "Working Smart with Technology" feature, websites are an important component of marketing your program. For many young families, if the program doesn't have a website, it isn't even considered as a possibility. With new no-cost or low-cost software, websites can be developed in house easily and inexpensively, or directors can contract with a professional developer to create the website. Regardless of who creates the website, it is imperative that the site reflects an understanding of quality (see **Table 16-3**).

Creating the website is one component of having an Internet presence. Equally as important is maintaining and updating the website with relevant information that keeps families and the public coming back to the site. One common mistake is to have

Table 16-3 Characteristics of a quality child care center website
Simplicity: Avoid busy webpage designs. Too much content on the page will frustrate the users and reduce the amount of time that they spend on the page.
Consistency: Effective webpages are consistent in design, navigation, writing style, and appearance throughout the pages of the website.
Accessibility: Webpages should be designed for the novice computer user. Avoid building websites that have complex features that are too sophisticated for the audience and their technology.
Credibility: For a website to become an important part of a comprehensive communication system, it must include current and relevant content. Users must be able to count on the accuracy of the information presented.
Navigation: Users need to be able to move throughout the webpage with ease. Links to other pages should work, and the number of clicks needed to access information should be minimal.
Appearance: The appearance of the page should be attractive with attention paid to color, font, and the balance of text, photos, and graphics. The amount of information on a page should be able to be viewed without scrolling.
Audience: The audience for the webpage needs to be determined at the beginning of the web-development process. The two most common audiences are current and prospective families. Prospective families are looking for slightly different information, which needs to be open and available to the public. It is possible to have a section of the website that is password protected to maintain confidentiality and Internet safety for children who are currently enrolled.
Source: Adapted from Wassom (2004).

a high-quality website developed without considering how the page will be maintained and who will maintain it. Sometimes it is better to select a less sophisticated webpage design so that the site can be maintained in house.

Where to market your program Traditionally, marketing a program and publicizing a program has been done through newspaper ads and radio announcements to reach a wide audience while a more limited population is reached through direct mailing of brochures or circulars, displays of window placards, door-to-door solicitation, and advertisements in local newspapers, church bulletins, and military newsletters. In the past, telephone book advertising was also successful.

Because of the impact of technology, many of these traditional vehicles now have less impact. Young families today rely more on new media and the Internet for information. Consider taking advantage of Internet advertising—the Yellow Pages does not have the impact that it once did. *New media* refers to on-demand access to content anytime and anywhere using digital devices such as smartphones, iPods, iPads, and other tools. New media allows families to access just the information they need at just the time they need it. The ability to have continuous and instant access to information through search engines and social networking sites makes such platforms as Google and Facebook important marketing tools.

New media also provides opportunities for interaction, so word-of-mouth marketing is an even more powerful tool. The directors who develop and maintain free Facebook sites for their programs are also providing a vehicle for families to talk about programs in ways that potential families are likely to interact with and trust. These new platforms can be frightening for many directors who would like to be more in control of the message being sent. However, like it or not, the advent of new media has shifted control to the consumer, who can provide feedback in a forum that is open for anyone to see. A director who is aware of how the program is being presented on Facebook or where the program appears on a Google search listing can impact the marketing message. By capitalizing on the everyday opportunities to communicate a consistent message during the day-to-day operations of the program, directors can

impact how current families describe the program for potential families on Facebook or on other new media vehicles.

Regardless of the vehicle used to advertise, be sure to consider the ethnic and cultural makeup of the audience, as well as reading levels and language skills, as you write and design promotional materials.

How to construct the message Constructing a message that resonates with the target audience is also important. Marston (2011) reminds us that generational differences should impact how information is presented (refer to **Table 16-2**):

> Understand X-ers take nothing at face value and will seek out their own information and referrals. Look at your marketing as an introduction that directs them to further information. Make sure your website is stocked with data and product specifications. Want to further your credibility with X-ers? Point them to an unbiased resource and show them you've got nothing to hide. Remember, these are the folks who were born in the Watergate era and grew up in an age of highly publicized scandals. Honesty is unexpected yet highly treasured. (Marston, 2011)

Likewise, millennials are accustomed to relying on peer feedback for credibility. If millennials are the targeted group, then an astute director might develop a program-sponsored Facebook site and encourage current families to provide feedback on their children's experiences. By being proactive and knowledgeable about the benefits and pitfalls of new media, the director can capitalize on the benefits of the tools while laying ground rules that can overcome some of the disadvantages. For example, if the Facebook site is established by the director, then he or she can provide guidance about confidentiality and respectful interactions. The owner of the site can also remove inappropriate comments and add prompts that direct the kind of feedback that is provided. New media has changed the marketing landscape; directors can choose to take advantage of these inexpensive and powerful marketing tools or not. However, ignorance of how the program is being portrayed through new media platforms can be the downfall of a program.

Making the Case for *Crafting the Word-of-Mouth Message* naeyc

Today, the families of young children are likely to be digital natives who rely heavily on social media to communicate and gather information. Word-of-mouth marketing is especially influential with digital natives because they have immediate access to online reviews of a myriad of services. If they want to know whether a restaurant or an early childhood program is "good," they type their question into a search box and reviews written by other digital natives pop up. Their understanding of good is not research based but is instead informed by their peers through social media. Effective directors understand how to use social media to inform the public about their services and do not leave their message to chance. They provide opportunities for an ongoing two-way stream of information using communication tools that appeal to today's parents. If a director wants families to understand what quality child care looks like, he or she provides information in short segments that can be read on a smartphone screen. Information is provided in a manner that can be downloaded, forwarded, and liked so that it can be shared with friends and family. Using photographs, short text segments, and video streams, the director shares information to questions that the audience may not know it had. The director is responsible for crafting the message and understanding the powerful tools that are available today to share that message.

16-1d • Marketing Materials

Marketing materials are a collection of products designed to meet established marketing goals. The marketing plan will help to determine the kinds of marketing products that will work with the target audience. In most situations, a variety of materials and platforms for dissemination is the most effective approach to achieve the desired outcome. With widespread availability of easy-to-use publishing software, many directors can create attractive and professional marketing materials—even those with limited computer skills. Many of the products designed for print materials can be adapted to digital formats, including websites. Because of the shift to new media, which requires immediate access to information, it is even more important to be proactive and have materials available to meet a variety of marketing needs. One strategy is to create a marketing tool kit that can be used to respond to a variety of marketing opportunities quickly and cohesively. Kalifeh (2011) suggests the following as marketing resources that directors can cultivate to become part of a marketing tool kit:

- print media (parent handbooks, business cards, brochures, press releases, advertisements, giveaways, etc.),
- electronic media (website, social networking, email),
- staff (an often overlooked marketing resource),
- parents (some of your best public relations specialists), and

Director's Corner

One frustration that my EC educators voiced programed on the parents' apparent lack of understanding about how an emergent and play-based curriculum could support the academic skills that children need to be ready for kindergarten. After lamenting this situation in several staff meetings, I asked my EC educators what they could do to help parents better understand what their children were learning. We realized that parents didn't really want to know about the importance of play, and that our efforts to convert them were having a negative effect on their views of our program. After some brainstorming, the EC educators decided to be proactive and started sharing evidence of the academic content that children learned in the context of play. While the children's experiences with a play-based and emergent curriculum remained the same, the way the program was framed for parents changed. We shifted our focus from selling the importance of play to showcasing what the children were learning during play. The weekly newsletter included examples of academic content learned. The parent communication board highlighted literacy and numeracy in the daily routine. The EC educators changed the bulletin boards outside of their classrooms to documentation boards and included work samples and photographs with notations about what the children had learned. We were amazed by the impact that communicating this consistent message had on parent perceptions of what children were learning. It also had a positive effect on our word of mouth marketing.

—Director of a university-affiliated child care program

- events (employer partnerships, school transition partnerships, open house, Kids' Day, legislative tours, parent appreciation, etc.) (p. 23).

Brochures and promotional materials The choice of words and the photographs used in the printed materials distributed by the program should reflect a subtle message of concern, respect, and appreciation for children and should express the philosophy behind the program's program.

Develop marketing materials that send a distinctive and powerful message. They must define your specialties and exactly what you offer that sets you apart from your competitors. The fundamentals of "quality care," "developmentally appropriate practice," and "trained, caring staff" are descriptive but not distinctive. Brainstorm with staff, parents, board members, and consultants about how you are different, and put down some sample statements that will tell that story in the materials that you develop, such as the following:

- soft, cozy spaces in a homelike environment (use pictures if possible);
- innovative, cutting-edge social or emotional focus; and
- family-centered practice that treats the family, child, and teacher as a unit.

Find unique ways to identify your program with a logo that appears on all business cards, stationery, ads, and so on. Use of a particular *tagline* with the logo can become your mark of distinction. In marketing circles, this is called *branding*. It is something potential clients recognize and remember. Taglines give a quick and easily remembered clip of what a program is about. For example,

- "Where Every Child Is Special"
- "We Strengthen Children Emotionally and Academically"
- "Child Care That Nurtures Our Future"

Keep in mind that you are endeavoring to attract the attention of the current generation of young parents, many of whom are generation Xers, millennials, or gen Zers. Select techniques and content for the marketing materials that appeal to and entice these target generational groups. For eye appeal and influence, consider the following:

- use color and emotion in taglines and photos,

- mix pictures and graphics (a photo of an EC educator and child, a parent event, your accreditation credential),
- bullet the benefits so there is a quick and easy way to sum up *what they will get from you*—a bit different from what you have to offer,
- quote testimonials from the current parent population, and
- use the talents of staff and parents to do creative marketing that will help you build your enrollment.

The content and appearance of brochures or fliers make a statement to parents. The words should be informative and spell out the philosophy of the program. The photographs or some creative, clever artwork should convey, in less obvious ways, that the program's staff is professional and creative. It is the creative design of these materials that will attract attention, and attention is the first step to generating interest. The message for parents should be clear: Any child who is sent to this program will share in the professionalism and creativity of the staff. When unsolicited letters from parents are available, using statements from those letters in brochures or publicity releases is an excellent way to get your message across. Every detail of any mailing piece to be used for initial advertising or in response to inquiries about the program should be carefully scrutinized.

The director is responsible for the preparation and mailing of brochures, but other staff members as well as parents can contribute to the effort by providing artistic talents, access to a printer, or some other expertise. When a brochure is prepared, two major considerations are cost and content.

Costs vary depending on number, length, quality of paper, use of color, and use of photographs. Therefore, it is wise to discuss ideas for the brochure with a printer as soon as possible. Costs increase when the professionally done brochure includes photos or a logo that incorporates artwork, but it is these unique features that may be precisely what attracts the attention of prospective clients. The distinctive logo and tagline on every promotional piece becomes a familiar identifying symbol to potential customers. Money spent on an attractive brochure may be a good investment. Using a single color on heavyweight, standard-size paper will give a look of high quality yet keep the costs down. A brochure on standard-size paper in a

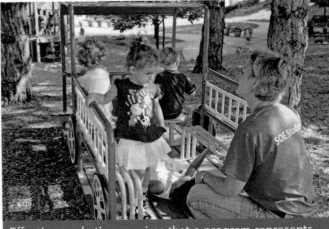

Effective marketing requires that a program represents what it does well. This image might be selected for marketing materials because it shows how children are engaged in a well-planned outdoor space with strong adult–child interaction and that this center is a university-affiliated program.

three-fold format that can be addressed on one side is economical and efficient. Check the size and weight so that mailing costs will be within the minimal limit for first-class postage rates.

If the brochure is to be used over a long period of time, it is wise to avoid including items that are subject to change such as the school calendar or the fee schedule. These variable items can be detailed in a short insert. The brochure itself should contain

Director's Corner

When it was time to make our logo more current, we worked very hard to choose one that communicated what we were about while also providing some brand recognition. We contacted a local university with a graphic design program and asked the program director if there was a class that was working on logo design. We were fortunate to be able to set up a competition in this class and had teams of students interview our program staff and examine our mission statement and handbooks. Teams designed a series of eight logos, which were voted on by staff and families through a Facebook website. We had great buy-in from families and staff and ended up with a very attractive logo for the cost of the competition prize, which was a gift card to an art supply store for each member of the winning team. The process was a win for all involved.

—*Director, private not-for-profit program*

information that remains constant from year to year. The following list includes some of the more stable items typically included in a brochure:

- name, address, and telephone number of the program;
- a map showing the location of the program;
- description of the program;
- sponsorship of the program;
- enrollment procedures and children served (ages, inclusive program, diversity, etc.); and
- the licensing or accreditation status of the program.

It is important to include the hours, days, and months for the program. The stability of the operational schedule will determine whether such information should go into the brochure itself or be part of the insert.

Programs sell services to families who seek solutions to concerns and have questions about quality child care. It is helpful to them when promotional materials cover all the services available at the program. Prospective customers, especially those with more than one child, will want to have information about availability of services such as before- and after-school care, summer programs for school-age children, care for the mildly ill child, and backup care for older children on school holidays or for the baby cared for at home when the regular caregiver is ill.

Other selling points to cover in promotional materials might include the following:

- accreditation by NAEYC, NACCP, NECPA, or the state's QRIS, if available;
- workshops;
- lending library;
- web address to help keep potential clients up to date on all program activities; and
- an email address to keep in touch with administrators.

Keep in mind that promotional materials are designed to tell prospective families that the program offers solutions for them and is there to help and support them and their children. Brochure space is limited, so details about program operation and range of services offered to families can be described in pamphlets or booklets available for those who call for more information or visit the program. A well-planned open house provides a special opportunity to share these additional materials and publicizes the best features of the program.

16-2 • Public Relations

As a director, it behooves you to take advantage of opportunities to invite reporters to the program so they can do newspaper or television pieces on your program. If you are affiliated with a large business or hospital, then its public relations staff may help you. Television and newspaper reporters may be interested in what is new at your program. If there is a new infant room opening or you have a new custom-designed playground, reporters and photographers will come to you. Other newsworthy items might be a new EC educator who signs for deaf children, installation of a ramp to accommodate children and adults with disabilities, or the use of senior citizen volunteers in the preschool classrooms.

Take advantage of the wave of interest that surrounds early learning and brain development in young children. When local reporters do a story on early learning, go to the reporter's webpage and contribute to his or her blog. Sometimes it is difficult to get the attention of busy reporters. Remember, if they have taken the time to write about a topic on their blogs, they will likely read the responses that their audience makes. Be sure to identify yourself and your program. Become a regular blog contributor and you get free publicity to an audience that is interested in the topic.

At community events that draw parents of young children, it is often useful to arrange to have a booth where a display of photos taken at the program and promotional materials will attract families who are interested in child care. Arrange for the director or a competent staff member who can answer questions and distribute admission applications to be available at these events. This is an excellent way to reach out to the community and capitalize on an opportunity to establish a personal contact with potential clients.

It is also worthwhile to get your message out to companies in the community as well as to individuals and community groups. The first wave of companies interested in addressing the child care needs of their employees typically were attracted to setting up on-site early childhood programs. However, some companies are more inclined to look to existing community EC programs where they can purchase slots, buy priority status, or negotiate for corporate group rates for their employees. Developing a professional presentation that is designed for use with corporate clients (Schulte, 2018) might include information about the impact of limited child care on the workforce (see **Figure 16-2**).

A lack of affordable quality child care has a significant impact on workforce participation and is a drain on U.S. employers' bottom lines:

- U.S. businesses lose approximately $4.4 billion annually from employee absenteeism resulting from child care breakdowns.

- Over a 6-month period, 45 percent of parents are absent from work at least once, missing an average of 4.3 days, because of child care breakdowns.

- In addition, 65 percent of parents' work schedules are affected by child care challenges an average of 7.5 times over a 6-month period.

- $28.9 billion in wages is lost annually by working families who do not have access to affordable child care and paid family and medical leave.

- Working mothers make up 40 percent of the workforce. When child care is not available, this workforce is affected; even a 10-percent decrease in availability of early childhood education reduces employment of single mothers by 3 to 4 percent and married women by 5 to 6 percent.

FIGURE 16-2
Adapted from Child Care Aware of America (2018, p. 9).

The program's image is an important consideration in all aspects of the public information and public relations efforts. The appearance of the physical setting and the behavior of personnel in that setting are fundamental factors in creating good public relations and sound relationships with the children and their parents. These factors are what convey professionalism and concern about children and families. The director serves as a model and encourages the staff to be mindful of their role as community advocates for children. Parents entering the building should see an interior prepared for use by children. Furthermore, parents should be greeted by a warm, caring person who expresses interest in them and in their children. A "Director's Coffee" once a month is a way to encourage parents to take a few minutes to chat before rushing off to work. When parents or others telephone the program, the person who answers must be pleasant, tactful, and knowledgeable.

An open house for parents who have made inquiries or have responded to your marketing efforts is a good way to expand the public relations program for the program. Remember to invite current parents, current staff members, and board members to these social events. An open house affords an opportunity for the staff to have an informal meeting with others who are interested in the program's activities. In the case of a new program, publicizing the open house can be part of the initial efforts at promotion. In the case of ongoing programs, staff and board members also will reap benefits from this kind of gathering because it provides a time for interaction and communication among adults who have common concerns and share an interest in the children attending the program.

When the program is opened to visitors, the environment should be prepared just as it would be for the children. In this way, you can demonstrate how a well-planned environment should look and also provide an opportunity for parents to participate and use available materials. What better way to give parents a feeling for what happens each day than to have them use the materials in the classrooms! In addition, slides, a scrapbook of photos, or a videotape or PowerPoint presentation of children actively participating in the classroom can give parents further insights into what a quality program can offer their children.

Planning for the open house is done by people who understand the lifestyles and expectations of the clients who are likely to show interest in the event. Careful and sensitive planning regarding the time of the event and the level of informality communicates to members of the community that the people at the program understand and care about them and their children.

Summary

The marketing plan for the program emerges from market research informed by the strategic planning process. Effective directors consider multiple factors when developing a marketing plan and can be informed by a carefully constructed SWOT analysis as well as by a sound understanding of the target audience. In today's technology-enhanced society, marketing must include both traditional print strategies and new media. Marketing materials for the program must be drafted and directed to the population that the program is designed to serve. Successful recruitment of children and families will depend on the content and dissemination of the promotional materials about the program as well as on the total public relations effort. Although written materials advertising the program must be planned carefully to attract the families to be served, the role of word-of-mouth advertising cannot be overlooked. To effectively market a program, the director must do the following:

- Identify the components of a well-developed marketing plan.

- Explain strategies that maximize public relations efforts.

TRY IT OUT!

1. Think about a program you have been in on a regular basis. You are sitting outside in the parking lot as parents arrive. Is the building inviting? Does it really welcome children and families? Now imagine yourself inside and observing the way children are greeted. Do adults stoop down and extend a friendly welcome to the children? Are parents recognized and called by name? As you walk farther into the building, how does it look? What sounds do you hear? How does it smell? The impressions you are reliving are the same impressions parents and children experience each day they enter the program. How do the answers to these questions impact the word-of-mouth marketing potential for this program?

2. Work with a team to complete a SWOT analysis using **Director's Resource 16-1**. Consider a program that a member of the team works for or is familiar with and then complete each of the four quadrants of your analysis. Describe how you would address the following:

   a. Strengths you can capitalize on to promote the program.
   b. Weaknesses that can be addressed or turned around and used as a marketing strategy.
   c. Look at the opportunities you have identified. How can they be incorporated into a marketing plan?
   d. Examine your threats. What marketing strategies can you use to reduce the threats?

Use these answers to identify what this program might include on a Facebook page. Consider children, families, and staff as you make your decision.

Director's Resource 16-1 ////
SWOT ANALYSIS CHART

STRENGTHS	WEAKNESSES
OPPORTUNITIES	THREATS

INTERPRETATION	HOW FINDINGS ARE ADDRESSED IN THE MARKETING PLAN
Which aspects of the SWOT analysis chart should be the focus of a marketing plan? Which are top priorities or can make the most impact on the success of the program?	
Strengths	
Weaknesses	
Opportunities	
Threats	

REFERENCES

Child Care Aware of America. (2018). *The U.S. and the high cost of child care: A review of prices and proposed solutions for a broken system.* Arlington, VA: Author. https://cdn2.hubspot.net/hubfs/3957809/COCreport2018_1.pdf

Farese, D. (2020). Web strategy. *Not Another Marketing Report.* Cambridge, MA: Hubspot. https://www.hubspot.com/state-of-marketing

Harms, T., Clifford, R. M., & Cryer, D. (2014). *Early childhood environment rating scale* (3rd ed.) (ECERS-3). New York, NY: Teachers College Press.

Harms, T., Cryer, D., Clifford, R. M., & Yazejian, N. (2017). *Infant/toddler environment rating scale* (3rd ed.). New York, NY: Teachers College Press.

Kalifeh, P. (2011, March–April). Marketing: No longer an afterthought. *Child Care Information Exchange,* 22–24.

Marston, C. (2011). Marketing to different generations: Choose your message wisely. International Association of Business Communicators.

Neese, B. (2020, April). Generational marketing myths from boomers to gen Z. *AdAge.* https://adage.com/article/jefferson/targeting-age-groups-understanding-generational-marketing/2246656

Schulte, B. (2018). The corporate case for child care. Slate. https://slate.com/human-interest/2018/02/the-corporate-case-for-childcare.html

Talan, T. N., & Jorde Bloom, P. (2011). *Program administration scale* (2nd ed.). New York, NY: Teachers College Press.

Wassom, J. (2004, March–April). Do they see what you see? Marketing to a new generation of child care buyers. *Child Care Information Exchange,* 6–8.

A NAEYC Code of Ethical Conduct and Statement of Commitment

The Code of Ethical Conduct is one of the five foundational documents developed by the National Association for the Education of Young Children (NAEYC) in concert with the early childhood profession. The purpose of the document is to support early childhood professionals as they face ethical dilemmas in their day-to-day practices. Because a high-quality, developmentally appropriate program must consider the often-conflicting needs of children, families, and staff, this position statement provides guidelines for decision-making. To read the NAEYC Code of Ethical Conduct and Statement of Commitment, visit the following link: https://www.naeyc.org/resources/position-statements/ethical-conduct

Appendix B

Statement on Developmentally Appropriate Practice (2020 Revision)

The NAEYC's revised Statement on Developmentally Appropriate Practice (2020) represents a significant emphasis on the contexts in which early childhood educators make decisions that result in developmentally appropriate practice. The fourth edition of this position statement focuses on the importance of social, cultural, and historical contexts that impact decision-making. More than in prior editions, "this broader view emphasizes the implications of contexts not only for each child, but also for all the adults (educators, administrators, and others) involved in any aspect of early childhood education" (p. 4).

This statement includes three core considerations that inform decision-making and include: (1) *commonality*, or what we understand about child development and learning that is typical for the age; (2) *individuality*, or "the characteristics and experiences that are unique to each child" (p. 7); and (3) *context*, or "everything discernible about the social and cultural contexts for each child, each educator, and the program as a whole" (p. 7).

The section that includes the *Principles for Development and Learning* has been revised and now includes a statement on the intentional use of technology and interactive media as a means of supporting young children's development and learning.

The emphasis on advancing equity in providing quality early childhood education for all children is woven throughout the document. The recommendations for implementing quality developmentally appropriate practice is directed toward schools, family child care homes, and other program settings; higher education and adult development; policy makers; and researchers.

To access the NAEYC Statement on Developmentally Appropriate Practice (fourth edition), go to https://www.naeyc.org/resources/developmentally-appropriate-practice

Advancing Equity in Early Childhood Education Position Statement

Advancing Equity in Early Childhood Education was adopted by the NAEYC Governing Board in 2019. This position statement is one of the five foundational documents developed by NAEYC with early childhood professionals to inform quality and developmentally appropriate practice for all young children. Because "all children have the right to equitable learning opportunity that help them achieve their full potential as engaged learners and valued members of society" (p. 1), this document includes important information for directors to help them understand the professional obligation to advance equity that all early childhood professionals must demonstrate. To read the position statement, Advancing Equity in Early Childhood Education, go to https://www.naeyc.org/resources/position-statements/equity

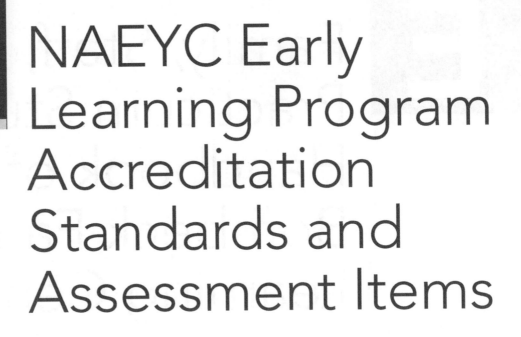

Appendix D

NAEYC Early Learning Program Accreditation Standards and Assessment Items

Revised in 2019, the NAEYC *Early Learning Program Accreditation Standards and Assessment Items* provide a comprehensive process for early childhood education programs to conduct self-evaluations. This continuous improvement process focuses on children, staff, partnerships, and administration and encompasses 10 standards ranging from relationships to staff competencies, preparation, and support to leadership and management. The NAEYC accreditation process is ongoing and serves as a standard of excellence. To learn more about the Early learning Program Accreditation Standards and Assessment Items, visit https://www .naeyc.org/accreditation/early-learning/tools

Appendix E

Family, Staff, and Practicum Student Handbook of the Bombeck Family Learning Center

Program handbooks are important documents designed to share policies and practices to those staff, families, and university students who may be completing a practicum experience at the site. Handbooks are designed to communicate the expectations and also serve as supporting documentation for early childhood education programs that are completing the NAEYC accreditation process.

The Bombeck Center Handbook was updated during the NAEYC accreditation process and includes many examples of the items that served as documentation. To view this sample handbook, go to the Digital Download section of the Student Companion Website. TeachSource Digital Download

Child Care Licensing Benchmark Project

ChildCare Aware of America recently completed the *Child Care Licensing Benchmark Project* (2020) in response to the 2014 reauthorization of the federal Child Care and Development Block Grant Act. This reauthorization includes new licensing requirements that served as a catalyst to standardize the benchmarks for healthy, safe, and high-quality early childhood programs. Before this project was completed, states developed their own licenses standards that required a wide range of quality standards. To learn more about the methodology of this project and review the benchmarks that were established, visit https://www.childcareaware.org/our-issues/research/child-care-licensing-benchmark-project/

Appendix G

Sources of Early Childhood Materials, Equipment, and Supplies

Albert Whitman & Company

250 South Northwest Highway, Suite 320
Park Ridge, IL 60068
(800) 255-7675
http://www.albertwhitman.com

Becker's School Supplies

1500 Melrose Highway
Pennsauken, NJ 08110-1410
(800) 523-1490
http://www.shopbecker.com

Broderbund Software

Navarre Corporation
384 Bel Marin Keys Blvd, Suite 150
Novato CA 94949
(800) 395-0277
http://www.broderbund.com

Candlewick Press

99 Dover Street
Somerville, MA02144
(617) 661-3330
http://www.candlewick.com

Cengage Learning, Inc.

10650 Toebben Drive
Independence, KY 41051
(800) 354-9706
http://www.cengage.com

Child Care Manager

Personalized Software
118 S. Main Street
Phoenix, OR 97535-0359
(800) 553-2312
http://www.childcaremanager.com

Childforms

110 Charleston Drive, Suite 106
Mooresville, NC 28117
(800) 447-3349
http://www.childforms.com

Children's Factory

510 S. McKinley Ave.
Union, MO 63084
Phone: 314.821.1441
https://www.childrensfactory.com/

Child Plus Software

303 Perimeter Center N
Suite 400Atlanta, GA 30346
(800) 888-6674
http://www.childplus.com

Clarion Books

Houghton Mifflin Harcourt
215 Park Avenue South
New York, NY 10003
(212) 420-5800
https://www.hmhbooks.com/

Community Playthings

2032 Route 213
Rifton, NY 12471
(800) 777-4244
http://www.communityplaythings.com

Custom Recreation

2190 North Cullen Avenue
Evansville, IN 47715
812-477-3052
http://www.customrecreation.com

Dick Blick Art Materials

PO Box 1267
Galesburg, IL 61402-1267
(800) 828-4548
http://www.dickblick.com

Didax Educational Resources Inc.

395 Main Street
Rowley, MA 01969
(800) 458-0024
http://www.didax.com

Discount School Supply

PO Box 6013
PO Box 734309
Chicago, IL
(606) 73-4309
(800) 627-2829
http://www.discountschoolsupply.com

Don Johnston Inc.

26799 West Commerce Drive
Volo, IL 60073
(800) 999-4660
http://www.donjohnston.com

Flagship Carpet

PO Box 1779
Calhoun, GA 30701
(800) 848-4055
http://www.flagshipcarpets.com

Growing Tree Toys

202 South Allen Street
State College, PA 16801
(800) 993-8697
http://www.growingtreetoys.com

Gryphon House Inc.

PO Box 10
6858 Leon's Way
Lewisville, NC 27023
(800) 638-0928
http://www.gryphonhouse.com

Hachette Book Group

237 Park Avenue
New York, NY 10017
(800) 759-0190
http://www.hachettebookgroup.com

HarperCollins Children's Books

HarperCollins Publishers
195 Broadway
New York, NY 10007 (212) 207-7000
http://www.harpercollinschildrens.com

Houghton Mifflin Harcourt Publishers

School Division (Pre-K through 8)
9205 South Park Center Loop
Orlando, FL 32819
(800) 269-5232
http://www.hmhco.com

Insect Lore

132 South Beech Avenue
Shafter, CA 93263
(800) 548-3284
http://www.insectlore.com

International Playthings Inc.

75D Lackawanna Avenue
Parsippany, NJ 07054
(800) 631-1272
http://www.intplay.com

John R. Green

400 Reed St.
PO Box 342
Clearfield, PA 16830-0342 (800) 354-9737
http://www.johnrgreenco.com

Jonti-Craft Inc.

PO Box 30
171 Highway 68
Wabasso, MN 56293
(800) 543-4149
http://www.jonti-craft.com

Kaplan Early Learning Company

1310 Lewisville-Clemmons Road
Lewisville, NC 27023
(800) 334-2014
http://www.kaplanco.com

Kohburg Early Childhood Educational Furniture

1926 West Holt Avenue
Pomona CA, 91768
(888) 718-8880
http://www.kohburg.com/

Lakeshore Learning Materials

2695 East Dominguez Street
PO Box 6261
Carson, CA 90895
Phone: (310) 537-8600
http://www.lakeshorelearning.com

Landscape Structures Inc.

601 7th Street South
Delano, MN 55328-0198
(800) 438-6574
http://www.playlsi.com

Learning Resources Inc.

380 North Fairway Drive
Vernon Hills, IL 60061
(800) 333-8281
http://www.learningresources.com

The Little Tikes Co.

2180 Barlow Road
Hudson, OH 44236-9984
(866) 855-4650
http://www.littletikes.com

Moment Path

https://www.momentpath.com/

Music Together LLC

225 Hopewell Pennington Road
Hopewell NJ 08525 (800) 728-2692
http://www.musictogether.com

Procare Software

3581 Excel Drive
Medford, OR 97504
(800) 338-3884
http://www.procaresoftware.com

Redleaf Press

10 Yorkton Court
St. Paul, MN 55117-1065
(800) 423-8309
http://www.redleafpress.org

Rhythm Band Instruments Inc.

PO Box 126
Fort Worth, TX 76102
(800) 424-4724
http://www.rhythmband.com

S+S Worldwide

75 Mill Street
Colchester, CT 06415
(800) 566-6678
http://www.ssww.com

Scholastic, Inc.

557 Broadway
New York, NY 10012
(800) 724-6527
http://www.scholastic.com

School Specialty

W6316 Design Drive,
Greenville, WI 54942
(888) 388-3224
http://www.schoolspecialty.com

Seedlings Braille Books for Children

PO Box 51924
Livonia, MI 48151-5924
(800) 777-8552
http://www.seedlings.org

SofterWare Inc.

132 Welsh Road, Suite 140
Horsham, PA 19044-2217
(215) 628-0400
http://www.softerware.com

Stress Free Kids

2561 Chimney Springs
Marietta, GA30062
(800) 841-4204
http://www.stressfreekids.com

Sunburst Technology

1501 N. Michael Drive
Wood Dale, IL 60191 (800) 321-7511
http://www.sunburst.com

Teachers College Press

1234 Amsterdam Ave.
New York, NY 10027
Phone: (212) 678-3929
http://www.teacherscollegepress.com

Terrapin Software

955 Massachusetts Avenue #365
Cambridge, MA 02139-3233
(800) 774-5646
http://www.terrapinlogo.com

Tree Blocks

(800) 873-4960
http://www.treeblocks.com

U.S. Toy Company

13201 Arrington Road
Grandview, MO 64030-1117
(800) 832-0224
http://www.ustoy.com

Director's Library of Early Childhood Professional Organizations and Information Sources

Periodicals

Early Childhood Professional Organizations and Information Sources

Administration for Children and Families

370 L'Enfant Promenade, SW
Washington, DC 20447
(202) 401-9200
http://www.acf.hhs.gov

American Academy of Pediatrics

141 Northwest Point Boulevard
Elk Grove Village, IL 60007-1098
(847) 434-4000
http://www.aap.org

American Association of Family & Consumer Sciences

400 North Columbus Street, Suite 202
Alexandria, VA 22314
(703) 706-4600
http://www.aafcs.org

American Association of School Administrators

801 North Quincy Street, Suite 700
Arlington, VA 22203
(800) 424-8080
http://www.aasa.org

American Council on Education (ACE)

One Dupont Circle, NW, Suite 800
Washington, DC 20036
(202) 939-9300
http://www.acenet.edu

American Educational Research Association (AERA)

1430 K Street, NW
Washington, DC 20005
(202) 238-3200
http://www.aera.net

American Federation of Teachers (AFT)

555 New Jersey Avenue, NW
Washington, DC 20001
(202) 879-4400
http://www.aft.org

American Medical Association

330 North Wabash
Chicago, IL 60611-5885
(800) 621-8335
http://www.ama-assn.org

American Montessori Society (AMS)

116 East 16th Street
New York, NY 10003
(212) 358-1250
http://www.amshq.org

American Speech-Language-Hearing Association

2200 Research Boulevard
Rockville, MD 20850-3289
(301) 296-5700
http://www.asha.org

Annie E. Casey Foundation

701 Saint Paul Street
Baltimore, MD 21202
(410) 547-6600
http://www.aecf.org

Appalachian Regional Commission

1666 Connecticut Avenue, NW, Suite 700
Washington, DC 20009-1068
(202) 884-7700
http://www.arc.gov

Childhood Education International (ACEI)

1875 Connecticut Ave., NW, 10th Floor
Washington, DC 20009
202-372-9986 • 1-800-423-3563
https://ceinternational1892.org/

Association for Early Learning Leaders

1250 S. Capital of Texas Hwy
Building 3, Suite #400
Austin, TX 78746
http://www.earlylearningleaders.org

Association for Library Service to Children-American Library Association

225 N Michigan Ave, Suite 1300
Chicago, IL 60601
1.800.545.2433
http://www.ala.org/alsc

Association for Supervision and Curriculum Development (ASCD)

1703 North Beauregard Street
Alexandria, VA 22311-1714
(800) 933-2723
http://www.ascd.org

Association Montessori International/USA

1421 Prince St, Ste 350
Alexandria, VA 22314
(585) 461-5920
http://amiusa.org/

Centers for Disease Control and Prevention

1600 Clifton Road N.E.
Atlanta, GA 30333
(800) 232-4636
http://www.cdc.gov

ChildCare Aware of America

1515 North Courthouse Road, 11th Floor
Arlington, VA 22201
(703) 341-4100
http://www.naccrra.org

Office of Child Care

U.S. Department of Health and Human Services
Administration for Children and Families
330 C Street, S.W., Washington, D.C. 20201
(202) 690-6782
http://www.acf.hhs.gov/programs/occ/

Child Care Education Institute

3059 Peachtree Industrial Boulevard, NW, Suite 100
Duluth, GA 30097
(800) 499-9907
http://www.cceionline.com

Child Care Information Exchange

17725 NE 65th Street, B-275
Redmond, WA 98052
(800) 221-2864
http://www.childcareexchange.com

Child Care Law Center

445 Church Street
San Francisco, CA 94114
(415) 558-8005
http://www.childcarelaw.org

Child Care Services Association

1829 East Franklin Street, Building 1000
P.O. Box 901
Chapel Hill, NC 27514
(919) 967-3272
http://www.childcareservices.org

Child Welfare League of America (CWLA)

727 15th Street, NW, Suite 1200
Washington, DC 20005
(202) 688-4200
http://www.cwla.org

Children's Book Council Inc.

54 West 39th Street, 14th Floor
New York, NY 10018
(212) 966-1990
http://www.cbcbooks.org

Children's Defense Fund

25 E Street, NW
Washington, DC 20001
(800) 233-1200
http://www.childrensdefense.org

Common Core State Standards Initiative

c/o National Governors Association
Hall of the States
444 N. Capitol Street, Suite 267
Washington, DC 20001-1512
(202) 624-5300
http://www.corestandards.org/

Council for Early Childhood Professional Recognition (CDA)

2640 16th Street, NW
Washington, DC 20009-3547
(800) 424-4310
http://www.cdacouncil.org

Council for Exceptional Children (CEC)

3100 Clarendon Blvd.
Suite 600
Arlington, VA, 22201-5332
(888) 232-7733
http://www.cec.sped.org

Council of Chief State School Officers

One Massachusetts Avenue, NW, Suite 700
Washington, DC 20001-1431
(202) 336-7000
http://www.ccsso.org

Division for Early Childhood—Council for Exceptional Children

3415 South Sepulveda Blvd.
Suite 1100, Unit 1127
Los Angeles, CA 90034
(310) 428-7209
http://www.dec-sped.org

Early Childhood Leadership Program

Bank Street College of Education
610 West 112th Street
New York, NY 10025
(212) 875-4400
http://www.bnkst.edu/graduate-school/academics
/programs/leadership-programs-overview/early
-childhood-leadership/

Education Development Center (EDC)

43 Foundry Avenue
Waltham, MA 02453-8313
(617) 969-7100
http://www.edc.org

Families and Work Institute

267 Fifth Avenue, 2nd Floor
New York, NY 10006
(212) 465-2044
http://www.familiesandwork.org

Foundation for Child Development

475 Riverside Drive, Suite 248
New York, NY 10115
(212) 867-5777
http://www.fcd-us.org

Head Start State Collaborative Project Center for Schools and Communities

275 Grandview Avenue, Suite 200
Camp Hill, PA 17011
(717) 763-1661
http://www.center-school.org

High/Scope Educational Research Foundation

600 North River Street
Ypsilanti, MI 48198-2898
(800) 587-5639
http://www.highscope.org

International Child Resource Institute

125 University Avenue, 2nd Floor, Southwest Suite
Berkeley, CA 94710
(510) 644-1000
http://www.icrichild.org

International Literacy Association

P.O. Box 8139
800 Barksdale Rd.
Newark, DE 19714-8139
(800) 336-7323
https://www.literacyworldwide.org/

McCormick Center for Early Childhood Leadership

National-Louis University
6200 Capitol Drive
Wheeling, IL 60090
(847) 947-5063
http://mccormickcenter.nl.edu/

National AfterSchool Association

2961A Hunter Mill Rd., #626
Oakton, VA 22124
(504) 903-9930
http://www.naaweb.org/

National Association for Bilingual Education

8701 Georgia Avenue, Suite 700
Silver Spring, MD 20910
(240) 450-3700
http://www.nabe.org

National Association for Family Child Care

700 12th Street NW Suite 700
Washington, DC 20005
http://nafcc.org

National Association for Gifted Children

1331 H Street NW, Suite 1001
Washington, DC 20005
(202) 785-4268
http://www.nagc.org

National Association for the Education of Young Children (NAEYC)

1313 L Street, NW, Suite 500
Washington, DC 20005
(800) 424-2460
http://www.naeyc.org

National Association for the Education of Young Children

Accreditation of Programs for Young Children
1313 L Street, NW, Suite 500
Washington, DC 20005
(800) 424-2460
http://www.naeyc.org/academy

National Association of Elementary School Principals

1615 Duke Street
Alexandria, VA 22314-3483
(800) 386-2377
http://www.naesp.org

National Association of State Boards of Education

123 North Pitt Street, Suite 350
Alexandria, VA 22314
703.684.4000
http://www.nasbe.org

National Association of State Directors of Special Education (NASDSE)

1800 Diagonal Road, Suite 600
Alexandria, VA 22314
(703) 519-3800
http://www.nasdse.org

National Black Child Development Institute (NBCDI)

8455 Colesville Road, Suite 910
Silver Spring, MD 20910
(202) 833-2220
Toll-Free: (800) 556-2234
http://www.nbcdi.org

National Board for Professional Teaching Standards

1525 Wilson Blvd., Suite 500
Arlington, VA 22209
(800) 228-3224
http://www.nbpts.org

National Center for Children in Poverty

Bank Street Graduate School of Education
610 West 112th Street
New York, NY 10025
(646) 284-9600
http://www.nccp.org

National Center for Education in Maternal and Child Health

Georgetown University
Box 571272
Washington, DC 20057-1272
(877) 624-1935
http://www.ncemch.org

National Child Care Association (NCCA)

2020 National Child Care Association
P.O. Box 2948,
Merrifield, VA 22116
877-537-NCCA (6222)
https://nationalchildcare.org/

National Coalition for Campus Children's Centers

188 Front Street
Suite 116-104
Franklin, TN
37064
916-790-8261
http://campuschildren.org

National Early Childhood Program Accreditation (NECPA)

P.O. Box 2948
Merrifield, VA 22116
Phone: 855-706-3272
http://www.necpa.net

National Education Association (NEA)

1201 16th Street, NW
Washington, DC 20036-3290
(202) 833-4000
http://www.nea.org

National Head Start Association

1651 Prince Street
Alexandria, VA 22314
(703) 739-0875
http://www.nhsa.org

National Institute of Child Health and Human Development (NICHD)

Eunice Kennedy Shriver National Institute of Child Health and Human Development (NICHD)
31 Center Drive
Building 31, Room 2A32
Bethesda, MD 20892-2425
(800) 370-2943
http://www.nichd.nih.gov

National Latino Children's Institute

1112 East Buckeye Road
Phoenix, Arizona 85043
800.948.6605
http://www.nlci.org

National Parent Teacher Association

1250 North Pitt Street
Alexandria, VA 22314
(800) 307-4781
http://www.pta.org

National Resource Center for Health and Safety in Child Care and Early Education

13120 E. 19th Ave., Mail Stop F541
P.O. Box 6511
Aurora, CO 80045
(800) 598-5437
http://nrckids.org

National Women's Law Center

11 Dupont Circle, NW, Suite 800
Washington, DC 20036
(202) 588-5180
http://www.nwlc.org

North American Montessori Teachers Association (NAMTA)

846 E 6th Avenue
Helena, MT 59601
(206)9196349
http://www.montessori-namta.org

Office of Child Care's Child Care Technical Assistance Network (CCTAN)

c/o Administration for Children and Families
370 L'Enfant Promenade, SW
Washington, DC 20447
(202) 401-9200
http://www.acf.hhs.gov

Office of Indian Education

c/o Office of Elementary and Secondary Education
400 Maryland Avenue, SW
Washington, DC 20202
(202) 401-0113
http://www2.ed.gov/about/offices/list/oese/oie/index.html

Office of Minority Health

U.S. Department of Health and Human Services
The Tower Building
1101 Wootton Parkway, Suite 600
Rockville, MD 20852
(800) 444-6472
http://minorityhealth.hhs.gov

Office of Special Education and Rehabilitation Services (OSERS)

U.S. Department of Education
400 Maryland Avenue, SW
Washington, DC 20202-7100
(202) 245-7459
http://www2.ed.gov/about/offices/list/osers/osep/index.html

Parent Cooperative Preschools International (PCPI)

P.O. Box 230327
Portland, OR 97281
(800) 636-6222
http://www.preschools.coop

Save the Children Federation

501 Kings Highway East, Suite 400
Fairfield, CT 06825
(800) 728-3843
http://www.savethechildren.org

Society for Research in Child Development (SRCD)

1825 K Street N.W., Suite 325
Washington, D.C. 20006
(202) 800-0677http://www.srcd.org

United Way of America

701 North Fairfax Street
Alexandria, VA 22314
(703) 836-7100
http://www.unitedway.org

U.S. Consumer Product Safety Commission

4330 East West Highway
Bethesda, MD 20814
(800) 638-2772
http://www.cpsc.gov

U.S. Department of Agriculture

1400 Independence Avenue, SW
Washington, DC 20250
(202) 720-2791
http://www.usda.gov

U.S. Department of Education

400 Maryland Avenue, SW
Washington, DC 20202
(800) 872-5327
http://www.ed.gov

Zero to Three National Center for Infants, Toddlers and Families

1255 23rd Street, NW, Suite 350
Washington, DC 20037
(202) 638-1144
http://www.zerotothree.org

Periodicals

Exchange Magazine

Exchange Press Inc.
7700 A Street
Lincoln, NE 68510 (800) 221-2864
http://www.childcareexchange.com
(Published as part of Child Care Information Exchange)

Childhood Education

Childhood Education International
1875 Connecticut Ave., NW
10th Floor
Washington, DC 20009
202-372-9986
1-800-423-3563
http://www.acei.org/childhood-education

Early Childhood Education Journal

Published by Springer
233 Spring Street
New York, NY 10013
(800) 777-4643
http://www.springer.com/education+%26+language/learning+%26+instruction/journal/10643

Early Childhood Research Quarterly

Elsevier Publishing
225 Wyman Street, Waltham, MA 02144
(781) 663-5200
http://www.journals.elsevier.com/early-childhood
-research-quarterly/

Early Developments

Frank Porter Graham Child Development Institute
University of North Carolina at Chapel Hill
105 Smith Level Rd
Chapel Hill, NC 27516
http://www.fpg.unc.edu/resources/early
-developments-archive

Education Week

Editorial Projects in Education Inc.
6935 Arlington Road
Bethesda, MD 20814
(800) 346-1834
http://www.edweek.org/ew/index.html?intc=thed

Eric Project

c/o Computer Science Corporation
655 15th Street, NW, Suite 500
Washington, DC 20005
(800) 538-3742
http://www.eric.ed.gov

Exceptional Children

Council for Exceptional Children
3100 Clarendon Blvd. Suite 600
Arlington, VA, 22201
(888) 232-7733
http://www.cec.sped.org

Growing Child

P.O. Box 2505
Lafayette, IN 47996
(800) 927-7289
http://www.growingchild.com

ExtendED Notes

P.O. Box 10
6848 Leon's Way
Lewisville, NC 27023
(888) 977-7955
http://www.extendednotes.com

InfoWorld

501 Second Street
San Francisco, CA 94107
(415) 572-7341
http://www.infoworld.com

MacWorld

501 2nd Street
San Francisco, CA 94107
http://www.macworld.com

PC Magazine

Ziff-Davis Media Inc.
28 East 28th Street, 11th Floor
New York, NY 10016
(800) 289-0429
http://www.pcmag.com

PC World

PCW Communications Inc.
501 2nd Street
San Francisco, CA 94107
http://www.pcworld.com

Reading Today and Reading Teacher

International Reading Association Inc.
800 Barksdale Road
P.O. Box 8139
Newark, DE 19714-8139
(800) 336-7323
http://www.reading.org

ReSource

High-Scope Educational Research Foundation
600 North River Street
Ypsilanti, MI 48198-2898
(800) 587-5639
http://www.highscope.org

Teaching Young Children

National Association for the Education of Young
Children
1313 L Street, NW, Suite 500
Washington, DC 20005
(800) 424-2460
http://www.naeyc.org/tyc

Young Children

National Association for the Education of Young Children
1313 L Street, NW, Suite 500
Washington, DC 20005
(800) 424-2460
http://www.naeyc.org/yc/

Young Exceptional Children

Division for Early Childhood/Council for Exceptional Children
3415 S. Sepulveda Blvd., Suite 1100, Unit 1127
Los Angeles, CA 90034
(310) 428-7209
http://www.dec-sped.org

Zero to Three

National Center for Infants, Toddlers, and Families
1255 23rd Street, NW, Suite 350
Washington, DC 20037
(202) 638-1144
http://www.zerotothree.org

Media

Arlitt Instructional Media

c/o Purdy Productions
6851 Steger Drive Cincinnati, OH 45237
(513) 821-1785
http://cech.uc.edu/centers/arlitt/arlitt_instructional
_media.html
These videos from the Arlitt Child & Family Research and Education Center at the University of Cincinnati provide numerous clips of evidence-based practices and curriculum being implemented in the classroom.

Center on the Developing Child at Harvard University

50 Church Street, 4th Floor
Cambridge, MA 02138
(617) 496-0578
http://developingchild.harvard.edu/
The Center on the Developing Child provides numerous online videos related to various aspects of development and learning.

Child Development Media, Inc.

5632 Van Nuys Boulevard, Suite 286
Van Nuys, CA 91401
(800) 405-8942

http://www.childdevelopmentmedia.com
Child Development Media offers a wide selection of videos related to child development, early childhood education, and early intervention.

Child Trauma Academy

5161 San Felipe, Suite 320
Houston, TX 77056
(281) 816-5604
http://childtrauma.org
The Child Trauma Academy is a nonprofit research, service, and education collaborative addressing the needs of children who have experienced or who are at risk for maltreatment. They make available both print and visual media, including many free resources, related to this issue.

Davidson Films Inc.

P.O. Box 664
Santa Margarita, CA 93453
(888) 437-4200
http://www.davidsonfilms.com
Davidson Films supplies videos and DVDs featuring many of the most well-known thinkers who have influenced early childhood education. Its "Giants" series includes Piaget, Elkind, Montessori, Ainsworth, and Bandura.

National Association for the Education of Young Children

1313 L Street, NW, Suite 500
Washington, DC 20005
(800) 424-2460
http://www.naeyc.org
NAEYC offers many videos, some in DVD format, that address nearly every aspect of early childhood education, including curriculum, developmentally appropriate practice, diversity, literacy, children with disabilities, play, and child development.

Program Development Associates

32 Court Street, 21st Floor
Brooklyn, NY 11201
(800) 876-1710
http://www.disabilitytraining.com
This company supplies multimedia training and educational resources on numerous disability-related topics.

Index